NEW MEXICO

STEVEN HORAK

Contents

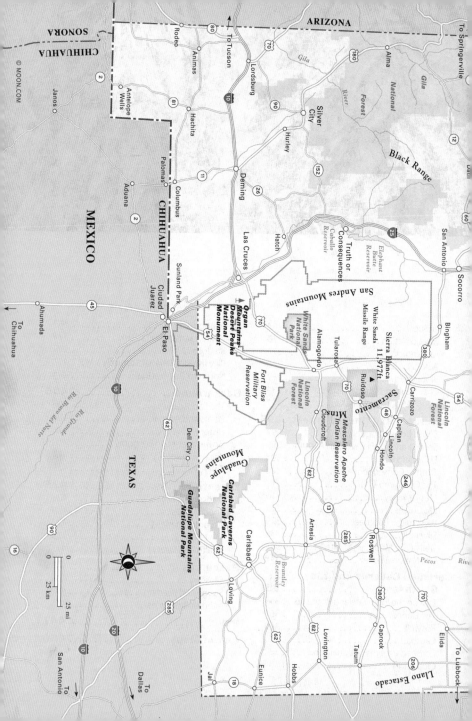

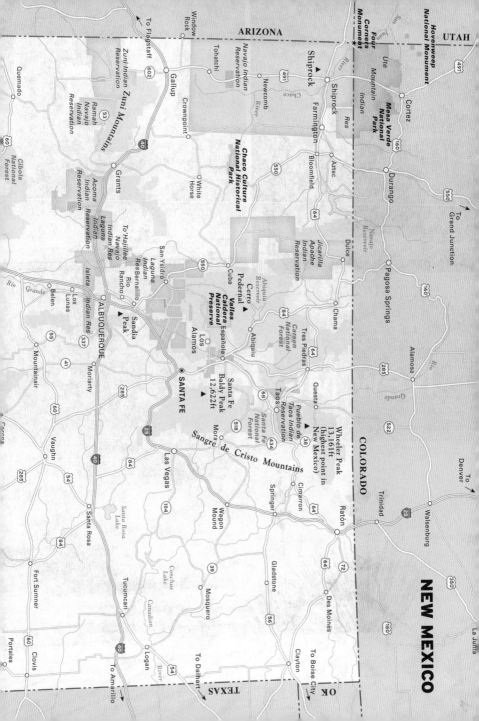

DISCOVER

New Mexico

There's a reason it's called the Land of Enchantment. The smells alone would be entrancing enough: lilacs in spring, petrichor after summer monsoons, green chiles roasting at farmer's markets in fall, and fragrant piñon crackling in woodstoves and kiva fireplaces. Listen, too, and you'll hear what makes the state special: Western tanagers warble in the trees, coyotes howl in the night, and the deep boom of drums and jingle of bells resound at pueblo ceremonies. And that green chile adds a distinct taste to everything—it finds its way onto hamburgers and pizzas and even into bagels and beer.

But none of that matches the majesty of what you see: austere mesas, sandstone canyons, meadows blanketed in wildflowers, and snowcapped mountain peaks. Straight above is a vast sky colored turquoise—just like the locally crafted jewelry. At night, stars, so close you can almost touch them, paint the Milky Way. It's a lot to take in, and many visitors to New Mexico understandably feel disoriented—and perhaps as well by the dizzying altitude, which soars over 13,000 feet at its highest point.

New Mexico is a sort of alternate world, one that lives by different rules. Santa Fe is an adobe-looking utopia where the economy seems to thrive

Clockwise from top left: the holiday season in Santa Fe; radio telescope at the Very Large Array; cow skull; cherry pie in Pie Town; blooming prickly pear; yucca at White Sands National Park.

magically on nothing but art and politics. Los Alamos is a city of scientists on a hill with a secret that changed the world, and half of Roswell, it seems, is still obsessed with an alleged UFO crash there in 1947. The state is home to some of the oldest settlements in the country and also to the world's first spaceport for tourists. There are communities named Truth or Consequences and Pie Town.

Visitors might need time to adjust—to the altitude, certainly, and maybe also to the laid-back attitude. But there's a point of entry for everyone. Outdoor adventurers can hike for an hour or a week, along mountainsides thick with yellow-leafed aspens, and camp on surreal gypsum dunes. Culture mavens thrive in Santa Fe, with its world-class art scene and an eclectic calendar of international film and music. History buffs can explore the ruined civilization at Chaco Canyon, spy ruts dug by thousands of passing wagon wheels on the Santa Fe Trail, or bunk down under a buzzing neon motel sign along Route 66.

At the end of the day, you can always pull yourself back into the present with a cold margarita and *carne adovada* with a kick—but there's no guarantee you'll shake off New Mexico's spell.

Clockwise from top left: red rocks near Ghost Ranch; the historic enclave of Mesilla in Las Cruces; San Geronimo Church at Taos Pueblo; the Classical Gas Museum in Embudo.

10 TOP EXPERIENCES

1 **Take in extraordinary landscapes:** Explore the undulating gypsum dunes of White Sands National Park (pictured, page 394), the vast green valleys of Valles Caldera National Preserve (page 145), the mesmerizing underground world of Carlsbad Caverns (page 382), and the eerie telescope-studded Plains of San Agustín (page 301).

2 **Journey back to the Wild West:** Visit old forts, count bullet holes in saloon ceilings, and trace the fortunes of prospectors in ghost-town graveyards (page 23).

3 **Hike, bike, or ski ...** Or even go caving or diving. New Mexico has got you covered (page 26).

>>>

4 **Explore Taos Pueblo:** Seemingly rising organically from the earth, these stepped adobe buildings make up the oldest continually inhabited community in the United States (page 174).

<<<

5 **Feast on Southwest cuisine:** In New Mexico, the food is as creative as the art and as distinctive as the landscape (page 25).

>>>

6 **Go gallery hopping in Santa Fe:** Art is life in Santa Fe—and **Canyon Road** is its beating heart (page 100).

<<<

7 Hit the road: Head out on a two-week road trip to really explore the state (page 20) or take shorter scenic drives (page 22).

>>>

8 Experience Native American culture: The historic culture of the pueblos can be awe inspiring, but the living culture is just as memorable (pages 28, 60, 138, 188, and 253).

<<<

9 Raft the Rio Grande: From the surging waters of the Taos Box to the gentle currents downstream, the Rio Grande offers a wide range of rafting opportunities (page 183).

>>>

10 **Go for a balloon ride:** Take a colorful trip into New Mexico's endless blue sky (page 52).

Planning Your Trip

Where to Go

Albuquerque

A modern Western city, Albuquerque sprawls over 189 square miles at the base of the **Sandia Mountains**. It's proud of its **Route 66** style, and it's also preserving **farmland** along the **Rio Grande** and redesigning itself as a green city. Head north to Santa Fe via the ghost towns of the **Turquoise Trail**, the hot springs in the **Jemez Mountains**, or the eerie **Kasha-Katuwe Tent Rocks National Monument.**

Santa Fe

New Mexico's picturesque capital has a human scale and a golden glow (partly from the loads of money spent here). **Museums** are a major draw—for state history, folk art, and more—as are the scores of **galleries.** Outside of town are the cliff dwellings at **Bandelier National Monument;** the solitary wilderness of the **Valles Caldera;** the red rock scenery of **Abiquiu,** which inspired painter Georgia O'Keeffe; and **Los Alamos,** birthplace of the A-bomb.

Taos and North Central New Mexico

Taos melds artists, spiritual seekers, and ski bums—plus centuries-old Spanish and American Indian families. Make time to enjoy the **atmosphere,** cultivated in coffee shops and creative restaurants. A good day drive is the **Enchanted Circle,** a loop of two-lane roads with **Wheeler Peak,** the highest in New Mexico, at the center. Or head over the mountains to **Chama,** home to a historic steam train that forges the pass into Colorado.

Motor through New Mexico on Route 66.

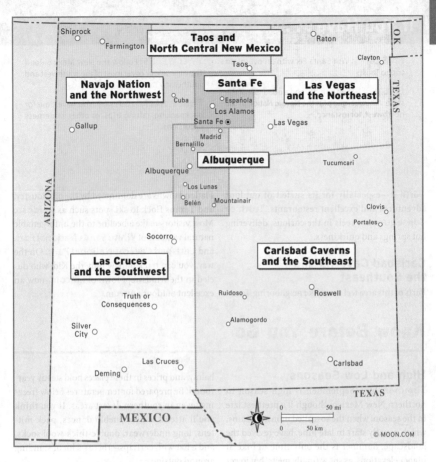

Shiprock
Farmington

**Taos and
North Central New Mexico**

Raton

Clayton

Taos

**Navajo Nation
and the Northwest**

Cuba

Santa Fe

Española
Los Alamos

Gallup

Santa Fe ◉

**Las Vegas
and the Northeast**

Las Vegas

Madrid
Bernalillo

Albuquerque

Albuquerque

Tucumcari

Los Lunas
Belén   Mountainair

Clovis

Portales

Socorro

**Carlsbad Caverns
and the Southeast**

**Las Cruces
and the Southwest**

Truth or
Consequences

Ruidoso

Roswell

Silver
City

Alamogordo

Las Cruces

Deming

Carlsbad

TEXAS

MEXICO

0   50 mi

0   50 km

© MOON.COM

ARIZONA

OK

TEXAS

Las Vegas and the Northeast

Past the Pecos Mountains, **Las Vegas,** aka
Meadow City, is a well-preserved historic town,
often used as a Western film set. From there the
terrain, where the **Santa Fe Trail** once ran, is all
short-grass prairie, once the western edge of the
Dust Bowl. To get a view, drive the spiral road
up **Capulin Volcano,** and then soar up to the
mountain towns of **Raton** and **Cimarron** and
through the gorgeous **Valle Vidal.**

Navajo Nation and the Northwest

Stark volcanic landscapes, lonesome roads,
tall mesas, and the multicolored hoodoos of

the **Bisti/De-Na-Zin Wilderness**—this is
some of the most dramatic desert terrain in
the state, along with its oldest cultures. This
is where the Ancestral Puebloans flourished
in **Chaco Canyon,** the Acoma live in **Sky
City,** and where **Gallup** is the self-proclaimed
American Indian capital.

Las Cruces and the Southwest

This corner of the state has both the rugged **Gila
Wilderness** and the mesmerizing **Chihuahuan
Desert.** It's a long drive between the river-fed
farmland around **Las Cruces** and colorful,
artsy **Silver City,** tucked in the mountains, but

If You Have . . .

- **FIVE DAYS:** Visit Santa Fe, with an overnight trip to Taos.

- **ONE WEEK:** See one city and a quadrant of the state: Albuquerque plus the Navajo Nation in the northwest, for instance.

- **TWO WEEKS:** Follow the New Mexico Road Trip itinerary, or cover most of the southwest and southeast.

- **THREE WEEKS:** Go crazy: You have time for backpacking, rafting trips, or other wilderness excursions.

worth it—especially for its surfeit of outdoor adventures and excellent restaurants. **Truth or Consequences** reels in the curious, delivering hot springs and quirkiness.

Carlsbad Caverns and the Southeast

Parts of this area feel more like neighboring Texas: Flatland towns are dominated by the oil industry, and Texans flock to ski spots such as **Ruidoso.** Most visitors make a beeline to the unforgettable natural wonders of **White Sands National Park** and **Carlsbad Caverns National Park.** On the way, you can track outlaw Billy the Kid, who dueled in the windswept town of **Lincoln,** now an excellent outdoor museum.

Know Before You Go

High and Low Seasons

Summer, June-September, is high season in northern New Mexico, though it's prettiest late in the season, when the so-called monsoon rains, which usually start in late June, have revived the landscape. Summer is the only time to hike at higher elevations, as snow finally melts, but lower elevations are baking and sleepy. Be prepared for a temperature drop from the 90s to as low as the 60s after sunset, especially outside of cities—and bring an umbrella.

Fall is the most beautiful time across the state, with crisp temperatures, clear skies, and brilliant leaves in the mountains. For New Mexico's most temperate season, pack a sweater and a windbreaker to keep out the nighttime chill.

Winter is busy (and pricier) in ski towns like Taos, but traditional celebrations preceding Christmas are magical. Many sights are closed or have limited hours, however. Towns at lower elevations, such as Las Cruces and Carlsbad, remain balmy, and prices in these places hold steady year-round. Be prepared for temperatures below freezing, even in southern desert areas. If you think you'll attend winter pueblo dances, pack mittens, long underwear, double-thick wool socks, and a hat with earflaps—there's a lot of standing around outside.

The cheaper **shoulder seasons** are March-May, and, to a lesser extent, November, before ski season starts. Spring is perhaps the harshest time in the state. Weather can be extreme, switching from snowfall and mud to dry, hot winds (pack boots for rural or muddy areas, and a clean pair of shoes for around town). But it is generally the best season for river rafting.

Be prepared for a **wide range of temperatures** whenever you go, and always pack sunglasses, sunscreen, and a brimmed hat. Local "formal" wear is only clean jeans and boots; when visiting churches and pueblos, women should cover their shoulders.

Advance Reservations

New Mexico is mostly a just-show-up kind of place, but a few attractions require some forethought.

Attending a ceremonial dance is worth planning a trip around. Dances are held at New Mexico pueblos year-round. Check the schedules for those near Albuquerque (page 60) and Santa Fe (page 138), as well as for Taos (page 188) and Zuni, Laguna, and Acoma Pueblos (page 253) in advance.

The Georgia O'Keeffe Home (page 150) in Abiquiu is open to guided tours mid-March through November. Book at least a month in advance.

Online ticket sales for the Santa Fe Opera (page 116) start in October for the following July and August summer season. Book in the winter for the best seat selection.

Book a hotel 6-8 months ahead if you plan to visit during Santa Fe's Spanish Market (July) and Indian Market (August), Albuquerque's International Balloon Fiesta (October), and Santa Fe's Christmas.

Visiting the extraordinary land art *The Lightning Field* (page 303) requires advance overnight reservations (May-Oct., $150-250 pp). Booking for the season starts in March; if your preferred dates are full, ask to be put on a waiting list.

Museum Pass

A New Mexico Museum CulturePass ($25) is good for 12 months and grants onetime access to 15 state-run museums and historic sites. This includes four Santa Fe institutions—the New Mexico Museum of Art, the New Mexico History Museum, the Museum of Indian Arts & Culture, and the Museum of International Folk Art—as well as two in Albuquerque (the National Hispanic Cultural Center and the Natural History Museum), and the Coronado and Jemez historic sites. It also covers attractions farther afield, in Las Cruces, Alamogordo, and more.

New Mexico Road Trip

You could conceivably explore New Mexico for a month or so, seeking out ever more obscure locales, but a two-week road trip gives enough time to appreciate the distinct character of the cities and enjoy the more isolated treats that taking the back roads affords. This itinerary involves a lot of driving to cover the state's most scenic routes, but you'll still have plenty of opportunity for leisurely lunches and on-the-ground activities.

Day 1
Albuquerque
Arrive at Albuquerque's Sunport airport; transfer to a hotel in the city or one of the rural-feeling bed-and-breakfasts in the North Valley. Have drinks and dinner in **Nob Hill.**

Day 2
Albuquerque to Gallup
150 MILES; 3 HOURS
Visit the **Indian Pueblo Cultural Center,** then head west to **Acoma Pueblo.** Lunch in Grants and stay the night in **Gallup.**

Day 3
Gallup to Abiquiu
220 MILES; 4.5 HOURS
Get an early start for the long, bumpy ride along the dirt road to **Chaco Culture National Historical Park.** When you're done exploring, grab a late lunch at **El Bruno's** in Cuba, then take Highway 96 over the mountains to **Abiquiu,** where you'll spend the night.

Ghost Ranch

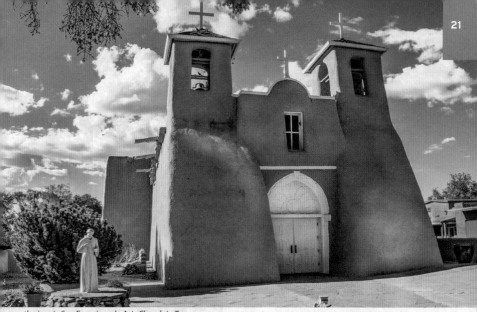

the iconic San Francisco de Asis Church in Taos

Day 4
Abiquiu to Santa Fe
95 MILES; 2.5 HOURS

If you like hiking, explore Abiquiu's red rocks at **Ghost Ranch** or drive down the road to **Bandelier National Monument.** If you prefer the city, head straight in to **Santa Fe** and the excellent museums around the plaza. In either case, stay the night there, at the classic **La Fonda** or the Native American-owned **Hotel Santa Fe.**

Day 5
Santa Fe

Take in Santa Fe's contemporary culture, with shopping, gallery-hopping, or a visit to the description-defying **House of Eternal Return.** Round out a colorful day with dinner at **Café Pasqual's.**

Day 6
Santa Fe to Taos
75 MILES; 2 HOURS

Head to **Taos** via the high road, with stops at the **Santuario de Chimayó,** where you can also pick up some delicious tamales, and in the villages of **Truchas** and **Las Trampas.** Settle into your hotel in **Taos** after a de rigueur margarita at the **Adobe Bar.**

Day 7
Taos

Start with an early visit to **San Francisco de Asis Church,** followed by breakfast at **Michael's Kitchen.** Then head to the **Taos Art Museum** for background on the town's art scene. Spend the afternoon at **Taos Pueblo,** followed by a local-produce dinner at **The Love Apple.**

Day 8
Taos to Las Vegas
150 MILES; 3 HOURS

Drive the first leg of the **Enchanted Circle,** turning east at Eagle Nest to reach **Cimarron.** Lunch at **Blü Dragonfly Brewing,** then head down to **Las Vegas** via I-25. Check in at the **Plaza Hotel,** and walk up Bridge Street and over to **The Skillet** for dinner.

Best Drives

There's hardly a bad road in New Mexico, but these drives are outstanding.

- **Turquoise Trail** (55 miles, 1.5 hours) — From Albuquerque to Santa Fe, **Highway 14** offers great vistas around every curve and ghost towns to break up the drive (page 78).

- **Jemez Mountain Trail** (32 miles, 1 hour) — **Highway 4** through Jemez Springs to the Valles Caldera is especially good in fall, with yellow aspens highlighted against red rock (page 82).

- **U.S. 84** (93 miles, 1 hour 45 minutes) — North of Santa Fe, ascend through the red rocks of **Abiquiu** (page 148), then past the Brazos Cliffs near **Tierra Amarilla** (page 200).

- **La Frontera del Llano Scenic Byway** (26 miles, 30 minutes) — Highway 39 zigzags across the northeastern plains, from Roy to Abbott, with pronghorns and ruined homesteads along the way (page 230).

- **Highway 72** (37 miles, 1 hour) — This tiny road between Raton and Folsom soars over the bucolic **Johnson Mesa** (page 237).

- **U.S. 180** (98 miles, 2 hours) — From Silver City to Reserve, this highway passes largely through the **Gila National Forest** (page 348).

- **Sunspot Highway** (17 miles, 30 minutes) — Highway 6563 winds south from Cloudcroft to

signs for I-40 and Historic Route 66

Sunspot National Solar Observatory, with White Sands visible below (page 386).

- **Historic Route 66** (350 miles, 7 hours) — Pieces of I-40 frontage road and more remote detours make up the decommissioned Mother Road, passing vintage Americana motels, diners, and more along the way (pages 250 and 355).

Day 9
Las Vegas to Carlsbad
270 MILES; 4.5 HOURS

Today is a long day of driving, but you'll pass through pretty old villages like **Villanueva** and the plains around **Vaughn.** Have a late lunch in **Roswell,** and visit the **International UFO Museum & Research Center** or the **Anderson Museum of Contemporary Art.** Drive down to Carlsbad for dinner at **Danny's Place BBQ** and bunk down at **Trinity Hotel & Suites.**

Day 10
Carlsbad to Cloudcroft
180 MILES; 3.5 HOURS

Head out early to **Carlsbad Caverns National Park.** From there, drive west up into the mountains to **Cloudcroft.** Kick back and take in the view at the **Western Bar & Café,** before settling in for the night at the **Burro Street Boardinghouse.**

Day 11
Cloudcroft to Las Cruces
90 MILES; 1.5 HOURS

Head west to **White Sands National Park,** winding up in **Las Cruces** that evening. Tour historic **Mesilla** on foot and enjoy an evening meal at **La Posta.**

Day 12
Las Cruces to Albuquerque
225 MILES; 3.5 HOURS

Drive up I-25 to return to Albuquerque, stopping in **Truth or Consequences** for coffee and a snack and a dip in the hot springs. Plan on a green-chile cheeseburger for lunch at the **Owl Bar & Café** in San Antonio. You should be in Albuquerque by nightfall—check out the scene downtown.

Days 13-14
Albuquerque

Take it easy on Day 13, and take one last look at the Southwestern scenery, either with a **hot-air balloon ride** at dawn or a tram ride to **Sandia Peak** at sunset.

On Day 14, fuel up for your flight with breakfast at **The Frontier,** where you can also grab some house-made tortillas to take home.

A Week in the Wild West

Gunslingers, cattle rustlers, and Apache warriors made New Mexico a colorful, if violent, place in the 19th century, and relics of that frontier lifestyle are still visible everywhere. History buffs can visit old forts, count bullet holes in saloon ceilings, and trace the fortunes of prospectors in ghost-town graveyards. Though the major cities have their share of history, this route takes you away from the modern centers and into emptier quarters. It can be expanded with a stop in Santa Fe or a more leisurely pace up to Las Vegas (Highway 3, which connects I-40 to I-25, for instance, is exceptionally pretty, if a bit out of the way).

Day 1
Arrive in Albuquerque. Take in the western sunset at the base of the **Sandia Peak Tramway,** in the foothills, and then come back to the center of the city for dinner at the appropriately named and Western-themed restaurant **The Frontier.** Bed down at the **Los Poblanos Historic Inn,** amid horse farms in the North Valley.

Day 2
Head southeast to **Mountainair** and the rustic-bizarre **Shaffer Hotel;** you'll also pass the **Salinas Pueblo Missions.** By mid-afternoon, you should be in **Lincoln,** where Billy the Kid earned his greatest notoriety. Tour the buildings here, and then settle in for the evening at the **Wortley Hotel.**

Day 3
After breakfast, you're headed north to **Fort Sumner** to see Billy the Kid's grave and a memorial to Navajo internment in the 1860s. Take an afternoon dip in the **Blue Hole** in Santa Rosa to fortify yourself for the last leg of the drive, to **Las Vegas,** where you'll stay and dine at the grand **Plaza Hotel.**

Day 4
Tour the Meadow City's historic buildings in the morning, with lunch at **Abraham's Tiendita,** then head for sprawling **Fort Union National Monument** in the afternoon—the slanting sun should highlight the ruts of the **Santa Fe Trail** off to one side. Return to Las Vegas for the evening.

Day 5
I-25 north takes you to **Raton,** where you turn east to **Capulin Volcano National Monument,** which affords a commanding view over the plains. Loop back via **Folsom** (site of numerous train robberies) and the awesome, empty expanse

the Wortley Hotel in Lincoln

of **Johnson Mesa.** Have a late lunch in Raton at **Enchanted Grounds** and then cruise on to **Cimarron,** where you'll spend the night in the spooky **St. James Hotel.**

Day 6

Depending on your interests, hang out in Cimarron in the morning until the **Old Aztec Mill Museum** opens, or make a beeline through dramatic Cimarron Canyon to **Eagle Nest** and on to **Taos.** The long way around the **Enchanted Circle** yields the best views and takes you past abandoned **Elizabethtown,** site of the state's first gold rush. In **Red River,** the scene is livelier:

Bars play both kinds of music (country *and* western). Spend the night in Taos at the **Historic Taos Inn** or **Hotel La Fonda de Taos.** Both wear their years well.

Day 7

Drive south back to Albuquerque via the **low road** and, if you have the time, the **Turquoise Trail**—stop in **Cerrillos,** which has been used as a Western film set, and eat at the **Black Bird Saloon,** which looks like one. If you don't have to meet a flight out, plan on stopping in **Madrid,** too, for a burger or a beer at the **Mine Shaft Tavern.**

Green Chile and So Much More

BEST TRADITIONAL NEW MEXICAN

"Red or green?" is the official state question, the dilemma diners face when they order anything that can be drowned in an earthy red-chile sauce or a chunky, vegetal green one. Hint: Choose "Christmas" if you can't decide.

- **Mary & Tito's Café:** An Albuquerque institution, this family restaurant was named a James Beard American Classic in 2009. Red chile is the star here (page 68).

- **Pueblo Restaurant:** In the category of restaurants in a gas station, this one in San Felipe Pueblo is a winner: big enchilada platters, as well as pueblo favorites like blue-corn mush (page 87).

- **Tia Sophia's:** The alleged inventors of the breakfast burrito, in Santa Fe (page 123).

- **Zuly's:** A dreamy rich, deep red sauce bathes enchiladas and burritos at this café in the bucolic village of Dixon (page 155).

- **El Bruno's:** The restaurant in Cuba processes all of its green chile by hand (page 291).

posole at the Pueblo Restaurant in San Felipe Pueblo

- **Big D's Downtown Dive:** An outpost of gourmet fast food in Roswell, this place does a succulent burger, with garlic fries on the side (page 375).

BEST GREEN-CHILE CHEESEBURGER

- **Bang Bite:** The wait is more than worth it at this orange food truck that draws long lines with its signature roasted five-chile blend burger (page 125).

- **Santa Fe Bite:** This casual restaurant grinds its own meat and shapes its enormous—and fabled—burgers by hand (page 130).

- **Sugar's:** If you're taking the low road to Taos, don't miss out on a juicy green-chile cheeseburger at this beloved Embudo institution (page 153).

- **Laguna Burger:** Devotees regularly drive to Laguna Pueblo for these GCCBs made from fresh, never frozen meat (page 252).

- **Owl Bar & Café:** A twofer in the village of San Antonio: not only the old-school Owl, but rival Buckhorn Burgers is right across the street (page 304).

BEST LOCAL AND ORGANIC

- **Vinaigrette:** This "salad bistro" in Santa Fe and Albuquerque grows its own greens on a Tesuque farm and can vouch for every ingredient on its menu (page 64).

- **Campo:** The restaurant at historic farm inn Los Poblanos serves a few perfect dishes each evening; overnight for the full farm-life experience in Albuquerque (page 68).

- **Café Pasqual's:** A Santa Fe institution, serving New Mexican and international dishes with organic ingredients since the late 1970s (page 123).

- **The Love Apple:** At this candlelit New Mexican bistro, a chalkboard displays the sourced ingredients: Tucumcari cheese, Pecos beef, and more (page 191).

- **Revel:** Laidback and welcoming, this Silver City gem serves creative comfort food using ingredients sourced from the surrounding region (page 341).

Outdoor Adventures

Marked by jagged mountains, endless and impossibly blue skies, and flora that endures against all odds, New Mexico has a primal beauty that can impact you to your core. Snowcapped peaks loom over arid deserts, and you can spot hardy animals, odd birds, and stunning rock formations everywhere in between. The sheer vastness of the scenery is intoxicating; the adventures that await you here are suitably epic.

Every corner of the state holds activities that can give you a lifetime of memories, but due to long driving distances, you're better off focusing your exploration on a specific part of the state. This way, you'll spend less time in the car and more time immersing yourself in the landscape.

Albuquerque
Hot-Air Ballooning

As you drift silently over Albuquerque, unmatched views open up in all directions—there's simply no better way to take in the **Sandia Mountains** and the **Rio Grande.**

Santa Fe
Hiking and Snowshoeing in the Valles Caldera National Preserve

The pristine backcountry of the 13-mile-wide **Valles Caldera National Preserve** beckons with mountain streams, thick alpine forests, and herds of elk grazing seemingly endless lush meadows. Whether you're planning a **day hike** in summer or a **snowshoe** trek in winter, every season is beautiful here.

Taos and North Central New Mexico
Rafting the Taos Box

Steep canyon walls loom alongside the 16 miles of surging waters of the **Taos Box;** the only way out is to negotiate the increasingly wild rapids that provide thrills and gasps in equal measure.

hot-air ballooning over Albuquerque

Carlsbad Caverns

Hiking and Skiing at
Taos Ski Valley

With bunny slopes and double black diamond runs, this **world-class ski resort** has it all, including stunning scenery and a **German beer garden** to boot. **Hiking trails** offer access to the beautiful mountain vistas in summer.

Navajo Nation and
the Northwest
Trekking in the Bisti/
De-Na-Zin Wilderness

Top-heavy **hoodoos**—precarious, windswept sandstone towers—are the hallmark of this barren landscape south of Farmington. There are **no trails** and **no services,** and virtually no other hikers, so come prepared with plenty of water, a compass, and an appreciation for solitude.

Las Cruces and the Southwest
Stargazing at the
Cosmic Campground

With some of the clearest skies in North America, just about anywhere outside of the

larger population areas in New Mexico is ideal for **stargazing.** To get the fullest picture of the **Milky Way,** set up camp and admire the breathtaking view at the **Cosmic Campground,** an International Dark Sky Sanctuary nestled in the southwestern part of the state.

Biking in the Organ
Mountains-Desert Peaks
National Monument

Miles of **single tracks** and **dirt roads** against a backdrop of some of the most rugged desert terrain in the state make this relatively new national monument a top destination for **mountain bikers** in the southern part of the state. From technical challenges to scenery that never fails to induce wonder, this vast protected area has it all.

Carlsbad Caverns and
the Southeast
Diving and Swimming
in the Blue Hole

It's not often you see scuba divers replete with an oxygen tank and fins in the middle of the desert, but it's fair to say the **Blue Hole** is no ordinary **dive spot.** Clear and temperate year-round, the pool is over 80 feet deep and fed by a natural spring. Whether or not you'd like to gear up at the adjacent dive shop, it's a great spot for a **swim**—particularly on a scorching summer afternoon.

Walking in White Sands National Park

A **sunset walk**—especially one led by a ranger—is one of the more magical ways to take in this impossibly white landscape and learn how it formed. Take time as well to hike the mesmerizing **Alkali Flat Trail** into the heart of the park, where waves of **gypsum dunes** undulate into the distance.

Caving in Carlsbad Caverns National Park

Go deeper—literally—than the average day-tripper by signing up for the hardcore **Spider Cave** tour, on which you'll wiggle through tiny tunnels into lofty halls. The park supplies helmets and headlamps, but it's BYOB: bring your own batteries. Handily, the temperature underground holds steady year-round; just book ahead during peak summer months.

Native New Mexico, Ancient and Modern

The culture that developed before the arrival of the Spanish in the 16th century can be experienced across the state in pueblos, in settlements long since abandoned, and in excellent museums that hold some of the state's finest treasures. Definitely try to schedule around a dance ceremony at a pueblo, as you'll see the living culture. If you're serious about purchasing art and jewelry, you may want to time your visit with the **Santa Fe Indian Market,** which takes place every August and showcases more than 1,100 artisans. But you'll also have a chance to buy directly from craftspeople in Zuni, Acoma, Crownpoint, and Santa Fe. If you have plenty of time to explore, you could also head south of Albuquerque to the Salinas Pueblo Missions, the Gila Cliff Dwellings, and the Bosque Redondo Memorial at Fort Sumner.

Albuquerque

The **Indian Pueblo Cultural Center** should be your first stop, for its good museum and information on all the American Indian settlements. Also pay a quick visit to **Petroglyph National Monument,** to see ancient rock carvings, and **Coronado Historic Site,** to see inside a painted kiva. The **Hyatt Regency Tamaya** resort nearby is owned by Santa Ana Pueblo.

Acoma Pueblo

West of Albuquerque, this dramatic **fortress village** atop a mesa is accessible only by **guided tour.** At the base is an excellent **cultural museum,** which displays the pueblo's specialty, delicate white pottery painted with fine black lines. You can grab Indian fry bread or lamb stew here, or have lunch down the road in Grants.

Zuni Pueblo

This is the only pueblo where you can stay overnight, at the **Inn at Halona.** It's also the source of beautiful jewelry. Take a walking tour of the **mission church,** with its resplendent kachina murals, and check out the **A:shíwi A:wan Museum and Heritage Center.** The dance ritual **Shalako,** in late November or early December, is amazing, but you must book at the inn many months ahead.

Gallup

Hosting a huge annual powwow, **Gallup** has the largest native population in the state, as well as the small **Navajo Code Talkers Museum.** Visit on a Saturday, for the funky and diverse **flea market.** About an hour's drive away is **Crownpoint,** which hosts a monthly rug auction—a must-visit even if you don't intend to buy anything.

Blue Swallow Motel in Tucumcari

"Get your kicks," advises Nat King Cole's classic anthem of the Mother Road. Though officially decommissioned, Route 66 (now traced by I-40) is still alive in New Mexico in the form of neon signs and cruising culture. And even off that iconic highway, many parts of the state foster nostalgia for the mid-20th century.

DRIVE-IN MOVIE MAGIC

Hit the road, preferably in a convertible, to enjoy good old-fashioned fun like a **drive-in movie theater** in Las Vegas (summers only). The car is still king in Clovis, where you'll find original **drive-ins,** such as Foxy, complete with carhops—this is the way burgers and fries were meant to be eaten.

ROCKIN' HISTORY

Clovis is also where 1950s crooner Buddy Holly recorded his early hits—check out the **Norman & Vi Petty Rock & Roll Museum,** or plan a trip for the September **Clovis Draggin' Main Music Festival.** Hot-rod fans can see one of Elvis's Caddies at **B-Square Ranch** in Farmington (the taxidermy museum here also seems like a relic of another age).

DESSERT DETOURS

Capture the real spirit of a road trip by heading out U.S. 60 to remote **Pie Town,** so named because it served intrepid motorists sweets in the 1930s. Several cafés keep this slice (pun intended) of Americana alive with mixed berry, chocolate cream, and more at the ready. In Portales, **Pat's Twin Cronnie** burger stand is famous for its peanut butter milkshake.

MOTOR LODGES

The best legacy of the Route 66 is the motels. Relive the era at the evocative **El Vado Motel** in Albuquerque. In Tucumcari, tuck yourself into 1939 at the **Blue Swallow Motel** or the slightly newer **Motel Safari,** or at **El Rancho Hotel & Motel** in Gallup, which hosted Ronald Reagan and other Western movie stars. Farther afield, in Raton, the **Maverick Motel** is meticulously preserved, and the **Budget Host Melody Lane Motel** has vintage saunas in the rooms. In Truth or Consequences (a town named for a 1950s radio show), the owners of **Blackstone Hotsprings** have decorated rooms as homages to *The Twilight Zone* and Lucille Ball. Sleep tight, and dream of the charm of yesteryear.

Sometimes New Mexico feels like an entirely different planet. Here's where to see the state at its most eccentric.

TRUTH OR CONSEQUENCES

From its attention-grabbing name (a 1950 publicity stunt) to its downtown of hot baths, odd shops, and the labyrinthine Geronimo Springs Museum, this is a small town with more than its share of character.

MADRID

It's pronounced MAD-rid, which gives you an idea about this ghost-town-turned-gallery-strip's wacky residents, who have brought the place back from the dead since the 1970s. South of here is Tinkertown Museum, a miniature wonderland whittled from wood, cobbled together from bottle caps and bits of string.

SANTA FE AND TAOS

Poll your fellow hot-tubbers at Ten Thousand Waves about their past lives, or ask your neighbor at the World Cup coffee shop if he can hear the "Taos hum." Take a trip to another dimension at the House of Eternal Return, or check out the Greater World Earthship Development, an off-the-grid outpost where the buildings crafted from beer cans and tires look straight off a *Star Wars* set.

Greater World Earthship Development

LOS ALAMOS

This mesa-top town is where the atomic bomb was devised and scientists still toil in secrecy; museums here present different takes on what that impact means. Round out your visit to "the Hill" with a trip down south to Trinity Site, where the bomb was first tested in July 1945; it's open to visitors only two days a year.

ROSWELL

Ever have cryptic dreams about green creatures with big heads and long, skinny arms? You'll feel right at home at the International UFO Museum & Research Center, where alien visitations are treated as a matter of course. The work at the outstanding Anderson Museum of Contemporary Art depicts all manner of alternate realities.

PLAINS OF SAN AGUSTÍN

If Roswell gets you in the mood to peer into the solar system, cruise out to this installation of radio telescopes that make up The Very Large Array. They don't actually receive messages from across the galaxy, but the images they take of deep space are illuminating all the same.

Bandelier National Monument

Shiprock and Farmington

Head into the Navajo Nation via U.S. 491, passing the Toadlena Trading Post, which displays beautiful rugs. Shiprock offers another chance at a flea market, or traditional mutton stew at the fast-food joints—or hold out until Farmington and AshKii's Navajo Grill. Farmington is usually the base for visiting Chaco Culture National Historical Park, a little over two hours south—though you'll get more out of the experience by camping at the site under starry skies.

Taos

Like Acoma, Taos Pueblo has endured for centuries and is inhabited to this day. If your visit doesn't coincide with a ceremonial dance there, stop by the Kachina Lodge in the early evening to see a demonstration performance (summer only)—but better to stay the night across the road at El Pueblo Lodge, a well-tended motel.

Santa Fe

Check out the modern arts scene at the Museum of Indian Arts & Culture and the Museum of Contemporary Native Arts, as well as several galleries representing pueblo artists. And don't miss the jewelry vendors under the *portal* at the Palace of the Governors. A short drive away are the ruins at Bandelier National Monument and the Puyé Cliff Dwellings, where Santa Clara residents lead the tours.

Albuquerque

As a tourist destination, Albuquerque has long labored in the shadow of the arts colonies to the north, but times are changing—and rightly so. The Duke City is fun, down-to-earth, and affordable.

If Santa Fe is the "City Different" (a moniker Albuquerqueans, or *Burqueños*, razz for its pretentiousness), then New Mexico's largest city, with a population of 900,000 in the greater metro area, is proudly the "City Indifferent," unconcerned with fads and fanciful facades.

The city does have its pockets of historic charm—they're just not visible from the arteries of I-40 and I-25, which intersect in the center in a graceful tangle of turquoise-trimmed bridges. Albuquerque was founded three centuries ago, its cumbersome name that of a Spanish

Highlights

Look for ★ to find recommended sights, activities, dining, and lodging.

★ **ABQ Trolley Co.:** The best city tour in the state, aboard an open-sided, faux-adobe tram-on-wheels, with the lively, knowledgeable owners sharing Albuquerque lore (page 37).

★ **KiMo Theatre:** A fantasia of Southwestern decorative styles, this former cinema is one of the few examples of Pueblo Deco style. Restored and run with city money, it's the showpiece of downtown (page 42).

★ **Sandia Peak Tramway:** Zip up the world's longest single-cable tram to the crest of the mountain that looms over the east side of Albuquerque. At the top, you'll get a vertigo-inducing view across the whole metro area and out to the hazy western horizon (page 48).

★ **Petroglyph National Monument:** Basalt boulders throughout the city's West Mesa are covered with several thousand fine rock carvings etched centuries ago by the ancestors of the local Pueblo people (page 48).

★ **Ballooning:** In the American hot-air balloon capital, enjoy a dawn flight—or at least witness hundreds of brightly colored balloons take part in the wildly popular Balloon Fiesta (page 52).

★ **Tinkertown Museum:** An enthralling collection of one man's lifetime of whittling projects, this folk-art exhibit delights kids and adults alike (page 79).

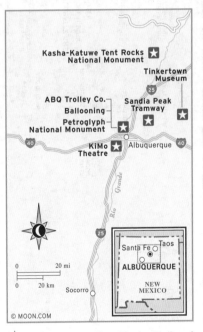

★ **Kasha-Katuwe Tent Rocks National Monument:** Break up the otherwise unremarkable freeway drive to Santa Fe with a hike in this eerie canyon landscape marked by dozens of bleached-white conical formations (page 86).

Albuquerque

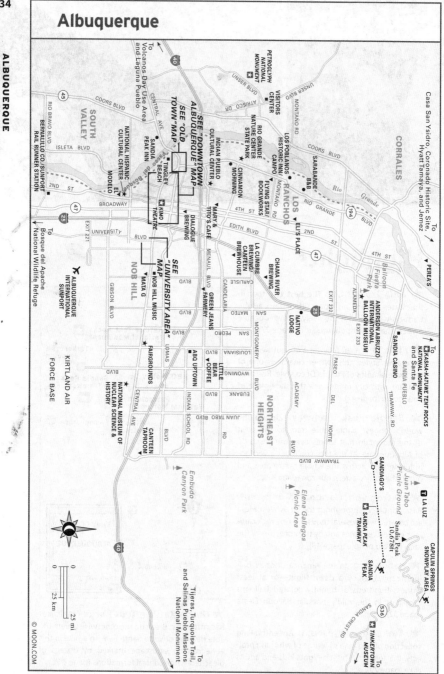

To Volcanos Day Use Area and Laguna Pueblo

PETROGLYPH NATIONAL MONUMENT

VISITORS CENTER

UNSER BLVD

COORS BLVD

CENTRAL AVE

SOUTH VALLEY

RIO BRAVO BLVD

BERNALILLO CO./SUNPORT RAIL RUNNER STATION

ISLETA BLVD

MODELO

2ND ST

BROADWAY

UNIVERSITY

EXIT 21

To Bosque del Apache National Wildlife Refuge

ALBUQUERQUE INTERNATIONAL SUNPORT

KIRTLAND AIR FORCE BASE

NATIONAL HISPANIC CULTURAL CENTER

SANDIA PEAK INN

EL TINGLEY BEACH

KIMO THEATRE

SEE "OLD TOWN" MAP

SEE "DOWNTOWN ALBUQUERQUE" MAP

INDIAN PUEBLO CULTURAL CENTER

DIALOGUE BREWING

MARY & TITO'S CAFE

CINNAMON MORNING

FLYING STAR/ BOOKWORKS

RIO GRANDE NATURE CENTER STATE PARK

LOS POBLANOS HISTORIC INN/ CAMPO

MONTAÑO RD

4TH ST

EDITH BLVD

MENAUL BLVD

SEE "UNIVERSITY AREA" MAP

NOB HILL

NOB HILL MUSIC

MATA G

GREEN JEANS FARMERY

LA CUMBRE BREWING / CANTEEN BREWHOUSE

CHAMA RIVER BREWING

CARLISLE BLVD

CANDELARIA

SAN MATEO

SAN PEDRO

LOUISIANA BLVD

GIBSON BLVD

FAIRGROUNDS

LOMAS

ABQ UPTOWN

LITTLE BEAR COFFEE

INDIAN SCHOOL RD

EUBANK BLVD

JUAN TABO BLVD

WYOMING BLVD

NATIONAL MUSEUM OF NUCLEAR SCIENCE & HISTORY

CENTRAL AVE

CANTEEN TAPROOM

Casa San Ysidro, Coronado Historic Site, Hyatt Tamaya, and Jemez

To Kasha-Katuwe Tent Rocks National Monument and Santa Fe

CORRALES

LOS RANCHOS

Rio Grande

194

COORS BLVD

RIO GRANDE BLVD

SARABANDE B&B

ELI'S PLACE

2ND ST

4TH ST

47

PEREA'S

Balloon Fiesta Park

ANDERSON ABRUZZO INTERNATIONAL BALLOON MUSEUM

ALAMEDA

EXIT 232

EXIT 233

25

NATIVO LODGE

PASEO DEL NORTE

ACADEMY BLVD

NORTHEAST HEIGHTS

TRAMWAY BLVD

To Sandia Casino

SANDIA PUEBLO

TRAMWAY RD

Juan Tabo Picnic Ground

LA LUZ

SANDIAGO'S

SANDIA PEAK TRAMWAY

Sandia Peak 10,678ft

SANDIA PEAK

CAPULIN SPRINGS SNOWPLAY AREA

Embudo Canyon Park

Elena Gallegos Picnic Area

SANDIA CREST RD

536

TINKERTOWN MUSEUM

To Tijeras, Turquoise Trail, and Salinas Pueblo Missions National Monument

N

0   25 km

0   25 mi

© MOON.COM

nobleman (hence its nickname, the Duke City but its character the product of later eras: the post-1880 downtown district; the University of New Mexico campus, built in the early 20th century by John Gaw Meem, the architect who defined Pueblo Revival style; and Route 66, the highway that joined Albuquerque to Chicago, Illinois, and Los Angeles, California, in 1926.

Spread out on either side of the Rio Grande, from volcanic mesas on the west to the foothills of the Sandia Mountains along the east, Albuquerque has accessible hiking and biking trails that run through diverse landscapes. In the morning, you can stroll under centuries-old cottonwood trees near the wide, muddy river; in the afternoon, you can hike along the edge of a windswept mountain range with views across the vast empty land beyond the city grid. And at the end of the day, you'll see Albuquerque's most remarkable feature, the dramatic light show on the Sandia Mountains—Spanish for "watermelon," for the bright pink hue they turn at sundown.

The city is also an excellent base for exploring the many interesting pueblos and natural attractions nearby. In the Manzano Mountains southeast of town, for instance, lie a series of ruined pueblos, last inhabited during the early years of the Conquest. The road that links them also winds past a canyon known for its fall colors and a historic hotel in a distinctly New Mexican style.

Albuquerque is also just an hour's drive to Santa Fe, with easy day trips or scenic drives through the mountains in between. The most direct is I-25, which cuts through dramatic rolling hills; take a short detour to Kasha-Katuwe Tent Rocks National Monument, where pointed white rocks tower above a narrow canyon. Beginning east of Albuquerque, the historic Turquoise Trail winds along the back side of the Sandias, then through the former mining town of Madrid, resettled as an arts colony, with galleries occupying the

cabins built against the black, coal-rich hills. The most roundabout route north is along the Jemez Mountain Trail, a scenic byway northwest of Albuquerque through the brick-red rocks surrounding Jemez Pueblo, then past natural hot springs.

PLANNING YOUR TIME

Precisely because it's not so full of must-see historic attractions, Albuquerque fares best as the primary focus of a trip, so you have time to enjoy the natural setting, the food, and the people. It makes financial sense, too: Your money will go further here than it will farther north, especially when it comes to hotels, which offer great value and don't dramatically hike rates for **summer** high season, as is standard in Taos and Santa Fe. Ideally, you would spend a leisurely **three days** here, soaking up a little Route 66 neon, enjoying the downtown entertainment, hiking in the Sandias, taking scenic drives, and bicycling along the Rio Grande.

But if you're also planning to visit other parts of the state, it is difficult to recommend more than a **couple of days** in Albuquerque—preferably on the way out, as the city's modern, get-real attitude is best appreciated after you've been in the adobe dreamland of Santa Fe for a bit. Spend a day cruising the neighborhoods along Central Avenue, and for a last dose of open sky, take the tramway up to Sandia Peak and hike along the Crest Trail. At the end of your trip, the altitude will likely be more manageable.

In the city proper, the weather for most of the year is enjoyable. **Winters** are mild in the low basin around the river, though the Sandias often get heavy snow. Note that a **summer** day here can be 5-10°F hotter than father north, though, as elsewhere in the state the heat of July and August is usually broken by heavy afternoon rainstorms. And because Albuquerque is seldom at the top of tourists' lists, there's never a time when it's unpleasantly mobbed.

Previous: Albuquerque International Balloon Fiesta; Kasha-Katuwe Tent Rocks National Monument; Sandia Peak.

HISTORY

Albuquerque was established in 1706 as a small farming outpost on the banks of the Rio Grande, where Pueblo Indians had been cultivating crops since 1100, and named after a Spanish duke. Decades later, the Villa de San Felipe de Alburquerque (the first "r" was lost over the years) flourished as a waypoint on the Camino Real trade route.

The city began to transform in 1880, when the railroad arrived, two miles from the main plaza—this sparked the growth of "New Town" (now the downtown business district) and drew tuberculosis patients, who saw the city's crisp air as beneficial. By 1912, these patients made up nearly a quarter of the state's population.

More modernization and growth came from Route 66, which was laid down Central Avenue in the 1930s, and the establishment of Sandia National Labs in 1949, in response to the escalating Cold War. Tourism boomed (and neon signs buzzed on), and new streets were carved into the northeast foothills for lab workers' tract homes. In the 1940s, the population exploded from 35,000 to 100,000; by 1959, 207,000 people lived in Albuquerque.

Growth has been steady ever since, and recent development has been spurred by a growing film industry and other technical innovations. Subdivisions have spread across the West Mesa, and small outlying communities have become suburbs—though portions along the river retain a village feel that's not too far from the city's roots as a farming community three centuries back.

ORIENTATION

Albuquerque's greater metro area covers more than 100 square miles, but visitors will likely see only a handful of neighborhoods, all linked by Central Avenue (historic Route 66), the main east-west thoroughfare across town. The new Albuquerque Rapid Transit (ART; www.brtabq.com) has significantly upgraded and enhanced bus options along Central Avenue, though with fewer lanes available, travel times by car can be a bit longer.

A few blocks from the Rio Grande, which runs north-south through the city, the Old Town makes for an ideal introduction to the city. The best museums are clustered here, and the area exudes history without feeling overly manufactured. East from Old Town lies downtown, with most of the city's bars and clubs, along with the bus and train depots. Central continues under I-25 and past the University of New Mexico campus, followed by the lively Nob Hill district, which occupies about 10 blocks of Central. Taking Louisiana Boulevard NE north from here will bring you through the largely nondescript shopping district known as Uptown. After this, the rest of Albuquerque blurs into the broad area known as the Northeast Heights; the main attractions up this way are hiking trails in the foothills and the Sandia Peak Tramway. The other notable parts of town—technically, separate villages—are Los Ranchos de Albuquerque and Corrales. These are two districts in the North Valley— the stretch of the river north of Central—that contain a few of the city's better lodging options; from Old Town, head north on Rio Grande Boulevard to reach Los Ranchos, then jog west over the river and north again to Corrales.

To keep your bearings, remember that the mountains run along the east side of the city. Street addresses are followed by the city quadrant (NE, NW, SE, SW); the axes are Central and 1st Street. When locals talk about "the Big I," they mean the relatively central point where I-40 and I-25 intersect.

Sights

Most sightseeing destinations are along or near Central Avenue (historic Route 66), with the remaining sights scattered elsewhere in the greater metro area.

OLD TOWN

Until the railroad arrived in 1880, this wasn't just the old town—it was the *only* town. The labyrinthine old adobes have been repurposed as souvenir emporiums and galleries; the city's major museums are nearby on Mountain Road. Despite the chile-pepper magnets and cheap cowboy hats, the residential areas surrounding the shady plaza retain a strong Hispano flavor, and the historic **Old Town** buildings have a certain endearing scruffiness—they're lived-in, not polished.

★ ABQ Trolley Co.

To cruise the major attractions in town and get oriented, put yourself in the hands of the excellent locally owned and operated **ABQ Trolley Co.** (800 Rio Grande Blvd. NW, 505/240-8000, www.abqtrolley.com)—even

if you're not normally the bus-tour type. The difference here is, first of all, in the bus itself: in summer, a goofy faux-adobe open-sided trolley-bus; in winter, a stealthy black van. But much more important are the enthusiastic owners, who give the tours themselves. Their love of the city is clear as they wave at pedestrians and tell stories about onetime Albuquerque resident and Microsoft founder Bill Gates.

All tours depart from the Hotel Albuquerque at Old Town. The 120-minute **standard tour** (11am and 1pm daily, $30) runs through downtown and some off-the-beaten-track old neighborhoods, passing many TV and movie locations. There's also a periodic *Breaking Bad* tour (4 hours, six-person minimum, $65) that remains a big draw—book well in advance for this. Or join one of the monthly nighttime theme tours—such as The Hopper, a brew-pub crawl—that draw locals as well. Buy tickets online to guarantee a spot; the tickets also get you discounts around town, so it's good to do this early in your visit.

The ABQ Trolley Co. offers a great introduction to the Duke City.

Old Town

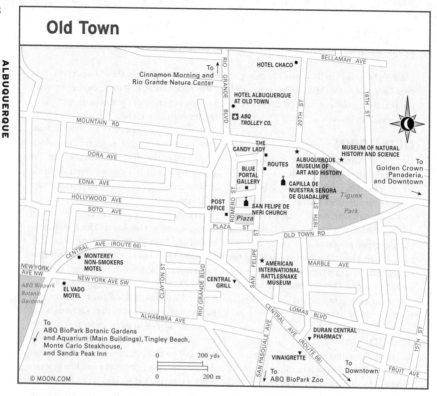

ABQ BioPark

The earnest **ABQ BioPark** (505/768-2000, www.cabq.gov/biopark, 9am-5pm Mon.-Fri., 9am-6pm Sat.-Sun. June-Aug.) is made up of several components, linked by park-land along the river. On the riverbank just west of Old Town (2601 Central Ave. NW) are an **aquarium** and **botanical gardens.** The aquarium is small but well stocked, with a giant shark tank and displays on underwater life from the Gulf of Mexico and up the Rio Grande. The well-conceived adjoining gardens include a desert hothouse, a butterfly habitat, a Japanese garden, a garden railroad, and a surprisingly compelling "BUGarium" full of insects in close approximations of their natural habitats. The gardens also include the 10-acre **Rio Grande Heritage Farm,** a re-creation of a 1930s operation with heirloom apple orchards and rare types of livestock,

such as Percheron horses and Churro sheep, in an idyllic setting near the river. The whole facility is of course very kid friendly, but in the desert rose garden, there's a pleasant **mini café** where you can enjoy a glass of wine, too.

A few blocks away is the **zoo** (903 10th St. SW), which you can reach from the aquarium via a miniature train. While not exactly ground-breaking, the zoo recently received an update, which included several enclosures receiving up-grades and the introduction of a sleek so-called Penguin Chill. Throughout the zoo there's plenty of space for kids to run around; aside from the new penguin exhibit, the window into the gorilla nursery is probably the most fascinat-ing. Tickets for each section (zoo or aquarium/gardens) are $14.50, and a combo ticket for entry to all three, which includes the mini-train ride, is $22. Ticket booths close 30 minutes before the attractions' closing times.

Breaking Bad

The Candy Lady tempts *Breaking Bad* viewers with bags of blue treats.

Walter White and Jesse Pinkman may be gone from television (at least, neither have yet to appear in the *Breaking Bad* prequel *Better Call Saul*), but their legacy lives on in Albuquerque. The AMC show about a high school chemistry teacher turned meth cook, *Breaking Bad* was originally written for a California setting, but production moved to Albuquerque following tax incentives. It was a happy accident, and unlike other productions shot here anonymously, *Breaking Bad* was explicitly down with the 505.

Dedicated fans can book the "BaD Tour" with the **ABQ Trolley Co.** (800 Rio Grande Blvd. NW, 505/240-8000, www.abqtrolley.com, Mar.-Nov., 4 hours, $65)—though its standard route passes a few filming locations as well. The bike rental company **Routes** (404 San Felipe St. NW, 505/933-5667, www.routesrentals.com, $60) offers "Biking Bad" tours every other Saturday.

A few other sights around town include:

- The **Dog House** hot dog stand, with its exceptionally fine neon sign, is at 1216 Central Avenue Southwest, near Old Town.

- **Los Pollos Hermanos** is actually Twisters, at 4257 Isleta Boulevard Southwest, but the PH logo is painted on the wall outside.

- Walt and Skyler's **A1A Car Wash** is at Menaul and Eubank (9516 Snow Heights Circle NE, for your GPS).

- **The Grove** (600 Central Ave. SE), where Lydia loved her Stevia too well, is a popular café downtown.

As souvenirs of your Albuquerque visit, **Great Face & Body** (123 Broadway SE, 505/430-5053) sells "Bathing Bad" blue bath salts. **The Candy Lady** (424 San Felipe St. NW, 505/243-6239), which cooked the prop "meth" for a few episodes, sells its blue hard candy in zip-top plastic bags.

Better Call Saul's ties to the city are just as strong, though Jimmy McGill (aka Saul) and his escapades have not yet been immortalized with an exclusive tour.

The land between the zoo and aquarium, on the east bank of the river, south of Central, is **Tingley Beach** (1800 Tingley Dr. SW, sunrise-sunset, free), 18 acres of paths and three ponds for fishing; you can also rent paddleboats ($14/hr) here and relax at the small café (late May-early Sept.).

Albuquerque Museum of Art and History

The **Albuquerque Museum of Art and History** (2000 Mountain Rd. NW, 505/243-7255, www.cabq.gov/museum, 9am-5pm Tues.-Sun., $6) has a permanent collection ranging from a few choice Taos Society of Artists members to contemporary work by the likes of Nick Abdalla, whose sensual imagery makes Georgia O'Keeffe's flower paintings look positively literal. The history wing covers four centuries, with emphasis on Spanish military trappings, Mexican cowboys, and Albuquerque's early railroad years. Free guided tours run daily around the sculpture garden, or you can join the informative **Old Town walking tour** (11am Tues.-Sun. mid-Mar.-mid-Dec.). The museum has free admission Saturday afternoon (after 2pm) and Sunday morning (9am-1pm), as well as the third Thursday night of the month, when it's open until 8:30pm.

American International Rattlesnake Museum

You'd never guess that a small storefront just off the plaza houses the largest collection of live rattlesnakes in the world. An outsized gift shop tempts at the entrance to the **American International Rattlesnake Museum** (202 San Felipe St. NW, 505/242-6569, www.rattlesnakes.com, 10am-6pm Mon.-Sat., 1pm-5pm Sun. June-Aug., $5); press past the snake swag to view the live critters in the back. You'll also see some fuzzy tarantulas and Gila monsters; the enthusiastic staff are usually showing off some animals outside to help educate the phobic. In the off-season, September-May, weekday hours are 11:30am-5:30pm (10am-6pm Sat., 1pm-5pm Sun.).

Capilla de Nuestra Señora de Guadalupe

One of the nifty secrets of Old Town, the tiny adobe **Capilla de Nuestra Señora de Guadalupe** (404 San Felipe St. NW) is tucked off a small side alley. It's dedicated to the first saint of Mexico; her image dominates the wall facing the entrance. The dimly lit room, furnished only with heavy carved seats against the walls, is still in regular use (although, unfortunately, a fire put an end to lit votive candles, and the image of the Virgin was repainted in a more modern style). Despite the building's diminutive size, it follows the scheme of many traditional New Mexican churches, with a clerestory that allows sunlight to shine down on the altar.

¡Explora!

A 50,000-square-foot complex adjacent to the natural history museum, **¡Explora!** (1701 Mountain Rd. NW, 505/224-8300, www.explora.us, 10am-6pm Mon.-Sat., noon-6pm Sun., adults $10, children $6) is dedicated to thrilling—and educating—with science. Its colorful geodesic-dome top reflects the enthusiastic and engaging tone within; inside, more than 250 interactive exhibits demonstrate the scientific principles behind everything from high-wire balancing to gravity. Since this is the desert, a whole section is dedicated to water, where kids can build a dam using Lego pieces.

Museum of Natural History and Science

The **Museum of Natural History and Science** (1801 Mountain Rd. NW, 505/841-2800, www.nmnaturalhistory.org, 9am-5pm daily) is a large exhibit space containing three core attractions: a **planetarium** and observatory, a wide-format **theater** screening the latest vertigo-inducing nature documentaries, and an **exhibit** of Earth's geological history. Admission is $8 to the

---

1: Capilla de Nuestra Señora de Guadalupe 2: San Felipe de Neri Church

main exhibit space (children $5) or $7 each for the planetarium and the theater, though there are discounts if you buy tickets to more than one.

The museum section devotes plenty of space to the crowd-pleasers: dinosaurs. New Mexico has been particularly rich soil for paleontologists, and several species that once lived in the area now known as the Bisti Badlands are on display, such as *Coelophysis* and *Pentaceratops*. In addition, the *Startup* exhibit details the early history of the personal computer in Albuquerque and elsewhere. The show was funded by Paul Allen, who founded Microsoft here with Bill Gates, *then* moved to Seattle, Washington.

San Felipe de Neri Church

Established in 1706 along with the city itself, San Felipe de Neri Church (2005 N. Plaza St. NW) was originally built on what would become the west side of the plaza—but it dissolved in a puddle of mud after a rainy season in 1792. The replacement structure, on the north side, has fared much better, perhaps because its walls, made of adobe-like *terrones* (sun-dried bricks cut out of sod) are more than five feet thick. As they have for two centuries, local parishioners attend Mass here, which is conducted three times a day, once in Spanish.

Like many religious structures in the area, this church received a late-19th-century makeover from Eurocentric bishop Jean-Baptiste Lamy of Santa Fe. Under his direction, the place got its wooden folk Gothic spires, as well as new Jesuit priests from Naples, who added such non-Spanish details as the gabled entrance and the widow's walk. The small yet grand interior has brick floors, a baroque gilt altar, and an elaborate pressed-tin ceiling with Moorish geometric patterns. A tiny museum (9:30am-5pm Mon.-Sat., free), accessible through the gift shop, contains some historic church furnishings.

DOWNTOWN

Albuquerque's downtown district, along Central Avenue between the train tracks and Marquette Avenue, was once known as bustling New Town, crowded with mule-drawn streetcars, bargain hunters, and wheeler-dealers from the East Coast. At Central Avenue and 4th Street, two versions of Route 66 intersect. When the original highway was commissioned in 1926, the road from Chicago to the West Coast ran along 4th Street; after 1937, the route was smoothed so that it ran east-west along Central. The route brought more business, but spread it through the city: In the 1950s and 1960s, shopping plazas farther east in Nob Hill and the Northeast Heights drew business away from downtown. By the 1970s, the neighborhood was a wasteland of government office buildings. Thanks to an aggressive urban-renewal scheme, downtown has regained some of its old vigor, and Central is now a thoroughfare best known for its bars.

By day there aren't many attractions to detain you, but you can join a walking tour with Albuquerque Tourism & Sightseeing Factory (219 Central Ave. NW, 505/200-2642, www.atsfworks.com), the friendly, informed crew that also runs the city trolley tours. Walks are currently limited to the Albucreepy (1.5 hours, $22), a nighttime ghost tour.

★ KiMo Theatre

Albuquerque's most distinctive building is the KiMo Theatre (423 Central Ave. NW, 505/768-3522 or 505/768-3544, www.cabq. gov/kimo). In 1927, local businessman and Italian immigrant Carlo Bachechi hired Carl Boller, an architect specializing in movie palaces, to design this marvelously ornate building. Boller was inspired by the local adobe and native culture to create a unique style dubbed Pueblo Deco—a flamboyant treatment of Southwestern motifs, in the same vein as Moorish- and Chinese-look cinemas of the same era. The tripartite stucco facade

Downtown Albuquerque

is encrusted with ceramic tiles and Native American iconography (including a traditional Navajo symbol that had not yet been appropriated by WWII Germany's Nazi Party when the KiMo was built).

To get the full effect, take a self-guided tour (noon-6pm Wed.-Sat., noon-3pm Sun.) of the interior to see the cow-skull sconces and murals of pueblo life; enter through the business office, just west of the ticket booth.

Occidental Life Building

On Gold Avenue at 3rd Street, the one-story Occidental Life Building is another of Albuquerque's gems, built in 1917 by H. C. Trost, whose work defines downtown El Paso, Texas. With its ornate facade of white ceramic tile, it looks a bit like the Doge's Palace in Venice rendered in marshmallow fluff. After a 1933 fire, the reconstructing architects added even more frills, such as the crenellations along the top. The entire building is surfaced in white terra-cotta; the tiles were made in a factory in Denver, Colorado, that sprayed the ceramic glaze onto concrete blocks, each individually molded and numbered, and the blocks were then assembled in Albuquerque according to an overall plan. (The building is owned by local-boy-made-good Jared Tarbell, a cofounder of Etsy, the online craft site. Tarbell's high-tech toy- and art-manufacturing company and event space, Levitated, is located nearby, on Silver Avenue at 7th Street.)

Museums

Production value is basic at the storefront Holocaust and Intolerance Museum (616 Central Ave. SW, 505/247-0606, 11am-3:30pm Tues.-Sat., free), but the message is compelling. Displays cover not just World War II, but also the Armenian genocide, actions against Native Americans, and a new permanent exhibit on African Americans and slavery. Nearby, the surprisingly detailed three-story Telephone Museum (110 4th St. NW, 505/841-2932, 10am-2pm Mon., Wed., and Fri., $2) is worth a visit—if

you happen to get there during its laughably narrow open time.

The Wheels Museum (1100 2nd St. SW, 505/243-6269, www.wheelsmuseum.org, donation) is dedicated to Western transportation, with a special focus on trains—fitting its location in the city rail yard. It displays some great interviews with former workers in the old Santa Fe workshops. At the time of writing, the place was under development with no set hours; call for regular hours. It is somewhat reliably open during the Rail Yards Market (777 1st St. SW, www.railyardsmarket.org, 10am-2pm Sun. May-Oct.), however; model-train fans will be well rewarded.

Recently relocated to the opulent eyeful that is Zachary Castle, the Turquoise Museum (400 2nd St. SW, 505/247-8650, https://turquoisemuseum.com, tours 11am and 1pm Mon.-Sat., $21) now occupies a setting much more suited to its collection. Exhibits present the geology and history of turquoise, along with legendary trader J. C. Zachary's beautiful specimens from all over the world. But most folks can't help but think how this relates to all the jewelry they plan to buy. So come here to learn the distinction between "natural" and "real" turquoise and arm yourself for the shopping ahead. The castle, built by one of Albuquerque's most successful businesswomen, is worth a visit alone. Admission is by guided tour only (1.5 hours).

THE UNIVERSITY AND NOB HILL

When it was established in 1889, what's now the state's largest university was only a tiny outpost on the far side of the railroad tracks. Surrounding the campus, which sprawls for blocks, is the typical student-friendly scrum of cheap-pizza places and dilapidated bungalow rentals. To the east along Central is Nob Hill, a thriving neighborhood developed around a shopping plaza in the late 1940s and still showing that decade's distinctive style in marquees and shop facades.

The University Area

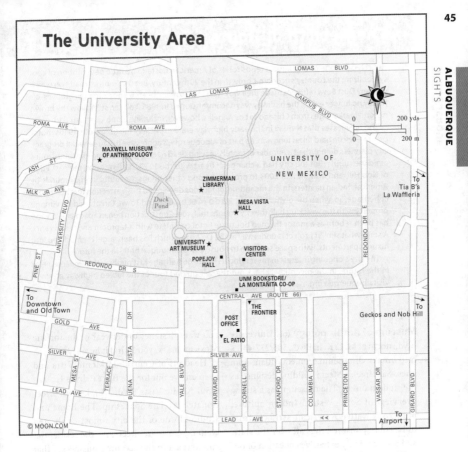

The University of New Mexico

Approximately 25,000 students are enrolled at the **University of New Mexico** (UNM) campus, the core of which is bounded by Central Avenue and University Boulevard. The school's oldest buildings are a distinct pueblo-inspired style, commissioned in the early 1900s by college president William George Tight. Trustees later fired Tight in part for his non-Ivy League aesthetics, but the style was in motion. Pueblo Revival pioneer John Gaw Meem carried on the vision through the 1940s, and even with contemporary structures now set among the original halls, it's still a remarkably harmonious vision, uniting the pastoral sanctuary feel of the great East Coast campuses with a minimalist interpretation of native New Mexican forms.

Visitors can park in a complex just inside the UNM campus across from Cornell Street. The info center, where you can pick up a detailed map, is in the southwest corner of the structure. Just across the way, the **University Art Museum** (203 Cornell Dr. NE, 505/277-4001, http://artmuseum.unm.edu, 10am-4pm Tues.-Fri., 10am-8pm Sat., $5 donation) displays treasures from the permanent fine art collection of more than 30,000 pieces from all over the globe.

Elsewhere on the grounds, you'll see such classic Meem buildings as **Mesa Vista Hall** and **Zimmerman Library**. Rest up at the bucolic duck pond, then head for the **Maxwell**

The Rebirth of Route 66

Route 66 is one of the biggest repositories of American nostalgia, a little neon ribbon of cool symbolizing the country's economic growth in the 20th century. But the "mother road," on which so many Dust Bowl refugees made their way west and so many beatniks got into their grooves, officially no longer exists; the highway was decommissioned in 1985. You can still follow the brown historic-marker signs from Chicago to Los Angeles, however, including along **Central Avenue.**

The businesses that thrived in the early highway era—especially the numerous 1940s motor courts—fell on hard times long ago. As part of Albuquerque's aggressive urban-renewal program, city planners demolished a number of motels, leaving dead neon signs standing like tombstones amid the rubble. But the city had a change of heart with the 1939 **De Anza**, on the east edge of Nob Hill, and bought it in 2003 to protect, among other things, beautiful interior murals by American Indian painters. In the meantime, *Burqueños* developed fresh affection for their neon-lit heritage. So, when the owner of the **El Vado Motel,** near Old Town, threatened his vintage property with the wrecking ball, the city bought that, too. Construction began apace and El Vado has been reborn as a motor-themed boutique hotel complete with a taproom and restaurants. A somewhat similar project is underway at the De Anza, which has been largely remodeled into luxury apartments, with space set aside to house a small boutique hotel in the future.

The city's ongoing interest in preserving its Route 66 heritage just might yield similar rebirths in the future. In the meantime, check out the self-guided tour of the fabled highway at www. visitalbuquerque.org.

Museum of Anthropology (off University Blvd., north of M. L. K. Jr. Blvd., 505/277-4405, http://maxwellmuseum.unm.edu, 10am-4pm Tues.-Sat., free), a Meem building designed as the student union. The museum has a strong overview of Southwestern Indian culture, numerous Native American artifacts from university-sponsored digs all over the state, and a surprisingly extensive collection of objects depicting cultures from around the world.

Nob Hill

At Girard Street, a neon-trimmed gate marks the start of the **Nob Hill** district, which extends east along Central Avenue about 10 blocks to Washington Boulevard. The area began to grow after 1937, when Route 66 was rejiggered to run along Central. The Nob Hill shopping plaza, at Central and Carlisle, signaled the neighborhood's success when it opened as the glitziest shopping district in town a decade later. The area went through a slump from the 1960s through the mid-1980s, but it's now lined with brightly painted facades and neon signs, making it a lively district where the quirk factor is high—whether you want designer underwear or an antique Mexican mask, you'll find it here.

Head off of Central on Monte Vista and keep an eye out for the **Bart Prince House** (3501 Monte Vista Blvd. NE), known affectionately as The Spaceship. The home and studio of one of the city's most celebrated contemporary architects, it's the residential counterpart to the eccentric businesses that flourish in this area.

NORTH VALLEY

The stretch of the river north of Central is one of Albuquerque's prettier areas, shaded with cottonwoods and dotted with patches of farmland. The scenic route through North Valley is Rio Grande Boulevard; the commercial strip is 4th Street.

Indian Pueblo Cultural Center

Just north of I-40 from Old Town, the **Indian Pueblo Cultural Center** (2401 12th St. NW, 505/843-7270, www.indianpueblo.org, 9am-5pm daily, $8.40) is a must-visit before heading to any of the nearby Indian communities. The horseshoe-shaped building (modeled after the Pueblo Bonito ruins in Chaco Canyon in northwestern New Mexico) houses a large museum that traces the history of the first settlers along the Rio Grande. Renovated in 2016, it is illustrated with some beautiful artifacts and showcases distinctive craftwork from each pueblo.

The central plaza hosts **dance performances** (11am and 2pm Sat.-Sun. Apr.-Oct., noon Sat.-Sun. Nov.-Mar.), one of the only places to see them outside of the pueblos themselves. The extensively stocked gift shop is a very good place to buy pottery and jewelry; you can also have a lunch of stew and fry bread at the Pueblo Harvest Café. Don't miss the south wing, which contains a gallery for contemporary art. At the information desk, check on ceremony schedules and get directions to the various pueblos.

Rio Grande Nature Center State Park

Explore a secluded wetland landscape at the **Rio Grande Nature Center State Park** (2901 Candelaria St. NW, 505/344-7240, www.emnrd.state.nm.us, 8am-5pm daily, $5/car). The sleek, concrete **visitors center** (10am-5pm daily) houses an exhibit on water conservation and river ecology, while just beyond is a comfortable glassed-in "living room," where you can watch birds on the pond from the comfort of a lounge chair, with the outdoor sounds piped in through speakers.

Outside, several **paved trails** run across irrigation channels and along the river, shaded by towering cottonwoods. In the spring and fall, the area draws all manner of migrating birdlife. Borrow binoculars from the staff if you want to scout on your own, or join one of the frequent **nature walks** (including full-moon tours) that take place year-round.

Los Ranchos and Corrales Scenic Byway

For a pretty drive (or bike ride) through historic villages that have been all but consumed by greater Albuquerque, head north from Old Town on Rio Grande Boulevard; you first reach **Los Ranchos,** then cross the river at Alameda to Corrales Road (Hwy. 448) and continue north up the west bank. This Corrales Scenic Byway still holds pockets of pastoral calm, a practical melding of old agricultural heritage with modern suburban trappings.

The only real sights are in central **Corrales,** two blocks west of Hwy. 448. The folk Gothic **Old San Ysidro Church** (505/897-1513, 1pm-4pm Sat.-Sun. June-Oct.) stands where the center of the village was in 1868, when its bulging adobe piers were first constructed. Every spring, the church gets a fresh coat of mud from the community. Across the road, **Casa San Ysidro** (973 Old Church Rd., 505/898-3915, www.cabq.gov/museum, guided tours $5) was the home of obsessive collectors Alan and Shirley Minge. While they lived in the place, 1952-1997, they heated with firewood and squirreled away New Mexican antiques and craftwork. It is a lovingly preserved monument to a distinct way of life. The Albuquerque Museum gives **tours** (10:30am, noon, and 1:30pm Tues.-Sat. June-Aug.) of the interior with its beautiful brickwork and wood carving; tours are less frequent September-November and February-May (9:30am and 1:30pm Tues.-Fri., 10:30am, noon, and 1:30pm Sat.). You can just show up, but it's a good idea to call to confirm the times.

ALBUQUERQUE METRO AREA

Beyond Central Avenue, Albuquerque is largely a haze of nondescript houses and shopping centers built during the 1960s and later—decades one local journalist dubbed the city's Asphalt Period. A few sights are well worth seeking out, however.

National Hispanic Cultural Center

Just south of downtown (but not quite walking distance), the modern **National Hispanic Cultural Center** (1701 4th St. SW, 505/246-2261, www.nhccnm.org) lauds the cultural contributions of Spanish speakers the world over. It has had a positive influence in the down-at-the-heels district of Barelas (even the McDonald's across the street mimics its architecture), but numerous houses—occupied by Hispanics, no less—were demolished for its construction. One woman refused the buyout, and her two small houses still sit in the parking lot, a kind of exhibit of their own.

The central attraction is the **museum** (10am-5pm Tues.-Sun., $6), which shows work ranging from the traditional *bultos* and *retablos* by New Mexican craftspeople to contemporary painting, photography, and even furniture by artists from Chile, Cuba, Argentina, and more. If you can, visit on Saturday or Sunday, when the *torreón* (tower) is open (noon-5pm) to show Frederico Vigil's amazing fresco *Mundos de Mestizaje,* a decadelong project depicting the many strands—Arab, Celtic, African—that have contributed to Hispanic culture today.

Adjacent to the museum is the largest Hispanic genealogy library in existence, as well as the giant **Roy E. Disney Center for Performing Arts.**

National Museum of Nuclear Science & History

The spiffy **National Museum of Nuclear Science & History** (601 Eubank Blvd. SE, 505/245-2137, www.nuclearmuseum.org, 9am-5pm daily, $12) covers everything you wanted to know about the nuclear era, from the development of the weapon on through current energy issues. Exhibits cover the ghastly elements of the atomic bomb, but also wonky tech details (check out the display of decoders set in suitcases for emergency deployment) and pop-culture artifacts, such as "duck and cover" films from the Cold War. Don't miss the beautiful posters by Swiss American artist Erik Nitsche. The adjoined nine-acre Heritage Park offers close-up views of a vast collection of missiles, jets and rocket launchers.

★ Sandia Peak Tramway

The longest tramway of its type in the world, the **Sandia Peak Tramway** (505/856-7325, www.sandiapeak.com, $1 parking, $25 round-trip, $15 one-way) whisks passengers 2.7 miles and 4,000 feet up, along a continuous line of Swiss-made cables. The ride from Albuquerque's northeast foothills to the crest takes about 15 minutes; the view of the cityscape and beyond along the way can be breathtaking. It's a convenient way to get to the ski area in winter, too, and in summer and fall, you can hike along the ridgeline a few miles to the visitors center. The old restaurant at the top has been demolished to make way for a new one due to open in 2019. The service runs frequently year-round (9am-9pm daily June-Aug., 9am-8pm Wed.-Mon., 5pm-8pm Tues. Sept.-May)—but check the website for periodic maintenance closures in fall and spring.

At the base of the tram, there's a small, free museum about skiing in New Mexico, and even from this point, the view across the city is very good. The remodeled Mexican restaurant here, **Sandiago's** (38 Tramway Rd. NE, 505/856-6692, 11am-9pm Mon., Wed.-Sun., 4:30pm-9pm Tues., $14-28), has morphed into a sophisticated choice for a sunset margarita—the cucumber spritzer is especially refreshing in the summer months.

★ Petroglyph National Monument

Albuquerque's west side is marked by the black boulders of **Petroglyph National Monument,** some of which are the canvas for 20,000 carved lizards, birds, and assorted other beasts. Most of the images, which were created by chipping away the dark "varnish" of the volcanic rock to reach the paler stone beneath, are 400-700 years old, while others may date back three millennia. A few later examples of rock art include Maltese crosses

1: Sandia Peak Tramway 2: Petroglyph National Monument

1

2

made by Spanish settlers and initials left by explorers (not to mention a few by idle teenagers in more recent years).

Stop in first at the **visitors center** (Unser Blvd. at Western Tr., 505/899-0205, www. nps.gov/petr, 8am-5pm daily) for park maps, flyers on flora and fauna, and general orientation. From here, you will have to drive to the major trails that crisscross the monument's 7,500 acres: **Boca Negra Canyon,** a short, paved loop and the only fee area ($1/car on weekdays, $2 on weekends); **Piedras Marcadas Canyon,** a 1.5-mile unpaved loop; and **Rinconada Canyon,** an out-and-back hike (2.2 miles round-trip) that can be tedious going in some spots because the ground is sandy. The clearest, most impressive images can be found here, in the canyon at the end of the trail. Everywhere in the park area, keep an eye out for millipedes, which thrive in this environment; dead, their curled-up shells resemble the spirals carved on the rocks—coincidence?

For the best overview (literally) of this area's geology, head for the back (west) side of the parkland, the **Volcanoes Day Use Area** (9am-5pm daily), where three cinder cones mark Albuquerque's western horizon. Access is via Atrisco Vista Boulevard (exit 149) off I-40; turn right (east) 4.3 miles north of the highway at a dirt road to the parking area.

From this vantage point, you can look down on the lava "fingers" that stretch east to form the crumbled edges of the escarpment where the petroglyphs are found. The fingers were formed when molten rock flowed between sandstone bluffs, which later crumbled away. The volcanoes were last reported emitting steam in 1881, though a group of practical jokers set smoky fires in them in the 1950s, briefly convincing city dwellers of an impending eruption. But the peaks are not entirely dead: Patches of green plants flourish around the steam vents that stud the hillocks, particularly visible on the middle of the three volcanoes.

Anderson Abruzzo Albuquerque International Balloon Museum

Boosters of Albuquerque's hot-air balloon scene—which has been flourishing since the first rally in 1972—include locals Ben Abruzzo, Larry Newman, and Maxie Anderson, who in 1978 made the first Atlantic crossing by balloon in the *Double Eagle II* helium craft. Abruzzo and Anderson also crossed the Pacific and set a long-distance record (5,678 miles) in the *Double Eagle V.*

These pioneers are honored at the so-called **BaMu** (9201 Balloon Museum Dr. NE, 505/768-6020, www.balloonmuseum.com, 9am-5pm Tues.-Sun., $6), in Balloon Fiesta Park just off Alameda Boulevard. The displays are a great mix of historical background, interactive physics lessons, and inspiring footage of record-setting balloon ventures. As long as you don't dwell too long on the zeppelin exhibit, complete with china and tableware from the *Hindenburg,* you may come away sufficiently inspired by the grace of balloons to seek out a ride in one yourself.

Coronado Historic Site

Though named for Spanish explorer Francisco Vásquez de Coronado, who camped on this lush riverside spot during his 1540 search for gold, the **Coronado Historic Site** (485 Kuaua Rd., Bernalillo, 505/867-5351, 8:30am-5pm Wed.-Mon., $5) is actually a Native American relic, the partially restored pueblo of Kuaua (Tiwa for "evergreen"), inhabited between 1300 and the early 1600s. The centerpiece is one of the partially sunken kivas, or ceremonial chambers, inside which murals of life-size human figures and animals were discovered in the 1930s. The images were carefully salvaged, then reproduced in the kiva by Velino Herrera (Ma Pe Wi), a member of a key group of early American Indian figurative painters who also painted murals in the U.S. Department of the Interior in Washington DC.

Albuquerque's Hot-Air History

How did it come to be that one of the most iconic sights in Albuquerque is the pairing of Darth Vader and Yoda, each several stories tall, floating in front of the Sandias? Albuquerque, it turns out, enjoys the world's most perfect weather for navigating hot-air balloons. A phenomenon called the Albuquerque Box, created by the steep mountains adjacent to the low river bottom, enables pilots to move at different speeds at different altitudes, and even to backtrack, if necessary. Combine that with more than 300 days of sunshine per year, and it's no wonder that now more than 700 balloons convene each October to show off their colors and compete in precision flying contests.

The city's air currents were discovered to be friendly to balloons for the first time in 1882. That was when an adventurous bartender piloted a hydrogen-filled craft into the sky as part of the New Town's Fourth of July celebrations, much to the delight of the assembled crowd, which had waited almost two days for *The City of Albuquerque*, as the balloon was dubbed, to fill. "Professor" Park Tassell, the showman pilot, went aloft alone and landed successfully; the only mishap was that a ballast sandbag was emptied on a spectator's head.

Ninety years passed, and in 1972, Albuquerque again drew attention to this venerable pursuit. This was the year the first balloon fiesta was held, with 13 aircraft participating. The gathering, a rudimentary race, was organized as a publicity stunt for a local radio station's 50th-anniversary celebration. The spectacle drew 20,000 people, most of whom had never even seen a hot-air balloon before—but within a few short years, the event was internationally renowned, and the **Balloon Fiesta** has been a hugely popular annual event ever since.

With Herrera's reproductions in place, this is the only opportunity to witness the usually protected, sacred space of a kiva close to how it originally appeared. And once you've seen the complete images, it's easier to pick out the representations on the original frescoes mounted in the visitors center—some of the oldest examples of indigenous art on display anywhere in the United States.

Join a tour of the kiva, if possible—the guides add a lot to the story. On occasional weekends, there are traditional craft and music demonstrations as well. And even if none of that is going on, this is a beautiful spot for a picnic. Facing the river and the mountains, with the city hidden from view behind a dense screen of cottonwoods, you get a sense of the lush, calm life along the Rio Grande in the centuries before the Spanish arrived. To reach the monument, exit I-25 in Bernalillo and head west on Highway 550; Kuaua Road is on your right, before the Santa Ana Star casino.

Gruet Winery

Spanish missionaries planted the first vineyards in North America in New Mexico in the 17th century, and the industry persisted until a series of floods finally wiped out the vines by the 1920s. So New Mexico's current wine scene, while strong, is still somewhat young. One of the state's best wineries, **Gruet** (8400 Pan American Fwy. NE, 505/821-0055, www. gruetwinery.com, 10am-7pm Mon.-Sat., noon-6pm Sun.) began producing its excellent sparkling wines (the Gruet family hails from Champagne, France) only in 1987; look out especially for its nonvintage sparkling rosé, which is delicious and affordable. The tasting room serves five pours for $7; **tours** of the winery are at 2pm.

Sports and Recreation

From the river basin up to mountain peaks, Albuquerque has plenty to keep you active in the outdoors for days on end. Late summer (after rains have started and fire danger is past) and fall are the best times to head to the higher elevations on the Sandia Mountains. Once the cooler weather sets in, the scrub-covered foothills and the bare, rocky West Mesa are more hospitable. The valley along the Rio Grande, running through the center of the city, is remarkably pleasant year-round: mild in winter and cool and shady in summer. As everywhere in the desert, always pack extra layers of clothing and plenty of water before you set out, and don't go charging up Sandia Peak (10,678 feet above sea level) your first day off the plane.

TOP EXPERIENCE

★ BALLOONING

For most people, the Balloon Fiesta is a spectator event, but the truth is you can go up, up, and away yourself just about any day of the year, thanks to the ideal conditions nearly always present around Albuquerque. A trip is admittedly an investment (and you have to wake up well before dawn for sunrise trips), but there's no other ride quite like it and the views can forever change how you see the city. One of the longest established operations is **Rainbow Ryders** (505/823-1111, www.rainbowryders.com, from $139 pp). Typically, you're up in the balloon for about an hour, depending on wind conditions, and you get a champagne toast when you're back on solid ground.

HIKING

Between the West Mesa and the East Mountains, there are plenty of day hikes to choose from. The least strenuous is the *bosque* (the wooded area along the Rio Grande), where level paths lead through groves of cottonwoods, willows, and olive trees. The **Rio Grande Nature Center State Park** (2901 Candelaria St. NW, 505/344-7240, www.rgnc.org, 8am-5pm daily, $3/car) is the best starting point for any walk around the area.

On the east side, the easiest approach to the mountains is to take the tram to **Sandia Peak** or drive up the east face of the mountain via scenic byway Highway 536, aka the Crest Road, to the **Sandia Crest Visitor Center** ($3/car). The 1.6-mile **Crest Trail** links the two points (tram and visitors center), with possible smaller loops in between. The views are fantastic, and the river-stone Kiwanis Cabin, a Civilian Conservation Corps project on a cliff edge, makes a nice picnic destination about halfway along.

In the fall, a hike in **Fourth of July Canyon,** in the Manzano Mountains east of the city, is a wonderful place to see the leaves changing color.

For a little elevation gain, head to the Sandia foothills, ideal in the winter but a little hot in the summertime. The best access is at **Elena Gallegos Picnic Area** (7am-9pm daily Apr.-Oct., 7am-7pm daily Nov.-Mar., $1 weekdays, $2 weekends), east of Tramway Boulevard and north of Academy, at the end of Simms Park Road.

The foothills are also the starting point for the popular but tough **La Luz Trail,** a 7.5-mile ascent to the Sandia Crest Visitor Center. The trail has a 12 percent grade at certain points, and passes through four climate zones (pack lots of layers) as you climb 3,200 vertical feet. Near the top, you can take a spur that leads north to the Sandia Crest observation point or continue on the main trail south to the ski area and the Sandia Peak Tramway, which you can take back down the mountain.

1: hot-air ballooning 2: Rio Grande Nature Center State Park 3: Routes, which rents bikes in Old Town and runs city cycling tours

Birding on the Peak

In the dead of winter, Sandia Peak does not seem hospitable to life in any form, much less flocks of delicate-looking birds the size of your fist, fluffing around cheerfully in the frigid air. But that's precisely what you'll see if you visit right after a big snowfall. These are rosy finches, a contrary, cold-loving variety (sometimes called "refrigerator birds") that migrate from as far north as the Arctic tundra to the higher elevations of New Mexico, which must seem relatively tropical by comparison.

What's special about Sandia is that it draws all three species of rosy finch, which in turn draws dedicated birders looking to add the finches to their life lists, and it's one of the few places to see them that's close to a city and accessible by car. So, if you see the finches—they're midsize brown or black birds with pink bellies, rumps, and wings—you'll probably also spy some human finch fans. But they might not have time to talk, as it's not unheard-of for the most obsessive birders—those on their "big year," out to spot as many species as possible in precisely 365 days—to fly in to Albuquerque, drive to the crest, eyeball the finches, and drive right back to the airport again.

Ideally, you'd have someone pick you up at the bottom, because the 2.5-mile trail from the tram back to the trailhead has no shade. (You might be tempted to take the tram up and hike down, but the steep descent can be deadly to toes and knees.) The La Luz trailhead ($3/car) is at the far north end of Tramway Boulevard, just before the road turns west.

BIKING

Albuquerque maintains a great network of paved trails in the city, and the mountains and foothills have challenging dirt tracks. The most visitor-friendly bike store in town is Routes (404 San Felipe St. NW, 505/933-5667, www.routesrentals.com, 8am-7pm Mon.-Fri., 7am-7pm Sat.-Sun. Mar.-Oct., 9am-6pm Mon.-Fri., 8am-6pm Sat.-Sun. Nov-Feb., $20/4 hours, $35/day), which rents city cruisers, mountain bikes, and more at its handy location in Old Town; pickup and drop-off from hotels is free. It also runs fun daylong bike tours along the Rio Grande (from $50), and rents snowshoes ($20/day) in the winter.

Road Biking

Recreational cyclists should look no farther than the river, where the Paseo del Bosque, a 16-mile-long, completely flat biking and jogging path, runs through the Rio Grande Valley State Park. The northern starting point is at Alameda/Rio Grande Open Space (7am-9pm daily Apr.-Oct., 7am-7pm daily Nov.-Mar.) on Alameda Boulevard. You can also reach the trail through the Rio Grande Nature Center State Park (www.rgnc.org, 8am-5pm daily, $3/car), at the end of Candelaria, and at several other major intersections along the way. For details on this and other bike trails in Albuquerque, download a map from the city's bike info page (www.cabq.gov/bike), or pick up a free copy at bike shops around town.

Corrales, in the far North Valley, is also good for an afternoon bike ride: The speed limit on the main street is low, and you can dip into smaller side streets and bike along the acequias.

A popular and more challenging tour is up to Sandia Peak via the Crest Road on the east side—you can park and ride from any point, but cyclists typically start somewhere along Highway 14 north of I-40, then ride up Highway 536, which winds 13.5 miles along increasingly steep switchbacks to the crest. The New Mexico Touring Society (www.nmts.org) lists descriptions of other routes and organizes group rides.

Mountain Biking

Mountain bikers can take the Sandia Peak Tramway to the ski area, then rent wheels ($60/day) to explore the 30 miles of wooded trails. Bikes aren't allowed on the tram, though, so if you have your own ride, you can drive around the east side of the mountain.

Also on the east side of the mountains, a whole network of trails leads off Highway 337 (south of I-25), through **Otero Canyon** and other routes through the juniper-studded Manzanos. Or stay in the city and ride the popular 16-mile long **Trail 365**, which covers a nice mix of terrain without being too difficult; access it via the Elena Gallegos Open Space Park. The trail is part of the **Sandia Foothills Trails**, a vast network of dirt tracks all along the edge of the Northeast Heights. Locals built a small but fun BMX terrain park at **Embudo Canyon;** park at the end of Indian School Road.

SWIMMING

Beat the heat at the **Rio Grande Pool** (1410 Iron Ave. SW, 505/848-1397, noon-5pm daily June-mid-Aug., $2.50), Albuquerque's nicest public place to take a dip; the outdoor 25-meter pool is shaded by giant cottonwoods.

WINTER SPORTS

Sandia Peak Ski Area (505/242-9052, www. sandiapeak.com, $55 full-day lift ticket) is open mid-December-mid-March, though it often takes until about February for a good base to build up. The 10 main trails, serviced by four lifts, are not dramatic, but they are good and long. The area is open daily in the holiday season, then Wednesday-Sunday for the rest of the winter.

Sandia Peak also has plenty of opportunities for cross-country skiing. Groomed trails start from **Capulin Springs Snow Play Area** (9:30am-3:30pm Fri.-Sun. in winter, $3/ car), where there are also big hills for tubing and sledding. Look for the parking lot nine miles up Highway 536 to the crest. Farther up on the mountain, **10K Trail** is usually groomed for cross country skiers, as is a service road heading south to the upper tramway terminal; the latter is wide and relatively level, good for beginners. For trail conditions, call or visit the Sandia **ranger station** (505/281-3304) on Highway 337 in Tijeras.

SPAS

Betty's Bath & Day Spa (1835 Candelaria Rd. NW, 505/341-3456, www.bettysbath.com) is the place to get pampered, whether with a massage and a facial or with an extended dip in one of two outdoor communal hot tubs. One is co-ed and the other for women only; both have access to dry saunas and cold plunges—a bargain at just $14. Private reservations are available most evenings.

Closer to downtown, **Albuquerque Baths** (1218 Broadway NE, 505/243-3721, www.abqbaths.com) has similar facilities, though only one communal tub, which is solar-heated; the sauna is done in Finnish cedar. The reasonable rates ($18/two hours) include the use of robes and sandals, and massages are available, too.

SPECTATOR SPORTS

Minor-league baseball thrives in Albuquerque, apparently all because of some clever name: The so-so Dukes petered out a while back, but a fresh franchise, under the name of the **Albuquerque Isotopes,** has been drawing crowds since 2003. It's hard to judge whether the appeal is the cool **Isotopes Park** (1601 Avenida Cesar Chavez NE, 505/924-2255, www.albuquerquebaseball.com), the whoopee-cushion theme nights, or just the name, drawn from an episode of *The Simpsons*. Regardless, a summer night under the ballpark lights is undeniably pleasant; it helps that you can usually get good seats for $15.

Burqueños also go crazy for UNM Lobos **basketball,** packing the raucous University Arena, aka **The Pit** (Avenida Cesar Chavez at University Blvd., 505/925-5626, www. golobos.com).

Albuquerque's newest sports team is **New Mexico United** (505/209-7529, www. newmexicoutd.com), which played its inaugural season in 2019 in the United Soccer League's second division. Matches are played at Isotopes Park from spring until fall, with most tickets ranging $13-39. As the state's only professional soccer team, the club has quickly gathered an enthusiastic following.

Entertainment and Events

NIGHTLIFE

Albuquerque's drinking dens can host a remarkable cross section of subcultures, and even the most chic-appearing places could see a Sandia National Laboratories physicist and a veteran Earth Firster propping up the bar next to well-groomed professionals.

That said, the city's main bar and club scene, in a few square blocks of downtown, can feel a bit generic, with free-flowing beer specials for non-choosy students. It ends in a rowdy scene after closing time on weekends, when crowds spill out onto several blocks of Central that are closed to car traffic. So, although this area does have a few good bars, you'll find more interesting entertainment elsewhere.

Downtown

The **Hotel Andaluz lobby** (125 2nd St. NW, 505/923-9080) touts itself as "Albuquerque's living room"—hotelier Conrad Hilton's original vision for the place—and it's a comfy spot to sip cocktails and nibble tapas, especially if you reserve one of the six private booths ("Casbahs") on the weekend. **Ibiza** (4pm-11pm Sun.-Thurs., 4pm-1am Fri.-Sat.), its rooftop bar, is a sleek and cozy spot to watch the sunset over drinks.

A great spot to watch the Sandia Mountains turn pink at sunset, the **Apothecary Lounge** (806 Central Ave. SE, 505/242-0040, 3pm-10:30pm Sun.-Thurs., 3pm-midnight Fri.-Sat.) is the rooftop bar at the Parq Central hotel in East Downtown. Fitting with the historic atmosphere of the hotel, the bar specializes in vintage cocktails.

The best all-purpose casual bars downtown are at the same address. Upstairs, **Anodyne** (409 Central Ave. NW, 505/244-1820, 4pm-2am Mon.-Sat., 7pm-midnight Sun.) is a long, wood-floored room filled with pool tables and thrift-store sofas. Choose from more than a hundred beers, and get some quarters to plug in to the good collection of pinball machines.

Happy hour is 4pm-8pm Monday-Thursday, and until 9pm on Friday. Downstairs, the more cavernous **Sister** (505/242-4900, www.sisterthebar.com, 11am-2am Mon.-Sat., 11am-midnight Sun.) has tacos, live bands, and more pinball.

The University and Nob Hill

In the Nob Hill shopping plaza, **Gecko's** (3500 Central Ave. SE, 505/262-1848, 11am-late daily) is a good place for finger food (anything from taquitos to buttermilk onion rings) and a drink in the sidewalk seats. Sporting its own breezy patio, the venerable **O'Niell's** (4310 Central Ave. SE, 505/255-6782, 11am-midnight Sun.-Thurs., 11am-1am Fri.-Sat.) is a great Irish pub that draws a varied crowd, whether for the quiz nights or weekend folk bands; the kitchen is open until 11pm. There's a second location in the Northeast Heights with the same hours (3301 Juan Tabo Blvd. NE, 505/293-1122).

THE ARTS

It's no stretch to say Albuquerque has the liveliest theater scene in the Southwest, with dozens of troupes in action. The standbys are the black box **Vortex Theatre** (2900 Carlisle Blvd. NE, 505/247-8600, www.vortexabq.org), running since 1976, and the more standard repertory **Albuquerque Little Theatre** (224 San Pasquale St. SW, 505/242-4750, www.albuquerquelittletheatre.org), founded in 1930 and performing in an intimate 500-seat Works Progress Administration-era building. Up in the North Valley, the **Adobe Theater** (9813 4th St. NW, www.adobetheater.org) has been running in some form since 1957. A recent renovation has spruced the place up, and its full calendar features performances based on the works of nationally-known playwrights as well as collaborative pieces by local artists.

The 70-seat **Cell Theatre** (700 1st St. NW, www.liveatthecell.com) is home to the

Albuquerque Beer Culture

Burque's beer scene is a lively one, with taprooms regularly putting on some of the city's best events and enticing with new drafts and food pairings; naturally, the *Albuquerque Journal* has a dedicated Brews News beat. These are some of the best spots in town; for more, see the New Mexico Brewers Guild (www.nmbeer.org). For car-free sampling, check out The Hopper trolley tour (www.abqtrolley.com; last Friday evening of the month; $20) that stops at four or five breweries.

just a few of New Mexico's many craft beers

- **Il Vicino** (3403 Central Ave. NE, 505/266-7855, 11am-11pm Sun.-Thurs., 11am-11pm Fri.-Sat.): This Nob Hill pizza parlor, the original of the three locations now in Albuquerque, has been brewing its own beer since 1994 and has a large brewing facility, the Canteen Brewhouse, at 2381 Aztec Road Northeast (noon-10pm Mon.-Thurs., noon-11pm Fri.-Sat., noon-10pm Sun.). There's also a Canteen Taproom serving the same brews with close-up views of the Sandias (427 Tramway Blvd. NE, 505/200-2344, 11am-11pm Mon.-Sat., noon-10pm Sun.).

- **Kellys Brew Pub** (3222 Central Ave. SE, 505/262-2739, 11am-10pm Mon.-Thurs., 11am-11pm Fri., 8am-11pm Sat., 8am-10pm Sun.): Another long-established Nob Hill brewery, set in an old car showroom. Great outdoor seating.

- **Matanza** (3225 Central Ave. NE, 505/312-7305, 4pm-10pm Mon., 11:30am-10pm Tues.-Thurs., 11:30am-midnight Fri.-Sat., 11am-10pm Sun.): A cornerstone of the Nob Hill scene, with 100 craft beers on tap and tasty "sangwiches," other bar food with New Mexican flair, and a popular Sunday brunch.

- **Marble Brewery** (111 Marble Ave. NW, 505/243-2739, noon-midnight Mon.-Sat., noon-10:30pm Sun.): Pleasantly out of the downtown fray, with a dog-friendly outdoor area featuring eclectic bands. There's also the Marble Taproom in Northeast Heights (9904 Montgomery Blvd NE, 505/323-4030, noon-midnight Mon.-Sat., noon-10:30pm Sun.).

- **Dialogue Brewing** (1501 1st St. NW, 505/585-1501, 4pm-10pm Mon., 4pm-11pm Tues.-Thurs., 2pm-11:45pm Fri., noon-11.45pm Sat., 2pm-10pm Sun.): Funky and friendly brewery that fosters a strong community feel and showcases works by local artists. Beers on tap range from a Belgian ale to a dry stout.

- **Boese Brothers** (601 Gold Ave. SW, 505/382-7060, 3pm-midnight Sun.-Mon., 3pm-midnight Tues.-Thurs., 3pm-2am Fri., 1pm-2am Sat., 3pm-10pm Sun.): This downtown brewery, opened in 2015, is big and lively, usually with six house brews on tap.

- **Tractor Brewing**: This popular place has three locations near central Albuquerque: its brewery, in the industrial area north of downtown (1800 4th St. NW, 505/243-6752, 3pm-late Mon.-Thurs., 1pm-late Fri.-Sat., 1pm-midnight Sun.), an airy bar in Nob Hill (118 Tulane St. SE, 505/433-5654, noon-midnight Sun.-Thurs., noon-2am Fri.-Sat.), and an outpost in Four Hills (13170-C Central Ave. SE, 505/554-2462, 11am-midnight Sun.-Thurs., 11am-2am Fri.-Sat.). All three have low-fi live music.

- **La Cumbre Brewing** (3313 Girard Blvd. NE, 505/872-0225, noon-late daily): La Cumbre is in a fairly isolated industrial area, with only the occasional food truck for sustenance, but locals love this beer.

long-running FUSION, a theater company of professional union actors. It often runs recent Broadway dramas.

A more avant-garde group is the two-decade-old Tricklock (110 Gold Ave. SW, 505/414-3738, www.tricklock.com), which develops physically oriented shows at its "performance laboratory" downtown. It also hosts an international theater festival (in Jan. and Feb.). The neighboring Box Performance Space (114 Gold Ave. SW, 505/404-1578, www.theboxabq.com) hosts various improv groups and satirical comedians, and it conducts workshops.

Also see what Blackout Theatre (505/672-8648, www.blackouttheatre.com) is up to—it doesn't have its own space, but it mounts interesting shows in interesting places: improv Dickens, for instance, or an interactive alien invasion commemorating the UFO incident at Roswell. Other groups of note include the Duke City Repertory Theatre (505/797-7081, www.dukecityrep.com) and Mother Road Theatre Company (505/243-0596, www.motherroad.org).

CINEMA

Century 14 Downtown (100 Central Ave. SW, 505/243-9555, www.cinemark.com) and AMC Albuquerque 12 (3810 Las Estancias Way SW, 505/544-2360, www.amctheatres.com) both devote most of their screens to blockbusters, while the latest indie and art films are shown at The Guild (3405 Central Ave. NE, 505/255-1848, www.guildcinema.com), a snug single screen in Nob Hill.

LIVE MUSIC

Albuquerque's arts scene graces a number of excellent stages. The most beautiful is the city-owned KiMo Theatre (423 Central Ave. NW, 505/768-3544, www.cabq.gov/kimo), often hosting locally written plays and dance, as well as the occasional musical performance and film screening.

Bigger classical and folkloric acts perform at the Roy E. Disney Center for Performing Arts at the National Hispanic Cultural Center (1701 4th St. SW, 505/724-4771, www.nhccnm.org), a modernized Mesoamerican pyramid that contains three venues, the largest of which is a 691-seat proscenium theater. This is the place to catch a performance by visiting or local flamenco artists—with the National Institute of Flamenco headquartered in Albuquerque, there's often someone performing.

UNM's Popejoy Hall (UNM campus, 505/277-3824, http://popejoypresents.com/) hosts the New Mexico Symphony Orchestra (which also plays at the Rio Grande Zoo in the summer).

A more intimate classical event is Chatter Sunday (505/234-4611, www.chatterabq.org, 10:30am Sun., $15). Originally known as Church of Beethoven, this chamber-music show aims to offer all the community and quiet of church, with none of the religious overtones. It takes place at the funky coffeehouse The Kosmos (1715 5th St. NW), part of a larger warehouse-turned-art-studios complex. The "service" lasts about an hour, with two musical performances, interspersed with a poem and a few minutes of silent contemplation. It's all fueled by free espresso.

Flamenco enthusiasts should check the schedule at Casa Flamenca (401 Rio Grande Blvd. NW, 505/247-0622, www.casaflamenca.org) in Old Town. The dance school in an old adobe house hosts a monthly tablao, in which local teachers and visiting experts perform.

For rock concerts, the biggest venue in town is Isleta Amphitheater (5601 University Blvd. SE, www.isletaamphitheater.net), with space for some 12,000 people. The next step down is one of the Albuquerque-area casinos, the ritziest of which is Sandia Casino (I-25 at Tramway, 800/526-9366, www.sandiacasino.com), which has a 4,000-seat outdoor amphitheater. Isleta Casino (11000 Broadway SE, 505/724-3800, www.isleta.com), not to be confused with the amphitheater, has a smaller indoor venue, as does Laguna Pueblo's Route

1: KiMo Theatre 2: Sunshine Theater

Ceremonial Dances

This is an approximate schedule for dances at Albuquerque-area pueblos. Pueblo feast days are always on the same date and generally open to all, but seasonal dances (especially Easter and other spring rituals) can vary, and are sometimes closed to visitors. Confirm details and start times with the Indian Pueblo Cultural Center (505/843-7270, www.indianpueblo.org) before setting out.

- **January 1:** Jemez: Los Matachines; Kewa (Santo Domingo): corn dance
- **January 6:** Most pueblos: various dances to honor new tribal officials
- **Easter:** Most pueblos: various dances
- **May 1:** San Felipe: Feast of San Felipe
- **Memorial Day weekend:** Jemez: craft show and powwow
- **June 13:** Sandia: Feast of San Antonio
- **June 29:** Santa Ana and Kewa (Santo Domingo): Feast of San Pedro
- **July 14:** Cochiti: Feast of San Bonaventura
- **July 26:** Santa Ana: Feast of Santa Ana
- **August 2:** Jemez: Feast of Santa Persingula
- **August 4:** Kewa (Santo Domingo): Feast of Santo Domingo
- **August 10:** Jemez: Pueblo Independence Day and Fair
- **August 15:** Zia: Feast of the Assumption of Our Blessed Mother
- **August 28:** Isleta: Feast of San Agustín (ends September 4)
- **Labor Day:** Kewa (Santo Domingo): craft market
- **November 12:** Jemez: Feast of San Diego
- **December 12:** Jemez: Los Matachines
- **December 25:** Santa Ana, Kewa (Santo Domingo), and Zia: various dances
- **December 26-28:** Kewa (Santo Domingo): corn dance; also dances at most other pueblos

66 Casino (14500 Central Ave. SW, 866/352-7866, www.rt66casino.com).

Also see what's on at **El Rey Theater** (620 Central Ave. SW, 505/510-2582, https://elreylive.com) and **Sunshine Theater** (120 Central Ave. SW, 505/764-0249, www.sunshinetheaterlive.com)—both converted movie houses, they have excellent sightlines. **Outpost Performance Space** (210 Yale Blvd. SE, 505/268-0044, www.outpostspace.org) books very good world music and dance acts. To catch touring indie rockers or the local crew about to hit it big, head to the very professional **Launchpad** (618 Central Ave. SW, 505/764-8887, www.launchpadrocks.com).

FESTIVALS AND EVENTS

The city's biggest annual event is the **Albuquerque International Balloon Fiesta** (505/821-1000, www.balloonfiesta.com, $10), nine days in October dedicated to

New Mexico's official state aircraft, with more than 700 hot-air balloons of all colors, shapes, and sizes gathering at a dedicated park on the north side of town, west of I-25. During the fiesta, the city is packed with "airheads," who claim this is the best gathering of its kind in the world. If you go, don't miss an early morning mass ascension, when the balloons glow against the dark sky, then lift silently into the air in a great wave. Parking can be a nightmare—take the park-and-ride bus, or ride a bike (valet parking available!).

In April is the equally colorful **Gathering of Nations Powwow** (505/836-2810, www. gatheringofnations.com), the largest tribal get-together in the United States, with more than 3,000 dancers and singers in full regalia from over 500 tribes coming together at the Tingley Coliseum and Expo New Mexico. Miss Indian World earns her crown by showing off traditional talents such as spearfishing or storytelling.

The eclectic and never dull two-day world-music fest **¡Globalquerque!** (www. globalquerque.com) runs in mid-September. It draws top-notch pop and traditional performers from around the world as well as plenty of international arts and crafts and cuisine. Concerts take place at the National Hispanic Cultural Center.

Just after Labor Day, the state's agricultural roots get their due at the **New Mexico State Fair** (www.exponm.com): two weeks of fried foods, prizewinning livestock, midway rides, and really excellent rodeos, which often end with shows by country music legends.

In early November, don't miss the **Marigold Parade** (505/363-1326, www. muertosymarigolds.org), celebrating the Mexican Day of the Dead and general South Valley pride. The parade is a procession of skeletons, cars bedecked in flowers, and a little civil rights activism.

For the **winter holiday season,** the city is trimmed with luminarias (paperbag lanterns), especially in Old Town and the Country Club neighborhood just to the south. The Albuquerque Botanic Garden (www.cabq.gov/culturalservices/biopark/garden) is decked out with holiday lights and model trains for much of December, and ABQ Ride, the city bus service, offers a bus tour around the prettiest neighborhoods on Christmas Eve.

Shopping

Old Town and its environs are where you can pick up traditional American Indian jewelry and pottery for very reasonable prices, while **Nob Hill** is the commercial center of Albuquerque's counterculture, with body-piercing studios adjacent to comic book shops next to herbal apothecaries.

OLD TOWN

The galleries and gift shops around the plaza can blur together after just a little bit of browsing, but the **Blue Portal Gallery** (2107 Church St. NW, 505/243-6005, 11am-3pm Tues.-Thurs., Fri.-Sat. 10am-4pm, 1pm-4pm Sun.) is a nice change, with well-priced and often very refined arts and crafts, from quilts to woodwork, by Albuquerque's senior citizens. And the **street vendors** set up on the east side of the plaza are all artisans selling their own work, at fair prices.

For a great selection of interesting New Mexico gifts and books, as well as local herbal treatments, visit **Duran Central Pharmacy** (1815 Central Ave. NW, 505/247-4141, 8:30am-7pm Mon.-Fri., 8:30am-3pm Sat., 9am-3pm Sun.), just outside Old Town.

DOWNTOWN

An emporium of American Indian goods, **Skip Maisel's Indian Jewelry & Crafts** (510 Central Ave. SW, 505/242-6526, 9am-5pm Mon.-Sat.) feels like a relic from downtown's

The Albuquerque Art Scene

When it comes to art, the Duke City may not have the buzz or the wealth that's concentrated farther north in Santa Fe, but it does have DIY energy, refreshing diversity, and a long history, thanks to the highly respected fine arts program at the University of New Mexico. On the first Friday of every month, the citywide Artscrawl (www.artscrawlabq.org, 5-8pm) keeps galleries and shops open late in Nob Hill, Old Town, and downtown. The rest of the time, check out these arts spaces and galleries:

- **Exhibit/208** (208 Broadway SE, www.exhibit208.com, 10am-4pm Thurs.-Sat.): Work by full-time artists, some well-known in the state. Openings are usually the second Friday evening of the month.

- **516 Arts** (516 Central Ave. SW, 505/242-1445, www.516arts.org, noon-5pm Tues.-Sat.): Polished downtown space with numerous international artists.

- **Harwood Art Center** (1114 7th St., 505/242-6367, www.harwoodartcenter.org, 9am-5pm Mon.-Thurs., 9am-4pm Fri.): Classes, exhibits, and special events, all with a strong community connection.

- **Mariposa Gallery** (3500 Central Ave. SE, 505/268-6828, 11am-6pm Mon.-Sat., noon-5pm Sun.): In Nob Hill, long established (since 1974) and eclectic, with jewelry, fiber art, and other crafts.

- **Matrix Fine Art** (3812 Central Ave. SE, 505/268-8952, 10am-4pm Tues., 10am-6pm Wed.-Sun.): In east Nob Hill, showing only New Mexico artists, usually figurative.

- **Richard Levy Gallery** (514 Central Ave. SW, 505/766-9888, 11am-4pm Tues.-Sat.): Ed Ruscha or John Baldessari alongside emerging artists.

- **Tamarind Institute** (2500 Central Ave. SE, 505/277-3901, tamarind.unm.edu, 9am-5pm Mon.-Fri.): Long-established and nationally renowned lithography center; gallery on the second floor shows expert prints.

- **Tortuga Gallery** (901 Edith Blvd. SE, 505/369-1648, www.tortugagallery.org, hours vary): Music, poetry, and more, with a super-grassroots vibe.

heyday. Whether you want a warbonnet, a turquoise-studded watch, or deerskin moccasins, it's all here in a vast, overstocked shop with kindly salespeople. Don't miss the beautiful murals above the display windows and in the foyer; they were painted in the 1930s by local Indian artists such as Awa Tsireh, whose work hangs in the New Mexico Museum of Art in Santa Fe.

Set in the old Santa Fe workshops south of downtown, **Rail Yards Market** (777 1st St. SW, www.railyardsmarket.org, 10am-2pm Sun. May-Oct.) is a festive gathering of arts and crafts, produce, snacks, and live music. It's a good place to shop for offbeat souvenirs—and

it's a great chance to see inside the majestic old buildings where locomotives for the Santa Fe line were built from the ground up.

THE UNIVERSITY AND NOB HILL

Among the various quirky boutiques in this area, of particular note is **Nob Hill Music** (3419 Central Ave. NE, 505/266-4200, noon-6pm Tues.-Thurs. and Sun., noon-8pm Fri.-Sat.), hands down the city's best record store. Flipping through vinyls here is imminently satisfying and can quickly transport you to an increasingly bygone era. And on the east edge of Nob Hill is a slew of **antiques marts.**

NORTH VALLEY

For excellent crafts, head to **Shumakolowa Native Arts** (2401 12th St. NW, 505/843-7270, www.indianpueblo.org, 9am-5:30pm daily), the shop at the Indian Pueblo Cultural Center. Not only are prices reasonable, but the staff is happy to explain the work that goes into various pieces.

Los Poblanos Farm Shop (4803 Rio Grande Blvd. NW, 505/938-2192, 9am-5pm daily) sells soaps, bath salts, and lotions scented with the organic lavender grown in the adjacent field. It also stocks an excellently curated selection of garden gear, books, kitchen supplies, and locally made snacks.

ALBUQUERQUE METRO AREA

Every Saturday and Sunday, Albuquerque's **flea market** (505/315-7661, $5 parking) takes place at the fairgrounds (enter at Gate 1, on Central just west of Louisiana). It's an interesting outlet where you can pick up anything from new cowboy boots to loose nuggets of turquoise; socks and beef jerky are also well represented. Stop off at one of the myriad food stands for a snack—refreshing aguas frescas (fruit juices, in flavors such as watermelon and tamarind) and Indian fry bread are the most popular. It allegedly starts at 7am, but most vendors get rolling around 9am and go until a little after 4pm.

If you're looking for central one-stop mall shopping, your best bet is **ABQ Uptown** (505/792-1929), where stores like the North Face, Lush, Anthropologie, and Apple are chock-a-block at the intersection of Louisiana Boulevard NE and Indian School Road NE.

Food

Albuquerque has a few dress-up establishments, but the real spirit of the city's cuisine is in its lower-rent spots where dedicated owners follow their individual visions. The more traditional New Mexican places tend to be open only for breakfast and lunch, so plan accordingly.

OLD TOWN

Aside from the few recommended here, the restaurants in the blocks immediately adjacent to the Old Town plaza are expensive and only so-so; better to walk another block or two for real New Mexican flavor, or drive a short way west on Central.

New Mexican

Look behind the magazine rack at ★ **Duran Central Pharmacy** (1815 Central Ave. NW, 505/247-4141, 9am-6:30pm Mon.-Tues., 9am-8pm Wed.-Sun., $9, cash only), and you'll find an old-fashioned lunch counter. Regulars pack this place at lunch for all the New Mexican staples: huevos rancheros, green-chile stew, and big blue corn enchilada plates.

Mexican

In a shady Old Town courtyard, **Backstreet Grill** (1919 Old Town Rd. NW, 505/842-5434, 11am-9pm daily, $12) is a great place to rest your tourist feet and enjoy a New Mexican craft beer, and maybe a green chile pizza with avocado and pine nuts. For a fuller menu, though, you're better off elsewhere.

Cafés

Inside the Albuquerque Museum, **Slate Street Café** (2000 Mountain Rd. NW, 505/243-2220, 10am-2:30pm Tues.-Fri. and Sun., 10am-3:30pm Sat., $8-14) is great for coffee and cupcakes, as well as more substantial breakfast and lunch entrées, such as a seared salmon club with applewood bacon. Its larger, original location is at 515 Slate Ave. NW (505/243-2210).

A 10-minute walk from Old Town, **Golden Crown Panadería** (1103 Mountain Rd. NW, 505/243-2424, 7am-8pm Tues.-Sat.,

10am-8pm Sun., $4-16) is a real neighborhood hangout that's so much more than a bakery. Famous for its green-chile bread and *bizcochitos* (the anise-laced state cookie), it also does pizza with blue-corn or green-chile crust, to take away or to eat at the picnic tables out back. Wash it down with a coffee milkshake.

Diners

Built on the bones of an old fast-food joint, **Central Grill** (2056 Central Ave. SW, 505/554-1424, 6:30am-4pm Mon.-Fri., 6:30am-3pm Sat.-Sun., $7) still makes quick food, but with a fresher, more homemade feel. Like a good diner should, it serves breakfast all day, and real maple syrup is an option. Its daily special plate is usually a solid deal, with a main like a grilled tortilla burger plus sides and a drink for around $10.

Fresh and Local

Founded in Santa Fe, ★ **Vinaigrette** (1828 Central Ave. SW, 505/842-5507, 11am-9pm daily, $9-18) is an excellent "salad bistro" with more substantial plates than you might imagine—its apple-cheddar chop with arugula is especially satisfying and it has sandwiches such as a Reuben and tuna melt. It's a welcome spot of healthy eating around Old Town.

Steak

With a brown, windowless cinderblock facade and a package-liquor store in the front, **Monte Carlo Steakhouse** (3916 Central Ave. SW, 505/831-2444, 11am-10pm Mon.-Sat., $9-29) doesn't do itself any favors winning over new customers. That said, it's a wondrous time machine, lined with vintage Naugahyde booths and serving good, hearty food, with scant care for calorie counts. The prime-rib special Thursday-Saturday, a softball-size green-chile cheeseburger, and marinated pork kebab all come with delicious hand-cut fries. Greek ownership means you get a tangy feta dressing on your salad and baklava for dessert. And even though there's a full bar, you're still welcome to buy wine from the package store up front and have it with your dinner, for a nominal markup.

Italian

It's not necessarily a destination from elsewhere in the city, but **Old Town Pizza Parlor** (108 Rio Grande Blvd. NW, 505/999-1949, 11am-9pm Mon.-Sat., 11am-8pm Sun., $9-15) is an unpretentious, kid-friendly place to eat in Old Town, with generously topped pizzas, ultra-creamy pastas, dense calzones, and cheesy garlic fingers. The back patio is a welcomed bonus.

DOWNTOWN

While there's no shortage of bars and coffee shops in this area, there's not exactly a huge selection of places when it comes to finding a sit-down meal; thankfully, there are a few solid options.

New Mexican

Even though it's in the middle of Albuquerque's main business district, ★ **Cecilia's Café** (230 6th St. SW, 505/243-7070, 7am-2pm Mon.-Fri., 7:30am-2pm Sat.-Sun., $8-12) feels more like a living room than a restaurant. Maybe it's the woodstove in the corner—as well as the personal attention from Cecilia and her daughters and the food that's clearly made with care. The rich, dark-red chile really shines, elevating dishes such as a chorizo burrito, chicken enchiladas, and a sopaipilla burger.

Cafés

Breakfast and lunch are served throughout the day at the inviting **Café Laurel** (1433 Central Ave. NW, 505/259-2331, 9am-3pm Tues.-Fri., Sat.-Sun. 9am-2pm, $7-9), where you can choose from a long list of mouthwatering sandwiches, quiches, sweet and savory crepes, and salads; the "Burque Turkey"—roast turkey, Swiss cheese, avocado mash, and green chile on grilled sourdough is divine.

Fresh and Local

Past the railroad tracks in EDo (East Downtown), ★ **The Grove** (600 Central

Ave. SE, 505/248-9800, 7am-4pm Tues.-Sat., 8am-3pm Sun., $6.25-13.50) draws devoted diners with its dedication to local and organic ingredients, big front windows facing Central, and a screened-in patio. The chalkboard menu features creative salads (mixed greens, roasted golden beets, asparagus, and almonds is one combo) as well as sandwiches and cupcakes; hearty breakfast dishes, such as pancakes with crème fraiche and poached eggs, are served all day.

There are a number of **farmers markets** throughout the city; one of the largest is downtown at Robinson Park on Central Avenue at 8th Street (7am-noon Sat. May-Aug., 8am-1pm Sept.-Nov.). For other markets around the city, visit www.farmersmarketsnm.org.

Italian

A popular hangout for urban pioneers in the EDo neighborhood, ★ **Farina Pizzeria** (510 Central Ave. SE, 505/243-0130, 11am-9pm Mon., 11am-10pm Tues.-Sat., 5pm-9pm Sun., $10-19) has exposed brick walls and a casual vibe. The pies come out of the wood-fired oven suitably crisp-chewy and topped with seasonal veggies. Make sure you get a cup of the Gorgonzola-crème fraîche-chive dip for your crusts—it's the upscale version of the ranch dressing that's more commonly offered. Sun.-Tues. there are pint-and-pizza combo specials as well.

Spanish

Chef James Campbell Caruso made his name in Santa Fe as a maestro of Spanish cuisine. His Albuquerque outpost, **Más Tapas y Vino** (125 2nd St. NW, 505/923-9080, 6am-3pm and 5pm-9:30pm Sun.-Thurs., 6am-3pm and 5pm-10pm Fri.-Sat., $6-15 tapas, $26-39 mains), in the Hotel Andaluz, shows off many of his best dishes, but it's not quite as chummy as his other restaurants. If you're not also visiting Santa Fe and want a creative bite of Iberian goodness, including grilled octopus and vegetarian paella, though, consider this a possible special-occasion meal. It also has happy hour from 4pm to 6pm daily.

Thanks to the large student population, this area has several great and varied spots to grab a cheap bite; Nob Hill has some upscale options, too.

New Mexican

You haven't been to Albuquerque unless you've been to ★ **The Frontier** (2400 Central Ave. SE, 505/266-0550, 5am-1am daily, $5-10), across from UNM. Everyone in the city passes through its doors at some point; pick a seat in one of the five Western-themed rooms and watch the characters file into the place. You'll want some food, of course: a green-chile-smothered breakfast burrito filled with crispy hash browns, or a juicy hamburger, or one of the signature cinnamon rolls, a deadly amalgam of flour, sugar, and some addictive drug that compels you to eat them despite all common sense.

Near the university, **El Patio** (142 Harvard Dr. SE, 505/268-4245, 8am-9pm Mon.-Sat., 11am-9pm Sun., $8-15) is the kind of old-reliable place that ex-locals get misty-eyed about after they've moved away. The green-chile-and-chicken enchiladas are high on many citywide-favorites lists and the Sunrise Burger—a hamburger with egg and bacon—makes a great case for kicking off your day with a large meat patty. It doesn't hurt that the setting, in an old bungalow with a shady outdoor space, feels like an extension of someone's home kitchen. The menu is more vegetarian-friendly than most New Mexican joints, including burrito and enchilada options. There's also a location just east of the Rio Grande (3851 Rio Grande NW, 505/433-4499, 11am-9pm Tues.- Thurs., 9am-9pm Fri.-Sun.).

Cafés

Step in to **Flying Star Café** (3416 Central Ave. SE, 505/255-6633, 7am-9:30pm Sun.-Mon., 7am-9:30pm Tues.-Thurs., 7am-10pm Fri.-Sat., $11), and you'll likely be mesmerized by the pastry case, packed with triple-ginger cookies, lemon-blueberry cheesecake, and fat éclairs. But try to look up to appreciate the all-encompassing menu: Asian noodles, hot and cold sandwiches, mac-and-cheese, and enchiladas sit alongside salads, Buddha bowls, and shrimp tacos. The food isn't always quite as great as it looks, but with speedy service and locations all over town, it's a handy place to zip in or to lounge around (Wi-Fi is free).

Great single-source coffee, attentive baristas, and a smartly designed space give the Nob Hill institution ★ **Humble Coffee** (4200 Lomas Blvd. NE, 505/289-9909, 6am-6pm Mon.-Fri., 7am-6pm Sat.-Sun.) plenty of reasons to boast—the selection of fresh pastries and savory breakfast burritos only add to its considerable appeal.

Pick up goods for a picnic at **La Montañita Co-Op** (3500 Central Ave. SE, 505/265-4631, 7am-10pm daily), where fresh breakfast burritos, sandwiches and salads are all the rage; look as well in the dairy section for samples of locally made cheese. You can make your own smoothie and grab a cup of coffee in the Market inside the **UNM Bookstore** (2301 Central Ave. NE, 505/277-9586, 8am-5pm Mon.-Fri.), across from The Frontier.

Waffles sweet or savory are the thing at **Tia B's La Waffleria** (3710 Campus Blvd. NE, 505/492-2007, 8am-2pm daily, $8-11.25), set in a funky old house with front and back patios. Of course, you can get a blue-corn waffle with eggs and scorching chile or layer your waffle with smoked salmon or ham and cheese. The adventurous can build their own, too.

Asian

The food at **Street Food Asia** (3422 Central Ave. SE, 505/260-0088, 11am-9pm Sun.-Thurs., 11am-10pm Fri.-Sat., $11-15.50) may not be as mind-blowing as it is in Asia, but there's something about its interior, with various cooking stations and lots of plastic, that does conjure a Bangkok mall food court. You can order noodles and other staples prepared in Thai, Vietnamese, Malaysian, and other styles; an authentic shaved-ice-and-bean dessert often comes free.

French

Sleek and modern **Frenchish** (3509 Central Ave. NE, 505/433-5911, 5pm-9pm Tues.-Sat., $18-32) has quickly built a reputation for serving French classics that look as good as they taste, and their personal touches shine on dishes such as a sautéed trout with capers and a braised pheasant pasta. The menu's not extensive and all the better for its focus. The three-course prix-fixe with a four-ounce filet is a bargain for $25.

A cozy restaurant with ample old-world charm, **P'tit Louis** (3218 Silver Ave. NE, 505/314-1110, 5:30pm-10pm Tues.-Wed., 11am-2:30pm and 5:30pm-10pm, Thurs.-Sat., 11am-2:30pm Sun.) serves familiar French fare such as steamed mussels, steak frites, and onion soup. There's little in the way of surprises, but the execution is first-rate and the atmosphere can't be beat. Don't leave without trying the perfectly executed crème brûlée, sure to give your meal a blissful closure.

Latin American

Guava Tree Café (118 Richmond Dr. SE, 505/990-2599, 11am-4pm Mon.-Sat., 11am-3pm Sun., $4.75-13) is a cheerful place serving succulent Cubano sandwiches, as well as pan-Central-American treats such as arepas and coconut flan, plus tropical fruit juices. It's very vegetarian-friendly, and the daily set lunch ($12.50) is a match for ravenous appetites.

Vegetarian

Mata G (116 Amherst Dr. SE, 505/266-6374, 10am-6pm Mon.-Sat., 10am-4pm Sun., $6-12.50) specializes in homemade and ready-to-eat vegetarian sandwiches, salads, and soups. There are plenty of tasty options to choose from—try the tempeh wrap, which is stuffed with vegan pork sausage, black pepper tempeh, and macaroni. There's also a hot bar with a focus on a different international cuisine daily.

1: Campo 2: Humble Coffee 3: Green Jeans Farmery 4: The Grove

NORTH VALLEY

New Mexican

For New Mexican food with a strong American Indian influence, hit the **Pueblo Harvest Café** (2401 12th St. NW, 505/724-3510, 7am-9pm Mon. Sat., 7am-4pm Sun., $9-26), at the Indian Pueblo Cultural Center. The menu has standard burgers and fries, but specialties such as a buffalo meat loaf with a mango chipotle glaze and a mutton stew are rich and earthy and hard to find elsewhere. Breakfast is also good, with blue-corn chicken and waffles and a flavorful eggs Benedict among the standouts. There's live music Friday and Saturday evenings, as well as Sunday around noon.

★ **Mary & Tito's Café** (2711 4th St. NW, 505/344-6266, 9am-6pm Mon.-Thurs., 9am-8pm Fri.-Sat., $6-12) is *the* place to go for *carne adovada,* the dish of tender pork braised in red chile, which is irresistible in what the café calls a Mexican turnover (a stuffed sopaipilla). The meat is flavorful enough to stand alone, but the fruity, bright-red-chile sauce, flecked with seeds, is so good you'll want to put it on everything. This place is such a local icon, seemingly untouched since the 1980s (note the dusty-rose vinyl seats), it won a James Beard America's Classics award. Sadly, both Mary and Tito have passed on now, leaving the place ripe for a decline in standards; so far, though, it is holding strong.

Out in Corrales, dependable **Perea's Tijuana Bar and Restaurant** (4590 Corrales Rd., 505/898-2442, 11am-2pm Mon.-Sat., $7) is open only for lunch, but if you know you'll be out this way, try to fit it in. Everything's home-cooked, from Frito pie to *carne adovada,* and the underrated green-chile cheese-burger oozes flavor.

Cafés

There are two branches of **Flying Star** up this way: one in Los Ranchos (4026 Rio Grande Blvd. NW, 505/344-6714, 6:30am-9pm Mon.-Sat., 7am-9pm Sun., $11) and another in Corrales (10700 Corrales Rd., 505/938-4717, 6:30am-9:30pm Sun.-Thurs., 6:30am-10pm Fri.-Sat., $11).

La Montañita Co-Op (2400 Rio Grande Blvd. NW, 505/242-8800, 7am-10pm daily) is a great spot to stock up on picnic goodies before outings along the river.

Fresh and Local

The restaurant at Los Poblanos Historic Inn, ★ **Campo** (4803 Rio Grande Blvd. NW, 505/344-9297, 7:30am-10:30am Mon.-Tues., 7:30am-10:30am and 5pm-9pm Wed.-Fri., 7:30am-11:30am and 5pm-9pm Sat.-Sun., $26) has been relocated to a restored dairy building and the new site is a perfect extension of a menu steeped in farm to table ethos. Local ingredients are featured heavily in menus that change seasonally; expect flawless takes on traditional New Mexican dishes with some Mediterranean influences. For breakfast, that means meals such as chilaquiles and shakshuka—poached eggs in a heavily spiced tomato sauce—while dinner can feature meals such as lavender chicken breast with winter squash and a lamb merguez. The adjoining bar is open daily from 4pm-5pm.

Firmly ensconced as one of the city's best and most inventive restaurants, ★ **Fork & Fig** (6904 Menaul Blvd. NE, 505/881-5293, 11am-8pm Mon.-Thurs., 11am-9pm Fri.-Sat.) was founded by Josh Kennon, a Le Cordon Bleu-trained chef from Deming, a few hours south of the city. His background and New Mexican heritage are reflected in unpretentious and irresistible sandwiches, burgers, salads, and wraps, such as The Fig, a burger with truffle fig aioli, bacon, and carmelized Swiss cheese, and a full-flavored Reuben with green-chile slaw. The atmosphere is industrial and modern, yet casual; reserve ahead if possible, as the space is compact and the word has long been out.

Featuring local and organic ingredients, **Seasonal Palate** (7600 Jefferson St. NE #2, 505/369-1046, 7:30am-2:30pm Mon.-Fri., $5-13) is a sunny bistro with a concise menu of refreshing salads, sandwiches, and soups. The kale super salad with grilled shrimp is a steal at $9.50, while the veggie burger on a pretzel bun will tempt carnivores. For dessert, the homemade double-chocolate brownies are far too decadent to pass up.

Indian

Venerable **Annapurna's** (5939 4th St. NW, 505/254-2424, 8am-9pm Mon.-Sat., 10am-8pm Sun., $6.25-13) for some remains the city's de facto vegetarian option, partly due to its three branches, but mostly because of its extensive menu of meat-free dishes, such as the Yogi Bowl—veggies with rice or quinoa, a *dosa* crepe, and yogurt or chutney sauce.

ALBUQUERQUE METRO AREA

Great places to eat are scattered all over the city, often in unlikely looking strip malls. These places are worth making a trip for, or will provide a pick-me-up when you're far afield.

New Mexican

Cruise down by the rail yards south of downtown to find **El Modelo** (1715 2nd St. SW, 505/242-1843, 7am-7pm daily, $3-8.60), a local go-to for a hangover-curing *chicharrón* burrito, chile-smothered spareribs, or tamales for the whole family—you can order a single tamale or a whole platter of food. Because it's really a front for a tortilla factory, the flour tortillas are also particularly tender. If the weather's nice, grab a seat at a picnic table outside and watch the freight trains go by.

Just two blocks from the National Hispanic Cultural Center, popular **Barelas Coffee House** (1502 4th St. SW, 505/843-7577, 7:30am-3pm Mon.-Fri., 7:30am-2:30pm Sat., $7) is potentially confusing to the first-timer: The attraction is not coffee, but chile—especially the red, which infuses hearty, New Mexican standards such as posole, *chicharrones,* and *menudo.* The restaurant occupies several storefronts, and even then, there's often a line out the door at lunchtime. But it's worth the wait—this is timeless food.

Cafés

In Northeast Heights, **Little Bear Coffee** (2632 Pennsylvania St. NE, 505/917-8902, 6am-9pm Mon.-Fri., 7am-7pm Sat.-Sun.) features multi-roast pour overs and methodically prepared drinks. The modern interior is simple and unfussy with open seating. In the warmer months, the covered patio is a great place to linger for an hour or two. If you like doughnuts, you're in luck; you can pair your drink with Bristol Donuts' finest—perhaps the most revered doughnuts in the city.

Fresh and Local

For one-stop noshing, head to **Green Jeans Farmery** (3600 Cutler Ave. NE, www.greenjeansfarmery.com, hours vary by store), a kind of outdoor food court and general hangout spot built from shipping containers. Pick from tacos, big sandwiches, artisanal pizza, espresso, ice cream, and an outpost of Santa Fe Brewing. It draws a nice cross section of the city's denizens.

Asian

Can't decide what kind of food you're craving? Cruise the aisles of **Talin Market World Food Fare** (88 Louisiana Blvd. SE, 505/268-0206, 8:30am-8pm Mon.-Sat., 9am-7pm Sun.), a megamarket near the fairgrounds that's stocked with items from Bombay to the United Kingdom. Its Asian stock is the largest, though, and you can get a variety of hot Laotian, Korean, and Filipino lunch items from the small cafeteria section in one corner and sweets such as pumpkin custard from the bakery. There's also a bubble-tea joint next door, and the parking lot draws a few food trucks.

Just across the parking lot from Talin is the excellent Vietnamese café **Coda Bakery** (230-C Louisiana Blvd. SE, 505/232-0085, 8:30am-6pm Mon.-Sat., 10:30am-5pm Sun., $5), which specializes in banh mi sandwiches (try the peppery meatball) and also serves chewy-sweet coconut waffles and other treats.

Accommodations

Albuquerque isn't quite a tourist mecca, which means you can find some great-value hotels; you'll pay substantially less here than you would in Santa Fe for similar amenities, for example. The only time you'll need to book in advance is early October, during Balloon Fiesta (when prices are usually higher).

UNDER $100

Funky and affordable, the **Mother Road Hostel** (1012 Central Ave. SW, 505/835-5943, https://motherroadhostel.com), formerly the Route 66 Hostel, is in a century-old house midway between downtown and Old Town. It's hardly modern and minimalist, but it's clean enough and the new management is exceedingly helpful. Upstairs, along creaky-wood hallways, are private rooms ($35-50) with various configurations. Downstairs and in the basement area are single-sex dorms ($27 pp). Guests have run of the kitchen, and there's a laundry room and a place to lounge. The most useful city bus lines run right out front.

Central Avenue is dotted with motels, many built in Route 66's heyday. Almost all of them are unsavory, except for **Monterey Non-Smokers Motel** (2402 Central Ave. SW, 505/243-3554, www.nonsmokersmotel.com, $79 s, $85 d), which is as practical as its name implies. The place doesn't really capitalize on 1950s kitsch—it just offers good-value rooms bereft of frills or flair. One large family suite has two beds and a foldout sofa. The outdoor pool is a treat, the laundry facilities are a nice bonus, and the location near Old Town is convenient.

A family-run motel on the west side, just over the river from Old Town, ★ **Sandia Peak Inn** (4614 Central Ave. SW, 505/831-5036, www. sandiapeakinnnm.us, $69 d) is named not for its proximity to the mountain, but its view of it. It's certainly the best value in this category, offering large, spotless rooms, all with bathtubs, fridges, microwaves, and huge TVs. Continental breakfast is included in the rate, and the proprietors

are positively sunny. There's a small indoor pool and free Wi-Fi throughout.

On the north side of town, **Nativo Lodge** (6000 Pan American Fwy. NE, 505/798-4300, www.nativolodge.com, $89 d) is convenient for the Balloon Fiesta, an early start to Santa Fe, or a cheap off-airport rental-car pickup, as a Hertz office is within walking distance. The price is great for this level of comfort and style, with several rooms designed by local American Indian artists. Request a room in the back so you're not overlooking I-25.

$100-150

The exceptionally tasteful ★ **Downtown Historic Bed & Breakfasts of Albuquerque** (207 High St. NE, 505/842-0223, www.albuquerquebedandbreakfasts.com, $139 d) occupies two neighboring old houses on the east side of downtown, walking distance to good restaurants on Central in the EDo (East Downtown) stretch. Heritage House has more of a Victorian feel, while Spy House has a sparer, 1940s look—but both are nicely clutter-free. Two outbuildings are private suites.

The stately and very reasonably priced ★ **Bottger Mansion** (110 San Felipe St. NW, 505/243-3639, www.bottger.com, $115 d) is smack in the middle of Old Town, making this an excellent central choice. The seven themed rooms are nicely appointed, and most are fairly spacious and include a queen- or king-size bed. Breakfasts are generous, and the owners are quick to provide insight into area attractions.

Lovingly restored, ★ **El Vado Motel** (2500 Central Ave SW, 505/361-1667, https:// elvadoabq.com, $137 d) captures the Route 66 charm of the original incarnation with several touches that elevate it well beyond a standard roadside motel. Centered around a large courtyard and pool, the surprisingly spacious rooms

1: Los Poblanos Historic Inn 2: Bottger Mansion

Bottger Mansion Bed and Breakfast

110

and open spaces are brightly decorated, with viga ceilings and several cheerful nods to its history throughout. Its Plaza hosts local musicians and art markets in summer and there's a taproom onsite as well as a handful of small eateries and a coffee shop.

$150-250

The heart of **Cinnamon Morning** (2700 Rio Grande Blvd. NW, 505/345-3541, www. cinnamonmorning.com, $125 s, $159 d), in the North Valley, about a mile north of Old Town, is its lavish outdoor kitchen, with a huge round dining table and a fireplace to encourage lounging on nippier nights. Rooms are simply furnished, with minimalist Southwestern detail—choose from three smaller rooms in the main house, each with a private bath, or, across the garden, a two-bedroom guesthouse ($249) and a casita ($169) with a private patio and a kitchenette.

At Albuquerque's nicest place to stay, you don't actually feel like you're anywhere near the city. ★ **Los Poblanos Historic Inn** (4803 Rio Grande Blvd. NW, 505/344-9297, www. lospoblanos.com, $210 d) sits on 25 acres, the largest remaining plot of land in the city, and the rooms are tucked into various corners of a sprawling ranch built in the 1930s by John Gaw Meem and beautifully maintained and preserved—even the huge, old kitchen ranges are still in place, as are murals by Taos artist Gustave Baumann and frescoes by Peter Hurd. In the main house, the guest rooms are set around a central patio and retain their old wood floors and heavy viga ceilings. Newer, larger rooms have been added and fit in flawlessly—deluxe rooms have a very light Southwest touch, while the farm suites have a whitewashed rustic aesthetic, accented by prints and fabrics by modernist designer Alexander Girard, of the folk-art museum in Santa Fe. There's also a saltwater pool and a gym, as well as extensive gardens. The included breakfast is exceptional, as is dinner at the onsite restaurant.

Set in the original AT&SF railroad hospital and sporting a storied past, the stylishly **Parq Central** (806 Central Ave. SE, 505/242-0040, www.hotelparqcentral.com, $161 d), opened in late 2010. The rooms are a bit small but feel light and airy thanks to big windows and gray and white furnishings, with retro chrome fixtures and honeycomb tiles in the bath. The hospital vibe is largely eradicated, though whimsical vitrines in the halls conjure old-time medical treatments, and the rooftop bar sports a gurney. Perks include free parking, a decent continental breakfast, and an airport shuttle.

A beautiful relic of early 20th-century travel, ★ **Hotel Andaluz** (125 2nd St. NW, 505/242-9090, www.hotelandaluz.com, $169 d) was first opened in 1939 by New Mexico-raised hotelier Conrad Hilton. It received a massive overhaul in 2009, keeping all the old wood and murals but updating the core to be fully environmentally friendly, from solar hot-water heaters to a composting program. The neutral-palette rooms are soothing and well designed, with a little Moorish flair in the curvy door outlines. The place is worth a visit for the lobby alone; check out the exhibits from local museums on the 2nd-floor mezzanine.

One of the city's newer hotels and on the edge of Old Town, **Hotel Chaco** (2000 Bellamah Ave, 866/505-7829, www.hotelchaco.com, $209 d) stands out in terms of its size, scope and the execution of its heavy Southwestern influences, with muted colors and earth tones, vigas, *latillas,* and works by Native American artists featured in public spaces and guest rooms. A rooftop restaurant and lounge, pool, and sleek and well-appointed fitness center round out the high-end touches; a daily all-inclusive resort fee is added one for use of many of the amenities.

North of the city, on Santa Ana Pueblo land, **Hyatt Regency Tamaya** (1300 Tuyuna Tr., Santa Ana Pueblo, 505/867-1234, www. hyattregencytamaya.com, $207 d) is a pretty resort. Rooms aren't always maintained as well as they could be, but even the standard ones are quite large, with either terraces or balconies. Three outdoor heated swimming pools and a full spa offer relaxation; the more active can play golf or tennis, take an archery class, or attend an evening storytelling program with a pueblo member.

Information and Services

TOURIST INFORMATION

The Albuquerque Convention and Visitors Bureau (800/284-2282, www.visitalbuquerque. org) offers the most detailed information on the city, maintaining a kiosk on the Old Town plaza (303 Romero St., 10am-6pm daily May-Oct., 10am-5pm daily Nov.-Apr.) and a desk at the airport near the baggage claim (9:30am-8pm Sun.-Fri., 9:30am-4pm Sat.). The **City of Albuquerque** website (www.cabq.gov) is very well organized, with all the essentials about city-run attractions and services.

Books and Maps

In the North Valley, **Bookworks** (4022 Rio Grande Blvd. NW, 505/344-8139, 9am-6pm daily) has a large stock of New Mexico-related work as well as plenty of other titles, all recommended with the personal care of the staff.

The **University of New Mexico Bookstore** (2301 Central Ave. NE, 505/277-5451, 8am-5pm Mon.-Fri.) maintains a good stock of travel titles and maps, along with state history tomes and the like. In summer, it closes an hour earlier on weekdays.

Local Media

The *Albuquerque Journal* (www.abqjournal. com) publishes cultural-events listings in the Friday entertainment supplement. On Wednesday, pick up the new issue of the free weekly *Alibi* (www.alibi.com), which will give you a hipper, more critical outlook on city goings-on, from art openings to city council debates. The free monthly *Local Flavor* (www. localflavormagazine.com) covers food topics.

Radio

KUNM (89.9 FM) is the university's radio station, delivering eclectic music, news from NPR and PRI, and local-interest shows, such as *Singing Wire*, where you'll hear traditional Native American music as well as folk and country and western.

KANW (89.1 FM) is a project of Albuquerque Public Schools, with an emphasis on New Mexican music, particularly mariachi and other music in Spanish. It also hosts a Saturday-night old-time-country show, and the most popular NPR programs.

Tune into **KHFM** (95.5 FM), Albuquerque's classical public radio station, to hear about classical music events going on around the city.

SERVICES

Banks

Banks are plentiful, and grocery stores and pharmacies increasingly have ATMs inside. Downtown, look for **New Mexico Bank & Trust** (320 Gold Ave. SW, 505/830-8100, 9am-4pm Mon.-Thurs., 9am-5pm Fri.). In Nob Hill, **Wells Fargo** (3022 Central Ave. SE, 505/255-4372, 9am-5pm Mon.-Thurs., 9am-6pm Fri., 9am-1pm Sat.) is on Central at Dartmouth. Both have 24-hour ATMs.

Post Offices

Most convenient for visitors are the **Old Town Plaza Station** (303 Romero St. NW, 505/242-5927, 11am-4pm Mon.-Fri., noon-3pm Sat.), **Downtown Station** (201 5th St. SW, 505/346-1256, 9am-4:30pm Mon.-Fri.), and an office near **UNM** (115 Cornell Dr. SE, 505/346-0923, 8am-5pm Mon.-Fri.).

Internet

The city's free **wireless hotspots** are listed at www.cabq.gov/wifi; many businesses around town also provide service.

Getting There and Around

AIR

Albuquerque International Sunport (ABQ, 505/244-7700, www.cabq.gov/airport) is a pleasant single-terminal airport served by all major U.S. airlines. It's on the south side of the city, just east of I-25, about four miles from downtown. It has free wireless Internet access. Near baggage claim is an info desk maintained by the convention and visitors bureau.

Transit from the airport includes **bus Route 50** ($1), which runs to the Alvarado Transportation Center downtown (Central and 1st St.) every half hour 7am-8pm, and on Saturday every hour and 10 minutes 9:45am-6:50pm; there is no Sunday service. The ride takes about 25 minutes.

Less frequent, but free, the **Airport Connection shuttle** (aka city bus **Route 250**) runs weekdays only (9:10am, 4:01pm, 5:09pm, and 6:10pm) to the downtown Alvarado Transportation Center. The schedule is timed to meet the Rail Runner train to Santa Fe, departing about 30 minutes later. Another free weekday bus (Route 222) runs to the Bernalillo Rail Runner stop, though this is less convenient for visitors. Verify online at www.riometro.org, as the train schedule can change.

TRAIN

Amtrak (800/872-7245, www.amtrak.com) runs the Southwest Chief through Albuquerque. It arrives daily in the afternoon from Chicago and Los Angeles. The depot shares space with the Greyhound terminal, downtown on 1st Street, south of Central Avenue and the Alvarado Transportation Center.

The **Rail Runner** (866/795-7245, www.riometro.org) connects downtown Santa Fe with Albuquerque and continues as far south as Belén. The main stop in Albuquerque is downtown, at the Alvarado Transportation Center, at Central and 1st Street. If the not-so-frequent schedule fits yours, it's fantastic service to or from Santa Fe, but within Albuquerque, the system doesn't go anywhere visitors typically go. If you ride, keep your ticket—you get a free transfer from the train to any city bus.

BUS

Greyhound (800/231-2222, www.greyhound.com) runs buses from all major points east, west, north, and south, though departures are not frequent. The **bus station** (320 1st St. SW, 505/243-4435) is downtown, just south of Central Avenue. Cheaper *and* nicer are the bus services that cater to Mexicans traveling across the Southwest and into Mexico, though they offer service only to Las Cruces and Denver; **El Paso-Los Angeles Limousine Express** (2901 Pan American Fwy. NE, 505/247-8036, www.eplalimo.com) is the biggest operator, running since 1966.

With the city bus system, **ABQ Ride** (505/243-7433, www.cabq.gov/transit), it's possible to reach all the major sights along Central Avenue, but you can't get to the Sandia Peak Tramway or anywhere in the East Mountains. The most tourist-friendly bus line is Route 66 (of course), along Central Avenue, linking Old Town, downtown, and Nob Hill; service runs until a bit past 1am on summer weekends. The double-length red **Rapid Ride** buses (Route 766) follow the same route but stop at only the most popular stops. The fare for all buses, regardless of trip length, is $1 (coins or bills; no change given); passes are available for one ($2), two ($4), and three ($6) days and can be purchased on the bus. The D-Ride bus is a free loop-route bus around downtown that runs weekdays 6:30am-5:30pm.

CAR

From Santa Fe, Albuquerque is 60 miles (one hour) south on I-25; from Las Cruces, it is 225 miles (a little more than three hours) north on I-25. From Denver, the drive takes about 6.5

hours (445 miles); Phoenix is about the same distance west on I-40.

All the major car-rental companies are in a single complex adjacent to the airport, connected by shuttle bus. **Hertz** and **Enterprise** offer service at the Amtrak depot (really, just a refund for the cab ride to the airport offices). Hertz's two other city locations are usually less expensive because you bypass the airport service fee; if you're renting for more than a week, the savings can offset the cab fare. The prominent ride-sharing companies **Uber** (www.uber.com) and **Lyft** (www.lyft.com) both operate in Albuquerque.

BIKE

Albuquerque's **bike-route system** (www.cabq.gov/bike) is reasonably well developed, the terrain is flat, and the sun is usually shining. Rent bikes from **Routes** (404 San Felipe St. NW, 505/933-5667, www.routesrentals.com, 8am-7pm Mon.-Fri., 7am-7pm Sat.-Sun. Mar.-Oct., 9am-6pm Mon.-Fri., 8am-6pm Sat.-Sun. Nov.-Feb., $15/hour, $35/day). You can also try the **bike-sharing program** (www.zagster.com/abq, $3/1.5 hours) that covers downtown and Old Town. If you think you might use the bikes more than one day, applying for the monthly pass ($15) may be a better deal.

Outside Albuquerque

Albuquerque is encircled by some of the state's top attractions, many of which are less than an hour away. Southeast of the city, a winding mountain road brings you to the ruined **Salinas Pueblo Missions,** intriguing remnants of early Conquest history. To the east off I-40 is the start of one of three routes to Santa Fe, the **Turquoise Trail,** which leads through proudly independent communities still exhibiting vestiges of New Mexico's mining past. An equally scenic route north is the much more circuitous **Jemez Mountain Trail,** which passes a dramatic landscape marked by red rocks and hot springs. The most direct route north, on I-25, brings you to the windswept **Kasha-Katuwe Tent Rocks National Monument** and its otherworldly formations.

SALINAS PUEBLO MISSIONS NATIONAL MONUMENT

The **Salinas Pueblo Missions** are a trio of ruined pueblos (**Quarai, Gran Quivira,** and **Abó**) southeast of Albuquerque, on the plains on the far side of the Manzano Mountains. The eerily affecting foundations and frames of the mission churches, built by the pueblo residents under pressure from Franciscan brothers in the early years of the Conquest, stand starkly amid the other remnants of nearby buildings. The drive here also passes one of the area's most beautiful fall hiking spots, a few very old Hispano villages, and the little town of Mountainair.

Allow the better part of a day for a leisurely drive. The whole loop route, starting and ending in Albuquerque, is about 200 miles, and straight driving time is about four hours. From Albuquerque, take I-40 east to exit 179, to the village of Tijeras (Scissors, for the way the canyons meet here), established in the 1850s. Turn south on Highway 337.

Tijeras

Kick your tour off right with a stop for breakfast at **Roots Farm Café** (11784 Hwy. 337, 505/900-4118, 7am-4pm Mon., Wed.-Fri., 8am-4pm Sat.-Sun., $6), a cozy cabin space run by a couple who also own a farm up the road. In high season, their produce shapes a menu that often changes daily. The coffee is exceptionally good.

Fourth of July Canyon

After you pass through the Spanish land grant of Chililí, Highway 337 runs into Highway 55—make a right and head to Tajique, then turn onto Forest Road 55 to reach **Fourth of**

Outside Albuquerque

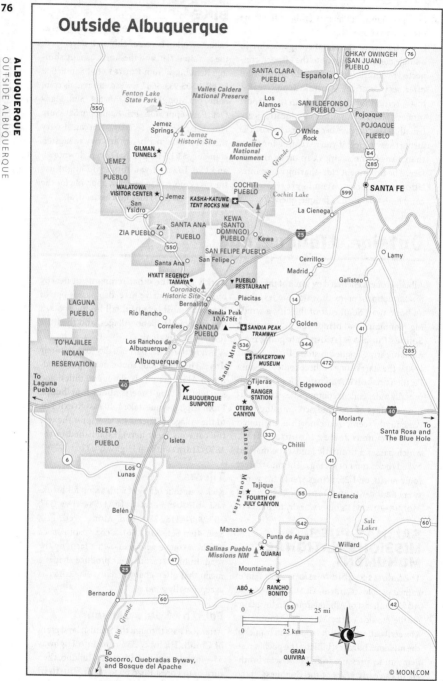

© MOON.COM

July Canyon. The area in the foothills of the Manzanos, seven miles down the dirt road, is well worth a detour in late September and early October, when the red maples and oak trees turn every shade of pink, crimson, and orange imaginable. (Surprisingly, the place got its name not for this fireworks-like show of colors, but for the date an Anglo explorer happened across it in 1906.) The canyon is also pretty in late summer, when the rains bring wildflowers. You can explore along the short **Spring Loop Trail** or **Crimson Maple Trail,** or really get into the woods on **Fourth of July Trail** (no. 173), which wanders into the canyon 1.8 miles and connects with **Albuquerque Trail** (no. 78) to form a 4.4-mile loop.

Technically, Forest Road 55 continues on to rejoin Highway 55 farther south, but after the **Fourth of July campground** ($7/site), the road is not always maintained and can be very rough going. It's wiser to backtrack rather than carry on, especially if you're in a rental car.

Quarai

The first ruins you reach are those at **Quarai** (505/847-2290, www.nps.gov/sapu, 9am-6pm daily June-Aug., 9am-5pm daily Sept.-May, free), a pueblo inhabited in the 14th-17th centuries. Like the other two Salinas pueblos, Quarai was a hardscrabble place with no natural source of water and very little food, though it did act as a trading outpost for salt, brought from small salt lakes (*salinas*) farther east. When the Franciscans arrived, they put more than the usual strain on this community. The 400 or so Tiwa speakers nonetheless were pressed to build a grand sandstone-and-adobe mission, the most impressive of the ones at these pueblos.

The priests also found themselves at odds with the Spanish governors, who helped protect them but undermined their conversion work by encouraging ceremonial dances. At the same time, raids by Apaches increased because any crop surplus no longer went to them in trade, but to the Spanish. *And* there were terrible famines 1663-1670. No wonder,

then, the place was abandoned even before the Pueblo Revolt of 1680. Only the mission has been excavated; the surrounding hillocks are all pueblo structures.

Mountainair

Highway 55 meets U.S. 60 in the village of **Mountainair,** once known as the Pinto Bean Capital of the World. It's less booming now, but you can still pick up a pound of local beans at the **B Street Market** (204 W Broadway St., 505/847-2223) grocery store.

You'll find the **Salinas Pueblo Missions Visitors Center** (505/847-2585, www.nps. gov/sapu, 8am-5pm daily) on U.S. 60, west of the intersection—though it offers not much more information than what's available at the small but detailed museums at each site. The **Mountainair ranger station** (505/847-2990, 8am-noon and 12:30pm-4:30pm Mon.-Fri.) is here as well; coming from the north, follow signs west off Highway 55 before you reach the U.S. 60 intersection.

Mountainair is also home to the weird architectural treasure that is the **Shaffer Hotel** (103 Main St.), a 1923 Pueblo Deco confection with a folk-art twist, built by one Clem "Pop" Shaffer, who had a way with cast concrete—look for his name in the wall enclosing the little garden. (Similar stonework of his can also be spotted in the garden at Los Poblanos in Albuquerque.) The place is closed these days, but with a new owner, rumors of it reopening are gaining pace; if it does, peek in the hotel dining room to admire the ceiling, Shaffer's masterpiece of carved and painted turtles, snakes, and other critters.

For food, stop at bustling **Alpine Alley** (210 N. Summit Ave., 505/847-2478, 6am-2pm Mon.-Fri., 8am-3pm Sat., $8), just north of the main intersection on Highway 55. The menu features freshly baked treats, tasty soups, and creative sandwiches; many of the items were inspired by the regular crew that settles in at the café for long periods.

Gran Quivira

South from Mountainair 26 miles lies Gran

Quivira—a bit of a drive, and you'll have to backtrack. On the way, about one mile south of town, you'll pass another Pop Shaffer creation, **Rancho Bonito,** his actual home. As it's private property, you can't go poking around, but from the road you can see a bit of the little log cabin painted in black, red, white, and blue. (If you happen to be in Mountainair in May for its art tour, the house is open then.)

Where Highway 55 makes a sharp turn east, **Gran Quivira** (505/847-2770, www. nps.gov/sapu, 9am-6pm daily June-Aug., 9am-5pm daily Sept.-May, free) looks different from the other two Salinas pueblos because it is built of gray San Andres limestone slab and finished with plaster that was painted with symbols. It's the largest of the three, and once was home to an estimated population of 1,500-2,000. The array of feathers and pottery styles found here indicate the community was devoted to trade. Like the people of Abó, the residents spoke Tompiro, and the Spanish dubbed them Los Rayados, for the striped decorations they wore on their faces. They appear to have outwardly accepted the Franciscan mission after the first sermon was preached here in 1627. But they took their own religion literally underground, building hidden kivas underneath the residential structures even as they toiled on two successive missions ordered by the Catholics. Nonetheless, the place was deserted by 1671, after more than one third of the population had starved to death.

Abó

From Gran Quivira, drive back the way you came and turn west on U.S. 60 in Mountainair to reach **Abó** (505/847-2400, www.nps.gov/sapu, 9am-6pm daily June-Aug., 9am-5pm daily Sept.-May, free), nine miles on. This was the first pueblo the Franciscans visited, in 1622; the mission here, constructed over more than 60 years, shows details such as old wood stairs leading to the choir loft. (The Franciscans were so dedicated to re-creating the Catholic church experience here in the desert that they brought in portable pipe organs and trained their converts to sing.)

Abó is also notable for the placement of its kiva, right in the center of the *convento* (the compound adjoining the mission) and apparently dating from the same period. This suggests that the local populace came to some agreement with the priests, though no archaeologist or historian has been able to find proof of this. The excellent condition of all of these ruins is due in part to the efforts of the family that owned the land from the mid-19th century. One member, Federico Sisneros, is buried near the mission, at his request.

From Abó, continue west through the mountain pass, then down into the long, flat Rio Grande Valley on U.S. 60. It runs straight into I-25 at Bernardo, but if you're heading back to Albuquerque, you can take Highway 47 northwest to Belén, about 25 miles closer to the city.

THE TURQUOISE TRAIL

This scenic back route to Santa Fe, along the east side of the Sandias and up across high plateaus, revisits New Mexico's mining history as it passes through a series of former ghost towns. From Albuquerque, it's about 70 miles and can be driven straight through in 1.5 hours.

Take I-40 east from Albuquerque to exit 175. For hiking maps of the area, bear right to go into the village of Tijeras and the **Sandia ranger station** (11776 Hwy. 337, 505/281-3304), and to gas up if you need it—it's one of the last stops until just south of Santa Fe. Go left to continue directly to the junction with Highway 14, the beginning of the Turquoise Trail.

East Mountains

The four-lane road heads north through alternating communities of old Spanish land grants and modern subdivisions collectively referred to as the East Mountains. Despite a few strip malls, the area still has a distinct identity from the city; one hub of mountain culture is the **Burger Boy** in the community of Cedar Crest (12023 Hwy. 14, 505/281-3949, 7am-7pm Mon. and Wed.-Sat., 8am-4pm Sun.,

The Turquoise Trail

© MOON.COM

$8). Its green-chile cheeseburger can hold its own against the state's best, plus the restaurant offers a range of breakfast and lunch specials. Don't miss the paintings, inside and out, of founding owner Green Chili Bill, by Ross Ward.

In Sandia Park is a large triangle intersection—to the left is Highway 536, the so-called **Crest Road** up to Sandia Peak, a beautiful winding drive through steadily thinning forests until you reach the exposed top of the mountain, more than 10,000 feet above sea level and more than 5,500 feet above the center of Albuquerque. At the peak is the Sandia Crest Visitor Center ($3/car), and the 1.6-mile **Crest Trail** along the rim.

★ Tinkertown Museum

Just 1.5 miles up the Crest Road is **Tinkertown Museum** (121 Sandia Crest Rd., 505/281-5233, www.tinkertown.com, 9am-6pm daily Apr.-Oct., $4), a temple to the ambitious use of downtime. Artist **Ross Ward,** a certified circus-model builder and sign painter who learned his trade making banners for carnivals, was also a master whittler and creative engineer who built, over 40 years, thousands of miniature figures and dioramas out of wood, clay, and found objects. Some of the scenes are even animated with tiny pulleys and levers: A man with a cleaver chases chickens in a circle; circus performers soar; the blacksmith's bellows huff and puff.

Much of the building is Ward's creation as well—undulating walls made of bottles and studded with odd collectibles, for instance. The museum, ever bulging at its seams, even took over a neighbor's 35-foot wooden boat. Ward died in 2002; his family keeps up the museum, and even though it's no longer growing as it used to, it remains a remarkable piece of pure American folk art.

Golden

Back on Highway 14, continue north through rolling hills and ever-broader skies. After 15 miles, you reach the all-but-gone town of **Golden,** site of the first gold strike west of the Mississippi, in 1825. All that's left now is a handful of homes, an attractive adobe church, and **Henderson Store** (10am-3:30pm Tues.-Sat.), open since 1918. It's largely given over to Indian jewelry and pottery, and antique trinkets line the upper shelves. The house across the road, bedecked with thousands of colored bottles, is worth a quick look.

Madrid

Thirteen miles beyond Golden, and about midway along the drive to Santa Fe, **Madrid** (pronounced MAD-rid) is a ghost town back from the dead. Built by the Albuquerque & Cerrillos Coal Co. in 1906, it once was home to 4,000 people, but by the end of World War II, when natural gas became the norm, it was deserted. By the late 1970s, a few of the sway-backed wood houses were squatted by hippies willing to live where indoor plumbing was barely available.

Over the decades, Madrid was slowly reborn. Portable toilets are still more common than flush models, but the arts scene has flourished along with a strong off-grid mindset, and a real sense of community pervades the main street, which is lined with galleries and pretty painted bungalows. In 2006, the village was the setting for the John Travolta film *Wild Hogs*, and the set-piece café built for the production (now a souvenir shop) has become a minor pilgrimage site for bikers. While you're in the area, tune in to local radio station KMRD, 96.9 FM.

The best place in Madrid to learn more about its history is the **Old Coal Town Museum** (2846 Hwy. 14, 505/473-0743, www.themineshafttavern.com, hours vary Sat.-Sun., $5), which can be unfortunate, given its nebulous opening hours and the less-than-attentive care of its collection. When it's open, you can wander among sinister-looking machine parts and old locomotives.

FOOD AND ACCOMMODATIONS
The **Mine Shaft Tavern** (2846 Hwy. 14, 505/473-0743, www.themineshafttavern.com, 11:30am-8pm Sun.-Thurs., 11:30am-9pm

Fri.-Sat., $8-15) is a vibrant remnant of Madrid's company-town days, where you can belly up to a 40-foot-long pine-pole bar. Above it are murals by local artist Ross Ward, who built the Tinkertown Museum in Sandia Park. "It is better to drink than to work," reads the Latin inscription interwoven among the mural panels, and certainly everyone in the bar, from long-distance bikers to gallery-hoppers, is living by those encouraging words. It serves solidly satisfying "New Mexico roadhouse cuisine," though that belies its award-winning Mad Chile Burger. It is, as the name suggests, not for those with delicate palates.

For morning coffee, pastries and local gossip, hit **Java Junction** (2855 Hwy. 14, 505/438-2772, www.java-junction.com, 7:30am-close daily), which also rents a comfy **suite** on its second floor ($129 d, breakfast included).

For more substance, head straight to ★ **The Hollar** (2849 Hwy. 14, 505/471-4821, 11am-9pm daily May-Sept., 11am-7pm Mon.-Wed., 11am-9pm Thurs.-Sun. Oct.-Apr., $9-16), which has excellent Southern standards such as shrimp po'boys and fried okra and several New Mexican dishes, too. The green tomatoes and goat cheese are both local—and there's a dedicated menu for dogs. The outside patio makes for a great place to linger in summer.

Cerrillos

Though the source of turquoise that has been traced to Chaco Canyon, Spain, and Chichén Itzá in Mexico's Yucatán Peninsula, **Cerrillos** hasn't been gallery-fied the way Madrid, its neighbor down the road, has—even if many residents are wealthy escapees from Santa Fe. Representing old-time Cerrillos is the combo petting zoo-trading post **Casa Grande** (17 Waldo St, 505/438-3008, 9am-5pm daily, $2), with some llamas and goats, plus turquoise nuggets and taxidermied jackalopes, and the

---

1: Tinkertown Museum 2: the excavated kiva at Abó 3: Cerrillos, which has been used as a Western film set 4: the former ghost town of Madrid

barest ghost of a dive bar, **Mary's** (15-A First St., erratic hours), filled with cats and serving primarily as the package liquor store. New-look Cerrillos is next door at **Cerrillos Station** (15-B First St., 505/474-9326), a rather swank shop, gallery, dance studio, and spa. Opposite Mary's is Cerrillos's liveliest and newest joint, the ★ **Black Bird Saloon** (29 Main St., 505/438-1821, 10am-7:45pm Thurs.-Sat., Sun. 10am-3pm, $9-15). Friendly and oozing a rustic Wild West vibe, the saloon offers plenty of local brews to wash down creative dishes such as roast lamb with a yogurt sauce on naan and an elk burger with blueberry mustard.

For some of the smoothest horseback rides around, visit the long-running **Broken Saddle Riding Co.** (505/424-7774, www.brokensaddle.com, $85 for two hours) on the edge of **Cerrillos Hills State Park** (head north across the railroad tracks, www.emnrd.state.nm.us, $5/car), which has more than 1,000 acres of rolling hills and narrow canyons that are also ideal for hiking and mountain biking.

North to Santa Fe

After ascending from the canyons around Cerrillos onto a high plateau (look out for pronghorn), you're on the home stretch to Santa Fe. Before you get there, you'll be tempted by one more dining option, the **San Marcos Café** (3877 Hwy. 14, 505/471-9298, 8am-2pm daily, $10), which shares space with a working feed store where chickens and the occasional peacock roam the yard. Hearty meals are served in a country-style dining room (complete with potbellied stove); breakfast customarily starts with fresh cinnamon buns and from there can include homemade chicken sausage and a variety of egg dishes.

Five miles farther, off the west side of the road, is the **"Old Main" State Penitentiary** (4337 Hwy. 14, www.cd.nm.gov), site of a vicious riot in 1980 that is still counted as one of the worst in American history. The state corrections department offers surprisingly detailed and thought-provoking **tours** ($15

of the old facility on Saturday in summer and early fall.

If you're heading into central Santa Fe, take the on-ramp to I-25 north (signs point to Las Vegas) to the Old Pecos Trail exit, and follow signs as it eventually merges with the Old Santa Fe Trail and ends at the plaza. This is faster and prettier than continuing straight in on Highway 14, which turns into Cerrillos Road, a particularly slow and non-scenic route to the plaza.

THE JEMEZ MOUNTAIN TRAIL

Beginning just northwest of Albuquerque, the **Jemez** (HAY-mez) **Mountain Trail** is a beautiful drive through Jemez Indian Reservation, the Santa Fe National Forest, and the **Valles Caldera National Preserve**. It's the least direct way of getting to Santa Fe—from Albuquerque, it covers about 140 miles, and you wind up near Los Alamos and must backtrack a bit south to reach the city. But anyone in search of natural beauty will want to set aside a full day for the trip, or plan an overnight in **Jemez Springs**, especially in the fall, when the aspen leaves are gold against the red rocks.

The drive begins on U.S. 550, northwest out of the satellite town of Bernalillo, just west of I-25. (Stop here for gas, if necessary—stations are few on this route.) At the village of San Ysidro, bear right onto Highway 4, which forms the major part of the route north.

Jemez Pueblo

This community of some 1,800 tribal members was settled in the late 13th century, and Highway 4 runs through the middle of the 89,000 acres it still maintains. Before the Spanish arrived, the Hemish (literally, "the people," and which the Spanish spelled *Jemez*) had established more than 10 large villages in the area. **Jemez Pueblo** is quite conservative and closed to outsiders except for holidays. Because Jemez absorbed members of Pecos Pueblo in 1838, it celebrates two feast days, San Diego (November 12) and San Persingula

(August 2), as well as Pueblo Independence Day (August 10), commemorating the Pueblo Revolt of 1680. It's also the only remaining pueblo where residents speak the Towa language, the rarest of the related New Mexico languages (Tewa and Tiwa are the other two).

The pueblo operates the **Walatowa Visitor Center** (575/834-7235, www.jemezpueblo.com, 8am-5pm daily Apr.-Dec., 10am-4pm Wed.-Sun. Jan.-Mar.), about five miles north of San Ysidro. You might miss it if you're gawking off the east side of the road at the vivid red sandstone cliffs at the mouth of the **San Diego Canyon;** from April-October, another, tastier distraction is the Indian fry bread and enchiladas sold by roadside vendors. The center has exhibits about the local geology and the people of Jemez and doubles as a ranger station, dispensing maps and advice on outdoor recreation farther up the road. You can take a one-mile guided hike ($5) up into the red rocks; it's a good idea to call ahead and arrange a time.

Gilman Tunnels

Blasted in the 1920s for a spur of a logging railroad, the two narrow **Gilman Tunnels** over scenic Highway 485 make a good excuse to drive up this narrow road and through a dramatic canyon. Look for the turn left (west) off Highway 4, a couple of miles after the Walatowa Visitor Center, after mile marker 9; the tunnels are about five miles along. After the tunnels, the road turns to dirt and heads into the national forest. (Sturdy vehicles can make a big loop around via Fenton Lake, rejoining Highway 4 north of Jemez Springs.)

Jemez Springs

A funky old resort town where hippies and Jemez Pueblo residents meet, **Jemez Springs** is a collection of little clapboard buildings tucked in the narrow valley along the road. As the most convenient place to indulge in the area's springs, which have inspired tales of miraculous healing since the 1870s, the town makes for a nice afternoon pause or an overnight getaway. **Giggling Springs** (Hwy.

4, 575/829-9175, www.gigglingsprings.com, 11am-sunset Mon. and Wed.-Sun., $25/one hour, $40/two hours, $100/day) has a spring-fed pool enclosed in an attractively landscaped flagstone area right near the Jemez River; reserve ahead, as occupancy is capped at 10. The **Jemez Springs Bath House** (Hwy. 4, 575/829-3303, www.jemezspringsbathhouse.com, 10am-6pm Mon.-Tues. and Thurs.-Sat., 10am-5pm Sun., $12/25 minutes, $18/50 minutes), in one of the original historic buildings, is operated by the village. (The source is in a gazebo next door—check out the mineral buildup!) Here, the springs have been diverted into eight concrete soaking tubs—a bit austere, but with a cool historic vibe. Reserve ahead here, too; massages and other spa treatments are available. The most natural springs (expect some algae) are on the riverside at the **Bodhi Manda Zen Center** (Hwy. 4, 575/829-3854, www.bmzc.org, 9am-4pm Wed.-Sun., $10 donation); payment is cash only and on the honor system.

If you're planning to explore the wilderness and missed the Walatowa Visitor Center at Jemez Pueblo, you can stop at the **Jemez Ranger District office** (Hwy. 4, 575/829-3535, 8am-4:30pm Mon.-Fri.) for info; it's on the north edge of town.

FOOD AND ACCOMMODATIONS

The **Bodhi Manda Zen Center** (Hwy. 4, 575/829-3854, www.bmzc.org) has its own hot pools, rents bare-bones rooms ($70 pp), and offers vegetarian meals to guests. Another bargain place to stay, with a few more amenities, is the **Laughing Lizard Inn** (Hwy. 4, 575/829-3108, www.thelaughinglizard.com, $75 d, $110 suite); its four simple but pretty rooms, plus one suite, open onto a long porch. Just across the street, **Jemez Mountain Inn** (Hwy. 4, 575/829-3926, www.jemezmtninn.com, $85 d) is slightly plusher, and its rooms a bit quieter, as they're back from the road. Hot springs are within easy walking distance.

Next door to the Laughing Lizard, ★ **Highway 4 Coffee** (17478 Hwy. 4, 575/829-4655, 8am-3pm Mon., Tues., and

Thurs., 8am-11am Wed., 8am-4pm Fri. and Sun., 8am-7pm Sat., $6-11) has a great selection of pastries and hearty homemade lunches—there's plenty of coffee, too, of course. For dinner, the only place open all the time is **Los Ojos Restaurant & Saloon** (17596 Hwy. 4, 575/829-3547, 11am-midnight Mon.-Fri., 8am-midnight Sat.-Sun., $10), where horseshoes double as window grills, tree trunks act as bar stools, and the atmosphere hasn't changed in decades. Burgers and the steak burrito are the way to go. The kitchen shuts around 9pm, and bar closing time can come earlier if business is slow, so call ahead in the evenings.

Jemez Historic Site

Just north of Jemez Springs, you pass the **Jemez Historic Site** (Hwy. 4, 575/829-3530, 8:30am-5pm Wed.-Sun., $5), a set of ruins where ancestors of the present Jemez people settled more than 700 years ago and apparently lived until 1694 or so, when Diego de Vargas returned after the Pueblo Revolt. The old pueblo, named Giusewa, has almost entirely dissolved; as at the Salinas Pueblo Missions south of Albuquerque, the attraction is the Franciscan convent and church. Built starting around 1620, it has been partially reconstructed, enough to show how the architecture—a floor that sloped up to the altar, a unique octagonal bell tower—created maximum awe in the local populace. If you pay $7 admission, you can also visit **Coronado State Monument,** on the north edge of Albuquerque, on the same or next day. If you're in the area in early to mid-December, check for the date of the **Light Among the Ruins,** during which hundreds of *farolitos* are lit at the site and traditional Native American dances take place in front of a bonfire.

A couple of curves in the highway past the monument, you reach the rocks of **Soda Dam** off the right side of the road. The pale, bulbous mineral accretions that have developed around this spring resemble nothing so much as the top of a root beer float, with a waterfall crashing through the middle. You can't really get in the water here, but it's a good photo op.

Hot Springs

Outside Jemez Springs, you pass two other opportunities to soak in hot water. Five miles north, where the red rocks of the canyon have given way to steely-gray stone and Battleship Rock looms above the road, is the start of the East Fork Trail (no. 137)—there's a dedicated parking lot just north of the picnic area. From here, the hike up the trail to **McCauley Warm Springs** is a bit more than two miles, mostly uphill; follow the trail until it meets a small stream flowing down from your left (north), then walk up the creek about 0.25 mile to the spring, which has been diverted so it flows into a series of pools, only 85°F at most points. (You can also reach the springs from the other direction along East Fork Trail, parking at Jemez Falls, farther north on Highway 4; from here, the hike is downhill—but of course a slog back up.)

More accessible are **Spence Hot Springs,** about two miles north of Battleship Rock, between mile markers 24 and 25. Look for a loop parking area on the east side of the road (if it's full, there is another lot a short way north along the highway). The 0.5-mile trail down to the river is wide and well tended, but then it's a bit more strenuous heading up the steep hillside to two sets of 100°F pools with milky-blue mineral water.

Hiking

Several trails run through the Jemez, but damage from the 2011 Las Conchas Fire has made some less scenic. Portions of **East Fork Trail** (no. 137) are still quite nice, however. The route runs between Battleship Rock (on the southwest end) and Las Conchas (on the northeast), crossing Highway 4 at a convenient midpoint. If you head south from the highway parking area (about 3 miles after

---

1: Gilman Tunnels, off the Jemez Mountain Trail **2:** Coronado State Monument **3:** Light Among the Ruins at the Jemez Historic Site

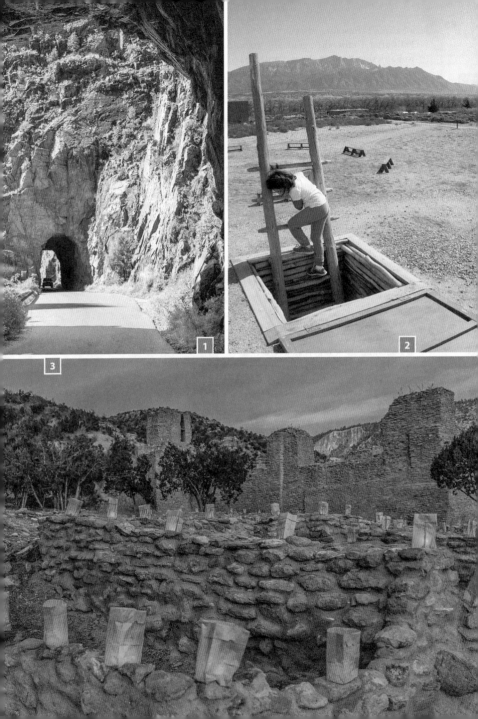

a hairpin turn southeast), you reach Jemez Falls after 1 mile, then gradually descend to Battleship Rock in about 6 miles, passing McCauley Springs on the way. Heading north from the highway is fine, too, following a stream through a pine forest, though near the end of 4.5 miles, you approach the burned area.

THE INTERSTATE TO SANTA FE

The most direct route north from Albuquerque to Santa Fe is along I-25, a one-hour drive without stops. The road, which passes through the broad valley between the Sandia and Jemez mountain ranges, is not as scenic as the more meandering routes, but it does cross wide swaths of the undeveloped pueblo lands of Sandia, San Felipe, and Kewa (formerly Santo Domingo).

Kewa (Santo Domingo)

The pueblo of **Kewa** (505/465-2214, www. santodomingotribe.org) is a short drive from exit 259, via Highway 22. Formerly known as Santo Domingo, this Keresan-speaking community of 2,500 people has been here since the 1200s. If you're going to Kasha-Katuwe Tent Rocks anyway, you'll pass a freshly repainted old-time curio stand, the **Santo Domingo Trading Post** (by the Rail Runner station stop). Then it's worth a short detour west on Indian Service Route 88, to the center of the pueblo, to see the whitewashed village church, its facade adorned with two large horses. Set against the red earth here, it's a vivid image— but remember, no photography is allowed on pueblo land.

To continue to Kasha-Katuwe Tent Rocks, backtrack to Highway 22; the Indian service route to Cochiti does not go through.

★ Kasha-Katuwe Tent Rocks National Monument

A bit west of I-25, **Kasha-Katuwe Tent Rocks National Monument** (Forest Rd. 266, 505/331-6259, 7am-7pm daily mid-Mar.-Oct., 8am-5pm daily Nov.-mid-Mar.,

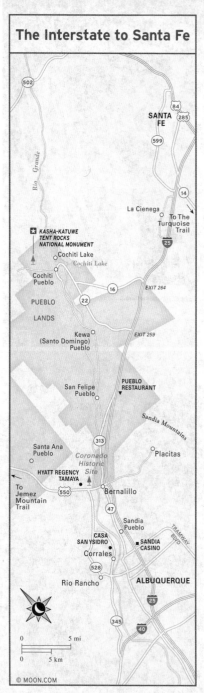

The Interstate to Santa Fe

© MOON.COM

$5/car) is one of the region's most striking natural phenomena. The wind-whittled clusters of volcanic pumice and tuff do indeed resemble enormous tepees, some up to 90 feet tall. To reach the area, continue past Kewa Pueblo and head northwest toward Cochiti Pueblo on Highway 22. After about 15 miles, turn south in front of Cochiti Dam. In less than two miles, in the middle of the pueblo, turn right on Indian Service Route 92.

From the monument parking area, you have the choice of two short trails: An easy, relatively flat loop runs up to the base of the rocks, passing a small cave, while a longer option runs 1.5 miles into a narrow canyon where the rock towers loom up dramatically on either side. The latter trail is level at first, but the last stretch is steep and requires a little clambering. Even if you just want to take a quick peek and don't intend to hike, don't come too late in the day: The gates (close to the junction with Highway 22) are locked one hour before official closing time.

To get back to the freeway without backtracking, continue northeast on Highway 22, which makes a sharp turn at the base of Cochiti Dam (turn left, or north, and you'll reach Cochiti Lake, a popular summer destination for boaters). Follow Highway 22 back southeast, then take Highway 16 to rejoin the interstate at exit 264.

Food

At exit 252, hop off for a meal at the ★ Pueblo Restaurant (26 Hagen Rd., 505/867-4706, 6am-9pm daily, $8), adjacent to the Black Mesa Casino and inside the San Felipe Travel Center and past a short hall of dinging slot machines. Its broad diner menu offers spaghetti and meatballs as well as New Mexican favorites. The pueblo dishes, such as posole with extra-thick tortillas, are excellent. Dig in alongside pueblo residents, day-trippers, and long-haul truckers.

Santa Fe

Over 400 years since its founding as a remote

Spanish outpost, Santa Fe remains proudly and blissfully quite unlike anywhere else in the country.

Indeed, this small cluster of mud-colored buildings in the mountains of northern New Mexico seems to subsist on dreams alone, as this city of 70,000 has a larger proportion of writers and artists than any other community in the United States. Art galleries are ubiquitous—one famous half-mile stretch of road has over 80 alone—and lots packed with film crews are increasingly common sights. In all, nearly half the city is employed in the larger arts industry. (Cynics would lump the state legislature, which convenes in the capitol here, into this category as well.)

Highlights

Look for ★ to find recommended sights, activities, dining, and lodging.

★ **Canyon Road Galleries:** The heart of Santa Fe's art scene is a visual smorgasbord, no more so than when it's packed with potential collectors, window-shoppers, and party hoppers on summer Friday nights (page 100).

★ **Museum of International Folk Art:** In the main exhibition hall, all the world's crafts, from Appalachian quilts to Zulu masks, are jumbled together in an inspiring display of human creativity (page 103).

★ **Meow Wolf Art Complex:** Meow Wolf's immersive House of Eternal Return expands the mind—and the definition of art—in Santa Fe. It's an immense amount of fun (page 105).

★ **Ten Thousand Waves:** As much a part of Santa Fe's identity as a centuries-old adobe, this Japanese-styled spa is the ultimate mountain getaway (page 112).

★ **Violet Crown:** It's more than just a movie theater, with dinner and drinks you can savor while catching the latest blockbuster, smart homages to cinema's heyday, and a sun-kissed, railroad-themed space (page 116).

★ **Santa Fe Indian Market:** The amount and quality of Native American artwork on display during this late-summer celebration is staggering, but it's the opportunity to interact with some of the Southwest's most seminal artists that makes this event truly special (page 118).

★ **Bandelier National Monument:** Spend a day exploring the once-hidden valley of Frijoles Canyon, where ancestors of today's Pueblo people constructed an elaborate city complex with cliffside cave homes (page 143).

★ **Valles Caldera National Preserve:** You're more likely to spot elk herds than groups of hikers in the lush meadows and pristine

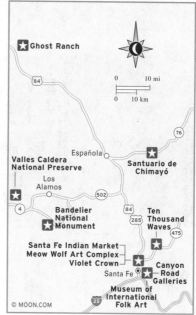

backcountry of this massive crater, where you can also mountain bike and snowshoe under the stars (page 145).

★ **Ghost Ranch:** This spread's dramatic red cliffs and windblown pinnacles inspired Georgia O'Keeffe. Take the iconic landscape in on horseback or hike to Chimney Rock for a sweeping view of Abiquiu and the Pedernal (page 152).

★ **Santuario de Chimayó:** Faith is palpable in this village church north of Santa Fe, known as "the Lourdes of America," thanks to the healing powers attributed to the holy dirt found here (page 156).

Santa Fe

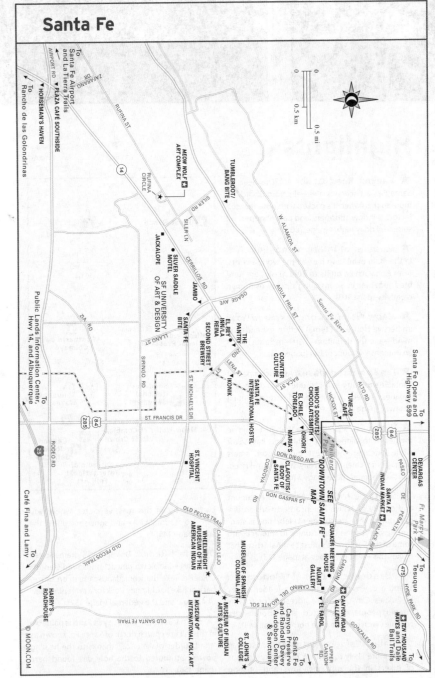

To Santa Fe Airport, and La Tierra Trails
▼ PLAZA CAFE SOUTHSIDE
AIRPORT RD

▼ HORSEMAN'S HAVEN

To Rancho de las Golondrinas

14

RUFINA ST

ZAFARANO DR

MEOW WOLF ART COMPLEX ✚
RUFINA CIRCLE ★

TUMBLEROOT/ BANG BITE ▼

SILER RD
SILER LN

W ALAMEDA ST

AGUA FRIA ST

OSAGE AVE

Santa Fe River

Santa Fe Opera and Highway 599

ALTO RD

HICKOX ST

■ JACKALOPE
SILVER SADDLE MOTEL ■
SF UNIVERSITY OF ART & DESIGN
CERRILLOS RD
▼ JAMBO

2A RD

LLANO ST

SIRINGO RD

ST MICHAELS DR

ST. FRANCIS DR

84
285

28A RD

RODEO RD

Public Lands Information Center, Hwy 14, and Albuquerque

25

To Café Fina and Lamy

▼ HARRY'S ROADHOUSE

OLD SANTA FE TRAIL

OLD PECOS TRAIL

ST VINCENT HOSPITAL ✚

SANTA FE BITE ▼
EL REY INN LA REINA ▼
THE PANTRY ▼
SECOND STREET BREWERY ▼
2ND ST
LENA ST
IKONIK ●
COUNTER CULTURE ●
BACA ST

SANTA FE INTERNATIONAL HOSTEL

EL CHILE TOREADO ●

WHOO'S DONUTS/ CHOCOLATESMITH ■
OHORI'S ▼

MARIA'S ▼
CLAFOUTIS ▼
BODY OF SANTA FE ●

DON DIEGO AVE
CORDOVA RD
DON GASPAR ST

TUNE-UP CAFÉ ●

RAILYARD PARK
SEE "DOWNTOWN SANTA FE" MAP

285
84

SANTA FE INDIAN MARKET ✚

PASEO DE PERALTA

DEVARGAS CENTER ■

Ft. Marcy Park

PALACE AVE

QUAKER MEETING HOUSE ●

NÜART GALLERY ■

CANYON RD

CAMINO DEL MONTE SOL

MUSEUM OF SPANISH COLONIAL ART ●

WHEELWRIGHT MUSEUM OF THE AMERICAN INDIAN ●

CAMINO LEJO

MUSEUM OF INTERNATIONAL FOLK ART ✚

MUSEUM OF INDIAN ARTS & CULTURE ✚

ST. JOHN'S COLLEGE ★

EL FAROL ▼
CANYON ROAD GALLERIES ●

Santa Fe Canyon Preserve and Randall Davey Audubon Center & Sanctuary

UPPER CANYON RD

GONZALES RD

475

To Tesuque

TEN THOUSAND WAVES and Dale Ball Trails ✚

HYDE PARK RD

To Santa Fe Canyon Preserve and Randall Davey Audubon Center

0   0.5 mi
0   0.5 km

The city fabric itself is a by-product of this creativity—many of the "adobe" buildings in the distinctive downtown area are in fact plaster and stucco, built in the early 20th century to satisfy an official vision of how Santa Fe should present itself to tourists. And the mix of old-guard Spanish, Pueblo Indians, groovy Anglos, and international jet-setters of all stripes has even developed a soft but distinct accent—a vaguely continental intonation, with a vocabulary drawn from the 1960s counterculture and alternative healing.

What keeps Santa Fe grounded is its location, tucked in the foothills of the Sangre de Cristos. The mountains are never far, even if you're just admiring the view from your massage table at a Japanese-style spa or dining at an elegant restaurant on mushrooms sourced from secret high meadows. You can be out of town and at a trailhead in 10 minutes, skiing down a precipitous slope in 30, or wandering among the ochre-colored hills you've seen in Georgia O'Keeffe's paintings of Abiquiu in 60. East of the city is the Pecos Wilderness Area, a couple hundred thousand acres studded with summits such as the 12,600-foot Santa Fe Baldy and 13,100-foot Truchas Peak.

Santa Fe's history is intrinsic to that of the Southwest; what took place here echoed across the region and farther east, too. It's the second-oldest city in the United States (after St. Augustine, Florida), and it's surrounded by pueblos that have been inhabited since well before the Spanish arrived, alongside remnants of older settlements, such as the cliff dwellings in Bandelier National Monument. As the capital of the Spanish territory of Nuevo México, Santa Fe was a far-flung outpost, a gateway to the wilder, emptier lands to the north. And it still is, with two scenic routes running north to Taos: The high road winds along mountain ridges, while the low road follows the Rio Grande.

PLANNING YOUR TIME

Santa Fe is an ideal destination for a **three-day weekend.** Add another day or two to take a day hike outside of town or make the drive to Taos, Los Alamos, or Abiquiu. **Summer** is high season, no more so than during Spanish Market and Indian Market, in July and August, respectively. This is also when the gallery scene is in full swing; plan to be in the city on a Friday night, when the Canyon Road galleries have their convivial openings.

In **fall,** the city is much calmer and offers beautiful hiking; the hills are greener and dense groves of aspen trees on the Sangre de Cristo Mountains turn bright yellow. As in the rest of New Mexico, **spring** and **early summer** can be hot and windy, but the city is still pleasant, as lilacs bloom in May, tumbling over adobe walls and filling the air with scent. **Winter** is cold and occasionally snowy, but cloudy days are few. Late December in Santa Fe is a special time, as houses and hotels are decked with *farolitos* (paper-bag lanterns) and Canyon Road is alight with bonfires on Christmas Eve. After this, in January and February, hotel prices tend to drop dramatically, as the few tourists in town are here only to ski.

HISTORY

Around 1609, La Villa Real de la Santa Fé (The Royal City of the Holy Faith) was established as the capital of Spain's northernmost territory in the New World. The Camino Real, the route that connected the outpost with Mexico, ended in the newly built plaza. Mexico's independence from Spain in 1821 marked a shift in the city's fortunes, as the new government opened up its northernmost territory to outside trade, via the Santa Fe Trail, from Missouri.

When the railroad arrived in nearby Lamy in 1880, it spurred what's still Santa Fe's lifeblood: tourism. Loads of curious Easterners

---

Previous: hiking among chamisa shrubs near the Santa Fe ski basin; The Teahouse on Canyon Road; Meow Wolf Art Complex.

New Mexico Culture Pass

A **museum pass** ($30) good for 12 months grants onetime access to all 15 state-run museums and historic sites. This includes four Santa Fe institutions—the New Mexico Museum of Art, the New Mexico History Museum, the Museum of Indian Arts & Culture, and the Museum of International Folk Art—as well as two in Albuquerque (the National Hispanic Cultural Center and the Museum of Natural History and Science), and the Coronado and Jemez historic sites. It also covers attractions farther afield, in Las Cruces, Alamogordo, and more—great if you're a state resident or you're already planning a longer return visit within the year.

flocked in. In 1912, a council of city planners decided to promote Santa Fe as a tourist destination and preserve its distinctive architecture. By 1917, the Museum of Fine Arts (now the New Mexico Museum of Art) had opened, and the first Indian Market was held in 1922, in response to the trend of Anglos collecting local arts and crafts.

Decades later, Santa Fe played a minor part in events that would shape the future of humanity. In 1943, the building at 109 East Palace Avenue became the "front office" and only known address for Los Alamos, where the country's greatest scientists were developing the atomic bomb under a cloud of confidentiality. But the rational scientists left little mark. Right-brain thinking has continued to flourish, and the city is a modern, evolving version of its old self, an outpost of melding cultures still drawing artists and an increasing number of adventurers looking to explore the mountainous landscape.

ORIENTATION

Santa Fe is compact, with most of its major sights within walking distance from the central plaza. You're likely to spend much of your time within the oval formed by **Paseo de Peralta,** the main road that almost completely encircles the city's core. On its southwest side it connects with **Cerrillos Road,** a wide avenue lined with motel courts, shopping plazas, and chain restaurants. Compared with the central historic district, it's unsightly, but there are some great local places to eat here, as well as the few inexpensive hotels in town.

Sights

DOWNTOWN
Santa Fe Plaza

When Santa Fe was established around 1609, its layout was based on Spanish laws governing town planning in the colonies—hence the central plaza fronted by the Casas Reales (Palace of the Governors) on its north side. The **Santa Fe Plaza** is still the city's social hub, and the blocks surrounding it are rich with history. In the center of the plaza is the **Soldiers' Monument,** now also a monument to how history gets rewritten. On the original panel, dedicated in 1867 to those who died in "battles with [. . .] Indians in the territory of New Mexico," the word "savage" was excised in the 1970s, following a debate about the word. One activist took it upon himself to chisel out the word himself, even as some Pueblo leaders thought the word should stand, on the logic that it could accurately describe the way in which Native people fought the Spanish at the time. Another, later panel has been modified, too, as "rebel," referring to Southern forces in the Civil War, has been cut away. Then next to it all is yet another plaque, apologizing for the whole mess.

Along the north side, under the *portal* of the **Palace of the Governors,** is one of the more iconic sights of Santa Fe: American Indians from all over New Mexico selling their craft work as they've been doing since the 1930s. More than 500 vendors are licensed to sell here after going through a strict application process that evaluates their technical skills. Every morning the 69 spots, each 12 bricks wide, are doled out by lottery. Expect anything from silver bracelets to pottery to *heishi* (shell bead) necklaces to freshly harvested piñon nuts. It's a great opportunity to buy directly from a skilled artisan and learn about the work that went into a specific piece.

New Mexico History Museum and Palace of the Governors

Opened in 2009, the **New Mexico History Museum** (113 Lincoln Ave., 505/476-5200, www.nmhistorymuseum.org, 10am-5pm daily May-Oct., 10am-5pm Tues.-Sun. Nov.-Apr., $12) was intended to give a little breathing room for a collection that had been in storage for decades. Oddly, though, it feels like few actual objects are on display. The permanent exhibits give a good overview, but if you're already familiar with the state's storied past, you might not find much new here.

Your ticket also admits you to the adjacent **Palace of the Governors,** the former seat of Santa Fe's government, and a generally more compelling display. An unimposing building constructed in 1610, it's been the site of several city-defining events. Diego de Vargas fought the Indian rebels here room by room when he retook the city in 1693; ill-fated Mexican governor Albino Pérez was beheaded in his office in 1837; and Governor Lew Wallace penned *Ben Hur* here in the late 1870s. The exhibits showcase some of the most beautiful items in the state's collection: trinkets and photos from the 19th century, as well as the beautiful 18th-century Segesser hide paintings, two wall-size panels of buffalo skin. These works, along with the room they're in (trimmed with 1909 murals of the Puyé cliffs) are worth the price of admission. In a couple of the restored furnished rooms, you can compare the living conditions of the Mexican leadership circa 1845 to the relative comfort the U.S. governor enjoyed in 1893.

The museum has **free admission** every Friday (5pm-8pm) May-October, and the first Friday of the month in winter. **Walking tours** depart from the blue gate on the Lincoln Avenue side of the New Mexico History Museum at 10:15am (Mon.-Sat. mid-Apr.-mid-Oct., $10), covering all the plaza-area highlights in about two hours.

New Mexico Museum of Art

Famed as much for its facade as for what it contains, the **New Mexico Museum of Art** (107 W. Palace Ave., 505/476-5072, www. nmartmuseum.org, 10am-5pm daily May-Oct., 10am-5pm Tues.-Sun. Nov.-Apr., $12) is dedicated to work by New Mexican artists. Built in 1917, it is a beautiful example of Pueblo Revival architecture, originally designed as the New Mexico pavilion for a world expo in San Diego, California, two years prior. The curvaceous stucco-clad building combines elements from the most iconic pueblo mission churches—the bell towers, for instance, mimic those found at San Felipe. Inside, the collection starts with Gerald Cassidy's oil painting *Cui Bono?*, on display since the museum's opening in 1917 and still relevant, as it questions the benefits of pueblo tourism. Look out for an excellent collection of Awa Tsireh's meticulous watercolors of ceremonial dances at **San Ildefonso Pueblo,** alongside works by other local American Indian artists.

On your way out, don't miss the adjacent **St. Francis Auditorium,** where three artists adorned the walls with art nouveau murals depicting the life of Santa Fe's patron saint. It's rare to see a secular style—usually reserved for languorous ladies in flowing togas—used to render such scenes as the apotheosis of Saint Francis and Santa Clara's renunciation, and the effect is beautiful.

As at the history museum, Friday evenings (5pm-7pm) are **free admission** in summer;

Downtown Santa Fe

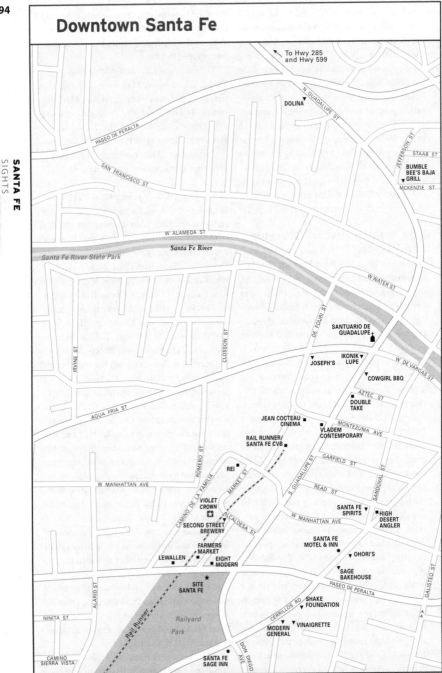

To Hwy 285
and Hwy 599

N GUADALUPE ST

DOLINA

PASEO DE PERALTA

SAN FRANCISCO ST

JEFFERSON ST
STAAB ST

BUMBLE
BEE'S BAJA
GRILL

MCKENZIE ST

W ALAMEDA ST

Santa Fe River

Santa Fe River State Park

W WATER ST

DE FOURI ST

SANTUARIO DE
GUADALUPE

IRVINE ST

CLOSSON ST

W DE VARGAS ST

IKONIK
LUPE

JOSEPH'S

COWGIRL BBQ

AGUA FRIA ST

AZTEC ST
DOUBLE
TAKE

JEAN COCTEAU
CINEMA

MONTEZUMA AVE

VLADEM
CONTEMPORARY

RAIL RUNNER/
SANTA FE CVB

GARFIELD ST

ROMERO ST

S GUADALUPE ST

SANDOVAL ST

REI

MARKET ST

W MANHATTAN AVE

READ ST

VIOLET
CROWN

CAMINO DE LA FAMILIA

ALCALDESA ST

SANTA FE
SPIRITS

HIGH
DESERT
ANGLER

SECOND STREET
BREWERY

W MANHATTAN AVE

SANTA FE
MOTEL & INN

OHORI'S

FARMERS
MARKET

LEWALLEN

EIGHT
MODERN

SAGE
BAKEHOUSE

ALARID ST

SITE
SANTA FE

PASEO DE PERALTA

GALISTEO ST

NINITA ST

Rail Runner

Railyard
Park

CERRILLOS RD

SHAKE
FOUNDATION

MODERN
GENERAL

VINAIGRETTE

CAMINO
SIERRA VISTA

DON DIEGO AVE

SANTA FE
SAGE INN

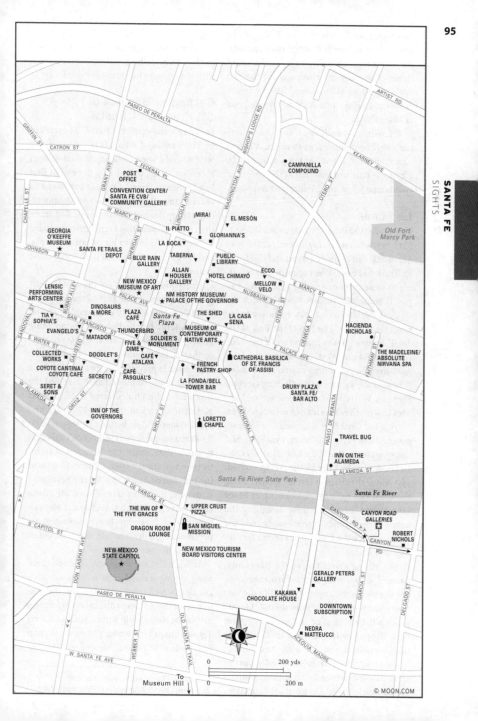

ARTIST RD

PASEO DE PERALTA

CATRON ST

KEARNEY AVE

CHAPELLE ST

GRIFFIN ST

GRANT AVE

S FEDERAL PL

BISHOP S LODGE RD

WASHINGTON AVE

OTERO ST

CAMPANILLA COMPOUND

POST OFFICE

CONVENTION CENTER/ SANTA FE CVB/ COMMUNITY GALLERY

W MARCY ST

¡MIRA!

EL MESÓN

Old Fort Marcy Park

GEORGIA O'KEEFFE MUSEUM

JOHNSON ST

IL PIATTO

LA BOCA

GLORIANNA'S

SANTA FE TRAILS DEPOT

SHERIDAN ST

TABERNA

PUBLIC LIBRARY

BLUE RAIN GALLERY

ALLAN HOUSER GALLERY

HOTEL CHIMAYÓ

ECCO

MELLOW VELO

E MARCY ST

NEW MEXICO MUSEUM OF ART

W PALACE AVE

NM HISTORY MUSEUM/ PALACE OF THE GOVERNORS

NUSBAUM ST

OTERO ST

LENSIC PERFORMING ARTS CENTER

BURRO ALLEY

DINOSAURS & MORE

PLAZA CAFÉ

Santa Fe Plaza

THE SHED

LA CASA SENA

CIENEGA ST

E PALACE AVE

HACIENDA NICHOLAS

FAITHWAY ST

SANDOVAL ST

SAN FRANCISCO ST

TIA SOPHIA'S

E WATER ST

GALISTEO ST

EVANGELO'S

MATADOR

THUNDERBIRD

FIVE & DIME

SOLDIER'S MONUMENT

MUSEUM OF CONTEMPORARY NATIVE ARTS

THE MADELEINE/ ABSOLUTE NIRVANA SPA

COLLECTED WORKS

DOODLET'S

CAFÉ ATALAYA

CATHEDRAL BASILICA OF ST. FRANCIS OF ASSISI

COYOTE CANTINA/ COYOTE CAFÉ

SECRETO

CAFÉ PASQUAL'S

FRENCH PASTRY SHOP

DRURY PLAZA SANTA FE/ BAR ALTO

SERET & SONS

LA FONDA/BELL TOWER BAR

PASEO DE PERALTA

W ALAMEDA ST

ORTIZ ST

INN OF THE GOVERNORS

LORETTO CHAPEL

TRAVEL BUG

SHELBY ST

CATHEDRAL PL

INN ON THE ALAMEDA

E ALAMEDA ST

Santa Fe River State Park

Santa Fe River

E DE VARGAS ST

S CAPITOL ST

THE INN OF THE FIVE GRACES

UPPER CRUST PIZZA

CANYON RD

CANYON ROAD GALLERIES

DON GASPAR AVE

DRAGON ROOM LOUNGE

SAN MIGUEL MISSION

ROBERT NICHOLS

CANYON RD

NEW MEXICO STATE CAPITOL

NEW MEXICO TOURISM BOARD VISITORS CENTER

GARCIA ST

DELGADO ST

PASEO DE PERALTA

GERALD PETERS GALLERY

WEBBER ST

OLD SANTA FE TRAIL

KAKAWA CHOCOLATE HOUSE

DOWNTOWN SUBSCRIPTION

ACEQUIA MADRE

NEDRA MATTEUCCI

W SANTA FE AVE

0   200 yds

To Museum Hill

0   200 m

© MOON.COM

November-April, only the first Friday of the month is free. Free docent-led **tours** around the museum run daily; call for the latest times. The museum also runs art-themed **walking tours** ($10) around the city center at 10am Monday; June-August, they also run at 10am Friday.

Planning is underway for the museum's new contemporary art annex, Vladem Contemporary, scheduled to open in 2020 in a historic Railyard building at the corner of Guadalupe Street and Montezuma Avenue.

La Fonda

La Fonda (100 E. San Francisco St., 505/982-5511, www.lafondasantafe.com), at the corner of East San Francisco Street and Old Santa Fe Trail, has been offering respite to travelers in some form or another since 1607, and it still hums with history—even though the stacked Pueblo Revival place you see today dates from 1920. "The Inn at the End of the Trail" boomed in the early years of the trade route across the West, and also in the later gold-digging era, with a casino and saloon. It hosted the victory ball following General Stephen Watts Kearny's takeover of New Mexico in the Mexican-American War. During the Civil War it housed Confederate general Henry Hopkins Sibley. Lynchings and shootings took place in the lobby. In the 1920s, La Fonda got a bit safer for the average tourist, as it joined the chain of Harvey Houses along the country's railways, and architect Mary Jane Colter (best known for designing the hotels at the Grand Canyon) redesigned the interior. Since the 1960s, it has been a family-owned hotel.

Something about the waxed tile floors, painted glass, and heavy furniture convey the pleasant clamor of hotel life the way many more modern lobbies do not. Guests pick up their keys at an old wood reception desk, drop their letters in an Indian-drum-turned-mailbox, and chat with the concierge below a poster for Harvey's Indian Detour car trips. Also look around—including up on the mezzanine level—at the great art collection.

La Plazuela restaurant, in the skylight center courtyard, is a beautiful place for a meal (with good brunches), and the bar is timeless, with live country music many nights.

Cathedral Basilica of St. Francis of Assisi

Santa Fe's showpiece **Cathedral Basilica of St. Francis of Assisi** (131 Cathedral Pl., 505/982-5619, www.cbsfa.org, 9:30am-4:30pm Mon.-Sat., free), towering at the end of East San Francisco Street, was built over some 15 years in the late 19th century by domineering Bishop Jean-Baptiste Lamy. For more than three decades, the Frenchman struggled to "elevate" the city to European standards, and his folly is exemplified in this grandiose cathedral.

Lamy looked down on the locals' religious practices, as the cult of the Virgin of Guadalupe was already well established, and the Penitente brotherhood was performing public self-flagellation. He also disliked their aesthetics. How could a person possibly reach heaven while praying on a dirt floor inside a building made of mud? Lamy assessed the tiny adobe church dedicated to St. Francis of Assisi, which had stood for 170 years, and decided he could do better. Construction on his Romanesque revival St. Francis Cathedral began in 1869, under the direction of architects and craftsmen from Europe. They used the old church as a frame for the new stone structure, and then demolished all of the adobe, save for a small side chapel. Lamy ran short of cash, however—hence the stumpy aspect of the cathedral's facade, which should be topped with domed towers.

Inside is all Gothic-inspired light and space and glowing stained-glass windows, with a gilt altar screen installed in 1987, for the centennial of the building's dedication. It features primarily New World saints, such as Kateri Tekakwitha, a 17th-century Mohawk woman beatified in 1980 and canonized in 2012 (her

1: Cathedral Basilica of St. Francis of Assisi
2: Loretto Chapel 3: New Mexico Museum of Art

statue also stands outside the cathedral). She is depicted with a turtle, representing her membership in the Turtle Clan.

The salvaged adobe chapel is to the left of the altar. It is dedicated to the figure of La Conquistadora, a statue brought to Santa Fe from Mexico in 1625, carried away by the retreating Spanish during the Pueblo Revolt, then proudly reinstated in 1693 and honored ever since. She glows in her shimmering robes, under a heavy viga ceiling. Lamy, who died in 1888, probably shudders in his crypt in front of the main altar.

On your way out, check the great cast-bronze doors—they're usually propped open, so you'll have to peer behind to see the images depicting the history of Catholicism in New Mexico. One plaque shows the Italian stoneworkers constructing the cathedral, and another shows families fleeing from attack in 1680—a rare depiction of the Pueblo Revolt that's sympathetic to the Spanish.

Museum of Contemporary Native Arts

Occupying two floors in the city's former post office, the Museum of Contemporary Native Arts (108 Cathedral Pl., 505/983-8900, www.iaia.edu, 10am-5pm Mon. and Wed.-Sat., noon-5pm Sun., $10) is the showcase for students, professors, and alumni of the prestigious Institute of American Indian Arts. The shows can be hit or miss; if your time is limited, the Museum of Indian Arts & Culture is a better bet. The gift shop stocks items with a good blend of modern and traditional styles.

Loretto Chapel

Initiated by Bishop Lamy in 1873, the Loretto Chapel (207 Old Santa Fe Tr., 505/982-0092, www.lorettochapel.com 9:30am-5pm Mon.-Sat., 10:30am-5pm Sun., $3) was the first Gothic structure built west of the Mississippi. Its beautiful interior has a great story to match, although the recording broadcast inside (the place was desanctified in

1971) explaining all this on an endless loop is slightly maddening.

The chapel's decorative elements reflect Lamy's fondness for all things European: the stations of the cross rendered by Italian masons, the harmonium and stained glass windows imported from France. Even the stone from which it was built was hauled at great expense from quarries 200 miles south.

What draws the eye is the elegant spiral staircase leading to the choir loft. Made entirely of wood, it makes two complete turns without a central support pole. It was built in 1878 by a mysterious carpenter who appeared seemingly at the spiritual behest of the resident Sisters of Loretto. The carpenter toiled in silence for six months, the story goes, then disappeared, without taking any payment. He was never heard from again—though some historians claim to have tracked him down to Las Cruces, where he met his end in a bar fight.

San Miguel Chapel

The San Miguel Chapel (401 Old Santa Fe Tr., 505/983-3974, www.sanmiguelchapel.org, 10am-4pm Mon.-Sat., $1, free silent worship 5pm-7pm Thurs.) is a sturdy adobe building where Mass is still said in Latin at 2pm on Sunday. It is the oldest church structure in the United States, and it's set in Barrio de Analco, the city's oldest residential neighborhood, at the head of De Vargas, the oldest street. The church was built starting in 1610, and then partially reconstructed a century later, after it was set aflame in the Pueblo Revolt. Its stone buttresses are the product of a desperate attempt to shore up the sagging walls in the late 19th century.

The interior is snug and whitewashed, with a restored altar screen that had been covered over in house paint for decades. The late 18th-century work is attributed to the anonymous Laguna Santero, a Mexican artist who earned his name from the intricately carved and painted screen at the Laguna Pueblo church, near Albuquerque. The screen functions as an enormous picture frame, with both oil paintings and *bultos* (painted wood statues of saints) inserted in the openings. In front of the altar, cutouts in the floor reveal the building's original foundations.

The old church bell, set at the back of the church, is said to have been cast in Spain in 1356. It was brought to the New World and installed at San Miguel in the early 19th century, and it hums beautifully even when tapped.

New Mexico State Capitol

A round building with an entrance at each of the cardinal points, the 1966 New Mexico State Capitol (491 Old Santa Fe Tr.) mimics the zia sun symbol used on the state flag. In the center of the rotunda is a mosaic rendition of the state seal: the Mexican brown eagle grasping a snake and shielded by the American bald eagle. Don't forget to look up at the stained glass skylight, with its intricate Indian basket-weave pattern.

But the real attraction of the Roundhouse, as the building is commonly known, is its excellent but often overlooked art collection (505/986-4614, www.nmcapitolart.org, 8am-5:30pm Mon.-Fri., also Sat. June-Aug., free), with works by the state's best-known creatives. You'll find paintings and photographs in the halls on every floor, in the upstairs balcony area of the senate, and in the 4th-floor Governor's Gallery.

Oh, and the building is used for legislating—though not particularly often (beginning on the third Tuesday in January, for 30 days in even-numbered years, and 60 days in odd). When house and senate meetings are in session, visitors are welcome to sit in the galleries and watch the proceedings.

Georgia O'Keeffe Museum

Opened in 1997, the Georgia O'Keeffe Museum (217 Johnson St., 505/946-1000, www.okeeffemuseum.org, 10am-5pm Sat.-Thurs., 10am-7pm Fri., $13), northwest of the plaza, honors the artist whose name is inextricably bound with New Mexico. The contrarian member of the New York avantgarde ("Nothing is less real than realism," she

famously said) started making regular visits to the state in the 1920s, and then moved to Abiquiu full-time in 1949, a few years after the death of her husband, photographer Alfred Stieglitz.

Many of O'Keeffe's finest works—her signature sensuous, near-abstract flower blossoms, for instance—have already been ensconced in other famous museums, so it's best to temper expectations accordingly. That said, the exhibits provide an intimate look at the artist's life not easily seen elsewhere, as they draw on the work that she kept, plus ephemera and other work her foundation has amassed since her death in 1986. Often the space is given over to exhibitions on her contemporaries or those whose work she influenced or admired.

The museum offers a variety of walking tours, most notably a Walk & Talk tour of the museum daily at 3pm ($40) and an in-depth look at O'Keeffe's home and studio at Ghost Ranch in Abiquiu ($35-45).

Cross of the Martyrs and Old Fort Marcy Park

Sitting at the top of a hill overlooking downtown Santa Fe, the white Cross of the Martyrs is a memorial to the Spanish settlers who were killed in the Pueblo Revolt. It's not a strenuous walk, and the bird's-eye view from the hilltop is excellent.

Behind the cross is Old Fort Marcy Park, site of the first American fort in the Southwest, though today there are no signs of it remaining. Built in 1846 by General Kearny, the fort was then abandoned in 1894, and the land was disused for several decades. The path up to the cross begins on Paseo de Peralta just east of Otero Street.

CANYON ROAD AND THE EASTSIDE

This narrow mostly one-way street southeast of the plaza epitomizes "Santa Fe style," or at least the ritzy side of it. The galleries are the primary draw, but it's worth heading a bit off the main drag, too. There's a city parking lot at the east (upper) end of the road and public parking near the bottom just north off **Canyon Road** on Delgado Street. Public **restrooms** (9:30am-5:30pm daily) are near the west end, in the complex at 225 Canyon Road, behind Meyer Gallery.

TOP EXPERIENCE

★ Canyon Road Galleries

The intersection of Paseo de Peralta and Canyon Road is ground zero for the city's **art market**. This is the beginning of a 0.5-mile strip that contains more than 80 galleries. In the summer, Canyon Road is a solid mass of strolling art lovers—pro collectors and amateurs alike. It's especially thronged on summer Fridays, when most galleries have an open house or an exhibition opening, from around 5pm until 7pm or 8pm.

Hard to believe, but the street wasn't always chockablock with thousand-dollar canvases. Long ago, it was farmland, irrigated by the "Mother Ditch," Acequia Madre, which still runs parallel one block to the south. Starting in the 1920s, transplant artists settled on this muddy dirt road, and the area gradually came to be associated with creative exploits. Eventually the art market really boomed in the 1980s. While those days have long since passed and many of the road's galleries seem to be in the throes of a never-ending game of musical chairs, it remains an enthralling stretch with some real gems.

In addition to the galleries and a few of the city's best restaurants, you'll also pass the mid-19th-century house **El Zaguán,** which contains the offices of the **Historic Santa Fe Foundation** (545 Canyon Rd., 505/983-2567, www.historicsantafe.org, 9am-noon and 1:30pm-3pm Mon.-Fri., free). Named for its long internal hallway (*zaguán*), the building was the home of a local merchant, James L. Johnson, from 1854, and then occupied by several other city bigwigs after he lost his fortune in 1881. Its **garden** (9am-5pm Mon.-Sat.), laid out in the late 19th century, is a lovely place to rest in the summer.

Camino del Monte Sol

To get some sense of what the neighborhood was like before the gallery era, walk south on **Camino del Monte Sol,** which is still residential—though decidedly tonier now than in centuries past. Turning off Canyon Road, you'll cross Acequia Madre, shaded by cottonwoods and channeling water through the city. Farther up the road, starting at No. 558, is a clutch of homes first inhabited in the 1920s by Los Cinco Pintores, the band of young realist painters who called themselves the "five little nuts in five mud huts." (Will Shuster is the best known of the five today, in part because he started the Zozobra tradition; Walter Mruk, Fremont Ellis, Joseph Bakos, and Willard Nash were the other four.)

Cut east on Camino Santander, then north on Camino San Acacio and northwest on Camino Don Miguel to find **Johnnie's Cash Store** (420 Camino Don Miguel, 505/982-9506, 8am-5:30pm Mon.-Fri. 9am-4pm Sat.), a little relic of a corner store, complete with a swinging screen door and a steamer full of famous homemade tamales.

Cristo Rey Catholic Church

Head beyond the shops and through a residential stretch to the far north end of Canyon Road to see John Gaw Meem's enormous and recently renovated **Cristo Rey Catholic Church** (1120 Canyon Rd., 505/983-8528). Built of 180,000 adobe bricks around a steel frame, the church opened in 1940 but looks as if it could be much older. Inside is a dramatic mid-18th-century baroque stone altarpiece, salvaged from La Castrense, the military chapel that used to occupy the south side of the plaza.

GUADALUPE AND THE RAILYARD

This neighborhood southwest of the plaza developed around the depot for the rail spur

---

1: the view from the Cross of the Martyrs
2: Santuario de Guadalupe 3: SITE Santa Fe
4: Canyon Road

It's Not *All* Adobe

Santa Fe's distinctive look is the product of stringent building codes that define and maintain "old Santa Fe style," from the thickness of walls (at least eight inches) to the shade of stucco finish, in only "brown, tan, or local earth tones." But look closely, and you'll see some variations. **Colonial** is the term applied to adobe (or adobe-look) buildings, usually one story, with their typical rounded edges and flat roofs supported by vigas, the long crossbeams made of single tree trunks. The style mimics one developed by the Spanish colonists in the 16th, 17th, and 18th centuries, based on their previous experience with adobe architecture and forms they saw in the pueblos.

In the 19th century, when New Mexico became a U.S. territory and the railroad could carry new building materials, timber-frame houses came into fashion. These so-called **territorial** buildings were often two stories tall, with balconies, and trimmed with brick cornices and Greek revival details, such as fluted wood columns and pediments above windows. The Catron Building, on the northeast corner of the plaza, is a fine example of the style developed in this period.

In the early part of the 20th century, the **Pueblo Revival** style was the product of architects like John Gaw Meem and Isaac Rapp, who admired the pueblo mission churches and Spanish colonial adobes for their clean-lined minimalism. Because they used frame construction, Pueblo Revival buildings could be taller: Rapp's New Mexico Museum of Art towers on the northwest corner of the plaza, and Meem's additions to the La Fonda hotel make it five stories. The trend coincided with an aggressive tourism campaign and the development of a comprehensive look for the city, and in the process many territorial houses were simply covered over in a thick layer of faux-adobe plaster. The result is not really true to history, but the city planners achieved their goal: Santa Fe looks like no other city in the United States.

from the main line at Lamy. Now it's the terminus for the Rail Runner from Albuquerque. The clutch of cafés and shops here are more casual and local, and generally lighter on the adobe look, as **Guadalupe Street** is just outside the most stringently policed historic zone.

South of the train depot, the focus of much of the city's efforts at enlivening its downtown core is the **Railyard** (www.railyardsantafe.com), a mixed-use district where former warehouses and workshops have been adapted to new business. As well as holding the city's excellent farmers market, it's also home to the best theater in the state. The south side of this area is the green space of **Railyard Park,** nicely landscaped with local grasses and fruit trees.

Santuario de Guadalupe

Built 1776-1796, the **Santuario de Guadalupe** (417 Agua Fria St., 505/983-8868, 9am-noon and 1pm-4pm Mon.-Sat., free) is the oldest shrine to the Virgin of Guadalupe in the United States. The interior is spare, in

front of a Mexican baroque oil-on-canvas altar painting from 1783. Mass is still said regularly, and a museum in the small anteroom displays relics from earlier incarnations of the building, such as Greek-style columns carved in wood. In winter, the church is closed on Saturday.

SITE Santa Fe

Fronted by a striking, angular facade, the modern exhibition space of **SITE Santa Fe** (1606 Paseo de Peralta, 505/989-1199, https://sitesantafe.org, 10am-5pm Thurs. and Sat., 10am-7pm Fri., noon-5pm Sun., $10) shows edgy art year-round, with installations often taking over the whole interior (and sometimes exterior). In July and August, it's also open on Wednesday, and entrance is free on Friday and Saturday until noon, when the farmers market is on, kitty-corner across the train tracks. A recent renovation and expansion dramatically increased its footprint and its visual impact, as well as adding a 200-seat auditorium and a coffee bar.

El Museo Cultural de Santa Fe

Dedicated to Hispanic culture in New Mexico and beyond, El Museo Cultural de Santa Fe (555 Camino de la Familia, 505/992-0591, www.elmuseocultural.org, 1pm-5pm Tues.-Sat., donation) is a grassroots effort in a surprisingly massive warehouse space that has room for installations, live theater, and more. It often hosts special events outside of normal museum hours.

Lannan Foundation Gallery

The influential Lannan Foundation, which funds art projects in Marfa, Texas, and an excellent speaker series in Santa Fe, among many other creative endeavors, operates the Lannan Foundation Gallery (309 Read St., 505/954-5149, noon-5pm Sat.-Sun.). In two adjacent houses, it displays selections from the family's ever-expanding trove of contemporary art, usually with an eye toward social justice.

MUSEUM HILL

These museums on the southeast side merit the trip from the plaza area. It's a short drive, or you can take the "M" route bus or the free Santa Fe Pick-Up shuttle, optionally strolling back downhill to the center, about a 30-minute walk.

Museum of Spanish Colonial Art

The museum of the Spanish Colonial Arts Society (750 Camino Lejo, 505/982-2226, www.spanishcolonial.org, 10am-5pm daily June-Aug., 10am-5pm Tues.-Sun. Sept.-May, $8) exhibits a strong collection of folk art and historical objects dating from the earliest Spanish contact. One-of-a-kind treasures—such as the only signed *retablo* by the 19th-century *santero* Rafael Aragón—are shown alongside more utilitarian items from the colonial past, such as silk mantas, wool rugs, and decorative tin. New work by contemporary artisans is also on display—don't miss Luis Tapia's meta-*bulto*, *The Folk-Art Collectors.*

Museum of Indian Arts & Culture

The excellent Museum of Indian Arts & Culture (710 Camino Lejo, 505/476-1250, www.miaclab.org, 10am-5pm daily May-Oct., 10am-5pm Tues.-Sun. Nov.-Apr., $12) is devoted to Native American culture from across the country. Cornerstone exhibit *Here, Now and Always* traces the New Mexican Indians from their ancestors on the mesas and plains up to their present-day efforts at preserving their culture. It displays inventive spaces (looking into a Housing and Urban Development-house kitchen on the reservation, or sitting at desks in a public schoolroom), sound clips, and stories. Another wing is devoted to contemporary art, while the halls of craft work display gorgeous beaded moccasins, elaborate headdresses, and more. The gift shop has beautiful jewelry and other tidbits from local artisans.

★ Museum of International Folk Art

A marvelous hodgepodge, the Museum of International Folk Art (708 Camino Lejo, 505/476-1200, www.internationalfolkart.org, 10am-5pm daily May-Oct., 10am-5pm Tues.-Sun. Nov.-Apr., $12) is one of Santa Fe's biggest treats—if you can handle visual overload. In the main exhibition space, some 10,000 folk-art pieces from more than 100 countries are on permanent display, hung on walls, set in cases, even dangling from the ceiling, juxtaposed to show off similar themes, colors, and materials. The approach initially seems jumbled but in fact underscores the universality of certain concepts and preoccupations. Join a guided tour (10:30am, 11:30am, and 2pm) to learn all the details.

A separate wing is dedicated to northern New Mexican Hispano crafts (a good complement to the Museum of Spanish Colonial Art) and a lab area where you can see how pieces are preserved. Temporary exhibits take up the rest of the space, usually with colorful interactive shows. Don't skip the gift shop, which stocks some smaller versions of the items in the galleries.

Wheelwright Museum of the American Indian

In the early 1920s, Mary Cabot Wheelwright, an adventurous East Coast heiress, made her way to New Mexico, where she met a Navajo medicine man named Hastiin Klah. Together they devised the **Wheelwright Museum of the American Indian** (704 Camino Lejo, 505/982-4636, www.wheelwright.org, 10am-5pm daily, $8), which opened in 1937 as the House of Navajo Religion. The mission has since incorporated all Native American cultures, with exhibits of new work by individual artists rotating every few months. The building is modeled after a traditional Navajo hogan, with huge timbers supporting the eight-sided structure, and a new wing (added in 2015) is dedicated to Southwestern jewelry. The basement gift shop is a re-creation of a 19th-century trading post, which would feel like a tourist trap if it weren't for the authentically creaky wood floors and the beautiful antique crafts on display. The museum offers guided **tours** (10:30am, 11:30am, and 2pm).

Santa Fe Botanical Garden

Opened in 2013, the 14-acre **Santa Fe Botanical Garden** (715 Camino Lejo, 505/471-9103, www.santafebotanicalgarden.com, 9am-5pm daily Apr.-Oct. $10, 11am-3pm Thurs.-Sun. Nov.-Mar., $7) is still growing, and until all three of its planned areas are open and flourishing, only really curious gardeners are likely to consider it worth the price of admission. The plantings emphasize drought-tolerant plants, including a garden thriving on zero irrigation and an orchard containing peach, apple, and cherry trees. To get the most out of your visit, take a guided tour at 10am or 2pm.

The gardens also maintain a wetland preserve near Rancho de las Golondrinas, just outside of the city, with free walking tours (by appointment) on weekends, May through October.

SANTA FE METRO AREA

New Mexico National Guard Museum

One of three small museums in a single complex a bit out of the center, the **New Mexico Military Museum** (1050 Old Pecos Tr., 505/474-1670, www.newmexicomilitarymuseum.com, 10am-4pm Tues.-Sat., free) began as a homegrown memorial for soldiers in the Bataan Death March of World War II. It was a particular tragedy in New Mexico because most of the state's national guardsmen, drafted as the 200th Coast Artillery, were among the more than 70,000 U.S. and Filipino soldiers subject to torture, malnourishment, random execution, and three years' imprisonment. Of the 1,800 who started in the regiment, fewer than 900 came home, and a full one-third of those men died in the first year back. The troops' experience is recalled with newspaper clippings, maps, and testimonials. The museum also contains Civil War memorabilia and exhibits on Native American contributions in U.S. wars, such as the Choctaw and Navajo code talkers of World War I.

Santa Fe Children's Museum

Kids can have tons of hands-on fun at the **Santa Fe Children's Museum** (1050 Old Pecos Tr., 505/989-8359, 10am-6pm Tues.-Wed., Fri.-Sat., 10am-6:30pm Thurs., noon-5pm Sun., www.santafechildrensmuseum.org, $7.50 adults, $5 children). Fitting for New Mexico, pint-size looms give kids a chance to learn to weave. Then there are the globally appealing bits: a giant soap-bubble pool, face painting, fun-house mirrors, and a dazzling collection of bugs. On Thursdays after 4pm, admission is free.

Center for Contemporary Arts

Behind the Children's Museum, the long-established **Center for Contemporary Arts** (1050 Old Pecos Tr., 505/982-1338, www.ccasantafe.org, noon-5pm Thurs.-Sun., free) has been mounting multimedia art shows and screening films since 1979. (An early James

Turrell Skyspace is on the grounds here; unfortunately, it is now in disrepair and not open to visitors, though the center aspires to restore it.) The center is a nice alternative to the slicker gallery spaces and usually a good spot to check the pulse of younger resident artists.

★ Meow Wolf Art Complex

The anchor of the emerging Siler-Rufina neighborhood, the **Meow Wolf Art Complex** (1352 Rufina Circle, 505/395-6369, https://meowwolf.com, 10am-8pm Sun.-Thurs., 10-10pm Fri.-Sat., $20) features an ethereal permanent exhibition dreamed up by a Santa Fe-based art collective. Giving life to a massive and long-shuttered space once occupied by a bowling alley, the 20,000-foot multilevel **House of Eternal Return** consists of a bewildering mix of kaleidoscopic rooms and nooks, each loosely building on an evolving narrative of the melding of real and otherworldly dimensions. Equally immersive and ambitious, the Victorian house holds the kinds of unexpected and multilayered surprises that reward multiple visits. It's great for both kids and adults, and you'll want to block out at least two hours, if not four; lines can be quite long during peak hours.

In addition to the permanent exhibit, the complex also contains the **David Loughridge Learning Center,** used by Meow Wolf's nonprofit educational outreach program, a gallery space that features the works of local artists, and a music venue that quickly established itself as one of the best spots in town to catch live acts. The art collective has broadened its ambitions, with fantastical exhibitions planned in Denver and Las Vegas.

Rancho de las Golondrinas

About a 15-minute drive southeast, **Rancho de las Golondrinas** (334 Los Pinos Rd., 505/471-2261, www.golondrinas.org, 10am-4pm Wed.-Sun. June-Sept., $6), the "Ranch of the Swallows," is Santa Fe's equivalent of Colonial Williamsburg, a 200-acre museum where staff members in period costumes demonstrate crafts and other aspects of early New Mexican history. The core of it is a restored Spanish colonial *paraje,* a way station on the Camino Real, and outbuildings contain a blacksmith shop, a schoolhouse, mills, and even a rebuilt Penitente *morada* (the docent who works here is a Penitente himself and may sing some of the group's hymns).

The ranch hosts big to-dos (entrance fees typically $10-15), including a wine festival in early July, a celebration of Mexican culture in late July, a lively renaissance fair in September, among other things. It's a good idea to pack your own picnic; there's a basic café at the ranch, but it's open only on weekends. Allow a few hours to see the whole place. In April, May, and October, the museum is open on weekdays for guided tours by appointment; call 505/471-2261 to make arrangements. In these shoulder months, the ranch is also occasionally open for special theme weekends.

Lamy

Probably worth the drive only if you're a rail fan, this village is little more than a depot with an attached restaurant, though it is a mighty fine place to step off Amtrak's Southwest Chief. Across the road, the **Lamy Railroad & History Museum** (151 Old Lamy Tr., 505/466-1650, noon-4pm Sat.) is a sprawling Old West saloon and dining room (known as Legal Tender) that doubles as a treasure trove of old railroading days; there's even a model train set. The place has a spotty record of opening, so call ahead if you plan to make the trip.

Take Old Las Vegas Highway (or I-25) southeast out of Santa Fe; six miles out of town, turn south on U.S. 285. After six miles, turn left for the last bumpy mile to Lamy.

Sports and Recreation

It's no accident *Outside* magazine has its offices here. After work and on weekends, Santa Feans leave the town to the tourists and scatter into the surrounding mountains on foot and bike—and in winter, on skis and snowboards. You'll find something to do all four seasons, though hikes above the foothills shouldn't be attempted until mid-May at least (and not until you're acclimated to the altitude). If you're in town in the fall, don't miss the aspen leaves turning, usually in mid-October. The access route for activities in the Sangre de Cristos is winding Highway 475—it starts out from the north side of Santa Fe as Artists Road, then the name changes to Hyde Park Road, and farther north it's Ski Basin Road.

Information, Guides, and Gear
Just off Highway 14, immediately south of I-25, the **Public Lands Information Center** (301 Dinosaur Tr., 505/954-2002, www.publiclands.org, 8am-4:30pm Mon.-Fri.) is the best starting point for any planning. The staff will also know the latest status on areas affected by wildfires or floods. **Outspire!** (505/660-0394, www.outspire.com) runs guided full- and half-day outings—hiking in summer, snowshoeing in winter. **Santa Fe Mountain Adventures** (505/988-4000, www.santafemountainadventures.com) offers guided mountain biking trips of varying difficulty levels between 4-6 hours in and around Santa Fe; they also lead guided hikes and 4x4 outings.

For gear, visit **REI** (500 Market St., 505/982-3557, 10am-8pm Mon.-Fri., 10am-7pm Sat., 11am-6pm Sun.) in the Railyard district.

HIKING
Some of the best hiking trails in the state can be reached by just a short drive or bike ride

1: Meow Wolf Art Complex 2: Rancho de las Golondrinas

from the center of Santa Fe. Even in the height of summer, none of them feels particularly overcrowded, meaning you can enjoy some seriously gorgeous scenery in relative solitude. The trails in this section are ordered based on their distance from downtown.

Santa Fe Canyon Preserve
For an easy saunter in town, head for **Santa Fe Canyon Preserve**, a 190-acre patch of the foothills managed by **The Nature Conservancy** (505/988-3867). The preserve covers the canyon formed by the now-diverted Santa Fe River. An easy interpretive loop trail leads around the marshy area for 1.5 miles, passing the remnants of the dam and winding through dense stands of cottonwoods and willows. The trailhead is on Cerro Gordo Road, just north of its intersection with Upper Canyon Road. The area is open only to people on foot—no mountain bikes and no pets.

Randall Davey Audubon Center & Sanctuary
Birders of course will want to start a hike here, but even general visitors will be intrigued by the house of artist **Randall Davey** (1800 Upper Canyon Rd., 505/983-4609, 8am-4pm Mon.-Sat., $2 suggested donation) and two pretty trails that lead into the forest and canyons behind. The beautifully painted back rooms of the house are open for a guided **tour** ($5) at 2pm every Friday, and a free guided bird walk departs from the parking lot at 8am every Saturday.

Sun Mountain
The two-mile round-trip trail up solitary **Sun Mountain** (elev. 7,920 feet) sets off from a small roadside parking area 2.2 miles southeast of Paseo de Peralta on Old Santa Fe Trail. The start of the hike is fairly flat, passing through shaded woods, before beginning a sharp ascent. After 0.25 mile, the trail

Scenic Drive: Fall Foliage

With its evergreens and scrub trees, New Mexico doesn't seem a likely spot for a vivid display of fall colors. But the deciduous trees that flourish here—aspen, maple, cottonwood—are wild pockets of color against the rocky landscape, often bright gold against red rocks. You don't have to drive far to see the colors, which are usually at their peak in mid-October.

From Santa Fe, just drive up **Highway 475** (the road to the ski basin), where pullouts are positioned for the best vistas of the many colorful aspen stands; the pullout at the aptly named Aspen Vista trailhead is one of the best. Abiquiu's dramatic rock formations are also a good backdrop for cottonwoods.

From Albuquerque, head to the east face of the **Sandia Mountains** and up the road to the peak, stopping off at Cienega Picnic Area and Las Huertas Picnic Area, about midway up the mountain. Or head southeast to the Manzano Mountains, where **Fourth of July Canyon,** with maple leaves turning shades of pink and crimson, is a beautiful color show. The area

Aspen Vista Trail in fall

around Jemez is especially nice, with the cottonwoods contrasting with red canyon walls, though when you get close to Valles Caldera National Preserve, you hit wildfire damage.

From Taos, the entire **Enchanted Circle** drive passes through various patches of color.

---

emerges on Sun Mountain's exposed western flank, where a series of switchbacks pass by yucca, cholla, and prickly pear. From the top, a little over 900 feet from the trailhead, sweeping panoramas take in the city's orderly grid below and an arc of jagged Sangre de Cristo summits to the east.

Atalaya Mountain

One of the most accessible trails in the Santa Fe area (you can take the M city bus to the trailhead on the campus of St. John's College) is also one of the more challenging. The mostly-shaded hike heads up to a **9,121-foot peak,** starting out as a gentle stroll along the city's edge, then becoming increasingly steep, for a round-trip of approximately 6 miles. Allow about four hours for the full up-and-back.

Aspen Vista

The most popular trail in the Sangre de Cristos is probably **Aspen Vista.** It is well traveled in fall, as the promised views of golden aspen groves are spectacular. In the densest spots, when the sun is shining through the leaves, the air itself feels yellow. Though at a high elevation, the hike is reasonably easy, on a service road with a gradual slope. The full length is 11.5 miles, but it's the first 2.5 miles that are the most aspen-intense. A little under 4 miles in, you get a great view of Santa Fe below; this makes a good turnaround point for a two-hour hike. Look for the parking area on the right of Ski Basin Road (Hwy. 475), just under 13 miles up the road from town.

Raven's Ridge

This is another local favorite, though not too heavily traveled, with great views of Santa Fe Baldy (elev. 12,622 feet)—while you're busy slogging up and over several peaks yourself. The trail starts at the Winsor trailhead (no. 254) in the Santa Fe ski area parking lot, but when you reach the wilderness boundary fence, the **Raven's Ridge Trail** heads to the right along the outside of the fence. The trail shows up on only one local map (Drake Mountain Maps' *Map of the Mountains of Santa Fe*), but it's easy to follow once you're up there. When in doubt, just head uphill: You'll bag Deception, Lake, and Tesuque peaks in a total of seven miles and with a top elevation of 12,409 feet, returning to the ski area parking lot by walking down along the Tesuque chairlift. But this final stretch isn't particularly scenic, so you may want to take in only one or two of the peaks (Lake Peak, the second you reach, is the highest) and then retrace your steps.

Rio en Medio

The serene Rio en Medio Trail (no. 163) begins north of Tesuque and parallels a clear stream to a series of waterfalls and then up some rather strenuous switchbacks to a large meadow that's filled with wildflowers in springtime. From the trailhead to the first cascade is 1.7 miles. The meadow is at the 3.5-mile mark, where you'll probably want to turn around, for a hike that will take a total of four or five hours.

To reach the trailhead, drive north out of Santa Fe on Washington Avenue, which becomes Bishops Lodge Road (Highway 590). Drive straight through the village of Tesuque and then turn right in less than a mile onto Highway 592, passing the Four Seasons along the way and following signs for the village of Rio en Medio. In the village, which you reach after 6.5 miles, the road turns into County Road 78-D, an unpromising-looking dirt track that winds through front yards for 0.8 mile before ending in a small parking area. A forest road carries on from there for a short stretch, and then the trail proper heads off to the right and down along a stream. As parking is limited, hiking the trail in off-peak hours is advisable.

BIKING

Mountain bikers have fantastic outlets close to Santa Fe, while those who prefer the open road will love the challenges in the winding

highways through the mountains north of the city. There are several reliable bike shops in and around town. Two of the best are Broken Spoke (1426 Cerrillos Rd., 505/992-3102, 10am-6pm Mon.-Fri., 10-5pm Sat.) and Bike N Sport (524 W. Cordova Rd., 505/820-0809, 10am-6pm Mon.-Fri., 10-5pm Sat.). Both provide a full range of bike services, including tune-ups and repairs.

For bike rentals, Mellow Velo (132 E. Marcy St., 505/995-8356, 10am-6pm Mon.-Fri., 10am-5pm Sat., 10am-3pm Sun., from $30/day), just off the plaza, stocks cruisers for around town as well as deluxe mountain and road bikes. It's also an excellent resource of area rides.

Mountain Biking

A local classic and the gentlest introduction to mountain biking around Santa Fe, the Santa Fe Rail Trail starts as a paved path in the Railyard Park, then turns to dirt outside the city limits, following a relatively easy route along the railroad tracks to Lamy. The trail is about 12.5 miles one-way; except for a grade near I-25, it's fairly level.

The Dale Ball Trails are the heart of the city's mountain biking scene: 22 miles of single-track routes for both hikers and mountain bikers, winding through stands of piñon and juniper in the Sangre de Cristo foothills. Two trailheads give access to the North, Central, and South Sections of the trail. From the northern trailhead, on Sierra del Norte (immediately off Highway 475 after mile marker 3), the North Section trails vary a bit in elevation, but the Central Section (south from the parking area) is more fun because it's a longer chunk of trails. The southern trailhead, on Cerro Gordo just north of its intersection with Canyon Road, gives access to the Central Section and the South Section, which is for advanced riders only. Note that the trail that starts at the southern trailhead lot, part of the Santa Fe Canyon Preserve, is for foot traffic only—ride your bike 0.1 mile down Cerro Gordo to the start of the Dale Ball system.

In the rolling hills west of the city, **La Tierra Trails** are for biking, hiking, and horseback riding—though it's the two-wheel crew who makes the most use of them, especially after work, when the day is cooler (there's not much shade out here). There are three trailheads, all interconnected by various loops; the more technical ones are clearly marked. Take Highway 599, the bypass road around the city, north out of the city for about 3.5 miles and turn right onto Camino La Tierra. The parking lot for the trailhead is a quarter of a mile down on the right.

A bit farther out of town is the immensely popular **Winsor Trail** (no. 254), a catchall that covers a great range of scenery and terrain and presents a few challenges, too. Heading up, there are few deadly steep ascents, so it's tiring but not impossible, and you'll rarely have to hike-a-bike; you're rewarded with a long, joyful downhill run. The trailhead is in Tesuque: Take Washington Avenue north out of the center of Santa Fe, continuing as it becomes Bishops Lodge Road (Highway 590). After not quite four miles, turn right onto County Road 72-A, also signed as Big Tesuque Canyon. There are two small pullout areas for parallel parking, and the trail starts about 0.1 mile up the road from the second parking area—the first 0.5 mile is through private land.

Road Biking

Make sure you're acclimated to the altitude before you set out on any lengthy trip and stay hydrated—road biking typically means little shade and long distances in between resupply points. Shoulders aren't a given; it's especially important to ride single file. The area's best tour, along the **High Road to Taos,** will take you through some of the area's highest elevations. Starting in Chimayó shaves some not-so-scenic miles off the ride and gives you a reasonable 45-mile jaunt to Taos.

A less taxing ride can be had by taking Washington Avenue north from downtown. After 0.25 miles it becomes Bishops Lodge Road (Highway 590) and descends into the shady village of **Tesuque.** Past Tesuque the road continues as Highway 591 before turning

into Frontage Road, just past the Highway 285 overpass. The stretch along Frontage Road before it ends near the Buffalo Thunder Casino is not as scenic as the earlier portion, but it is generally blissfully free of traffic.

The annual **Santa Fe Century** (www.santafecentury.com) is the biggest organized riding event in the state, taking place mid-May. The course runs a 104-mile loop south down the Turquoise Trail and back north via the old farm towns in the Galisteo Basin, southeast of Santa Fe. There's also a Gran Fondo version that pits you against the clock and other riders as well as more manageable 25- and 50-mile rides.

ROCK CLIMBING

To polish your **rock climbing** skills or get tips on nearby routes, talk to the experts at **Santa Fe Climbing Center** (3008 Cielo Court, 505/986-8944, www.climbsantafe.com, noon-9pm Mon., 9am-9pm Tues., Thurs., and Fri., noon-10pm Wed., noon-8pm Sat., 10am-6pm Sun.). You can play around on the walls at the gym ($16 for a day pass) or sign up for a guided group trip to a nearby climbing site (starting at $70 for half a day).

RAFTING

With the **Rio Grande** within easy reach of Santa Fe, some of the best rafting opportunities in the country are close at hand. Snowmelt runoff determines the peak spring times for many of the runs—including the challenging 17-mile-long **Taos Box**—though it has much less of an impact throughout the summer months, when the water levels are more constant. One of the more popular trips is the **Racecourse**, an adrenaline-packed half-day adventure near Pilar. A succession of Class III rapids with names such as The Maze and The Narrows provide plenty of white-knuckle moments. There are more mellow trips, too, particularly in the Lower Gorge and the Orilla Verde Recreation Area, where it's easy to float carefree.

1: the Santa Fe Rail Trail, an introduction to mountain biking around Santa Fe **2:** rafting the Rio Grande

The Rio Chama offers mostly gentle outings through the heart of O'Keeffe Country, with some Class III rapids as well. Half-day and full-day trips on both rivers are offered by longtime outfitters **Kokopelli Rafting Adventures** (1401 Maclavia St., 505/983-3734, https://kokopelliraft.com, from $64).

FISHING

Trout teem in the Rio Chama, northwest of Santa Fe, in the streams of **Valles Caldera National Preserve,** and in pockets of a few lesser-known rivers north of the city. The fly shops the **High Desert Angler** (460 Cerrillos Rd., 505/988-7688, www.highdesertangler.com, 8am-6pm Mon.-Sat., 11am-4pm Sun.) and **The Reel Life** (526 N. Guadalupe St., 505/995-8114, www.thereellife.com, 8am-7pm Mon.-Fri., 8am-6pm Sat., 8am-5pm Sun.), in the DeVargas Center, sell gear and can also arrange guided day-trips to nearby waters (from $350 for two).

GOLF

Marty Sanchez Links de Santa Fe (205 Caja del Rio Rd., 505/955-4400, www.linksdesantafe.com) is a "water-aware" course that uses indigenous grasses and other plants to minimize water use. It offers great views of the mountains as you tour the 18 holes designed by Baxter Spann; there's also "The Great 28," an additional par-3 nine-holer that's exceptionally challenging. With five sets of tees, the course is good for both beginners and experts. Greens fees start at $23 for nine holes, and there are discounts after 2pm.

WINTER SPORTS

Sixteen miles northeast of town in the Santa Fe National Forest, **Ski Santa Fe** (Hwy. 475, 505/982-4429, www.skisantafe.com, $80 full-day lift ticket, $36 full equipment rentals) is a well-used day area with over 80 trails of varying difficulty, including quite a few challenging runs. Along with its impressive cross-section of trails, another major selling point is that there are virtually no lines on any of the seven lifts.

Exclusively for cross-country skiers, the groomed **Norski Trail** (also known as Trail #255) starts about 0.25 mile before the Ski Santa Fe parking lot, off the west side of Hwy. 475. The standard route is about 2 miles, winding through the trees and along a ridgeline, and you can shorten or lengthen the tour by taking various loops and shortcuts, as long as you follow the directional arrows counterclockwise.

Just seven miles out of town along the road to the ski basin, **Hyde Memorial State Park** (740 Hyde Park Rd., 505/983-7175, www.emnrd.state.nm.us) has a couple of nicely maintained sledding runs, and some shorter cross-country ski and snowshoeing routes.

For gear, **Cottam's Ski Shop** (740 Hyde Park Rd., 505/982-0495, from 7:30am daily in ski season) is the biggest rental operation in the area, handily located at the entrance to Hyde Memorial State Park.

In town, the knowledgeable **Alpine Sports** (121 Sandoval St., 505/983-5155, 10am-6pm daily) specializes in winter apparel and equipment.

SPAS
★ Ten Thousand Waves

A Santa Fe institution, **Ten Thousand Waves** (3451 Hyde Park Rd., 505/982-9304, www.tenthousandwaves.com, 9am-9:30pm Mon. and Wed.-Thurs., 1pm-9:30pm Tues., Fri.-Sun. 9am-10:30pm Jan.-June, 9am-10:30pm Wed.-Mon., 1pm-10:30pm Tues. July-Oct.) is a traditional Japanese-style bathhouse that melds seamlessly into the mountainside above town. Featuring two big communal pools, it also has five smaller private ones tucked among the trees; many have adjoining cold plunges and saunas. The place also offers full day-spa services, with intense massages and luxe facials and body scrubs. Prices are relatively reasonable, starting at $28 for unlimited time in the public baths and $119 for 50-minute massages. In the winter (Nov.-June), the baths open at 10:30am (at 2pm Tues.) and close earlier on weeknights.

Other Spas

The relaxed and welcoming atmosphere of **Body of Santa Fe** (333 W. Cordova Rd., 505/986-0362, www.bodyofsantafe.com, 8:30am-7pm daily) has helped it earn a devoted following—and its affordable treatments (massages from $85/hour) help, too. There's also an on-site studio offering yoga and pilates classes (from $16) daily.

In town, **Absolute Nirvana Spa** (106 Faithway St., 505/983-7942, www.absolutenirvana.com, 10am-6pm Mon.-Thurs., 10am-8pm Fri.-Sun.) runs a "green" operation with a Balinese inspiration for many of its treatments and massages (from $120/hr). Afterward, you can relax in the gardens with a cup of tea and some organic sweets from the adjacent tearoom.

South of the city and down the road from Rancho de Las Golondrinas, **Sunrise Springs** (242 Los Pinos Rd, 505/780-8145, www.sunrisesprings.ojospa.com, 10am-8pm daily) is suited for those looking to truly get away. Spread over 70 idyllic acres, the spa includes yoga and fitness studios, outdoor pools, soaking tubs, hot tubs, and an art studio. A comprehensive list of services and packages is offered, including hot stone massages ($135 for 50 minutes) and various forms of bodywork.

SPECTATOR SPORTS

The **Santa Fe Fuego** (www.santafefuego.com), a baseball team that puts the minor in minor league, plays at Fort Marcy Park, just north of the plaza area, mid-May-early August. It's part of the incredibly scrappy Pecos League (www.pecosleague.com), established in 2011 and fielding 12 teams from around the Southwest, California, Texas, and Kansas.

SPORTS FACILITIES

For bargain yoga classes, swimming in a 25-yard indoor pool, and other activities close to the plaza, stop in at the **Fort Marcy Recreation Complex** (490 Bishops Lodge Rd., 505/955-2500, www.santafenm.gov, 6am-8:30pm Mon.-Fri., 8am-4pm Sat., $5).

Genoveva Chavez Community Center (3221 Rodeo Rd., 505/955-4000, www.chavezcenter.com, 5:30am-9:45pm Mon.-Thurs., 5:30am-7:45pm Fri., 8am-7:45pm Sat., 9am-5:45pm Sun., $7) is the city's biggest recreational facility. It has a large swimming pool with a slide and a separate lap pool (both are indoors); basketball and racquetball courts; a gym; and a year-round ice rink.

The city's only outdoor pool—and with the crowds you might expect—is **Bicentennial Pool** (1121 Alto St., 505/955-4779, www.santafenm.gov, $3), open late May-early September.

Entertainment and Events

NIGHTLIFE

With breezy summer evenings and a populace that always seems to be able to knock off work a little early, Santa Fe typically favors happy hour over late-night carousing.

Bars and Clubs

Longtime city haunt the **Dragon Room Lounge** (406 Old Santa Fe Tr., 505/983-7712, 4pm-midnight Tues.-Sun.) is so dim you might not notice at first the huge tree growing up from the left side of the bar. Guys in cowboy hats chat with mountain bikers and dressed-up cocktail drinkers. There's live music Tuesday, Thursday, and Saturday.

South of the city center, **Maria's** (555 W. Cordova Rd., 505/983-7929, 11am-10pm daily) has gained a devoted following by serving impeccably balanced margaritas, with fresh lime and nearly any brand of tequila you can imagine. About 1.5 miles to the south on Cerrillos Road and inside El Rey Court, hip and unpretentious ★ **La Reina** (1862 Cerrillos Rd., 505/982-1931) is *the* place to go for mezcal and tequila-tinged cocktails; there's also a good selection of draft beers, wines, and sakes for good measure.

Open-Air Bars

For a perfectly perched sunset drink, get to the Bell Tower Bar (100 E. San Francisco St., 505/982-5511, 11am-sunset daily May-Oct.) early if you can, as this spot on the rooftop at La Fonda fills up fast. It's usually packed with tourists, but the view over the plaza is inspiring.

If there's no room at the Bell Tower, the next best spot for plaza views is Thunderbird (50 Lincoln Ave., 505/490-6550, 11:30am-9pm, 11:30am-10pm Fri.-Sat.), which has a 2nd-floor porch. At happy hour (4pm-6pm), margaritas are $6.

A couple of blocks to the east, spacious Bar Alto (228 E. Palace Ave., 505/982-0883, 2pm-10pm Mon.-Fri, noon-midnight Sat.-Sun.), spreads out alongside the rooftop pool of the Drury Plaza Hotel. Service can be uneven, but the setting can't be beat; the fire pits and comfy lounge chairs are nice touches, too. There are daily drink specials, with happy hours from 3pm-6pm.

The mellow patio scene at Cowgirl BBQ (319 S. Guadalupe St., 505/982-2565, 11:30am-midnight Mon.-Thurs., 11am-1am Fri.-Sat., 11am-11:30pm Sun.) gets started early, with happy hour kicking off at 3pm and lasting until 6pm, with two-for-one apps and $4 margaritas. It's good later, too, with live music many nights.

On Canyon Road, stalwart El Farol (808 Canyon Rd., 505/983-9912, 11am-10pm Sun.-Thurs., 11am-11pm Fri.-Sat.) is the gallerists' after work hangout, with outside seating on a creaky wooden *portal* and a back patio.

A strong selection of over 30 craft ales is on tap at the Violet Crown (1606 Alcaldesa St., 505/216-5678, 10:30am-11pm daily), which offers one of the more scenic views in the Railyard and a great starting point to a night out in the district.

The grungier side of Santa Fe is on display at Evangelo's (200 W. San Francisco St., 505/982-9014, 3pm-2am Mon.-Fri., 2:30pm-2am Sat., 2pm-midnight Sun.), where soul and blues bands take the small stage at the back. When there's no band, there's room at the pool tables, plus no shortage of crusty characters. On the opposite corner, those who descend the stairs to the basement-level Matador (116 W. San Francisco St., entrance on Galisteo St., 505/984-5050, 5pm-2am daily) will find a good cross section of Santa Fe's younger artists, among other renowned drinkers, in the bar's dark and decidedly grungy environs. If there's not a live band, there's punk rock on the stereo to match the concert posters on the walls.

A few downtown restaurants have standout bars and merit a visit alone even if you're not looking for a meal. The upscale rooftop Coyote Cantina (132 Water St., 505/983-1615, 11:30am-11pm daily, May-Oct.) of the Coyote Café has one of the liveliest scenes around the plaza, while the snug bar at Geronimo (724 Canyon Rd., 505/982-1500, 5:30pm-9:30pm daily) is a good place to put your feet up after a Canyon Road cruise. La Casa Sena (125 E. Palace Ave., 505/988-9232, 11am-10pm daily) is set in a truly dreamy garden courtyard; order a cocktail and an appetizer and enjoy the eye candy.

Breweries

Local operation Second Street Brewery brews stouts, bitters, IPAs, and other beers on tap in a chummy, semi-industrial atmosphere, sometimes backed up by a band. There are multiple locations: the original site that gave it its name (1814 2nd St., 505/982-3030, 11am-10pm Mon.-Thurs., 11am-11pm Fri.-Sat., noon-9pm Sun.), the more central branch in the Railyard (1607 Paseo de Peralta, 505/989-3278, 11am-10pm Mon.-Thurs., 11am-11pm Fri.-Sat., noon-9pm Sun.) with a patio area, and another in the heart of the Siler-Rufina neighborhood (2920 Rufina St., 505/954-1068, 11am-midnight Mon.-Sat., noon-midnight Sun.). Happy hour is 4pm-6:30pm daily.

Cozy Duel Brewing (1228 Parkway Dr., 505/474-5301, noon-midnight Mon.-Sat.,

1pm-8pm Sun.) focuses mainly on Belgian-style beers—Duel's potent saison is a standout—with a few other options on tap as well. An eclectic selection of live acts performs regularly on the small stage, and the menu features items filling sandwiches and tasty finger food.

On the southern outskirts of the city, venerable **Santa Fe Brewing Company** (35 Fire Pl., 505/424-3333, 11am-10pm Mon.-Fri., Sat 11am-9pm 2pm-8pm Sun.) is the oldest brewery in New Mexico. The small taproom has more than a dozen crafted beers, including its popular Happy Camper IPA and Santa Fe Gold lager as well as seasonal varieties. Saturday **tours** (noon) provide an excellent glimpse behind the scenes of the onsite brewery.

There's no lack for choice at **Tumbleroot** (2791 Agua Fria St., 505/780-5730, 4pm-10pm Mon.-Thurs. 4pm-midnight Fri., noon-midnight Sat. noon-10pm Sun.), a ten-minute drive west of the plaza, where you can choose from IPAs, pale ales, lagers, stouts, and quite a few others. Where this locals' favorite really stands out, however, is with its selection of spirits—it's also a distillery—and its shaded outdoor patio set in a semicircle around a koi pond. There's live music most night and a couple of food trucks parked outside, including the stellar **Bang Bite**.

Cocktail Lounges

While most Santa Fe bars stick to margaritas, **Secreto Lounge** (210 Don Gaspar Ave., 505/983-5700, 4pm-midnight Mon.-Thurs., noon-midnight Fri.-Sat., noon-10pm Sun.) is up on the cutting edge of cocktail culture. Its "garden to glass" menu uses only fresh herbs and other seasonal ingredients in such drinks as the Ginny Juice, a lemonade, orange juice, and vodka concoction with a serious kick. Of course, it still does a margarita or two: Its Agave Way is a pseudo-margarita that's spicy and sweet, with black grapes. Happy hour (4pm-7pm Mon.-Fri.) is worth planning around, as it knocks the price down to $7 or so, and you can sit out in the loggia of

the Hotel St. Francis and watch the passing parade.

Intimate and ornately designed, **Tonic** (103 E. Water St., 505/982-1189, www.tonicsantafe. com, 5pm-3am Mon.-Sat.) unabashedly evokes a bygone era. Sip on sophisticated cocktails—several of which are fairly elaborate—and enjoy the art deco flourishes steps from a jazz quartet.

Boozehounds will also want to drop by the tasting room of **Santa Fe Spirits** (308 Read St., 505/780-5906, 3pm-8:30pm Mon.-Thurs., 3pm-9pm Fri.-Sat.), a relaxed place to sample all the local distiller's products. Order a full flight, or enjoy a showcase drink such as the Whiskeyrita, which features the distiller's unaged Silver Coyote whiskey, or a simple gin and tonic with its aromatic, sage-infused gin.

Live Music

El Mesón (213 Washington St., 505/983-6756, 5pm-11pm Tues.-Sat.) has live music five nights a week, with a particularly devoted crew of regulars for tango on Tuesdays. You can order traditional tapas or bigger dishes from El Mesón's excellent dinner menu, or just join in the dancing on the small wood floor.

The Bridge (37 Fire Pl., 505/557-6182), Santa Fe Brewing Company's indoor and larger outdoor performance spaces, hosts touring bands and local acts across the lot from the taproom.

THE ARTS
Performing Arts

Set in a 1931 Moorish curlicue palace, the **Lensic Performing Arts Center** (211 W. San Francisco St., 505/988-1234, www.lensic. com) is Santa Fe's showpiece venue, with 820 seats and an eclectic wide-ranging schedule. The six-week-long summer **Santa Fe Chamber Music Festival** (www.sfcmf.org) holds events here, with performances nearly every day July-August. The chamber orchestra **Santa Fe Pro Musica** (505/988-4640, www.santafepromusica.com) also performs at the Lensic, fall-spring, as well as in Loretto Chapel and other intimate venues.

George R. R. Martin in Santa Fe

Santa Fe has been home to the wildly celebrated author George R. R. Martin since long before readers and HBO viewers were devouring his epic tales of warring nobles, zombie armies, and dragons in a land called Westeros. The author is quick to profess his love for the city—and green chile—and that affection is writ large around town. He restored and reopened the Jean Cocteau Cinema, giving Santa Fe its most eclectic theater—the kind of place where obscure 1970s horror movies can be seen on the big screen alongside Italian film classics. Part of the impetus behind the theater was to provide "The City Different" with something different—a compelling late-night diversion unlike anything else in town. That desire was likely also a contributing factor in his decision to back the Meow Wolf Art Complex. Now a runaway success, the complex was anything but a surefire hit when the idea to fund it was presented to Martin by its directors. It's hard to imagine the project getting off the ground without his support.

Though Martin is busy writing the latest book in his *A Song of Ice and Fire* series and helping HBO to create *Game of Thrones* spinoffs, he continues to give back to Santa Fe. His latest venture is The Stagecoach Foundation (stagecoachfdn.org), a nonprofit formed in 2017 to support Santa Fe's growing presence in the film industry as well as in the fields of education and technology. Its headquarters include space for film productions. Perhaps the White Walkers will someday come to the high desert . . .

If you think opera is all about tuxes, plush seats, and too-long arias, give the Santa Fe Opera (U.S. 84/285, 505/986-5900, www.santafeopera.org) a chance. Half the fun is arriving early to "tailgate" in the parking lot, which involves gourmet goodies, lots of champagne, and time to mill around and check out other attendees' bolo ties. Then there's the show itself, featuring the country's best singers, who treat this as their "summer camp" July-August. The elegant 2,000-plus-seat open amphitheater is beautiful at sunset; pack blankets to ward off the chill later on. If you have kids to entertain, time your visit for bargain-priced "family nights" or a special dress rehearsal with extra info to introduce young ones to the art form.

Cinema

★ VIOLET CROWN

Santa Fe's take on the Austin, Texas, beloved cinema and the Railyard's biggest draw, the Violet Crown (1606 Alcaldesa St., 505/216-5678, https://santafe.violetcrown.com) offers the most well-rounded and enjoyable movie-watching experience around. Select from a full snack and dinner menu and an extensive beer and wine list and settle into cushy seats to watch the latest blockbusters, hand-picked indies, and one-night-only showings of film classics.

OTHER CINEMAS

The delightful Jean Cocteau Cinema (418 Montezuma Ave., 505/466-5528, www.jeancocteaucinema.com, 2pm-10pm daily) gets press because of its owner, resident author George R. R. Martin, but it's a real treat on its own. The 120-seat theater oozes art-house charm and shows eclectic offerings and hosts readings for an appreciative local audience. It also holds a small bar area where you can order a pint, and cocktails such as a Jon Snow Cone and splurge on signed *Game of Thrones* merchandise.

Santa Fe University of Art and Design also has an excellent theater, The Screen (1600 St. Michael's Dr., 505/473-6494, www.thescreensf.com). The curator brings in quality first-run independent films along with repertory gems. Additionally, the CCA Cinematheque (1050 Old Pecos Tr.,

---

1: Violet Crown **2:** International Folk Art Market **3:** Jean Cocteau Cinema **4:** Lensic Performing Arts Center

1

2

3

4

505/982-1338, www.ccasantafe.org) has a film program with an emphasis on international titles and music documentaries.

Lectures

The **Lannan Foundation Lecture Series** (www.lannan.org, 505/986-8160) is run by a Santa Fe-based organization funding international writers and socially active artists. The program brings major writers and intellectuals to the Lensic for fascinating interviews and conversation. Events usually sell out quickly—check the schedule a couple of months before your visit.

The **Southwest Seminars Series** (www.southwestseminars.org, 505/466-2775) runs weekly year-round. Speakers are anthropologists, archaeologists, and other researchers with a special interest in the history and people of the region. Talks take place nearly every Monday (50 weeks a year) at 6pm at the Hotel Santa Fe (1501 Paseo de Peralta).

FESTIVALS AND EVENTS

★ Santa Fe Indian Market

Approaching its centennial mark, the city's biggest annual event is held in late August, when 100,000 visitors come for the **Santa Fe Indian Market** (505/983-5220, www.swaia.org). Centered on the plaza, the massive showcase of Native American art features more than 1,200 artisans selling jewelry, pottery, weaving, and more. The biggest crowds wander amongst the numerous stalls over the weekend, though there are celebratory events leading up to it.

Other Events

One of the earliest events in Santa Fe's festival season and a relative newcomer, the **InterPlanetary Festival** (interplanetaryfest.org) takes place in and around the Railyard Park over a weekend in mid-June and features screenings of science fiction classics and documentaries, panel discussions

and podcasts on all manner of extraterrestrial and more earthbound subjects—and book signings, too.

One weekend in mid-July, the **International Folk Art Market** (505/992-7600, www.folkartalliance.org) showcases traditional crafts from all over the globe, often from the artists in person. It's set up on Museum Hill so that the center of the city is not disrupted. On Sunday, tickets are cheaper than Friday and Saturday, and vendors are ready to make deals.

In late July, **Spanish Market** (505/982-2226, www.spanishcolonial.org) takes over the plaza with traditional New Mexican woodwork (especially santos), weaving, and furniture.

Alongside, the upstart **Indigenous Fine Art Market** (www.indigefam.org), based at Railyard Park, emphasizes more contemporary work. It's all a bit of a frenzy, but festive, due to free music and dance performances in the week leading up to the market itself.

After the bustle of summer tourism, locals celebrate the arrival of fall with the weeklong **Fiesta de Santa Fe** (505/204-1598, www.santafefiesta.org), which has been celebrated in some form since 1712. It begins with a re-enactment of Diego de Vargas's *entrada* into the city, then a whole slew of balls and parades, including the Historical/Hysterical Parade and a children's pet parade—eccentric Santa Fe at its finest. The kickoff event is usually the **Burning of Zozobra** (855/969-6272, www.burnzozobra.com), a neo-pagan bonfire; the schedule has fluctuated a bit but typically falls on the Friday before Labor Day. Some downtown businesses close for some fiestas, particularly on Zozobra day.

Held in early September in the Farmers Market Pavilion, relative newcomer **Green Chile Cheeseburger Smackdown** (ediblesmackdown.com) is the definitive showcase for all things green-chile cheeseburger. Judges and the public take on the tough task

The Burning of Zozobra

Every fall a raucous chant fills the air in Santa Fe's Fort Marcy Park: "Burn him! Burn him! Burn him!" It's the ritual torching of Zozobra, a 50-foot-tall marionette with long, grasping arms, glowering eyes, and a moaning voice. In the weeks before the event, Old Man Gloom, as he's commonly known, is stuffed with divorce papers, pictures of his ex, hospital gowns, and other anxiety-inducing scraps. Setting Old Man Gloom aflame is intended to purge these troubles, clearing the way for a fresh start.

This Santa Fe tradition sounds like a medieval rite, but it dates only from the 1920s, when artist Will Shuster—a bit of a local legend who's also credited with inventing piñon-juniper incense and starting the tradition of city-wide bonfires on Christmas Eve—wanted to lighten up the heavily Catholic Fiesta de Santa Fe. Shuster, who had moved to Santa Fe in 1920 to treat his tuberculosis, was inspired by the Mummers Parade from his native Philadelphia, as well as the Yaqui Indians in Tucson, Arizona, who burn Judas in effigy in the week before Easter. A 1926 *Santa Fe New Mexican* article describes the spectacle Shuster developed, with the help of the Kiwanis Club:

Zozobra

> Zozobra . . . stood in ghastly silence illuminated by weird green fires. While the band played a funeral march, a group of Kiwanians in black robes and hoods stole around the figure. . . . [Then] red fires blazed at the foot . . . and leaped into a column of many colored flames. . . . And throwing off their black robes the spectators emerged in gala costume, joining an invading army of bright-hued harlequins with torches in a dance around the fires as the band struck up "La Cucaracha."

Shuster oversaw Zozobra nearly every year until 1964. In the late 1930s, actor Errol Flynn, in town with Olivia de Havilland and Ronald Reagan to film *The Santa Fe Trail,* set Zozobra aflame. A few years later, during World War II, the puppet was dubbed Hirohitlomus, a stringing together of abbreviated names of the enemy leaders. In 1950, Zozobra appeared on the New Mexico state float in the New Year's Day Rose Bowl parade and won the national trophy.

Although Zozobra now has a Twitter account and accepts worries-to-burn online, the spectacle is roughly unchanged, with dozens of white-clad children playing "glooms," followed by a "fire dancer" who taunts Zozo until he bursts into flame; fireworks cap off the event. It's a raucous spectacle, attended by a great cross section of New Mexicans. But anyone leery of crowds may prefer to watch from outside the perimeter of the ball field; the streets above and to the east of Fort Marcy Park provide a great vantage point and less intense experience.

of tasting and choosing the best green-chile cheeseburger around—perhaps not surprisingly, it's a hugely popular event.

The **Santa Fe Mountain Fest** (www. velonewmexico.org/sfmf) features a full slate of events centered around bikes or beer—and occasionally both—in and around the city over a weekend early September. Clip in for challenging and more leisurely area rides and kick back with craft ales during concerts in the Railyard Park.

In late September, foodies flock to the city for the **Santa Fe Wine and Chile Festival** (505/438-8060, www.santafewineandchile. org), five days of tastings and special dinners at various venues around town.

Shopping

Even people who clutch their purse strings tight may be a little undone by the treasures for sale in Santa Fe. The rational approach would be to consider the most expensive shops more as free museums. (The cheapest, on the other hand, are stocked with made-in-China junk and are eternally on the brink of "going out of business" and should be avoided.) Several souvenir shops and a few influential galleries are clustered around the plaza. Canyon Road is lined with a bewildering number of galleries, though there can be a certain sameness to many of them. South Guadalupe Street and surrounding blocks have more funky and fun boutiques. If you buy too much to carry, **Pak Mail** (369 Montezuma Ave., 505/989-7380) can ship your treasures home safely; it even offers free pickup from hotels.

ART GALLERIES

The densest concentration of artwork is on Canyon Road, though it can seem a bit crowded with Southwestern kitsch. Summer hours are given here; in the winter, most galleries are closed at least Monday and Tuesday.

Local Artists

In the convention center, the **Community Gallery** (201 W. Marcy St., 505/955-6705, 10am-5pm Tues.-Fri., 9:30am-4pm Sat.) is run by the Santa Fe Arts Commission and always has a wide mix of work on display.

Contemporary

Santa Fe's contemporary scene isn't always easy to find, with the notable exception being **LewAllen** (1613 Paseo de Peralta, 505/988-3250, 10am-6pm Mon.-Fri., 10am-5pm Sat.), fittingly across the street from SITE Santa Fe. One of the Railyard's longtime draws, the vast industrial space holds a strong collection of well-conceived exhibitions. A couple of doors down, **TAI Modern** (1601 Paseo de

Peralta, 505/984-1387, 9:30am-5:30pm Mon.-Sat., 11am-4pm Sun.) focuses on colorful, abstract, and pop art.

A rare spot for abstraction on Canyon Road, **Nüart Gallery** (670 Canyon Rd., 505/988-3888, 10am-5pm daily) also showcases a wide variety of international artists, with a focus on magic realism.

North of Santa Fe, in the village of Tesuque, the bronze foundry **Shidoni** (1508 Bishops Lodge Rd., 505/988-8001, 9am-5pm Mon.-Sat.) has two large gardens full of metalwork sculpture, open from sunrise to sunset every day; its foundry, which ran for over 25 years, is now closed. Immediately adjacent, **Tesuque Glassworks** (1510 Bishops Lodge Rd., 505/988-2165, 9am-5pm daily) functions as a co-op with a range of glass artists using the furnace and displaying their work. To get to Tesuque, head north out of Santa Fe on Washington Avenue, which becomes Bishops Lodge Road; Shidoni is on the left side of the road.

Native American and Southwestern

Near Canyon Road, **Gerald Peters Gallery** (1011 Paseo de Peralta, 505/954-5700, 10am-5pm Mon.-Sat.) and **Nedra Matteucci Galleries** (1075 Paseo de Peralta, 505/982-4631, 9am-5pm Mon.-Sat.) are the biggies when it comes to Taos Society of Artists and other Western art, though both have contemporary artists, too. Even if nothing inside hits the spot, the one-acre sculpture garden and ponds in back of Nedra Matteucci are a treat. Smaller **Robert Nichols Gallery** (419 Canyon Rd., 505/982-2145, 10am-5pm Mon.-Sat., 11am-5pm Sun.) specializes in Native American pottery, including some with whimsical, boundary-pushing sensibilities.

Near the plaza, **Allan Houser Gallery** (125 Lincoln Ave., 505/982-4705, 10am-5pm Mon.-Sat.) showcases the work of the

Santa Fe for Kids

Doodlet's

In addition to the **Santa Fe Children's Museum** (1050 Old Pecos Tr., 505/989-8359, 9am-5pm Wed., 10am-6:30pm Thurs., 10am-5pm Fri.-Sat., noon-5pm Sun., www.santafechildrensmuseum. org, $7.50), the following are fun options:

· **Bee Hive** (328 Montezuma Ave., 505/780-8051, 10:30am-5:30pm Mon.-Sat., noon-4pm Sun.): A lovingly curated kids' bookstore, often with story time on Saturdays.

· **Dinosaurs & More** (137 W. San Francisco St., 505/988-3299, 10:30am-5:30pm Mon.-Thurs., 10:30am-6pm Fri.-Sat., 10:30am-5pm Sun.): The owner can tell a story about nearly every meteorite, fossil, and geode in the place.

· **Doodlet's** (120 Don Gaspar St., 505/983-3771, 10am-5:30pm Mon.-Sat., 10am-5pm Sun.): A totally absorbing corner shop filled with bits and bobs for kids and adults, from toy accordions to kitchen tchotchkes.

Southwest's best-known Native sculptor; it also maintains a sculpture garden south of the city near Cerrillos, with visits by appointment. In the Railyard, **Blue Rain Gallery** (544 S. Guadalupe St., 505/954-9902, 10am-6pm Mon.-Sat.) showcases work from many pueblo residents, such as Tammy Garcia's modern takes on traditional Santa Clara pottery forms—she sometimes renders bowls in blown glass or applies the geometric decoration to jewelry.

CLOTHING AND JEWELRY

On the plaza, **Santa Fe Dry Goods** (53 Old Santa Fe Trail, 505/983-8142, 10am-5:30pm Mon.-Sat. 11am-5pm Sun) has a wide-ranging collection of high-end women's clothing and accessories, including jewelry, bags, and shawls; it also sells stylish home decor items. Nearby ¡Mira! (101 W. Marcy St., 505/988-3585, 10:30am-5:30pm Mon.-Sat.) has a hip mix of clothes and housewares, with T-shirts by local designers ("Fanta Se" in the old Santa Fe Railroad logo, say) as well as cool imports from far flung locales such as Ghana. Just down the block, **Glorianna's** (55 W. Marcy St., 505/982-0353, 10am-4:30pm Mon.-Tues. and Thurs.-Sat., often closed for lunch 1pm-2pm) is a treasure trove of beads, packed to bursting with veritable eggs of raw turquoise, trays of glittering Czech glass, and ropes of African trade beads.

The city's best consignment shop is Double Take (321 S. Guadalupe St., 505/989-8886, 10am-6pm Mon.-Sat.), a sprawling two-story space with an excellent selection of boots and cowboy hats, as well as cool clothing, rodeo-themed 1950s sofas, Fiestaware, and plenty more.

GIFT AND HOME

Santa Fe icon Seret & Sons (224 Galisteo St., 505/988-9151, 9am-5pm Mon.-Fri., 9am-6pm Sat., 9:30am-5pm Sun.) deals in finely woven rugs, antique doors, and large-scale wooden creations from its cavernous warehouse just south of the plaza.

For funky folk art that won't break the bank, head for the equally gigantic Jackalope (2820 Cerrillos Rd., 505/471-8539, 9am-6pm daily), crammed with mosaic-topped tables, wooden chickens, Mexican pottery vases, and inexpensive souvenirs. Sharing the space is a community of prairie dogs—a good distraction for children while adults cruise the breakables.

OPEN-AIR MARKETS

As much a quirky fashion show and social scene as a shopping event, the Santa Fe Flea (2904 Rufina St., 505/982-2671,) convenes vintage aficionados, fine artists, crafty folks, and "tailgate traders" of miscellaneous oddities. In recent years the market has moved annually for the warmer months; call first to confirm the current location. In winter, many of the vendors move indoors to El Museo Cultural (555 Camino de la Familia, 8am-3pm Sat.-Sun. late Nov.-Apr.) at the Railyard complex.

In the Santa Fe Farmer's Market Pavilion, the Railyard Artisan Market (1607 Paseo de Peralta, www.artmarketsantafe.com, 10am-4pm Sun.) showcases locally crafted goods, such as blown glass, ceramics, blankets, jewelry, and clothing. The selection is better in the shoulder seasons, when fewer competing craft fairs siphon off vendors.

SWEET TREATS

Todos Santos (125 E. Palace Ave., 505/982-3855, 10am-5pm Mon.-Sat., noon-4pm Sun.) adds the sweet smell of chocolate to the air in Sena Plaza. The closet-size shop has the perfect (if short-lived) Santa Fe souvenir: *milagros,* the traditional Mexican Catholic prayer charms shaped like body parts, rendered in Valrhona chocolate and covered in a delicate layer of gold or silver leaf. If you prefer nuts and chews, head to longtime candy vendor Señor Murphy (100 E. San Francisco St., 505/982-0461, 10am-5pm daily) for some "caramales" (chewy balls of caramel and piñon nuts wrapped up in little corn husks) and other New Mexico-inspired sweets.

Food

Dining is one of Santa Fe's great pleasures. For its size, the city supports a dazzling range of excellent restaurants, some nationally recognized and others simply revered by locals. Sure, you can get a cheese-smothered, crazy-hot plate of green-chile-and-chicken enchiladas, but there's so much more from across the globe to choose from. Top-notch Southwestern, Italian, French, Mediterranean, and—of course—New Mexican fare can all be had within walking distance of the plaza; drive a little farther out and the options open up exponentially.

DOWNTOWN

The ring formed by Alameda Street and Paseo de Peralta contains some classic Santa Fe spots, plus a few hidden treats. On the plaza itself, the carnitas cart and the fajitas cart are institutions, too—and the Chicago hot dog stand, when it's set up, gets strong votes for authenticity.

New Mexican

The Shed (113½ E. Palace Ave., 505/982-9030, 11am-2:30pm and 5pm-9pm Mon.-Sat., $17) has been serving up platters of enchiladas since 1953—bizarrely, with a side of garlic bread. But that's just part of the tradition at this colorful, comfortable, marginally fancy place that's as popular with tourists as it is with longtime residents. There are perfectly decent distractions like lemon-garlic shrimp and fish tacos on the menu, but it's the red chile you should focus on. Reservations are essential throughout the summer.

Mexican

The specialty at **Bumble Bee's Baja Grill** (301 Jefferson St., 505/820-2862, 11am-8:30pm daily, $4.50) is Baja-style shrimp tacos, garnished with shredded cabbage and a creamy sauce, plus a spritz of lime and your choice of house-made salsas. The seafood stew is also delicious, as are the fried-fresh tortilla chips and that Tijuana classic, Caesar salad. Don't leave without indulging in the churros dipped in chocolate sauce.

Fresh and Local

Open since the late 1970s, ★ **Café Pasqual's** (121 Don Gaspar St., 505/983-9340, 8am-3pm and 5:30pm-9:30pm daily, $29) has defined its own culinary category, relying almost entirely on organic ingredients. Its breakfasts are legendary, but the food is delicious any time of day. Expect nearly anything on the menu, such as smoked-trout hash or Yucatán-style *huevos motuleños* for breakfast and grilled filet mignon with Portobello mushrooms or mole enchiladas for dinner. Call ahead for a reservation or brace yourself for the inevitable line, as the brightly painted dining room seats only 50.

Cafés

Adorned with handsome maps denoting international coffee trade routes, **35° North** (60 E. San Francisco St., 505/983-6138, 7am-5pm daily), on the second floor of The Arcade and overlooking Water Street, serves up some of the best espressos around the plaza as well as a filling and energizing "Latitude Adjustment"—coffee blended with grass-fed butter, coconut oil, and MCT oil.

Café Atalaya (66 E. San Francisco St., no phone, 8am-6pm Mon.-Thurs., 8am-8pm Fri.-Sat., 9am-6pm Sun., $4) boasts a prime people-watching spot overlooking the Plaza, though the real draw is a stellar selection of both savory and sweet crepes, including green chile chicken, smoked salmon, caramel with toasted pecans, and a simple but exquisite lemon sugar offering. Salads, soup, and a smattering of gelatos complete the menu.

The **French Pastry Shop** (100 E. San Francisco St., 505/983-6697, 6:30am-5pm daily, $5) has been doling out sweet crepes, buttery pastries, croques monsieurs, and chewy baguette sandwiches for more than 40 years. Early mornings attract a fascinating crew of Santa Fe regulars.

Ecco (128 E. Marcy St., 505/986-9778, 7am-9pm Mon.-Thurs., 7am-10pm Fri., 8am-10pm Sat., 8am-8pm Sun., $3) is packed with coffee junkies in the mornings, giving way to gelato lovers later in the day; choose from nearly 100 flavors of the cold treat, including banana rum, fig and walnut, and chocolate cabernet.

With its white walls, cozy furnishings, and tempting pastry case, it's easy to imagine strolling upon ★ **Dolina** (402 N. Guadalupe St., 505/982-9394, 7am-2:30pm Mon.-Sat., 8am-2:30pm Sun., $8.50) in the Slovakian countryside, which is not surprising given it's where the café's owner was born. In addition to a truly mouthwatering selection of baked goods, the menu focuses on a mix of Eastern European and New Mexican breakfast and lunch staples such as paprikash, stuffed schnitzel, and breakfast burritos. Soups, including Hungarian goulash, and salads round out the choices.

Diners

★ **Tia Sophia's** (210 W. San Francisco St., 505/983-9880, 7am-2pm Mon.-Sat., 8am-1pm

Sun., $9) is one of the last places around the plaza that feels untouched by time and tourists, serving no nonsense New Mexican plates to a slew of regulars without a touch of fuss or fusion—so authentic, in fact, the kitchen claims to have invented the breakfast burrito decades back.

Plaza Café (54 Lincoln Ave., 505/982-1664, 7am-9pm daily, $11) may look shiny and new, but it's a city institution where residents have long come to read the paper and load up on coffee and great renditions of New Mexican and American diner favorites. This is no greasy spoon, though—the piñon blue-corn pancakes are fluffy and fresh, the posole is perfectly toothsome, and the chicken-fried steak is a plateful of comforting goodness. There's another, far larger and livelier outpost on the **southside** (3466 Zafarano Dr., 505/424-0755, 8am-9pm Sun.-Thurs., 8am-10pm Fri.-Sat.).

For just about the most casual lunch around, stop in at the **Five & Dime General Store** (58 E. San Francisco St., 505/992-1800, 8:30am-9pm Mon.-Fri and Sun., 8:30am-10pm Sat., $5), on the plaza. In this former Woolworth's where, allegedly, the Frito pie was invented (Frito-Lay historians beg to differ), the knickknack shop has maintained its lunch counter and still serves the deadly combo of corn chips, homemade red chile, onions, and shredded cheese, all composed directly in the Fritos bag. Eat in, or, better still, lounge on the plaza grass—and don't forget the napkins.

Spanish

Cozy, creative-tapas joint **La Boca** (72 W. Marcy St., 505/982-3433, 11:30am-10pm daily, little plates $7-16) tempts with a strong selection of Spanish staples, such as olives stuffed with jamón serrano, gilled octopus, and bruschetta; the wine list, heavy on South American and Mediterranean vintages, is stellar as well. The little plates can add up fast, unless you're at La Boca 3pm-5pm weekdays, when there's a selection for half price. Reserve, ideally, and go early if you're sensitive to noise.

Italian

Off the plaza, next to Mission San Miguel, **Upper Crust Pizza** (329 Old Santa Fe Tr., 505/982-0000, 11am-10pm Sun.-Thurs. and Sat., 11am-11pm Fri., $14) is a slice of old-school Santa Fe, with a nice, creaky front porch, often with a live country crooner. Choose from regular, whole-wheat, or gluten-free crust and several specialty pizzas, or build your own. Piping-hot calzones and big super-fresh salads round out the menu.

Locals head to amber-lit and intimate **Il Piatto** (95 W. Marcy St., 505/984-1091, 4:30pm-9pm Sun.-Tues., 11:30am-9pm Wed.-Sat., $25) for understated Italian and a neighborly welcome from the staff, who seem to be on a first-name basis with everyone in the place. Hearty pastas such as pappardelle with duck are served in generous portions—a half order will more than satisfy lighter eaters. This is a great central spot to take a breather from enchiladas and burritos, without breaking the bank.

GUADALUPE AND THE RAILYARD

An easy walk from the plaza, the Railyard and a few surrounding blocks hold some of the better, quirkier dining options in town.

New Mexican

The cousin of downtown's The Shed, **La Choza** (905 Alarid St., 505/982-0909, 11am-2:30pm and 5pm-9pm Mon.-Sat., $11.75-$20) has a similar creative New Mexican menu but is more of a local's hangout and has a livelier atmosphere; in the summer months, it's especially packed after the workday ends. Count on well-executed New Mexican fare, such as a posole stew and a filling chile relleno. The location in the Railyard district makes it a handy destination if you're coming to Santa Fe by train—just walk back along the tracks a few blocks.

Fine Dining

The understated exterior of Chef Charles Dale's ★ **Bouche Bistro** (451 W. Alameda

Food Trucks

Bang Bite

Slowly but surely, Santa Fe's food truck scene is gaining traction, and these days not only are there are several to choose from, but they can be counted on for some of the tastiest meals in the city. Food trucks are now fixtures at major events around town, though many pull up at the same spot throughout the week. Though Meow Wolf doesn't draw as many food trucks as it once did, it's still a reliable spot, particularly for **Taqueria Gracias Madre** (505/795-6397), which serves chicken and beef tacos. For mouthwateringly good burgers, including one with sharp cheddar, bacon, and maple bacon jam, stop by the neon orange ★ **Bang Bite** (2791 Agua Fria St., 505/469-2345), west of downtown in the parking lot of the Tumbleroot brewery. Also sporting a bright orange hue, **Palate** (2601 Cerrillos Rd., 505/386-6343) has a menu made almost entirely of po'boys and tacos. It's a curious combination, to be sure, but the execution is flawless, as evidenced by a cornmeal shrimp po'boy and a flash-fried avocado taco. **El Chile Toreado** (805 Early St., 505/500-0033, 8:15am-3pm Mon.-Fri., 8:15am-2pm Sat., $7), just east of Cerrillos Rd., delivers a cilantro-tinged green salsa that is a near-mystical experience. Its carnitas may be the best in town; it also serves excellent breakfast burritos—get one with Mexican chorizo. **Santafamous** (501 Old Santa Fe Trail, 505/269-2858) focuses mainly on tacos—try one stuffed with sweet potatoes, dates and topped with a honey chipotle cream and you might forsake all others. One of the city's longest-running food trucks remains one of its best: **Santa Fe Barbecue** (600 Old Santa Fe Tr., 505/573-4816), where you'll need a bib and a big appetite to handle pulled pork, beef brisket, and baby back pork ribs slathered with a barbecue sauce not soon forgotten. Of course, as food trucks are mobile by nature, it's good to call ahead to find out current locations.

St., 505/982-6297, www.bouchebistro.com, 5:30pm-9:30pm Tues.-Sat. $17-$38) belies one of Santa Fe's most sumptuous dining experiences. Rich earth tones, warm lighting, and elegant decor complement a menu filled with French classics, such as a navarin-styled lamb stew, black mussels in white wine, and hanger steak with *pomme frites*. For dessert, choose from a slew of decadent offerings, including crème brûlée and lemon meringue tart.

Whether you want hearty bar food or an ethereal creation that will take your taste buds in new directions, Chef Joseph Wrede delivers at his lovely, candlelit space ★ **Joseph's** (428 Agua Fria St., 505/982-1272, www. josephsofsantafe.com, 5pm-10pm Sun.-Thurs.,

5pm-11pm Fri.-Sat., $16-44). Wrede's best dishes are vegetable-centric, though not necessarily vegetarian, such as a poblano relleno with a garlic sauce and grilled asparagus. But he's also into local meats, so carnivores will find a beef tenderloin, green chile, and potato stew, and a seemingly simple lamb patty that may be the state's best green-chile cheeseburger. Book ahead if you can, or try for a seat at the bar. And whatever happens, don't miss the duck-fat ice cream.

Fresh and Local

If you're on green-chile-and-cheese overload, head to ★ Vinaigrette (709 Don Cubero Alley, 505/820-9205, 11am-9pm Mon.-Sat., $14) and dig into a big pile of fresh greens. The so-called salad bistro uses largely organic ingredients from its farm in Nambé, in imaginative combos, such as a highbrow taco salad with chorizo and honey-lime dressing. The setting is pure homey Santa Fe, with tea towels for napkins, iced tea served in canning jars, and local art on the whitewashed walls. There's a shaded patio, too. Next door, you'll first see the same owner's faux farm shop and café, Modern General (637 Cerrillos Rd., 505/930-5462, 8am-5pm Mon.-Sat., 9am-4pm Sun., $7), which is also good, with its simple menu of juices, avocado toast, a few other breakfasts all day, and exquisite Czech kolaches—pastries with all manner of sweet fillings. Vinaigrette is in the building behind that.

Just outside the Paseo de Peralta loop, the ★ Tune-Up Café (1115 Hickox St., 505/983-7060, 7am-10pm Mon.-Fri., 8am-10pm Sat.-Sun., $8) is a homey two-room joint that locals love, whether for fish tacos or a suitably Santa Fe-ish brown-rice-and-nut burger. The place is especially packed during weekend brunches, when early morning outdoor adventures are recapped over heaping plates of fruit compote-stuffed French toast and steak and eggs.

The popular ★ Santa Fe Farmers Market (1607 Paseo de Peralta, 505/983-4098, www.santafefarmersmarket.com, 7am-1pm Tues. and Sat. late May-Nov., 8am-1pm Sat. Dec.-mid-May) is a buzzing social scene and a great place to pick up fresh local produce and treats as well as souvenir chile *ristras*. It's in a market hall in the Railyard complex, off Paseo de Peralta near Guadalupe Street; from late May to November the stalls spill out along the nearby train tracks and the landmark water tower.

Burgers and Barbecue

All things Texan are the specialty at Cowgirl BBQ (319 S. Guadalupe St., 505/982-2565, 11am-11pm Sun.-Thurs., 11am-11:30pm Fri.-Sat., $8.50-19)—think mesquite-smoked baby back ribs, chile with cheese and jalapeño cornbread, and barbecued chicken. It's a kitsch-filled spot that's as friendly to kids as it is to margarita-guzzling, barbecued-rib-gnawing adults. For non-meat-eaters, there are more options than you might expect, including an ooey-gooey butternut squash casserole comes with a salad on the side. Both carnivores and veggies can agree on the flourless chocolate cake with red chile and the ice cream "baked potato."

An outdoor burger joint that's so good people flock to it even in winter, Shake Foundation (631 Cerrillos Rd., 505/988-8992, 11am-7pm Mon.-Thurs., 11am-8pm Fri. and Sat., 11am-6pm Sun., $3.95-7.50), serves undersized beef, lamb, and turkey burgers (order a double if in doubt) on lavishly buttered buns; there's also a melt-in-your-mouth fried oyster sandwich with red-chile mayo. The eatery's dense, namesake drinks come in "adobe mud shakes," with ice cream made from New Mexico dairy. Seats in the shade are in short supply; plan accordingly in the heat of a summer afternoon.

Cafés

Make room in your morning for an almond croissant from ★ Sage Bakehouse (535 Cerrillos Rd., 505/820-7243, 7:30am-2:30pm Mon.-Sat., $5). Washed down with a mug of coffee, these butter-soaked pastries will have

---

1: the Santa Fe Farmers Market 2: Izanami

you set for hours. Before you leave, pick up some sandwiches for later—classics such as egg salad on sourdough and smoked turkey and cheddar on the bakery's excellent homemade whole wheat crust. And maybe a pecan-raisin wreath. And a chocolate-chip cookie, too.

A few steps away, **Ohori's Coffee, Tea & Chocolate** (505 Cerrillos Rd., 505/988-9692, 7am-6pm Mon.-Sat., 8am-4pm Sun.), is Santa Fe's small-batch coffee epicure; its dark-as-night brew makes Starbucks seem weak. With few seats, it's not so much a place to linger long but rather one at which to appreciate a clear attention to detail. There's a roomier location at 507 Old Santa Fe Tr. next to the Kaune's market (8am-7pm Mon.-Sat.).

CANYON ROAD AND THE EASTSIDE

Gallery hopping on Canyon Road can make you hungry—and it's all uphill from the road's terminus at Paseo de Peralta. Fortunately, there are a few places where you can fill up on caffeine to get you going and find a satisfying meal at the day's end.

Fine Dining

Elegant **Geronimo** (724 Canyon Rd., 505/982-1500, 5:30pm-9pm daily, $27-52) is consistently rated one of Santa Fe's best restaurants, and it's easy to see why. Standouts on the menu include an elk tenderloin, grilled rack of lamb and seared scallops; the service is impeccable, too.

Spanish

One of the oldest restaurants in the country, **El Farol** (808 Canyon Rd., 505/983-9912, noon-3pm and 5pm-9pm Sun.-Thurs., noon-3pm and 5pm-10pm Fri.-Sat., $8-36) is Canyon Road's liveliest nightspot. There's usually lots of action in the bar area, including frequent live flamenco, but it's the outside seating, under a creaky wooden *portal* and on a back patio, that really makes this historic adobe one of the better places in town to settle in for an evening. Pair drinks with numerous hot and cold tapas, such as *patatas bravas* and Spanish olives with anchovies and roasted peppers or opt for larger plates, including its popular house paella.

Cafés

For a morning brew, stroll over to **Downtown Subscription** (376 Garcia St., 505/983-3085, 7am-6pm daily), an airy coffee shop buzzing with locals and stocked with a bewildering selection of magazines. In the warmer months, enjoy your drink in the shaded garden in the back.

Chocolate devotees should consider ★ **Kakawa Chocolate House** (1050 E. Paseo de Peralta, 505/982-0388, 9:30am-6pm Mon.-Sat., noon-6pm Sun., $4) an essential—and educational—stop. It elevates hot chocolate to an art form, specializing in historically accurate drinks based on Mesoamerican and medieval European recipes. Complete your indulgence with decadent bite-size chocolates as well as dense dark-chocolate brownies. It's in a tiny adobe house with a kiva fireplace; when the temperature drops in winter, there's no place better to settle in.

Located near the top end of Canyon Road, **The Teahouse** (821 Canyon Rd., 505/992-0972, 9am-9pm daily, $12) is the ideal place to put your feet up after a long art crawl. Choose from an incredibly long list of teas from around the world, many of which are prepared in a variety of ways. There are also vittles such as mixed greens with cranberries, pecans, and feta and a deliciously hearty bowl of oats, black rice, buckwheat groats, and maple cream for breakfast. The service could be euphemistically described as "very Santa Fe" (i.e., forget about a quick meal), but the teas and food are unquestionably worth it.

CERRILLOS ROAD

This commercial strip south of the plaza isn't Santa Fe's most scenic stretch, but you'll find some great culinary gems out this way and along various side streets.

New Mexican

Long appreciated for its dazzling list of margaritas, **Maria's** (555 W. Cordova Rd., 505/983-7929, 11am-10pm daily, $10.25-$17.95) is well worth settling into for a meal of hearty New Mexican classics, starting with a genuinely hot table salsa and chips. Both red and green are sold here, and the tamales are exceptionally rich and creamy (even the vegetarian ones!).

A welcoming, no-frills family diner, **The Pantry** (1820 Cerrillos Rd., 505/986-0022, 6:30am-8:30pm Mon.-Sat., 7am-8:30pm Sun., $9) has been slinging eggs, pancakes, and chile since 1948; breakfast is served all day. There's a lunch counter up front, but regulars request the back room.

The decision of which chile to slather your breakfast burrito with is not one to be taken lightly at the ★ **Horseman's Haven** (4354 Cerrillos Rd., 505/471-5420, 8am-8pm Mon.-Sat., 8:30am-2pm Sun., $8), home to some of the hottest green chile in Santa Fe. It picks and mixes chile varieties to offer a couple of consistent grades that are doled out generously with filling plates of old-school New Mexican fare. Like all good chile purveyors, the café is in an unassuming box of a building next to a gas station, and it takes cash only.

French

In an incongruous location adjacent to Body of Santa Fe, ★ **Clafoutis** (333 W. Cordova St., 505/988-1809, 7am-4pm Mon.-Sat., $5-12.50) still oozes a laid-back Parisian charm and tempts with the sweet smells of crepes, bruschettas, and croissants. The *croque madame* is as delectable as ever and the beignets can still be ordered by the bagful; the salads, including one with smoked salmon and toasted almonds, don't disappoint either.

African

Just next to Hobby Lobby in a strip mall, ★ **Jambo** (2010 Cerrillos Rd., 505/473-1269, 11am-9pm Mon.-Sat., $11) has a menu of spicy, earthy food that's well priced and consistently satisfying. The menu features primarily Indian-inflected dishes from East Africa—lentil stew spiked with chile and softened with coconut, for instance—as well as Caribbean and Moroccan stews.

Asian

Attached to a Quality Inn, **Lu Lu's** (3011 Cerrillos Rd., 505/473-9898, 11am-9pm Mon.-Thurs. and Sun., 11am-9:30pm Fri.-Sat., $8-17) serves some of the most satisfying Chinese food around. Count on familiar pleasures such as sweet and sour chicken and kung pao, but don't overlook several standout house specialties, including a generous Royal Seafood Pot—scallops, crabmeat, shrimp, fish, and vegetables in a white-wine sauce.

Cafés

One of the most dangerous addresses in Santa Fe is an inconspicuous duplex with **Whoo's Donuts** (851-B Cerrillos Rd., 505/629-1678, 7am-3pm daily, $2) and **ChocolateSmith** (851-A Cerrillos Rd., 505/473-2111, 10am-5:30pm Mon.-Sat., noon-5pm Sun.). Bear right for organic maple bacon and orange cardamom cream doughnuts; bear left for intense hand-dipped truffles.

Catering to green thumbs and green tea drinkers alike, ★ **Opuntia** (922 Shoofly St., 505/780-5796, 8am-8:30pm Mon.-Sat., 8am-4pm Sun., $9-16) tempts with potted plants to take home and healthy food and drinks to fill up on. Breakfast dishes include an omelet featuring seasonal ingredients, while later in the day choose from a bewildering array of flavorful bowls and tasty toasts—the one with sautéed mushrooms, roasted garlic, kale and reggiano cheese is especially savory.

Counter Culture (930 Baca St., 505/995-1105, 8am-3pm Sun.-Mon., 8am-8pm Tues.-Sat., $12) is generally a locals-only scene, well liked for its catchall menu (including carne asada, Vietnamese banh mi sandwiches, and tire-size cinnamon buns), its casual-industrial vibe, and its outdoor patio where kids can run around.

Tucked away in the heart of Lena Street's industrial lofts, airy ★ Iconik (1600 Lena St., 505/428-0996, 7:30am-7pm Mon.-Sat., 8am-5pm Sun.) is worth seeking out for its heady mix of top-notch pour-overs and drips, bagel sandwiches, and smart decor. It's a large communal space with comfy couches set against a backdrop of coffee-roasting equipment, and features occasional live music. The company also operates the café inside the bookstore Collected Works (202 Galisteo St., 505/988-4226, 8am-6pm daily) and the newer Iconik Lupe (314 S. Guadalupe St., 505/428-0996, 7am-5pm Mon.-Sat., 8am-5pm Sun.), a sun-kissed spot with a shaded patio off Agua Fria.

Diners

Longtime burger connoisseurs may remember Bobcat Bite, just outside the city. It closed in 2013, becoming ★ Santa Fe Bite (1616 St. Michael's Dr., 505/438-0328, 7am-9pm Tues.-Sun., $13)—an even better incarnation, now in a more spacious locale off Cerrillos. The 10-ounce green-chile cheeseburgers, made from beef ground fresh every day and served on a home-baked bun, remain worthy of a pilgrimage. There's plenty more now, too, including a bulging patty melt, big salads, and, on Friday, fish-and-chips.

SANTA FE METRO AREA

Classic American

On the frontage road for I-25, Harry's Roadhouse (96 Old Las Vegas Hwy., 505/989-4629, 7am-9:30pm daily, $10-$24.50) is an easy detour off the freeway (exit at Old Santa Fe Trail). The pretty patio is usually buzzing, there's a full bar, and the diner-style menu includes everything from fried catfish with grits to turkey meat loaf to pizza, plus coconut cream pie. Expect a line and a packed parking lot; reserve ahead, if possible.

Fresh and Local

For a calmer, more wholesome vibe, keep driving down the road to Café Fina (624 Old Las Vegas Hwy., 505/466-3886, 7am-3pm Mon.-Wed., 7am-3pm and 5:30pm-8:30pm Thurs.-Sat., 7am-3pm Sun., $10), also easily accessible at exit 290 off I-25. This is a casual order-at-the-counter place, with a short but flavor-packed menu (including ricotta pancakes, migas, and grilled salmon tacos) from mostly locally grown ingredients.

Italian

Handsome and welcoming ★ El Nido (1577 Bishop's Lodge Rd., 505/954-1272, 5pm-10pm Mon.-Sat., $18-39) serves up refined and hearty fare in a historical Tesuque adobe. The seasonal menus are smorgasbords of smoked and grilled creations, such as shrimp skewers on a couscous salad, grilled Scottish salmon, and steak frites; there are also exquisite pasta dishes and several wood-fired pizzas to choose from. Though portions are substantial, think twice about skipping dessert.

Asian

The restaurant at Ten Thousand Waves, Izanami (3451 Hyde Park Rd., 505/428-6390, 11:30am-10pm Wed.-Mon., 5pm-10pm Tues., $4-22), melds old Japan and new without feeling like a theme restaurant. On the menu, there's pickled burdock root and grilled avocado, as well as wagyu-beef burgers and sake-braised mushrooms in a butter sauce, served in small plates to share. The dining room has a rustic mountain-lodge feel, with an optional shoes-off tatami-mat seating area. Throw in arguably the most extensive sake menu in the Southwest and surprisingly reasonable prices, and it's one of Santa Fe's cooler places to eat, whether you make the drive up for dinner or just wander over after your bath.

Accommodations

Santa Fe offers some great places to stay, but few are particularly cheap. Prices quoted for the bigger hotels are standard rack rates; chances are, you'll find substantially lower ones by calling or booking online, at least at the higher-end properties. Prices spike in July and August, often up to holiday rates. If you're coming for Indian Market or Christmas, try to book several months in advance. On the other hand, despite ski season, rates are often quite low in early December, January, and February.

UNDER $100

As hostels go, **Santa Fe International Hostel** (1412 Cerrillos Rd., 505/988-1153, www.hostelsantafe.com) is best appreciated with rose-colored glasses firmly in place, viewed as an old-school hippie project (it *is* run as a nonprofit). The dorms ($20 per person) and private rooms ($25 s, $35 d) are dim, and cleanliness can be spotty, as you're relying on the previous guests' efforts as part of the required daily chores. The kitchen has free food, but you have to pay for Internet access ($2/day), and everything is cash only.

For camping, the closest tent sites to the center are at **Hyde Memorial State Park** (Hwy. 475, 505/983-7175, www.emnrd.state.nm.us), about eight miles northeast of the city, with both primitive ($10) and developed sites with electricity ($14).

Possibly the best lodging deal in Santa Fe, the **Quaker Meeting House** (630 Canyon Rd., 505/983-7241, www.santafefriends.org, $65 d) rents a guest apartment with a kitchenette. It's a small space, and it has a three-night minimum, but the location on Canyon Road can't be beat. Payment is cash or check only.

Wedged in among the chain hotels on Cerrillos, the self-described kitschy ★ **Silver Saddle Motel** (2810 Cerrillos Rd., 505/471-7663, www.santafesilversaddlemotel.com, $68

d) plays up the retro charm. Cozy rooms may be pretty basic and have cinder-block walls, but they're decked out with Western accoutrements and kept clean—and the price, which includes breakfast, can't be beat. A handful of later-built rooms have a little more space to spread out.

$100-150

The bones of ★ **Santa Fe Sage Inn** (725 Cerrillos Rd., 505/982-5952, www.santafesageinn.com, $130 d) are a standard highway motel, but the super-clean rooms are done in sharp, modern red and black, with Southwestern rugs hung on the walls. Little touches such as free Wi-Fi, plush beds, and an above-average breakfast (fresh bagels, fruit, yogurt, and more) make this an excellent deal. The place even has a swimming pool. It's still walking distance to the center, and it's right across the street from the Railyard Park and the farmers market. The onsite restaurant, Social Kitchen is a good spot for a drink and a casual meal after a day out.

Built around a 1936 motor court, the recently renovated ★ **El Rey Court** (1862 Cerrillos Rd., 505/982-1931, www.elreycourt.com, $106 d) counts as one of the more charming motels in Santa Fe. Though it has been expanded over the years, its character remains intact, and it has been meticulously kept up and adjusted for modern standards of comfort, with beautiful gardens, a big swimming pool, a hot tub, and a sauna. The 86 rooms, spread over 4.5 acres, vary considerably in style (and in price), from the oldest section with snug adobe walls and heavy viga ceilings to airier rooms with balconies. Guests get a voucher for breakfast at the Pantry, a nice old-timey restaurant next door. The only drawback is that the plaza is too far to walk, but a city bus stops right outside.

One of the best options off the plaza, **Hotel Chimayó** (125 Washington Ave.,

505/988-4900, www.hotelchimayo.com, from $149 d) is a great value, though not everyone will like its folksy style, done up with wooden crosses and striped rugs from its namesake village. Upstairs rooms have private balconies, and some suites have fireplaces. Free downtown walking tours are included in the rate.

$150-200

Santa Fe Motel & Inn (510 Cerrillos Rd., 505/982-1039, www.santafemotel.com, $159 d) is a good budget option close to the center, with rooms done up in simple, bright decor that avoids motel sameness despite the generic layout. A few kitchenettes are available, along with more-private casitas with fireplaces. Lots of nice touches—such as bread from the Sage Bakehouse across the street along with the full breakfast—give the place a homey feel without the tight quarters of a typical bed-and-breakfast.

East of the plaza, two exquisite bed-and-breakfasts under the same ownership offer two kinds of style: The six rooms at **Hacienda Nicholas** (320 E. Marcy St., 505/986-1431, www.haciendanicholas.com, $155 d) have a tasteful Southwestern flavor, decorated with a few cowboy trappings and Gustave Baumann prints. Most rooms have fireplaces and there's also a spacious suite ($245) and a cottage ($225). Across the street, **The Madeleine** (106 E. Faithway St., 505/982-3465, www.madeleineinn.com, $155 d) occupies a wood Victorian, with antique furniture offset by rich Balinese fabrics throughout its seven rooms. At both spots, breakfasts show the same attention to sumptuous detail, with items such as blue-corn waffles and a Southwestern frittata.

$200-250

The 100-room **Inn of the Governors** (101 W. Alameda St., 505/982-4333, www.innofthegovernors.com, $199 d) isn't flashy on the outside, but inside it has a personable only-in-Santa-Fe feel, starting with the afternoon "tea and sherry hour," when guests are plied with free drinks and *bizcochitos*. The inn's unique profit-sharing system may account for the exceptionally nice staff. Breakfast is generous, parking is free (unheard-of elsewhere downtown), and there's even a tiny pool. Rooms in the Governors Wing are quietest. The attached Del Charro Saloon serves the best-value meals and margaritas around the plaza.

Owned by Picurís Pueblo, ★ **Hotel Santa Fe** (1501 Paseo de Peralta, 800/825-9876, https://hotelsantafe.com, $219 d) is a successful amalgam of Native American cultural touchstones and Southwestern décor and a thoroughly enjoyable place to stay. The standard rooms are a bit small—it's worth upgrading to the junior suite. If you book online, rates for the exceedingly high-end Hacienda wing—where the huge rooms all have fireplaces and butler service—are a steal compared to the other luxury options in town. Amenities include a large outdoor pool, spa, and the contemporary Amaya restaurant, which serves mostly New Mexican dishes.

Inn on the Alameda (303 E. Alameda St., 505/984-2121, www.innonthealameda.com, $209 d) is an ideal choice for those who want adobe style *and* space, and its location near Canyon Road is handy for galleryhoppers. The big rooms have triple-sheeted beds, wireless Internet access, and overstuffed armchairs that are only lightly dusted with Southwestern flair; most also have a patio or balcony. Gas fireplaces are usually an additional $20. The continental breakfast spread is generous, and there's a wine-and-cheese hour every afternoon.

Downtown's newest and largest property, **Drury Plaza Santa Fe** (828 Paseo de Peralta, 505/424-2175, www.druryhotels.com, $259 d) has a somewhat corporate feel, but it occupies a sprawling historic hospital complex behind the St. Francis Cathedral—a convenient location at a pretty good price for amenities that include a rooftop pool and bar, full breakfast, and free afternoon drinks. Rooms are a little small but comfortably furnished.

A short walk from the plaza, the handsome **La Posada** (330 E Palace Ave, 505/986-0000, www.laposadadesantafe.com, $205 d) offers a full range of high-end amenities, including an outdoor pool, a fitness center, and a popular spa. The decor is decidedly Southwestern throughout but not over the top, with earth tones and vigas beams in common areas and guest rooms, the latter of which can vary in size. Some rooms have kiva fireplaces and face out on to the pool; all exude an understated elegance.

A rental condo is a great option if you have a family or group, and those at **Campanilla Compound** (334 Otero St., 800/828-9700, www.campanillacompound.com, $247) are especially nice, with whitewashed walls, fireplaces, and Mexican-tiled kitchens. Each unit has plenty of space inside and out, with a private patio or porch, and, thanks to the location on a hill, some have excellent views of the city and the sunset. There's a three-night minimum in summer, and two nights the rest of the year.

Secluded and wonderfully restful, ★ **Houses of the Moon** (3451 Hyde Park Rd., 505/992-5003, www.tenthousandwaves.com, $215 d), the guest cottages at Ten Thousand Waves spa, are real gems. Some have more of a local feel, with viga ceilings and kiva fireplaces, while others are straight from Japan, both samurai era and contemporary anime. Some larger suites have kitchens. Rates include a suitably organic granola breakfast and Japanese teas, as well as free access to the communal and women's tubs.

OVER $250

The iconic, family-owned **La Fonda** (100 E. San Francisco St., 505/982-5511, www.lafondasantafe.com, $259 d) has been offering respite to travelers in some form or another since 1607. A recent renovation has lightened up its guest rooms considerably but also spoiled the impeccable historic feeling in the public areas. The whole place feels more generic and modern as a result, though many rooms do have original folk art, and a few have *latilla* ceilings and kiva fireplaces—along with all the necessary luxuries, such as pillow-top beds. You can soak up most of the place's atmosphere in the public areas, of course, but the location couldn't be better. It helps to have flexible dates—in periods of high demand, the rates can spike to exorbitant levels. Even if you don't stay here, do at least take a spin through the lobby and the mezzanine—there are still traces of the 1920 designs by Mary Colter (best known for the hotels at the Grand Canyon), and some great paintings.

The singular Relais & Chateaux property **The Inn of the Five Graces** (150 E. De Vargas St., 505/992-0957, www.fivegraces.com, from $395 d) can transport you to exotic lands—for at least slightly less than a plane ticket. Outside, it looks like a typical historic Southwestern lodge, a collection of interconnected adobe casitas on Santa Fe's oldest street. But inside, the 24 sumptuous suites are done in the style of an opium dream: antique Turkish kilims, heavy wooden doors, mosaics, and handcrafted furnishings—all courtesy of the boho-style dealers Seret & Sons. Amenities include a Tibetan-themed spa and the most stylish fitness center around. Rates include full breakfast, delivered to your room, if you like.

Information and Services

TOURIST INFORMATION

The **Santa Fe Convention and Visitors Bureau** (800/777-2489, www.santafe.org) hands out its visitors guide and other brochures from offices at the **convention center** (201 W. Marcy St., 8am-5pm Mon.-Fri.), at the small **plaza kiosk** next to the First National Bank (66 E. San Francisco St., 10am-6pm daily) and at the **Rail Runner depot** (401 S. Guadalupe St., 9am-5pm Mon.-Sat.); the depot office is also open for the same hours Sunday May-October. The New Mexico Tourism Department runs a **visitors center** (491 Old Santa Fe Tr., 505/827-7336, www.newmexico.org, 8am-5pm Mon.-Fri.) near San Miguel Mission.

For info on the outdoors, head to the Bureau of Land Management's comprehensive **Public Lands Information Center** (301 Dinosaur Tr., 505/954-2002, www.publiclands.org, 8am-4:30pm Mon.-Fri.), just off Highway 14 (follow Cerrillos Road until it passes under I-25). You can pick up detailed route descriptions for area day hikes, as well as guidebooks, topo maps, and hunting and fishing licenses.

Books and Maps

Santa Fe has several particularly good bookshops in the center of town. **Travel Bug** (839 Paseo de Peralta, 505/992-0418, 7:30am-5:30pm Mon.-Sat., 11am-4pm Sun.) specializes in maps, travel guides, and gear—and has good coffee and baked goods to munch on while you plan your next adventure. For more general books, **Collected Works** (202 Galisteo St., 505/988-4226, 10am-8pm Mon.-Fri., 10am-7pm Sat., 10am-6pm Sun.) is the place to go for a trove of local-interest titles. **REI** (500 Market St., 505/982-3557, 8am-8pm Mon.-Sat., 8am-6pm Sun.) is well stocked with area outdoor guides and hiking maps.

Local Media

The *Santa Fe New Mexican* is Santa Fe's daily paper. On Friday, it publishes events listings and gallery news in its *Pasatiempo* insert. For left-of-center news and commentary, the *Santa Fe Reporter* is the free weekly rag, available in most coffee shops and cafés.

Radio

KBAC (98.1 FM), better known as Radio Free Santa Fe, is a dynamic community station with eclectic music and talk. Tune in Friday afternoons for news on the gallery scene. Another public station is **KSFR** (101.1 FM), run by Santa Fe Community College.

SERVICES

Banks

First National Santa Fe (62 Lincoln Ave., 505/992-2000, 8am-5pm Mon.-Fri.) is on the west side of the plaza.

Post Office

Santa Fe's **main post office** (120 S. Federal Pl., 505/988-2239, 8am-5:30pm Mon.-Fri., 9am-4pm Sat.) is conveniently just north of the plaza, near the district courthouse.

Laundry

Most self-service laundries are on or near Cerrillos Road. Nearer to the center is **Solana Laundromat** (949 W. Alameda, 505/982-9877, 7am-8pm daily). It also has drop-off service.

Getting There and Around

AIR

Santa Fe Municipal Airport (SAF, 121 Aviation Dr., 505/955-2900), west of the city, receives direct flights from Dallas and Phoenix (seasonal) with American Airlines, and from Denver with United. Typically, fares are better to the Albuquerque airport (ABQ), an hour's drive away.

Sandia Shuttle Express (888/775-5696, www.sandiashuttle.com) does hourly pickups from the Albuquerque airport 4:45am-6:45pm and every 90 minutes 8pm-12:30am and will deliver to any hotel or B&B ($33 each way) or drop off passengers at 269 W. Water St.

TRAIN

The Rail Runner (866/795-7245, www.riometro.org) goes from Albuquerque to downtown Santa Fe—the final stop is at the rail yard in the Guadalupe district (410 S. Guadalupe St.). The ride takes a little over 90 minutes and costs $10, or $11 for a day pass, and the last train back to Albuquerque leaves at 9pm weekdays, 10:14pm Saturday, and 8:10pm Sunday.

Amtrak (800/872-7245, www.amtrak.com) runs the Southwest Chief once a day through Lamy, 18 miles south of Santa Fe. It's a dramatic place to step off the train—with little visible civilization for miles around, it feels like entering a Wild West movie set. Trains arrive from Chicago and Los Angeles in the afternoon, and Amtrak provides a shuttle van to the city.

BUS AND SHUTTLE

Santa Fe Pick-Up (505/231-2573, www.santafenm.gov, every 10 minutes 6:30am-5:30pm Mon.-Fri., 8:30am-5:30pm Sat., 10am-5:30pm Sun., free) is a service for tourists, with two routes covering all the main sights. It's free and runs more frequently than the regular city bus. The main circuit starts and ends in front of Jean Cocteau Cinema, on Montezuma Avenue just north of the Rail Runner depot, and it stops at the capitol, the St. Francis Cathedral, four points on Canyon Road, Museum Hill, and a few other tourist-friendly spots around town. From the capitol, the second route runs a loop up Canyon Road and out to Museum Hill.

For Cerrillos Road, you can use Route 2 on the city bus system, Santa Fe Trails (505/955-2001, www.santafenm.gov), from the handy central depot on Sheridan Street northwest of the plaza. Buses on all routes are not terribly frequent, every 20 minutes at the most. Fare is $1, or you can buy a day pass for $2, payable on board with exact change.

CAR

Having a car in Santa Fe itself is not necessary, though with a car day trips become that much more feasible. Bear in mind that street and garage parking is limited and expensive in the city's center. Hertz, Budget, Avis, and Thrifty all have branches on Cerrillos Road.

From Albuquerque to Santa Fe, it's a straight shot north on I-25 for 65 miles; you'll reach Santa Fe in about an hour.

Coming from Taos, allow 1.5-2.5 hours, depending on whether you come on the low road (on Hwy. 68 and U.S. 84/285, via Española), via Ojo Caliente (mostly on U.S. 285), or on the high road (mostly on Hwy. 76, via Truchas).

Less than an hour's drive from Santa Fe are six-century-old ruins of Ancestral Puebloan culture at **Bandelier National Monument,** and the 20th-century atomic developments in **Los Alamos,** home of the Manhattan Project. **Abiquiu,** best known as O'Keeffe Country, is a landscape of rich red rocks bisected by the tree-lined Rio Chama, while green is the predominate color of the endless valleys of the **Valles Caldera National Preserve,** an hour to the northwest of Santa Fe.

The most popular outing from the city is to **Taos**—and even the route there is filled with compelling diversions. The main options are the **low road** along the Rio Grande or the **high road** that passes through tiny mountain villages. You can also take a more roundabout route through **Ojo Caliente,** a village built around hot springs.

THE PUEBLOS

Between Santa Fe and Taos lie seven **pueblos,** each occupying their own patches of land with their own tribal governments. Unlike scenic Taos Pueblo, these are not notable for their ancient architecture and, with a few small exceptions, do not have any tourist attractions. Some pueblos are closed to visitors all or part of the year, but do make the trip on feast days or for other ceremonial dances if you can.

Tesuque and Pojoaque

Just north of Santa Fe, the highway overpasses are decorated with the original Tewa names of the pueblos. **Tesuque** (Te Tesugeh Owingeh, "village of the cottonwood trees") is marked by **Camel Rock,** a piece of sandstone on the west side of the highway that has eroded to resemble a creature that looks right at home in this rocky desert. The "mouth" of the camel broke off in early 2017, but that hasn't stopped the curious from making the quick stop along Highway 285.

A few miles farther north, the Pojoaque-managed **Poeh Museum** (78 Cities of Gold Rd., 505/455-5041, www.poehcenter.org, 9am-5pm Mon.-Fri., 10am-4pm Sat., free) occupies a striking old-style adobe building just off the highway. It shows (and sells) local artwork, as well as a permanent installation relating the **Pojoaque** people's path (*poeh*) through history.

Pojoaque's no fuss outpost of the popular local chain **El Parasol** (30 Cities of Gold Rd., 505/455-7185, 8am-9pm Mon.-Sat., 9am-5pm Sun., $5) has a long menu of recognizable and dependable New Mexican fare, including *chicharrón* burritos, arroz con pollo, and shredded beef tostados.

San Ildefonso

Best known for its black-on-black pottery (first by María Martinez and her husband, Julian, and now from a number of skilled potters), the pueblo of **San Ildefonso** is off Highway 502, on the way to Los Alamos. Of all the pueblos just north of Santa Fe, it's the most scenic, with even its newer houses done in faux-adobe style, and the main plaza shaded by giant old cottonwoods. You must first register at the **visitors center** (off Hwy. 502, 505/455-3549, 8am-5pm Mon.-Fri., $10/car), then proceed on foot. There is a small **museum** (8am-4:30pm daily), which is really just an excuse to walk across the village. The only other attractions are pottery shops—which are interesting even if you're not in the market, as it's a chance to peek inside people's homes and chat a bit.

Santa Clara

On the land of **Santa Clara** (Kha P'o, or Shining Water), on Highway 30 south of Española, are the beautiful **Puyé Cliff Dwellings** (888/320-5008, www. puyecliffdwellings.com), which were occupied until the early 1600s. They're accessible only by guided tour, and a slightly expensive one at

Outside Santa Fe

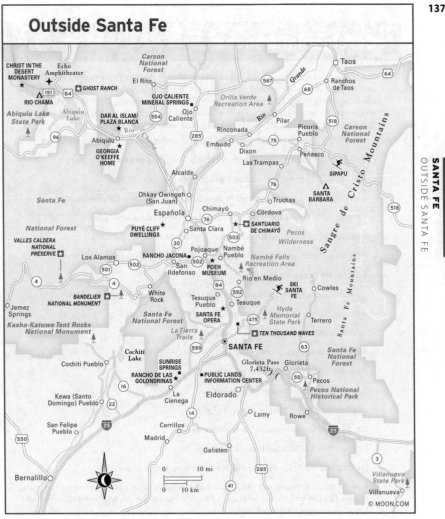

Center—better recognized as a gas station on Highway 30—marks the turn to the cliffs; you can buy your tickets here (preferred, so they know you're coming) or up the road at the site. **Tours** run on the hour 9am-5pm daily April-September; the rest of the year, tours run 9am-2pm.

that: $20 for a one-hour walk either along the cliffside or the mesa top, or $35 for both. But tour leaders come from the pueblo and connect the ancient ruins with current culture in an intimate and fascinating way.

At the base of the cliffs is a stone building from the Fred Harvey Indian Detour days of the early 1900s, when carloads of intrepid visitors would trundle off the train and out to these exotic sights; it now houses a small museum. The Puyé Cliffs Welcome

Getting There

From downtown Santa Fe, northbound Guadalupe Street turns into U.S. 84/285,

Ceremonial Dances

This is an approximate schedule for dances at pueblos in the Santa Fe area. Pueblo feast days are always on the same date and generally open to all, but seasonal dances (especially Easter and other spring rituals) can vary, and are sometimes closed to visitors. Confirm details and start times—usually afternoon, but sometimes following an evening or midnight Mass—with the **Indian Pueblo Cultural Center** (505/843-7270, www.indianpueblo.org) before setting out.

- **January 1:** Ohkay Owingeh (San Juan): cloud or basket dance; Picurís: various dances

- **January 6:** Picurís: various dances; Nambé: buffalo, deer, and antelope dances

- **January 22:** San Ildefonso: vespers and firelight procession at 6pm

- **January 23:** San Ildefonso: Feast of San Ildefonso, with buffalo and deer dances

- **January 25:** Picurís and Ohkay Owingeh (San Juan) : Feast of San Pablo

- **February 2:** Picurís: various dances for Candlemas (Día de la Candelaria)

- **February, first or second weekend:** Ohkay Owingeh (San Juan): deer dance

- **Easter:** Most pueblos: various dances

- **June 13:** Ohkay Owingeh (San Juan), Santa Clara, and Picurís: Feast of San Antonio

- **June 24:** Ohkay Owingeh (San Juan): Feast of San Juan Bautista

- **July 4:** Nambé: celebration at the waterfall

- **July 25:** San Ildefonso: Feast of Santiago

- **August 9-10:** Picurís: Feast of San Lorenzo

- **August 12:** Santa Clara: Feast of Santa Clara

- **September 8:** San Ildefonso: corn dance

- **October 4:** Nambé: Feast of San Francisco de Asís

- **November 12:** Tesuque: Feast of San Diego

- **December 12:** Pojoaque: Feast of Nuestra Señora de Guadalupe

- **December 24:** Picurís and Ohkay Owingeh (San Juan): torchlight procession at sundown, followed by Los Matachines; Tesuque and Nambé: various dances, beginning after midnight Mass; San Ildefonso: various dances

- **December 25:** San Ildefonso, Ohkay Owingeh (San Juan), Picurís, and Tesuque: various dances

- **December 26:** Ohkay Owingeh (San Juan): turtle dance

- **December 28:** Picurís: children's dances to celebrate Holy Innocents Day

which runs north through Tesuque in 5 miles and Pojoaque in 15 miles. Though this stretch of casinos and tax-free cigarette shops isn't particularly scenic, don't be tempted to race through it—the area is a major speed trap.

To reach San Ildefonso, turn off U.S. 84/285 in Pojoaque at the exit for Highway 502 to Los Alamos; the turn for the pueblo is about 6 miles ahead on the right. From San Ildefonso, you can continue to Santa Clara by turning north on Highway 30; the cliff dwellings are 7 miles ahead on the left. The slightly more direct route to Santa Clara is via Española, following signs for Highway 30; the total drive from the edge of Santa Fe is about 23 miles.

LOS ALAMOS

Unlike so many other sights in New Mexico, which are rooted in centuries of history, **Los Alamos,** home of the atomic bomb, is a product of the modern age. You may spend only a few hours here, visiting the museum and admiring the view from this high plateau, but you'll still sense an atmosphere quite unlike anywhere else in New Mexico. If you can, visit on a weekday, as more businesses are open; weekends are especially sleepy in this town that draws specialized commuters from around the state—and even beyond.

During World War II, the army requisitioned an elite, rugged boys' school on a remote New Mexico mesa in order to build a top-secret laboratory for development of the nuclear bomb. It was home for a time to J. Robert Oppenheimer, Richard Feynman, Niels Bohr, and other science luminaries. The Manhattan Project and its aftermath, the Cold War arms race, led to the establishment of **Los Alamos National Laboratory** (LANL). Only in 1957 did the onetime military base become an actual public town; it's now home to about 18,000 people (if you count the "suburb" of White Rock, just down the hill on Highway 4). The highway up the mountainside is wider than it used to be, but the winding ascent to the mesa of "Lost Almost"—as the first scientists dubbed their officially nonexistent camp—still carries an air of the clandestine. The town can be visually jarring—there is no adobe to be found and the streets have names such as Trinity Drive (named after the first test of a nuclear weapon)—a feeling only enhanced by the dramatic landscape surrounding it.

The town is spread over four long mesas that extend like fingers from the mountain behind. Highway 502 arrives on a middle mesa, depositing you on Central Avenue and the main downtown area. The northernmost mesa is mostly residential, while the southernmost mesa is occupied by LANL and two routes running back down the mountain and connecting with Highway 4.

Los Alamos Historical Museum

Though the manufactured feel of Los Alamos would lead you to believe otherwise, the area's history began long before the construction of LANL. See what the area was like pre-Manhattan Project at the fascinating, recently renovated **Los Alamos Historical Museum** (1050 Bathtub Row, 505/662-4493, www.losalamoshistory.org, 9am-5pm Mon.-Fri., 10am-4pm Sat.-Sun., $5), set in an old building of the Los Alamos Ranch School, the boys' camp that got the boot when the army moved in. The exhibits cover everything from relics of the early Tewa-speaking people up to juicy details on the social intrigue during the development of "the gadget," as the A-bomb was known. Volunteer docents lead two-hour **walking tours** (11am Mon., Fri., and Sat., $10) from the museum late May-early October; if you miss this, pick up a brochure for a self-guided walk.

In front of the museum is **Fuller Lodge Art Center** (2132 Central Ave., 505/662-1635, 10am-4pm Mon.-Sat., free), originally the ranch school's dining room and kitchen. It usually has a community art exhibit downstairs, plus a room upstairs restored to the era when schoolteachers bunked here. The architect John Gaw Meem built the structure in 1928, handpicking more than 700 pine poles to form the walls, and designing

Los Alamos

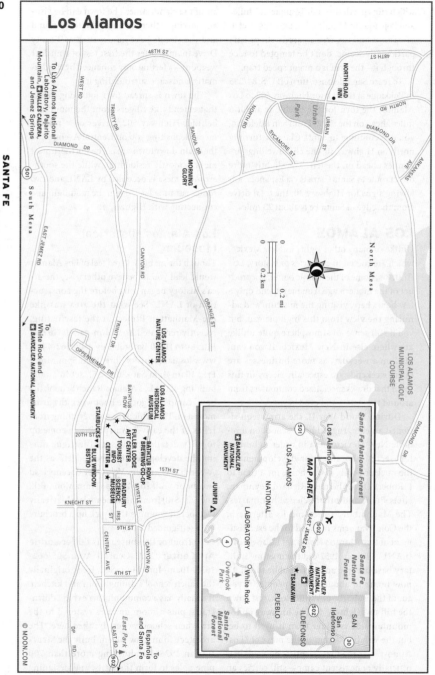

To Los Alamos National Laboratory, Pajarito Mountain, ◆VALLES CALDERA, and Jemez Springs

48TH ST

48TH ST

NORTH ROAD INN

NORTH RD

NORTH RD

DIAMOND DR

Urban Park

SYCAMORE ST

URBAN ST

ARKANSAS AVE

DIAMOND DR

WEST RD

TRINITY DR

SANDIA DR

DIAMOND DR

MORNING GLORY ▼

CANYON RD

ORANGE ST

North Mesa

LOS ALAMOS MUNICIPAL GOLF COURSE

South Mesa

EAST JEMEZ RD

0   0
0   0.2 km
0   0.2 mi

North Mesa

To White Rock and ◆ BANDELIER NATIONAL MONUMENT

OPPENHEIMER DR

TRINITY DR

LOS ALAMOS NATURE CENTER ▼

BATHTUB ROW

LOS ALAMOS HISTORICAL MUSEUM ▼

STARBUCKS ▼

20TH ST

★ FULLER LODGE ART CENTER

TOURIST INFO CENTER ■

▼ BATHTUB ROW BREWING CO-OP

▼ BLUE WINDOW BISTRO

15TH ST

MYRTLE ST

★ BRADBURY SCIENCE MUSEUM

KNECHT ST

IRIS ST

9TH ST

CENTRAL AVE

CANYON RD

4TH ST

East Park ▼

DP RD

EAST RD

To Española and Santa Fe

502

© MOON.COM

Inset map

Santa Fe National Forest

501

Los Alamos

✈

502

East Jemez Rd

MAP AREA

◆ BANDELIER NATIONAL MONUMENT

JUNIPER △

LOS ALAMOS NATIONAL LABORATORY

4

Overlook Park

○ White Rock

▲ TSANKAWI

502

BANDELIER NATIONAL MONUMENT ◆

SAN ILDEFONSO PUEBLO

San Ildefonso ○

30

SAN

Santa Fe National Forest

Santa Fe National Forest

To Santa Fe

Tribal Economies in the Gaming Age

North of Santa Fe on U.S. 84/285, Cities of Gold Casino looms beside the road, a sight that would have dazzled any conquistador in search of El Dorado. While it's showing its age, it was the first of the pueblo casinos, and a much-debated project within the community of Pojoaque before it opened in the 1990s. Casinos were effectively permitted by the federal Indian Gaming Regulatory Act in 1988 and then legalized in New Mexico in 1994.

The main argument in Pojoaque for getting into the industry was a need for cash and jobs in communities that had virtually no industry. At the time, up to 72 percent of pueblo residents were jobless, and the average income in many communities was less than $10,000 per year—almost inconceivably below national standards. Now, Pojoaque boasts close to zero unemployment as well as attractive apartment housing and a beautifully appointed museum funded by casino profits (including the Buffalo Thunder Resort, opened in 2008).

Many other nearby Rio Grande-area pueblos have followed with their own projects, including, most recently, Tesuque whose eponymous casino opened in November 2018 to much fanfare. Sleek and modern with a design that complements the nearby Santa Fe Opera, the casino is indicative of many pueblos' willingness to embrace the possibilities the gaming industry affords.

More remote pueblos have taken different strategies, however. Small and somewhat conservative Picurís voted against its own gambling palace; the elders did eventually agree to co-owning the Hotel Santa Fe, a venture initiated by a few Anglo entrepreneurs who aimed to capitalize on a unique relationship with a pueblo. Jemez Pueblo attempted to open a casino in southern New Mexico, far from its own land, but its application was denied at the federal level in 2011.

Puebloans and Anglos alike complain about the aesthetics of the gaudy, brightly lit casinos, and others worry about the apparent loss of tradition that goes along with courting lowest-common-denominator tourism. But for many pueblo people who, previously, had been considered to be not much more than a scenic backdrop in New Mexico—a mute patch of "local color"—there's no incongruity at all. As George Rivera, the governor of Pojoaque, has put it, "You don't have to be poor to have your culture."

the cowboy-silhouette light fixtures in the main hall.

The museum is just west of the main street, Central Avenue—you'll see Fuller Lodge on Central, with the museum set back behind it.

Bradbury Science Museum

Set up by Los Alamos National Laboratory, the Bradbury Science Museum (1350 Central Ave., 505/667-4444, www.lanl.gov/museum, 10am-5pm Tues.-Sat., 1pm-5pm Sun.-Mon., free) on the miracles of atomic energy has the feel of an upper-grade science fair, with plenty of buttons to push and gadgets to play with. There's also an air of a convention sales booth—the museum's mission is definitely to sell the public on LANL's work and nuclear technology in general, though a public forum corner gives space to opposing views. More interesting are the relics of the early nuclear age: Fat Man and Little Boy casings, gadgetry from the Nevada Test Site, and the like.

Atomic City Van Tours (505/662-2547, www.atomiccitytours.com, 1:30pm daily Mar.-Oct., available on advance arrangement Nov.-Feb., $25) leave from the parking lot in front of the museum. The 1.5-hour tour is a good way to see more of the town, which is otherwise a bit difficult to navigate, and learn some of the history. Call ahead to reserve. If you can't make the set tour time, you can download a short self-guided tour from the website; this route takes the free city bus to the main part of LANL, pointing out town landmarks along the way.

Recreation

The mountain behind Los Alamos is recovering from the 2011 Las Conchas Fire, but the canyons below Los Alamos were untouched, and are laced by numerous top-notch hiking and mountain biking trails, easily accessible from the town's main roads. Pick up a map and get recommendations from the visitors center or the smartly designed **Los Alamos Nature Center** (2600 Canyon Rd., 505/662-0460, www.peecnature.org, 10am-8pm Tues., 10am-4pm Wed. and Fri.-Mon., free), which also is a good place to get to know the plants and animals in the area.

The dramatic **Canyon Rim Trail** skirts the edge of Los Alamos Canyon for 1.5 miles; it provides the best vantage point for appreciating the town's setting atop the finger-like mesas. The trailhead is located along Hwy 502, just shy of two miles east of the town center; count on about 45 minutes to hike to the paved trail's end and back. There are further spectacular views in White Rock, 15 minutes to the southeast, where the **White Rock Rim Trail** runs three miles along the cliff edge—you'll have suburban tract homes to your back and a dizzying canyon out in front of you. Even if you don't much feel like a hike, stop by where the walk starts in Overlook Park, just for the view of the Rio Grande; follow signs from Highway 4 at the first stoplight in town. You can also take a strenuous hike into the gorge along the **Red Dot Trail,** which passes a few petroglyphs on its way down to the Rio Grande; follow signs from Highway 4 for Overlook Park, at the back end of a subdivision.

A bit of a locals' secret, **Pajarito Mountain** (397 Camp May Rd., 505/662-5725, www.skipajarito.com, 9am-4pm Fri.-Sun. and holidays) offers good skiing and snowboarding for relatively cheap ($49/full day), with six lifts giving access to bunny slopes as well as double-black-diamond trails. The area is just a few miles west of Los Alamos, off Highway 501.

Food

Los Alamos is not exactly bursting with restaurants, and many are open weekdays only. For breakfast and lunch, the family-run **Morning Glory** (1377 Diamond Dr., 505/662-4000, 6am-4pm Mon.-Fri., 7am-1pm Sat., $5) has tasty breakfast burritos, filling lunch specials, such as chicken-fried steak, and a tempting selection of homemade doughnuts and baked goods.

Blue Window Bistro (1789 Central Ave., 505/662-6305, 11am-2:30pm and 5pm-8:30pm Mon.-Fri., 5pm-9pm Sat., $18) is the fanciest restaurant in town, which in Los Alamos still doesn't mean too fancy. It's a colorful, bustling place; it often feels as if the entire town is crammed inside. Food is typical fresh American: huge salads and hot sandwiches for lunch, creative pasta and steaks in the evening. If you're headed back down the hill for the night, it's not worth staying for dinner, but if you're here overnight, it's your best option.

Tucked away at the end of a small strip mall, **Bathtub Row Brewing Co-Op** (163 Central Park Square, 505/500-8381, 2pm-10pm Mon.-Wed., 2pm-11pm Thurs., noon-11pm Fri.-Sat., noon-10pm Sun.) pours pints of its own brews, such as excellent brown and blonde ales, and select offerings from other New Mexico breweries. It's especially lively when the laboratory's day ends.

Starbucks on Central Avenue (1801 Central Ave., 505/661-0100, 4:30am-8pm Mon.-Fri., 6am-8pm Sat., 5:30am-7pm Sun.) is the only café in town and is notable just for the deeply scientific conversations on which you can eavesdrop.

Accommodations

The few hotels in Los Alamos cater primarily to visiting engineers, though it's a handy place to bunk if you want to get an early start at Bandelier and the Valles Caldera. The chain hotels are functional; the best of the few remaining options is the **North Road Inn** (2127 North Rd., 505/662-3678, www.northroadinn.com, $94 d), a converted apartment complex in a quiet residential area that has large rooms (some are suites with kitchenettes). Those on the upper level are a bit more private.

Information

Stop at the recently relocated **tourist info center** (475 20th St., 505/662-8105, www.

visitlosalamos.org, 9am-5pm Mon.-Fri., 9am-4pm Sat., 10am-3pm Sun.), adjacent to Ashley Pond, for maps and advice on hikes. There's another office in **White Rock** (115 Hwy 4, 505/672-3183, 8am-6pm daily, 10am-2pm daily in winter), en route to Bandelier. The comprehensive events calendar at www.fyilosalamos.com is the best source of the latest happenings.

Getting There

Los Alamos is 36 miles (45 minutes by car) from downtown Santa Fe via U.S. 84/285 north to Highway 502 west. From Española, it's 20 miles (30 minutes) west on Highway 30 to Highway 502. There is an airport (LAM, www.lam.aero), but the city no longer has commercial service.

★ BANDELIER NATIONAL MONUMENT

One of New Mexico's most entrancing ancient sites, **Bandelier National Monument** (www.nps.gov/band, $20/car) comprises 23,000 acres of wilderness, including the remarkable Frijoles Canyon, lined on either side with "cavates"—rooms carved by the Ancestral Puebloans that served as their homes—while the remnants of a massive settlement from the 16th century occupy the valley floor. Though signs of human settlement in the canyon date back over 10,000 years, it is these dwellings and the foundations of kivas that were central to Ancestral Puebloan society that the park is most known for today. Several of the cavates are just a short walk from the visitors center—it's possible to climb inside some of them—and there's a network of much longer trails that wend deeper into the canyon, the mesa and the backcountry.

Bandelier gets so busy in summer that mid-May-mid-October the park is accessible only by shuttle bus from the visitors center in White Rock. The best way to avoid crowds is to arrive early on a weekday, if possible. Another approach is to join a torch-lit, silent **night walk** ($6) into Frijoles Canyon; they're typically on Friday nights, but call the visitors center or check online for the schedule.

In the park, another **visitors center** (505/672-3861, 9am-6pm daily mid-May-mid-Oct., 9am-4:30pm mid-Oct.-mid-May) has a museum and the usual array of maps and guides. If you're interested in wildflowers, pick up a Falls Trail guide, as it has good illustrations of what grows in the area. Rangers run free **guided walks** around the main loop a few times a day, or you can pick up the trail guide for $1.

Main Loop Trail and Alcove House Trail

A paved walkway leads out the back of the visitors center into Frijoles Canyon, passing the ruins of the major settlements—or at least the ones that have been thoroughly excavated. You first reach **Tyuonyi** (chew-ON-yee), a circle of buildings that was settled for about 200 years, beginning in the 1300s. Built of bricks cut from tuff (the volcanic rock that makes up most of the area) and adobe plaster, some of the 250 rooms at one time stood several stories tall.

The trail then goes up next to the cliffs, dotted with small caves dug out of the soft stone, and to **Long House,** the remnants of a strip of condo-style buildings tucked into the rock wall. Paintings and carvings decorate the cliff face above. If you're here near sunset, keep an eye on the **bat cave** near the end of the strip, home to thousands of the flying mammals.

Continue another 0.5 mile to the **Alcove House,** accessible by 140 feet of ladders. It's well worth the climb up, if you can handle heights.

Frey Trail

The 1.5-mile **Frey Trail** used to be the main route to Frijoles Canyon, before the access road was built by the Civilian Conservation Corps in the 1930s. Descending from **Juniper Campground** (just off Highway 4 northwest of the park access road), it's a nice approach to the area, offering great views over Tyuonyi

and a general sense of what it must have been like to "discover" the canyon. The trail has no shade, however, so it's best hiked early in the day. The shuttle bus can drop you at the trailhead, so you can hike down, then ride back to the depot.

Tsankawi

Well before you reach the main entrance to Bandelier, you pass **Tsankawi** on the east side of Highway 4. (This area is accessible by car year-round.) Unique pottery excavated in this separate section, disconnected from the main park, suggests that it was inhabited by a different people from those who settled in Frijoles Canyon, and some sort of natural border seems to have formed here, despite a shared cliff-dwelling culture: Today the pueblos immediately north of the Bandelier area speak Tewa, while those to the south speak Keresan. A 1.5-mile loop, with ladders to climb along the way, leads past unexcavated ruins, cave houses, and even a few petroglyphs.

Camping

Juniper Campground ($12), just inside the park's northern border, is usually open year-round, with 94 sites. There are no hookups or showers. No reservations are taken, but it's usually not full. The scenery up on the plateau is a bit bleak, due to the 2011 fire, but you will get an early start on the day if you overnight here.

Getting There

Bandelier is 45 miles (one hour) from downtown Santa Fe via U.S. 84/285 north to Highway 502 and Highway 4 west. From Jemez Springs, it's 41 miles (one hour) via Highway 4 east.

Mid-May-mid-October, access to the park is via free **shuttle bus** only. The service departs from the **White Rock visitors center** (Hwy. 4) every 20 or 30 minutes between 9am

1: a cliffside dwelling at Bandelier National Monument **2:** a view at Bandelier National Monument **3:** Valles Caldera National Preserve

and 3pm; before or after that time, you can enter the park by car.

White Rock is a 40-minute drive from Santa Fe via U.S. 84/285 north to Highway 502 and Highway 4 west. From Jemez Springs, it's about an hour's drive via Highway 4 north and east (but you'll have to drive past the Bandelier entrance, and double back in the shuttle bus). The bus also stops at the Frey Trail trailhead en route to the main park.

★ VALLES CALDERA NATIONAL PRESERVE

Spreading out for 89,000 acres to the north of Highway 4, **Valles Caldera National Preserve** (575/829-4100, www.nps.gov/vall, $20/car) is a series of vast green valleys, rimmed by the edges of a volcano that collapsed into a massive bowl millennia ago. At the center is rounded Redondo Peak (11,254 feet). The surrounding meadows are home to herds of elk; the view down into the caldera from Highway 4 when the elk spread out in front of Redondo Peak can be breathtaking. The land has been carefully managed since it was converted from a ranch in 2000, and it is not heavily visited—it's easy to get out into the wilderness and feel utterly alone under the dome of the sky.

To get oriented, drive in two miles to the **Valle Grande Contact Station** (8am-8pm daily mid-May-Sept., 9am-5pm daily Oct.-mid-May), where you can get a hiking map and the latest trail conditions. A full roster of guided activities is available in winter and summer, including group day hikes, elk sightseeing, and full-moon snowshoeing in winter. There is no **camping** available in the preserve.

Hiking and Mountain Biking

Hiking in the preserve no longer requires reservations or is confined to specific days, and there are several trails to choose from. From the contact station, an hour-long trail offers a quick introduction to the preserve. Follow the loop west around the bases of Redondo Peak and neighboring Redonito (10,898 feet) for a relatively flat hike that bisects a few of the preserve's many creeks; short spurs can be tacked on. Further in the preserve, the trails along the slopes of Cerros del Abrigo (10,332 feet) and Cerros Santa Rosa (9,701 feet) are more challenging and heavily forested.

Many of the preserve's hiking trails are also open to **mountain bikers,** but perhaps the most enjoyable ride can be had by simply following the main dirt road that winds through the preserve to the northwest for approximately 10 miles, crossing through rolling grasslands along the way. As cattle still graze on the land in summer, be prepared to negotiate slow-moving herds.

Winter Activities

Over 25 miles of trails are available for **snowshoeing** and **cross-country skiing;** you can also blaze your own trail into the snowy backcountry. The Contact Station hands out maps for winter activities and is also the staging point for guided outings, including skiing and snowshoeing under the moonlight.

Getting There

Valles Caldera is a scenic, and at times hair-raising, 30-minute drive west from Los Alamos along Highway 501 and Highway 4. From Valles Caldera, continuing west on Highway 4 will bring you to Jemez Springs in 30 minutes; driving east on Highway 4 will take you to Bandelier National Monument in about 20 miles.

If you're carrying on to Santa Fe, it's another hour's drive (about 40 miles). Continue on Highway 4 through the town of White Rock and join Highway 502. This leads to U.S. 285, which then goes south to the capital.

ESPAÑOLA

Midway between Santa Fe and Taos, **Española** lacks the glamour or scenery of its neighbors. The town of 10,000 is unquestionably rough around the edges, but don't let that deter you from some of the best New Mexican food in the state. And although it doesn't have much in the way of its own sights (except for the ubiquitous lowriders), it is at a convenient crossroads.

Plaza de Española

Clustered around this public space are the town's museums. The tiny **Bond House Museum** (706 Bond St., 505/747-8535, 1pm-3:30pm Mon.-Wed., noon-4pm Thurs.-Fri., free), built at the turn of the 20th century by a Canadian family that established the Española Mercantile, devotes half its space to artwork and the other small room to various historic artifacts. Down the hill, past the replica Alhambra fountain, is the **Misión Museum,** a replica of the town's original mission church, furnished with traditional craft work from around the valley. It is open sporadically—ask at the Bond House if no one is around.

Chimayó Trading Post

No, you haven't made a wrong turn—you're still in Española. The **Chimayó Trading**

Post (110 Sandia Dr., 505/753-9414, 10am-4pm Wed.-Mon.), on the west side of the main highway, relocated here in the 1930s, after several decades at its original location in Chimayó. Now it's a listed landmark, as one of the last remaining historic trading posts, and it has everything you'd expect: creaky wood floors, dim lighting, and a jumbled stock of treasures and bric-a-brac that includes Chimayó rugs, as well as Nepalese silver jewelry; cut-tin candleholders, made locally; skeins of handmade wool yarn; postcards; and even free coffee. The remaining elderly owner (one of a pair of airline employees, back in the real jet-set age) is no longer seriously replenishing his stock, but there are still some nifty finds. Hours can be a bit erratic.

Santa Cruz de la Cañada Church

Midway through Española, take a right turn at Highway 76 to reach the village of Santa Cruz, established in 1695. The sizable Santa Cruz de la Cañada Church (varied hours, free) that's here now (turn left at the traffic light after one mile) dates from 1733, and its altar screen is another colorful work attributed to the Laguna Santero, who also painted the reredos at San Miguel Mission in Santa Fe and the church at Laguna Pueblo. It is dated 1795 but was completely painted over—with the same images—in the mid-19th century, presenting a particular challenge to preservationists, who cleaned and restored the piece in 1995. Each panel presents a different combination of the original artist's work and the fresh paint applied half a century later.

Food

Tucked away underneath a stand of cottonwood trees, takeout stand El Parasol (603 Santa Cruz Rd., 505/753-8852, 7am-9pm Mon.-Sat., 8am-8pm Sun., $5) has a no-nonsense Spanglish menu ("pollo with guacamole taco") of cheap and delicious New Mexican classics. It's an ideal pit stop for those taking the high road to Taos; there are a few picnic tables if you want to linger in the shade.

Next door and one of the forerunners of New Mexican cuisine, El Paragua (603 Santa Cruz Rd., 505/753-3211, 11am-9pm Mon. & Wed.-Thurs., 11am-9:30pm Fri.-Sat., 11am-8pm Sun., $12) has been offering similar staples and much more besides for over 50 years, including a baked salmon filet, lamb chops, and beef flautas quesadillas.

Diner-style JoAnn's Ranch O Casados (938 N. Riverside Dr., 505/753-1334, 8am-9pm daily, $10) does all-day breakfast, plus good and inexpensive enchiladas, fajitas, and more. The red chile is rich and mellow, and you can get half orders of many dishes.

Warm and friendly and nearly always jam packed during lunch, La Cocina (415 S. Santa Clara Bridge Rd., 505/753-3016, 7am-8pm Mon.-Thurs., 7am-8:30pm Fri.-Sat., 8am-3pm Sun., $11) does all the New Mexican classics, including sopaipilla tacos and a combination plate with enchiladas, a tamale and posole.

Easily missed, Blue Heron Brewing Company (100 Hwy. 503, 505/747-4506, 4pm-9pm Wed.-Thurs., 4pm-10pm Fri., noon-10pm Sat., noon-8pm Sun., $11) serves some of the best pizza and ales around; snack on appetizers such as beer-battered fries and salt-crusted pretzels with beer mustard. Beers on tap rotate but typically include Blue Heron's red ale, IPA, stout, and Scottish ale. The taproom occasionally hosts live music and has frequent game nights.

Accommodations

Española is not an obvious choice for staying overnight, but it has some hotels that are so nice, you might rethink your itinerary. They can be especially handy after a night at the Santa Fe Opera, when all the traffic toward Santa Fe is backed up—but the road north is wide open; as well, you'll get more bang for your buck staying here than in Santa Fe. The ★ Inn at the Delta (243 Paseo de Oñate, 505/753-9466, www.innatthedelta.biz, $110 s, $140 d) is a beautiful, rambling adobe complex built by a longtime Española family. The positively palatial rooms are decorated with locally made furniture, and each has a fireplace, a porch, and a jetted tub. Rates include breakfast.

A project of the local pueblo, the **Santa Claran Hotel Casino** (460 N. Riverside Dr., 877/505-4949, www.santaclaran.com, $90 d) also has spacious rooms, tastefully done in subdued grays and browns. Perks include fridges, laundry machines, and satellite TV.

South of town, a couple of minutes off the road to Los Alamos, ★ **Rancho Jacona** (277 County Rd. 84, 505/455-7948, www.ranchojacona.com, $150 d) is a working 35-acre farm dotted with a dozen casitas, each with a kitchen and space for 2-11 people. You'll likely get some fresh eggs for breakfast, and kids can frolic in the pool. There's a two-night minimum.

Getting There

Española is about a 35-minute drive from central Santa Fe via U.S. 84/285 north. Leaving Española, take Highway 68 (also called Riverside Drive) north from here to Taos (45 miles), or cross over the Rio Grande and continue on U.S. 84 to Abiquiu (22 miles) or U.S. 285 to Ojo Caliente (25 miles). From an intersection in the middle of Española, Highway 76 leads east to Chimayó (8 miles), then to Truchas and the other high-road towns on the way to Taos. From the old main plaza on the west side of the Rio Grande, Highway 30 is the back road to Los Alamos (20 miles).

OJO CALIENTE

Twenty-six miles north of Española on U.S. 285, **Ojo Caliente Mineral Springs** (50 Los Banos Dr., 505/583-2233, www.ojocaliente.ojospa.com, 9:30am-10pm daily) is effectively the center of a tiny settlement that built up around the hot springs here. Established in 1916, it's now a somewhat posh resort. The various paved pools ($24 Mon.-Thurs., $38 Fri.-Sun., $20/$32 after 6pm) have different mineral contents, and there's a mud area with rich local clay, as well as private soaking tubs and a full spa. It's a pretty little place, set up

against sandstone bluffs; try to go on a weekday, as it gets busy on weekends.

The handsome onsite **Artesian Restaurant** (7:30am-11am, 11:30am-2:30pm and 5pm-9:30pm), with its creative use of local ingredients, is worth a visit alone. The hotel rooms at the resort ($169 d, no shower; $209 d, full bath) are no great value (although rates do include access to the springs); there are cottages ($199) and handsome suites ($319) to choose from as well. Camping ($40) is also an option; try to choose a shaded site near the river. **The Inn at Ojo** (11 Hwy-414, 505/583-9131, www.ojocaliente.com, $145 d), just down the road, is a better value; breakfast is included.

Just behind the springs, the one-mile **Posi Trail** leads into public land; centuries-old pottery shards are visible along the route. The longer **Mica Mine** trail wends its way through a scenic landscape of cacti and arroyos, ultimately reaching its eponymous destination after two miles. The resort office has trail maps on these trails and others in the area.

Getting There

Ojo Caliente is 50 miles from downtown Santa Fe, about an hour's drive north on U.S. 84/285, then U.S. 285 east where it splits, north of Española. From Española, allow a 30-minutes driving time. From Abiquiu, avoid backtracking by going through El Rito; take Highway 554 north to Highway 111 north, coming out on U.S. 285 a few miles north of Ojo Caliente. This route takes about 45 minutes.

From Ojo Caliente, you can continue 41 miles to Taos (about a one-hour drive). Follow U.S. 285 north for 10 miles, then turn right (east) on Highway 567. In nine miles, Highway 567 ends at a T-junction; turn left (north) on Taos County Road and continue about eight miles. You will meet U.S. 64 about one mile west of the Rio Grande Gorge; Taos is to the right (east).

ABIQUIU

Northwest of Española, along U.S. 84, the valley formed by the Rio Chama is one of the

Ancient Egypt in New Mexico

"Adobe," the word for the sun-dried mud bricks the Spanish used to build their houses for the first few centuries they lived in New Mexico, is derived from Arabic (al-tub), which in turn comes from Coptic, a language with its roots in Pharaonic Egypt. The etymology came full circle in 1980, when an Egyptian architect named Hassan Fathy came to Abiquiu to build an adobe mosque and madrassa, as the cornerstone of **Dar al Islam,** a newly established community of American-born Muslims.

Fathy was a lifelong champion of vernacular architecture, especially of adobe. He drew international interest in the 1940s, when he built the village of New Gourna near Luxor in Egypt. Modernists scoffed at his use of mud brick, but it provided cheap, efficient, even elegant housing, which residents could help construct and, later, make their own repairs to.

By the time the Dar al Islam community hired him in 1980, Fathy was in his eighties, but he nonetheless came to New Mexico to help personally with the mosque construction. It was his first and only commission in North America, and he was excited to work so near the pueblos, where, he noted, the proportions of the mud bricks were nearly the same as those that make up the Temple of Hatshepsut. He brought with him two Nubian assistants and hired a team of locals to help.

An awkward culture clash ensued. Fathy had been built up as an expert to New Mexican *adoberos,* who resented the deference, especially when he was wrong. In particular, they saw that his construction was not adapted to the cold climate, and he used techniques that could not be applied after he left. The minaret proved too expensive, and a plan to build individual homes in Dar al Islam had to be scrapped because modern building codes required framing in adobe structures.

The innovations Fathy did bring are lovely, though: arched doorways and roofs, and—best of all—the signature adobe domes and barrel vaults that the architect had derived from ancient Nubian temples. The gentle curves of the complex's roofline and its rounded, whitewashed interior spaces echo the nearby Plaza Blanca hills, so the building seems beautifully integrated into its natural surroundings—even though it differs from its Spanish-style adobe neighbors.

most striking landscapes in northern New Mexico. Lush greenery on riverbanks clashes with bright-red mud; roaming sheep and cattle graze by the roadside. The striated hills represent dramatic geological shifts, from purple stone formed in the dinosaur era 200 million years ago to red clay formed by forests, then gypsum from sand dunes, then a layer of lava only eight million years old. Far more recently, **Abiquiu** became inextricably linked with the artist Georgia O'Keeffe, who made the place her home for more than 40 years, entranced by the glowing light and dramatic skyline.

Although Abiquiu often refers to the whole river valley, the unofficial town center is **Bode's** (21196 U.S. 84, 505/685-4422, 6:30am-7pm Mon.-Thurs., 6:30am-8pm Fri., 7am-8pm Sat., 7am-7pm Sun.), pronounced BO-deez. This long-established general store also has gas, breakfast burritos, pastries and green-chile cheeseburgers (11:30am-3pm daily), fishing licenses and tackle, camping gear, and local crafts. In winter, it closes earlier on weekends.

Up the hill opposite Bode's is the actual **village of Abiquiu,** established in 1754 by *genízaros* (Hispanicized Indians) through a land grant from the Spanish Crown. Georgia O'Keeffe's house forms one side of the old plaza; on the other is the Santo Tomás de Abiquiu Church, built in the 1930s after the community opted for the legal status of village rather than pueblo. Past O'Keeffe's house is the village *morada,* dramatically set on a hilltop. You're not really welcome to poke around, however—the village maintains a privacy policy similar to those of the pueblos. So, it's best to visit on a guided tour of the house, or come on the village's feast day, for Santa Rosa de Lima, on the weekend closest to August 25.

Poshuouinge Ruin Trail

About two miles south of Abiquiu proper, on the west side of the road, the 0.5-mile **Poshuouinge Ruin Trail** leads to an ancestral Tewa site, literally the "village above the muddy river," inhabited only AD 1420-1500—why it was abandoned is unclear. The village contained about 137 rooms, as well as surrounding field grids, though there's not much to see today (thorough excavations took place in 1919, and it has been left to melt away since then). Nonetheless, it's a good place to get out and stretch your legs and take in the view from the hilltop.

Georgia O'Keeffe Home

The artist's main residence, where she lived 1949-1984, fronts the small plaza in the village center of Abiquiu. The **Georgia O'Keeffe Home** (505/685-4539, www.okeeffemuseum. org) is open for hour-long guided tours mid-March-November. The price, even for the basic tour, can seem a bit steep, but for fans of modernism of any kind, it's a beautiful place to see. The rambling adobe, parts of which were built in the 18th century, is a great reflection of O'Keeffe's aesthetic, which fused the starkness of modernism with an organic sensuality. If you're on a budget, console yourself with the fact that in many ways the surrounding landscape evokes O'Keeffe's work at least as much as her home does—and stop at Ghost Ranch, for more (and cheaper) info on the painter.

The schedule varies by month, but there are five **tours** ($40) daily on Tuesday, Thursday, and Friday. June-October, tours are also on Wednesday and Saturday. A Wednesday- and Friday-night "behind-the-scenes" tour ($65) includes a visit to O'Keeffe's fallout shelter, among other things. Tours depart from the Abiquiu Inn on U.S. 84; you must make reservations at least a month in advance.

Dar al Islam and Plaza Blanca

In another chapter of New Mexico's long utopian history, a few American converts established **Dar al Islam** (342 County Rd. 0155, 505/685-4515 ext. 21, www.daralislam.org, 10am-4pm Mon.-Fri., free), an intentional religious community, in 1980. It was meant to be a place in which Muslims—some 30 families to start with—could practice their religion in every aspect of life, from education to food. The group set up a ranch and built the Abiquiu Inn and a few other local businesses, but the village concept eventually foundered. More recently, Dar al Islam has been reinvented as a retreat center that's open to visitors.

Anyone interested in architecture will want to see the adobe mosque by Egyptian architect Hassan Fathy, all organic, sinuous lines; the view from the hilltop across the Chama River valley is a beautiful one, too. The head of the center requests that visitors dress modestly (arms, legs, and cleavage covered) and be quiet, so as not to disturb classes or workshops in session. Stop at the office first (back a bit and to the right of the parking area) to introduce yourself.

The community's land, some 8,500 acres, also includes the towering gypsum formations of **Plaza Blanca** (White Place). The eerie space, bleached as bones, was recorded in a series of Georgia O'Keeffe paintings, and it has also been used for numerous movie shoots. Two main trails lead down from the parking area.

Coming from the south, the community is accessible via Highway 554, which runs east from U.S. 84, just south of Abiquiu (follow signs for El Rito). Immediately after crossing the Chama River, turn left on County Road 0155. Continue 3.2 miles and turn right through a wooden gate made of telephone poles. Coming from the north on U.S. 84, look for County Road 0155, which is unpaved here, just north of Bode's; the wooden gate will be on the left, 2.3 miles on, shortly after the paving starts. Once through the gate, the road forks after less than a mile: To the left is the entrance to Dar al Islam; to the right, Plaza Blanca.

1: Plaza Blanca **2:** Ghost Ranch

Abiquiu Lake and the Pederal

An Army Corps of Engineers dam project in the late 1950s-early 1960s created the 4,000-acre Abiquiu Lake, with fingers running into the canyons all around. The view coming in is marred by the power station, but past that the water glimmers at the base of the flat-topped mountain Pedernal ("Flint") Peak, the distinctive silhouette that found its way into so many of O'Keeffe's paintings. ("It's my private mountain," she often said. "God told me if I painted it often enough, I could have it.") The overly paved Riana campground (505/685-4561, www.recreation.gov) at the lake is open year-round, but water and electric hookups ($16) are available from mid-April to mid-October. There's also a small beach suitable for swimming.

★ Ghost Ranch

Ghost Ranch (U.S. 84, 505/685-1000, www.ghostranch.org, welcome center 8am-9pm daily), a 21,000-acre retreat owned by the Presbyterian Church, is best known because Georgia O'Keeffe owned a small parcel of the land and maintained a studio here. In the science world, it's also known as the place where, in 1947, paleontologists combing the red hills discovered about a thousand skeletons of the dinosaur Coelophysis ("hollow form," for its hollow, birdlike bones), the largest group discovered in the world.

The grounds are open to day visitors ($5 suggested donation) for hiking. The best trek, which takes about two hours round-trip, is to Chimney Rock, a towering landmark with panoramic views of the entire area. Don't be daunted—the steepest part of the trail is at the start—but do slather on the sunscreen, as there's no shade on this route. Box Canyon is an easier, shadier, all-level walk that's about four miles round-trip. Kitchen Mesa Trail, which starts at the same point, is much more difficult, requiring some scrambling to get up the cliffs at the end (though you could hike the easy first two-thirds, then turn around).

Visitors can also see the Florence Hawley Ellis Museum of Anthropology and the Ruth Hall Museum of Paleontology (both 9am-5pm Mon.-Sat., 1pm-5pm Sun., $5), which display the local finds, including remnants of the prehistoric Gallina culture from the ridge above the valley and an eight-ton chunk of Coelophysis-filled siltstone in the process of being excavated. In summer, both museums are also open 1pm-5pm on Sunday.

Guided tours (various times, $25-35) of the ranch grounds run mid-March-November, on various topics, from local archaeology to movie settings. One walking tour visits O'Keeffe's painting spot in the red Chinle hills behind the ranch. Horseback rides ($85) are another option, visiting various spots key to O'Keeffe's painting life.

Christ in the Desert Monastery

Thirteen miles up a winding dirt road, the Benedictine Christ in the Desert Monastery (Forest Rd. 151, 575/613-4233, www.christdesert.org, 8am-6pm Sun.-Fri.) is said to be the remotest monastery in the Western Hemisphere. The drive follows the Chama River through a lush valley, ending at a striking modern church designed in 1972 by the woodworker and architect George Nakashima to blend in with the dramatic cliffs behind. Most of the outbuildings are straw-bale construction, running on solar power, and the monks grow much of their food and brew their own Belgian-style beer, Monks Ale (look for it at Bode's in Abiquiu). A gift shop next to the modern church sells various monastery products. The annual hop harvest, in late August, is a convivial event that draws volunteers from all over. Look for Forest Road 151 off the west side of U.S. 84, north of Ghost Ranch.

For a hike with a view across the valley and the red rocks, Rim Vista trail (no. 15) is a good route, climbing up to a mesa in about 2.3 miles one-way. The trailhead is less than 1 mile in on Forest Road 151, off the north side of the road; turn right, then bear right at the fork and park after 0.25 mile. The trail is best in spring and fall, as there is not much shade here.

Echo Amphitheater

The bandshell-shaped rock formation **Echo Amphitheater** ($2/car) is a natural wonder of acoustics and a great place to let kids run around and yell to their hearts' content. A short, paved trail from the parking area leads up to the Echo Canyon overlook; there are also several pleasant picnic areas tucked in the brush. It's just over three miles north of Ghost Ranch on U.S. 84, a couple hundred feet from the road.

Food and Accommodations

The **Abiquiu Inn** (21120 U.S. 84, 505/685-4378, www.abiquiuinn.com) functions as the area's visitors center. Lodging ($170 d) consists of some pretty casitas ($250) at the back of the property near the river, and a cluster of motel rooms closer to the front (request one facing away from the road). Two economy rooms ($110) are well kept but best for early risers, as there are skylights over the beds. The inn's restaurant, **Café Abiquiu** (7am-9pm daily, $14) serves a nice mix of traditional New Mexican and more creative food, with especially good breakfasts. When the temperatures warm, the adjacent outdoor seating area, La Terraza, is a wonderful spot for a meal.

You can also stay at **Ghost Ranch** (U.S. 84, 505/685-4333, www.ghostranch.org) when it's not full for retreats, in various room options. The cheapest are cabins with a shared bath ($74 s, $89 d, with breakfast), which are an especially good deal for solo travelers. Private-bath rooms ($119 s, $139 d) have fine views over the valley. You can also camp (sites from $25) in a canyon. Rates for rooms (but not campsites) include breakfast, and day visitors can take simple meals (noon-1pm and 5pm-6pm) at the dining hall.

Christ in the Desert Monastery (Forest Rd. 151, 801/545-8567, www.christdesert.org) offers wonderful accommodations (two-night minimum) for a suggested donation ($70 to $150), which includes all meals. At the 11.5-mile mark on the same road abutting the river, the **Rio Chama Campground** (no fee), with several shaded sites, is p[...] Abiquiu Lake if you really want t[...] from it all.

Getting There

Abiquiu is about 50 miles (one h[...] downtown Santa Fe; take U.S. 84/[...] for 26 miles to Española. From Espa[...] tinue on U.S. 84 north for 23 miles t[...] From Taos, it's about 70 miles, or [...] via El Rito or Ojo Caliente.

LOW ROAD TO TAOS

Following the winding Rio Gran[...] the mountains is the highlight of [...] north, mostly along Highway 68. [...] begins just beyond Española, pass[...] narrowing canyon and finally emerg[...] point where the high plains meet t[...] tains. This dramatic arrival makes it [...] route for heading north to Taos; you[...] loop back south via the high road.

Embudo and Dixon

The village of **Embudo** is really ju[...] in the river where the Chili Line railr[...] Denver, Colorado, used to stop (the o[...] is across the river). But it offers an un[...] treat in the form of the roadside C[...] **Gas Museum** (1819 Hwy. 68, 505/8[...] free), a front yard filled with old ser[...] tion accoutrements. If the gate is o[...] owner is probably home, and you c[...] inside and take a stroll around the [...] to see a beautiful collection of ne[...] and restored gas pumps. A short wa[...] ★ **Sugar's** (1799 Hwy. 68, 505/85[...] 11am-5pm Thurs.-Sun., $6), a small [...] trailer, doles out seriously big, bib[...] food, such as barbecued brisket burr[...] takeout only, but there are a few plast[...] tables where you can sit down.

If you're into wine, keep an eye ou[...] various wineries just north of here[...] (2075 Hwy. 68, 505/579-4441, 10a[...] Mon.-Fri., 10am-8pm Sat., noon-7p[...] May-Sept., 10am-6pm Mon.-Sat., no[...] Sun. Oct.-Apr., standard tasting $8) i[...]

main highway, and La Chiripada (505/579-4437, 11am-5pm Mon.-Sat., noon-5pm Sun.) is down Highway 75 a few miles, in the pleasant little town of Dixon, known for its dense concentration of artists, organic farmers, and vintners. The convivial farmers market runs early June-early November on Wednesdays (3:30pm-6:30pm) in front of the co-op, and, on the first full weekend in November, check out the long-running Dixon Studio Tour (www.dixonarts.org), which showcases over 25 area galleries. A good year-round reason to make the turn is ★ Zuly's (234 Hwy. 275, 505/579-4001, 8:30am-3pm Tues.-Thurs., 8:30am-7pm Fri., 9am-7pm Sat., $8), serving strong coffee and classic New Mexican food with a bit of a hippie flair; hours cut back slightly in winter.

Pilar

Beginning just south of the village of Pilar and stretching several miles north, Orilla Verde Recreation Area (Hwy. 570, www.blm.gov, $3/car) is public land along either side of the Rio Grande, used primarily as a put-in or haul-out for rafting, but you can camp on the riverbanks as well. There are seven campgrounds in Orilla Verde; Petaca and Taos Junction have the best sites ($9/night), while Pilar and Río Bravo have electric hookups.

Running about 1.2 miles one-way along the west edge of the river, the Vista Verde Trail is an easy walk with great views and a few petroglyphs to spot in a small arroyo about one-third of the way out. The trailhead is located on the other side of the river, 0.5 mile up the hill from the Taos Junction Bridge off the dirt road Highway 567 (turn left off Hwy. 570 in Pilar, then follow signs into Orilla Verde). Stop first on the main highway at the Rio Grande Gorge Visitors Center (Hwy. 68, 575/751-4899, 8:30am-4:30pm daily June-Aug., 10am-3pm daily Sept.-May) for maps and other information.

Across the road, Pilar Yacht Club (Hwy. 68, 575/758-9072, 8am-6pm daily mid-May-Aug., 9am-2pm daily Apr.-mid-May and Sept.-Oct.) is the hub of local activity, selling tubes for lazy floats, serving New Mexican staples and diner food to hungry river rats, and functioning as an office for a couple of outfitters.

Getting There

The low road is more direct than the high road to Taos, and has fewer potential diversions. Driving the 70 miles from downtown Santa Fe to Taos (on U.S. 84/285 and Hwy. 68), with no stops, takes about 1.5 hours. There are no gas stations between Española and Taos.

HIGH ROAD TO TAOS

Chimayó, Córdova, Truchas, Las Trampas, Peñasco—these are the tiny villages strung, like beads on a necklace, along the winding highway through the mountains to Taos. This is probably the area of New Mexico where Spanish heritage has been the least diluted—or at any rate relatively untouched by Anglo influence, for there has been a long history of exchange between the Spanish towns and the adjacent pueblos. The local dialect is distinctive, and residents can claim ancestors who settled the towns in the 18th century. The first families learned to survive in the harsh climate with a 90-day growing season, and much of the technology that worked then continues to work now; electricity was still scarce even in the 1970s, and adobe construction is common.

To casual visitors, these communities, closed off by geography, can seem a little insular, but pop in at the shops and galleries that have sprung up in a couple of the towns, and you'll get a warm welcome. During the High Road Art Tour (www.highroadnewmexico.com), over two weekends in late September, modern artists and more traditional craftspeople, famed particularly for their

---

1: Christ in the Desert Monastery 2: Santuario de Chimayó 3: Sugar's, a worthwhile detour on the low road to Taos

wood-carving skills and blanket weaving, open their home studios.

The route starts on Highway 503, heading east off U.S. 84/285 just north of Pojoaque.

Chimayó

From Nambé Pueblo, Highway 503 continues to a T-junction; make a hard left onto Highway 98 to descend into the valley of Chimayó, site of the largest mass pilgrimage in the United States. During Holy Week, the week before Easter, some 50,000 people arrive on foot, often bearing large crosses. At their journey's end is a small church, seemingly existing in a time long since passed, that holds an undeniable pull.

★ SANTUARIO DE CHIMAYÓ

The pilgrimage tradition began in 1945, as a commemoration of the Bataan Death March, but the **Santuario de Chimayó** (Hwy. 98, 505/351-9961, www.holychimayo.us, 9am-6pm daily May-Sept., 9am-5pm daily Oct.-Apr.) had a reputation as a miraculous spot from its start, in 1814. It began as a small chapel, built at the place where a local farmer, Bernardo Abeyta, is said to have dug up a glowing crucifix; the carved wood figure was placed on the altar. The building later fell into disrepair, but in 1929, the architect John Gaw Meem bought it, restored it, and added its sturdy metal roof; Meem then granted it back to the archdiocese in Santa Fe.

Unlike many of the older churches farther north, which are now seldom open, Chimayó is an active place of prayer, always busy with tourists as well as visitors seeking solace, with many side chapels and a busy gift shop. (Mass is said weekdays at 11am and on Sunday at 10:30am and noon year-round.) The approach from the parking area passes chain-link fencing into which visitors have woven twigs to form crosses, each set of sticks representing a prayer. Outdoor pews made of split tree trunks accommodate overflow crowds, and a wheelchair ramp gives easy access to the church.

But the original adobe *santuario* seems untouched by modernity. The front wall of the dim main chapel is filled with an elaborately painted altar screen from the first half of the 19th century, the work of Molleno (nicknamed "the Chile Painter" because forms, especially robes, in his paintings often resemble red and green chiles). The vibrant colors seem to shimmer in the gloom, forming a sort of stage set for Abeyta's crucifix, Nuestro Señor de las Esquípulas, as the centerpiece. Painted on the screen above the crucifix is the symbol of the Franciscans: a cross over which the arms of Christ and Saint Francis meet.

Most pilgrims make their way directly to the small, low-ceilinged antechamber that holds *el pocito,* the little hole where the glowing crucifix was allegedly first dug up. From this pit they scoop up a small portion of the exposed red earth, to apply to withered limbs and arthritic joints, or to eat in hopes of curing internal ailments. (The parish refreshes the well each year with new dirt, after it has been blessed by the priests.) The adjacent sacristy displays handwritten testimonials, prayers, and abandoned crutches; the figurine of Santo Niño de Atocha is also said to have been dug out of the holy ground here as well. (Santo Niño de Atocha has a dedicated chapel just down the road—the artwork here is modern, bordering on cutesy, but the back room, filled with baby shoes, is poignant.)

CHIMAYÓ MUSEUM

The only other official sight in the village is the tiny **Chimayó Museum** (Plaza del Cerro, 505/351-0945, www.chimayomuseum.com, 10am-4pm Wed.-Sat. May-Aug., free), set on the old fortified plaza. It functions as a local archive and displays a neat collection of vintage photographs. Look for it behind Ortega's Weaving Shop.

FOOD AND ACCOMMODATIONS

The family-owned ★ **Rancho de Chimayó** (County Rd. 98, 505/351-4444, www.ranchodechimayo.com, 11:30am-8:30pm Tues.-Sun. $7.50-$21) has earned a James Beard America's Classics award for its great local food, such as sopaipilla relleno (fried bread

Walk On, Santo Niño

In northern New Mexico, the figure of Santo Niño de Atocha is a popular one. This image of Jesus comes from a Spanish legend, when the Christians were battling the Moors in the medieval period. Around 1300, the Muslims took a number of prisoners after a brutal battle in Atocha, near Madrid, and would not allow the captives' families to visit them. After many desperate prayers on the part of Atocha's Christian women, a mysterious child appeared, carrying food and water, to care for the prisoners. The populace guessed that it must be the child Jesus—thus Santo Niño de Atocha became the patron saint of prisoners, and he is depicted carrying a pail for bread and a gourd for water and wearing a large hat emblazoned with a scallop shell, the symbol of pilgrims.

In Chimayó alone, Santo Niño de Atocha is installed in the main church and in a separate 1857 chapel just a block away. He is seen now as a broader intercessor not just for those imprisoned, but also for the chronically ill. New Mexicans have developed a unique folk practice, placing baby shoes at the Santo Niño's feet, on the assumption that his own have worn out while he was walking in the night.

stuffed with meat, beans, and rice), shrimp pesto green-chile enchiladas, and green-chile stew. Enjoy your meal on a beautiful terrace—or inside the old adobe home by the fireplace in wintertime. The place is also open for breakfast on weekends (8:30am-10:30am), and it rents seven rooms (from $69 s, $79 d) in an old farmhouse across the road.

Beyond the Rancho de Chimayó's hacienda, the surrounding area holds a few good options for staying overnight. Not far from the church, off County Road 98, Rancho Manzana (26 Camino de Mision, 505/351-2227, www.ranchomanzana.com, from $72) has a rustic-chic feel, with excellent breakfasts, cozy casitas and much larger lofts. En route to Española, Casa Escondida (64 County Rd. 100, 505/351-4805, www.casaescondida.com, $122 s, $153 d) is a polished country hideaway with nine colorful Southwest-style rooms and a big backyard with lots of birdlife.

Córdova

From Chimayó, turn right (east) on Highway 76 to begin the climb up the Sangre de Cristo Mountains. Near the crest of the hill, about three miles along, a small sign points to Córdova, a village best known for its austere unpainted santos and *bultos* done by masters such as George López and José Dolores López. Another family member, Sabinita López Ortiz (9 County Rd. 1317, 505/351-4572, variable hours), sells her

work and that of five other generations of woodcarvers. Castillo Gallery (181 County Rd. 80, 505/351-4067, variable hours) mixes traditional woodwork with more contemporary sculpture.

Truchas

Highway 76 winds along to the little village of Truchas (Trout), founded in 1754 and still not much more than a long row of buildings set against the ridgeline. On the corner where the highway makes a hard left north is the village *morada,* the meeting place of the local Penitente brotherhood.

Head straight down the smaller road to reach Nuestra Señora del Rosario de las Truchas Church, tucked into a small plaza off to the right of the main street. It's open to visitors only June-August—if you do have a chance to look inside the dim, thick-walled mission that dates back to the early nineteenth century, you'll see precious examples of local wood carving. Though many of the more delicate ones have been moved to a museum for preservation, those remaining display an essential New Mexican style—the sort of "primitive" thing that Bishop Lamy of Santa Fe hated. They're preserved today because Truchas residents hid them at home during the late 19th century. Santa Lucia, with her eyeballs in her hand, graces the altar, and a finely wrought crucifix hangs to the right, clad in a skirt because the legs have broken off.

Just up the road is **Cordova's Handweaving** (32 County Rd. 75, 505/689-1124, variable hours Mon.-Sat.), an unassuming wooden house that echoes with the soft click-clack of a broadloom, as this Hispano family turns out subtly striped rugs in flawless traditional style, as it has done for generations. Prices are quite reasonable.

Las Trampas

Farther north on Highway 76, the village of **Las Trampas** was settled in 1751, and its showpiece, **San José de Gracia Church** (generally 10am-4pm Sat.-Sun. June-Aug.), was built nine years later. It remains one of the finest examples of New Mexican village church architecture. Its thick adobe walls are balanced by vertical bell towers; inside, the clerestory at the front of the church—a typical design—lets light in to shine down on the altar, which was carved and painted in the late 1700s. Other paradigmatic elements include the *atrio*, or small plaza, between the low adobe boundary wall and the church itself, utilized as a cemetery, and the dark narthex where you enter, confined by the choir loft above, but serving only to emphasize the sense of light and space created in the rest of the church by the clerestory and the small windows near the viga ceiling.

As you leave the town heading north, look to the right—you'll see a centuries-old acequia that has been channeled through a log flume to cross a small arroyo.

Picurís Pueblo

One of the smallest pueblos in New Mexico, **Picurís** is also one of the few Rio Grande pueblos that has not built a casino. Instead, it capitalizes on its beautiful natural setting, a lush valley where bison roam and aspen leaves rustle. You can picnic here and fish in small but well-stocked Tu-Tah Lake. The **San Lorenzo de Picurís Church** looks old, but it was in fact rebuilt by hand in 1989, following the original 1776 design, a process that took eight years; it recently underwent

a restoration that lasted several years. As at Nambé, local traditions have melded with those of the surrounding villages, and the Hispano-Indian Matachines dances are well attended on Christmas Eve. Start at the **visitors center** (575/587-2519, 9am-5pm Mon.-Sat.) to pick up maps and pay a suggested donation. The pueblo is a short detour from the high road proper: At the junction with Highway 75, turn west, then follow signs off the main road.

Peñasco

Peñasco is best known to tourists as the home of ★ **Sugar Nymphs Bistro** (15046 Hwy. 75, 575/587-0311, 11am-3pm Mon.-Thurs. 11am-8pm Fri.-Sat., 10am-3pm Sun., $12), a place with "country atmosphere and city cuisine," where you can get treats such as grilled vegetable tacos, green chile cheeseburgers, grilled trout, and staggering wedges of triple-layered chocolate cake. The adjoining **Peñasco Theatre** (www.penascotheatre.org) hosts quirky music and theatrical performances June-September. In winter, restaurant hours are more limited, so call ahead.

This is also the northern gateway to the **Pecos Wilderness Area**—turn on Forest Road 116 to reach Santa Barbara Campground and the Santa Barbara Trail to Truchas Peak, a 23-mile round-trip that requires advance planning. Contact the **Española ranger district office** (1710 N. Riverside Dr., 505/753-7331, 8am-4:30pm Mon.-Fri.) or the one in the town of Pecos for conditions before you hike.

Sipapu

Detouring right (east) along Highway 518, you reach **Sipapu** (Hwy. 518, 800/587-2240, www.sipapunm.com), an unassuming, inexpensive ski resort—really, just a handful of casitas (from $74), an adobe house (from $109) and campsites ($12) at the base of a 9,255-foot mountain. Cheap lift tickets ($45

1: Truchas **2:** San José de Gracia Church in Las Trampas

full-day) and utter quiet make this a bargain getaway.

Returning to the junction, continue on to Taos via Highway 518, which soon descends into a valley and passes **Pot Creek Cultural Site** (575/587-2255, 9am-4pm Wed.-Sun. late June-early Sept.), a mildly interesting diversion for its one-mile loop trail through Ancestral Puebloan ruins from around AD 1200.

You arrive in Taos at its southern end—really, in Ranchos de Taos, just north of the San Francisco de Asis Church on Highway 68. Turn left to see the church, or turn right to head up to the town plaza and to Taos Pueblo.

Getting There

From downtown Santa Fe, the high road to Taos is about 90 miles. Follow U.S. 84/285 north for 17 miles to Pojoaque. Turn right (east) on Highway 503, following signs for Nambé Pueblo; turn left where signed, onto County Road 98, to Chimayó, then left again on Highway 76. In about 30 miles, make a hard left onto Highway 518, and in 16 miles, you'll arrive in Ranchos de Taos, just north of the church and about 3 miles south of the main Taos plaza. The drive straight through takes a little more than two hours; leave time to dawdle at churches and galleries, take a hike, or have lunch along the way.

Taos and North Central New Mexico

Adobe buildings cluster around a plaza. Snow-
capped mountains beckon. Art galleries, organic bakeries, and yoga studios proliferate. But the town of Taos is anything but a miniature Santa Fe.

It's more isolated, reached by two-lane roads along either the winding mountain-ridge route or the fertile Rio Grande Valley, and it has a less polished, more tied-to-the-earth feel. The glory of the landscape, from looming Taos Mountain to the blue mesas dissolving into the flat western horizon, can be breathtaking. The mysticism surrounding Taos Pueblo is intense, as is the often-wild creativity of the artists who have lived here. No wonder people flock here on pilgrimages: to the hip-deep powder at Taos Ski Valley, to the San Francisco de Asis Church that

Highlights

Look for ★ to find recommended sights, activities, dining, and lodging.

★ **Taos Art Museum at Fechin House:** In the early 1930s, Russian artist Nicolai Fechin designed his home in a fusion of Tartar, Spanish, and American Indian styles. His and other artists' paintings hang inside (page 170).

★ **Mabel Dodge Luhan House:** This idiosyncratic home once hummed with artists drawn to Taos by a freethinking woman from New York City, birthing a thriving counterculture (page 171).

★ **San Francisco de Asis Church:** With its massive adobe buttresses and rich earthy glow, this 350-year-old Franciscan mission is one of the most recognizable in the world, thanks to its frequent depiction in paintings and photographs (page 174).

★ **Taos Pueblo:** The stepped adobe buildings at New Mexico's most remarkable pueblo seem to rise organically from the earth. Don't miss the ceremonial dances performed here, about eight times a year (page 174).

★ **Hiking in Taos Ski Valley:** As the road wends ever higher, trailheads beckon, providing access to mountain vistas and some of the most stunning backcountry in the state—not to mention its highest peak (page 181).

★ **Rafting the Rio Grande Gorge:** As jaw-dropping as this 800-foot-deep channel cut through the rock to the west of Taos looks from above, it can't compare to the thrill of rafting its Class III and Class IV rapids (page 183).

★ **Cumbres & Toltec Scenic Railroad:** Ascending the pass through the Rockies into

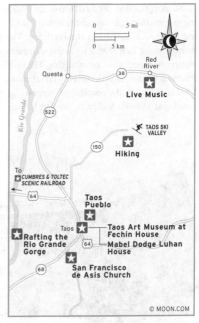

Colorado on this rumbling old steam train, soot and wind in your hair, you'll feel like you've climbed to the top of the world (page 202).

★ **Live Music in Red River:** Though the alpine setting might seem incongruous, the little village of Red River has a surprisingly strong country and bluegrass scene. Catch live acts at packed 1950s-era venues that ooze character (page 209).

Georgia O'Keeffe painted, to the ranch where D. H. Lawrence lived. Then they wind up staying. The person pouring your coffee at the café just might have a variation on this story.

Taos has long been associated with artists and writers—and, recently, Hollywood types—but this doesn't translate to wealth and exclusivity. Hispano farmers in Valle Valdez are sustained by acequia-fed farm plots as they have been for centuries. The same goes for residents of old Taos Pueblo, the living World Heritage Site that still uses no electricity or running water. Add to that a strong subculture of ski bums, artists, off-the-grid eco-homesteaders, and spiritual seekers, and you have a community that is more loyal and dedicated to preserving its unique way of life than perhaps any other small town in the western United States.

Jump the Taos Gorge on U.S. 64 west out of town for a beautiful drive over the mountains to Tierra Amarilla, where sheepherding continues as it has for centuries. North from here, you're nearly at the Colorado state line in Chama, best known as the depot for a scenic steam train.

North and east from Taos, the so-called Enchanted Circle byway loops around Wheeler Peak, the highest mountain in New Mexico at 13,161 feet. Unlike the rest of northern New Mexico, the area was settled primarily by miners and ranchers in the late 19th century. Along the way, you can stop at a mining ghost town, a moving Vietnam veterans' memorial, and a couple of less extreme ski resorts, each with their own character—including one with a thriving music scene.

PLANNING YOUR TIME

Taos's busiest tourist season is summer, when a day can be spent gallery-hopping and museum-going, then settling in to watch the afternoon thunderheads gather and churn, followed by the sun setting under lurid red streaks across the broad western mesas. Wintertime gets busy with skiers November-April, but as they're all up on the mountain during the day, museums scale back their hours, and residents reclaim the town center, curling up with books at the many coffee shops. Taos Pueblo closes to visitors for up to 10 weeks in February and March. By May, the peaks are relatively clear of snow, and you can hike to high meadows filled with wildflowers. Fall is dominated by the smell of wood smoke and the beat of drums, as the pueblo and the rest of the town turn out for the Feast of San Geronimo at the end of September.

From Santa Fe, it's possible to visit Taos as a day trip—as plenty of people do in the summertime—but you'll get a better sense of the place if you stay overnight. A three- or four-night visit gives you time for an afternoon at Taos Pueblo, a couple of mornings at galleries and museums, a hike or skiing, and a day tour of the Enchanted Circle.

For Chama, you can easily make the drive from Taos and back in a day, though if you plan to ride the train, you'll have to get an early start or book a hotel there. As for the Enchanted Circle, the 84-mile loop is typically done as a day trip. By no means attempt to visit Taos and do the Enchanted Circle loop in a single day—you'd be terribly rushed, and this is hardly the spirit of Taos.

HISTORY

The first human inhabitants of the area at the base of Taos Mountain were Tiwa-speaking descendants of the Ancestral Puebloans (also called Anasazi) who migrated from the Four Corners area around AD 1000. Taos (how Spaniards heard the Tiwa word for "village") was a thriving village when Spanish explorers, part of Francisco de Coronado's crew, passed through in 1540. By 1615, settlers had arrived. By the mid-18th century, Taos was the hub of a large trade in beaver pelts, which drew French fur trappers, Mexican traders, and local settlers to swap meets.

Previous: an adobe house in Taos; Taos Ski Valley; shop door in downtown Taos.

Taos and North Central New Mexico

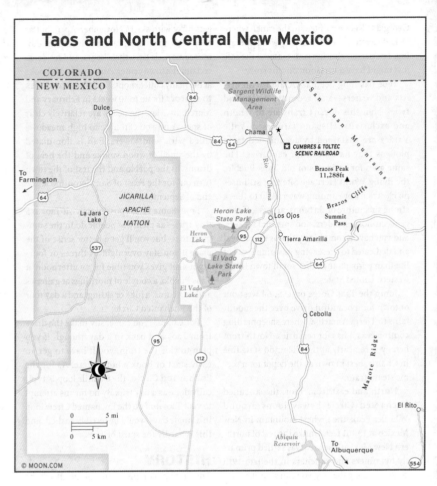

COLORADO
NEW MEXICO

Dulce

Sargent Wildlife
Management
Area

84

Chama

CUMBRES & TOLTEC
SCENIC RAILROAD

To
Farmington

64

JICARILLA
APACHE
NATION

La Jara
Lake

537

84 64

Rio Chama

San Juan Mountains

Brazos Peak
11,288ft

Brazos Cliffs

Heron Lake
State Park

Los Ojos

Summit
Pass

Heron
Lake

95 112

Tierra Amarilla

64

El Vado
Lake State
Park

El Vado
Lake

Cebolla

95

112

84

Magote Ridge

0   5 mi
0   5 km

Abiquiu
Reservoir

To
Albuquerque

El Rito

554

© MOON.COM

But in 1879, the railroad arrived in Raton, bumping Taos from its position as a trading hub. Fortunes began to turn nearly two decades later, in 1898, when Bert Geer Phillips and Ernest Blumenschein, two painters on a jaunt from Denver, Colorado, "discovered" Taos after their wagon wheel snapped near town. They established the Taos Society of Artists (TSA) in 1915, making names for themselves as painters of the American West and a name for Taos as a destination for creative types. In the 1960s, creativity took a turn to the communal, with groups such as the New Buffalo commune in Arroyo Hondo— an inspiration for Dennis Hopper's film *Easy Rider*. The culture clash at first was fierce, but in the decades since, hippies (and their richer relatives, ski bums) have become part of the town's most basic fabric.

ORIENTATION

The area referred to as Taos encompasses a few nearby communities as well. Arriving via the low road, on Highway 68, you pass first through **Ranchos de Taos;** it's connected to **Taos Plaza** by Paseo del Pueblo Sur, a

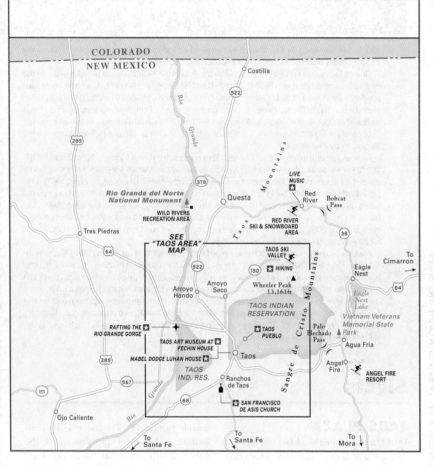

commercial stretch abutted by chain stores and cheap motels. The intersection with Kit Carson Road (U.S. 64) is the center of town proper (Taos Plaza is just west); for **parking**, there's a pay lot at the light, or a free lot a few blocks farther east on Kit Carson.

Heading north past Kit Carson, the road becomes Paseo del Pueblo Norte. It curves west after 0.5 mile, and a smaller road continues north about two miles to **Taos Pueblo**. Paseo del Pueblo Norte carries on through what is technically the separate village of El Prado, then to a four-way intersection that will forever be known to locals as "the old blinking light," even though the flashing yellow signal was replaced with a newfangled three-color traffic light in the 1990s. Here U.S. 64 shoots **west to the Rio Grande,** and Highway 522 leads northwest to the outlying village of **Arroyo Hondo,** then to Questa and the Enchanted Circle. Highway 150 goes north to **Arroyo Seco,** and eventually to **Taos Ski Valley** and the slopes of Kachina Peak.

Taos: Fact and Fiction

Just as San Francisco de Asis Church has inspired countless painters and photographers, the people of Taos have found their way into novels and short stories.

One of Taos's more revered figures is **Padre Antonio Martinez,** a popular priest in the mid-1800s who clashed with **Bishop Jean-Baptiste Lamy** in Santa Fe. As a result, some Taos residents aren't fond of Willa Cather's *Death Comes for the Archbishop* (New York: Vintage, 1990), even if it is a classic. The 1927 novel is based on the mission of Lamy, with sympathy for his efforts to straighten out "rogue" Mexican priests like Martinez. The padre gets more balanced coverage in *Lamy of Santa Fe* (Middletown, CT: Wesleyan University Press, 2003), a Pulitzer Prize-winning biography by Paul Horgan.

Famous Western novelist Frank Waters, a Taos resident for almost 50 years, fictionalized **Edith Warner,** a woman who ran a small café frequented by Los Alamos scientists while they developed the nuclear bomb. *The Woman at Otowi Crossing* (Athens, OH: Swallow Press, 1987) is his portrait of a woman who seeks isolation in the New Mexico wilderness but is drawn back into the world through the largest event of her time. The novel is fairly true to life, but a biography, *The House at Otowi Bridge: The Story of Edith Warner and Los Alamos* (Albuquerque: University of New Mexico Press, 1973), is stricter with the facts. It's by Peggy Pond Church, who lived at Los Alamos for 20 years before the area was taken over by the government.

Another Taos writer, **John Nichols,** earned acclaim for his 1974 comic novel *The Milagro Beanfield War* (New York: Owl Books, 2000), later made into a film by Robert Redford. The war of the title is an escalating squabble in a tiny village over the acequia, the type of irrigation ditch that's still used in Valle Valdez and other agricultural communities in the area. But if you think it takes comic melodrama and a star such as Redford to make irrigation interesting, look into the beautiful and fascinating *Mayordomo: Chronicle of an Acequia in Northern New Mexico* (Albuquerque: University of New Mexico Press, 1993), **Stanley Crawford**'s memoir about his term as "ditch boss" in the valley where he runs his garlic farm.

Sights

TAOS PLAZA

Taos Plaza, enclosed by adobe buildings with deep *portales,* is easy to miss if you just cruise through on the main road—it's just west of the intersection with Kit Carson Road. Once an informal area at the center of a cluster of settlers' homes, the plaza was established around 1615 but destroyed in the Pueblo Revolt of 1680. New homes were built starting in 1710, as defense against Comanche and Jicarilla raiders. Before long a series of fires gutted the block-style buildings, so the structures that edge the plaza all date from around 1930—and unfortunately virtually all are now filled with rather cheesy souvenir shops.

On the plaza's north side, the **Old Taos County Courthouse** contains a series of Works Progress Administration-sponsored murals painted in 1934 and 1935 by Emil Bisttram and a team of other Taos artists. The door is usually open when the farmers market is on, but not reliably so at other times. Still, it's worth a try: Enter on the ground floor through the North Plaza Art Center and go upstairs, toward the back of the building. On the south side, the **Hotel La Fonda de Taos** harbors a small collection of D. H. Lawrence's "erotic" paintings (10am-6pm daily, guided $6, unguided $3, free to guests). The nine paintings are tame by today's standards, but they flesh out (no pun intended) the story of the writer's time in Taos, some of which is described in his book *Mornings in Mexico.*

In the center is a **monument** to New Mexicans killed in the Bataan Death March of World War II. The U.S. flag flies day and

Taos Area

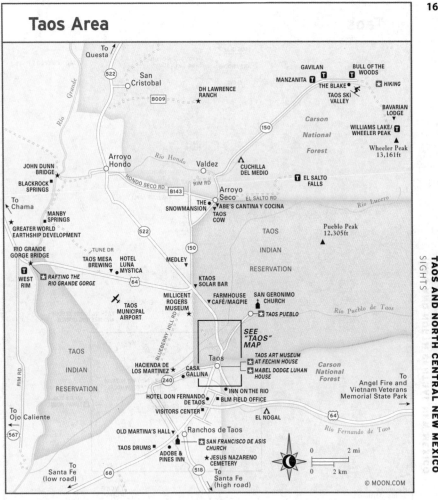

night, a tradition carried on after an incident during the Civil War when Kit Carson and a crew of his men nailed the flag to a pole and guarded it to keep Confederate sympathizers from taking it down.

In front of the historic La Fonda hotel, a large bronze **statue of Padre Antonio Martinez** gestures like a visionary. This local hero produced the area's first newspaper, *El Crepúsculo de la Libertad* (The Dawn of Freedom), which later became the *Taos News;* he also established a co-ed school, a seminary, and a law school. Bishop Jean-Baptiste Lamy in Santa Fe criticized his liberal views, especially after Martinez defied Lamy's call for mandatory tithing, and Lamy later excommunicated him. Martinez continued to minister to locals at a chapel in his house until his death in 1867. The statue's enormous hands suggest his vast talent and influence in the town.

Harwood Museum of Art

The **Harwood Museum of Art** (238 Ledoux St., 575/758-9826, www.harwoodmuseum.

Taos

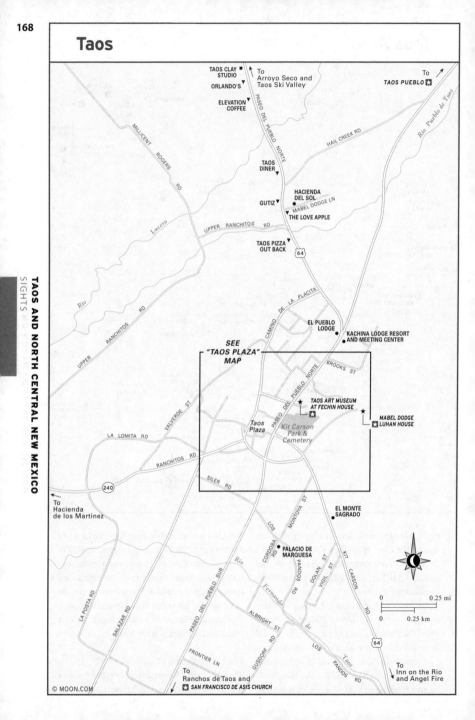

TAOS CLAY STUDIO
ORLANDO'S
ELEVATION COFFEE
To Arroyo Seco and Taos Ski Valley
To TAOS PUEBLO
Rio Pueblo de Taos
MILLICENT ROGERS RD
PASEO DEL PUEBLO NORTE
HAIL CREEK RD
TAOS DINER
HACIENDA DEL SOL
GUTIZ
MABEL DODGE LN
THE LOVE APPLE
Lucero
UPPER RANCHITOS RD
TAOS PIZZA OUT BACK
64
Rio
UPPER RANCHITOS RD
CAMINO DE LA PLACITA
EL PUEBLO LODGE
KACHINA LODGE RESORT AND MEETING CENTER
SEE "TAOS PLAZA" MAP
BROOKS ST
VALVERDE ST
PASEO DEL PUEBLO NORTE
TAOS ART MUSEUM AT FECHIN HOUSE
Taos Plaza
MABEL DODGE LUHAN HOUSE
Kit Carson Park & Cemetery
LA LOMITA RD
RANCHITOS RD
240
SILER RD
To Hacienda de los Martinez
EL MONTE SAGRADO
LOS
MONTOYA ST
LA POSTA RD
SALAZAR RD
PASEO DEL PUEBLO SUR
Rio
CORDOBA RD
PALACIO DE MARQUESA
PANDOS GD
DOLAN ST
VIGIL ST
KIT CARSON RD
Fernando
ALBRIGHT ST
de
GUSDORF RD
FRONTIER LN
LOS
Taos
PANDOS RD
64
To Ranchos de Taos and SAN FRANCISCO DE ASIS CHURCH
To Inn on the Rio and Angel Fire

0   0.25 mi
0   0.25 km

© MOON.COM

Taos Walking Tour

The major sights around Taos Plaza are listed in the order of a potential walking tour. Stroll quickly to get oriented, or take your time and visit the museums along the way. Either way, you'll pass a few other historical spots as well.

Starting on **Taos Plaza,** walk out the southwest corner to **Ledoux Street** and the museums (such as the **Harwood Museum of Art**). Make a short jog left (southwest) down Lower Ranchitos Road to **La Loma Plaza.** Return to Ranchitos, and then turn left into **Padre Martinez Lane,** where the influential pastor lived until his death in 1867. At the end of the street, turn right and walk to Camino de la Placita, then turn left.

After a couple of blocks, turn right (east) on **Bent Street,** passing **Governor Bent House and Museum,** home of the first American governor, Charles Bent. At Paseo del Pueblo Norte, turn left and walk to **Taos Art Museum at Fechin House,** at least to admire the structure. Backtrack and enter **Kit Carson Park** to find the **cemetery** where many Taos notables are buried. Cut out the back of the park, past the baseball diamonds to Morada Lane—at the end is the **Mabel Dodge Luhan House.**

Take Morada Lane back to **Kit Carson Road,** passing the **Couse-Sharp Historic Site** and the **Kit Carson Home.** Turn right (west) to get back to Paseo del Pueblo, passing Carson's home on the way. Another right turn gets you to a well-deserved drink at the **Taos Inn.**

org, 10am-5pm Wed.-Fri., noon-5pm Sat.-Sun., $10), set in the sprawling Pueblo Revival-style home of the Harwood patrons, tells the story of Taos's rise as an art colony, beginning with Ernest Blumenschein's fateful wagon accident, which left him and his colleague Bert Phillips stranded in the tiny town in 1898.

Modern Taos painters are represented in changing exhibit spaces upstairs and down, and it's interesting to see the same material—the mountain, the pueblo, the river, local residents—depicted in different styles over time. Also upstairs is a small but good assortment of Hispano crafts, including some beautiful 19th-century tinwork and a couple of santos by Patrocinio Barela, the Taos wood-carver who modernized the art in the 1930s. A separate back wing is dedicated to seven ethereal abstractions by painter Agnes Martin; a local teacher offers yoga in the gallery every Wednesday. The Arthur Bell Auditorium hosts concerts and artist talks.

E. L. Blumenschein Home

Ernest Blumenschein, one of the founding fathers of the Taos Society of Artists, moved into what is now the **E. L. Blumenschein Home** (222 Ledoux St., 575/758-0505, www.

taoshistoricmuseums.org, 11am-4pm Mon.-Tues. and Fri.-Sat., noon-4pm Sun., $8) in 1919 with his wife, Mary Shepherd Greene Blumenschein, also an accomplished artist. The house's decoration largely reflects her taste, from the sturdy wood furnishings in the dining room to the light-filled studio and the cozy wood-paneled library.

The original rooms of the house feature rotating exhibits, while other rooms, including the "Green Room," are hung with works by their contemporaries, including a beautiful monotype of Taos Mountain by Oscar E. Berninghaus. The main bedroom, entered through a steep arch, is decorated with Mary's lush illustrations for *The Arabian Nights.* Throughout, you can admire the variety of ceiling styles, from rough-hewn split cedar (*rajas*) to tidy golden aspen boughs (*latillas*).

La Loma Plaza

To see what Taos Plaza looked like before the souvenir-shop economy, stroll down Lower Ranchitos Road and turn on Valdez Road to reach **La Loma Plaza.** The center of a fortified settlement created by 63 Spanish families in 1796, the ring of adobe homes around a central open space is dusty and little changed

Taos Plaza

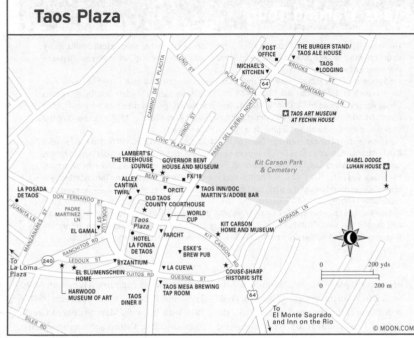

through the centuries. Exit the plaza by continuing uphill and bearing right—this takes you past La Loma's tiny old chapel and onto paved San Antonio Street, which leads downhill and back to Lower Ranchitos.

Governor Bent House and Museum

This dusty little backroom exhibit space is odd and not well cared for, but worth a visit if it happens to be open (the posted hours aren't always maintained). The **Governor Bent House and Museum** (117 Bent St., 9am-5pm daily May-Sept. 10am-4pm Oct.-Apr., $3) is the former residence of Charles Bent, who, following the onset of the Mexican-American War, was appointed the first governor of the territory of New Mexico in 1846, based on his extensive experience as a Western trader (he and his brother had built Bent's Fort, an important trading center in southern Colorado). But Bent died in 1847, at the hands of an angry mob dissatisfied by the new U.S. government.

Amid the slightly creepy clutter, which includes a malevolent-looking ceremonial buffalo head and photos of Penitente rituals from an old *Harper's* magazine, is the very hole in the very wall that Bent's family quickly dug to escape while Bent tried to reason with the murderous crowd. The back room only gets stranger, with weird taxidermy (including an eight-legged lamb), sinister early 1900s doctor's instruments, and lots of old guns. The place may feel like an antiques store where nothing's for sale, but it still gives a surprisingly good overview of the period.

★ Taos Art Museum at Fechin House

This sunny space, the former home of artist and wood-carver Nicolai Fechin, is a showcase not only for a great collection of paintings, but also for Fechin's lovely woodwork. When the Russian native moved to Taos in 1927, hoping to cure his tuberculosis, he purchased seven acres of land, including the small, two-story

Taos Art Museum at Fechin House (227 Paseo del Pueblo Norte, 575/758-2690, www. taosartmuseum.org, 10am-5pm Tues.-Sun. May-Oct., 10am-4pm Nov.-Apr., $10). He proceeded to hand-carve the lintels, staircases, bedsteads, and more, in a combination of Russian Tartar and local styles. His blending of traditions is flawless and natural—a small altar, also in the dining room, is set with Orthodox icons but could just as easily hold local santos.

The permanent collection rotates through three times a year, so the collection varies at any given time. One thing you can count on is that all will be eclectic: Victor Higgins's 1936 *Indian Nude* recalls Paul Gauguin, while Dorothy Brett's *Rainbow and Indians* from 1942 is more enamored of the powerful landscape. One room is dedicated to Fechin's own portrait work, characterized by broad, dynamic brushstrokes and a canny eye for distinctive facial features. After all the work Fechin did on the house, he stayed in Taos only six years, when his wife divorced him. He moved on to Los Angeles with his daughter, Eya (her sunny study, on the ground floor, contains the child-scale furniture that her father made for her). After her father died in 1955, Eya, by then practicing psychodrama and dance therapy, returned to live in the studio (the back building that also houses the gift shop) and helped establish the main house as a museum.

Kit Carson Park and Cemetery

A shady sprawl of gravestones in a corner of **Kit Carson Park** (211 Paseo del Pueblo Norte, north of the Taos Inn), the **cemetery** was established in 1847 to bury the dead from the Taos Rebellion, a melee incited by wealthy Spanish landowners and Catholic priests anxious about their loss of influence under the Americans. Mobs killed New Mexico's first American governor, the veteran merchant Charles Bent, as well as scores of other Anglo landowners in the area. The cemetery earned its current name when the bodies of Carson and his wife were moved here in 1869, according to his will.

Many of Taos's oldest families, particularly the merchants of the late 1800s, are buried here. Mabel Dodge Luhan had been a close friend of the trader Ralph Meyers, and they often joked about being buried together. When Mabel died in 1962, a few years after Ralph, writer Frank Waters recalled their wishes and suggested that Meyers's grave be scooted over to make room for Mabel. She was the last person to be buried in the cemetery, in 1962, and her grave is squeezed into the far southwest corner. Other local luminaries at rest here include Padre Antonio Martinez, who stood up to Catholic bishop Lamy, and an Englishman named Arthur Manby, whose grave actually stands outside of the cemetery proper, due to his lifetime of shady business deals, land grabs, and outright swindles perpetrated in town. Manby was found beheaded in his mansion in 1929, and the unsympathetic populace was happy to attribute the death to natural causes.

The park itself is a popular picnic and barbecue spot in summer, when it also holds concerts by local and national acts.

★ Mabel Dodge Luhan House

Now used as a conference center and B&B, the **Mabel Dodge Luhan House** (240 Morada Ln., 575/751-9686, http://mabeldodgeluhan. com, 9am-7pm daily, free) is open to curious visitors as well as overnight guests. Knock at the main building first; the caretaker will give you a history brochure for a self-guided tour around the public areas of the house.

Mabel Dodge, a well-off, freethinking woman who had fostered art salons in New York City and Florence, Italy, decamped to Taos in 1916, following her third husband. Eventually she got married again, to Taos Pueblo member Tony Luhan, and her name became inextricably linked with Taos's 20th-century history, thanks to all the budding artists and writers she encouraged to visit. Novelist D. H. Lawrence dubbed Taos

"Mabeltown," and figures as grand and varied as actress Greta Garbo, writer Willa Cather, photographer Ansel Adams, artist Georgia O'Keeffe, poet Robinson Jeffers, and psychiatrist Carl Jung made the long trek to her home.

Bordering the Taos reservation, the house was built to Luhan's specifications starting in 1918. Unsurprisingly, given her artistic taste, she exercised a firm hand in its design. Alongside a small original structure—a low row of adobe rooms that were already a century old at that point—she added a three-story main building, topped with a huge sunroom open on three sides. This, and the similarly glass-enclosed bathroom on the 2nd floor, scandalized her neighbors, the pueblo residents.

One of them, however, didn't seem to mind: Tony Luhan, the foreman of the construction project, became her next husband. But Mabel's custom love nest brought out some latent prudery even in D. H. Lawrence, who objected to the curtainless bathroom windows; to soothe his sensibilities, if not Mabel's, he painted colorful swirls directly on the glass.

Couse-Sharp Historic Site

Tours of the **Couse-Sharp Historic Site** (146 Kit Carson Rd., 575/751-0369, www. couse-sharp.org, 10am-5pm daily, May-Oct., donation) are by appointment and during open houses (3pm-5pm, first Sat. of the month June-Oct.), but it is well worth arranging to see the interior of painter Eanger Irving Couse's home and studio. Couse, a friend of E. L. Blumenschein's, came to Taos in 1902 with his wife, Virginia, and spent the summers here, working as a figurative painter, until he died in 1936.

Not only has the Couse home and garden been meticulously kept up, as has adjacent property owned by friend and fellow painter Joseph Henry Sharp, but the tours are led by Couse's granddaughter and her husband, who have a wealth of stories to share. And not only

artists will be intrigued; Couse's son, a mechanical engineer who developed mobile repair vehicles, built a vast machine shop here.

Kit Carson Home and Museum

Old photographs, memorabilia, and assorted trinkets from the frontier era conjure the spirit of the legendary scout at the **Kit Carson Home and Museum** (113 Kit Carson Rd., 575/758-4945, www. kitcarsonhomeandmuseum.com, 10am-5pm daily Mar.-Oct., noon-4:30pm daily Nov-Feb, $10), where he lived with his third wife, Josefa Jaramillo, from 1843 until they both died in 1868.

The definitive mountain man, Carson was of the most acclaimed of the many solitary scouts, trackers, and trappers who explored the American West. He was an intrepid adventurer who, after a childhood on the barely settled edge of Missouri, joined a wagon train headed down the Santa Fe Trail; he arrived in Taos in 1826. His talent for tracking, hunting, and translating from Spanish and various Indian languages soon put him in high demand. Whether he was scouting for John C. Frémont as the explorer mapped the trails west to Los Angeles or serving as an officer in the Civil War or, less heroically, forcing the Navajos on the Long Walk to Fort Sumner, he called Taos home.

Taos Inn

Distinguished by its large glowing thunderbird sign, the **Taos Inn** (125 Paseo del Pueblo Norte, 575/758-2233, www.taosinn. com) was as central to previous generations of Taoseños's lives as it is now. Granted, today it's the hotel bar that everyone goes to, but starting in the 1890s, it was the home of T. P. Martin, Taos's first and only county doctor, who had a reputation for accepting chickens or venison from his poorer patients in lieu of cash. His home looked out on a small plaza and a well—which has since been covered over and made into the hotel lobby.

1: Taos Plaza 2: Mabel Dodge Luhan House
3: Governor Bent House and Museum 4: Kit Carson Park and Cemetery

HACIENDA DE LOS MARTINEZ

The word *hacienda* conjures a sprawling complex and fields, but the reality in 19th-century Taos was quite different, as seen at the carefully restored 1804 **Hacienda de los Martinez** (708 Hacienda Rd., off Lower Ranchitos Rd., 575/758-1000, www.taoshistoricmuseums.org, 10am-5pm Mon.-Sat., noon-5pm Sun. Apr.-Oct., 10am-4pm Mon. and Thurs.-Sat., noon-4pm Sun. Nov.-Mar., $8), one of the last remaining homes of its kind in the Southwest. Its builder and owner, Don Antonio Severino Martinez, was a prominent merchant who hosted the Taos trade fairs at the hacienda and eventually became the mayor of Taos in the 1820s. His oldest son was Padre Antonio Martinez, the valley leader who clashed with the French bishop Jean-Baptiste Lamy.

If you plan to visit just Hacienda de los Martinez and the E. L. Blumenschein Home, ask about discounted admission to both places for $12 (as opposed to $8 each).

Despite the family's high social standing, life was fairly rugged, cramped, and dangerous. The 21 simple rooms arranged around two courtyards allowed room for sleeping, cooking, and protection against raids. Some of the spaces have been furnished to reflect their original use; others are dedicated to exhibits, such as an interesting display on slavery in the area, and a wood carving of Doña Sebastiana, Lady Death, with her glittering mica eyes, in the collection of Penitente paraphernalia. During the spring and summer, local craftspeople are on hand to demonstrate weaving, blacksmithing, and the like in the house's workshops; in the fall, the trade fair is reenacted over a weekend.

★ SAN FRANCISCO DE ASIS CHURCH

Just as photographs of the Great Pyramid of Cheops seldom show the sprawl of modern Cairo crowding up to its base, **San Francisco de Asis Church** (east side of U.S. 68 in Ranchos de Taos, 575/758-2754, 10am-4pm daily, Mass 8am, 9:30am, and 11:30am Sun., donation) as depicted in, say, Georgia O'Keeffe's paintings and Ansel Adams's photographs, is a shadow-draped fortress isolated on a hilltop. In fact, the iconic church, completed in the early 19th century as a Franciscan mission, is at the center of a plaza, ringed with buildings.

It's easy to see what has fascinated so many artists: the clean lines, the shadows created by the hulking buttresses, the adobe bathed in the sun's glow. The church is living architecture, as much a part of the earth as something raised above it. As with every traditional adobe structure, it must be refinished every year with a mix of clay, sand, and straw; it is then coated with a fine layer of water and sand, and buffed with sheepskin. This happens over two weeks in June, during which the church is open only at lunchtime and on Sunday.

Inside, the whitewashed walls are covered with the stations of the cross; two Spanish Colonial *reredos* decorate the altars. In the **parish hall** (9am-3:30pm Mon.-Fri., $3) is the 1896 painting *The Shadow of the Cross*, an eight-foot-high canvas in which the figure of Christ can be seen to luminesce—allegedly miraculously.

★ TAOS PUEBLO

Even if you've been in New Mexico for a while and think you're inured to adobe, **Taos Pueblo** (575/758-1028, www.taospueblo.com, 8am-4:30pm Mon.-Sat., 8:30am-4:30pm Sun., 8:30am-4pm daily in winter, closed for 10 weeks Feb.-Mar., $16) is an amazing sight. Two clusters of multistory mud-brick buildings make up the core of this village, which claims, along with Acoma Pueblo, to be the oldest continually inhabited community in the United States. The current buildings, annually repaired and recoated with mud, are from the 1200s, though it's possible that all their constituent parts have been fully replaced several times since then.

Dennis Hopper in Taos

In 1968, a Taos Pueblo elder told Dennis Hopper, "The mountain is smiling on you!" No wonder the *Easy Rider* actor and real-life renegade claimed the town as what he called his "heart home." His early years here were wild: He's notorious for having ridden his motorcycle across the roof of the Mabel Dodge Luhan House, which he bought in 1969. Over the decades, he mellowed just a bit, and Taos locals came to think of him as one of their own. In 2009, as part of a 40th-anniversary celebration of the Summer of Love, the Harwood Museum mounted an exhibit of his photography and paintings, along with works by some of his compatriots from that era.

Hopper died not long after, in 2010. His funeral was held at the San Francisco de Asis Church, and attended by fellow *Easy Rider* actors Peter Fonda and Jack Nicholson. Following Pueblo tradition, Hopper was buried in a pine box under a dirt mound, in the nearby **Jesus Nazareno Cemetery.** Fans can pay their respects there. To find it, take Highway 518 south; about 0.25 mile along, turn left (east) on Espinoza Road. The cemetery is a short way from here, off the left side of the road. From the main gate, Hopper's grave is near the back, on the right-hand side.

About 150 people (out of the 1,900 or so total Taos reservation residents) live here year-round. These people, along with the town's designation as a United Nations Educational, Scientific, and Cultural Organization (UNESCO) World Heritage Site, have kept the place remarkably as it was in the pre-Columbian era, save for the use of adobe bricks (as opposed to clay and stone), which were introduced by the Spanish, as the main structural material. The apartment-like homes, stacked upon each other and reached by wooden ladders, have no electricity or running water, though some use propane gas for heat and light.

You are free to explore, but be mindful not to intrude on private space: Enter only buildings that are clearly marked as shops, and stay clear of the ceremonial kiva areas on the east side of each complex. These round structures form the ritual heart of the pueblo, a secret space within an already private culture.

You're welcome to wander around and enter any of the craft shops and galleries that are open—a good opportunity to see inside the earthen structures and to buy some of the distinctive Taos pottery, which is only lightly decorated but glimmers with mica from the clay of this area. These pots are also renowned for cooking tender beans. On your way out of the pueblo, you may want to stop in at the **Oooonah Art Center** (575/779-9566, 1pm-5pm daily Oct.-Apr.), whose gallery displays the work of pueblo children and adults enrolled in its craft classes.

San Geronimo Church

The path from the Taos Pueblo admission gate leads directly to the central plaza, a broad expanse between Red Willow Creek (source of the community's drinking water, flowing from sacred Blue Lake high in the mountains) and **San Geronimo Church.** The church, built in 1850, is perhaps the newest structure in the village, a replacement for the first mission the Spanish built, in 1619, using forced Indian labor. The Virgin Mary presides over the room roofed with heavy wood beams; her clothes change with every season, a nod to her dual role as the Earth Mother. (Taking photos is strictly forbidden inside the church at all times and, as at all pueblos, at dances as well.)

The older church, to the north behind the houses, is now a cemetery—fitting, given its tragic destruction. It was first torn down during the Pueblo Revolt of 1680; the Spanish rebuilt it about 20 years later. In 1847, it was again attacked, this time by U.S. troops sent in to quell the rebellion against the new government, in retaliation for the murder of Governor Charles Bent. The counterattack brutally outweighed what had sparked it. More than 100 pueblo residents, including women and children, had taken refuge inside the church when

the soldiers bombarded and set fire to it, killing everyone inside and gutting the building. Since then, the bell tower has been restored, but the graves have simply intermingled with the ruined walls and piles of dissolved adobe mud. All of the crosses—from old carved wood to newly finished stone—face the sacred Taos Mountain.

EL PRADO AND WEST ON U.S. 64

Millicent Rogers Museum

A dashing, thrice-married New York City socialite and designer, Millicent Rogers visited Taos in 1947 after breaking things off with actor Clark Gable. After moving to Taos, she brought Southwestern fashion to national attention, as she modeled Navajo-style velvet broomstick skirts, concha belts, and pounds of silver-and-turquoise jewelry for photo spreads in *Vogue* and *Harper's Bazaar*. Though she died just six years after she arrived in Taos, at the age of 51, she managed to accumulate a fantastic amount of local art. The **Millicent Rogers Museum** (1504 Millicent Rogers Rd., 575/758-2462, www.millicentrogers.org, 10am-5pm daily Apr.-Oct., 10am-5pm Tues.-Sun. Nov.-Mar., $10) was established by her son, Paul Peralta-Ramos, and is set in the warren of adobe rooms that make up her former home.

Her belongings form the core collection, with flawless pieces of pottery, rugs, baskets, and jewelry—both local works and her own designs. Peralta-Ramos also contributed his own collection, including beautiful pieces of Navajo rugs and Hispano devotional art. An entire gallery is devoted to the work of San Ildefonso potter Maria Martinez. Aside from the works' individual beauty, they make an excellent broad introduction to the crafts of the area, from ancient times to modern. But it's not all rooted in local culture: Rogers's goofy illustrations of a fairy tale for her children fill the last room. The gift shop here is particularly thorough and includes beautiful vintage jewelry and circa-1900 rugs.

1: Rio Grande Gorge 2: San Francisco de Asis Church 3: Taos Pueblo

Rio Grande Gorge

Heading west on U.S. 64 from its intersection with Highway 150 and Highway 522, you pass the Taos airstrip on the left; then, after a few more miles, the ground simply drops away. This is the **Rio Grande Gorge** (also called the Taos Gorge), plunging at its most vertigo-inducing point 800 feet down into malevolent-looking basalt. The river courses below, but it's not just millions of years of rushing water that have carved out the canyon—seismic activity also caused a rift in the earth's surface. The crack extends north to just beyond the Colorado state line and south almost to Española.

The elegant, unnervingly delicate-looking bridge that spans it was built in 1965 to supplement entrepreneur John Dunn's rickety old toll crossing eight miles north. Critics mocked the newer structure as "the bridge to nowhere" because the highway on the western bank had yet to be built, but the American Institute of Steel Construction granted it the Most Beautiful Steel Bridge award in 1966. At 650 feet above the river, the cantilever truss was a stunning engineering feat; it is still the seventh-highest bridge in the United States. On either side of the bridge is the stretch of white water called the Taos Box, two words that inspire wild tales in any seasoned river-runner. This series of Class III and IV (and occasionally class V, if the water is high) rapids is the best place for rafting in New Mexico.

A pedestrian path along the bridge brings the depths below you into extremely sharp relief; viewing the gorge from here at sunset with the mountains looming in the backdrop can make for a stunning end to the day. On the west side of the gorge is a rest area, and the start of the **West Rim Trail,** running south from the parking lot and yielding great views of the bridge to the north.

Greater World Earthship Development

If you brave the slender gorge bridge and continue a mile or so west on U.S. 64, you soon see some whimsically curved and creatively stuccoed houses along the right side of the road. These are Earthships: modular, low-priced homes that function entirely on collected rainwater and wind and solar power. Although they look like fanciful hobbit homes or Mars colony pods, Earthships are made of rather common stuff: The walls, built into hillsides for efficient heating and cooling, are stacks of used tires packed with rammed earth, while bottles stacked with cement and crushed aluminum cans form front walls and colorful peepholes.

Greater World is the largest of three local all-Earthship subdivisions and headquarters of the architecture office that developed the design. The **Earthship visitors center** (2 Earthship Way, 575/613-4409, www. earthship.com, 9am-5pm daily in summer, 10am-4pm daily in winter, $8) is the most unconventional model home and sales office you'll ever visit. You can take the self-guided tour of a basic Earthship and watch a video about the building process and the rationale behind the design. If you're hooked, you can, of course, get details on buying a lot in the development or purchasing the plans to build your own place elsewhere. Or try before you buy: You can stay the night in an Earthship here, starting at $140. Look for the green building on the right, 1.5 miles past the bridge.

HIGHWAY 150

Arroyo Seco

When Taos's downtown core becomes too overrun for your liking, it's a good time to make for the village of **Arroyo Seco,** reached by driving past El Prado on U.S. 64 and heading north on Highway 150. This cluster of buildings at a bend in the road to the ski valley feels very much of another era. Sure, there's art up here, too, but this diminutive community, though only a half-hour drive from the Taos Plaza, maintains an even more laidback and funky attitude than

Taos—if such a thing is possible. It has been a retreat for decades: Frank Waters, celebrated author of *The Man Who Killed the Deer* and *The Woman at Otowi Crossing,* lived here off and on from 1947 until his death in 1995.

"Downtown" Arroyo Seco, all one block of it, has grown up around the bend in the road and **La Santísima Trinidad Church,** set back from Highway 150 on the left. The church, built in 1834, has adobe walls that are alarmingly eroded in patches, but it sports a cheery red-metal roof; the spare traditional interior is decorated with *bultos* and *retablos,* but the doors are often locked. Secular pursuits in this area are more surefire draws: a fine bar and general store, for instance, and El Salto Falls, up the mountain a bit.

The Rim Road

As Highway 150 continues, the road to the ski valley eventually makes a hard right, and the so-called rim road heads to the left, along the canyon edge. It gives a great view of **Valle Valdez** below, where tidy farm plots are set along Rio Hondo and the traditional acequia irrigation that has been used here for more than four centuries. In typical modern real-estate distribution, the not-so-well-off native *Taoseños* value their fertile soil, while wealthy *arrivistes* (actress Julia Roberts, most famously) have claimed the swoon-inducing views on the rim road, which was developed only in the later part of the 20th century. On the north side of the valley, the ritzy Turley Mill development is built on the site of a still that produced powerful bootleg hooch known as "Taos lightning" from the 1700s to 1847. (Also glossed over in the development: The still was burned and its owner and customers killed during the uprising against Governor Bent.) The area is now home to former defense secretary Donald Rumsfeld and other occupants of million-dollar casitas.

1: the Greater World Earthship Development
2: Arroyo Seco

New Mexico's Communes

Something about New Mexico's vast empty spaces inspires utopian thinking, as if the landscape were a blank slate, a way to start from scratch and do things right. Spanish settlers felt it in the 16th century. Gold miners banked on it in the 1800s. And in the 1960s, freethinkers, free-lovers, and back-to-the-landers fled crowded cities and boring suburbs to start communities such as the Hog Farm and the New Buffalo commune, both near Taos. For a while, New Mexico was the place to be: Actor Dennis Hopper immortalized New Buffalo in his film *Easy Rider,* singer Janis Joplin chilled out in Truchas, and author Ken Kesey drove his bus, *Further,* through the state. At the end of the decade, some 25 communes had been established.

In most of the rest of the United States, these experimental communities and their ideals were just a brief moment of zaniness—their legacy appears to be Hog Farm leader Wavy Gravy's consecration on a Ben & Jerry's label. But in New Mexico, many of the ideals set down by naked organic gardeners and tripping visionaries took root and sprouted in unexpected ways. Yogi Bhajan, a Sikh who taught mass kundalini yoga sessions in New Mexico in 1969, later became a major contributor to the state economy through all the businesses he established. Buddhist stupas dot the Rio Grande Valley, the product of Anglo spiritual seekers working with Tibetan refugees brought to New Mexico by Project Tibet, cofounded by John Allen, who also ran the commune Synergia Ranch near Santa Fe. Allen was also instrumental in building Biosphere 2, the experimental glass dome in the Arizona desert—probably the most utopian vision yet to have sprouted in New Mexico.

Taos Ski Valley

Highway 150 winds relentlessly up through Hondo Canyon, the steep mountain slopes crowded with tall, dense pines that in winter disappear into a wreath of clouds. The paved road ends at the still-growing village of **Taos Ski Valley;** from there it's another two miles along a rough dirt road to the Wheeler Peak and Williams Lake trailhead. When you get out of the car at the village and take in the vertiginous view up to Kachina Peak (elevation 12,481 feet and often white-capped even in July), you'll see why it inspires legions of reverential skiers every winter, when an average of 305 inches of snow falls on the mountain—almost 10 times the amount they get down in town.

For decades, it was *only* skiers here. Snowboarders were banned, allegedly because the slopes were too steep—more than half the trails are rated expert level, and many of them are left ungroomed. The mountain was opened to all in 2008, and the ski valley's ambition has grown with each passing year.

In the summer, the village is increasingly the site of a burgeoning mountain social scene with occasional live music, and Hondo Canyon's many trails make for good hiking or picnicking. The road is dotted on either side with picnic areas and campgrounds—Cuchilla del Medio is a particularly nice area for a picnic. The **visitors center** (575/776-1413, www.taosskivalley.com) in the ski area parking lot stocks trail descriptions and maps.

Sports and Recreation

The wild setting presses in all around Taos, and the mountains frame every town view. Downhill skiing is the main draw in the winter, but snowshoeing and Nordic skiing are also wildly popular. In summer, peak-baggers will want to strike out for Wheeler, the state's highest, and mountain bikers should seek out—but not underestimate—the adrenaline rush that is descending the nearby dedicated trails in the ski valley. Not quite as intense, but no less dramatic, is the ride along the Rio Grande Gorge. In the waters below, kayakers and rafters challenge the churning rapids of the legendary Taos Box (late May and early June, with winter runoff, are the most intense season for this).

Information

Stop in at the **Carson National Forest Supervisor's Office** (208 Cruz Alta Rd., 575/758-6200, 8am-4:30pm Mon.-Fri.) for booklets on recommended trails and maps. Just down the street, the **Bureau of Land Management Taos Field Office** (226 Cruz Alta Rd., 575/758-8851, 8am-4:30pm Mon.-Fri.) can help with rafting or camping trip prep, with plenty of maps and brochures.

The **Taos Youth and Family Center** (407 Paseo del Cañon, 575/758-4160, 8:30am-6pm daily) has a big indoor pool, as well as an ice-skating rink and skate park. Hours are limited in fall and winter.

Sudden thunderstorms are common in summer, as are flash floods and even freak blizzards. Well into May, snow can blanket higher passes, so wherever you go, always carry more warm clothing than you think you'll need. Carry plenty of water with you—your adventures are taking place at over 7,000 feet, after all—and don't skimp on the sunscreen, even when it's below freezing.

HIKING

With Taos Mountain and Wheeler Peak in the backyard, you can ramble along winding rivers or haul up 2,000 feet in less than four miles. Be prepared for a cold snap or storm at any time, and don't plan on anything before May—it takes that long for the snow to thaw. You can still hit white stuff in the alpine meadows well into summer. If you'd like to lighten your load and enjoy unique animal companionship to boot, contact **Wild Earth Llama Adventures** (800/758-5262, www.llamaadventures.com), which runs day hikes with lunch ($125), as well as multiday treks (from $425). What follows are just a few of the many trails worth seeking out.

In town, **Mudd N Flood** (103 Bent St., 575/751-9100) is a great spot to fill any last-minute gear needs before hitting the trails.

West Rim Trail

Accessed via the rest area adjacent to the Rio Grande Gorge Bridge, approximately 20 minutes northwest of the center of Taos, the **West Rim Trail** offers dramatic views throughout its roughly ten-mile length. Hugging the rim of the gorge, the trail is fairly flat and easy to negotiate, with good opportunities to see bighorn sheep along the sides of the gorge. Spurs near the halfway point can be tacked on and bring you down closer to the river.

★ Taos Ski Valley

Highway 150 winds through Hondo Canyon, the paved road ending at the village of **Taos Ski Valley.** The **visitors center** (575/776-1413, www.taosskivalley.com) in the ski area parking lot off Thunderbird Road stocks trail descriptions and maps.

Just before the parking lot for the ski area, **Gavilan Trail** (no. 60) begins at the north side of the road. It's plenty steep but leads to a high mountain meadow. The route is five miles round-trip, or you can connect with other trails once you're up on the rim.

It's another two miles along a rough dirt road to the Wheeler Peak and Williams Lake trailhead. **Wheeler Peak Summit Trail** (no. 67), which scales New Mexico's highest mountain in about four miles (one-way), requires no technical skill, but it's a fairly relentless ascent and should not be undertaken lightly. The first two miles of the route are on the relatively easy and popular **Williams Lake Trail** (no. 62), which starts near the end of Twining Road, a narrow dirt road that leads out of the top of the Taos Ski Valley parking lot. After looking down on the aquamarine waters of Williams Lake (11,040 feet) and negotiating a rocky stretch, the trail is straightforward. Aim to begin your hike early in the morning to avoid afternoon thunderstorms (and to time your return with a well-earned pint at the Bavarian Lodge). In summer, on the night of the full moon, there's a free guided **moonlight hike** to Williams Lake, starting at 7:30pm; check the schedule at www.taosskivalley.com.

If all that sounds too strenuous, in summer you can take the **chairlift** (10am-4pm Thurs.-Mon. June-Aug., $18) up to the top of the mountain, then wander down any of several wide, well-marked trails, all with stunning views.

El Salto Falls

Some theorize that the mysterious "Taos Hum"—the faint, low drone that many in the area claim to hear—emanates from the caves at **El Salto Falls** (575/776-2371, $5), a scenic spot on a patch of private land in Arroyo Seco. That mystery aside, the series of waterfalls (the tallest drops 200 feet) is an iconic Taos natural landmark, and an easy hike or a challenging one, depending on just how much you'd like to see. Save this hike for dry weather, unless you have a four-wheel drive—the road is rough when muddy or snowy.

In Arroyo Seco, take El Salto Road east (go straight where Highway 150 makes a hard right); after about a mile is a sign on the left asking visitors to pay. Leave cash in the honor box on the porch of the green house just off the road, and fill out a waiver and a permit to place on your dashboard. Continue driving another 0.7 mile and bear left; from here, it's 0.9 mile up to a green gate and small parking area. Walk in, following the road as it curves left, then bearing right. This leads in just a few minutes to the lowest, largest cave and the first waterfall—though most of the year, it is often just a trickle. Intrepid hikers can climb up to the right of the cave, to ever-smaller falls and notches in the cliff face.

BIKING

Gearing Up (616 Paseo del Pueblo Sur, 575/751-0365, 10am-6pm Mon.-Sat., noon-5pm Sun.) rents mountain and hybrid bicycles starting at $55 per day. If you're bringing your bicycle with you, consider having it shipped here. The shop will reassemble it and have it waiting when you arrive.

Mountain Biking

Taos has several great trails for mountain biking. A popular ride close to town is **West Rim Trail** along the Rio Grande Gorge, either from the gorge bridge up to John Dunn Bridge, about 15 miles round-trip, or from the gorge bridge south to the Taos Junction Bridge near Pilar, about 18 miles out and back. Either way, you'll have great views and fairly level but rugged terrain. For some serious downhill action, **Taos Ski Valley** offers mountain biking in summer and early fall; the fee-based **Northside** (daily, late June-Oct., $10) contains several exhilarating trails suited for intermediate to advanced riders; the Alpine Wildflower Loop (10.3 miles) offers the best introduction and some of the most dramatic scenery in the area. The 3.6-mile Berminator route, which sets off from the top of the Taos Ski Valley, is a wildly bouncy and heart-pounding descent from 12,500 feet.

Road Biking

For road touring, the pleasant 25-mile loop from Taos through Arroyo Hondo and Arroyo Seco, with no steep grades, is a good way to get adjusted to the altitude. Head north up Paseo del Pueblo Norte, straight through the intersection at Highway 150, then, in Arroyo Hondo, turn right onto County Road B-143. Cross Highway 230, and you arrive in Arroyo Seco, behind The Snowmansion. Turn right on Highway 150 to loop back to Taos.

For a longer road challenge, take on the 84-mile Enchanted Circle—even better if you do so with more than 1,000 fellow riders. Held in September, the Enchanted Circle Century Tour (575/754-3104, www.redriver.org), the four-decade-old ride kicks off in Red River and is marked by grueling climbs and hairpin descents.

RAFTING AND STAND-UP PADDLEBOARDING

★ Rafting the Rio Grande Gorge

The Taos Box, the 16-mile stretch of the Rio Grande between the John Dunn Bridge and Pilar, provides the most exhilarating rafting in New Mexico, with Class III and Class IV rapids with ominous names like Boat Reamer and Screaming Left-Hand Turn. The river mellows out south of the Taos Box, then leads into a shorter Class III section called the Racecourse—the most popular run, usually done as a half-day trip. Beyond this, in the Orilla Verde Recreation Area around Pilar, the water is wide and flat, a place for a relaxing float with kids; you can flop in an inner tube if you really want to chill. North of the John Dunn Bridge and accessed only by hiking 1.25 miles down the La Junta trail in the Wild Rivers Recreation Area, is another highly rated run called La Junta. It's usually done as a half-day outing and offers some of the best opportunities to see bighorn sheep.

Los Rios River Runners (575/776-8854, www.losriosriverrunners.com) leads trips to all these spots as half-day outings ($54), day trips (from $105), and overnight trips (from $325). Another outfitter, Far Flung Adventures (575/758-2628, www.farflung.com), can add on rock climbing and horseback riding (half-day trips from $58; full-day Lower Gorge trip with horseback riding $158). With both organizations, you can choose whether you want a paddle boat—where you're actively (and sometimes strenuously) paddling—or an oar boat, where guides row, and you can sit back. Far Flung Adventures and New Mexico River Adventures (800/983-7756, www.newmexicoriveradventures.com) also offer stand-up paddleboarding half-day and full-day trips (from $70) on the tamer sections of the Rio Grande. As these outings can be tailored based on skill level, they are suited for those new to the sport as well as those with more experience. All gear is included.

The best month to be on the river is late May-late June, when the water is high from mountain runoff; if the snowmelt is particularly extensive, that period typically extends by a few weeks.

ROCK CLIMBING

From popular rock-climbing spots such as the basalt Dead Cholla Wall in the Rio Grande Gorge to the more traditional routes at Tres Piedras, Taos is a climber's dream. One of the most impressive pitches is at Questa Dome, north of Taos on Highway 378, where the flawless granite on the Questa Direct route is graded 5.10 and 5.11. And climbers are not limited to the summer, as winter sees some terrific ice climbs at higher elevations. Taos Mountain Outfitters (113 N. Plaza, 575/758-9292, www.taosmountainoutfitters.com, 9am-6pm Mon.-Wed., 9am-8pm Thurs.-Fri., 9am-8pm Sat., 10am-6pm Sun.) can provide maps, ropes, and more details. For climbing lessons and guided climbs (from $220 for a half day), contact Mountain Skills (575/776-2222, www.climbtaos.com) in Arroyo Seco.

SKIING AND SNOWBOARDING

Taos Ski Valley (866/968-7386, www.skitaos. org, $101 full-day lift ticket) is a mecca for downhill skiing and snowboarding, with an enticing mix of demanding and accessible runs coupled with spectacular mountain scenery and first-class facilities. The resort is open late November-first weekend in April, with over 110 trails served by 15 lifts, and snowmaking capacity on all beginner and intermediate areas in dry spells. Having opened a lift to just shy of the 12,481-foot Kachina Peak—making it some of the highest lift-served terrain in North America—much of the focus is currently on improving and expanding the beginner area. Devotees of hike-to terrain still have areas dedicated to them, including a 35-acre tree-skiing area. The highly regarded Ernie Blake Snowsports School (866/968-7386) is one of the best places to learn the basics or polish your skills. Group (from $75) and private lessons (full day $175) are available; rates are cheaper in the afternoon for the latter.

For cross-country skiing and snowshoeing, Enchanted Forest (575/754-6112, www.enchantedforestxc.com, $18 full-day pass), between Elizabethtown and Red River on the Enchanted Circle loop, offers miles of groomed trails. There are also easy ski access points in the Carson National Forest—at Capulin Campground on U.S. 64, for instance, five miles east of Taos, and along Manzanita Trail in Hondo Canyon on Highway 150, four miles before the ski valley.

The family-run Cottam's Ski Shop (207-A Paseo del Pueblo Sur, 575/758-2822, 7:30am-7pm Mon.-Fri., 7:30am-8pm Sat.-Sun.) has the area's biggest stock of rental skis, snowboards, and snowshoes. The shop also sells everything else you'll need to get out and enjoy the snow; there's another location at the ski valley (575/776-8719) and one at the Angel Fire ski resort (575/377-3700).

1: the Williams Lake Trail 2: Taos Ski Valley in winter 3: rafting the Rio Grande

HOT SPRINGS

Two spots along the Rio Grande have natural pools of warm water, by-products of the seismic upsets that formed the gorge. They're popular with locals, and clothing is optional. Don't crowd in if several people are already in the spring, and never leave trash behind.

The easier location to reach is Blackrock Springs, accessible by a 0.25-mile hike. From the intersection with U.S. 64, head north on Highway 522 about six miles to where the road dips; immediately after the bridge, turn left on County Road B-005, which runs along the north side of the small Rio Hondo and past the New Buffalo commune. The road crosses the water, then climbs a hill and descends again, toward the Rio Grande. Cross the old John Dunn Bridge to reach the west side, then turn left and park at the first switchback. Hike down the rocks and downstream to the two pools.

Also called Stagecoach Springs, Manby Springs are at the edge of the river where the stage road used to meet a bridge and cross to the west side of the gorge. The hike down is on the old road, now quite rocky, and takes about 20 minutes. (In the late afternoon, keep an eye out for bighorn sheep near the trail.) To find the parking area, take U.S. 64 four miles west, just past the airport, and turn right on Tune Drive; follow this to the end, approximately another four miles. The old road is off the southwest side of the parking area.

FISHING AND HUNTING

Taos's mountain streams and lakes teem with fish. The feisty cutthroat trout is indigenous to Valle Vidal, north of Questa, or you can hook plenty of browns in the wild waters of the Rio Grande. Eagle Nest Lake and Cabresto Lake (northeast of Questa) are both stocked every year. If you'd like a guide to show you where to cast, Cutthroat Fly Fishing (575/776-5703, www.cutthroatflyfishing. com) and The Solitary Angler (866/502-1700, www.thesolitaryangler.com) are two knowledgeable operators (half-day trips from $175). Stop at the tidy Taos Fly Shop (338

Paseo del Pueblo Sur, 575/751-1312, taosfly-shop.com) for tackle and info on flows and other conditions.

Elk are the primary target in hunters' rifle scopes, but you can also bag mule deer, bear, and antelope; **High Mountain Outfitters** (575/751-7000, www.huntingnm.com) is one of the most experienced expedition leaders.

Visit the website of the **New Mexico Department of Game and Fish** (www.wildlife.state.nm.us) for details on seasons, permits, and licenses.

Entertainment and Events

Taos is a small town: no glitzy dance clubs, no bars where you're expected to dress up. Nighttime fun is concentrated in places where, even after just a couple of visits, you'll get to know the regulars. The various town-wide celebrations—including music and dancing on the plaza on summer Thursdays—draw a good cross section of the population.

NIGHTLIFE
Bars and Clubs
Starting around 5pm, the **Adobe Bar** (125 Paseo del Pueblo Norte, 575/758-2233, 11am-10pm daily), in the lobby of the Taos Inn (look for the neon thunderbird sign), is where you'll run into everyone you've seen over the course of the day, sipping a Cowboy Buddha ($12) or some other specialty margarita—the best in town. Mellow jazz or acoustic guitar sets the mood from 7pm. To give hotel residents a break, the bar closes at 10pm.

Wood-paneled **Eske's Brew Pub** (106 Des Georges Ln., 575/758-1517, 3pm-9pm Mon., noon-9:30pm Tues.-Thurs., 11am-10pm Fri.-Sat., 11am-9:30pm Sun.) is across from the plaza, tucked back from the southeast corner of the intersection of Paseo del Pueblo Sur and Kit Carson Road. It serves its house-made beer and barley wine to a chummy après-ski crowd, and there's often live music. You're in New Mexico—you should at least *try* the green-chile ale.

Everyone's default late-night spot is **The Alley Cantina** (121 Teresina Ln., 575/758-2121, 11:30am-midnight Mon.-Sat.,

11am-11pm Sun.). This warren of interconnected rooms (one of which is supposedly the oldest in Taos . . . but don't they all say that?) can be potentially baffling after a few drinks. There's shuffleboard for entertainment if you're not into the ensemble onstage, whose name usually ends in "Blues Band"; a cover of $5-10 applies on weekends. The kitchen is open until 11pm.

Wine and Cocktails
Softly lit **The Treehouse Lounge** (123 Bent St., 575/758-1009, 2:30pm-close daily), located on the upper floor of Lambert's, is Taos's most sophisticated late-night option, with a full bar and no shortage of creative cocktails ($10). Happy hour ($6) is 2:30pm-6pm.

On the plaza, the wine shop **Parcht** (103 E. Plaza, 575/758-1994, 2pm-9pm Tues.-Sat.) pops the cork on a dozen bottles a night, offering glasses and tastings along with perfectly paired small plates, such as pear slices with bleu cheese and honey. It's popular with both the après-work and après-ski sets.

Live Music
The **KTAOS Solar Bar** (9 Hwy. 150, 575/758-5826, www.ktao.com, 3pm-9pm Mon.-Thurs., 3pm-11pm Fri.-Sat., 11am-9pm Sun.), the social scene of the KTAO radio station, is a solar-powered smorgasbord of beers, burgers, and spectacular mountain views. You can peek into the radio studios, or dance on the lawn out back, in front of the large stage that hosts major shows. Happy hour (4pm-6pm) sees drinks as low as $3, and kids are usually welcome, with plenty of room to play.

What to Expect at Pueblo Dances

Visiting a pueblo for a ceremonial dance or feast-day celebration is one of the most memorable parts of a trip to New Mexico. But it's important to remember that a pueblo dance is not at all for the benefit of tourists. It is a ceremony and a religious ritual, not a performance—you are a guest, not an audience.

Keep this in mind as a guide to your own behavior. Applause is not appropriate, nor is conversation during the dance. Queries about the meaning of the dances are generally not appreciated. Never walk in the dance area, and try not to block the view of pueblo residents. The kivas, as holy spaces, are always off-limits to outsiders. During feast days, some pueblo residents may open their doors to visitors, perhaps for a snack or drink—but be considerate of others who may also want to visit, and don't stay too long. Photography is strictly forbidden at dances (sometimes with the exception of Los Matachines, which is not a religious ritual). Don't even think about trying to sneak a shot with your smartphone, as tribal police will be more than happy to confiscate it.

On a practical level, be prepared for a lot of waiting around. Start times are always approximate, and everything depends on when the dancers are done with their kiva rituals. There will usually be a main, seasonal dance—such as the corn dance at the summer solstice—followed by several others. If you go in the winter, dress warmly, but in layers. Ceremonies often start inside the close-packed, overheated church, and then dances often proceed outside in the cold.

If your style is cramped by old adobes, head out to **Taos Mesa Brewing** (20 ABC Mesa Rd., 575/758-1900, www.taosmesabrewing.com, noon-10pm daily), on U.S. 64 opposite the airport, where there's plenty of room to groove. The metal Mothership looms like a far-flung Burning Man theme camp, and the entertainment roster is suitably eclectic, with everyone from grizzled blues masters to major global artists performing outside (cover from $5 some nights). The crowd is all of Taos's younger hippies, plus hops aficionados of all stripes. The menu features tacos and a couple of filling house-made veggie burgers (from $10) and naturally showcases their own brews, including several IPAs and a potent Scottish ale. More centrally, the company's "in town" **tap room** (201 Paseo del Pueblo Sur, 575/758-1900, 11am-11pm daily) also hosts bands and fuels the crowd with pizza.

Finally, check the schedule at **Old Martina's Hall** (4140 Hwy. 68, 575/758-3003, www.oldmartinashall.com) for special events in this renovated old adobe theater. It may not get as wild as back in the days when Dennis Hopper owned the joint, but the new wooden dance floor is a treat.

THE ARTS

Given the high concentration of artists of all stripes, it's no surprise that Taos's theater scene is so rich for such a small town. Check at the **Taos Center for the Arts** (133 Paseo del Pueblo Norte, 575/758-2052, www.tcataos.org) to find out what shows may be on; the group also organizes chamber music performances and film screenings at the adjacent Taos Community Auditorium (145 Paseo del Pueblo Norte, 575/758-4677).

SMU in Taos (6580 Hwy. 518, 575/758-8322, www.smu.edu/taos) organizes a summer lecture series at its Fort Burgwin campus about seven miles east of Ranchos de Taos. The Tuesday night gatherings (from 7pm, free), late May-mid-August, bring noted historians, anthropologists, authors, and others with an interest in the Southwest.

The Storyteller (110 Old Talpa Canyon Rd., 575/751-4245, www.storyteller7.com) shows first-run films on seven screens, with an occasional arty option.

FESTIVALS AND EVENTS

Late spring marks the unofficial start of Taos's festival season. The nascent **Monolith**

Ceremonial Dances at Taos Pueblo

In addition to the Feast of San Geronimo, ceremonial dances are open to visitors. This is only an approximate schedule—dates can vary from year to year, as can the particular dances. Contact the **pueblo** (505/758-1028, www.taospueblo.com) for times, or check the listings in the Tempo section of *The Taos News* for that week.

Every night May-October, there are demonstration dances at the **Kachina Lodge** (413 Paseo del Pueblo Norte)—a little touristy, but nice if your trip doesn't coincide with a dance at the pueblo itself.

- **January 1:** Turtle dance
- **January 6:** Deer or buffalo dance
- **Easter:** Various dances
- **May 3:** Feast of Santa Cruz, corn dance
- **June 13:** Feast of San Antonio, various dances
- **June 24:** Feast of San Juan, corn dance
- **July 25-26:** Feast of Santiago and Santa Ana, corn dances and footraces
- **September 29-30:** Feast of San Geronimo
- **December 24:** Sundown procession and bonfire
- **December 25:** Various dances

on the Mesa (www.monolithonthemesa.com), held in mid-May on three stages at Taos Mesa Brewing, sees some of the best regional psych and space rockers—and a few national ones, too—descending on Taos; of course, there's plenty of locally crafted beer to be had as well.

Things get into full swing in July, beginning with the loopy creativity of the **Arroyo Seco Fourth of July parade,** and then, in the second week, the **Taos Pueblo Powwow** (www.taospueblo.com), a major get-together of Pueblo Indians and tribal members from around the country. Try to be there for the Grand Entry, the massive opening procession. The event takes place at the powwow grounds in El Prado near the Overland Sheepskin store. The next weekend, the town turns out for the **Fiestas de Taos** (www.fiestasdetaos.com), a three-day celebration of Santiago de Compostela and Santa Ana, with a parade,

food and crafts booths on the plaza, and the crowning of the Fiestas Queen.

In mid-August, Santa Fe's Meow Wolf takes its otherworldly art on the road to Kit Carson Park, where it hosts **Taos Vortex** (www.taosvortex.com), a wildly popular weekend-long music festival and immersive experience. Expect to catch a few big-name indie acts and step into installations that are likely to leave you wondering long after you've headed home.

Taos galleries put out their finest at the **Taos Fall Arts Festival** (TFAF, www.taosfallarts.com), a 10-day-long exhibition in late September and early October that shows the works of more than 150 Taos County artists. Taking place at roughly the same time is the three-day-long **Taos Environmental Film Festival,** which is supported by the TFAF and showcases select documentaries on the environment at the Taos Community Auditorium.

Taos's biggest annual festivity (for which many local businesses close) is the **Feast of San Geronimo,** the patron saint assigned to Taos Pueblo by the Spanish when they built their first mission there in 1619. The holiday starts the evening of September 29 with vespers in the pueblo church and continues the next day with footraces and a pole-climbing ritual. Hacienda de los Martinez usually reenacts a 19th-century Taos trade fair, with mountain men, music, and artisans' demonstrations.

On the first weekend in October, the **Taos Wool Festival** (www.taoswoolfestival.org) has drawn textile artists as well as breeders since 1983. Admire the traditional Churro sheep or an Angora goat and then pick up a fleece or scarf made from its wool.

In winter, the glow of luminarias and torchlight on snow produces a magical effect. On the first weekend in December, the **tree-lighting ceremony** on the plaza draws the whole town, and the rest of the season sees numerous celebrations, such as the reenactments of the Virgin's search for shelter, called Las Posadas, which take place at Our Lady of Guadalupe Church west of the plaza on the third weekend in December. At the pueblo, vespers is sung at San Geronimo Church on Christmas Eve, typically followed by a children's dance. On Christmas Day, the pueblo hosts either a deer dance or the Spanish Matachines dance.

The end of winter sees the town hosting the Sundance of short film gatherings, the **Taos Shortz Film Fest** (www.taosshortz. com), which screens 150 films from around the globe over one weekend in March.

Shopping

ARTS AND CRAFTS

In the Overland Ranch complex about three miles north of the plaza, **Magpie** (1405 Paseo del Pueblo Norte, 781/248-0166, 11am-5:30pm Tues.-Sat.) promises "wonderful things for your nest." The owner, a Taos native returned from living on the East Coast, has selected a colorful array of handcrafted furniture, pottery, handmade jewelry, and more, nearly all produced by Taos residents.

Taos Drums (3956 Hwy. 68, 800/424-3786, 9am-5pm Mon.-Fri., 10am-5pm, Sat., 11am-5pm Sun.) is a giant shop and factory dedicated to making Taos Pueblo-style percussion instruments, from thin hand drums to great booming ones, out of hollow logs. Trying out the wares is encouraged. The shop is located on the west side of the highway five miles south of the plaza.

Taos Clay Studio (1208 Paseo del Pueblo Norte, 719/304-4850, 10am-5pm daily), in El Prado, is a homegrown affair. Local artists turn the ceramics at the on-site studio; classes are available, too (individual lessons from $125).

GIFT AND HOME

Fx18 (103-C Bent St., 575/758-8590, 11am-6pm Mon.-Sat., noon-5pm Sun.) has a great selection of assorted goodies, including groovy housewares, lively kids' stuff, and nifty stationery. The selection of contemporary Southwest-style jewelry is particularly good.

Tap into Taos's environmental ethic at **Seconds Eco Store** (120 Bent St., 575/751-4500, 10am-6pm daily May.-Oct., 10am-5pm daily Nov.-Apr.), with nifty upcycled and green goods, such as earrings made of skis and circuit boards turned key chains.

Up Highway 150, **Arroyo Seco Mercantile** (488 Hwy. 150, 575/776-8806, 10am-5:30pm Mon.-Sat., 11am-5pm Sun.) is the town's former general store, now a highly evolved junk shop that has maintained the beautiful old wood-and-glass display cases. Its stock ranges from the practical (books on passive-solar engineering and raising llamas) to the frivolous, with lots of the beautiful, like antique wool blankets.

TOYS

Taos is also home to an exceptionally magical toy store, the nonprofit Twirl (225 Camino de la Placita, 575/751-1402, www.twirltaos.

org, 10am-6pm daily). Tucked in a series of low-ceilinged adobe rooms, it's crammed with everything from science experiments to wooden trains to fairy costumes. Even the kiva fireplace gets a fantastical 1,001 Nights treatment, and it has the best playground in town out back—it even includes a handcrafted hobbit house.

Food

Taos has no shortage of restaurants that can deliver memorable meals. At one of the New Mexican places, try some posole—it's more common here than in Albuquerque or Santa Fe, often substituted for rice as a side dish alongside pinto beans. Also—especially given the hiking and skiing opportunities nearby—don't overlook the breakfast burrito. This unfussy combo of scrambled eggs, green chile, hash browns, and bacon or sausage in a flour tortilla commonly wrapped in foil makes for the perfect meal on the go. Most restaurants close relatively early, and many smaller places don't take plastic—so load up on cash and get seated by 8pm. You'll need reservations for the more upscale restaurants on the weekends, but the whole scene is relatively casual.

CENTRAL TAOS
New Mexican

A small, festively painted place on the north side of town, the family-run ★ Orlando's (1114 Don Juan Valdez Ln., 575/751-1450, 10:30am-2:30pm and 5pm-8:30pm Mon.-Thurs. and Sun., 10:30am-2:30pm and 5pm-9pm Fri.-Sat., $7-14) is invariably the first restaurant named when the question of the best chile comes up. It enlivens all of the New Mexican classics, such as tamales, tostados, and chiles rellenos, most of which are satisfying and freshly made. A standout is the green-chile chicken enchiladas, and the pozole is quite good, too—perfectly firm, earthy, and flecked with oregano. The restaurant is

always busy, but a fire pit outdoors makes the wait more pleasant on cold nights.

Mexican

Tiny ★ La Cueva (135 Paseo del Pueblo Sur, 575/758-7001, 10am-3pm daily, $7-14) looks like a New Mexican restaurant at first glance, as it has all the usual green-chile-smothered dishes. But its owners are from south of the border and round out the menu with fantastically fresh and homemade-tasting dishes such as chicken mole enchiladas and a heaping steak and relleno, as well as exceptionally savory beans. Breakfasts are especially inexpensive. They now serve beer and wine as well.

Fine Dining

Sitting down for dinner at Byzantium (112 Camino de la Placita, 575/751-0805, 5:30pm-9:30pm Sun.-Mon. & Thurs.-Sat., $19-39) feels not unlike stumbling upon the environs of a secret gastronomic society, with its dim lighting, low vigas-beam ceilings, and, most of all, exquisitely prepared dishes. The menu is lean, but varied and full of difficult choices, such as a shrimp potpie and a pork tenderloin with pear sauce. It's a small space; reservations are recommended.

Set inside a cozy adobe house, Lambert's (123 Bent St., 575/758-1009, 11:30am-2:30pm and 5:30pm-9pm Mon.-Sat., 5:30pm-9pm Sun., $23-38) is a Taos favorite, long a popular choice for celebrations and special occasions.

Its New American menu is a bit staid, but everything is executed perfectly. The filet mignon in a peppercorn demi glace is fantastic; less obvious, but equally gratifying, is the zucchini pasta with arugula pesto and oyster mushrooms. The summer Sunday brunch (11:30am-2:30pm) is well worth it for the shrimp and cheddar grits alone. A full liquor license means good classic cocktails, which you can also enjoy upstairs at The Treehouse Lounge (11:30am-close daily).

Fresh and Local

★ The Love Apple (803 Paseo del Pueblo Norte, 575/751-0050, 5pm-9pm Tues.-Sun., $9-18) wears its local, organic credentials on its sleeve, and the food delivers in simple but powerful flavor combinations for less than you'd expect. The menu is seasonal, with dishes such as a baked tamale with a red-chile mole sauce and chicken confit taco with green-chile coconut creamed corn. There's an extensive wine list, too. Set inside a thick-walled adobe chapel dating back to the early 19th century, the place oozes atmosphere, with candles glimmering softly against whitewashed walls. It's one place in town where reservations should be considered essential, and in an old-school move, it only accepts cash.

Burgers

★ The Burger Stand (401 Paseo del Pueblo Norte, 575/758-5522, 11am-11pm daily, $9) is an outpost of a Kansas restaurant—but it fits right in in Taos, in large part because it makes not one but two killer veggie burgers. We recommend the one topped with feta cheese, pickled green beans, and toasted almonds. The beef and lamb burgers are great, too, and decked out in similarly creative ways. The same can be said for the fries, which come in a whopping seven varieties; try a basket tossed in a white truffle oil. It doesn't hurt that the restaurant's set inside the lively Taos Ale House, where there's a strong beer selection, and it's open relatively late.

Italian

Taos Pizza Out Back (712 Paseo del Pueblo Norte, 575/758-3112, 11am-9pm Mon.-Thurs. & Sun., 11am-10pm Fri.-Sat., $8-23) serves up the best pie in town, using mostly local and organic ingredients. Sure, you can design your own pizza, but there's little need to with specialty options such as marinated chicken, peppers, onions, and garlic with a honey chipotle chile sauce and smoked mozzarella or basil pesto, green chile, smoked mozzarella, feta, roasted garlic, and fresh tomatoes.

Breakfast and Lunch

A down-home, wood-paneled family restaurant, Michael's Kitchen (304-C Paseo del Pueblo Norte, 575/758-4178, 7am-2:30pm daily, $8) is filled with chatter, the clatter of dishes, and the sense that your fellow patrons have been here many times before. It's famous for New Mexican breakfast items like huevos rancheros and blue-corn pancakes with pine nuts, served all day, but there's quite a bit more on the extensive menu. "Health Food," for instance, is a double order of chile-cheese fries and there are blintzes, deli sandwiches, and a handful of steak dishes, too. The front room is devoted to gooey doughnuts, Frisbee-sized cinnamon rolls, and pie.

Taos Diner (908 Paseo del Pueblo Norte, 575/758-2374, 6:30am-2:30pm daily, $10) is as straightforward as its name. Still, there is a pleasant surprise: Much of the enchiladas, egg plates, pancakes, and the like is prepared with organic ingredients. Plus, the largely local scene provides good background theater to your meal—the servers seem to know everyone. There's a second outpost, Taos Diner II (216-B Paseo del Pueblo Sur, 575/751-1989, 7am-2:30pm daily), just south of the plaza.

Euro-Latino might be the best catch-all term for the menu at ★ Gutiz (812-B Paseo del Pueblo Norte, 575/758-1226, http://gutiztaos.com, 8am-3pm Tues.-Sun., $8-16), which borrows from France and Spain and adds a dash of green chile. Start your day with a chocolate croissant or an impressive tower of scrambled eggs and spinach. Lunch sees traditional croques monsieurs, grilled chicken with hummus sandwiches, and paella that doesn't skimp on the scallops, shrimp, clams, and mussels.

Set in bucolic gardens with a view of Taos Mountain, **Farmhouse Café** (1405 Paseo del Pueblo Norte, 575/758-5683, 8am-4pm daily, $7-17) is a beautiful spot to revive over a hearty salad, veggie shepherd's pie, or a bison burger. There are several gluten-free options, too, including a shepherd's pie and a chocolate-peanut-butter crispy-rice bar. Service can be a little spotty, but the meals are worth the wait.

Just west of the plaza, **El Gamal** (112 Doña Luz St., 575/613-0311, 9am-5pm Mon.-Wed., 9am-9pm Thurs.-Sat., 11am-3pm Sun., $5-12) brings the best of Israeli street food to Taos, with *shakshuka* (spicy scrambled eggs) and boiled bagels for breakfast and falafel and *sabich* (hummus, eggplant, and egg) sandwiches at lunch, washed down with a fizzy yogurt soda.

In the Taos Inn, elegant **Doc Martin's** (125 Paseo del Pueblo Norte, 575/758-1977, 11am-3pm and 5pm-9pm Mon.-Fri., 7:30am-2:30pm and 5pm-9:30pm Sat.-Sun., $8-28) is fine at dinner, but weekend brunch is when the kitchen really shines—especially on dishes such as the Kit Carson (poached eggs on yam biscuits topped with red chile and cheddar cheese), bagel with house-cured salmon, and blue-corn waffles. The lunch menu is also tasty and doesn't reach the comparatively high dinner prices.

Cafés

★ **Elevation Coffee** (1110 Paseo del Pueblo Norte, 575/758-3068, 6:30am-4pm daily, $3) boasts the best coffee in town without a whiff of snobbery—in fact, its knowledgeable baristas are some of the friendliest around. The fancifully designed mochas are as tasty as they look, while the pour-overs are consistently on the mark. Grab a seat with your drink and admire the art; there's a small patio, too. Cash only.

The location of **World Cup** (102 Paseo del Pueblo Norte, 575/737-5299, 7am-7pm daily, $3) on the corner of the plaza makes it a popular pit stop for both tourists and locals—the latter typically of the drumming, dreadlocked variety, lounging on the stoop.

Markets

If you're planning a picnic or a meal in, stop at **Cid's Grocery** (623 Paseo del Pueblo Norte, 575/758-1148, 8am-8pm Mon.-Sat.) for great takeout food, as well as freshly baked bread and a whole range of organic and local goodies, from New Mexican wines to fresh elk steaks.

The excellent **Taos Farmers Market** (www.taosfarmersmarket.org, 8am-12:30pm Sat.) takes place on the plaza mid-May-late October. As well as fresh produce and meats, vendors sell prepared food and locally made gifts such as honey, jams, and spices.

RANCHOS DE TAOS

Just off the plaza near the church, **Ranchos Plaza Grill** (6 St. Francis Plaza, 575/758-5788, 11am-3pm and 5pm-8:30pm Tues.-Sat., 8am-3pm Sun., $11) is a casual spot, known for its red-chile *caribe*, made from crushed, rather than ground, chiles. New Mexican dishes fill the menu, and the sopaipillas are gargantuan.

Across the road from the turn to St Francis de Asis, **Old Martina's Hall** (4140 Hwy. 68, 575/758-3003, www.oldmartinashall.com, 11am-3pm and 4pm-9pm Tues.-Thurs., 11am-3pm and 4pm-11pm Fri.-Sat., 10am-2pm Sun., $12-22), a once-derelict adobe theater with a soaring ceiling that has been lovingly redone, is a wonderfully welcoming place with a menu of sophisticated regional standbys as well as more than a few surprises. There is green chile, but it's dialed down and accentuates rather than overtakes. The surf & turf is excellent, as is the jasmine rice with veggies in a red curry sauce. It's more casual for lunch ($10 for sandwiches).

TAOS PUEBLO

On the road to the center of Taos Pueblo, **Tiwa Kitchen** (328 Veterans Hwy., 575/751-1020, 11am-4pm Wed.-Mon., $9-17) is a friendly, family-run place that specializes in Pueblo food, much of which is laced with chile. The hearty lunch options include stuffed fry bread and a red chile beef and vegetable stew; for dessert there are homemade baked goods to choose from, including a decadent chocolate squash cake.

ARROYO SECO

A creaky, old, all-purpose general store/diner/saloon, ★ **Abe's Cantina y Cocina** (489 Hwy. 150, 575/776-8643 7am-5pm Mon.-Fri., 7am-1:30pm Sat., $4) has earned fans from all over for serving a breakfast burrito that is both cheap and immensely satisfying. There's a full menu of tacos and green-chile cheeseburgers, an impressive beer list featuring several top-notch regional ales, and a nice shaded back patio. Don't miss the sweet, flaky empanadas next to the cash register in the store.

For coffee and ice cream head next door to **Taos Cow** (485 Hwy. 150, 575/776-5640, 7am-6pm daily, $3-9.50), a chilled-out coffee bar par excellence, with writers scribbling in one corner and flute players jamming in another. But it's the ice cream that has made the Taos Cow name (you'll see it distributed all around town, and elsewhere in New Mexico

and Colorado). The most popular flavors are tailored to local tastes: Café Olé blends cinnamon and Mexican chocolate chunks in its coffee ice cream, while Cherry Ristra is cherry with piñon nuts and dark chocolate. There are plenty of breakfast options, too, including a bagel sandwich with lox, cream cheese, and capers.

The husband-and-wife chef team at the restaurant, bar, and wine shop **Medley** (100 N.M. 150, 575/776-8787, 4pm-9pm Mon.-Fri., 10am-2pm and 3pm-9:30pm Sat.-Sun., $17-38) have cooked all over the world. Their menu mixes eclectic global flavors (chili, curry, aioli, saffron) with New American staples such as roasted red peppers. The food is great, if not flawless—even the bread plate is worthy of a lengthy post-dinner recap—and the atmosphere is casual.

TAOS SKI VALLEY

For nourishment in the ski village, fortify yourself with a green-chile cheeseburger or a bowl of smoky-hot green-chile stew at the **Stray Dog Cantina** (105 Sutton Pl., 575/776-2894, 8am-9pm daily in winter, 11am-9pm daily in summer, $12), which gets busy after 3pm, when tired skiers come down from a day on the slopes. In the summer, it's

Stray Dog Cantina

an especially nice destination for a drive, as you can sit on the deck and listen to the river flow by.

More adventurous drivers should head for ★ Bavarian Lodge (100 Kachina Rd., 575-776-8020, 11:30am-9pm daily in ski season, $15), way up Twining Road near the southeast edge of the ski area and Kachina Lift 4. You'll need four-wheel drive in winter; in summer, the huge and recently expanded front deck is a lovely place to have a stein of ale (served by actual German speakers) in the pines, though note that it's typically open only around the weekend (11:30am-close Thurs.-Sun.). The menu is hearty Wiener schnitzel and spaetzle; the bread pudding with pretzel pieces is as dense as it sounds—and delicious, too.

Accommodations

Taos hotels can be overpriced, especially at the lower end, where there are few reliable bargains. But because Taos is awash in centuries-old houses, bed-and-breakfasts have thrived. For those skeptical of B&Bs, don't despair: The majority have private bathrooms, separate entrances, and not too much country-cute decor. Certainly, just as in Santa Fe, the Southwestern gewgaws can be applied with a heavy hand, but wood-burning fireplaces, well-stocked libraries, hot tubs, and big gardens make up for that.

For better deals, consider staying outside of Taos proper. Arroyo Seco is about a half-hour drive from the plaza, and rates here and in Ranchos de Taos can be a little lower. In the summer, the lodges in the ski valley cut prices by almost half—a great deal if you want to spend time hiking and don't mind driving for food and entertainment.

CENTRAL TAOS
Under $100
Not a hotel at all, but simply a clutch of well-maintained one- and two-bedroom private casitas, Taos Lodging (109 Brooks St., 575/751-1771, www.taoslodging.com, $75 studio) is in a quiet, convenient block about a 10-minute walk north from the plaza. Here, eight cottages, arranged around a central courtyard, have assorted floor plans, but all have porches, full kitchens, living rooms, and fireplaces as well as access to a shared outdoor hot tub. The smallest, a 350-square-foot studio, sleeps two comfortably; the largest ($140 for two) sleep up to six. The same group manages two additional properties nearby, for those who want a larger condo.

The Kachina Lodge Resort and Meeting Center (413 Paseo del Pueblo Norte, 575/758-2275, https://kachinalodge.com, $86), a sprawling former Best Western property, has seen better days and is in need of improvements—cosmetic and otherwise—but it is a dependable and well-run option with more character than most in this price bracket. Rooms are comfortable and nicely decorated, though dated, with basic amenities.

$100-150
Of the various motels on the south side, none is excellent—and most are not memorable in a good way, for that matter—but Hotel Don Fernando (1005 Paseo del Pueblo Sur, 575/751-4444, https://tapestrycollection3.hilton.com/tc/hotel-don-fernando, $111 d) is a cut above. Reopened in 2018, the hotel has more than 120 rooms spread throughout six buildings. Rooms are generally bright and cheerful, though not all have benefitted equally from the renovation. There's a medium-sized pool and fitness center.

In addition to being a tourist attraction, the Mabel Dodge Luhan House (240 Morada Ln., 575/751-9686, www.mabeldodgeluhan.com, $116 d) also functions as a homey bed-and-breakfast. Even the least expensive rooms, in a 1970s outbuilding, feel authentically historic and cozy, with wood floors and antique furniture. In the main house, Mabel's original bedroom ($220) is the grandest (you can even sleep in her bed). The pick of the 21 rooms, though—if you don't mind waking at the crack of dawn—is the upstairs solarium ($145), which is gloriously sunny, with gorgeous views of the mountain. Either way, you'll feel a little like you're bunking in a museum (which means those who want modern amenities like air-conditioning should look elsewhere). Breakfast is a cut above standard B&B fare.

Of the two landmark hotels in town, **Hotel La Fonda de Taos** (108 S. Plaza, 575/758-2211, www.lafondataos.com, $149 d) has a few more modern perks, such as gas fireplaces in some rooms and mostly reliable Wi-Fi. As can be expected of an older hotel, rooms tend to be on the small side, and you're certainly paying a premium for its history. Its location can't be beat if you're looking for something central—plus, it can feel quite grand opening your balcony doors over the plaza (though you may also be subjected to predawn street-cleaning noise).

Walking distance from the plaza, **El Pueblo Lodge** (412 Paseo del Pueblo Norte, 575/758-8700, www.elpueblolodge.com, $137 d) is a budget operation with nice perks such as a full breakfast and free use of barbecue grills. The cheerful rooms vary from a snug nook in the oldest adobe section to new, slick motel rooms complete with gas fireplaces. Those in the 1960s motel strip are a good combo of atmosphere and amenities. The grounds are pleasant and shaded, with a hot tub and a heated pool in the summertime.

★ **Inn on the Rio** (910 E. Kit Carson Rd., 575/758-7199, www.innontherio.com, $129 d) might be more accurately called Motel on the Creek. But what a motel: Each of the 12 thick-walled rooms has been decorated with rich colors and retro Western details. The vintage wall heaters, still cranking from the old motor-court days, keep the rooms as toasty as a fireplace would. A hot tub and summer-only pool between the two wings, plus luxe sheets

and locally made bath gels, are nice upgrades. Pair this with longtime resident owners and a great morning meal, and you have all the benefits of a bed-and-breakfast without the feeling that you have to tiptoe in late at night. Rates are lower on weekdays in summer.

$150-200

Everything at **Hacienda del Sol** (109 Mabel Dodge Ln., 575/758-0287, www.taoshaciendadelsol.com, from $160 d) is built in relation to Taos Mountain. With this view, even the smallest of the 11 rooms in the adobe complex feel expansive. The style is cozy without being too oppressively Southwestern. Once owned by Mabel Dodge Luhan, the house was where she often put up guests; perks like plush robes and kiva fireplaces make it feel homey; some rooms have skylights.

The seven rooms at the central **Dreamcatcher** (416 La Lomita Rd., 575/758-0613, www.dreambb.com, from $150 d) look out on to a pretty courtyard with hammocks. Three of the rooms are attached to the main house, while the four others are split between two cute casitas. All are thoughtfully designed and appointed and evoke the region; think warm earth tones, wood furniture, and Native American rugs and artwork; some have kivas as well.

The **Historic Taos Inn** (125 Paseo del Pueblo Norte, 575/758-2233, www.taosinn.com, $199 d), established in 1936 in the former home of the town doctor, like La Fonda, has long been intertwined with the town's past and present, though it is cozier and slightly overpriced. Rooms in the main building have more character and are cheaper (about $129 in high season); in the courtyard section or other outbuildings, you may get a kiva fireplace. All 44 rooms offer free Wi-Fi and access to the onsite fitness center and yoga studio.

Decorated with an artist's eye, the five bright and colorful guest cottages at **Casa Gallina** (613 Callejon, 575/758-2306, www.casagallina.net, from $195 d) showcase beautiful handicrafts from Taos and around the globe. All are well appointed and cared for

and the kitchens can be stocked with occasional goodies from the garden and eggs from resident hens (they're also pressed into service for the fresh and delicious breakfasts).

A somewhat storied and star-crossed luxury hotel, **El Monte Sagrado** (317 Kit Carson Rd., 575/758-3502, www.elmontesagrado.com, $189 d) is owned by the excellent New Mexico company Heritage Hotels and Resorts, which enlivened the overall look and restored some of its eco-friendly infrastructure. The hotel has eclectic style in the Global Suites ($499 and up), but entry-level Taos Mountain rooms, while a little generic with their white linens and dark wood, are reasonably priced and have balconies. The grounds are immaculate, and there's a lovely spa.

Over $250

Palacio de Marquesa (405 Cordoba Rd., 575/758-4777, www.marquesataos.com, $259 d) is an exquisite eight-room inn, also run by Heritage Hotels and Resorts. The rooms have an air of what might be called pueblo minimalism: dark viga ceilings, with white walls, white leather chairs, and marble baths. What could come off as too austere is warmed up with pops of color, skylights, and kiva fireplaces. Rooms are dedicated to Taos women of influence, such as Mabel Dodge Luhan and Agnes Martin. Spa services and the option of a made-to-order breakfast delivered to your room add to the cocoon-like feel.

ARROYO SECO
Under $100

The best bargain option in the area is **The Snowmansion** (Hwy. 150, Arroyo Seco, 575/776-8298, www.snowmansion.com). Conveniently set midway to the Taos Ski Valley in bustling "downtown" Arroyo Seco, this cheerful place offers bunks in dorm rooms ($38) and private rooms (from $74). In the summer, you can also camp (from $30)

and nosh on veggies from the hostel garden. But as the name suggests, winter sports fanatics are the main clientele, and if you don't want to be woken by skiers racing for the Chile Line bus outside, opt for an individual cabin with shared bath ($65).

TAOS SKI VALLEY
Over $250

When ★ **The Blake** (116 Sutton Pl., 575/776-8298, www.skitaos.com, $275) opened in February 2017, it was the clearest signal yet of the Taos Ski Valley's intent to position itself squarely among the top ski resorts in the West. A model of sustainability and replete with thoughtful touches and features, the property at once pays homage to the ski valley's European roots and proudly displays the area's Native American and Southwestern influences. Rooms vary in size from two queen beds or a king to lavish 1400-square-foot suites. All are handsomely designed and include access to a hot tub, pool, spa services, and breakfast at the onsite 192 at The Blake restaurant. Hitting the slopes from here couldn't be any easier—there's a ski lift outside the doors and a full equipment shop onsite.

RANCHOS DE TAOS
$150-200

At the south edge of Ranchos de Taos, ★ **Adobe & Pines Inn** (4107 Hwy. 68, 575/751-0947, www.adobepines.com) is built around an 1830s hacienda, shaded by old trees and overlooking a lush garden. Of the eight rooms, six are quite large (from $239), with especially lavish bathrooms. But even the two smallest rooms ($133 and $145) have fireplaces—and everyone gets the exceptionally good breakfasts, with fresh eggs from the on-site chickens and veggies from the garden.

NORTH AND EAST OF TAOS
Under $100

Hotel Luna Mystica (25 ABC Mesa Rd., 575/977-2424, www.hotellunamystica.com,

1: Mabel Dodge Luhan House 2: The Blake

$90), conveniently located across the road from the Taos Mesa Brewing, offers cheerful accommodation in an assortment of vintage trailers from the 1950s and '60s—there's even one done up as a hostel (bunks $30). All are smartly appointed and comfortable, and the morning coffees from their decks can't be beat. There are also several dozen primitive campsites ($10) equipped with hammocks for some of the best stargazing around.

$100-150

Nestle into a snug sheepherder's cabin at **Taos Goji Eco Lodge** (Old State Rd. 3, 575/776-3971, www.taosgoji.com, $130 d), in the village of San Cristobal, 11 miles north of Taos. Blessedly devoid of Internet access and TVs, the 10 cozy and comfortable cabins, each over a century old, have wood stoves and kitchens, and the surrounding 40-acre farm is lively with sheep, goats, and chickens.

$150-200

For an only-in-Taos experience, stay the night in an **Earthship** (U.S. 64, 575/751-0462, www.earthship.com, from $185 d). Five of the curvy, off-the-grid homes are available, with room for up to six people in the largest one. Evoking a stay in a hobbit house with banana trees (in the south-facing greenhouse areas), you're out in the larger, all-Earthship subdivision, with great views of the mountain. And, yes, you'll have running water, a refrigerator, and all the other comforts. It's a bit of a drive from town (west of the Rio Grande), but it's well worth it. It's now also possible to stay in the Earthship that started it all ($140 d), a short drive east of the Taos Plaza.

Information and Services

TOURIST INFORMATION

A few miles south of the plaza, the **Taos Visitor Center** (1139 Paseo del Pueblo Sur, 575/758-3873, www.taos.org, 9am-5pm daily) is helpful, as long as you don't show up right before closing time. Stop here for flyers and maps galore, free coffee, and the thorough weekly news and events bulletin (also posted online), which includes gallery listings, concerts, festivals, and more.

Books and Maps

Op.cit. (124-A Bent St., No. 6 Dunn House, 575/751-1999, 10am-6pm daily) stocks new and used books, local titles, and maps, and hosts author readings.

Local Media

The *Taos News* comes out every Thursday; its Tempo entertainment section covers music, theater, and film listings. Many hotels offer free copies of Tempo to their guests. The *Albuquerque Journal North*, which covers northern New Mexico, publishes daily.

Radio

While you're in town, don't miss tuning in to **KTAO** (101.9 FM), a solar-powered local radio station. The musical programming is broad, and you're sure to learn interesting tidbits about the community as well.

SERVICES

Banks

US Bank (120 W. Plaza, 575/737-3540, 9am-5pm Mon.-Fri.), just off the southwest corner of the plaza, is the most convenient bank and ATM while on foot. The drive-through service at **Centinel Bank of Taos** (512 Paseo del Pueblo Sur, 575/758-6700, 9am-5pm Mon.-Fri.) is easily accessible from the main drag.

Post Offices

The Taos **post office** (710 Paseo del Pueblo Sur, 575/751-1801, 9am-1pm and 2pm-4:30pm Mon.-Fri.) is on the south side; there's another on the north side (318 Paseo del Pueblo Norte, 575/758-2081, 8:30am-5pm Mon.-Fri.).

Getting There and Around

CAR

From Santa Fe, the drive to Taos takes about 1.5 hours (70 miles) along the direct "low road" through the river valley (via Española, U.S. 84/285 to Hwy. 68). If taking the more circuitous "high road" (via Chimayó and Truchas, mostly on Hwy. 76), plan on at least 2 hours for the 80-mile drive.

From Albuquerque, add at least an hour's travel time for the 60-mile drive up I-25 (the most direct route) to Santa Fe.

Once in Taos, you will need a car to get to outlying sights but will also have to negotiate the frequent traffic jams on Paseo del Pueblo. There are paid parking lots close to the plaza, and a free one less than 0.25 mile down Kit Carson Road. Of the rental car options, Enterprise (1350 Paseo del Pueblo Sur, 575/758-5333, www.enterprise.com, 8am-6pm Mon.-Fri., 9am-noon Sat.) is the most convenient, a block south of the visitors center.

BUS AND SHUTTLE

For pickup at the Albuquerque airport, Taos Ski Valley Airport Shuttle (800/776-1111, www.skitaos.com, $80 one-way from town, $165 one-way from the ski valley) runs a shuttle two times a day (12:30pm and 3:30pm). Allow at least 2.5 hours for travel time; reservations are required.

From Santa Fe, there's great weekend service from city-sponsored Taos Express (Route #305, 575/751-4459, www.taosexpress. com, $10 round-trip), which runs from Taos and back once on Saturday and Sunday, completing a loop in the morning and another in the afternoon. The one-way trip takes 1 hour and 50 minutes.

In Santa Fe, the bus picks up passengers near the Rail Runner main depot (Montezuma at Guadalupe) and at the South Capitol station (Sunday). In Taos, it drops off at Our Lady of Guadalupe parking lot, one block west of the plaza; going back south, it also picks up passengers at the Sagebrush Inn (1508 Paseo del Pueblo Sur). The schedule syncs with the Rail Runner's arrival in Santa Fe (and it can carry bicycles), making it a potentially seamless three-hour trip all the way from Albuquerque.

Within Taos, the Chile Line bus runs north-south from the Ranchos de Taos post office to the Taos Pueblo, approximately every 40 minutes 7:30am-5:30pm Monday-Friday. In town, it's free. Mid-December-April, a ski shuttle ($1 one-way) runs to Taos Ski Valley, with five buses daily making stops at key motels en route to the mountain; not all buses stop at all hotels. Contact Taos's transportation division (575/751-4459, www.taosgov.com) for maps and schedules.

The Road to Chama

U.S. 64 leads west out of Taos into an undulating landscape of thick patches of forest and open grassy plains interrupted sparingly by resolute ranching communities, most of which have long since passed their heyday. After winding through mountains, a dramatic descent brings you into the lush Chama Valley and the likeable town of Chama, a few miles from the border with Colorado.

TRES PIEDRAS

This settlement about 30 miles west of Taos is not much more than a handful of houses scattered around the crossroads of U.S. 64 and U.S. 285 and the welcoming Chili Line Depot Café (38429 U.S. 285, 575/758-1701, 8am-7pm daily, $7), just north of the intersection. With friendly staff, hearty burritos, and green-chile cheeseburgers, it's well worth the detour. Call

King Tiger and the *Mercedes*

The pastoral village of **Tierra Amarilla** gives little indication that it was once a battleground in the Chicano rights movement and the local Hispano fight for land-grant restitution. The Tierra Amarilla *merced* (land grant) was established in the 19th century, and when Nuevo México became a U.S. territory in 1848, the Treaty of Guadalupe Hidalgo specified it would be preserved. But cattle ranchers and the national forest system gradually appropriated it, so that, by the 1960s, many families in largely Hispano Rio Arriba County found themselves landless and subsisting on less than $1,500 per year.

Around this time, Reies López Tijerina, a charismatic activist in the growing Chicano movement, took up the land-grant cause. In 1967, he and more than 150 local men stormed the Tierra Amarilla courthouse, calling themselves the Political Confederation of Free City States and bearing a banner proclaiming "Give Us Our Land Back." Their plan was to make a citizen's arrest of the district attorney (DA). But the DA was nowhere around, the activists wound up taking everyone in the courthouse hostage, and 300 National Guard troops were called in. The incident made headlines across the country, and Tijerina was an overnight legend. The press dubbed him King Tiger, and he was praised in the ballad "El Corrido de Rio Arriba," penned within weeks by the band Los Reyes de Albuquerque.

Trials the next year were equally gripping: Tijerina wept on the witness stand, a lawman present at the raid turned up murdered, and even New Mexico's governor gave heartfelt testimony. Tijerina came away with a minimal sentence for second-degree kidnapping. He went on to lead the Chicano faction as part of Martin Luther King Jr.'s Poor People's Campaign.

In Tierra Amarilla, meanwhile, the battle lines became hopelessly tangled. With seed money from a generous donor, the Sierra Club announced in 1970 that it would donate a new "land grant" to the area, but it failed to materialize—perhaps because environmentalists soon were battling the local sheepherders over the effects of grazing. In 1995, a local shepherd successfully sued the Sierra Club for the never-applied donation, and the economic situation in the valley has somewhat improved. But many people must lease land on which to graze their sheep, resentments run deep, and the activism of King Tiger is still recalled with feeling.

ahead to check hours; the restaurant may close early if business is slow. It also has a couple of cozy guest rooms with breakfast and dinner included ($95).

TIERRA AMARILLA AND LOS OJOS

U.S. 64 climbs up and over the Brazos Mountains—the view from the pass takes in the sheer limestone of 3,000-foot-high cliffs to the north. Descending into the golden valley along the Rio Chama, you soon reach the junction with U.S. 84 and the village of Tierra Amarilla, off the east side of the highway. Most of the buildings have long been vacant and the limited places it had in recent years to grab a bite to eat or a cup of coffee have now closed.

Just a few miles north of Tierra Amarilla and west of the highway, Los Ojos is a two-block-long main street of adobe and Victorian wood-frame buildings, most connected in some way with **Ganados del Valle,** a cooperative established in 1983 to preserve the economy in the region, which, for hundreds of years, had been based on raising sheep and selling their products. But young people could no longer earn a living from this, and many of the most traditional weaving and spinning techniques had already been lost. The cooperative was gradually able to provide employment for dozens of artists, administrators, and sheepherders, and in 1990, one of its founders, Maria Varela, who got her start as a Chicana activist in the Student Nonviolent Coordinating Committee in the 1960s, earned a MacArthur "genius grant" for her efforts.

Once a Ganados project, though now a consignment shop, **Tierra Wools** (91 Main St., 575/588-7231, www.handweavers.com,

9am-6pm Mon.-Sat., 11am-4pm Sun. Apr.-Oct., 10am-5pm Mon.-Sat. Nov.-May) has become a pilgrimage site for anyone engaged in fiber arts. The shop showcases the work of local weavers—rugs, pillows, ruanas—as well as brilliantly dyed skeins of handwoven wool yarn from the hardy, four-horned Churro sheep, a breed the conquistadors introduced to New Mexico. If you're interested in the process, you can join a weeklong class ($625) or try your hand at it by the hour ($25). The last weekend in April, the **Spring Harvest Festival** involves demonstrations of sheep-shearing, hand-spinning, and more, along with music and other entertainment. The shop also offers two lodgings in a sweet rental **casita** (from $95), for those who'd like a taste of village life.

EL VADO LAKE AND HERON LAKE STATE PARKS

The two reservoirs west of Tierra Amarilla are nearly linked; **El Vado Lake State Park** (575/588-7247, www.nmparks.com, $5/car day use) is smaller but busier, as motorboats are permitted here, and it's a popular recreation spot, with large **campgrounds** (sites $10) at its south end (accessible via Hwy. 112, 17 miles southwest of Tierra Amarilla; the turnoff to the park is about 2 miles north of the village).

A 5.5-mile one-way hiking trail leads from Shale Point, north of all the campgrounds, up along the Rio Chama, across a bridge, up past Heron Dam, and into the south end of **Heron Lake State Park** (575/588-7470, www.emnrd. state.nm.us, $5/car day use), which is also accessible via U.S. 64/84 and Highway 95. This lake is much more sedate as boats can only operate at no-wake speeds, which also makes it popular for kayakers. During the week, free ranger-led hikes are available on request—ideally, call ahead to the visitors center to let the staff know you're coming. Scores of attractive **campsites** (sites from $8) line the park's southern and eastern shores.

Both lakes offer excellent trout and kokanee salmon fishing, though you'll need to arrange for a boat at **Stone House Lodge** (Hwy. 95, 575/588-7274, www.stonehouselodge.com, from $175/four hours), as there are no rentals at the lake itself; the lodge is about 14 miles west of the U.S. 64/84 turnoff. It also offers a range of places to spend the night, including barebones cabins (from $100) and trailers (from $150).

Rafting

The stretch of the Chama River from El Vado Dam to Abiquiu Lake is one of the state's more scenic rafting runs and can be done as a leisurely multiday trip. **Kokopelli Rafting Adventures** (505/983-3734, www. kokopelliraft.com) in Santa Fe and **Los Rios River Runners** (575/776-8854, www. losriosriverrunners.com) in Taos both run trips through these remote canyons; expect to pay about $115 for a one-day outing and $350 for a two-day trip.

CHAMA

A picturesque high-mountain town, **Chama** is the last population center of any size until you're well inside Colorado. With just 1,000 residents, the place has always been centered on the railroad that begins here and threads its way northeast between the mountains and over the state line to Antonito. Even if the steam train isn't your thing, you can drive north on Highway 17 for the views, though note that when the train isn't running, neither is much of the town; check for winter closures.

Chama is bordered on both sides by land belonging to the Jicarilla Apache. The tribe operates an elite hunting ranch south of town, The Lodge at Chama, that's a favorite politico getaway. But the natural attractions here are accessible to all—with the Rio Chama running right through town, you could theoretically walk out the front door of your (affordable) rental cabin, snag a trout, and cook it for dinner. On a day visit, the star of the show is the great steam train. If you stay a little longer, you'll have a chance to appreciate the remarkable vistas—particularly in the fall, when the mountains are blanketed with a thick patchwork of color.

★ Cumbres & Toltec Scenic Railroad

The biggest attraction in Chama is the historic steam-driven **Cumbres & Toltec Scenic Railroad** (888/286-2737, www.cumbrestoltec. com), which has been running 64 miles from Chama up to Antonito, Colorado, since 1880. It is now jointly owned by the two neighboring states and maintained as a sort of museum.

You can travel the route in several ways, depending on how long of an outing you want. The shortest ride is the four-hour Sunday Express, running only that day in summer. The year-round standard outing is from Chama to the midpoint, the ghost town of Osier, just over the state border—you hop off there, have lunch, stroll around, and get back on the train for the ride back down the pass (from $95 adults, $50 kids). The whole trip takes a little more than six hours. Hard-core rail fans can go the whole way to Antonito—stopping in Osier for lunch—and return to Chama by bus, which takes eight hours ($100 adults, $50 kids); this way, you'll get to see the dramatic Toltec Gorge, just north of Osier.

Trains run late May through August and less frequently from September to mid-October for autumn leaf season; there are limited runs in late December around the holidays on occasion as well. Reservations are advised, and you can choose from three classes of service (windows open in tourist class, which is fun, but soot from the steam engine can make things a little gritty). The hot lunch included in the ticket price is pretty generous, with turkey and all the standard vegetables, plus pie to finish.

You can also prowl around the depot and rail yards. Pick up a flyer at the station that identifies all the structures, as well as distinguishes between drop-bottom gondolas, flangers, and other specialized train cars.

Recreation

Elk are prevalent throughout the mountains around Chama, and in the fall, the elk's distinctive mating call, or bugle, can be heard. North of town, accessed at the end of Pine Street, the **Edward Sargent Wildlife Management Area** (575/476-8000, www. wildlife.state.nm.us) has a viewing spot just inside the borders of the reserve, overlooking a big basin where the animals often graze; the best times to spot them are at dawn and dusk. You can also hike into the center of the 20,000 acres, along the Rio Chama (for excellent fishing)—ask at the Chama visitors center for more information and other area hiking spots. If you want to hike or explore further, you'll need a Gaining Access into Nature (GAIN) permit, which you can pick up at the Chama Valley Supermarket (2451 S. Hwy. 84, 575/756-2545).

Food

For an honest steak and potato, plus grilled local trout and cold beer, head to the **High Country Restaurant & Saloon** (2289 S. Hwy. 17, 575/756-2384, 11am-10pm Mon.-Sat., 8am-10pm Sun., $10-20), a big wood-paneled operation that's popular with through-bikers as well as locals; the wait for your meal can be lengthy. The saloon hosts live music most nights, when the place can get a bit rowdy.

Across the street from the train yard, **Box Car Cafe** (425 Terrace Ave., 575/756-2706, 7am-2pm Sun.-Mon., Wed.-Sat. 7am-8pm. Apr.-Nov., $8) serves hearty breakfast burritos (smothered in piquant chile) and juicy burgers for lunch. The menu is fairly limited, but the food is good and priced well.

Choose from a full selection of New Mexican breakfast and lunch staples at the **Elk Horn Cafe** (2663 S. Hwy. 64, 575/756-2229, 7am-2pm Mon.-Fri., 7am-2pm Sat.-Sun.), where the portions are generous and the red chile does not disappoint.

Accommodations

Chama has a reasonable selection of places to stay. The south side of town is largely devoted to rustic riverside cottage operations. **Chama River Bend Lodge** (2625 Hwy. 64, 575/756-2264, www.chamariverbendlodge.

1: El Vado Lake 2: Rio Chama 3: the Cumbres & Toltec Scenic Railroad

com) offers clean, basic rooms in a motel-like strip (from $89 d), as well as cabins closer to the water (from $119). Neighboring **Vista del Rio Lodge** (2595 Hwy. 64, 575/756-2138, www.vistadelriolodge.com, $95 d) is one of the nicest in town. Spacious, rooms are furnished in a contemporary Southwest style and have modern bathrooms.

Up near the depot, the lodging is a bit less rustic. The pretty ★ **Chama Station Inn** (423 Terrace Ave., 575/756-2315, www.chamastationinn.com, May-mid-Oct., from $95 d) is just across from the train depot. Most of the nine rooms have wood floors, and all are decorated sparingly with country touches; the extra $10 for a deluxe room is well worth it, as it gets you a kiva fireplace, a graceful high ceiling, and a little more space.

Some of the least expensive beds can be found at **The Hotel** (501 S. Terrace Ave., 575/756-2416, www.thehotel.org, from $79 d), a 1930s building with small rooms that are nonetheless clean, and a pleasant throwback.

Campers will do well at the **Rio Chama RV Park** (U.S. 64, 575/756-2303, May-Oct.), on the north edge of town, where tent sites ($16) and RV sites (from $27) with hookups are nestled amid tall trees, and the river flows right by.

Information and Services

Chama's **visitors center** (575/756-2306, 9am-5pm daily) is located at the junction of U.S. 64/84 and Highway 17, on the southern edge of town. In addition to maps and other info (for the whole state), it also provides free Internet access and coffee.

JICARILLA APACHE NATION

The village of **Dulce** is the main town of the 750,000-acre **Jicarilla Apache Nation** (575/759-3242), which stretches north to the state line and south almost to the town of Cuba. The area is not the ancestral home-land of this band of Apache—originally, they had lived around the Platte and Arkansas Rivers in what is now central Colorado.

But they were pushed south by white settlers in the 19th century, eventually scattering to live with other tribes as far south and east as Tucumcari. The current reservation wasn't designated until 1887, when the band's numbers had dwindled to just 330 and the group had split into two factions. Although the land was hard-won, it proved fortunate when oil and gas were discovered on it in the 1930s. Profit from these resources, as well as a casino in Dulce and the luxurious Lodge at Chama, has made this a relatively prosperous reservation.

The tribe now numbers about 3,000 members, with 2,500 or so based in Dulce, 25 miles west of Chama on U.S. 64. The village is set in a high, grassy valley that feels hidden away from the rest of the world, with bison, cattle, and sheep grazing beneath the snowcapped Rockies. The **Jicarilla Cultural Affairs** (13533 U.S. 64, 575/759-1343, 8am-5pm Mon.-Fri., free) has a small museum that describes the role of buffalo, medicinal herbs, and other heritage. In a trailer south of the tribal head-quarters, the **Arts and Crafts Museum** (U.S. 64, 575/759-3242, 8am-5pm Mon.-Fri., free) is more of a shop, where you can also see people making the intricate baskets for which the tribe is known.

Recreation

Most visitors come here to hunt mule deer and elk on the reservation lands, or to fish in one of the many lakes; contact **Jicarilla Game and Fish** (575/759-3255, www.jicarillahunt.com) for rules and permits. **Stone Lake** ($5, or free with fishing and hunting licenses), 18 miles south of Dulce, has pretty campsites around its three miles of shoreline.

Festivals and Events

On the third week in July, the **Little Beaver Roundup** is a well-attended powwow and rodeo in Dulce that's open to visitors, and photography is permitted. Similar events, plus traditional footraces, mark **Go-Jii-Ya,** the tribe's feast day on September 15; it takes place at Stone Lake.

The Enchanted Circle

The Enchanted Circle, the loop formed by U.S. 64, Highway 38, and Highway 522, is named for its breathtaking views of the Sangre de Cristo Mountains, including Wheeler Peak. The area is a cultural shift from Taos, much of it settled by Anglo ranchers and prospectors in the late 1800s and currently populated by transplanted flatlander Texans enamored of the massive peaks. The main towns on the route—Angel Fire and Red River—are ski resorts. As the scenery is really the thing, you can drive the 84-mile route in a short day, with time out for a quick hike around Red River or a detour along the Wild Rivers scenic byway. If you like country music, you might want to plan to be in Red River for the evening.

Driving counterclockwise around the loop, as described below, gives you the arresting descent into the Taos Valley from Questa— not to be missed, if you can manage it. Avoid driving the circle on a Sunday and early in the week, as significantly more attractions and businesses are closed.

To start, head east out of Taos on Kit Carson Road, which turns into U.S. 64, winding along next to the Taos River and past numerous campgrounds and hiking trails. At Palo Flechado Pass, the road descends into the high Moreno Valley, a gorgeous expanse of green in early spring and a vast tundra in winter.

ANGEL FIRE

After about 20 miles, a right turn up Highway 434 leads to this tiny ski village, a cluster of timber condos at the base of a 10,600-foot mountain. In comparison with Taos Ski Valley, Angel Fire Resort (800/633-7463, www.angelfireresort.com, $77 full-day lift ticket) looks like a molehill, with a vertical drop of 2,077 feet. But it's friendly to families, has two freestyle terrain parks, and is the only place in the state for night skiing. For those with no snow skills at all, the 1,000-foot-long tubing hill provides an adrenaline rush.

In summer, the resort transforms itself with a full slate of activities on offer, though mountain biking is the clear highlight. Rightly acclaimed by regional riders, the Angel Fire Bike Park ($49/day) is larger than the nascent one at Taos Ski Valley and has more varied runs, including a handful that are suitable for beginners. Near the resort, the storied South Boundary Trail (no. 164) runs from a trailhead off Forest Road 76 south of Angel Fire. The route to Taos is about 5 vertical-seeming miles over the pass, then another 22 or so back to El Nogal trailhead on U.S. 64, a couple of miles east of Taos. Gearing Up (129 Paseo del Pueblo Sur, 575/751-0365) offers shuttle service ($55), so you can bike one-way.

The cool alpine waters of the resort's Monte Verde Lake are particularly appealing at the height of summer. Try your hand at stand-up paddleboarding ($20/hour) and fishing ($25/person), or enjoy the elaborate zipline course ($119). Off the slopes, Roadrunner Tours (Hwy. 434 in town, 575/377-6416, www.nancyburch.com) offers a variety of trail rides on horseback into the mountains.

Food

Before hitting the slopes, stop in at The Bakery & Cafe (3420 Mountain View Blvd., 575/377-3992, 7am-2:30pm daily, $7-11) for generous portions of tasty migas, biscuits and gravy, and chicken-fried steak and eggs.

Hail's Holy Smoked BBQ (3400 Hwy. 434, 575/377-9938, 7am-2pm Tues.-Sat., $5-16) proudly serves a no-nonsense Texas lunch, with smoked brisket, cowboy beans, and house-made desserts. Hail's does meat by the pound, too, and its breakfast options are pretty inexpensive.

If you're around for dinner, Angel Fired Pizza (3375 Mountain View Blvd., 575/377-22774, 11am-9pm daily, $8-20) is the place to

The Enchanted Circle

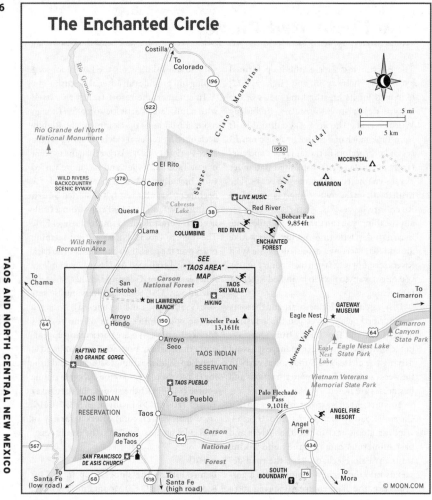

go. As well as several thin-crust whole wheat pizza specialties, it serves a green-chile carbonara and an unwieldy, but supremely tasty, meatball sub.

Information

The Angel Fire CVB maintains a **visitors center** (3365 Hwy. 434, 575/377-6555, www.angelfirefun.com, 9am-5pm daily) just south of the T-intersection with Angel Fire Road. The **Angel Fire Chamber of Commerce** (3407 Hwy. 434, 575/377-6353, www.

angelfirechamber.org, 9am-5pm Mon.-Fri.) has its own office where the lobby is open 24 hours, so you can pick up brochures and maps anytime.

VIETNAM VETERANS MEMORIAL STATE PARK

Back on U.S. 64, a little more than a mile past the turn for Angel Fire, a swooping white structure rises on the hill to your left. This is the **Vietnam Veterans Memorial** (575/377-2293, www.vietnamveteransmemorial.org,

8am-5:30pm daily; chapel open 24 hours), built by Victor "Doc" Westphall as a remembrance of his son David, who was killed in the war. When Westphall commissioned Santa Fe architect Ted Luna to design the graceful white chapel in 1968, it was the first such memorial dedicated to the casualties of Vietnam. An adjacent visitors center was built later and now holds a small but moving museum about the conflict and its aftermath. In the garden are a Huey helicopter and the graves of Victor Westphall and his wife, Jeanne.

EAGLE NEST

At the junction of U.S. 64 and Highway 38, Eagle Nest is a small strip of wooden buildings, all that's left of what was a jumping gambling town in the 1920s and 1930s, when bars hosted roulette and blackjack, and enterprising businesspeople would roll slot machines out onto the boardwalks to entice travelers en route to Raton and the train. The pretty lake here now is the main focus of fun, but there's also good hiking just east in Cimarron Canyon State Park.

Eagle Nest Lake State Park

East of U.S. 64, south of town, Eagle Nest Lake was created in 1918 with the construction of a privately financed dam on the Cimarron River. Today it's a pretty state park, stocked with trout, and a popular recreation spot year-round—the Fourth of July fireworks display and winter ice fishing are legendary. For the marina and visitors center (42 Marina Way, 575/377-1594, www.emnrd.state.nm.us, 8am-4:30pm daily, $5/car day use), look for the turn off U.S. 64 marked by a large RV park sign. Stop here for an exhibit on the dam, as well as camping ($10).

Enchanted Circle Gateway Museum

The Enchanted Circle Gateway Museum (U.S. 64, 575/613-3648, generally 10am-4pm Mon.-Sat., 11am-4pm Sun., donation), at the eastern edge of Eagle Nest, gives an overview of the good old days and often hosts events, such as a mountain-man rendezvous.

Food and Accommodations

The aptly named Among Friends (144 E. Therma Dr., 575/252-3253, 11am-2pm and 5-7pm Wed.-Sat., 11am-2pm Sun., $8) is a welcoming pizza shop that serves up immensely satisfying slices. Choose from a few specialties or pick your own toppings. The sandwiches are generous in size, and the freshly baked

Vietnam Veterans Memorial State Park

cinnamon rolls are worth saving room for—or ordering for the road.

During the week, the rustic **Cowboy's Corner** (50 Hwy. 38, 575/377-9525, 11am-2pm Mon.-Fri., $8) is a great spot for lunch and the views are tough to beat. There are sandwiches and wraps, but it's the burgers—think juicy and oversized patties with buns heated just right—that get the most acclaim.

Laguna Vista Lodge (51 Therma Dr., 575/377-6522, www.lagunavistalodge.com, $100-125 d) has standard motel rooms connected by a screened porch, as well as cabins and apartments with a view of the lake.

Information

The **Eagle Nest Chamber of Commerce** runs a **visitors center** (50 Therma Dr., 575/377-2420, www.eaglenestchamber.org, 8am-4pm Mon.-Fri. mid-May-mid-Oct.) with an enthusiastic staff and plenty of local and regional information.

ELIZABETHTOWN

Blink and you'll miss it: A small sign on the right side of the road 4.8 miles past Eagle Nest points to a left turn to the former gold rush site of **Elizabethtown,** the first incorporated village in New Mexico. When gold was discovered in 1866, it grew to more than 7,000 people, and then faded to nothing after a dredge-mining project failed in 1903. It's now a barely discernible ghost town, with the meager stone ruins of the Mutz Hotel, the former center of social activity. The only signs of life are, ironically, in the **cemetery,** which is still used by residents of Colfax County and contains graves dating as far back as 1880, and in the **museum** (505/312-3800, call for hours, donation suggested), which provides a surprisingly good sense of what life was like in the village's heyday.

RED RIVER

The ski village of **Red River** is a cluster of tidy rows of wooden buildings, all done up in Old West facades, complete with boardwalks and swinging saloon doors. Like Elizabethtown,

this was once a community of wild prospectors, but when mining went bust, the town salvaged itself by renting out abandoned houses to vacationers escaping the summer heat. Just when air-conditioning started to become widespread in the 1950s, the ski area opened, saving the town from a major slump. Red River still thrives, with a year-round population of only about 500.

The town hosts several outsized events throughout the year, including a rowdy **Memorial Day Motorcycle Rally,** a large Fourth of July parade, the **Enchanted Circle Century Tour** and the **Red River Folk Festival** (http://redriverfolk.com) in September, and a Mardi Gras street party; contact the **Red River Chamber of Commerce** (575/754-2366, www. redriver-chamber.org) for more details.

Skiing

Compared with Taos Ski Valley, **Red River Ski & Summer Area** (575/754-2223, www. redriverskiarea.com, $80 full-day lift ticket) may be a bunny hill, but it's nothing if not convenient: The trails run into town, so the two chairlifts are walking distance from anywhere in town.

Cross-country skiers should follow Highway 38 east of town, to the **Enchanted Forest** cross-country ski area (575/754-6112, www.enchantedforestxc.com, $20 full-day pass), which has more than 20 miles of groomed trails through the trees and up the mountainside. Nonskiers can rent snowshoes. And, for a special overnight experience, you can trek in to a **yurt** ($50-150, depending on season), nicely appointed with a woodstove. It's available year-round, and snowmobile delivery of your gear is an option in winter.

Hiking

The town abuts the back side of Wheeler Peak, so the ascents here are much more gradual, while still yielding dramatic views. Stop in at the **visitors center** (101 W. River St., 575/754-3030, www.redriver.org, 8am-5pm daily), in the town hall, for area maps and trail guides. The easy **Red River Nature Trail** can be accessed behind the conference center just past the covered bridge and runs one mile round-trip, with signs identifying plants and geological formations. The more demanding and scenic **Pioneer Creek Trail** (FR 485) starts next to the Arrowhead Lodge off Pioneer Street and follows an old mining road through the forest for 3.4 miles before ending at just over 10,000 feet; there are a few signs of long-closed silver and copper mines along the way.

West of town, Highway 38 leads past a number of trailheads that make for a good amble. **Columbine Trail** (no. 71), on the left (south), eight miles out (or about four miles east of Questa), at the back of the Columbine Campground, is the one to choose if your time is limited. The trail starts out easy, crossing Deer Creek, but soon climbs switchbacks that lead through a large aspen grove, then above the tree line to the ridge, a total of about five miles. As an incentive, wild berry bushes flourish alongside the trail in late summer. The right side of the road, however, is a little less scenic because a molybdenum mine has stripped a good chunk of the mountain.

In summer, you can ride the **Platinum Chairlift** ($21) to the ski area, where you can hike around the summit, grab a bite to eat on the deck of The Tip restaurant, and negotiate the steep trail back into town; it's also popular with experienced mountain bikers. The 360-degree views from the top are worth the trip up alone.

★ Live Music

Red River has a lively country music scene, heavily influenced by the Texans and Oklahomans who have long come here for vacation. "Outlaw country" singer and songwriter Michael Martin Murphey, whose song "The Land of Enchantment" is the official state ballad, has long been active in the music scene here, and he performs regularly July-first week of September at **Rockin' 3M Chuckwagon Amphitheater** (178 Bitter Creek Rd., 575/754-6280, 3pm-2am daily).

The barn-like Texas Reds holds two live music venues: the adjacent **Motherlode Saloon** (406 E. Main St., 575/754-6280, 6pm-2am daily) and the aptly named **Lost Love Saloon** (400 E. Main St., 575/754-2922, 4:30pm-9pm daily). Local rock and country acts take the stage at the former and make it the most rollicking place in town on weekends; the latter features more sedate country and western crooners throughout the week.

Bobcat Pass (1670 Hwy. 38, 575/754-2769, www.bobcatpass.com, 5pm Tues., Thurs., and Sat. mid-June-late Aug.) offers horseback rides by day (from $55) and hosts "cowboy evenings," which include a home-style steak dinner along with a night of singing and picking and a bit of poetry.

Food

The largest selection of lunch options on the Enchanted Circle is in Red River, but none of them is particularly memorable. Business turnover can be high here, but at least **Texas Reds** (400 E. Main St., 575/754-2922, 4:30pm-9pm Mon.-Thurs., 11:30am-3pm and 4:30pm-9pm Fri.-Sun., $15) is consistent; it packs 'em in with Texas-sized steaks and elk burgers in a wood-paneled Western-look room, the floors scattered with peanut shells.

For Tex-Mex, including gut-busting stuffed sopaipillas, **Sundance** (401 High St., 575/754-2971, 5pm-9pm daily, $13) is equally reliable—it's on the street uphill and parallel to the main drag.

For a quick in-and-out meal, **Dairy Bar** (417 E. Main St., 575/754-9969, 11am-10pm daily in summer, 11am-7pm Thurs.-Mon. in winter, $5) offers burgers, chile, quesadillas, and, of course, soft-serve ice cream.

Though the food—burgers, brats, and hot dogs—isn't exactly remarkable, the summit views from the deck of **The Tip** (Red River Ski and Summer Area, 575/754-2223, $7) warrant a stop alone.

The best place in town to stock up for a picnic and hike is the central **Der Market** (307 W. Main St., 575/754-2974, 7am-9pm daily).

Accommodations

Red River is an ideal base for exploring the Enchanted Circle's hiking and skiing options; there are plenty of choices, and most are pleasant and reasonably priced, if somewhat dated. **Golden Eagle Lodge** (1100 Main St., 575/754-2227, from $90), on the village's eastern edge, is one of the better representatives of what's on offer. It's a quaint, family-run place with various-sized apartments that are comfortable and well cared for.

Spread along the river, the Bavarian-themed **Alpine Lodge** (417 W. Main St., 575/754-2952, $115 d) is the best deal in the village. Accommodations range from nicely appointed rooms with balconies in the hotel to spacious log cabins that can fit up to twelve. The property has its own private park and you can even cast a line in the river out back.

Information

The chamber of commerce staffs a **visitors center** (101 W. River St., 575/754-3030, 8am-5pm daily) inside the town hall, off the north side of the main drag.

QUESTA

Arriving in **Questa,** at the junction of Highway 38 and Highway 522, it's hard not to get a sense you're back in Spanish New Mexico. The town, which now has a population of about 1,700, was established in 1842 and is still primarily a Hispano farming village, though a few Anglo newcomers have set up art spaces here. **Ocho** (8 Hwy. 38, 575/779-9357, gallery 11am-5pm Fri.-Sun.) is one; it hosts community music jams, yoga, and other events.

Across the road is the **visitors center** (Hwy. 38, 575/613-2852, www.questa-nm.com/visitor-center, 9:30am-5pm daily June-Aug.), though it has little to share. The heart of town, a few blocks back, is the 1841 **San Antonio Church,** which was restored in 2016

by volunteers over about eight years of night-and-weekend work.

Of the few places to grab a bite to eat, **The Wildcat's Den** (2457 Hwy. 522, 575/586-1119, 11am-6pm Mon.-Fri., 11am-4pm Sat., $7) is the best bet; its burgers are rightly revered by locals. For a meal more in line with Questa's roots, head north a bit to **My Tia's Café** (107 Hwy. 378, 575/586-2203, 11am-6pm Tues.-Fri., 9am-6pm Sat.-Sun., $7), which does New Mexican home cooking, including chiles rellenos and taco salads.

Wild Rivers Recreation Area

In 2014, the **Río Grande del Norte National Monument** (575/758-8851, www.blm.gov) was established, protecting the river from the Colorado state line to Pilar, south of Taos. Perhaps the wildest section of the land is found north of Questa, in the **Wild Rivers Recreation Area,** where the Red River meets the Rio Grande. Red-tailed hawks circle over gnarled, centuries-old piñon and juniper trees, and river otters thrive here, after their reintroduction in 2008. White-water **rafting** is popular in the Class III rapids of the Red River Confluence run; contact an outfitter in Taos.

The access road to the recreation area is three miles north on Highway 522 from the main Questa intersection, then west on Highway 378, which leads through the town of Cerro and to the area's **visitors center** (575/586-1150, 9am-6pm daily June-Aug., $3/car day use).

Steep **hiking** trails lead down into the gorge and along the river, so you can make a full loop, starting down from **La Junta Point,** then taking **Little Arsenic Trail** back up (about 4.5 miles total), or **Big Arsenic Trail** for a longer hike (6 miles). If you'd prefer not to descend (and, necessarily, ascend) the canyon, follow the more level 1.7-mile **Pescado Trail** along the Red River rim and gently down to the Red River Fish Hatchery.

Five developed **campgrounds** (but no RV hookups; $7/car) on the rim can be reached by car, or you can hike in to campsites by the river ($5).

TAOS AND NORTH CENTRAL NEW MEXICO
THE ENCHANTED CIRCLE

1: Motherlode Saloon in Red River 2: Alpine Lodge in Red River 3: Columbine Trail 4: cabin at the D. H. Lawrence Ranch

D. H. LAWRENCE RANCH

After Questa, the view opens up as you descend into Taos Valley, with mesas stretching far to the west. Five miles east on the rutted San Cristobal Road is the 160-acre **D. H. Lawrence Ranch** (575/776-2245, 10am-2pm Thurs.-Fri., 10am-4pm Sat. June-Oct.), also known as the Kiowa Ranch, where English writer and provocateur D. H. Lawrence lived in 1924 and 1925 with his wife, Frieda, and the painter Dorothy Brett. The ranch was closed to visitors for several years, but reopened in 2014, with a docent on-site to answer questions. Though there's not much to see, it is as good a reason as any to drive up a back road and into the fragrant pine forests. (Don't bother driving up on a closed day—the property is fully fenced and locked up.)

The 160-acre spread was a gift from Mabel Dodge Luhan—generous, but nonetheless a bare-bones existence, as you can see in the cabins the artists occupied. Lawrence soon returned to Europe, but Frieda stayed on. Years after the writer died of tuberculosis in France in 1930, Frieda exhumed and cremated his body and brought the ashes to New Mexico. This plan sparked anger among Lawrence's friends, including Mabel, who characterized Frieda's planned site for the ashes as "that outhouse of a shrine." Tales abound about how the ashes never made the trip. Some of the earliest visitors to pay their respects at the ranch include playwright Tennessee Williams and artist Georgia O'Keeffe, whose painting *The Lawrence Tree* was inspired by the view from the base of a gnarled pine in front of the Lawrences' cabin.

Coming from the north, turn left at the *second* sign for County Road B-009 (the first is in the town of San Cristobal). Coming up from Taos, look for the historical marker on the right side of the road, immediately before the turn.

Las Vegas and the Northeast

The northeast section of the state bridges central New Mexico and the great American plains. The alpine Pecos Wilderness forms a natural barrier east of Santa Fe, then the land levels out into a grassy vista stretching to the horizon.

This was the northern border for the Spanish, and only after Mexico gained its independence in 1821 were traders' wagon trains welcome to enter the area from Kansas. For the three decades when the Santa Fe Trail was at its peak of activity, then with the subsequent prosperity brought in by the railroad, northeastern New Mexico was a lively place.

Now, though, especially since the Dust Bowl ate away at the eastern edge, it's a relatively silent swath of territory, traversed mainly by ranchers, their cattle, and motorists. The latter usually stick to the

Highlights

Look for ★ to find recommended sights, activities, dining, and lodging.

© MOON.COM

★ **Las Vegas Plaza:** The heart of "Meadow City" is this grassy spread surrounded by grand territorial and old adobe buildings. It's so well preserved, it has been used frequently as a movie set—but it's blessedly free of souvenir shops (page 221).

★ **Montezuma Castle:** The glamour of the early railroad era is captured in this Queen Anne-style confection built as a resort hotel, now used as a college student center. Schedule a tour of the interior if possible, and don't miss the nearby hot springs (page 222).

★ **Clayton Lake State Park:** Stop by this oasis in the prairie to stand in—or at least near—the footsteps of giants. Dinosaurs left their immense tracks in the prehistoric mud here 100 million years ago (page 232).

★ **Capulin Volcano National Monument:** To get a great view across the plains, wind your way along the unnervingly narrow road that spirals up this perfectly round peak. You can also hike down into the crater (page 236).

★ **The Drive through Valle Vidal:** The lonely east-west traverse through Valle Vidal, marked by elk herds, snow-capped Sangre de Cristo peaks, and numerous creeks, is the best opportunity to see the untouched northern New Mexico wilderness as it once was (page 241).

★ **St. James Hotel:** The history of Cimarron, and its present social life, is intrinsically caught up with this old inn, the state's best 19th-century hotel (page 242).

interstate that runs north to Colorado, though a few stop to visit the town of Raton, at the base of a precipitous pass over the Rockies, or Cimarron, deeper in the mountains and that much more untouched by time. Just off I-25 in the lowlands, Las Vegas is the region's biggest center of activity. No bright lights and high rolling here, however: This Vegas is a college town with a population of about 13,600, a sedate place that's endured hard times. There's no adobe here—faux or otherwise. Its tree-shaded plaza is edged with colonial and Victorian buildings that manage to be well preserved without feeling like a theme park.

The other major landmark on the plains is Capulin Volcano, which was active 60,000 years ago. Its cinder cone rises a thousand feet above the surrounding land, and from its rim you can see the earth fall away to the edge of the Sangre de Cristo Mountains. This area may not exude the barren drama of New Mexico's western desert or the thrill of the rugged mountains, but these placid flatlands, interrupted by only a few roads and small towns, offer a sense of space and tranquility unmatched elsewhere in the state.

HISTORY

Dinosaurs traipsed through in the Early Cretaceous (most notably leaving footprints north of Clayton), and Comanche and other Plains Indians crisscrossed the area for hundreds of years before the Spanish arrived. But northeast New Mexico is even more indelibly marked by the Santa Fe Trail. The trade route proved to be the thin end of the wedge that opened up the West to American domination. First came goods from Missouri to the hungry market in Santa Fe (previously restricted to trading only with Spain), then came military supplies during the Mexican-American War, followed by homesteaders, prospectors, and entrepreneurs.

It was these prospectors who caused substantial trouble in the Rocky Mountains when, in 1866, gold was discovered not far from the northern branch of the Santa Fe Trail. Scores of hopeful miners flooded in—never mind the strike was on the Maxwell Land Grant, 1.7 million acres of private property. By the 1870s, a battle was brewing between the land-grant owners and the squatting miners. The resulting Colfax County War involved assassinations, lynchings, and Republican conspiracies in Santa Fe. Finally, an 1887 Supreme Court ruling gave squatters the boot, along with Spanish families who had been settled for generations. But by then, the railroad was bringing surer money than gold anyway—as well as another point of conflict. Anglo businessmen piled off the train in Raton and East Las Vegas, buying up land and earning the wrath of the Hispano shepherds who had been living in a much simpler economy for centuries.

Meanwhile, homesteaders on the plains northeast of Las Vegas had set the stage for another drama. Beginning in 1862, when the Homestead Act doled out 160-acre parcels to any family with enough nerve to take them, the would-be farmers struggled to work the thin topsoil that lay over limestone bedrock. They were able to displace the native Plains Indian tribes in many areas, but they had no defense against the drought that struck in the 1920s. Soon, this was the western edge of the Dust Bowl, where the sky turned black for days at a time and children died from inhaling the grit. It was an unrivaled economic and environmental disaster that emptied the region of all but the ranchers who had initially settled the area for the United States.

After many decades, the northern plains' fortunes finally turned again, with the discovery of carbon-dioxide fields and the expansion of cattle ranching. But the area remains sparsely populated, just as much of the former Maxwell Land Grant is still relative wilderness.

Previous: Fort Union National Monument; cows grazing on the grassy northern plains; Pecos National Historical Park.

Las Vegas and the Northeast

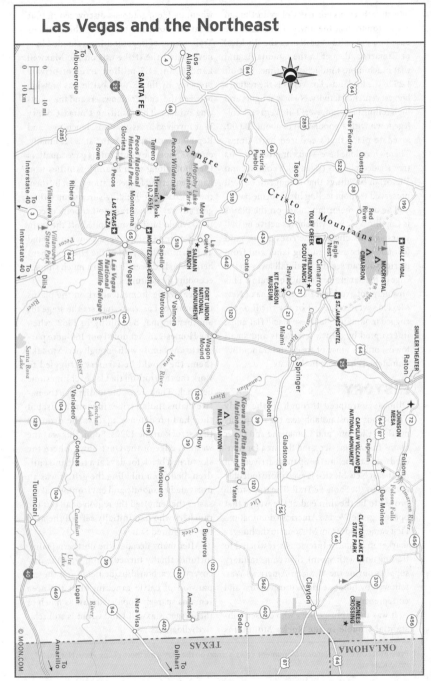

© MOON.COM

PLANNING YOUR TIME

On the surface, Clayton, Las Vegas, Raton, and Cimarron are all one-night towns, as there are few formal sights and little to do in the evenings. But you could easily settle down somewhere for a few days (Cimarron or Las Vegas are the strongest candidates) while you investigate the spaces in between, hiking, fishing, or just driving the pretty back roads. Aside from a detour to Pecos National Historical Park, the drive to Las Vegas on I-25 is a fairly dull one just for a day

trip from Santa Fe, but the town is a great diversion if you're staying awhile or heading farther into the plains. Few tourists make it all the way to Clayton, in the farthest corner. But if you think of it as a point of contrast with central, mountainous New Mexico, it can be a worthwhile journey. Winter can be harsh here: Tourist services in Raton and Cimarron are severely curtailed beginning in September and lasting through the end of April, and a cold snap in early fall is not uncommon.

Pecos and Villanueva

Santa Fe backs up against the 223,000 acres of the **Pecos Wilderness**, the second-largest nature reserve in New Mexico (after the Gila, in southwestern part of the state). The mountain streams seethe with trout, and elk ramble through emerald-green meadows. The heart of the wilderness is slowly recovering from the 2011 Pacheco Fire, but day visitors will find plenty to enjoy.

On the drive out on I-25, near exit 295, you pass the site of the westernmost Civil War battle in the United States, the **Battle of Glorieta Pass.** It raged March 26-28, 1862, part of a Confederate plan to invade the West with a force of Texans—a plan that was foiled in this decisive rout. The fight is reenacted here annually, and the property owner maintains a makeshift memorial and exhibit on the side of the highway.

PECOS

The wilderness's gateway is the former logging town of **Pecos,** where mountain men rub shoulders with alternative healers and monks; south of town are the ruins of **Pecos Pueblo,** the regional power before the Spanish arrived.

Pecos National Historical Park

When the Spanish made first contact with local people in 1540, Pecos was the largest

pueblo in the region, with a population of 2,000 living in and around four- and five-story stone buildings sealed with mud. In **Pecos National Historical Park** (Hwy. 63, 505/757-7241, www.nps.gov/peco, 8am-6pm daily June-Aug., 8am-4:30pm Sept.-May, free), the ruins of this complex community are accessible to visitors via a 1.5-mile interpretive trail that winds through the remnants of the Pecos Pueblo walls, a few restored kivas, and, most striking, the shell of a Franciscan mission. A free **guided walking tour** around the site runs Friday-Sunday in spring and daily at 10am in summer. Additional free **van tours** cover different aspects of local history; check the website for schedules. For a history of the pueblo, set aside twelve minutes for the video that runs on demand in the visitors center.

On a ridge looking out onto the plains to the northeast and the mountains behind, the park provides a beautiful view today; around AD 1100, when the area was being settled into the first villages, it also provided a livelihood. The ridge was part of a natural trade path between the Rio Grande farmers and the buffalo hunters of the Great Plains. Both groups met in Pecos, itself an agricultural community, to barter. What began as a series of small villages consolidated in the 14th century into a city, with a layout so orderly it appears to have been centrally planned, and by 1450, the fortress of Pecos was the major economic power in the area.

Perhaps it was the city's trading culture and relative worldliness that made the Pecos Indians welcome Spaniard Francisco Vásquez de Coronado and his men in 1540 with music and dancing rather than bows and arrows. Nearly 60 years later, Don Juan de Oñate visited the area and ordered a mission church built—a giant structure with six bell towers and buttresses 22 feet thick in some spots. The building was destroyed during the Pueblo Revolt, however, and the Pecos people dug a kiva smack in the middle of the ruined convent area—symbolic architecture, to say the least.

But the Spanish returned, and they were even welcomed and aided at Pecos. When they built a new church in the early 1700s, it was noticeably smaller, maybe as a form of compromise. But even as a hybrid Pueblo-Spanish culture developed, the Indian population was falling victim to disease and drought. When the Santa Fe Trail opened up in 1821, Pecos was all but empty, and in 1838, the last city dwellers marched to live with fellow Towa speakers at Jemez Pueblo, 80 miles west; their descendants still reside there today.

Pecos Wilderness

Stop in at the **Pecos ranger station** (Hwy. 63, 505/757-6121, 8am-4:30pm Mon.-Fri.) on the south end of Pecos town to get maps and information on trail conditions as well as the eight developed campgrounds. At this high elevation, summer temperatures are rarely above 75°F and can dip below freezing at night, so pack accordingly.

Highway 63 is the main access route into the wilderness, running north out of town along the Pecos River. If you've forgotten anything, you can probably get it at the long-running **Tererro General Store** (1911 Hwy. 63, 505/431-1132, 8am-5pm daily May-Sept.), about 13 miles along the two-lane road. The road then narrows and steadily rises, passing fishing access points and campgrounds.

With the change in the state's administration, there's been a renewed push by many locals to establish a Pecos Canyon State Park that would incorporate much of the area's attractions.

HIKING

About a mile after Mora campground on Highway 63 is the right turn for Forest Road 223, a rough road (ideally, for high-clearance cars only; proceed slowly) that leads 4.5 miles up to Iron Gate Campground and **Hamilton Mesa Trail** (no. 249), a fairly gentle 3.8-mile hike to a wide-open meadow on an elevated plateau—look for strawberries among the wildflowers.

At Cowles Ponds, a developed fishing area where a mining camp once stood, you can turn left off Highway 63 on Windsor Road to follow a paved one-lane road 1.5 miles to Panchuela campground, the start of **Cave Creek Trail** (no. 288). It's an easy 3.6-mile out-and-back that follows a small waterway up to some caves that have been carved out of the white limestone by the stream's flow. If you go past the caves, up a steep hillside, you reach an area burned in the 2013 Jaroso Fire; hiking here is not recommended, due to the danger of falling trees.

Continuing straight past Cowles on Highway 63 brings you in about three more miles to the scenic Jack's Creek campground and the **Jack's Creek Trail** (no. 257), a 12.5-mile out-and-back that ascends sharply at times to the Pecos Baldy Lake. All trails in this area require a $2 trailhead parking fee; additional fees apply for camping or picnicking, depending on the spot.

Food and Accommodations

For staying the night, the **Pecos Benedictine Monastery** (Hwy. 63, 505/757-6415, www. pecosmonastery.org, $66 d) maintains simple rooms with beautiful views; the rate is a suggested donation and includes continental breakfast and dinner. Several mountain lodges deeper in the forest, such as **Los Pinos Ranch** (505/757-6213, www.lospinosranch.

com, $145 pp), are typically open only in summer and offer multiday packages with all meals included and a variety of outdoor activities, including horseback riding.

At the main crossroads in Pecos, where Highway 50 meets Highway 63, **Frankie's at the Casanova** (12 Main St., 505/757-3322, 8am-2pm daily, 5:30pm-8:15pm Fri.-Sat., $9) is the town social center, set in an old adobe dance hall. The food, mainly New Mexican fare and diner staples, isn't always a hit, but it's worth a stop just to see the murals over the bar.

HIGHWAY 3 TO VILLANUEVA

From exit 323 off I-25, 14 miles southeast of Pecos, **Highway 3** is a beautiful drive south. The two-lane road meanders through a narrow valley with rich red earth cut into small farm plots, dotted by villages such as Ribera and El Pueblo dating to the late 18th century. Stop in **Villanueva,** the largest settlement along the road, at the area institution that is the family-run **Villanueva General Store** (1225 Hwy. 3, 575/421-2265, 8am-6:30pm Mon.-Sat., noon-5:30pm Sun.) for everything from Frito Pies to camping supplies and then visit the small but beautiful **Villanueva State Park** (575/421-2957, www.emnrd.state.nm.us, $5/car), which occupies a bend in the Pecos River against 400-foot-tall sandstone cliffs. It's rarely crowded—you'll probably have the 2.5-mile Canyon Trail to yourself. Spring comes early, filling trails with wildflowers by late April; fall is a burst of red scrub oak and yellow cottonwood leaves, in sharp contrast to the evergreens.

Las Vegas

The city in New Mexico that suffers most from misplaced expectations, Las Vegas is a quiet community about 50 miles northeast of Santa Fe. Its centerpiece is a tree-shaded plaza, and nearly a thousand registered historic buildings stand in the surrounding blocks.

Set near Starvation Peak—a landmark butte on the Santa Fe Trail—the city was a Spanish settlement well before it was a stop on the trade route. In the middle of town, the Gallinas River still marks the historic division between the 1835 settlement of Nuestra Señora de los Dolores de las Vegas (Our Lady of Sorrows of the Meadows) and the railroad boom town of East Las Vegas, begun in 1879. The old Hispano plaza-centered town and the new, largely Anglo community didn't merge until 1970—probably because for decades, East Las Vegas was huge, anarchic, and populated with cattle rustlers, scam artists, and outlaws like Doc Holliday, who owned a saloon here for a year. Poor relations between the two towns were exacerbated by fights over land use. A band of Hispano vigilantes called the Gorras Blancas (White Caps) went around snipping through Anglo fencing in the night, so that their sheep could continue to graze.

But the changes wrought by the railroad were irrevocable, and along with Anglo economic supremacy came telephones, an electric streetcar, an opera house, and other trappings of modern life. For a period in the late 19th century, "Meadow City" was the biggest metropolis between Missouri and San Francisco, with an opera theater and a huge Harvey House hotel, the Castañeda. Times changed again, and the Harvey House went derelict (though it reopened in 2019). The New Mexico Normal School, established during this early boom period to train teachers, is now the sleek Highlands University, and philanthropist Armand Hammer established a branch of the United World College system outside of town in the 1980s. Together, the two institutions cater to several thousand students, who give the town much of its life.

Las Vegas

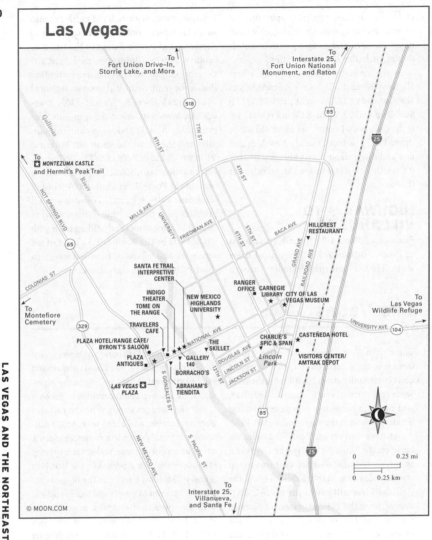

To
Fort Union Drive–In,
Storrie Lake, and Mora

To
Interstate 25,
Fort Union National
Monument, and Raton

518

85

7TH ST

8TH ST

25

Gallinas River

To ✚ MONTEZUMA CASTLE
and Hermit's Peak Trail

HOT SPRINGS BLVD

MILLS AVE

UNIVERSITY

4TH ST

FRIEDMAN AVE

6TH ST

5TH ST

BACA AVE

HILLCREST
RESTAURANT

65

GRAND AVE

RAILROAD AVE

COLONIAS ST

SANTA FE TRAIL
INTERPRETIVE
CENTER

RANGER
OFFICE

CARNEGIE
LIBRARY

CITY OF LAS
VEGAS MUSEUM

To
Montefiore
Cemetery

329

INDIGO
THEATER
TOME ON
THE RANGE

NEW MEXICO
HIGHLANDS
UNIVERSITY

To
Las Vegas
Wildlife Refuge

UNIVERSITY AVE

104

TRAVELERS
CAFE

NATIONAL AVE

CHARLIE'S
SPIC & SPAN

CASTEÑEDA HOTEL

PLAZA HOTEL/RANGE CAFE/
BYRONT'S SALOON

THE
SKILLET

DOUGLAS AVE

Lincoln
Park

VISITORS CENTER/
AMTRAK DEPOT

PLAZA
ANTIQUES

GALLERY
140

BORRACHO'S

LINCOLN ST

12TH ST

JACKSON ST

LAS VEGAS ✚
PLAZA

S GONZALES ST

ABRAHAM'S
TIENDITA

85

NEW MEXICO AVE

S PACIFIC ST

25

0   0.25 mi
0   0.25 km

To
Interstate 25,
Villanueva,
and Santa Fe

© MOON.COM

SIGHTS

The best way to explore Las Vegas and appreciate its historic architecture is on foot. Start on the old plaza and notice how the building styles and the street layouts change as you head east across Bridge Street, which leads toward the New Mexico Highlands University campus. Douglas Avenue, two blocks south, is the main shopping district on the east side; still farther east are the rail yards, now relatively derelict but at one time the liveliest part of town.

If Las Vegas looks vaguely familiar, maybe it's because you watched the 1984 Cold War scare flick *Red Dawn* too many times, or you're a fan of Tom Mix Westerns such as *The Tenderfoot's Triumph*. The city was the setting for scores of silent films shot in the early 20th century, as well as later productions such as *Easy Rider, All the Pretty Horses,* and *No Country for Old Men. Red Dawn* used the area most thoroughly; the "Calumet Says Howdy" mural just off Grand Avenue is a relic of the shoot.

You can pick up a thorough walking-tour guide from the visitors center or from the **Citizens' Committee for Historic Preservation** (116 Bridge St., 505/425-8803, www.lvcchp.org, 10am-3pm Mon.-Sat.). The pamphlet covers the plaza and outlying historic districts, each with a distinctive building style; some structures date back as far as 1846. The group also occasionally organizes tours inside many of the private homes.

★ Las Vegas Plaza

The large, tree-edged **Las Vegas Plaza** on the west side of town shows only a few remnants of the original Spanish settlement, which had been built entirely of adobe, in a defensive ring meant to be sealed off against Apache raids. Many buildings later got spruced up with territorial details when the railroad brought in bricks, tin cornices, and other modern details. **Desmarais House/Our Lady of Sorrows Parish Hall** (1810 E. Plaza) is one of the few older adobe structures (built before 1883), though the curvy roofline is a bit of 1930s whimsy. The old *acequia madre* (main irrigation ditch) runs along South Pacific Street, one block south of the plaza.

On the corner with Bridge Street, **Plaza Drugs** (178 Bridge St., 505/425-5221, 8am-6pm Mon.-Sat.) is a great old-school soda fountain and pharmacy. Sip a cherry-lime soda and check out the Lego model and the house-brand medicinal herbs, harvested nearby. Peek into **Plaza Antiques** (1805 Plaza St., 505/429-9447, 10am-6pm daily), on the opposite side of the plaza, for all manner of Southwestern and Victorian curios; in a town known for its antique shops, it's one of the more satisfying ones to browse.

Bridge Street

Bridge Street, which leads toward the Gallinas River, was built up in the mid-19th century and now mixes old and new: A tattoo parlor and galleries have filled the empty spaces near Popular Dry Goods, which deals in rodeo wear. **Gallery 140** (140 Bridge St., 505/425/1085, 1pm-4pm Tues.-Thurs. and Sat., 1pm-7pm Fri.), home of the Las Vegas Arts Council, features monthly themed exhibitions of local art, some crafty and some fine. The exhibits at the **Santa Fe Trail Interpretive Center** (116 Bridge St., 10am-3pm Mon.-Sat.) are heavy on historic photos and low on artifacts. But entrance is free, and the place is run by the local historic preservation group, members of which are happy to answer questions of all kinds.

East Las Vegas

New Mexico Highlands University occupies either side of the street once you cross the river. Up the hill and past the campus, you enter some of the finer residential districts, with many examples of beaux arts and Queen Anne architecture—the best is around **Carnegie Park** (4th St. and National Ave.). The park's green lawn surrounds the elegant domed **Carnegie Library** (500 National Ave., 505/426-3304, 8am-5pm Mon.-Fri., 8am-2pm Sat.), a mini-Monticello. Of the more than 2,500 libraries around the world funded by steel magnate and philanthropist Andrew Carnegie, it's one of the few that still houses the public library, and the only one of three in the state to have survived.

About five blocks south is Douglas Avenue, where the commercial buildings range from sleek 1940s storefronts to the enormous Romanesque **Masonic Temple** (514 Douglas Ave.) of 1895. Farther south still, **Lincoln Park** (Lincoln and 7th Sts.) is another square surrounded by gracious large homes.

Castañeda Hotel

Adjacent to the train station, the **Castañeda Hotel** is a onetime Harvey House dating back to 1898 and one of the Southwest's most historic properties. Shuttered in 1948, it underwent extensive renovations recently and—against all odds—is open for business once more. Kathy Hendrickson of

Southwest Detours (505/459-6987, www. southwestdetours.com) offers guided tours by appointment of the railroad-era monolith, the Plaza Hotel and of Montezuma Castle (from $20).

City of Las Vegas Museum and Rough Riders Memorial Collection

It takes almost more time to say the name of the **City of Las Vegas Museum and Rough Riders Memorial Collection** (727 Grand Ave., 505/426-3205, www.visitlasvegasnm. com/rough-rider-museum, 10am-4pm Tues.-Sat., $2 donation) than it does to tour it, but the exhibits are informative and based on well-chosen artifacts. It starts with a glass case of pots and baskets from the pre-Columbian era, but quickly gets to Vegas's glam years in the late 19th century, when the town supported two opera houses and had all the trappings of high society and general civilization, including the first telephone line in the state, installed in 1879.

One room is dedicated to souvenirs from Teddy Roosevelt's Rough Riders, the spirited regiment he led in the Spanish-American War of 1898. The soldiers, chosen for their skills with horses and guns, were volunteers from all over the West, with the majority from New Mexico; they chose Las Vegas as the site of their first reunion and continued to gather over the years, until the last soldier died in 1975.

Montefiore Cemetery

On the west edge of town, at the end of Colonias Street (you'll probably want to drive), the rambling **Montefiore Cemetery** is an interesting place to visit, especially the back corner, dedicated to the sizable Jewish population that settled here in the mid-1800s and set up stores and other trade operations. After walking around downtown, you'll recognize many of the names: Charles Ilfeld, for instance, and Samuel Nahm of the Stern & Nahm building on Bridge Street. The community established the first synagogue in the territory, Congregation Montefiore, in 1881, and although there are far fewer Jewish families left in Las Vegas today, it's influence is still strong.

★ Montezuma Castle

About six miles north of town (head north off the plaza on Hot Springs Blvd.), **Montezuma Castle** is a 90,000-square-foot architectural confection perched on the mountainside. The turreted Queen Anne-style building stands as a reminder of more glamorous travel days, when the Atchison, Topeka & Santa Fe Railroad envisioned an elite resort here, connected to the main line with a spur track. The firm of Burnham & Root (one of whose principals went on to make his name with the Chicago World's Fair complex of 1893) created the spectacular building, which opened to guests in 1885. But despite the patronage of Billy the Kid as well as American presidents, the place closed after less than 20 years. It later became the Montezuma Baptist College, then a Jesuit seminary for Mexican priests until 1972.

It was nearly in ruins when the **Armand Hammer United World College of the American West** (505/454-4221, www.uwc-usa.org) acquired it in 1981 and invested more than $10 million in its restoration. Historically accurate, but with modern touches such as vivid Dale Chihuly chandeliers, the interior is as lavish as the exterior—it's well worth seeing if your schedule allows. It is open to visitors only during free, student-led **tours,** on Saturday afternoons—call or check the website for the schedule.

Also on the college grounds is **Dwan Light Sanctuary** (505/454-4200), which *is* open to the public between 6am and 8pm daily. The serene meditation space is at its most remarkable during daylight, when it dazzles with prism installations by Charles Ross, an artist who is building an earthwork sculpture

---

1: Montezuma Castle **2:** Dwan Light Sanctuary
3: Hillcrest Restaurant **4:** Plaza Hotel

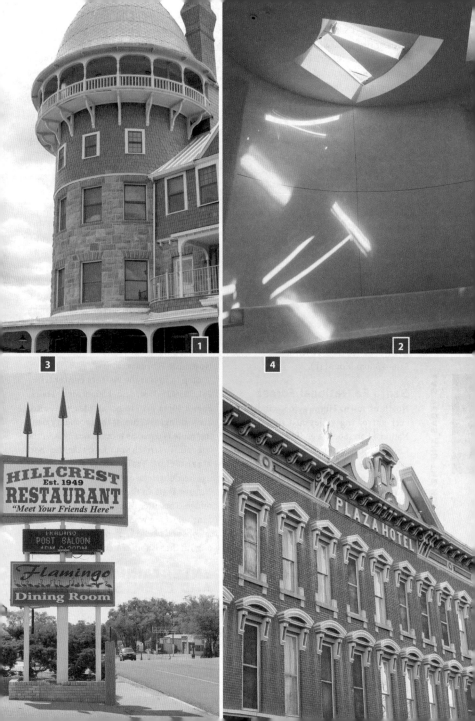

nearby called *Star Axis* (www.staraxis.org). Register first at the visitors booth.

What makes the drive up more worthwhile are the **Montezuma Hot Springs** (5am-midnight, free), the waters that first inspired the construction of the castle resort. The set of three pools is alongside Highway 65—just drive a half-mile past the main school entrance and look for signs and breaks in the guardrail on the right side. Those farthest along are the most appealing, terraced round concrete pools, screened from the road with a basic fence.

In the winter months, **Montezuma Pond**, just west of the campus, once froze solid enough for ice skating, but it is now too shallow. The pond was originally built by the hotel for ice harvesting; plans are afoot to dredge it and return it to its former dimensions.

SPORTS AND RECREATION

For maps and current conditions in the mountains, visit the **Pecos/Las Vegas Ranger District office** (1926 N. 7th St., 505/425-3534, 8am-4:30pm Mon.-Fri.).

Santa Fe National Forest

North of town, Highway 65 winds up an ever-narrowing valley just into Santa Fe National Forest before ending at **El Porvenir Campground,** a pretty patch of pine forest with 19 campsites ($8) near a stream shaded by ponderosas at the base of Hermit's Peak. **Hermit's Peak Trail** (no. 223) leads 9.5 miles to the 10,260-foot summit. The peak's name refers to wandering mendicant Giovanni Maria Agostini, who was born in Italy and traveled all over the Americas on foot. He walked from Kansas to Las Vegas with a wagon train in the 1860s and took up residence in a cave ministering to the sick; he eventually wound up in the Organ Mountains near Las Cruces, where he was mysteriously killed.

Storrie Lake State Park

Just a few miles north of town, **Storrie Lake State Park** (Hwy. 518, 505/425-7278, www.

nmparks.com, $5/car day use, $8/night camping) is heavily used for waterskiing and windsurfing. But as a place to camp, you can do much better, as it's rather barren, and campsites are so close to the highway that you hear the rush of traffic. As long as you're not hauling an RV, head instead toward Mora to **Morphy Lake State Park** (575/387-2328, www.nmparks.com, $5/car day use, $8/night camping), which is much more scenic and secluded.

Las Vegas National Wildlife Refuge

Southeast of town via Highway 104, the remarkably lush **Las Vegas National Wildlife Refuge** is part of a chain of wetlands cultivated to accommodate migratory birds. A number of bald eagles winter here, and Swainson's hawks and more than 10 other species of raptors pass through every fall. A rectangular eight-mile driving route cuts through the 8,672-acre area, passing **McAllister Lake.** The second half of the circuit is unpaved and can get quite muddy, and is closed entirely November-February.

Stop in first at the **visitors center** (Hwy. 281, 505/425-3581, 8am-4:30pm Mon.-Thurs., 8am-3:30pm Fri.) to get an idea what birds are visiting; ask, too, if the secondary driving route is open, as it occasionally is in the late fall. To stretch your legs, take the short **Meadowlark Trail,** a nature trail at refuge headquarters, or the 1.75-mile **Gallinas Nature Trail,** in the southwest corner of the refuge. The latter hike descends into a small canyon, where you can usually spot prairie falcons and swallows; register first (weekdays only) at the visitors center.

ENTERTAINMENT AND EVENTS

Even though it's a college town, Las Vegas isn't particularly rambunctious, and it rolls up its sidewalks entirely on Sunday.

Nightlife

In July and August, the plaza hosts live music on Friday afternoons (5:30pm-7:30pm), after which you could check out the **Fort Union Drive-In** (3300 7th St., 505/425-9934, Fri.-Sun. May-Sept.), a great little relic of cinematic history for $20 per carload. Downtown, **Indigo Theater** (146 Bridge St., 505/434-4444, www.indigotheater.rocks) is the town's first-run movie theater, a cheery, 51-seat space.

After the nightly movie, you could head to **Byron T's Saloon** (230 N. Plaza, 11am-midnight daily), the bar at the Plaza Hotel, which has big show windows overlooking the square and a great mix of local drinkers, craft beers, vintage cocktails, and live music.

One block east of the plaza, friendly **Borracho's** (139 Bridge St., 505/615-3561, 2pm-1:30am Tues.-Fri., noon-1:30am Sat., noon-9pm Sun.) heaves on the weekends with regulars who come for an impressive selection of house cocktails, such as the Chupacabra margarita—made from a potent green-chile infused tequila. New Mexican ales are exclusively on tap and there's frequent live music.

Festivals and Events

On the second Saturday evening of each month, Bridge Street gets lively with the town **Artwalk**, when galleries and shops are open late.

If you're in town over Fourth of July weekend, you'll see the **Fiestas de las Vegas**, when vendors of traditional foods (as well as fair staples like caramel apples) set up all around the plaza and down Bridge Street, and bands perform in the gazebo. Festivities last for five days, beginning with Mass at Our Lady of Sorrows Church, one block west of the plaza, and ending with the crowning of the Reina de las Fiestas.

In early August, **Heritage Week** (www. lvcchp.org) features activities across town that celebrate Las Vegas's history, including military reenactments, concerts, and guided tours, including of the Castañeda Hotel.

FOOD

Aside from the chains on Grand Avenue, dining choices are limited in Las Vegas, but there are a few gems.

New Mexican

Get goodies to eat in the park from **Abraham's Tiendita** (151 Bridge St., 505/425-0930, 9am-4pm Mon.-Fri., $3), a tiny storefront that doles out handheld treats, including empanadas, tamales, burritos, and sopaipillas. Look out for specials such as veggie Frito pies and tacos gordos.

Cafés

Charlie's Spic & Span Bakery and Café (715 Douglas Ave., 505/426-1921, 6:30am-6pm Mon.-Sat., 7am-3pm Sun., $6) is a roomy restaurant where the glass cases burst with monster-size éclairs, jelly doughnuts, and cinnamon buns. But the real specialty is the flour tortilla—be sure to get one with whatever you order, whether it's chile-smothered eggs (breakfast is served all day) or spicy green-chile stew, or even a green-chile cheeseburger. After tasting the delectably fluffy things, you'll be ruined for the supermarket variety, so pick up a to-go bag at the door.

On the plaza, the all-purpose **Travelers Café** (1814 S. Plaza, 505/426-8638, 7am-7pm Mon.-Sat., $5) is the place for a coffee, Wi-Fi, breakfast sandwich, and veggie-sandwich fix.

Diners

The Plaza Hotel's sunny **Range Cafe** (230 N. Plaza, 505/434-0022, 7am-9pm daily, $12), part of a New Mexico chain that's popular in Albuquerque, serves a nice mix of diner favorites, such as biscuits and gravy, country fried steak, and Caesar salad. There are quite a few New Mexican classics, too, and breakfast is served all day.

Up on the north side, not far from the freeway, the family-run diner **Hillcrest Restaurant** (1106 N. Grand Ave., 505/425-7211, 6am-9pm daily, $9) is a wonderful time capsule serving a wide swath of comfort food, from Americana (hot turkey sandwiches) to great New Mexican classics. Unsurprisingly, the local customers chat equally in Spanish and English.

One of Las Vegas' newer restaurants and one that has gone a long way toward livening up the town's dining and bar scene, ★ **The Skillet** (623 12th St., 505/563-0477, 11am-9pm Mon.-Wed., 11am-midnight Thurs.-Sun., $3-11) occupies an historic warehouse, though its original incarnation was as a food truck. An ethos of serving up meals that are quick and extremely tasty has endured, with a menu featuring tacos and burritos—the fish taco with cod, slaw, and sriracha mayo and a smoked chipotle brisket burrito are among the standouts. The bar tempts with a number of appealing house cocktails, including margaritas and beer cocktails, including an aptly named Beergarita.

ACCOMMODATIONS

Just about all of Las Vegas's hotels and motels are on North Grand Avenue. The newest chain operations are on the far end, at exit 347.

Las Vegas has three historic hotels. **El Fidel Hotel** (500 Douglas Ave., 505/425-6761, $45 s, $63 d) gets less press than its rival on the plaza, but you can't beat the price. Hotel rooms will appeal to those with basic tastes—who don't mind mismatched furniture and styles—but the small rooms are clean and the vast, tile-floor lobby is relaxing. You're also right next to an excellent restaurant, and there's pretty much always a vacancy.

If the budget allows, the ★ **Plaza Hotel** (230 N. Plaza, 505/425-3591, www.plazahotellvnm.com) is beautiful, the grandest building on the main square. The standard rooms ($89) are perfectly nice, but the deluxe rooms and suites ($129-149), in the original building, have the most atmosphere, with towering ceilings, velvet drapes, and stately antiques. Grab a seat on a colorful hand-painted chair—originals from La Fonda in Santa Fe—for coffee in the morning; full breakfast is served at an additional fee in the dining room.

Under the same ownership as the Plaza Hotel, the storied **Castañeda Hotel** (524 Railroad Ave, 505/425-3591, castanedahotel.org, from $129) reopened its doors to overnight guests in April 2019 for the first time in over 70 years. While finishing touches remain, extensive and tasteful renovations have breathed life into the property, which now rivals its sister hotel in town in terms of historical significance and handsome décor. At the time of publication, just over a dozen suites had been remodeled with period furnishings and modern amenities, with the remaining rooms available for stays in the coming months.

INFORMATION

The Las Vegas **visitors center** (500 Railroad Ave., 505/425-3707, www.visitlasvegasnm.com, 9am-5pm daily), run by the City of Las Vegas, occupies a tiny office in the former rail depot where Lincoln Street dead-ends at the tracks.

Tome on the Range (158 Bridge St., 505/454-9944, 10am-6pm daily) is an excellent bookstore, with a fine selection of local history and other Western lore, along with all the best sellers.

GETTING THERE

By car, Las Vegas is 65 miles (about 1 hour) east of Santa Fe via I-25, and 107 miles (1.5 hours) south of Raton. From Taos over the pass through Mora is 75 miles (nearly 2 hours).

Amtrak (800/872-7245, www.amtrak.com) stops at the nicely remodeled old train depot, with service once daily each way from Chicago and Los Angeles. As a weekend trip, you could take the train up from Albuquerque—it takes about three hours and costs $28. There is no Greyhound service.

Mora Valley

Highway 518 heads north from Las Vegas, along the Sangre de Cristo foothills. It eventually turns west to begin the ascent over the mountains—here you'll find the communities of La Cueva and Mora, which are culturally and historically linked with the Hispano towns on the other side of the range, such as Peñasco. A drive through here will take only a few hours (or the better part of a day, if you come during raspberry season), but several mountain retreats might entice you to stay awhile.

MORPHY LAKE STATE PARK

Gem-like Morphy Lake State Park (575/387-2328, www.emnrd.state.nm.us, $5/car) used to be one of the most difficult-to-reach parks in New Mexico. The narrow road up to the lake, off Highway 94 (turn in Sapello), has finally been paved, however. Once you get there, the lake is open only to rowboats or electric-engine craft, so the quiet isn't disturbed. The deep-blue water is stocked with trout and ringed with tall ponderosa pines, which provide shade for the campsites (no hookups; $8). At the time of publication the park was closed for renovation; call first to confirm that it has reopened.

LA CUEVA

At the junction of Highways 518 and 442, La Cueva is no longer a town, but a national historic site. It was settled as part of the Mora Land Grant in the early 19th century, and the old mill, built in the 1870s, still creaks and clanks as the *acequia* streams over the waterwheel, which generated electricity for nearby homes until 1949. To the northeast, the small adobe San Rafael Mission Church displays the French Gothic windows in vogue in 1862, when it was built. Salman Ranch (575/387-2900, www.salmanraspberryranch.com) occupies some of the La Cueva outbuildings,

and it has built beautiful rambling gardens inside the mill complex's old adobe walls. These are a wonderful place to stretch or enjoy a picnic in the summertime. The you-pick raspberry farm is open late August-mid-October, depending on the weather, as is a basic café to feed hungry pickers (11am-4pm Thurs.-Sun.). Year-round, the farm store (9am-5pm daily July-Dec., 9am-4pm Thurs.-Mon. Jan.-June) sells raspberry jam and vinegar, fresh berries (in season), and other local foodstuffs.

MORA AND CLEVELAND

The center of the 1835 land grant and of the lush valley, the town of Mora is also the county seat—though it's no bustling metropolis. Visitors often come for Tapetes de Lana (Hwy. 518, 575/387-2247, www.moravalleyspinningmill.com, 9am-5pm Mon.-Fri., 9am-4pm Sat., 10am-2pm Sun.), at the main intersection in Mora. Inside, locally spun yarn from the nearby mill, and handwoven rugs are for sale. Guided tours of the mill are available as well. The group works with Churro sheep and locally raised alpaca wool.

About a mile down the road in the neighboring village, the Cleveland Roller Mill Museum (Hwy. 518, 575/387-2645, www.clevelandrollermillmuseum.org, 10am-3pm Sat.-Sun. Memorial Day-Labor Day, $3) is a two-story adobe structure built around 1900 and kept in use until the mid-1950s. It doesn't look very impressive from the outside, but the building houses a complex system of heavy-duty machinery, from the massive steel rollers that crushed the wheat to the "sock dusters" that absorbed the potentially explosive flour dust. Everything's intact and put into use every Labor Day weekend for the annual Millfest, when there's also live music and arts and crafts booths.

Food and Accommodations

At the south end of Mora, **Hatcha's Café** (Hwy. 518 at Hwy. 434, 575/387-9299, 10:30am-7pm Mon.-Fri., 9am-2pm Sun., $8) does a mean green-chile stew and their blue corn enchiladas are baked just right and drip with melted cheese. If you visit in the summer, don't leave without trying their Hatcha's Crisp—ice cream with cinnamon sopaipilla pockets and your choice of topping.

Across from the Cleveland Roller Mill Museum, **Mora Inn & RV Park** (765 Hwy. 518, 575/387-5230, www.morainn.com) is a quiet spot to bunk for the night, though the motel rooms are worn and dated ($65 d); there are also campsites for RVs ($25) and tents ($10). It also has a cozy café, **Krystal's Korner Kafe** (7am-6:30pm Mon.-Fri., 7:30am-6:30pm Sat., 7:30am-3pm Sun., $7), where the pinto beans are especially good.

The Northern Plains

New Mexico's plains are a subtly shifting blanket of gold, brown, or green, depending on the season. This requires a certain mindset to appreciate. The trick is to stop craving switchbacks, vertigo-inducing vistas, and all the other adrenaline-fueled drama of the mountains. Then you'll find this area incredibly relaxing, as the low-hanging, little fluffy clouds spread out to the horizon. After a bit of driving, you'll begin to discern the smallest changes: a shimmer of silver where a certain grass flourishes, or the brief contrast afforded by a dark rock outcropping.

As pleasant as the views are, there's very little to do. The major public lands, the Kiowa and Rita Blanca National Grasslands, are virtually indistinguishable from the surrounding private ranches and offer little in the way of recreation. The whole area is home to herds of pronghorn, some elk, and thousands and thousands of cows, the lifeblood of the economy. It's modern cowboy country, but it's also scarred by the traumatic Dust Bowl years, when dirt lay in drifts up to the fence posts. Some of the older locals still recall those hard times. In the unreconstructed small towns, there are few galleries or other signs of modern gentrification. If you're interested in prehistoric goings-on, though, the place is fascinating. Dinosaurs roamed through the mud, and then so-called Folsom Man hunted bison during the last ice age; you can see the lingering evidence in several places.

FORT UNION NATIONAL MONUMENT

On a barren plain 80 miles from Santa Fe, **Fort Union National Monument** (Hwy. 161, 505/425-8025, www.nps.gov/foun, 8am-5pm daily June-Aug., 8am-4pm daily Sept.-May, free) was the largest military depot in the Southwest, located strategically where the two branches of the Santa Fe Trail joined. Built largely of adobe, the fort has melted away, leaving not much more than the outlines of the buildings; however, you can still get an idea just how vast the complex was, and the experience is heightened by audio clips that play in front of buildings like the jail and the latrine.

It took three tries to build the fort. The first, made of logs, was built in 1851 as a base for campaigns against Apache raiders, but it soon rotted away. A second was a star-shaped earthen fortification built in a hurry to defend against a rumored Confederate attack in 1861; fortunately, the Union triumphed in the Battle of Glorieta Pass, just a year later, and the troops could abandon the muddy hovel.

The third structure, the stone and adobe outlines of which are preserved today, had relatively luxurious officers' quarters and plenty of room for both a military post and a very busy supply depot for items on the trade route.

Along the Santa Fe Trail

Whether Bing Crosby is crooning about it, Ronald Reagan is riding along it, or a modern traveler is retracing it, the Santa Fe Trail has earned a certain golden glow in American popular culture. The route, which cut across the frontier from Missouri to the middle of New Mexico, was used for less than 60 years, but it has become one of the great symbols of American westward expansion, all bundled up with the era when the cowboy and his horse were the masters of the new land.

The trail holds up well under the pressure of symbolism, especially when you consider the effort it took to traverse its 900 miles. A certain entrepreneur named William Becknell is credited with making the first trading trip, in 1821, without even knowing yet that the Mexican government, newly independent from Spain, had opened the borders of Nuevo México to outsiders. When Becknell was welcomed in Santa Fe, rather than imprisoned, and made a profit of 2,000 percent on his first load of calico cloth, it wasn't long before wagons loaded with more than three tons of goods were groaning across the plains.

Not that it was easy money. On this highway, wagons took close to three months to make the trip. At the far edge of Kansas, traders had to make a choice: the slow-going Mountain Route through frigid Colorado and the brutal Raton Pass, or the level and easy Cimarron Cut-off, where wagon trains faced scarce water and attacks by Comanche and Apache raiders. The biggest wagon trains, bursting with everything from basic cotton cloth to fripperies like parasols and playing cards, had no choice but to take the latter. Despite the dangers, the traders forged on, driven by dreams of profit. In the process, they also carried the dreams of the expansionist United States—an abstract concept until the U.S. Army used the Santa Fe Trail for supply caravans when it went to war with Mexico in 1846.

So many tons of trade goods and, later, settlers to the new American territory were hauled along the plains that in places, the earth is still scored by wagon ruts. But even such an influential, profitable trail was not a permanent one. First the trail shortened as America's frontier border moved west, then the railroad displaced it entirely. But perhaps the very fact that the Santa Fe Trail was outmoded so quickly by more modern technology is what has fixed it so well in the American imagination.

But like so many settlements in New Mexico, Fort Union became obsolete when the railroad was laid through the state, and by 1891, after less than three decades of use, the massive installation was decommissioned.

Walk out northeast from the ruins to see the ghostly imprints of wagon ruts from the Santa Fe Trail—they're most visible early or late in the day. If able, try to time your visit for one of the special events that focus on what is above you rather than before you—the combination of fort remnants and so little light pollution makes for awe-inspiring night sky astronomy sessions and tours.

EAST FROM WAGON MOUND

Named for a rock outcropping that faintly resembles a Conestoga wagon, the small town at exit 387 on I-25 is the turning point for Roy—a pretty route to Clayton, preferable to U.S. 56 from Springer. There's not much here but a couple of gas stations, though on Labor Day weekend, Wagon Mound hosts **Bean Day** (http://beanday100.com), a harvest celebration more than a century old, with a bean cleaning party, rodeos, a free barbecue, and a big parade—bigger than the tiny downtown can hold, so it runs through twice.

Highway 120 to Roy

You're really getting off here for Highway 120, which heads east across flatlands that are often surprisingly green. Another surprise: the dip down into Canadian River Canyon, striated with red and white. The road then heads to **Roy**—home to not quite 250 people, giving it the dubious title of the largest town in Harding County. Its last claim to fame was that Western-swing bandleader Bob Wills penned "San Antonio Rose" here in 1927, as he worked as a barber by day. At the time, Roy was a shipping point for coal to Tucumcari and a major dry-ice manufacturing site, thanks to its location on top of the Bravo Dome carbon-dioxide field.

Places to eat around Roy are decidedly limited, which helps make **Lonita's Café** (275 Richelieu St., 575/485-0191, 11am-6pm Mon.-Fri., 8am-6pm Sat., 8am-2pm Sun.) that much more appealing. There are plenty of New Mexican dishes to choose from, as well as a satisfying chicken-fried steak and a belt-adjusting hot fudge pie for dessert.

La Frontera del Llano Scenic Byway

Although the drive from Wagon Mound is arguably more awe-inspiring, Highway 39, which runs north and south from Roy, is an *official* scenic route, a section of La Frontera del Llano Scenic Byway. To the south and east, the "Edge of the Plains" route goes to the cattle-ranching centers of **Mosquero** and **Bueyeros,** passing pink-striped buttes, a string of beautiful old churches, and dilapidated little bars. Mosquero, population 92, has become a colorful destination as high school students, overseen by artist Doug Quarles, have painted murals depicting Harding County history on several downtown storefronts. At Bueyeros, you can turn south to follow the byway to its end at Logan (near Ute Lake State Park and I-40), or head north to make a roundabout route up to Clayton.

Back at Roy, the byway follows the northern stretch of Highway 39 through the **Kiowa and Rita Blanca National Grasslands.** The 230,000 acres of short-grass prairie are federally managed to maintain the natural flora, so as to avoid a repeat of the 1930s devastation. The land is home to quail, bobcats, and lots of pronghorn, but don't expect pristine wilderness—cattle are still allowed to graze here. You can camp at one of the 12 primitive sites at **Mills Canyon,** 10 miles north of Roy on Highway 39, then about 9 miles west,

on Mills Canyon Road #600 where a narrow, rocky road leads 800 feet down into the canyon. A former commercial farm, the sheltered river bottom still harbors a few fruit trees, as well as wildlife such as mule deer and Barbary sheep, introduced in 1950. During dry summers, the campground can be closed due to fire danger—call the grasslands headquarters in Clayton (575/374-9652) to check the status before heading out. It can be a bone-jarring ride at times; a 4x4 vehicle is advised.

Highway 39, and the scenic byway, ends at Abbott (describing it as a "town" is generous), at the junction with U.S. 56—from here, it's virtually a straight shot east to Clayton.

SPRINGER

At the I-25 exit for U.S. 56, which runs directly to Clayton, the tiny town of Springer was formerly named Maxwell, for Lucien B. Maxwell, whose land grant covered all of Colfax County. It was also the county seat between 1882 and 1898 (Raton now holds the title). When political power moved away, so did most of the action. Now there's not much here except a handful of antiques stores, the largest and most obsessively organized of which is **Jespersen's Cache** (403 Maxwell Ave., 575/483-2349, by appointment only).

CLAYTON

Only 12 miles from Texas, Clayton is a place where most of the 3,000 people in town spend their days on horseback or otherwise engaged in the large cattle operations on the surrounding ranches and feedlots. (If the wind blows the wrong way, the smell is hard to ignore, though on a crisp autumn evening, there's a positive spin: You definitely get a sense of place.) By night, attention focuses on the gem of a vintage movie theater or the high school football stadium. The big annual event is the rodeo on Fourth of July weekend, and there are easily more churches than restaurants in town. In short, you're a long way from Santa Fe.

Clayton was established relatively late by New Mexican standards—in 1888, well after

Clayton

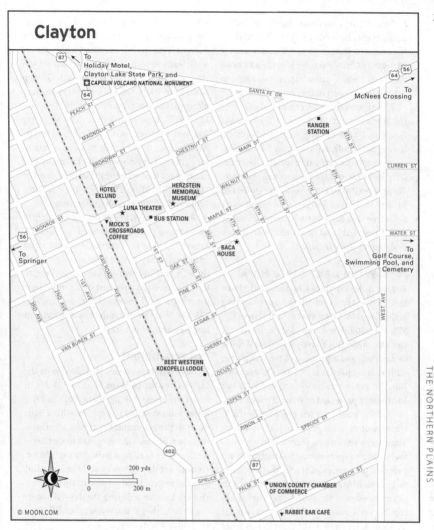

the railroad cut through. But it soon rocketed to notoriety as the place where outlaw Thomas "Black Jack" Ketchum met his end, two years after he was picked up for attempting to rob a train near Folsom.

Sights

Bone up on local history at the interesting **Herzstein Memorial Museum** (22 S. 2nd St., 575/374-2977, 10am-5pm Tues.-Sat. May-Oct., 10am-4pm Tues.-Sat. Sept.-Apr., free), a collection of local ephemera bequeathed to the town by a prominent shopkeeper. Spread over two floors of a stately 1919 Methodist church, the displays are kept sparkling and dust-free, with period furniture, clothing, and medical equipment alongside vitrines dedicated to local luminaries such as Cowgirl Hall of Famer and single mom Bernice McLaughlin. There's also a small but fascinating display on the Dust Bowl. Tucked away in a small hall are photographs of Black Jack Ketchum being hanged on the courthouse square in 1901, a grisly event that ended in his accidental beheading. Ketchum (both parts) is buried in the **cemetery** (Princeton Ave.), in the southeast corner of town. During winter, call ahead to make sure it's open during posted hours.

The thorough sightseer can also cruise the **Baca House** (320 Oak St.), where the fence and gate are the work of Dionicio Rodríguez, a folk artist known for his elaborate faux-bois cement creations, particularly in Brackenridge Park in San Antonio, Texas, as well as in Little Rock, Arkansas, and Memphis, Tennessee. The Oak Street work dates from the early 1940s, commissioned by a well-traveled land speculator who'd seen Rodríguez's work in Texas.

★ Clayton Lake State Park

Fifteen miles north of Clayton, sunk down just below the level of the surrounding plain, **Clayton Lake State Park** (Hwy. 370, 575/374-8808, www.emnrd.state.nm.us, $5/car, $8 camping) is a lovely haven for day use or camping and a prime spot for stargazing, with viewing parties at its Lake Observatory. But the real attraction is the **dinosaur footprints** preserved in stone at the east end of the lake, one of the few places such trackways are open to the public in the Southwest. Made some 100 million years ago in what was then mud, the approximate 500 footprints are part of a long series of tracks that stretches to Fort Collins, Colorado, a route that ran along the edge of an ancient sea. They're accessible via a quarter-mile-long recreational trail—look for signs to the right as you enter the park. Try to go early in the morning or in late afternoon, when the longer shadows make the prints stand out more clearly. The **visitors center** (8am-4:30pm daily) also has a small display about dinosaur life in this area.

Sports and Recreation

McNees Crossing gets frequent mention in tourist literature, but even true Santa Fe Trail enthusiasts will find the trail ford a bit underwhelming; look for the marker on Highway 406, east and north of Clayton. Better to head for another point in the **Kiowa and Rita Blanca National Grasslands** where a short walk leads to some better-preserved wagon ruts, as well as a ruined homestead. Getting to the unofficial trailhead requires zigzagging along dirt ranch-access roads. Head east on U.S. 64/56, then 13 miles north on Highway 406; turn left (west) on Campbell Road and go 3 miles, then north 1 mile to a small pullout for parking. On your way out of Clayton, you might want to stop at the grasslands' **ranger station** (714 Main St., 575/374-9652, 8am-12pm and 12:30pm-4:30pm) for a map.

Should you need to cool off, the **municipal swimming pool** (Water St., 575/374-8014, 8am-7:30pm daily summer) is a good-sized outdoor facility with a kiddie slide. It's on the east side of town—go through the gate to the armory and the airport. A nine-hole **municipal golf course** (4 Airport Park Rd., 575/374-9643) works on the honor system, so stop by any time to tee off.

Entertainment

If you're a vintage cinema buff, don't miss the **Luna Theater** (4 Main St., 575/374-2712), under the neon winking moon. Built in 1916, it was redone in 1935, complete with a ballroom in the basement. Pay the $7 admission regardless of what's showing, just to see the recently restored and positively glowing interior, set with art deco sconces and the beautiful original embroidered velvet curtain. You can also try knocking during the day—if someone's there, they'll show you around. Shows are Friday-Sunday only.

Food

The **Hotel Eklund** (15 Main St., 575/374-2551, 11am-1:30pm and 4:30pm-8pm Mon.-Wed., 10:30am-9pm Sat.-Sun., $10) is a major hub for lunch and dinner, and a great excuse to sit in the front saloon (though now, sadly,

1: Fort Union National Monument **2:** Mock's Crossroads Coffee in Clayton **3:** Hotel Eklund in Clayton **4:** dinosaur tracks dotting Clayton Lake State Park

the 1850s wood bar can only serve beer and wine). The menu has the usual mix of steaks ($15-25), New Mexican standards, and burgers, but a lot is made from scratch, including dangerously sweet desserts.

The other popular spot—which doesn't mean it's great—open for breakfast, too, is the Rabbit Ear Café (1201 S. 1st St., 575/374-3277, 10:30am-8pm Tues.-Thurs., 7am-8pm Fri.-Sat., $5-9). American cheese and white bread are cornerstones of the menu, but the chile is hot and the burritos are stuffed. Either way, it's a good slice of life in Clayton.

The other option is Mock's Crossroads Coffee (2 S. Front St., 575/374-5282, 7am-3pm Mon.-Fri., 8am-11am Sat., $4), a funky wood-paneled place in the old feed store that also happens to be an unlikely outpost of superb espresso and coffee drinks made with house-roasted beans. It serves a different sandwich, soup, and salad every day; breakfast burritos and biscuits and gravy are on offer in the morning and there's an ample selection of pastries.

Accommodations

Clayton has a remarkable number of fine places to sleep. Locally owned independent Holiday Motel (U.S. 87, 575/374-2558, $65 s, $79 d) is a gem, well kept and scrupulously clean. The owners are so enthusiastic, they fold the towels into elephants. It's on the northwest edge of town, about a quarter-mile out from the big bridge.

Downtown at the main crossroads, Hotel Eklund (15 Main St., 575/446-1939, www.hoteleklund.com, $99 d) is a three-story trove of history, with a cool saloon. Rooms are spare, with metal bedsteads, lace curtains, and clean bathrooms with honeycomb tiles and pedestal sinks. Rooms on the front (east) side are preferable to those on the west, to dampen freight-train noise. Rates include a hot breakfast, often with made-there quiche.

If you want a pool, head to Best Western Kokopelli Lodge (702 S. 1st St., 575/374-2589, www.bestwestern.com, $119 d). It's a million times nicer than it has to be, considering the feeble competition from the other chain hotels: big outdoor swimming area, wireless Internet, a free hot breakfast buffet, and plush, spacious rooms.

Information

The Clayton-Union County Chamber of Commerce (1103 S. 1st St., 575/374-9253, www.claytonnm.org, 9am-4pm Mon.-Fri. Sept.-May, 9am-4pm daily June-Aug.) has plenty of brochures, plus souvenir Dust Bowl postcards and free wireless Internet.

Getting There

By car, Clayton is 84 miles (1.5 hours) east along U.S. 56/412 from Springer at I-25, and about the same distance from Raton via U.S. 64/87. From Santa Fe, it's about 220 miles (3.5 hours).

Greyhound (800/231-2222, www.greyhound.com) runs through once a day, but only via Amarillo, Texas, dropping you off at the station (113 E. Walnut St., 575/374-6207, 8am-5pm Mon.-Fri.).

WEST TO RATON

U.S. 64/87 heads roughly northwest out of Clayton, another hypnotizing drive through golden prairie. The terrain changes a bit halfway along, as defunct volcanoes punctuate the horizon. The most distinctive is the perfectly conical peak of Capulin; a drive up to the top (an adventure in itself) gives you a break from all the flatness, as well as a stunning view.

From Capulin, you can detour north to the ghost town of Folsom, a starting point for two smaller, more scenic roads. Backtrack east along a rough byway through the washes and ridges strung along the border with Colorado, or keep heading west on Highway 72, which takes you across a dramatic high mesa, the perfect way to meet the mountains at Raton.

1: the view from Capulin Volcano 2: a lone church on the top of Johnson Mesa

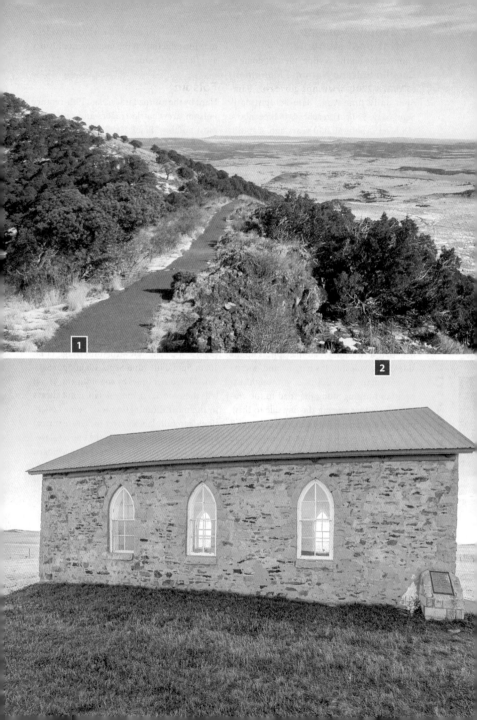

★ Capulin Volcano National Monument

Unmissable on the skyline, the soft dome of **Capulin Volcano National Monument** (575/278-2201, www.nps.gov/cavo, 8am-5pm daily June-Aug., 8am-4:30pm daily Sept.-May, $20/car) reaches 8,182 feet above sea level. About 60,000 years ago, Capulin spewed hot ash and rock into the air, which settled into an almost perfect cone—its top edge looks like a carefully opened soft-boiled egg. From the summit you can see more clearly how this whole region was shaped by volcanic activity, from the lava-topped mesas to the hulking Sierra Grande. The latter formation is another dormant volcano, about a million years old, that's also the largest lone mountain in the United States, covering 50 square miles and rising 2,200 feet above the surrounding plain. Ranger talks at the crater in summer at 11am and 1pm (free) can point out more details.

To reach the top of Capulin, you have to negotiate a two-mile road that spirals up the side of the volcano. It's narrow and doesn't have as many guardrails as you might expect (and hiking along the road to the crater is forbidden during the day due to this); put your steeliest driver in charge, and take it slow. It's much easier coming down, as you're on the inside lane. Keep an eye out for bald eagles at the top, and watch out for mule deer in the road around the base. The area at the top has limited parking, so if you're visiting in the busy months of July and August, go very early or late in the day, or you'll have to wait to drive up.

HIKING

At the summit, you can walk the quarter-mile **Crater Vent Trail** down into the crater, where steam vents are noticeable in the winter, as the surrounding patches are covered with greenery. A longer option is the paved one-mile **Crater Rim Trail**, which has a few fairly steep climbs and takes you around the volcano's circumference. Much less taxing and acrophobia inducing, is the **interpretive** trail near the visitors center, which provides a nice introduction to the monument's history and flora and fauna.

Folsom

Hard by the railroad tracks, late 19th-century Folsom drew cattle-traders and outlaws—most notably "Black Jack" Ketchum, whose gang held up trains three times here. In 1908, a flood demolished a good part of the town, and even claimed the life of the village telephone operator, who stayed at her post to warn residents of danger. Around the same time, floods also uncovered a collection of bison skeletons embedded with spear points in a wash west of town. When the site was excavated in 1927, the spear points were determined to be at least 10,000 years old—a shock to archaeologists, who'd previously thought American Indians had arrived on the continent only around 2000 BC.

In an old general store at the intersection of Highways 325 and 456, **Folsom Museum** (575/278-2122, www.folsomvillage.com, 10am-5pm daily June-Sept., 10am-5pm Sat.-Sun. May, other times by appointment, $1.50) tells these stories in more detail, if not always in the most illuminating way. Some collections (carefully labeled river rocks) are surreal and cryptic; others, such as the one on slave-turned-cowboy-and-accidental-archaeologist George McJunkin, are genuinely illuminating. Perhaps the best item is the odd diorama of the Ketchum hanging.

Dry Cimarron Byway

A network of rural highways stretching into Colorado and Oklahoma, this route roughly follows the path of the Dry Cimarron River, with Highway 456 as the backbone; it eventually winds up back in Clayton.

About 3.5 miles northeast of Folsom on Highway 456, on the right (southeast) side of the road, look for a pullout and a sign warning against swimming. A small trail leads a short way to **Folsom Falls**, where water pours directly out of the rock face. It's visible from the edge of the shallow canyon, but you'll need to clamber down the rocks to get to the water's edge.

From here, Highway 456 zigzags across the river bottom as it heads east. At the junction with Highway 370, you can drive south to Clayton Lake State Park, but if you continue east, you'll pass towering buttes dubbed Battleship and Wedding Cake. You then loop back to Clayton via Highway 406.

Johnson Mesa

If time (and weather—the road is often closed in winter due to snow) permits, don't skip the drive along Highway 72 out of Folsom, one of the most beautiful in New Mexico. The narrow paved byway dips and rises, roller-coaster-like, as it gradually climbs the foothills, and then you're deposited on the top of **Johnson Mesa,** a bucolic expanse of grazing land studded with smaller hills, including the perfectly round Red Mountain. At one point, the road passes close to the mesa edge, and you can see the land plunge away. About the only evidence of human habitation up here is a small stone church, **St. John's Methodist,** built in 1897. No one lives on the mesa regularly now, though a few hardy souls come up for the summer along with the livestock. If you drive this way at dusk, watch out for deer on the road, even on the outskirts of Raton.

The Rockies

Where the laden caravans of traders struggled through Raton Pass on the Santa Fe Trail's mountain route, drivers now zip up with ease. Raton is still a watering hole, but it sates visitors with fast-food restaurants and travel centers; go beyond the off-ramp economy to see the town's century-old core, laid out along the railroad depot. South and west of Raton, smaller Cimarron was another stopping point on the mountain route, and one that wears its history well.

RATON

The glowing red RATON sign on the hilltop on the northwest side of town suggests a bit more glitz than this mountain burg currently has. But traces of past glamour remain in the sturdy downtown, in the art deco fire station on North 2nd Street, for instance, the quirky castle facade of the El Raton Theatre, and the elegant Colfax County Building on North 3rd Street.

Raton is defined entirely by the mountain behind it. In 1866, an entrepreneur by the name of Richens Wootton took it upon himself to blast out a proper road through the mountains over Raton Pass, wide enough to accommodate wagon trains—then he set up a toll gate and charged Santa Fe Trail traders to come through. "Uncle Dick," as he was known, sold his road to the AT&SF Railroad for $1 and a lifetime grocery stipend. The railroad helped keep the town of Raton in money, too, and some wealth came from coal mining in the surrounding mountains, though nothing like the giddy get-rich-quick silver and gold mines in the south. All of this was enough to bring big theaters and the first public school in the state—though, like everywhere in the late 19th-century West, Raton had its fair share of lynchings, mob violence, and more.

Now it's more peaceful, overlooking the plains to the east, but with its heart in the Rockies. If you are just passing through, note that nearly everything shuts on Sunday—you'll be hard-pressed to find somewhere to eat outside of the usual chains.

Sights

The gem of 2nd Street is the rococo **Shuler Theater** auditorium (131 N. 2nd St., 575/445-4746, www.shulertheater.com), beautifully restored by the town and used for live performances. Visitors can tour the theater weekdays 9am-5pm when there's someone

Raton

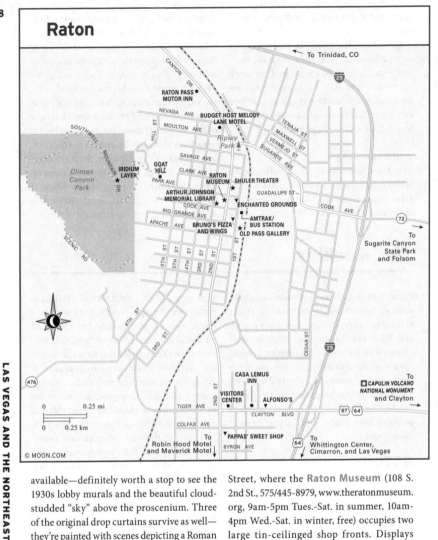

To Trinidad, CO

RATON PASS
MOTOR INN

BUDGET HOST MELODY
LANE MOTEL

Ripley
Park

GOAT
HILL

IRIDIUM
LAYER

Climax
Canyon
Park

RATON
MUSEUM

SHULER THEATER

ARTHUR JOHNSON
MEMORIAL LIBRARY

ENCHANTED GROUNDS

AMTRAK/
BUS STATION

BRUNO'S PIZZA
AND WINGS

OLD PASS GALLERY

To
Sugarite Canyon
State Park
and Folsom

CASA LEMUS
INN

VISITORS
CENTER

ALFONSO'S

CAPULIN VOLCANO
NATIONAL MONUMENT
and Clayton

To

PAPPAS' SWEET SHOP

To
Robin Hood Motel
and Maverick Motel

To
Whittington Center,
Cimarron, and Las Vegas

0   0.25 mi

0   0.25 km

© MOON.COM

available—definitely worth a stop to see the 1930s lobby murals and the beautiful cloud-studded "sky" above the proscenium. Three of the original drop curtains survive as well—they're painted with scenes depicting a Roman villa, the palisade cliffs near Cimarron, and Raton's Ripley Park. Building the theater was a bit of a battle, as the city council used money that had been earmarked for a new city hall. Later, the municipal auditorium was named in honor of the mayor who'd perpetrated the boondoggle, in a council resolution that was worded to effectively tell Raton residents, "See, we told you you'd love it."

The main thoroughfare for cars is 2nd

Street, where the **Raton Museum** (108 S. 2nd St., 575/445-8979, www.theratonmuseum. org, 9am-5pm Tues.-Sat. in summer, 10am-4pm Wed.-Sat. in winter, free) occupies two large tin-ceilinged shop fronts. Displays about the coal camps and other facets of local life are nicely presented, along with vintage dolls, works by Taos painters, and some good *santero* carvings in the front upstairs area.

Pick up a walking-tour brochure here or at the visitors center to guide you along 1st Street, Raton's **historic downtown** where the handsome old storefronts are trimmed in cast-iron garlands, graceful figureheads, and jutting cornices. Business isn't exactly booming, but there are a few antiques shops and the **Old Pass Gallery** (145 S. 1st St., 575/445-2052, 10am-4:30pm Tues.-Sat.), run by the local arts council. It occupies a renovated Wells Fargo office, and next door is the train depot, the only surviving building of a huge complex that used to manage the comings and goings of more than 60 trains a day.

You could also seek out the **Arthur Johnson Memorial Library** (244 Cook Ave., 575/445-9711, 1pm-6pm Mon., 10am-6pm Tues.-Wed. and Fri.-Sat., 10am-9pm Thurs.), between 2nd and 3rd Streets, a neoclassical structure built as a post office in 1917, then converted to a library under the Carnegie program. It houses a good collection of Southwest-themed art, including some of the early Taos artists.

By car, you can head up **Goat Hill,** where the RATON sign is perched; take Moulton Avenue west to Hill Street. This hill is geologically famous, as it has a visible stripe of iridium running through it—the stripe of detritus that marks the meteorite crash that ended the dinosaurs. Just before the top of the hill, bear right rather than left at the fork—this dirt road will carry you around the ridgeline a few miles to a marked spot (simply "Iridium Layer") and a scenic overlook.

Sports and Recreation

An eight-mile drive from Raton, **Sugarite Canyon State Park** (211 Hwy. 526, 575/445-5607, www.emnrd.state.nm.us, $5/car) encompasses 3,600 acres along either side of Chicorica Creek. In 2011, the Track Fire burned much of the large trees on the hillsides, making the campgrounds ($8 per site) and trails here less scenic than it once was, but Lake Maloya is still a charming destination for trout fishing and casual boating. From behind the visitors center, two miles up Highway 526, the **Coal Camp Trail** runs through the ruins of a mining settlement and up to two old mine shafts; a few longer trails lead up to the bluffs that line the road and one trails the lake's shoreline—ask at the visitors center for maps.

Hunting is a very big deal in the high mountains around Raton. **Whittington Center** (Hwy. 64, 575/445-3615, www.nrawc.org), a 52-square-mile complex established in 1973 by the National Rifle Association, is a starting point for many hunters. It's the largest gun club in the United States, offering classes for beginners and experts (from $300), target and skeet shooting at the range (from $20/day), plus real-life hunting for deer, pronghorn, and elk. There's also space for tent and RV camping (from $12) or simple cabins (from $40 d).

Entertainment

A quirky castle facade marks **El Raton Theatre** (115 N. 2nd St., 575/445-7008, www.elratontheatre.com, 7pm Thurs.-Sat., 4pm and 7pm Sun.), a movie palace built in 1929, now souped up with a digital projector for first-run films. If you want a peek inside during the day, just knock—if someone's free, they're happy to let you in and show you around.

Food

Raton's restaurants have limited opening hours, and if you don't plan well, you'll be relegated to the fast-food joints on Clayton Boulevard. For morning coffee, **Enchanted Grounds Espresso Bar** (111 Park Ave., 575/445-2129, 7am-4pm Mon.-Fri., 8am-2pm Sat.) is the place to go; it also serves breakfast burritos, egg sandwiches, and light lunches.

Pappas' Sweet Shop (1201 S. 2nd St., 575/445-9811, 10am-2pm Mon., 8am-2pm Thurs.-Sun., $7-12) bears mention just because it's the longest-running restaurant in town. In fact, the atmosphere can be a bit geriatric, but fair enough, since it's been going since 1923. It has a vintage soda fountain and American classics like chicken salad and an assortment of burgers and New Mexican fare such as stuffed sopaipillas and burrito plates on the menu.

Locally owned **Bruno's Pizza and Wings** (133 Cook Ave., 575/445-9512, 11am-8pm Mon. and Wed.-Thurs., 11am-9pm Fri.-Sat., noon-8pm Sun., $12) serves just what you'd

expect from the name, with solid and extensive takes on both paired with plenty of sports on the TVs.

Alfonso's (412 Clayton Rd., 575/445-8022, 8am-8:30pm Mon.-Sat., 9am-5pm Sun., $8) is open a little bit later than other places—though you'll be dining in one end of a Conoco gas station. The setup is fast-food-y, but the food is good, authentic Mexican.

Accommodations

Most chain motels are on Clayton Boulevard, which runs from exit 451 off I-25—but some of the old-time independent options here, at the north and south ends of town, will restore your faith in American roadside hospitality. On the north side, **Raton Pass Motor Inn** (308 Canyon Dr., 575/445-3641, www. ratonpassmotorinn.com, $70 d) is an excellent choice. The 1950s exterior sports jazzy green-and-salmon paint; inside, the 14 large rooms are each decorated with a theme befitting that era and include Wi-Fi, mini-fridges, and microwaves.

Just to the south, the ★ **Budget Host Melody Lane Motel** (136 Canyon Dr., 575/445-3655, www.budgethost.com, $53 d) is remarkable for its nifty slant-ceiling rooms, eight of which have a vintage steam sauna built into the tub, a real treat after a long drive. Rooms are meticulously clean and come with a continental breakfast.

On the south side of town, **Robin Hood Motel** (1354 S. 2nd St., 575/445-5577, www. robinhoodmotelusa.com, $72 d, open May-Sept. only) is yet another fine old-style inn, though a touch more up-to-date than others. Behind butter-yellow doors are fairly standard modern motel trappings, though the groovy original orange linoleum shows in some bathrooms. There's also a small outdoor pool.

At the southernmost edge, just by the I-25 on-ramp, the ★ **Maverick Motel** (1510 S. 2nd St., 575/445-3792, $45 s, $62 d) is the

1: Raton's stately Shuler Theater and El Raton Theatre **2:** view from Raton's Goat Hill **3:** Budget Host Melody Lane Motel in Raton **4:** the Old Aztec Mill Museum in Cimarron

greatest throwback of all, a block of 10 snug rooms straight from the 1940s, maintained by a man who seems stuck in that decade himself. Pale-blue chenille bedspreads, screen doors, and even an old soda machine will make you feel like you're sleeping in a museum, in the best way. Fair warning: That means no Wi-Fi, not even a website. But connoisseurs of Americana ought to pick up the phone and reserve, before the owner decides to retire.

If you prefer motels of a slightly more recent vintage, **Casa Lemus Inn** (350 Clayton Rd., 575/448-5538, www.casalemus.com, $89 d) is another decent option, with spacious and clean rooms. There's also a small outdoor pool in summer. Rates include a continental breakfast, and the Casa Lemus Restaurant, which serves passable steaks and diner fare, is in the parking lot.

Information

The **New Mexico Visitor Information Center** (100 Clayton Blvd., 575/445-3689, www.raton.info, 8am-5pm daily) is maintained by both the Raton Chamber of Commerce and the state tourism board.

Getting There

By car, Raton is 83 miles (1.5 hours) from Clayton (about 20 minutes longer if you go via Johnson Mesa). From Santa Fe, it's 175 miles (2.5 hours) via I-25, and 220 miles (3.25 hours) from Denver. Cimarron is 40 miles (45 minutes) away, and Taos is 95 miles (2 hours).

Amtrak (800/872-7245, www.amtrak. com) trains pull in to the historic depot on 1st Street once each day on the eastbound and westbound routes. The trip from Albuquerque takes just under 5 hours and costs $38. The only direct **Greyhound** (800/231-2222, www. greyhound.com) buses come in from Denver, Colorado, and Amarillo, Texas, and drop you off at the station (144 S. 1st St., 575/445-9071, 8am-9am and 11am-1pm daily).

★ Valle Vidal

South of Raton, U.S. 64 bears west, away from I-25 and deeper into the mountains. About

35 miles along (5 miles east of Cimarron) is the turn for Forest Road 1950. This dirt road is the only access route (and a circuitous one) to **Valle Vidal,** a 102,000-acre chunk of the Carson National Forest that straddles some of the highest peaks in the Sangre de Cristo range. For anyone seeking pristine wilderness, Valle Vidal is perhaps the last, best place to get a sense of what New Mexico was like before mining and ranching took off in the 19th century. The area is home to the state's largest elk herd, and its watershed is essential for the now-rare Rio Grande cutthroat trout.

Though little visited, it is probably one of the best-known public lands in New Mexico, as the area was the topic of strenuous debate from 1982, when Pennzoil traded the land to the National Forest Service in exchange for tax breaks, until 2006, when a long grassroots campaign finally got a law passed to prohibit mining and drilling for natural gas.

There are no services in the wilderness, very few trails, and only two formal camping areas with no services but toilets. Coming from U.S. 64, the first one you reach is **McCrystal Campground** (late May-Oct; $8), set on a flat plain with a few ponderosas providing shade; this is where people exploring on horseback often camp. If you want more privacy, head nine more miles to the 36 sites at the higher-elevation **Cimarron Campground** (late May-Oct; $9), which are tucked amid spruce and aspen trees; many trout-fishing creeks are right nearby. For current conditions and advisories (parts of the valley are closed seasonally to protect the elk), contact the **Questa Ranger District office** (575/586-0520), on the west side, which manages the whole area.

VERMEJO PARK RANCH

Formerly part of the Maxwell Land Grant, the 200,000 acres of **Vermejo Park Ranch** (575/445-3097, www.vermejoparkranch.com) belong to media mogul and conservationist Ted Turner. Guided hunting and fishing trips go from the swanky Costilla Lodge

(from $1500) or Casa Minor (from $525); other guesthouses, as well as Turner's former home, Casa Grande, are also available to rent. The land climbs from short-grass plains to 13,000-foot peaks, and wildlife includes Rocky Mountain elk, pronghorn, and black bear—as well as the North American bison Turner raises here.

CIMARRON

This community of less than a thousand people still feels like a 19th-century mountain town. A few times a year, the streets are filled with horses being driven to various pastures on the vast Philmont ranch that adjoins the community, and the assorted rivalries of the Colfax County War are spoken of as though they happened yesterday—perhaps because so much of the town's social life takes place at the old St. James Hotel, where the ceiling is pocked with bullet holes.

But more than this violent history, the wilderness is what defines Cimarron. Established in 1861 by Lucien Maxwell, the town was the most substantial settlement on the giant land grant that Maxwell would later own outright. The surrounding mountains (and all the wildlife they harbor) still press in close; when the sun starts to set and the stars glimmer overhead, you're reminded just how small the town is. Amid so much empty land, you have to wonder what all the fighting was about . . . and was that a bear rustling in the trees?

By day, you can visit a handful of galleries on 9th Street, one block north of U.S. 64 and the old *acequia,* or watch the fish jump in the Cimarron River. You can hike between granite cliffs or tour the mansion of the oilman who ran Philmont ranch and dedicated it to the Boy Scouts of America. But at the end of the day, you'll likely be back at the St. James, drinking a beer and talking about the past.

Sights
★ ST. JAMES HOTEL
The center of Cimarron's social life, past and present, is the **St. James Hotel** (Hwy. 21/61 S.

Collison Ave., 575/376-2664, www.exstjames. com), a beautifully maintained building that's as packed with legends, lore, and (perhaps) ghosts as it is with beautiful antiques and stuffed buffalo heads. Opened first as a saloon by a French chef named Henri Lambert (former employer: Abraham Lincoln) in 1872, the St. James became a Wild West playground bar none, with just about every famed outlaw passing through its swinging doors. Buffalo Bill Cody met Annie Oakley in the saloon, Jesse James always requested the same room, and Billy the Kid, "Black Jack" Ketchum, and Wyatt Earp all signed the guest register. Cimarron was considered calm and quiet when three days passed without the sound of gunfire in the St. James; bullets are still embedded in walls and ceilings, particularly in the main dining room.

Specifically, one act of the Colfax County War played out here, when in 1875 the ranch hand and freelance gunman Clay Allison killed Francisco Griego in alleged self-defense as Griego was seeking vengeance for the murder of his nephew, the constable Cruz Vega, whom Allison had lynched, in retaliation for his alleged participation in the murder of Franklin Tolby, a young minister who supported the rights of the local settlers. Sound complicated? It was, and it only got more so, as some 200 people were killed trying to settle the debate over who got to live on the Maxwell Land Grant.

All that history still feels very present in the chandelier-lit hallways lined with peeling wallpaper. Visitors are welcome to poke around on the ground floor, where some of the guestroom doors are left open. You can also pick up a walking-tour guide to other, far less preserved monuments in the "old town" part of Cimarron.

OLD AZTEC MILL MUSEUM
Round out the local history with a visit to the Old Aztec Mill Museum (220 W. 17th St., 575/376-2417, 10am-4pm Mon.-Sat., 1-5pm Sun., June-Aug., free), four floors of fun just across the street from the hotel. Built by Lucien Maxwell in 1864, the structure now houses Boy Scouts memorabilia, relics of the Colfax County War, and a two-headed calf.

You can also visit the cemetery, a short walk south on Highway 21, where the grave of settler-rights supporter Reverend Franklin Tolby sits alongside more recent (and longer-lived) Cimarron residents.

Cimarron Canyon State Park
West of town about 12 miles, straddling U.S. 64 and stretching nearly to Eagle Nest, Cimarron Canyon State Park (575/377-6271, www.emnrd.state.nm.us, $5/car) is known for its excellent trout fishing in the Cimarron River and its tributaries, as well as the dramatic granite palisades that form the canyon walls. Of the three established campgrounds, Maverick has the best sites ($10), though several spots are fairly close to the road. Backcountry camping is not permitted.

Hiking in and around the canyon is excellent, especially on Clear Creek Trail, a 7-mile out-and-back you can do in about three hours. The route runs along a creek and passes several small waterfalls while gaining about a thousand feet; it's particularly nice in the fall when the aspens turn yellow. Look for a signed pullout on the south side of the road, around mile marker 292. Running about 6 miles one-way, Tolby Creek Trail makes a longer outing, but most of the trek is pleasantly shaded and damp, ending in beautiful high meadows. This trail is not so clearly marked—you should double-check the route at the park office, across the highway from the trailhead at the western park boundary, just before you reach the town of Eagle Nest.

Food
Cimarron has few dining options. As usual, the main action is at Lambert's in the St. James Hotel (Hwy. 21, 575/376-2664, 7am-9pm daily, $6-28). The food—burgers, steaks, and burritos—is pretty standard, though there's no doubt it suits the dark paneling and evident fondness for taxidermy. The bar here

is open 11am-midnight, or "whenever the bartender gets tired of looking at people."

There are no pretenses at ★ **Blü Dragonfly Brewing** (301 E. 9th St., 575/376-1110, 11am-9pm Mon.-Thurs., 11am-10pm Fri.-Sat. May-Oct., 11am-8pm Mon.-Thurs., 11am-9pm Fri.-Sat. Nov.-Apr., $7-20): You're in for a no-fuss meat and potatoes meal, if the checkered tablecloths didn't give it away. The menu is a veritable carnivore's delight, with smoked meat sandwiches, brisket mac-and-cheese, pulled pork, and spare ribs—all easily among the best in the state. Wash the barbecued delicacies down with their own brews, including an IPA, stout, and blonde ale.

Eight miles up the road toward Raton, the **Colfax Tavern** (32230 U.S. 64, 575/376-2229, noon-10pm Mon.-Thurs., noon-11pm Fri.-Sat., noon-9pm Sun., $9) is better known as Cold Beer, due to these very words painted in extremely large letters on the front of the building. Monday is spaghetti night, its pizza gets praise, and bands play on weekends.

Accommodations

The **St. James Hotel** (Hwy. 21, 575/376-2664, www.exstjames.com) is the obvious pick here, even if the 12 rooms in the main building have been very gently remodeled in recent years. In most cases the floors still creak atmospherically, but the bathrooms, with small tubs, are shiny. Most have private baths (from $135), and a few share a more deluxe facility in the hall (from $85). If you can't live without a TV, phone, and air-conditioning, opt for one of the 10 modern rooms in the annex (from $99).

Just up the road, the excellent-value **Cimarron Inn & RV Park** (U.S. 64, 575/376-2268, www.cimarroninn.com) offers a different taste of history: Its main building is a converted old motel with snug, thick-walled rooms, each one in a different Western theme. Four small rooms ($49) are a steal for solo travelers or couples, while the eight larger rooms ($79 d) are divvied up like tiny apartments, so there's a wall separating beds. Families or groups might like the Cowboy Cabin ($120), which sleeps up to six people, or the Casita ($250), with room for a baker's dozen.

Information

Cimarron's **visitors center** (104 N. Lincoln Ave., 575/376-2417, www.cimarronnm.com, 10am-5pm Mon.-Sat., 1pm-5pm Sun. May-Aug., hours vary Sept.-Apr.) occupies a small house just off U.S. 64. You can pick up a

the St. James Hotel in Cimarron

walking-tour brochure here, along with other background info. To really get into the history of the place, you could take the **Legends by Lantern Light tour** (575/445-8373, www. legendsbylantern.com, 7:30pm Sat. in summer, $8) to hear the tales of local outlaws.

Getting There

From Raton, Cimarron is 40 miles southwest, about a 45-minute drive on U.S. 64. Taos is 55 miles away to the west, also on U.S. 64; the drive takes about 1.5 hours.

PHILMONT SCOUT RANCH

South out of Cimarron, Highway 21 takes the roundabout way back to Springer at I-25. The first leg roughly follows the old Santa Fe Trail route, passing the headquarters of **Philmont Scout Ranch** (575/376-2281, www.philmontscoutranch.org), the 137,000-acre spread that's now the property of Boy Scouts of America. More than a million scouts and leaders have ventured here since 1939. Practically an independent village, the place has its own post office, fire brigade, and hospital.

Visitors are welcome at the **National Scouting Museum** (575/376-1136, 8am-5:30pm daily June-Aug., 9am-5pm Mon.-Fri. Sept.-May, free), which was moved from its former location in Irving, Texas and opened at the Philmont Scout Ranch in May 2018. Over 600,000 artifacts commemorating the Boy Scouts of America occupy the squat modern structure, including gear, pottery, vintage patches, and historical photos. It's all very well presented, and its impact on current and former visiting Boy Scouts is palpable.

The grounds also hold the **Philmont Museum & Seton Memorial Library** (575/376-1136, 8am-5:30pm daily June-Aug., 9am-5pm Mon.-Fri. Sept.-May, free), which displays a history of the ranch, photos of the Santa Fe Trail, and the art collection of Ernest Thompson Seton, a cofounder of the Boy Scouts. Fans of lavish manors will want to make reservations with the Philmont Museum to see **Villa Philmonte** (call for tour schedule, free), the vacation home of Oklahoma oilman Waite Phillips, the Boy Scouts' benefactor. His Spanish Mediterranean manse was completed in 1927, and it's still chockablock with European antiques, as well as Waite's collection of Western paraphernalia.

Philmont Scout Ranch also manages the **Kit Carson Museum** (Hwy. 21, 575/376-1136, 8am-5pm daily June-Aug., free), about seven miles farther down Highway 21. The adobe building is near where Lucien Maxwell and his friend Kit Carson set up a camp in the late 1840s to deal with Santa Fe Trail traders (ruts are still visible where the trail crosses the Rayado River), and the museum re-creates life in that period, with costumed "mountain men" demonstrating how to fire a black-powder rifle, forge a horseshoe, and cook up a meal on a campfire.

Navajo Nation and the Northwest

American Indian culture is often relegated to

museums, its crafts and relics preserved behind glass or mounted on walls. But in New Mexico, especially in the northwestern part of the state, native traditions are lived every day.

The Navajo Nation, the largest reservation in the United States, occupies much of the northwest and stretches across 27,000 square miles into Arizona and Utah, while close by are the Puebloan communities of Acoma, Laguna, and Zuni. It's a vast area where visitors can appreciate a remarkable continuity of culture, from ancient ruins to contemporary powwows. The backdrop is a landscape of slablike mesas, jagged canyons, spired red-rock buttes—the sort of classic Southwestern scenery

Highlights

Look for ★ to find recommended sights, activities, dining, and lodging.

★ **Acoma Pueblo:** This windswept village atop a mesa west of Albuquerque is one of the oldest communities in the United States. Visit for the views as well as for the delicate black-on-white pottery made only here (page 252).

★ **Crownpoint Rug Auction:** Pick up a beautiful piece of handmade craftsmanship, and a good story while you're at it. This monthly auction in a Navajo village is a shopping event like no other (page 255).

★ **Nuestra Señora de Guadalupe Church:** Stunning murals decorate the white-washed walls of Zuni Pueblo's oldest adobe church. Colorful and intricately detailed, the kachinas look vividly real (page 260).

★ **Bisti/De-Na-Zin Wilderness:** Hiking this windswept landscape of dusty gray, red, and black stones is like taking a trip to another planet. There are no marked trails; instead rely on the weird mushroom-shaped rocks that have long been used as waypoints (page 275).

★ **Pueblo Bonito:** The largest set of ruins at **Chaco Culture National Historical Park,** this 12th-century complex was also the largest building in North America in pre-Columbian times, marking the center of a vast, complex network of trade and culture (page 287).

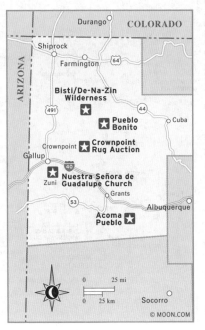

Navajo Nation and the Northwest

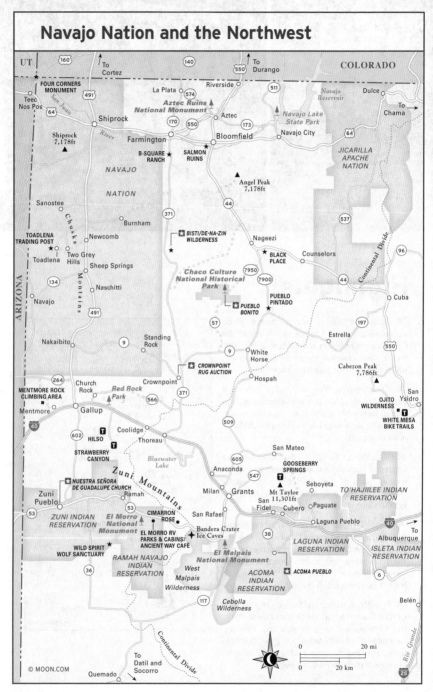

UT · To Cortez · To Durango · COLORADO
160 · 140 · 550

FOUR CORNERS MONUMENT
491
Teec Nos Pos
64
Shiprock
La Plata
574
Riverside
511
Navajo Reservoir
Dulce
To Chama

Aztec Ruins National Monument
170
550
Aztec
173
Navajo City
64
Navajo Lake State Park

JICARILLA APACHE NATION

Shiprock 7,178ft
San Juan River
Farmington
Bloomfield

B-SQUARE RANCH
SALMON RUINS

NAVAJO NATION

Angel Peak 7,178ft
44

Sanostee
371
Burnham
BISTI/DE-NA-ZIN WILDERNESS
Nageezi
Counselors
537

TOADLENA TRADING POST
Newcomb
BLACK PLACE
44
Continental Divide
96

Toadlena
Two Grey Hills
Sheep Springs
7950
7900
PUEBLO PINTADO
Cuba

134
Naschitti
Chaco Culture National Historical Park
PUEBLO BONITO

Navajo
491
57
Estrella
197

Nakaibito
9
Standing Rock
White Horse
550

CROWNPOINT RUG AUCTION
Hospah
Cabezon Peak 7,786ft
San Ysidro

264
Church Rock
Red Rock Park
Crownpoint
371
OJITO WILDERNESS
WHITE MESA BIKE TRAILS

MENTMORE ROCK CLIMBING AREA
Mentmore
566
509

40
Gallup
Coolidge
Thoreau
San Mateo
605

602
HILSO
Bluewater Lake
Anaconda
547
GOOSEBERRY SPRINGS
Seboyeta
TO'HAJIILEE INDIAN RESERVATION

STRAWBERRY CANYON
Milan
Grants
Mt Taylor 11,301ft
Cubero
Paguate

Zuni Mountains
NUESTRA SEÑORA DE GUADALUPE CHURCH
Ramah
San Fidel
Laguna Pueblo
40
To Albuquerque

Zuni Pueblo
53
EL MORRO NATIONAL MONUMENT
53
CIMARRON ROSE
San Rafael
38
LAGUNA INDIAN RESERVATION
ISLETA INDIAN RESERVATION

ZUNI INDIAN RESERVATION
EL MORRO RV PARKS & CABINS/ ANCIENT WAY CAFÉ
Bandera Crater Ice Caves

WILD SPIRIT WOLF SANCTUARY
RAMAH NAVAJO INDIAN RESERVATION
West Malpais Wilderness
EL MALPAIS NATIONAL MONUMENT
ACOMA PUEBLO
6

36
ACOMA INDIAN RESERVATION

117
Cebolla Wilderness
Belén

Continental Divide
To Datil and Socorro
Quemado
Rio Grande
25

0 · 20 mi
0 · 20 km

© MOON.COM

that has photographers, mountain bikers, and hikers all reaching for their gear.

The most common route around the area begins on I-40 west out of Albuquerque, toward Acoma Pueblo. A thousand-year-old settlement atop a natural fortress of stone, "Sky City" is one of the most striking spots in New Mexico, rivaling Taos for the title of oldest inhabited town in the United States. Farther on, Gallup is the self-proclaimed Indian capital of the world, a major business hub for more than a hundred years. Along with its old-fashioned trading posts, it's emerging as a great outdoor destination, thanks to some excellent trails and rock-climbing sites nearby.

Heading due north brings you into the heart of Diné Bikéyah (Navajo land) and past Shiprock, a great plume of volcanic stone sticking straight out of the plain that, like so many natural features in this area, is the subject of scores of legends and tales.

Just beyond the eastern border of the reservation, Farmington and neighboring Aztec are towns built by the petroleum industry. They're also one common base (Cuba, to the south, is the other) for exploring the biggest draw in the region: Chaco Canyon. This site is where, between AD 850 and 1250, the Ancestral Puebloans (Anasazi) built a nine-mile-long city, a metropolis that served as the ceremonial and religious capital for this influential culture.

HISTORY

Northwestern New Mexico shows evidence of human occupation as early as 8000 BC, but it was not until the middle of the 9th century AD that people really began to flourish here. At this point, the residents of Chaco Canyon started building homes above ground that grew into multistory blocks. Chaco was part of a network of communities as far north as Mesa Verde and as far south as Zuni, all displaying a similar architectural style and connected by skillfully engineered roads. For unknown reasons, though, people eventually left these towns and dispersed, some toward the Rio Grande, some to Zuni, and some onto the Hopi lands in what is now Arizona.

Meanwhile, bands of Navajo had migrated from northern climes into the desert a bit west of Chaco. No one has been able to pinpoint the date of their arrival here; the tribe's oral tradition says that Chaco was still inhabited, but archaeological evidence suggests the Navajo were not in their current territory until after Chaco was empty, around 1300, and perhaps not even until shortly before the Spanish made their first *entrada*, in 1540. In any case, the Navajo settled in quickly, and when the Spanish brought livestock, they added sheepherding—as well as raiding on horseback—to their already highly developed agricultural lifestyle.

Because the region was farther away from Santa Fe and the main trade routes, it avoided some of the worst suffering brought by early Spanish rule. Trouble began when the United States took control of the New Mexico territory in 1846, and optimistic homesteaders began flooding in. American expansionists also discovered rich mineral deposits in the Navajo homeland. The worst confrontations came in the 1860s, the era when federal Indian agent Kit Carson embarked on a scorched-earth campaign, burning crops, slaughtering sheep, and chopping down orchards. On the brink of starvation, the Navajo began to surrender in 1863, and Carson promptly marched them all, in the dead of winter, 400 miles southeast to Fort Sumner. Thousands died during "the Long Walk" and in the following years of captivity. They returned to a federally granted reservation in 1868. Much of modern Navajo history has involved wrangling with the federal government, private energy interests, and the neighboring Hopi people (in Arizona) over the use of coal and other natural resources.

Previous: stark landscape in the Four Corners region; trail at El Morro National Monument; the reconstructed great kiva at Aztec Ruins National Monument.

PLANNING YOUR TIME

The driving distances are not so great here, so you could cover this territory in as little as three days, staying one night in Zuni or Gallup and the next in Farmington. But this would leave you time to see only, say, Acoma Pueblo the first day, a long scenic drive including Four Corners the next, and the ruins at Chaco Canyon on the third. If you really want to appreciate how distinct this corner is from the rest of the state, four days will give you a little more time, also allowing for a hike or two. For anyone with more than a passing interest in ancient archaeological sites, Chaco can take a whole day, or even three. Mountain bikers and hikers could concentrate on the trails around Gallup—a great mix of mountains and rugged rock—and a couple of good places to hang out in town at night.

As there are few mountain ranges, a lot of the terrain in this region is devoid of shade. For outdoor activities, try to avoid the peak of summer. The lower elevations relative to the rest of the state mean that most of this area does not get heavy snow in the winter, but the road to Chaco—which can inflict a toll on cars in the best of weather—may be muddy.

Route 66: Albuquerque Toward Gallup

I-40 climbs west out of Albuquerque and heads straight across a plateau lined with flat mesas—archetypal Southwest scenery. Ancient Acoma Pueblo dominates one of these mesas, a veritable rock tower and an amazing place to visit and meet the people whose ancestors have lived here for nearly a thousand years. At the small town of Grants, you can turn south from the highway to enter the volcanic badlands of El Malpais; nearby is El Morro National Monument, a natural pool amid cliffs adorned with centuries-old graffiti. If you're on this loop on Highway 53, you'll next reach Zuni Pueblo, and Gallup (and I-40) is straight north from there.

Dedicated drivers can hop off the interstate and cruise a remote—sometimes winding—two-lane stretch of old Route 66, resurfacing at Laguna and then cruising parallel to I-40 almost to Gallup. Outside Albuquerque, take exit 126, heading south on Highway 6. Then turn right (southwest) on old Route 66. This road eventually meets, then crosses I-40, winding a bit, and eventually settling in as the frontage road up to exit 47, west of Thoreau.

LAGUNA PUEBLO

About 18 miles west of Albuquerque, I-40 crosses the border onto the 45 square miles of **Laguna Pueblo** (505/552-6654, www. lagunapueblo-nsn.gov), on which 7,000 Keresan-speaking Ka-waikah (Lake People) live in six villages. From the highway, the only impression you get of Laguna is its Dancing Eagle Casino, but if you have time, get off at exit 114 to visit the **San José Mission Church** (505/552-9330). Established in 1699 when the Laguna people requested a priest (unlike any other pueblo), it stands out for its stark white stucco coating, but this is a relatively recent addition, following a 19th-century renovation. It was mudded and whitewashed every year until the 1950s, when the boom in uranium mining in the area left no time for this maintenance; it's now sealed with stucco.

Inside, between a packed-earth floor and a finely wrought wood ceiling, the late-18th-century altar screen commands the room. It's the work of the so-called Laguna Santero, an unidentified painter who made the innovation of placing icons inside a crowded field of decorative borders and carved and painted columns, creating a work of explosively colorful

---

1: a rugged stretch of old Route 66 west of Albuquerque 2: view from Acoma's Sky City

1

2

folk art that was copied elsewhere in the region in subsequent decades.

The doors, and the small onsite gift shop, are usually open 9am-3pm daily (and after a 7am Mass).

Each of the six villages of Laguna celebrates its own feast day, and then the whole pueblo turns out at the church September 19 for the Feast of San José, one of the bigger pueblo events in the Albuquerque area.

Food

One of New Mexico's most acclaimed green-chile cheeseburgers is served at ★ **Laguna Burger** (Old Rte. 66, 505/552-1022, 6am-10pm daily, $5), at the 66 Pit Stop gas station at exit 114. The ragged patties are made of fresh, never frozen beef, the buns are toasted on the griddle, and the fries are hand-cut, with skins on. Still, the cheery staff's T-shirts wonder, "Is it the beef, or is it the love?" There's also a branch of Laguna Burger at exit 140, at the 66 Pit Stop north of the highway.

★ ACOMA PUEBLO

On the road to Acoma, you may feel as though you've crossed through a pass into a Southwestern Shangri-La, for none of this great basin is visible from the highway. Down in the valley, the route runs directly toward a flat-topped rock that juts up like a tooth.

Atop the rock is the original **Acoma Pueblo**, the village aptly known as **Sky City**. The community covers about 70 acres and is built largely of pale, sun-bleached adobe, as it has been since at least AD 1150. Only a hundred or so people live on the mesa top year-round, given the hardships of no running water or electricity. But many families maintain homes here, and the place is thronged on September 2, when the pueblo members gather for the **Feast of San Esteban.** The rest of the 2,800 Acoma (People of the White Rock, in their native Keresan) live on the valley floor, which is used primarily as ranchland.

Visiting Sky City

All visitors must stop at the **Sky City Cultural Center and Haak'u Museum** (Indian Rte. 23, 800/747-0181, www. acomaskycity.org, 8am-5pm daily Mar.-Oct., 9am-5pm Fri.-Sun. Nov.-Feb.) on the main road, which houses a café and shop stocked with local crafts, along with beautiful rotating exhibits on Acoma art and tradition. From here, you must join a **guided tour** ($25; first tour 9:30am and last tour 3:30pm mid-Mar.-Oct, first tour 9:30am and last tour 2:30pm Nov.-early Mar.), which transports groups by bus to the village. The road to the top is the one concession to modernity; previously, all goods had to be hauled up the near-vertical cliff faces. The tour lasts about 1.5 hours, after which visitors may return by bus or climb down one of the old trails, using hand- and footholds dug into the rock centuries ago. Definitely call ahead to check that the tours are running and verify times, as the pueblo closes to visitors periodically.

The centerpiece of the village is the **Church of San Esteban del Rey,** one of the most iconic of the Spanish missions in New Mexico. Built between 1629 and 1640, the graceful, simple structure has been inspiring New Mexican architects ever since. Its interior is, like many New Mexican pueblo churches, spare and simple, the white walls painted with rainbows and corn.

As much as it represents the pinnacle of Hispano-Indian architecture in the 17th century, the church is also a symbol of the brutality of Spanish colonialism, as it rose in the typical way: forced labor. The men of Acoma felled and carried the tree trunks for the ceiling beams from the forest on Mount Taylor, more than 25 miles across the valley, and up the cliff face to the village.

Acoma is well known for its pottery, easily distinguished by the fine black lines that sweep around the curves of often creamy-white vessels. On the best works, the lines are so fine and densely painted, they shimmer almost like a moiré. The clay particular to this area can be worked so thin that the finest pots

Ceremonial Dances

Feast days typically involve carnivals and markets in addition to dances. Dates can vary from year to year. Confirm details and start times—usually afternoon, but sometimes following an evening or midnight Mass—with the **Indian Pueblo Cultural Center** (505/843-7270, www.indianpueblo.org) before setting out. For the Navajo dances in Shiprock, check with the organizers of the **Northern Navajo Nation Fair** (505/368-4305, www. northernnavajonationfair.org).

- **February, first or second weekend:** Acoma (Sky City): governor's feast, various dances
- **February 19:** Laguna (Old Laguna): Feast of San José
- **Easter:** Most pueblos: various dances
- **May 7:** Acoma: Feast of Santa María
- **July 26:** Laguna (Seama): Feast of Santa Ana
- **August 10:** Acoma (Acomita): Feast of San Lorenzo
- **August 15:** Laguna (Mesita): Feast of the Assumption
- **September 2:** Acoma (Sky City): Feast of San Esteban
- **September 8:** Laguna (Encinal): Feast of the Nativity of the Blessed Virgin Mary
- **September 19:** Laguna (Old Laguna): Feast of San José
- **September 25:** Laguna (Paguate): Feast of Saint Elizabeth
- **Early October:** Shiprock: Yei Bichei dances
- **October 17:** Laguna (Paraje): Feast of Saint Margaret Mary
- **Thanksgiving:** Zuni: Christmas light parade; Acoma (Sky City): craft show
- **Late November/early December:** Zuni: Shalako
- **December 24:** Acoma (Sky City): luminaria display; Laguna (Old Laguna): dances after evening Mass
- **December 25-28:** Acoma (Sky City) and Laguna (Old Laguna): Christmas dances

will hum or ring when tapped. Throughout the tour, there are several opportunities to buy pieces. This can feel slightly pressured, but in many cases, you have the privilege of buying work directly from the artisan who created it.

Food and Accommodations

The cultural center contains the **Y'aak'a Café** (9am-2:30pm daily Mar.-Oct., $8), which serves earthy local dishes like lamb stew, Indian fry bread, and corn roasted in a traditional *horno* oven—as well as Starbucks coffee.

Acoma Pueblo operates the small-scale **Sky City Casino & Hotel** (888/759-2489, www.skycity.com, $89 d), also at exit 102. Its rooms are perfectly clean and functional, and there's an exercise room and a little pool.

GRANTS

This town of 8,000 has gone through several career changes since its start in the 1880s. It began as a railroad camp, but it soon grew into a lumber town, based on the rich forests of the Zuni Mountains to the south. In

Acoma vs. Oñate: Grudge Match

The early history of the conquistadors at Acoma was one of brutal back-and-forth attacks, each escalating in violence after the initial Spanish incursion. In a 1599 attack following many previous skirmishes, Don Juan de Oñate, the first governor of Spain's newest province, killed 800 people, leaving only 80 men alive in the hilltop village.

But Oñate was not content. He then brought his enemies into a makeshift court and tried them for the murder of 11 Spaniard soldiers. The sentence for the inevitable guilty verdict was that every male in Acoma over the age of 25 would have one foot cut off; everyone between the ages of 12 and 25 was pressed into slavery; and the children were sent to convents in Mexico.

Oñate was eventually recalled from his post and chastised for his actions. But in 1640, as if to add insult to injury, the Spanish friars presented the Church of San Esteban del Rey—built by Acoma slaves over more than a decade—to the maimed pueblo population as "restitution" for Oñate's cruelties. As a further gift of salvation, the friars publicly purged and hanged the village's spiritual leaders in the churchyard.

statue of Don Juan de Oñate by sculptor Reynaldo Rivera

Variations on this treatment happened up and down the Rio Grande, eventually inspiring the Pueblo Revolt of 1680. But Oñate's particular brand of viciousness is probably the most remembered. Shortly after a monument to the conquistador was erected north of Española in 1998, the right foot of the bronze statue turned up missing—someone had snuck in at night and sawed it clean off. An anonymous letter to newspapers stated that the act was "on behalf of our brothers and sisters at Acoma Pueblo." Rumor adds that the prankster vandals also left behind at the statue two miniature feet made of clay, attached to a shield inscribed with the words "The Agony of Defeat."

the 1940s, logging restrictions kicked in, and locals turned to farming, mustering the questionable boast of "carrot capital of the world."

But just a decade later, Grants reinvented itself as the much more au courant "uranium capital of the world," after a local sheepherder happened across some of that valuable ore on the edge of town. It turned out to be one of the largest uranium fields in the world. With the best ore depleted in the 1980s and the last mine closed in 1999, Grants is now retired, so to speak, but it welcomes guests for a meal and a story or two about its past before they carry on to Gallup or Albuquerque. Just to the north, Mount Taylor (elevation 11,305 feet) is a popular destination for hikers and back-country skiers.

Sights

Make time for the surprisingly good New Mexico Mining Museum (100 N. Iron Ave., 505/287-4802, 9am-4pm Mon.-Sat., $5), where you descend below the earth into a mock mine shaft. The narration from former miners gets pretty technical, but the narrow tunnels and clanking machinery give you a very real appreciation for the physical labor and risk involved in mining. The museum is on the west side of town, at the corner of Santa Fe Avenue, the main east-west drag.

On the west side of town, the Cibola Arts Council (1001 W. Santa Fe Ave., 505/287-7311, 1pm-5pm Tues.-Sat., free) shows local work and houses the Route 66 Vintage Museum, with postcards and other trinkets from Grants' motoring heyday. And flying geeks can check out the **Aviation History Museum** (505/287-4700, 9am-1pm Sat., free), built around a restored beacon for Midcontinental Airway, established by Charles Lindbergh in the 1920s. It's at the airport near Milan, west of I-40 between exits 81 and 79.

Hiking

Heading north out of town, 1st Street (Hwy. 547) turns into Roosevelt Avenue then Lobo Canyon Road, headed toward **Mount Taylor,** aka Tsoodzil (Turquoise Bead) to the Navajo, who count it as one of their nation's four sacred mountains (although it is not technically on the reservation). Just past mile marker 10 on Highway 547, **Coal Mine Campground** (505/287-8833, www.recreation.gov, May-Sept., $5) is thick with pines and has some nice shady sites, with a stream running nearby.

Just as the pavement on Highway 547 ends, a right turn onto gravel Forest Road 193 takes you five miles to the head of **Gooseberry Springs Trail** (no. 77). From here, you can hike 3.5 miles to the mountain's summit, at 11,301 feet. Although the elevation gain is 2,400 feet, it's not a very strenuous climb, and it delivers an incredibly rewarding view—on a clear day, you can see as far as the Arizona border. Allow about three hours for the round-trip.

Food and Accommodations

Few people stay the night here, as Grants is so close to Albuquerque, but it can be handy after the Crownpoint Rug Auction. Old-motel aficionados will appreciate the Route 66 gem that is **Southwest Motel** (1000 E. Santa Fe Ave., 505/287-2935, $35 s, $50 d), greeting visitors with a vivid neon sign and tidy little rooms with mini-fridges and desks.

A couple of blocks west, **El Cafecito** (820 E. Santa Fe Ave., 505/285-6229, 7am-8:30pm Mon.- Sat., $8) is a family-run restaurant with excellent red and green chile, as well as some non-spicy American standards to round out the menu.

For coffee, bagels, and a slice of home-made pie, **Coco Bean Café** (333 Nimitz Dr., 505/285-4143, 7am-6pm Mon.-Fri., 8am-3pm

Sat., 11am-4pm Sun., $4) is a good excuse to get off the main road through town. Look for Nimitz Drive on the east side, next to El Cafecito; turn north and follow the road as it curves and crosses a small bridge.

For a good, quick stop right off the interstate, the classic gleaming stainless-steel **Wow Diner** (1300 Motel Dr., 505/287-3801, 6am-midnight Tues.-Sun., $5.95-13.95) beckons from exit 79 (really Milan, just west of Grants). The menu has something for everyone, from pork *carnitas* to spinach salad to old-fashioned ice cream shakes. For breakfast on the go, pick up a bulging handheld breakfast burrito, which is a steal at $3.95.

Information

Definitely stop in at the helpful and attractive **El Malpais Visitor Center** (1900 E. Santa Fe Ave., 505/876-2783, 9am-5pm daily), just south of I-40 at exit 85. Pick up maps, brochures, and suggested driving routes and hiking tours for this corner of the state.

★ CROWNPOINT RUG AUCTION

The curiously named town of **Thoreau** (pronounced thu-ROO) at exit 53 inspires no Walden-style reveries, but it is the turnoff for one of the best shopping experiences in northwestern New Mexico. Twenty-five miles north is a small Navajo community, home of the **Crownpoint Rug Auction** (505/736-2130, https://crownpointrugauction.com), which has been connecting buyers and sellers from all around the region since 1968. Even if you have no interest in buying, it's a great cultural experience, and an opportunity to see some beautiful work up close.

The sales, in the elementary-school gym on the second Friday of the month (usually; check the website), draw casual shoppers as well as big gallery owners from Santa Fe. Jewelers and potters set up tables in the hall, and food is available in the school cafeteria. It's easy to find the school in the tiny town—turn left from Highway 371 and look for lots of parked cars. Rugs are on view 4pm-6:30pm; bidding

starts at 7pm and usually lasts until around 10pm. Often with more rugs on offer than customers, there's a good chance you'll find something you like for a reasonable price—a good 4- by 6-foot rug can go for $300 or so, and small sampler rugs can go for $30. Cash, credit cards, and checks are accepted as payment.

There's nowhere to stay in Crownpoint; Grants and Gallup are both about an hour's drive, and Farmington is due north on Highway 371, about an hour and a half away.

EL MALPAIS NATIONAL MONUMENT

The product of three volcanic events, the lava-strewn landscape of the **El Malpais National Monument** (505/783-4774, www.nps.gov/elma, free) is not exactly the barren terrain that *el malpaís* (el-mal-pie-EES, literally, "the badlands") suggests. A surprising amount of greenery has taken root in the millennia since the last eruption, between 2,000 and 3,000 years ago, and in the spring, wildflowers stand out against the jagged black rock. The lava fields are riven with deep, cave-like tubes that formed as the hot rock cooled. Some of the most scenic areas are along the monument's eastern border, where the lava meets red sandstone cliffs, as well as New Mexico's largest natural arch. Stay around at dusk to see bats fly out around El Calderon; there is a ranger-led talk twice a week in summer.

For those who just want a quick look, the easiest access point is **Sandstone Bluffs Overlook,** where, on a short walk along the edge of the eastern cliffs, you can admire the lava fields and see north to Mount Taylor. It's about 11 miles south from I-40 on Highway 117. Drive another 7 miles to reach **La Ventana Arch,** a great sandstone arch; a short trail leads to a scenic viewing spot.

If you'd like a longer hike or drive into the park, stop first at the **El Malpais Visitors Center** (1900 E. Santa Fe Ave., 505/876-2783,

9am-5pm daily), near I-40 at exit 85, midway between the two highways that access different parts of the badlands. National Park Service employees can give you detailed maps and current conditions, and from there you can decide whether to take Highway 53 or Highway 117 south into the monument area. The monument **information center** (505/783-4774, 9am-4pm Sat.-Sun. mid-June-Sept.) is less conveniently located on Highway 53, 23 miles south of I-40.

In addition to the hikes detailed below, there are more demanding but worthwhile places to explore outside the borders of the national park, in the BLM land designated **Cebolla Wilderness** (off the southeast border of the park) and **West Malpais Wilderness** (to the south and west)—ask at the visitors center for details on these areas as well.

Zuni-Acoma Trail

By far the most strenuous hike, the shadeless 7.5-mile **Zuni-Acoma Trail** cuts across the lava beds roughly along the path used for centuries by the Puebloans in this region. It's rough going because the ground is uneven and you have to keep your eye out for cairns, but if you're interested in the plants and animals that thrive in El Malpais, this can be a rewarding trek. The eastern trailhead is on Highway 117, before you reach La Ventana Arch; the western one is on Highway 53.

Lava Falls Area

For the best up-close look at the lava, head farther south on Highway 117 to the **Lava Falls Area.** Here you can still make out the swirls and eddies of the molten stuff as if it had cooled yesterday; the variety of shapes and textures is fascinating, as are the odd pockets of stunted trees that manage to flourish here. The three-mile route (a mile-long loop with a one-mile spur) is marked only by rock cairns, so bring a compass, as it's easy to get disoriented.

El Calderon Area

At **El Calderon Area** on Highway 53, a 3.8-mile loop trail heads up to the Continental

Divide, then around the edge of **El Calderon Cinder Cone**, a former lava vent. Calderon Crater, the oldest of the three lava flows that make up the area, dates back some 115,000 years—as a result, the rock is more weathered, and not the stark black found around younger McCartys Crater on the south side of the park. This is also the area where lava tubes are closest to the road—a short walk from the car reveals the entrance to **Junction Cave**, a tube that partially collapsed—you see a sliver of daylight on the other end. Farther up the trail is **Xenolith Cave**, a similar lava tube with odd rocks jumbled in with the lava; the famous **Bat Cave** (closed to hikers), less than a mile from the parking area, has a circling cloud of the nocturnal critters at sunset.

Big Tubes Area

The **Big Tubes Area**, a network of 17 miles of lava caves on the west side of the monument, has by far the weirdest terrain. Two caves are open here, Big Skylight and Giant Ice Cave. You'll need a high-clearance truck, as the road is often very rough, as well as headlamps (with extra batteries), sturdy boots, and heavy work gloves to protect your hands from the jagged rocks.

Ice Cave and Bandera Volcano

A family-run tourist attraction that was grandfathered in when El Malpais was made a national monument, the **Ice Cave and Bandera Volcano** (Hwy. 53, 505/783-4303, www.icecaves.com, 9am-7pm daily Mar.-Oct., $12) are an impressive natural sight, especially during the heat of summer, when you can descend from 90°F outside to 31°F underground, the chill emanating from a permanent layer of greenish ice at least 20 feet thick. Although the same phenomenon is visible elsewhere in El Malpais (for much less money), this is the most accessible spot, and generally more impressive. The other half of the attraction, Bandera Crater, 750 feet deep, is actually not much to look at—literally, just a big hole in the ground.

Accommodations

A few miles west of the Ice Cave off Hwy. 53, ★ **Cimarron Rose** (Hwy. 53, 800/856-5776, www.cimarronrose.com, from $145) is a delightful eco-friendly B&B smack in the middle of a forest in the Zuni Mountains. Choose from three spacious and rustic suites, each featuring large timbers, full kitchens, private outdoor areas, Wi-Fi, and fireplaces.

EL MORRO NATIONAL MONUMENT

This pocket of New Mexico may seem like relative wilderness today, but in fact, it has always been a fairly well-traveled route. The proof is at the **El Morro National Monument** (Hwy. 53, 505/783-4226, www.nps.gov/elmo, 9am-5pm daily, free), where Don Juan de Oñate carved his name in the bluff *(morro)* and darkened the inscription with lamp soot, as a way of passing the time while his men rested and horses drank at the natural pool formed by snowmelt. It's also a vivid image of the early Spanish power in the Southwest—Oñate made his mark in 1605, seven years after his first official colonizing mission, and two years before the English even set foot in the New World. In the centuries since, seemingly every celebrity of the American West, major and minor, has left a graffiti autograph: Don Diego de Vargas was here in 1692, early in his campaign to reclaim Nuevo México following the Pueblo Revolt of 1680. P. Gilmer Breckenridge, who led an experimental caravan of 25 camels from Texas to California, visited in 1857, and his compatriot, E. Pen Long, left a curlicue signature that gets the prize for best penmanship.

The half-mile **Inscription Loop Trail** is paved and leads first to the year-round pool at the base of the rocks, then along the cliff face. The longer you stare at the rocks, the more names—as well as figures, carved by the Zuni centuries earlier—pop out. The natural ground level has sunk over the centuries, too, so the graffiti crawls up the cliffs well above your head. For a spectacular view of the surrounding landscape, continue on up to the top of the bluffs on the Headland Trail. The loop, which takes another hour, passes alongside the Atsinna, the ruins of a small pueblo occupied by the Zuni in the 13th and 14th centuries.

Food and Accommodations

Just west of the national monument, El Morro RV Park & Cabins (Hwy. 53, 505/783-4612, www.elmorro-nm.com) is a great place to stay in the wilderness. Tent campsites are $15 per night, while tidy little cabins with queen and double beds start at $84; RV sites are $30. The on-site ★ Ancient Way Café (9am-5pm Sun.-Tues. and Thurs., 9am-8pm Fri.-Sat., $8) uses organic ingredients to make a nice assortment of tasty dishes, including brisket and beans and good veggie options; weekend dinners are one set entrée (pineapple pulled pork, for instance), and you should call to reserve. If you have a fondness for baked goods, this is the place to indulge—the seven-layer cookies are heavenly and there's an assortment of pies, too.

RAMAH

Twelve miles west of El Morro, Ramah (pronounced RAY-muh) was originally settled by Mormons, though it is now part of the Navajo reservation. The local Ramah Navajo Weavers Association, like the collective in Tierra Amarilla in northern New Mexico, has helped revive an economy based on sheep, particularly the old Churro breed. The settlement's history is told in the tiny Ramah Museum (505/783-4392, 10am-2pm Sat. June-Aug., donation); at the curve in town, turn north.

Wild Spirit Wolf Sanctuary

Just before you reach Ramah, you pass the turn for the long-running Wild Spirit Wolf Sanctuary (378 Candy Kitchen Rd., 505/775-3304, www.wildspiritwolfsanctuary.org, 10am-5pm Tues.-Sun., $10), where you can observe some 50 captive-bred wolves and wolf-dogs that would otherwise go homeless. Guided tours (required) run at 11:30am, 1:30pm, and 3:30pm; you can also sign up for more intimate tours (from $150). You can camp ($15 for tents or RVs) or stay the night in a cabin or house ($125-$250)—then you're here in the morning to help feed the animals (reserve ahead; $25 pp), and the evening howls from your nearby neighbors will certainly give you something to remember. Signs off Highway 53 point to Mountainview and Pine Hill; it's another 12 miles on Indian Route 125 and 120.

the Wild Spirit Wolf Sanctuary

Zuni Pueblo

Covering several hundred square miles and with a population of more than 10,000, Zuni is the largest of the pueblos in the state. For centuries, Zuni settlements were spread over a wide area; eventually people began to form large pueblos. The pueblo Halona:wa (Anthill), around which the modern town of Zuni is based, was established long ago, but did not become the center of population until 1692, after the Zuni people made a peace agreement with Don Juan de Oñate and gathered here. There is a splendid church to visit, and this is the only pueblo where you can stay overnight, giving a much better appreciation for the community.

Isolation from the Rio Grande-area pueblos has helped keep Zuni culture more distinct—its "olla maidens," for instance, perform a traditional dance with pots balanced on their heads. Zuni is also famous for its delicate inlay jewelry, called "needlepoint," in which the tiniest bits of turquoise, coral, and other stones are set in intricate patterns on a silver field; the texture almost resembles beadwork. Collectors also hold Zuni kachinas (figurines of spirit beings) and fetishes (tiny carved animals) in high esteem. If you're coming here to shop, avoid late June and late December, when a period of fasting called Deshkwi bans buying or selling.

SIGHTS

Register first at the visitors center (Hwy. 53, 505/782-7238, www.zunitourism.com, 8:30am-5:30pm Mon.-Fri., 10am-4pm Sat., noon-4pm Sun.), midway through town on the north side of the road. Here you can get information on artists' studios as well as arrange a number of tours, including the highly recommended walking tour around Old Zuni (Middle Village). Note that if you plan to take photos, pick up a photo permit (from $10) from the visitors center before you start exploring.

All tours require advance notice, but if you have a particular interest, they are a wonderful way of seeing a different side of Zuni. The visitors center can arrange a 2.5-hour artist workshop tour ($85 for up to four people), based on your preferred medium (pottery, silver, stone, woodcarving, etc.). Archaeological site visits are also available, to Hawikku, where ancestral Zuni lived and where Coronado thought one of the "Cities of Gold" might be, and to the Village of the Great Kivas, inhabited in the 11th century. Both are $85 for two people and require a week's notice.

★ Nuestra Señora de Guadalupe Church

The core of the historic area called the Middle Village is the Nuestra Señora de Guadalupe Church, where the walls, first erected in 1629 and rebuilt in 1692, are painted with larger-than-life Shalako figures and other elements of the Zuni tradition as they function in the four seasons. The brilliantly colored murals, created over more than 20 years beginning in 1970, are the work of one esteemed pueblo artist, Alex Seowtewa, and his sons. Together with the blankets and buffalo heads, this is one of the most syncretic churches in the state—a beautiful, fervent expression of faith over millennia.

The church is accessible only by guided tour (10am, 1pm, and 3pm Mon.-Sat., 1pm and 3pm Sun.), which departs from the Zuni visitors center. Theoretically, two separate tours are offered: one around the old town and one to the church, each for $20. But in practice, all visitors are usually lumped into a single tour of everything for $25. The whole combined tour takes a little over an hour.

A:shíwi A:wan Museum and Heritage Center

Zuni's small A:shíwi A:wan Museum and Heritage Center (2 E. Ojo Caliente Rd., 505/782-4403, www.ashiwi-museum.org, 9am-6pm Mon.-Fri., free) is fascinating. It tells the story of the Zuni people, from creation myths through more contemporary issues with archaeologists and other researchers, such as Frank Cushing, who brought the pueblo to broader attention in the 19th century and became a local hero for a time. Cushing's endeavors are portrayed in a few hilarious cartoons by a Zuni artist. Also on display are artifacts from the ancestral settlement of Hawikku, excavated in 1916. They had been whisked away to a basement in a branch of the Smithsonian; Zuni leaders negotiated for this selection to be returned, leaving the remainder to be better preserved at the Smithsonian.

The museum is just south of Highway 53: Turn at the major stop sign on the west end of town; the museum is at the next big intersection, on the northwest corner, across from Halona Plaza.

FESTIVALS AND EVENTS

The largest event of the year, the ritual of **Shalako** (also spelled Sha'la'ko) marks the end of the agricultural season and the beginning of winter in late November or early December. Although many of the prayers and dances take place in areas closed to visitors, it is still a remarkable time to visit the pueblo.

The Shalako, part of the extensive pantheon of kachinas, act as messengers between man and gods; when they depart the village, they are bearing the Zuni prayer for rain in the spring. For this ceremony, they are men who are elected each year to impersonate these godlike forces, and they spend the entire year preparing. The 24-hour ritual begins around noon, but the real excitement comes at dusk, when the figures descend from the sacred mesa south of town. With giant eagle-feather masks with goggle eyes and wooden beaks, they are frightening, noisy, 10-foot-tall creatures, an awesome sight as they swoop through the crowds and the bonfires, their beaks clacking and the drums pounding behind them.

Shortly after Shalako, the whole community gathers for the **Give-Away,** to thank the clans involved in the ritual, for which preparation is a massive expense. People bring specific gifts as well as all manner of unused items, from deer meat to refrigerators, which are redistributed according to need. Again, it's a ceremony that outsiders may not entirely get, but it's a festive time to be in town.

Other secular events throughout the year include the **Zuni Cultural Arts Expo,** in late July or early August; the **McKinley County Fair,** also in August; the **Ancient Way Fall Festival,** an arts and harvest festival all along Highway 53 in early October; and the **Holiday Arts Market,** in early December. The visitors center can confirm dates.

FOOD AND ACCOMMODATIONS

The main place to eat is the adjacent general store, **Halona Plaza** (1 Shalako Dr., 8am-9pm Mon.-Sat., noon-6pm Sun., 505/782-2470), where the deli counter serves up excellent fried chicken ($6) with smoky-hot red-chile sauce on the side—New Mexican fusion at its finest. There's a bit more of a social scene at night down at **Chu-Chu's** (1344 Hwy. 53, 505/782-2100, 11am-10pm, Mon.-Sat., $8), on the east end of the town, where there's pizza, subs, and a nice little patio. The food-curious should also stop in to **Paywa's Bakery** (noon-5pm Wed.-Fri.), down a dirt road opposite Chu-Chu's. The family-run operation bakes irresistible sourdough loaves and sweet pies in a giant adobe *horno*.

Unlike most pueblos, where visitors are welcome for the day or as casino customers, Zuni offers a unique opportunity to stay overnight and just soak up the atmosphere of the place: wood smoke, red dirt, and sparkling stars. The supremely comfortable ★ **Inn at Halona** (23-B Pia Mesa Rd., 505/782-4547, www.halona.com, from $75 d) is run by a family with century-old roots on the reservation. The older main house has five rooms (no. 4 upstairs is beautifully sunny, while the basement no. 5 is big yet cozy-feeling), but you might prefer the side house if you like to sleep late, because the scene in the main house's breakfast room can get pretty animated. Guests dig in to what seems like an endless array of breads, eggs, meats, and the signature blue-corn pancakes. Book well ahead if you plan to be in town during any special events.

Gallup

Initially just a wide spot along the railroad, Gallup took its name from the man who doled out cash in exchange for the coal that companies hauled in from the surrounding mines in the 1880s. By the 1920s, Gallup was known for its exceptionally pure coal, which meant higher wages for workers, who flooded in from Britain, China, Italy, Greece, and scores of other places, making the town a polyglot community from early on. The mining business has slowed, but at least a hundred trains still rumble through every day—it's a near-constant background noise, and as the freight loads cruise right through the center of town, you often have the disconcerting sensation of looking down a street and seeing the background in motion.

Gallup's other disconcerting effect is the sense you've stepped onto a movie set. The place was a popular Hollywood location from the 1930s on through the Route 66 heyday, and it's not hard to see why, what with the glowing neon, the red sandstone cliffs, and the jagged Hogback Mountains, which inspire visions of Wild West adventure. Less glamorously, in the 1970s and 1980s, Gallup struggled with high unemployment and astronomical rates of drunk driving and alcoholism. But one get-tough mayor started a turnaround, and now downtown is clean and lively, and the civic pride is palpable.

SIGHTS

The railroad and I-40 divide Gallup in two, and most of what appeals to visitors is on the south side. The historic downtown area is on Highway 66 and Coal Avenue, lined with the most notable buildings and shops. The far east and west ends of town, with their assortment of chain hotels and restaurants, cater to through travelers on the interstate.

You can cover most of Gallup's attractions on foot after parking downtown. Some of the best art is outdoors, in the many **murals** around town, some painted by the WPA in the 1930s and others put up in the 21st century. There's one dedicated to the Navajo code talkers on South 2nd Street just south of Highway 66, as well as a great modern one on the side of the city hall (Aztec Avenue at South 2nd Street) that evokes modern life in Gallup: kids in pickup trucks, road construction, and rodeo events.

McKinley County Courthouse

Downtown is anchored by the Pueblo Revival **McKinley County Courthouse** (207 W. Hill St.), one block south of Coal Avenue. If you ask nicely and it's a slow day, you can walk around inside the courthouse and admire the tile work, the punched-tin light fixtures, and the 2,000-square-foot WPA mural in the main courtroom. Painted by Lloyd Moylan, it's the largest surviving work from that period in the state.

Navajo Code Talkers Museum

Adjoining the chamber of commerce, the **Navajo Code Talkers Museum** (103 W. Hwy. 66, 505/722-2228, 8am-5pm Mon.-Fri., free) is a collection of memorabilia arranged in fluorescent-lit glass cases—ask the chamber employees to turn the lights on. No frills here: The room is mostly used for business meetings, but the collected papers, photographs, and clippings trace the use of the Navajo language as code through the fight. Given the importance of the code to the success of the U.S. campaign, it's a little depressing to realize this is one of the largest permanent exhibits on the subject. State lawmakers have made a recent push to fund the construction of a more expansive museum in Tse Bonito, about 30 minutes to the northwest of Gallup.

Gallup

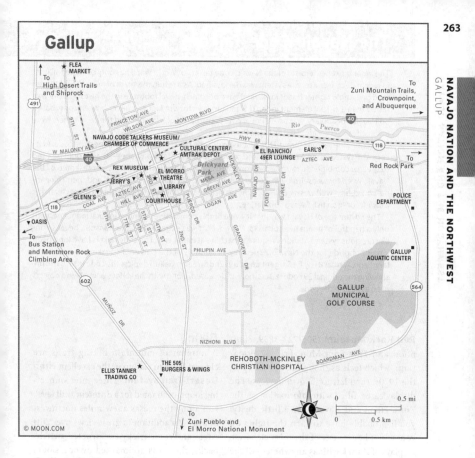

Gallup Cultural Center

The old Santa Fe Railway station has been converted into a well-used community arts center. Visitors will enjoy the upstairs **museum** (201 E. Hwy. 66, 505/863-4131, 8am-4pm Mon.-Fri., free). The nifty collection of dioramas—scenes involving model trains, a replica trading post—are accompanied by headphones to listen to a local's explanation of the scene. You'll also find a café, a visitors info desk, and a music and gift shop.

Between Memorial Day and Labor Day, free guided **walking tours** of downtown depart from here, usually at 10am daily.

Rex Museum

Like many small-town collections, the **Rex Museum** (300 W. Hwy. 66, 505/863-1363, 8am-3:30pm Mon.-Fri., $2 donation) is a hodgepodge, from roller skates to programs from the Inter-Tribal Indian Ceremonial. But perhaps it's most interesting to see the traces of the various immigrant groups that have settled in Gallup, from Chinese to Greeks.

Red Rock Park & Museum

East of town about six miles, **Red Rock Park** is Gallup's public party spot, with rodeo grounds and an outdoor amphitheater. It also has the surprisingly large

The Navajo Code Talkers

The ingenuity and heroism of the Navajo code talkers of World War II has only come to full light in recent decades, after the system was declassified. As a result, this team of more than 300 men (and one Anglo fighter fluent in Navajo) have become a novel footnote in the history of the war, rather than a crucial element in the U.S. military's victory. In fact, the never-broken code, based on Navajo vocabulary, was an essential part of the Battle of Iwo Jima, and the code talkers were involved in every Marine battle in the Pacific.

Twenty-nine recruits formed the first team of code talkers, who also developed the code. At its core, the system used Navajo words to represent letters of the alphabet—these could be used to spell, or combined to form larger words and concepts. For instance, w was represented by the Navajo word for weasel, *gloe-ih*. To say "when," the code talker said "weasel" and "hen": *gloe-ih-na-ah-wo-hai;* "will" was *gloe-ih-dot-sahi,* or "sick weasel." Military terms required more creativity: a *bish-lo,* or "iron fish," was a submarine.

The advantage of Navajo was that it was a highly complex yet completely oral language, with only a handful of nonnative speakers. Moreover, it was extremely fast to transmit, because unlike previous systems, it didn't require a machine at either end. The code talkers have long been a point of pride for the Navajo, especially as symbols of the power of speaking the ancestral language. A mural by Be Sargent on South 2nd Street in Gallup depicts the code in visual form, showing the original 29 code talkers, now all deceased, along with the various animals and objects used as keys in the code.

Red Rock Museum (505/722-3839, 8am-noon and 1pm-5pm Mon.-Fri., $2 donation), which feels as though it was set up in the 1970s, then left to its own devices. The display cases, filled with information on the Zuni, Hopi, and Navajo, are a little dusty; you'll probably have to turn the lights on yourself. It houses one of the most elaborate displays of Zuni kachinas anywhere—all the figurines labeled and their roles explained. There's also a model hogan (the traditional Navajo home) and a selection of local jewelry styles. Access the park via the frontage road (E. Hwy. 66), from exit 33 or exit 26 off I-40, then turn north on Highway 566.

SPORTS AND RECREATION

The city of Gallup has developed great trails on the nearby sandstone bluffs and in the ponderosa-covered Zuni Mountains. There's a lot to do in a relatively small area, and it's all fairly crowd-free. For additional details to what follows, see the **Gallup Real True website** (https://galluprealtrue.com), or pick up a comprehensive map from the chamber of commerce.

Biking

A number of mountain biking trails are close at hand to Gallup in the excellent **High Desert Trail System.** Three interconnecting loops, each rated for a different skill level, run along the mesas a few miles northwest of town. In addition to great views over cliff edges and some tricky constructed switchbacks, the trails are marked by occasional public art—so just when you think the weird rock formations are sculpture enough, you might look up to see a black steel bobcat peering down at you. The east trailhead, called Gamerco, is two miles north on U.S. 491, then left on Chino Loop; the gravel parking lot is on the left side of the road. The west-side trailhead is accessible via County Road 1, just west of exit 16 from I-40.

For shady forest biking, head to the **Zuni Mountain Trail System,** a patch of national forest southeast of Gallup. From exit 33 on I-40, Highway 400 runs south about six miles to Hilso Trailhead, the beginning of several climbs up through ponderosa

1: Gallup Cultural Center 2: Red Rock Park

forests and aspens; nearly all intersect up on the ridgeline, so you can come back a different way.

In town, **Brickyard Park** (700 E. Aztec Ave.) is a mountain-bike terrain park in Gallup's old clay quarry. Come here to practice your skills on dirt tracks and jumps.

Hiking

Hikers are also welcome on the High Desert and Zuni Mountain Trails, though two-wheelers have the right-of-way. In the latter area, **Strawberry Canyon Trail** is a shady, easy 1.5-mile hike up to a lookout tower, and it runs along a rough forest road, so there's room for both bikers and hikers. Follow Highway 400 past Hilso Trailhead, up to mile marker 0; just past the entrance to McGaffey Campground is a parking area on the right.

At two accessible trails close to town, you get the whole place to yourself. They both start in Red Rock Park: **Pyramid Rock Trail** is a 3-mile round-trip hike up to 7,487 feet, atop an aptly named butte. **Church Rock Trail** is 2.2 miles round-trip (a stem with a loop at the end)—it's less of a climb, working around the base of some dramatic spire-shaped rocks. An optional connector trail (1.3 miles) links the two routes, making a full hike of 3-4 hours.

Rock Climbing

A well-maintained public park east of town, **Mentmore Rock Climbing Area** has cliff faces between 40 and 70 feet high, with scores of routes spread over six different walls, along with quite a few bouldering options. At least some of the rocks get sun all the time, so it's climbable in the winter, but check the weather before heading out. The sandstone is fragile when wet, so local policy is to stay off the rocks for a couple of days after heavy rain. To get there, take exit 16 from I-40 and head west on Highway 66 for half a mile; turn north on County Road 1, then turn west after the bridge, on Mentmore Road, and follow the road straight as it turns to dirt; this ends in the parking area.

Swimming

Gallup Aquatic Center (620 S. Boardman Ave., 505/726-5460, $4) is a kid's dream, with curvy slides galore, cactus-shaped sprinklers, and even a "lazy river" setup; adults get a separate competition-size pool for laps. It's all indoors, but still a lot of fun.

ENTERTAINMENT AND EVENTS

On an average day, the streets of Gallup are not exactly hopping. You will notice a significant rush on weekends, though, as people from surrounding communities come into town to do business. Expect crowds during the two big annual events, a powwow and a balloon rally. The landmark **El Morro Theatre** (207 W. Coal Ave., 505/863-1250, www.elmorrotheatre.com) is downtown, built in 1926 in the Spanish colonial revival style. It's huge and a bargain for second runs of movies ($5). It also hosts local theater and music.

Nightlife

Gallup's past alcohol problems mean a somewhat subdued night scene. Still, one lively outpost is **Sammy C's Rock N Sports Pub & Grille** (107 W. Coal Ave., 505/863-2220, 11am-11pm Mon.-Thurs., 11am-1am Fri.-Sat., 10am-9pm Sun.), run by New Mexico sports-broadcasting legend Sammy Chioda. There's enough memorabilia on the walls to fill a museum, and there's no shortage of TVs and draft ales with which to take in the action.

Another option is **Coal Street Pub** (303 W. Coal Ave., 505/722-0117, 11am-10pm Sun.-Wed., 11am-11pm Thurs.-Sat.), which serves beer, wine, margaritas, and has a full food menu, too. There's often some kind of live music on the weekends.

The **49er Lounge** (1000 E. Hwy. 66, 5pm-1am daily) in the El Rancho Hotel specializes in margaritas, but you might not need them because the setting is dizzying enough—like the rest of the hotel, this place exudes an almost overwhelming aura of decaying Western glamour. Go early, as it tends to close before the posted time if business is slow.

Festivals and Events

Every night at 7pm between Memorial Day and Labor Day, Navajo, Hopi, and other **dance groups** perform in the plaza in front of the courthouse, for free.

For four days in late July or early August, Gallup hosts the **Inter-Tribal Indian Ceremonial** (www.gallupceremonial.com), which draws more than 20,000 participants from various tribes across the United States as well as Canada and Mexico. The main events are the pow wow and a an art show; other activities include a beauty pageant, rodeo, and lots of music and dancing.

The other big annual event is the **Red Rock Balloon Rally** (www.redrockballoonrally. com), on the first weekend in December. With about 200 participating hot-air balloons, it has been going strong since 1981, probably because the setting, against the vibrant sandstone at Red Rock Park, is unbeatable. The balloonists often need extra volunteers, so it's a good chance to get a free ride or join a chase crew—show up early and ask around.

SHOPPING

With a historic trading post or overstocked pawnshop seemingly every 10 feet, Gallup can be an exciting place to shop, or an overwhelming one, depending on your point of view. But even if you don't feel up to sifting through treasure troves of Navajo turquoise, the **trading posts,** some selling their wares for the better part of a century and still doing business primarily with the local Indian population, are worth a visit simply as another town attraction. They're stocked with everything from hand-spun skeins of wool to crisp new blue jeans, and of course, heaps and heaps of jewelry.

One of the oldest, most respected trading posts downtown is **Richardson's Trading Co. & Cash Pawn** (222 W. Hwy. 66, 505/722-4762, 9am-6pm Mon.-Sat.), where the warren of storefronts is permeated with the smell of old leather.

Another shopping hot spot is **City Electric Shoe Shop** (230 W. Coal Ave.,

505/863-5252, 9am-6pm Mon.-Sat.), where you can pick up a pair of street-ready moccasins in butter-soft suede or an embossed leather belt—both are made in a workshop in the basement.

On the south side, **Ellis Tanner Trading Co.** (1980 Hwy. 602, 505/863-4434, 8am-7pm Mon.-Sat.) has deep roots in Gallup; check inside for a huge mural by local artist Chester Kahn, honoring locals who have been good role models. You can pick up roasted piñon nuts, Diné-English children's books, vintage dance regalia, and more.

But perhaps the best shopping experience in town is at the **Gallup Flea Market** (340 9th St., 505/399-2166) every Saturday on the north side of town. It's a great swap meet where you can pick up anything from a beaded necklace to Native American charms to a bale of hay—not to mention all kinds of traditional foods. Vendors get rolling around 10am and wind things up in the mid-afternoon. To get there, head north on U.S. 491, then cut east to North 9th Street on West Jefferson Avenue.

FOOD

As with the hotels, all the chain places (and a couple of vintage diners) are near the freeway exits. You definitely get more local flavor, in every sense, if you venture downtown.

New Mexican

Family-owned, with a weather-worn neon sign, ★ **Jerry's Café** (406 W. Coal Ave., 505/722-6775, 8am-9pm Mon.-Sat., $8) has a crowd of dedicated followers (read: addicts) who drive miles for the stuffed sopaipillas, drenched in superhot red-chile sauce and jammed with different fillings depending on the meal. The place is tiny and often packed with courthouse employees during lunchtime, so arrive late or early.

It may not have the absolute best food in town, but **Earl's** (1400 E. Hwy. 66, 505/863-4201, 6am-8:30pm Mon.-Sat., 7:30am-3:30pm Sun., $8) has a timeless and welcoming atmosphere that can't be beat. Since 1947, it has been serving biscuits and gravy, Navajo tacos, and enchiladas. It's conveniently close to the east-side freeway exit, and gets packed after the Saturday flea market. You'll either love or hate the fact that local artisans go table to table selling their wares.

Even if you're not staying at the eponymous hotel, consider popping in for a perfectly good meal at the **El Rancho Restaurant** (1000 E. Hwy. 66, 505/863-9311, 6:30am-10pm daily, $11), where all the dishes are named after Hollywood stars. Burgers and New Mexican food are your best bets, including *atole* (cornmeal mush) for breakfast; the margaritas ($7 for "top shelf" with fresh lime juice) are dangerously strong.

Cafés

The **Gallup Coffee Company** (203 W. Coal Ave., 505/410-2505, 7am-8pm Mon.-Sat., 10am-4pm Sun., $7) has an old tin ceiling, contemporary photography on the walls, and a mellow atmosphere where Navajo artists and fleece-clad mountain bikers mingle. Evenings often see a set by a local singer-songwriter. The menu ranges from fresh salads and big sandwiches to a full breakfast.

With a nice small-town diner vibe, **Angela's Café** (201 E. Hwy. 66, 505/722-7526, 10:30am-3:30pm and 6pm-9pm Mon.-Fri., $9), in the cultural center in the former train station, serves burgers, big sandwiches on locally baked bread, and a good selection of craft beers to locals. Breakfasts include scones, crepes, and assorted egg dishes. In the evenings, there's occasionally acoustic music.

So dazzling is the baked good display at ★ **Glenn's Bakery** (901 W. Hwy. 66, 505/722-4104, 6am-8pm Mon.-Fri., 6am-6pm Sat., $3-10) that it's easy to be overwhelmed by the abundance of options before you. Thankfully, there's no wrong choice—just some of the best doughnuts anywhere and wonderfully flaky cinnamon rolls. If you need more than a sugar fix, settle in alongside locals reading the morning papers for breakfast burritos, pizza, or one of the daily specials, such as lamb stew.

Aside from the fact that all burgers are served well-done, **The 505 Burgers & Wings** (1981 Hwy. 602, 505/722-9311, 11am-8pm Mon.-Fri., 11am-5pm Sat., $9) is pretty good, with hand-cut fries, pretzel-bread buns, and nice fresh sides. With an almost entirely local clientele, it's a good glimpse of regular life in Gallup. Look for it on the corner of a small strip mall on the south side of town.

Middle Eastern

If you need a break from enchiladas and burgers, head straight to **Oasis** (1301 E. Hwy. 66, 505/863-8899, 11am-8:30pm Mon.-Thurs., 11am-9pm Sat.-Sun., $7), which serves top-notch Mediterranean meals, such as chicken and beef shawarmas, kabab sandwiches, filling vegetarian options, and homemade hummus. Look for it on Hwy. 66, two blocks west of Hwy. 602.

ACCOMMODATIONS

Look no further than ★ **El Rancho Hotel** (1000 E. Hwy. 66, 505/863-9311, www.elranchohotel.com, $80 d), one of the best places in New Mexico to get a taste of what tourism must've been like back when this was still the wild frontier. The lobby alone—worth a stop even if you're not planning to spend the night—is a Western fantasia of rustic wood paneling, furniture made of bull horns, a giant stone fireplace, and glossy photos of all the Hollywood actors who passed through the doors back in Gallup's heyday as a movie backdrop. (It helped that the man who built the place in 1937 was D. W. Griffith's brother.) Rooms named after Kirk Douglas, Ronald Reagan, and others are kitted out with wagon-wheel headboards and vintage bathroom tile; some even have back porches.

A separate motel wing has significantly less character but perfectly clean and functional rooms—rates here start at $95. Guests at both have access to a decent swimming pool, and there's wireless Internet access everywhere.

1: Richardson's Trading Co. & Cash Pawn **2:** Jerry's Café **3:** El Rancho Hotel

INFORMATION

Conveniently located right downtown, the staff at Gallup's **chamber of commerce** (106 W. Hwy. 66, 505/722-2228, www. thegallupchamber.com, 8:30am-5pm Mon.-Fri.) can answer just about any question. Memorial Day-Labor Day, it's also open 8:30am-5pm Saturday.

GETTING THERE

By car, Gallup is two hours (140 miles) west of Albuquerque on I-40, and nearly three hours (187 miles) east of Flagstaff, Arizona. From Farmington, it's a two-hour drive west, then south (120 miles).

Trains stop at Gallup's station on Highway 66 once a day, eastbound and westbound. From Albuquerque, the trip takes about 2.5 hours and costs $20, making it a pleasant option for a car-free outing. The station, which is used as the Multi-Cultural Center, is not staffed; you'll have to contact **Amtrak** (800/872-7245, www.amtrak.com) for tickets and train status.

Greyhound (800/231-2222, www. greyhound.com) serves Gallup from Albuquerque, with departures from a truck stop on the west side (3405 W. Hwy. 66, 505/863-9078) three times daily.

The truly adventurous traveler can hop a **Navajo Transit System** (928-729-4002, www.navajotransit.navajo-nsn.gov) bus to head out across the whole Navajo Nation; fare is a very reasonable $2 (note that the entire system operates on Mountain Standard Time). **Gallup Express** (505/722-0777, www. gallupexpress.com) runs around town and down to Zuni Pueblo.

Navajo Nation

Covering some 27,000 square miles in New Mexico, Arizona, and Utah, the Navajo Nation is the largest reservation in the United States, and with nearly 300,000 people claiming Navajo ancestry (about 175,000 of whom live on the reservation), the Navajo are the largest tribe in the country. They call themselves Diné (The People); the term Navajo came from Tewa via the Spanish, translating as "cultivated field," for which these settled people were already well known when the conquistadors met them.

Although the reservation was granted in 1868, the Navajo Nation didn't take on its current shape until decades later, when the eastern border was expanded through a series of complex land swaps with the U.S. government—the ruins at Chaco Canyon, for instance, are on federal land but surrounded by Navajo territory. This fringy edge, where reservation land alternates with private land in carefully delineated squares, is often referred to as the Checkerboard. Some portions of the reservation, such as Ramah, near Zuni, are completely separate from the rest of the "Big Rez."

The main route through New Mexico's Navajo land is U.S. 491 north from Gallup. Until 2003, the highway was known as U.S. 666, but the Department of Transportation reportedly got sick of the chronic sign theft and changed the number. It still hasn't completely shaken its nickname, the Devil's Highway, due to regular car crashes and tales of people being attacked by "skinwalkers" (Navajo shape-shifters) along its most remote stretches.

The drive north to Shiprock is beautiful but solitary, passing only a few chapter houses (reservation administrative centers) and the occasional hogan, the traditional Navajo ceremonial building. With their straight, faceted sides, hogans resemble the cliffs that often tower above them, and their doors always face east, toward the rising sun.

The terrain shifts to a sandy pink as you head north, punctuated by the Chuska Mountains, to the west on the border with Arizona, then the occasional mesa. Finally, there is the Shiprock formation, a dramatic spike that does look like a prow gliding through the sandy sea—or, as the Navajo see it, a "rock with wings" (Tsé Bit'a'í).

TOADLENA TRADING POST

The community of Two Grey Hills is widely considered the source of some of the finest rugs in the Navajo tradition, made of undyed wool carefully selected for its natural gray, brown, cream, and black, then woven into intricate geometric patterns rich with symbolic meaning. Some can be so thin and tightly woven, they resemble paper. The creaky old Toadlena Trading Post (505/789-3267, 9am-6pm Mon.-Sat., noon-5pm Sun. June-Sept., 9am-6pm Mon.-Sat. Oct.-May) near Newcomb is one of the main places where Two Grey Hills rugs are sold, and in addition to exquisite work for sale, it has a museum dedicated to skilled artisans of New Mexico. The exhibit changes periodically—typically every two years. It's a nice excuse to drive off the highway and into the foothills of the Chuskas.

On U.S. 491, look for the Shell station around mile marker 60; head west on the paved road, about 10 miles, and follow it as it turns south through the village of Toadlena. The trading post is on a small hill, a few curves after the road turns to dirt. From there, if you have a sturdy car, you can continue on the dirt road as it heads back southeast, passing through Two Grey Hills proper, where its own trading post (505/789-3270, 8am-6pm Mon.-Sat.) is less artfully arranged but also holds some treasures. Look for it just past the intersection with a paved road leading north. This northbound road drops you back on the paved Toadlena road, to connect to U.S. 491.

SHIPROCK

Not to be confused with Window Rock (the Navajo Nation capital in Arizona), the town of Shiprock is the largest community in the Navajo Nation, home to a little over 8,000 people. Diné College is also here, as well as a regional hospital and a major Bureau of Indian Affairs office. Visitors won't find a lot going on, though, unless they're in town for the flea market, in the parking lot at the intersection of U.S. 491 and U.S. 64—it's appealing not just for the random assortment of merchandise (CDs from Navajo rock bands, as well as crafts and jewelry) but also for the seriously traditional Navajo food, such as blue-corn mush and stewed sumac. If you're staying in Farmington, the flea market is definitely worth the short drive over. There are usually a few vendors there every day (8am to 5pm), but it's biggest and most interesting on Saturday.

The big annual event is Northern Navajo Nation Fair (505/368-4305, www.northernnavajonationfair.org), celebrated for more than a century. It happens the first weekend in October, when there's a major powwow, the Miss Northern Navajo pageant, a free barbecue, and a fry bread cook-off, as well as the nine-day Yei Bichei dance ritual.

The rest of the time, Shiprock is as good a place as any to fill up on gas and admire the view across the San Juan River and desert plateau. In the strip mall at the intersection with U.S. 64, look for Navajo Arts & Crafts Enterprise (505/488-0101, 9am-8pm Mon.-Sat., noon-6pm Sun.). It may not have the charm of an old trading post, but as a project of the Navajo Nation government, it's very well priced and shows some excellent work, along with books, music, and Western wear.

For the best vantage points of the Shiprock volcanic formation, about 15 miles southwest of the eponymous community, pull off along the drive south on U.S. 491 or, for a closer view, turn west off U.S. 491 onto Indian Service Route 13. Along this route, the peak will tower above you on your right as you draw closer to it. Note that hiking is not permitted on Shiprock nor is driving any of the dirt roads that approach its base.

Food

If you miss the **flea market,** you can get green-chile stew and fry bread tacos at **Mannings Thatsaburger** (U.S. 491, 505/368-4019, 7am-8pm daily, $7) and at **KFC** (U.S. 491, 505/368-4805, 10am-9pm Sun.-Thurs., 10am-10pm Fri.-Sat., $4). Honestly, everything is better at Mannings, but there is novelty value in subverting the fast-food establishment by marching up to the plastic KFC counter and ordering the local goods.

In the summer, keep an eye out for roadside vendors of fresh produce and "kneel down bread," fresh corn pudding steamed in corn husks.

FOUR CORNERS MONUMENT

In 2009, the **Four Corners Monument** (U.S. 160, 928/871-6647, 8am-7pm daily May-Sept., 8am-5pm daily Oct.-Apr., $5) where the state boundaries of New Mexico, Arizona, Utah, and Colorado all meet came under scrutiny, as analysis of old surveying techniques suggested that the point might be a good 2.5 miles off. But rebuttal from the National Geodetic Survey settled the matter, and the monument rests easy again. It's not much to see, though: it's recommended only for aficionados of roadside Americana, fans of Twister, and land surveyors.

It does at least provide an excuse to tour around the barren, butte-spiked lands up here, and you'll be wanting to get out and stretch your legs just about the time you pass by the entrance on U.S. 160. And what a stretch you'll get, as you put one limb in each state and pose for your travel companion's camera. There's also a gift shop, some fry bread vendors, and a short hiking trail for a view around the surrounding canyons. (And farther north on U.S. 160, just past the San Juan River, be sure to stop at the scenic overlook for another awesome view across the flatlands to Shiprock Peak.)

Shiprock volcanic formation

Farmington

The most common base for visiting the ruins at Chaco Canyon to the south, Farmington is a pleasant enough city in its own right, tidy and filled with parks. Even though (or perhaps in part because) it's set right against the border of the Navajo Nation, Farmington has a different feel from Shiprock, at least on the surface. The largely Anglo population of 45,000 prospers from coal, oil, and natural-gas deposits, and the nearby Four Corners Generating Station is a major employer. Still, keep your radio tuned to 89.7 FM (KUUT) for Native news and music, and stop off at a good Navajo diner—you get a taste of the true cultural mix here.

Farmington's first settlers, from England, were attracted by the fertile land around the confluence of the San Juan, La Plata, and Animas Rivers (the Navajo name for the area is Tótah, "the place where the waters meet"). The first well was drilled in the 1890s—but the investor was dismayed to hit gas rather than the water he'd been looking for. The Farmington Oil & Gas Co. was established in 1906, but it wasn't until 1922 that the industry got any attention, with a wildcat well in Hogback producing crude so pure that cars could run on the stuff, no refining necessary. In the meantime, though, Farmington's growth was based on the prosperous farms and orchards in the surrounding river valley. The 1950s marked the first true oil boom, and many of the orchards were plowed under to make room for new houses; another came in the 1970s, thanks to the limited supply from overseas.

SIGHTS

The town proper has only a handful of typical attractions that aren't likely to detain you for more than a few hours. The town of Aztec and the ruins there are just 30 minutes by car, so it's easy to hit the highlights in one day.

Farmington Museum

In the same building as the convention and visitors bureau, the **Farmington Museum** (3041 E. Main St., 505/599-1174, www. farmingtonmuseum.org, 8am-5pm Mon.-Sat., free) has some pretty slick exhibits, including a gee-whiz display, complete with video holograms, about the oil and gas industry—underwritten by major corporations, naturally. Once you get away from the hissing steam and chattering touch-screen games, you'll find more on Farmington's general history, as well as an interesting replica trading post and information on just how the posts' complex, usually cashless economies functioned.

B-Square Ranch

A 12,000-acre spread, **B-Square Ranch** (3901 Bloomfield Hwy./U.S. 64, www. bolackmuseums.com, 505/325-4275, tours by appointment only, 9am-3pm Mon.-Sat., free) is home to two of the weirdest (in a great way) museums in New Mexico. It's not the hunting trophies and electrical gizmos on display that are especially odd—it's the glimpse you get into the obsessive minds of the men behind them.

At the main ranch house, the **Bolack Museum of Fish & Wildlife** is the work of Tom Bolack, oilman and erstwhile lieutenant governor of New Mexico, who, until his death, was an outspoken environmentalist—and a passionate hunter. One-hour tours begin with Bolack's "big five" hunting trophies from Africa and carry on through a veritable menagerie of taxidermy, with over two thousand specimens from all over the globe, as well as tiger-skin rugs, elephant-foot spittoons, and specimen trays of Indonesian flying lizards. And then there's the whole display of marine life, including a stuffed shark.

On the other side of the property, Tom Bolack's son, Tommy, is steadily adding to the **Bolack Electromechanical Museum,**

Farmington

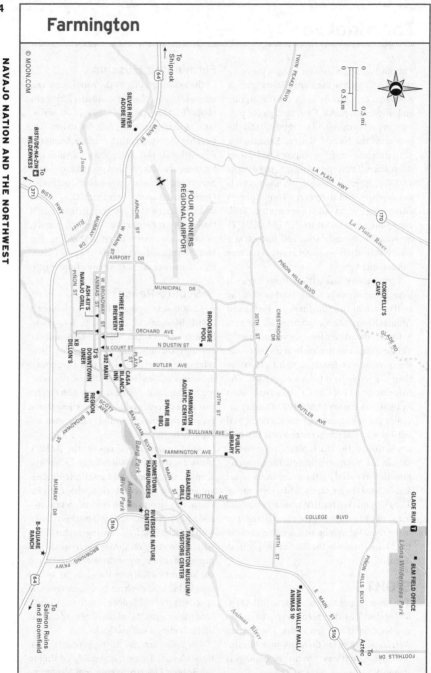

© MOON.COM

a jumbled but awesome array of obsolete or near-obsolete technology: electric meters, radio antennae, TV cameras, a vintage DC-3, and one of Elvis's Cadillacs. The walk through the collection takes two hours and is peppered with odd information about the family and Tommy's interests, which include country music and pyrotechnics (he sets off a massive display every Fourth of July).

The ranch driveway is immediately west of Browning Parkway, running south, marked by a small sign. Make reservations for tours at least a day ahead, and at least four days ahead for a Saturday tour.

Salmon Ruins & Heritage Park

Ten miles east of Farmington, the **Salmon Ruins** (6131 U.S. 64, 505/632-2013, www. salmonruins.com, 8am-5pm Mon.-Fri., 9am-5pm Sat.-Sun., $4) is not exactly the best place to contemplate the mysteries of the ancients, what with the traffic drone from the highway and the dilapidated mobile homes that clutter the view behind the 11th-century semicircular complex.

But the site is intriguing for this very reason: Here, the layers of accumulated culture include the present day, as well as homesteaders' cabins and a gnarled apple orchard planted in the 19th century. And even though the area feels crowded now, you can see why the spot, next to the San Juan River and towering cottonwoods, must have appealed to each wave of settlers. The buildings from the earliest period, between 1088 and 1263 (when the place was abandoned following a major fire), were probably built by colonists from Chaco, as they use the same masonry style and a similar layout. There are more than 300 rooms in a single large block.

The site includes the rough timber home of George Salmon, whose family helped preserve the ruins, as well as facsimile hogans, tepees, and other examples of local architecture over the millennia. The small **museum** here is also quite good, with its emphasis on tools and daily life. In the winter (Nov.-Apr.), the ruins don't open until noon on Sunday.

The **San Juan County Archaeological Research Center and Library,** based at Salmon Ruins, runs small-group tours around Chaco Canyon, the Bisti/De-Na-Zin Wilderness (Oct.-May), and some of the more obscure sites on Navajo land. Rates for an eight-hour outing, including a sandwich lunch, start at $390 for one or two people.

SPORTS AND RECREATION

With three rivers and dramatic sandstone formations nearby, as well as a few in-town parks, the Farmington area is good for getting out and about. For maps, permits, fishing licenses, and more information on these and other activities, stop in at the **BLM Farmington Field Office** (6251 College Blvd., 505/564-7600, 8am-5pm Mon.-Fri.).

★ Bisti/De-Na-Zin Wilderness

Some 41,000 acres of barren shale hills and weird rock formations, this wilderness area is about 30 miles south of Farmington, most directly accessible by Highway 371. You have to be self-sufficient to enjoy this place—there are no marked trails, no bicycles allowed, nor groups of more than eight people. You'll find no services, water, or information at the access points. But if you can commit a few hours to a hike (or better, camp on a moonlit night), you will find it one of the more fascinating terrains in the state. It's also relatively easy to navigate—as long as you stick to the ravines and washes that form natural paths. The larger formations and hills are good landmarks, though definitely bring a compass no matter which route you take.

The BLM-managed patch of land has two access points. The **Bisti** side (36.5 miles south on Hwy. 371, then 2 miles east on gravel Road 7297, then left at the T-intersection), which provides access to the **Alamo Wash,** is less than stunning when you get out of your car—you probably passed more intriguing hoodoos (wind-eroded pillars of sandstone) on the drive down. The land in front of the small parking area looks like poorly maintained

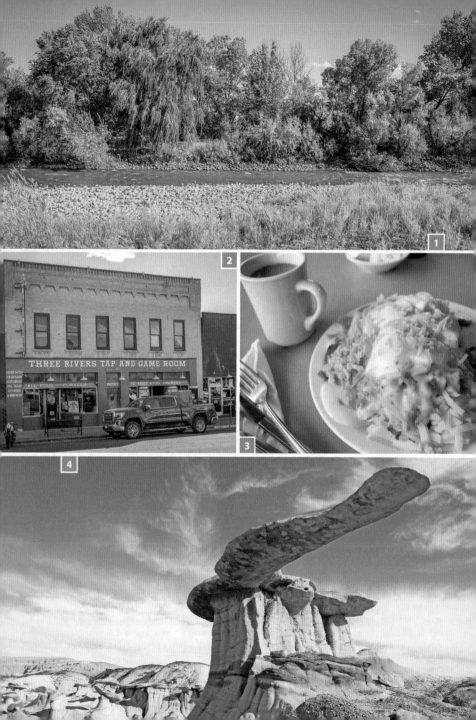

pavement, and the low hills resemble mud-caked elephants. Farther off, deep-red hills are a by-product of intensely hot coal fires millions of years ago.

Walk roughly southeast about 30 minutes (2 miles), and you're surrounded by precarious-looking towers of rock and undulating walls of ravines; another 1.5 hours due east from here, and you pass all of the best formations. Keep an eye out for fossils in the rocks and chunks of petrified wood on the ground.

The other access point, the De-Na-Zin side, is on County Road 7500, 13 miles east from Highway 371 and a little over 11 miles west of U.S. 550. The pull-off on the north side of the dirt road is marked only by a small sign that's easy to miss. Here, there's a marked trail for about three-quarters of a mile, through low scrub, to the Hunter Wash.

Hiking

The relatively wild-feeling Animas River Park runs along the riverbank on the east side of town, with trails winding through the trees. It's a pretty place for a morning run or a sunset stroll, and the paved waterside path, dotted with picnic tables, runs a full five miles. The easiest access to this walk is at Berg Park, on the west bank of the river, off Scott Avenue; on the east bank, the Riverside Nature Center (505/599-1422, 9am-6pm Tues.-Sat., free) opens onto more trails, as well as a village of fat prairie dogs. It's also open 1pm-5pm Sunday in spring and summer.

Mountain Biking

Local mountain bikers developed the BLM-managed Glade Run Recreation Area through the sandstone cliffs north of the city. It's the site of the venerable Road Apple Rally (505/599-1184, www.roadapplerally.com), which has run every October since 1981 (back then, competitors rode single-speed, fat-tire cruisers). You can do the rally route

1: Animas River Park 2: Three Rivers Brewery & Tap Room 3: an aptly named "pileup" at TJ's Downtown Diner 4: hoodoo in Bisti Wilderness

on your own, or one of several other loops through the foothills.

It's easy to get lost in the network of single-track and dirt roads—view trails at www.mtbproject.com. An expert at 505 Cycles (4301 E. Main St., 505/326-0429, 10am-6pm Mon.-Fri., 10am-5pm Sat.) should be able to get you oriented better. The Glade Run trails are also open to hikers, though bicyclists get the right-of-way.

ENTERTAINMENT AND EVENTS

Farmington turns in early—if you can't find fun at the places mentioned here, there's always the Animas Valley mall and Animas 10 multiplex cinema at 4601 East Main Street, on the north side of town.

Nightlife

Your best bet for a relaxed bar scene is Three Rivers Brewery & Tap Room (101 E. Main St., 505/325-6605, noon-11:30pm daily), where most people play pool while savoring pints of the house-made Chaco Nut Brown Ale and other brews. Also downtown, K. B. Dillon's (101 W. Broadway, 505/325-0222, 11am-10pm Mon.-Thurs., 11am-midnight Fri., 5pm-midnight Sat.) is a bit rowdier; there's a steakhouse attached, if you need something to soak up the beer.

Every Friday and Saturday afternoon in the summer, there's live music on the small square at the corner of Main Street and Orchard Avenue.

For a very mellow evening, chill out at the friendly board-game parlor Game Changers (217 W. Main St., 505/330-8479, 2pm-7pm Tues.-Thurs., 2pm-midnight Fri.-Sat., $5), which stocks some 450 games to play.

Festivals and Events

Farmington's main get-together is the Totah Festival (505/599-1174, 200 W. Arrington Ave., www.totahfestival.org), a Navajo art market held on Labor Day weekend in the Civic Center. The city also hosts the Connie Mack World Series (1101 N. Fairgrounds

Rd., $5) in late July and early August at Ricketts Park, the final contest of the youth baseball teams that aren't in the Little League.

FOOD

Meals in Farmington are rarely anything to write home about, but there are a few reliable options among the scores of fast-food outlets.

New Mexican

A rare opportunity to eat Navajo food, made by and for Navajo, the very popular **AshKii's Navajo Grill** (123 W. Broadway, 505/326-3804, 11:30am-4:30pm Mon.-Fri., $7) is a cheerful diner run by a family that once sold food at flea markets. All the favorites are here, with squash stew, Navajo tacos, fry bread, and mutton sandwiches and plates. Wash it down with Navajo tea (an herb called *cota*).

Tucked in the back of a Chevron station, **Habanero Grill** (2834 E. Main St., 505/324-9876, 6am-6pm Mon.-Sat, 8am-2pm Sun., $6) gets high marks for its made-to-order burritos and fajitas and imaginative dish names, such as the Junk Yard Dog—a burrito with green chile, chicken, ham, bacon, and cheese.

Cafés

Occupying a vast old lumber warehouse, **Artifacts Gallery** (302 E. Main St., 505/327-2907, 7:30am-3:30pm Mon.-Fri., 8am-2pm Sat., $3), is a wonderful spot to linger over a cup of coffee and indulge your creative pursuits. There's plenty of art to admire, occasional live music—and the coffee and pastries are top-notch, too.

The friendly staff at **Oso Grande** (2214 San Juan Blvd., 505/860-8086, 6:30am-3pm Mon.-Fri., 8am-1pm Sat., $3) serve a wide assortment of organic coffee drinks, including a few of their own creations. Don't leave without trying their dangerously-sized mini cinnamon doughnut rings.

Breakfast

For a breakfast guaranteed to fill you up head down to **TJ's Downtown Diner** (119 E. Main St., 505/327-5027, 5:30am-2:30pm Mon.-Fri.,

6am-12:30pm Sat., $9), where specialties include the One Car Pile Up, a towering concoction of biscuits and gravy plus green chile and eggs.

Burgers and Barbecue

Farmington's favorite burgers are made in the tiny white building that is **Hometown Hamburgers** (2133 E. Main St., 505/326-5580, 10am-10pm Mon.-Sat., 11am-6pm Sun., $5). With hand-cut fries and the option of a one-pound patty, it beats the chains in quality *and* quantity.

It's a little disorienting to walk into **Spare Rib BBQ** (1700 E. Main St., 505/325-4800, 11am-8pm Tues.-Sat., $9), which looks exactly like a roadside joint somewhere in the South—except the picnic tables are indoors, on carpeting. Hush puppies, sweet tea, and collard greens are all on the menu next to succulent pulled pork and deep-fried shrimp.

Brewhouse

In a stately old downtown block that once housed a drugstore and the daily *Times-Hustler,* the sprawling ★ **Three Rivers Brewery** (E. Main St.) takes up the better part of a block between Orchard and Commercial avenues, with a bar, brewery, sit-down restaurant, and pizzeria—all with separate menus and entrances along Main Street. The **Brewery & Eatery** (101 E. Main St., 505/324-2187, noon-midnight daily, $22), is a lovely old tin-ceilinged room, with an original soda fountain, serving house-made root beer for kids and real beer for grownups. The menu shows a love of drink with items like the super-marinated Drunken Steak. Sandwiches are fresh-tasting items like herbed chicken salad.

Next door is the bargain **Pizzeria** (107 E. Main St., 505/324-2197, noon-midnight daily, $8), where you can build your own pie with a stupendous array of toppings, from garlic-pistachio cream to homemade meatballs. From a brick oven, they're nice and crispy, and very reasonably priced. And if *that* doesn't satisfy, it also has a whole menu of New Mexican items, plus pinball and old arcade games to distract the kids.

Finally, you can toddle down to the **Tap Room** (113 E. Main St., 505/325-6605, noon-11:30pm daily) for a game of pool, or just a beer in the backyard.

ACCOMMODATIONS

Many of Farmington's visitors are here for work, which creates a market for decent hotels in all price brackets—though many are not especially cheap. You will find better deals in nearby Aztec. All the chain hotels are represented, on the east and north fringes of town.

Under $100

Independent **Region Inn** (601 E. Broadway, 505/325-1191, www.hotelsone.com, $71 d) matches all the chain hotels in amenities but charges less; there's free wireless Internet, and even an outdoor pool. Not far from downtown and the river walk along the Animas, the location is very convenient, and the on-site restaurant is not bad in a pinch.

$100-150

If you can find it, down a precipitous little gravel road just off U.S. 64 on the west side of town, **Silver River Adobe Inn** (3151 W. Main St., 505/325-8219, www.silveradobe. com, $115 d) makes a wonderful, natural oasis. The breakfast room, packed floor to ceiling with plants, overlooks the river, and the whole place has a pleasant, hand-built-in-the-1970s feel, complete with solar panels, as well as exposed adobe-brick walls in the two rooms and one suite.

In a quiet residential neighborhood, ★ **Casa Blanca Inn** (505 E. La Plata St., 800/550-6503, www.casablancanm.com, $119 d) encompasses three separate properties—humdrum split-level ranch homes on the outside, but completely transporting inside, with a tasteful and uncluttered mix of hand-carved furniture, brick and wood floors, and decorative treasures like Guatemalan bedspreads, Indian headboards,

and Chinese vases. The main "hacienda" has two separate garden areas and includes the Vista Grande suite, with a wraparound sun porch. Across the street are two smaller properties, with two rooms each suited for long-term rentals. Main Street is easy walking distance down the hill.

Over $150

For sheer novelty value, you can't beat **Kokopelli's Cave** (3204 Crestridge Dr., 505/860-3812, www.kokoscave.us, $340 d), a "luxury cave dwelling" in the cliffs on the north side of town. To get to your fully appointed, 1,650-square-foot home, you have to edge along a sandstone path down the side of a cliff face—only consider staying here if you can bring what you need in a backpack. All that said, once you're in, you'll probably stay in for a night or two ($290 per night). But with a full kitchen, a barbecue grill, a hot tub, and a deck with a pretty spectacular view, you're pretty well set. Note that it's closed December-February.

INFORMATION

The **Farmington Convention & Visitors Bureau** (3041 E. Main St., 505/326-7602, www.farmingtonnm.org, 8am-5pm Mon.-Sat.), in the same building as the Farmington Museum, is the place to pick up flyers, maps, and a comprehensive vacation guide.

GETTING THERE AND AROUND

By car, Farmington is three hours (180 miles) northwest from Albuquerque on U.S. 550 and two hours (120 miles) northeast from Gallup via U.S. 491 and Highway 371. It's a little over one hour (55 miles) south from Durango, Colorado, on U.S. 550, and just over 30 minutes east from Shiprock on U.S. 64.

Thanks to the oil and gas industry, **Four Corners Airport** (FMN, 1296 Navajo St., 505/599-1394), on the west side of town, currently offers charter flights only. National car-rental chains have branches at the airport.

Aztec

A half-hour drive northeast from Farmington, Aztec nearly counts as a suburb, but this town of 7,000 has its own character. Its pretty restored main street is lined with brick-front shops, including a giant historical museum.

SIGHTS

The scenery around here is a study in dusty tones, with white and beige rocks studded only with sagebrush and the occasional piñon tree—a stark backdrop for the Ancestral Puebloan ruins on the north side of town that are worth the visit for the great kiva alone.

Aztec Ruins National Monument

The "place by flowing waters" was misnamed Aztec by American settlers in the 19th century, who assumed people from central Mexico had established this place. **Aztec Ruins National Monument** (84 County Rd. 2900, 505/334-6174, www.nps.gov/azru, 8am-6pm daily in summer, 8am-5pm daily in winter, $5) doesn't have the dramatic setting of Chaco Canyon or Mesa Verde, but it's the best place to see Ancestral Puebloan (Anasazi) architecture if you can't make it to those more remote spots.

The main excavated area is only a portion of a larger city. When you're up on a high point looking over the surrounding ground, you'll see that the other "hills" are really unexcavated rubble. The cleaned-up **West Ruin** contains some 400 rooms, as well as a few nice details that show off the Ancestral Puebloans' knack for building. As you walk out of the visitors center and along the side wall of the great house, for instance, notice the band of green stone embedded in the wall, apparently an intentional bit of decoration. This is also a rather neat place to explore because you can go inside many of the rooms, some of which have their original ceilings: 800-year-old timber, insulated with mud-daubed twigs. The interior walls would have been plastered; some were painted as well.

But the really fascinating detail here is the fully reconstructed **great kiva**, a submerged room 40 feet across, the roof of which originally weighed 95 tons. Descending the stairs into the gloom, stepping onto the packed earth of the floor, you can easily imagine the whole community (or at least the men) gathered together for meetings and ceremonies.

Culturally, Aztec appears to have been first affiliated with Chaco Canyon; later, its construction style imitated that used at Mesa Verde in Colorado. It was occupied only for about two centuries and abandoned before 1300.

A number of burials found in the lower rooms led archaeologists to reexamine the long-held assumption that these buildings—and similar complexes at other Ancestral Puebloan sites—functioned like apartment blocks. According to that theory, lower rooms were most often used for storage. But here at Aztec, the ritually prepared bodies suggest that the rooms had a more specialized use, and that perhaps these stone buildings were dedicated to ceremonies and city administration, while people lived in outlying structures made of perishable materials that haven't stood the test of time.

The small **museum** addresses this issue, just one in the ever-changing field of archaeology, with a small item in one corner noting that the exhibits have yet to be updated to reflect the new ideas about the use of great houses. No matter, as the items on display are particularly interesting regardless of what theory they prop up. There's a shred of a woven reed mat, a portion of a blanket made of turkey feathers and rabbit fur, and an original ladder (rare, because they were so heavily used and usually left out in the elements), among other small comforts of life eight centuries ago.

Aztec Museum & Pioneer Village

The ultimate in small-town historical collections, the Aztec Museum & Pioneer Village (125 N. Main Ave., 505/334-9829, www.aztecmuseum.org, 10am-5pm Tues.-Sat. May-Oct., Wed.-Sat. Nov.-Apr., $5) certainly has the usual array of old telephone switchboards, vintage eyeglasses, and farming implements—but it has an enormous number of them, all obsessively laid out in what seems like an endless series of rooms. Then there's a beautiful "cyclorama," a huge, meticulously carved rotating diorama of Wild West scenery, as well as an annex devoted to gas-drilling history, including an unnerving exhibit on a nuclear fracking program in the late 1960s.

And finally, when you thought you were done browsing through the complete interior of an old barbershop and the large gun room, you go outside to find . . . an entire town. Set in orderly rows, all the usual Old West establishments are there, built at a slightly smaller scale: the sheriff's office, the one-room schoolhouse, the general store, the village doctor, even the church, which in this case was a real building from a nearby community that was moved here and scaled down to fit with the others. And of course, each building is kitted out with period-specific knickknacks.

SPORTS AND RECREATION

The mountain biking and hiking trail called Alien Run traces a route up Hart Canyon, past the site of an alleged UFO crash. It's a scenic bit of single-track, with a few patches of slick sandstone. There are 5-, 9-, and 16-mile routes, and about four miles in, a plaque marks the site where in 1948 the remnants of a 100-foot-wide disc were spotted, along with dead creatures resembling small humans. According to locals, the crash was swiftly followed by heavy-breathing military reps who whisked all the evidence away—though apparently the site does register a slightly abnormal amount of radiation. To reach the trailhead, take U.S. 550 north four miles, then turn right on County Road 2770. Follow this three miles to a left turn, then it's a half-mile up a hill and a right turn; the parking area is on the left.

There's an annual bike race (www.alienrun.com) on the trail in early May. The excellent Alien Bike Shop (200 S. Main Ave., 505/333-7919, 10am-6pm Tues.-Fri., 10am-5pm Sat.) can provide advice on local trails and gear.

FOOD AND ACCOMMODATIONS

The Bistro (122 N. Main Ave., 505/334-0109, 7am-2:30pm Mon.-Fri., 8am-noon Sat., $8) is across the street from the Aztec Museum. It offers good strong coffee, homemade pastries, and quiche. Much beloved local Thai restaurant ThanThip (104 S. Main Ave., 505/334-1234, 11am-9pm daily, $10) makes good curries and other standards.

At the Step Back Inn (103 W. Aztec Blvd., 505/334-1200, www.stepbackinn.com, $98 d), the rooms nod to the past with Victorian-style armoires and reproduction wallpaper; you get homemade cinnamon rolls at breakfast. For those on a budget, the motel-style Enchantment Inn (1800 W. Aztec Blvd., 505/334-6143, $58 s, $65 d) is an exceptionally great deal. It looks a little bare-bones outside, but the rooms are modern, solidly built, and clean, and there's even a pool.

INFORMATION

The Aztec Welcome Center (110 N. Ash St., www.aztecchamber.com, 505/334-9551, 8am-5pm Mon.-Fri.), run by the chamber of commerce, can answer all pressing questions.

GETTING THERE

Aztec is 16 miles (30 minutes) northeast of Farmington via Highway 516, and 9 miles (15 minutes) north of Bloomfield on U.S. 550.

Bloomfield

The town of Bloomfield, at the intersection of U.S. 64 and U.S. 550, is about the same size as Aztec but doesn't really present any strong reason for visitors to stop. It's the gateway to the best state park in the region, though.

ANGEL PEAK SCENIC AREA

Think of **Angel Peak Scenic Area** (free) as the cheater's version of Bisti/De-Na-Zin—a great place to take in northwestern New Mexico's unique geology, from the comfort of your car. The area gives you the big picture, down into a dramatic expanse of striated sandstone, rather than the ground-level view you get at Bisti. The landscape of peaks and pinnacles, carved by ancient rivers and millennia of wind, is a short drive south of Bloomfield, accessible by a road winding along the canyon edge for about six miles. Each turn yields new photo-worthy vistas; you'll also find several sets of picnic shelters. At the end of the road is a tidy primitive **campground** (no water) with nine sites.

From U.S. 550, 15 miles south of Bloomfield, turn east on County Road 7175.

NAVAJO LAKE STATE PARK

Approaching **Navajo Lake State Park** (36 Road 4110, 505/632-2278, www.emnrd.state. nm.us, $5/car), Highway 539 crosses the dam itself in an unnerving, guardrail-free swoop. The lake is the second largest in the state (after Elephant Butte), its 15,500 acres of water stretching like fingers up into Colorado; the glassy surface reflects the sky and year-round snow on the Rocky Mountains to the north. The main access point (of three) is **Pine Site,** just across the dam on Highway 511, with a visitors center and a large developed **campground** ($10, $14 with electric) that has great views over the lake, although it's somewhat removed from the water's edge. This entrance also leads to the main **marina,** offering boat rentals, a well-stocked general store and a cafe. This area can get pretty packed in the summertime, but the shoulder

the view into the canyon at Angel Peak Scenic Area

seasons can be beautifully empty. The alternate access to the lake is at Sims Mesa Site, on the east side via Highway 527, which has a significantly smaller camping area and can be a little quieter in high season.

Boating

Naturally for such a large lake—and especially one in the high desert—boating is wildly popular. The modern Navajo Lake Marina (1448 Hwy. 511, 505/632-3245, daily 8am-10pm June-Sept., daily 8am-5pm Oct.-May), in the Pine Site, is the place to go if you're interested in rentals, with options from paddleboards ($15/hr, two-hour minimum) and kayaks ($12/hr, two-hour minimum) to jet skis ($75/hr) and pontoon boats ($75/hr). The scene near the marina can be a little chaotic due the sheer number of people trying to get on the water, but as the lake is so large, it's pretty easy to find a tranquil spot all to yourself.

Fishing

The park encompasses a portion of the San Juan River that's renowned for its fishing: rainbow, cutthroat, and brown trout, as well as kokanee salmon and largemouth bass. The San Juan's "quality waters," as they're called, have special regulations: The first quarter mile after the dam is catch-and-release only, and in the next 3.5 miles, you may use only flies with a single barbless hook, and keep only one fish of 20 inches or more. There are pull-offs for riverbank access all along Highway 511. On the opposite bank (reached via Road 4280 off Highway 173) is pretty, tree-shaded Cottonwood Campground, with

nearly 50 sites. You can pick up a fishing license at the Navajo Lake Marina and at any of the lodges and guide shops in the community of Navajo Dam, at the junction of Highways 173 and 511.

SIMON CANYON

Technically not part of Navajo Lake State Park but accessible by the same road as Cottonwood Campground, Simon Canyon is BLM land that has been labeled an "area of critical environmental concern," due to the presence of golden eagles, prairie falcons, and other treasured species. Use is restricted to hikers and anglers, and the trails are not frequently used. The main hiking route, a 1.5-mile trail up through the canyon that runs due north where Road 4280 dead-ends, also passes a small Navajo defensive fort, built in the 18th century on a pillar of rock. To access the trail, pass the Cottonwood Campground and follow the dirt road to the trailhead.

ACCOMMODATIONS

The nicely appointed and very well-kept Best Western Territorial Inn & Suites (415 S. Bloomfield Blvd., 505/632-9100, www.bestwestern.com, $105 d) is the closest you can stay to Chaco Canyon without camping.

Just east of the last turn to Navajo Lake from U.S. 64, The Monastery of Our Lady of the Desert (10258 U.S. 64, 505/419-2938, www.ourladyofthedesert.org, $65 s, $80 d) has four spare and cozy retreat rooms. Guests are also given meals. The price is a suggested donation, and guests are encouraged to do some light chores.

Chaco Culture National Historical Park

One of New Mexico's greatest treasures, as well as a UNESCO World Heritage Site, **Chaco Culture National Historical Park** (505/786-7014, www.nps.gov/chcu, 7am-sunset, $20/car, good for seven days) is the most isolated attraction in the state and all the more memorable for it. Located in a long valley bordered with sheer cliff faces, Chaco was once home to more than 6,000 people. Its dramatic ruins, relatively untouched since the Ancestral Puebloans (Anasazi) departed sometime in the 13th century, are all accessible and rarely see the number of visitors you might expect. The opportunity to experience them in near solitude serves to heighten what a special place this is.

The long, bumpy and lonely ride to this hidden valley gives you time to get into the right frame of mind—you're turning back the calendar 800 years as you drive. Arriving via the more forgiving—comparatively speaking—northern route, you first see Chaco through a small pass in the reddish rocks, with the striking Fajada Butte directly in front of you. State politicians make periodic threats to pave the access roads to Chaco, but fortunately this has not yet come to pass.

Chaco has been at the center of a protracted battle to curb drilling on Bureau of Land Management (BLM) lands near the park. In the spring of 2019, legislation was introduced to permanently prevent the BLM from leasing federal land for the purpose of oil and gas drilling within a ten-mile radius of the site.

HISTORY

The first people to settle in Chaco Canyon arrived sometime between 5,000 and 10,000 years ago, but a distinctive Chacoan culture (also called Anasazi and Ancestral Puebloan) only developed around AD 850. In an arid valley with a harsh climate and very little water, the people of Chaco worked extremely hard to build a society that supported thousands

of residents and spread its influence all over the region.

Aerial surveys done in the 1980s revealed a network of roads connecting the settlements here with some 150 outlying communities, farms, and forests where timber was gathered. The roads were perfectly straight (even going up and over cliffs and mesas, rather than around) and up to 30 feet wide—a great deal of effort for a culture that did not have wheels or beasts of burden. Chaco was at the center of a sophisticated trade network, as shown by the tropical bird feathers, baby macaw skeletons, copper bells, and seashells, all from Mexico, that have been uncovered here. It is also likely that the people who lived here were from many different tribes and bands, rather than a single distinct culture—this would explain how today's Pueblo people, who all claim ancestry from here, speak a number of languages.

Far more impressive is the Chacoans' knack for large-scale construction, often taking into account solar and lunar alignments. They developed the **"core and veneer"** style of building, in which walls consisted of an inner mass of rubble faced with thin panels of sandstone, which had been chipped from the surrounding cliffs. With this sturdy technique, they raised the ceremonial complexes we now call **great houses,** which could be up to five stories tall. That the walls are thickest on the first floors, then taper at each subsequent level, suggests that the Chacoans had planned the construction before setting out, even though the growth of the largest great houses, such as Pueblo Bonito, took place over a couple of centuries.

Chacoan ceilings were another durable innovation. They were made of layers of wood stacked at right angles: First, whole tree trunks (which were dried before use, to reduce their weight), then thinner, stripped poles, then twigs, then scraps of juniper bark,

Chaco Culture National Historical Park

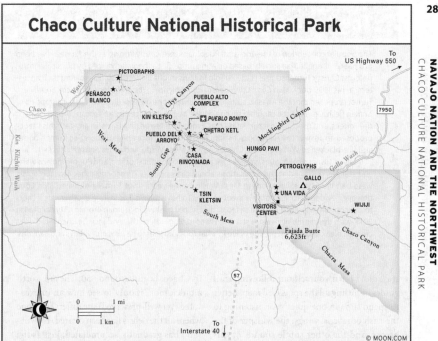

all smoothed over with a layer of plaster. Many of these roofs survive, nearly a thousand years later—even more impressive when you consider that most wood had to be carried in from the Chuska Mountains, 50 miles west.

The Chacoans' sophistication is also evident in the "sun daggers" discovered at the top of Fajada Butte. There, three rocks are positioned to allow light to fall in a particular pattern on a spiral drawn on a boulder behind. The sun falls on it differently according to the time of year. On the summer solstice, a dagger of light shone through the rocks directly across the center of the spiral; on the winter solstice, two daggers framed the spiral; and on the equinoxes, a smaller dagger of light marked a smaller spiral off to one side. The cycles of the moon are also reflected in shadows. Unfortunately, the rocks shifted in recent years, in part due to visitors wearing away the dirt at their base, and the daggers are no longer aligned; the butte is now closed off.

The pace of construction slowed in the 12th century, and by 1300 or so, the canyon seems to have been empty, and the Chacoans dispersed, some to what is now Hopi territory in Arizona, some south to Zuni, others to the Rio Grande pueblos. No one has determined for certain whether the migration was due to environmental degradation, attacks from outside, or some other factor, and every new archaeological discovery seems to open up more possibilities, rather than confirm any one theory.

VISITING THE PARK

Even if you're not a big fan of ruins, the remote setting makes the place well worth the drive for an afternoon visit, though bear in mind the rough dirt roads to access the park require time and patience to negotiate. If you're intrigued by ancient culture or wildlife, then you may want to allot several days, pitching a tent at the campground near the entrance to the valley. And regardless of how long you

The Anasazi and the Cannibalism Debate

The popular conception of the Ancestral Puebloans (previously known as the Anasazi) has been of a peaceful, egalitarian society based on agriculture. But a theory advanced by physical anthropologist Christy Turner suggests the Pueblo Indians might be better off disavowing their ancestors. In his 1999 book *Man Corn: Cannibalism and Violence in the Prehistoric American Southwest,* Turner proposed that the Anasazi culture was a violent one obsessed with ritual consumption of human flesh. Granted, the cannibalism could have been introduced by a Mexican culture, perhaps the Toltecs, and used against the Anasazi as a means of terrorizing them. In any case, his theory proposed an answer to a nagging question: What about all those piles of mangled human bones and fire-blackened skulls found at Chaco Canyon, Mesa Verde, and other Anasazi sites?

Many of Turner's colleagues were skeptical, if not downright shocked, and Pueblo Indians were, and still are, outraged at the accusations about their people. Turner and other archaeologists were banned from excavations in Mesa Verde. In the years since Turner published *Man Corn,* however, evidence to support his theory seems to have grown. For instance, other researchers found coprolites (preserved human feces) that tested positive for human proteins. Turner died in 2013, with the cannibalism issue still unanswered. Regardless, the evidence he uncovered does create a bleak and violent picture of life in what today appear to be peaceful valleys and canyons.

stay, don't burn yourself out following trail guides or hitting all the spots on a map. Better to spend time in one quiet spot, listening to the rush of ravens' wings, the whisper of the breeze, and the other subtle sounds of this now-empty place. Note that inside the park the roads are paved.

Visitors Center

Stop first at the visitors center (505/786-7014, 8am-5pm daily) to pay the entrance fee, pick up a map, find out what birds and animals have been spotted recently, and get a free backcountry permit if you think you'll be hiking. You can also join a ranger-led tour of Pueblo Bonito (free). If your schedule allows, time your visit with a Chaco Night Sky Program, a stargazing event three nights a week April-October that takes advantage of Chaco's location, more than 75 miles from any population center. Visitors can peer through a number of high-powered telescopes, and the sky positively glitters at night.

Una Vida

The small Una Vida ruins, accessible via a 1.6-mile trail behind the visitors center, represent the earlier phase of great-house building

in Chaco, begun around 850. They're worth a quick look, if only to see how an unexcavated (yet well-preserved) site differs from one where all the debris has been cleared. Blowing sand has gradually accumulated, just as the walls have slowly crumbled. You can see evidence of later occupation, probably by shepherds in the 19th century—the slabs of stone have been freshly piled up, in a different style from the original building. If you follow the trail behind the ruins, you'll see a few petroglyphs chiseled into the rock.

Camping

Before you reach the visitors center, Gallo Campground offers proximity to a nearby cliff dwelling and several petroglyphs as well as 49 sites (877-444-6777, www.recreation.gov, $15), water, restrooms, and a dump station for RVs. The closest hotels, all about a two-hour drive, are in Bloomfield and Farmington north on U.S. 550; Cuba, southeast on U.S. 550; and in Grants on I-40 to the south.

Note that no food is available in the park—no café, restaurant, or shop. You must stock up in Cuba, Farmington, or Grants. Of course, be sure you have enough gas for the drive in and out and the road around the park.

CANYON LOOP DRIVE

A nine-mile one-way loop runs up to the northwest end of the canyon and back, with parking areas near each great house.

Hungo Pavi

Like Una Vida, **Hungo Pavi** is one of the earlier complexes in the valley, built between 940 and 1040; also like the other ruins, it's largely unexcavated. If you're short on time, you can easily skip this, though the gentle curve of the back wall and the numerous tiny windows in it are rather striking.

Chetro Ketl

The defining element of **Chetro Ketl**, built over a century beginning around 1010, is its huge raised plaza. The elevated platform, some 12 feet high, required tons of packed earth and stone in its construction. With more than 500 rooms, it's the second-largest great house in Chaco. It also displays a long colonnaded wall—a very rare style in this region, and perhaps an idea borrowed from Paquimé, in northern Mexico, a city with which the Chacoans are known to have traded. You can also walk from Chetro Ketl to Pueblo Bonito (the next stop on the ruins road), along a flat, quarter-mile trail that passes clusters of petroglyphs on the canyon wall.

★ Pueblo Bonito

The largest complex in the canyon and the pinnacle of Chacoan engineering, **Pueblo Bonito** is thought to be the ceremonial heart of the ancient community. It began in the mid-800s as a sliver of an arc, a few rooms deep, and by the 12th century grew into a compound with more than 600 rooms, at least 30 kivas, and walls up to five stories tall in some sections. Roads lead straight to it from every smaller settlement in the area. The various masonry styles used in construction make it clear where the various phases begin and end, and where, for instance, an old wall and a new one converge to enlarge the arc. In some sections, the masonry is as regular as brick;

in others, you can see where worn stone has been reused.

The 0.6-mile trail leads first through an alarming array of sandstone boulders that seem to have just yesterday tumbled down from the cliff above. (In fact, they fell in 1941, crushing part of the compound.) The route then continues through the Pueblo Bonito complex, including some of the enclosed rooms, but it is hard to get a true sense of the scale of the place from the ground. If you have time and energy, hike to the mesa top via the Pueblo Alto trail.

Wetherill Cemetery

One of the few relics in this valley from a more recent era, the tiny **Wetherill Cemetery** near the end of the ruins road (look for a trail from Pueblo Bonito) is easily overlooked. It is the final resting place of Richard Wetherill, a Colorado rancher turned profiteering archaeologist. He was the first to bring Cliff Palace at Mesa Verde to national attention, and in 1896, the American Museum of Natural History hired him to dig up relics at Chaco Canyon. Wetherill is also credited with being the first to apply the name Anasazi to the people who inhabited the Four Corners area between the 9th and 12th centuries.

At that time, archaeology was only just developing as a science, and many academics in the field saw Wetherill—who worked on his own, removing pots and other valuable items as he pleased—as a threat to accurate study of these ancient places. It was irrelevant that Wetherill was often far more knowledgeable about the area and the culture than they were. Wetherill was disparaged as a "pot-hunter," and the Antiquities Act of 1906 was devised to designate national monuments and keep people like him out—Wetherill had actually staked a homestead claim on the land around Pueblo Bonito. He was operating a trading post there when he was shot and killed by a Navajo man in 1910. His wife, Marietta, is also buried here, along with several unnamed Navajo.

Pueblo del Arroyo

This is a beautiful spot in spring or summer during the rains, when the tall cottonwoods are thick from the water in the wash that gives **Pueblo del Arroyo** its name. The large, rounded stones used in many of the rooms indicate a slightly later construction than Pueblo Bonito and Chetro Ketl, which are built of the thin, regular, sharp-edged slabs that were easily collected from the mesa top. This stone was eventually used up, forcing a switch to the rounder, more irregular stone found here. For the most part erected in the early 12th century, the complex also displays some of the "tri-wall" construction that is more common in Mesa Verde.

Kin Kletso

If you've been noting the different styles of masonry throughout the various great houses, then you should also stop at **Kin Kletso,** at the far north end of the road, and a short walk from the parking lot. It displays the clearest example of what's dubbed the McElmo style of masonry (after the McElmo Valley in Colorado), associated with Mesa Verde. Its presence in Chaco Canyon is taken as an indication that the two communities were in regular contact (although now archaeologists debate who influenced whom). Whereas the best Chacoan stone walls incorporate thick rubble cores and exceptionally regular facing stones, McElmo masonry is characterized by a relatively thin rubble core and the use of large, rounded pieces of sandstone on the surface, chinked with tiny, irregular bits of rock. It was first used at Chaco in the early 1100s.

Casa Rinconada

Relatively isolated from the other great houses, **Casa Rinconada** is an enormous great kiva, meant to hold hundreds of people. Unlike other kivas, it stands alone, rather than as part of a larger complex, and it is aligned on a north-south axis with the great house of New Alto, on the opposite mesa top. It displays all the signature elements, from the wall niches to the two raised floor vaults, which may have been topped with wood to create large drums.

To visit just the kiva, bear right at the fork in the trail shortly after it begins. The trail then loops south, past a number of small villages, similar to the great houses, but on a much more limited scale. The oral histories of the contemporary Pueblo people—Zuni, Acoma, Hopi, etc.—all refer to Chaco Canyon as their ancestors' home; however, the Puebloans represent such a variety of languages and traditions that Chaco must have been home to a mix of peoples even then. Some archaeologists have proposed that these distinct villages near Casa Rinconada were inhabited by one of the different peoples.

HIKING

For all the longer hikes, you must have a permit, available from the visitors center, or, if you're indecisive, at the trailhead. There's no additional fee for the permit, and no limit on numbers—this is just a way for rangers to keep track of who's out in the wilderness.

Pueblo Alto

This 4.4-mile loop hike, which runs off the north end of the valley from behind Kin Kletso (park at Pueblo del Arroyo), is definitely the most worthwhile of the day hikes, as long as you can handle the first clamber up the cliff face to the canyon rim. From here, it's a level walk back along the mesa top to a point where you can peer down on Pueblo Bonito—the geometry of the buildings and the successive layers of development all pop into focus from this perspective. You can backtrack from the Pueblo Bonito overlook, which makes for a 2-mile hike, or carry on to the **Pueblo Alto Complex site.** The trail then passes by stairs and ramps the Anasazi carved in the cliffs, through a slot canyon, and back up to the mesa edge for a view over Chetro Ketl. You finish by climbing back down the same route to Kin Kletso. Allow between three and four hours for the full hike.

1: Pueblo Bonito 2: the ruins of Kin Kletso

Peñasco Blanco

From the Pueblo de Arroyo parking lot at the north end of the ruins road, this longer out-and-back leads to seldom-visited Chacoan and Navajo petroglyphs (rock carvings) and pictographs (paintings on the rock), and the unexcavated ruins of Peñasco Blanco, the third-largest great house in the canyon, with a unique oval layout. It's a bit of a drab hike just for this, but mostly level. The first batch of pictographs is 1.8 miles in. The whole hike, 7.4 miles round-trip, will take between four and six hours; it can be especially tiring due to the sandy ground along most of the route.

South Mesa

Parts of this 3.6-mile loop follow some old Chacoan roads, from near Casa Rinconada on the west side of the canyon to the unexcavated great house Tsin Kletsin, which appears to have been used as a lookout and signal post, as the view from its main kiva has sightlines to six other great houses. The trail first rises to the mesa top, about 450 feet, then descends through South Gap via one of the ancient roads. The full trip can take up to four hours, or you can just hike up to Tsin Kletsin and back in about two.

Wijiji

A perfectly flat hike (also accessible to bicyclists), this trail leads 1.5 miles through a natural wash to a great house from AD 1100. It's a piece of wholly planned architecture, apparently built in a single phase, unlike the other great houses in the area. Though relatively small, it is exceptional for its symmetry. Allow 2-3 hours.

PUEBLO PINTADO

A separate, unexcavated great house about 20 miles southeast of Chaco and technically part of the same park, Pueblo Pintado is recommended for completists only. If you come here after an extensive visit to Chaco, you will almost certainly wonder why you made the drive; however, if you happen to be going to nearby Crownpoint for the rug auction, then you might want to stop in.

GETTING THERE

The only way to reach Chaco is by car, and you should allow ample time for the drive—at least two hours from Farmington, Cuba, or Grants. There are two approaches: the better-used northern route from U.S. 550 and the often bumpier southern route, up from I-40. Some maps and GPS devices suggest that Highway 57 provides access to Chaco Canyon on the north side. It does not.

The northern route is from U.S. 550 near Nageezi, onto County Road 7900, which is paved. After eight miles you turn onto the smaller County Road 7950 (well signed), and the paving gives out. The full drive is 21 miles and takes no more than 45 minutes when conditions are good.

From the south, the main approach is via paved Highway 371 from Thoreau and Highway 9, then 20 miles on dirt Highway 57. But you'll want a high-clearance vehicle, and patience—the top practical speed on this bumpy road is 35 miles per hour at best. Call ahead (505/786-7014) to check conditions before taking this route.

U.S. 550 South to Bernalillo

The drive back south to the Albuquerque area is a scenic one, with a couple of possible stops in some lesser-visited wilderness areas.

THE BLACK PLACE

Fans of Georgia O'Keeffe may recognize the gray-black hills along U.S. 550, about two miles south of the junction with County Road 7900 (the turn to Chaco), the subject of several of her paintings. Off either side of the road around mile marker 111 is the so-called Black Place—shadowy arroyos, hollowed-out cliffs, and silvery buttes, just ripe for abstract painting.

CUBA

Forty-eight miles south of the turn to Chaco Canyon (County Road 7900), Cuba is a very small settlement, founded in the late 18th century, where you can get a filling meal and a good deal on a bed.

Food

Cuba's Hispano roots have yielded the exemplary ★ El Bruno's (6449 Main St., 575/289-9429, 11am-9pm daily, $12), where every fall a team of women hand-preps all the green chile (from Hatch, naturally) the restaurant will use for the rest of the year. In this season, you can order a bowl of "Hazel's green chile stew," which is really just a bowl of the stuff, barely seasoned with pork and tomato. The rest of the year, the chile works its way into stuffed sopaipillas, tamales, enchiladas, and sandwiches. Occasionally, the execution is off, but when it's good, it's great—and you can't really argue, as it's one of the few restaurants for miles around.

For a great to-go meal, Chaco Grill (6454 Main St., 575/289-0338, 6am-10pm daily, $4), at the gas station where the road curves northwest, offers excellent tamales, fry bread, and burritos—its basic bean-and-*chicharrón* is a dense amalgam of creamy, spicy, and crunchy.

Accommodations

Cuba is a handy place to sleep before or after visiting Chaco Canyon. On the north side of town, the Frontier Motel (6474 Main St., 575/289-3474, $69 s, $75 d) is a no-frills

You may recognize the Black Place from Georgia O'Keeffe's paintings.

bargain, with 33 rooms in two complexes, across the road from each other. Families will like the two-bedroom suite with a kitchen. If the Frontier is full, the next best option is Cuban Lodge (6332 U.S. 550, 575/289-3269, $65 d), on the south edge of town. It shows its age, but it is clean.

If you don't mind a winding drive, the B&B ★ Sueños Encantados (232 San Pablo Rd, off County Rd. 11, 575/249-7597, www. suenosencantados.com, $80 d) makes for a lovely rural retreat, out on an old adobe homestead about 6.5 miles off U.S. 550, just south of Cuba. To-go lunches are an option, which go a long way toward ensuring your Chaco trip starts off right.

Another neat remote option, especially good for groups or families, is Chaco Lodge Hacienda (200 Nacimiento Rd., 505/252-7488, www.chacolodgehacienda.com, $140 d), a private two-bedroom home about 30 minutes' drive southeast of Cuba.

CABEZON PEAK

West of U.S. 550, this 2,000-foot-tall "big head" butte is popular for rock climbing, or you can hike up to the peak for a view as far as Mount Taylor. According to Navajo legend, Mount Taylor represents a slaughtered giant whose head rolled to form Cabezon, while his blood settled into El Malpais. To reach the trailhead, turn west off U.S. 550 at County Road 279, about 20 miles north of San Ysidro. Then go 12 miles southwest to BLM Road 1114, which leads to the parking area in 3 miles.

OJITO WILDERNESS

The Ojito Wilderness, a landscape of stark, striped red hills, scored by rivulets of glittering white gypsum, is not quite as dramatic as the badlands of Bisti/De-Na-Zin, but it's much more accessible. The partial skeleton of the herbivore *Seismosaurus* was discovered here in 1979, and an eponymously-named trail leads to that canyon, where you can spot other fossils in the walls. The 3.5-mile long Hood Trail leads into the most picturesque section of hoodoos. From U.S. 550, turn onto Cabezon Road (County Road 26), south of San Ysidro, then bear left at the fork—the trailhead for Seismosaurus Trail is 10 miles in, on the left; Hoodoo Trail starts 11 miles on, also on the left.

On the way to Ojito (about 4 miles down Cabezon Road), you pass gray gypsum hills that are traced by White Ridge Bike Trails, 15 miles of single- and double-track. The system runs in two concentric loops. About a third of it, the "Dragon's Back" section, is exceptionally challenging, while the rest is fairly accessible to all riders. Although the trails were laid out for two-wheelers (and a stretch for horses), they're also open to hikers.

Both Ojito and Cabezon are managed by the BLM Rio Puerco field office in Albuquerque (100 Sun Ave. NE, 505/761-8700).

Las Cruces and the Southwest

South from Albuquerque along I-25, the New

Mexican landscape is dramatically split between the stark, scrubby Chihuahuan Desert and the lush green of the Rio Grande valley.

At the wildlife sanctuary in the Bosque del Apache, the river nurtures migratory birds, such as sandhill cranes. Elsewhere it feeds alfalfa fields, pecan orchards, and acre upon acre of green chile. The town of Hatch, which lends its name to the state's favorite chile variety, turns out tons of the stuff every year. And, appropriately, in the city of Las Cruces, New Mexico State University is best known for its agriculture program.

But beyond the reach of irrigation, the Chihuahuan Desert is the largest in North America, beginning around Socorro and stretching

Highlights

Look for ★ to find recommended sights, activities, dining, and lodging.

★ **The Very Large Array:** Spread across the plains west of Socorro, 27 giant radio telescopes gaze into deep space. See the massive white structures up close on a guided tour led by the knowledgeable staff (page 301).

★ *The Lightning Field:* An equally innovative, yet completely different, use of these central plains, Walter de Maria's mesmerizing sculpture requires a long drive and a 24-hour time commitment (page 303).

★ **Bosque del Apache National Wildlife Refuge:** Nothing quite prepares you for the sight of thousands of snow geese suddenly taking flight against the backdrop of a burnt orange sky at one of North America's premier birding destinations (page 304).

★ **New Mexico Farm & Ranch Heritage Museum:** Ancient tractors, actual livestock, and crafts demonstrations are among the attractions at this vast museum that tells the history of New Mexico in a practical yet fascinating way (page 321).

★ **Gila Cliff Dwellings National Monument:** Overshadowed by cliffside ruins elsewhere in the state, they're still enthralling in their own right and a fitting start to an adventure into the immense Gila Wilderness, the state's largest (page 345).

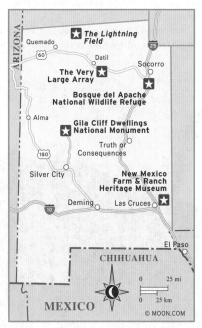

south all the way to Zacatecas in Mexico. From a car window, the view can be monotonous and dreary—no wonder Spaniards along the Camino Real trade route called this waterless stretch the Jornada del Muerto (Dead Man's Trail). Up close, though, the terrain is studded with a surprising variety of yucca and cactus, as well as roadrunners, jackrabbits, and coyotes. And when the scenery does shift, as in the Florida Mountains near Deming or at the strange outcroppings called the City of Rocks, it is all the more striking in this barren expanse.

Farther west rise the mountain ranges of the Continental Divide, where the ancient Mogollon people made their home—you can see their living spaces at the Gila Cliff Dwellings. Elsewhere in the Gila Wilderness, the largest reserve in the state, are remnants of the phenomenal, if short-lived, mining boom of the late 19th century. Silver City, on the southern edge of the Gila, has held up quite well, and now harbors a laid-back creative community that holds "Carpe mañana" as its unofficial motto.

Along the north side of the Gila Wilderness, the mountains level onto the Plains of San Agustín, a great empty bowl dotted with herds of pronghorn—as well as the giant white radio telescopes that make up the Very Large Array, a major space research center. This is ranch land, with an independent ethos held over from the rough-and-tumble mining days and range wars. Landowners in Catron County are required by law to carry a gun, and it's not uncommon to see folks swaggering around with full hip holsters. But even the most weather-beaten Westerner will sweeten up in Pie Town, where, just as you'd hope, you can get a fresh slice of America's favorite dessert.

HISTORY

This corner of New Mexico saw the first extensive human habitation in the American Southwest, with the Mogollon (moh-gui-YONE) and Mimbres cultures (named for the places in which relics of their culture were first discovered) settling here around AD 700. With the exception of the late-era Gila Cliff Dwellings and the remnants of a few pit houses, however, these ancient people left few traces. Around 1300, about the same time that the Ancestral Puebloans (Anasazi) left Chaco and Bandelier, the Mogollon abandoned their territory, for reasons that are still not clear. Presumably they moved east to the Rio Grande to meld with and expand the Pueblo culture that had just started there.

They were replaced (or perhaps edged out) by the Apache, a nomadic people spread across what's now Arizona, New Mexico, and northern Mexico. The Chiricahua and the Mimbres bands ranged over what's now the Gila Wilderness. Geronimo, the best-known Apache, said he was born on the Gila River in 1829. Their raiding culture put them at odds with the Mexican government, then the American one, which was keen to protect the gold miners who'd arrived in the new territory in the 1850s.

The U.S. Army was soon engaged in a small-scale war with the most tenacious Apache leaders, such as Cochise, Victorio, the woman fighter Lozen, and Mangas Coloradas (Red Sleeves). Instrumental in the fight was the African American cavalry, better known as the Buffalo Soldiers; they also helped build many of the forts in southern New Mexico. In the meantime, Apache women and children were being forced onto trains and resettled as far away as Florida and Alabama; the Chiricahua were the only American Indians who were not granted a reservation.

Geronimo finally surrendered in 1886, but violence continued. The mining boomtowns (now focused on silver) that sprang up were brutal, lawless places. The towns faded rapidly when silver currency was replaced

---

Previous: ocotillo flowers blooming in front of the Florida Mountains near Deming; Pie Town; petroglyph at the Gila Cliff Dwellings National Monument.

Las Cruces and the Southwest

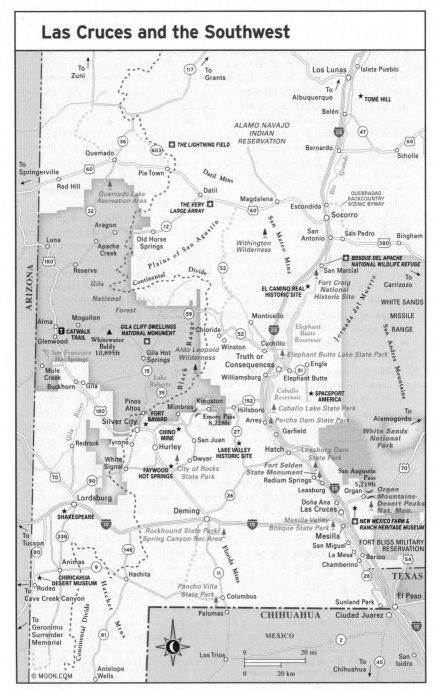

To Zuni

117 To Grants

Los Lunas ○ ○ Isleta Pueblo

To Albuquerque

★ TOMÉ HILL

Belén

36

603

☐ THE LIGHTNING FIELD

ALAMO NAVAJO INDIAN RESERVATION

Bernardo

47

60

Scholle

To Springerville

60

Quemado

Pie Town

Red Hill

Datil Mtns

Datil

Magdalena

60

Escondida

Socorro

QUEBRADAS BACKCOUNTRY SCENIC BYWAY

Quemado Lake Recreation Area

THE VERY LARGE ARRAY ☆

San Antonio ○ ○ San Pedro ○ Bingham

380

32

Aragon

12

Old Horse Springs

Plains of San Agustín

Withington Wilderness

San Mateo Mtns

Luna

Apache Creek

San Marcial

☆ BOSQUE DEL APACHE NATIONAL WILDLIFE REFUGE

To Carrizozo

Reserve

Continental

52

Divide

59

Monticello

Fort Craig National Historic Site ★

EL CAMINO REAL HISTORIC SITE ★

Gila

National

Forest

WHITE SANDS MISSILE RANGE

Mogollon

GILA CLIFF DWELLINGS NATIONAL MONUMENT ▲

Chloride

52

Elephant Butte Reservoir

25

Jornada del Muerto

San Andres Mountains

Alma

CATWALK TRAIL

Whitewater Baldy 10,895ft

Black Range

Aldo Leopold Wilderness

Winston

Cuchillo

Elephant Butte Lake State Park ▲

Glenwood

San Francisco Hot Springs

Gila Hot Springs

☆

Truth or Consequences

Williamsburg

51 Engle

Mule Creek

15

Lake Roberts

Caballo Reservoir

Elephant Butte

★ SPACEPORT AMERICA

To Alamogordo

Buckhorn ○ Gila

35

Kingston

152

Hillsboro

Caballo Lake State Park ▲

Pinos Altos

Mimbres

Gila River

Silver City

FORT BAYARD ★

Emory Pass 8,228ft

Arrey

Percha Dam State Park ▲

Garfield

White Sands National Park

180

CHINO MINE ★

San Juan

27

Hatch

Leasburg Dam State Park ▲

70

Redrock

Tyrone

Hurley

Dwyer

LAKE VALLEY HISTORIC SITE ★

Fort Selden State Monument

San Augustín Pass 5,719ft

Organ

White Signal

FAYWOOD HOT SPRINGS ★

City of Rocks State Park

26

Radium Springs

Leasburg

25

Organ

Organ Mountains-Desert Peaks Nat. Mon.

90

Lordsburg

Doña Ana

Las Cruces ★

NEW MEXICO FARM & RANCH HERITAGE MUSEUM

SHAKESPEARE ★

10

Deming

Rockhound State Park Spring Canyon Rec Area ▲

Mesilla Valley Bosque State Park ▲

FORT BLISS MILITARY RESERVATION

To Tucson

338

Mesilla

San Miguel

80

146

Florida Mtns

La Mesa ○ Berino

54

Animas

9

Hachita

11

Chamberino

28

TEXAS

CHIRICAHUA DESERT MUSEUM ★

Pancho Villa State Park

Sunland Park

El Paso

To Rodeo Cave Creek Canyon

81

Columbus

Palomas

CHIHUAHUA

Ciudad Juarez

10

To Geronimo Surrender Memorial

Continental Divide

Hatchet Mtns

MEXICO

2

Antelope Wells

Los Trios

0   20 mi

0   20 km

San Isidro

To Chihuahua

45

© MOON.COM

with the gold standard in 1893. Meanwhile, south of the mountains, the growing cattle-ranching industry had its own share of vicious infighting, which consumed big business-men, mercenary cattle rustlers, hit men, and every politician in the southern flatlands; assassinations were not uncommon. And the small town of Columbus, on the border with Mexico, was all but demolished by Pancho Villa in a 1916 raid.

These early battles have moved to the courtroom, where preservationists face off against cattle ranchers. Citing the long-term damage caused by overgrazing, environmentalists have successfully sued to take more wilderness acreage out of ranchers' control. Long-standing debates—over reintroduction of the Mexican gray wolf, for instance—have yet to be resolved, making the contrast all the more stark between deep-rooted families who've lived on and worked the land for generations and transplants who've moved here for the natural beauty.

PLANNING YOUR TIME

Given the driving distances, it's difficult to visit New Mexico's southwest if you're also interested in Santa Fe or other northern destinations. You're better off focusing on this area exclusively, perhaps even flying in to El Paso and working your way north, rather than driving down from Albuquerque. You can lounge around Truth or Consequences for a couple of days, and Las Cruces and Silver City both merit a long weekend, though you could get the spirit of each place in a day. What will interest most visitors is the Gila Wilderness, where hiking and relaxing in hot springs can occupy a day or a week.

Relatively speaking, the plains west of Socorro hold less appeal, but it's nice to at least cruise through this ranching area if you can (and it does complete a logical driving loop), as it's a sharp contrast to the hippie-holdover outlook in Silver City. Likewise, Deming and points west could be left off an arts- or hiking-focused itinerary. As largely empty land, studded by occasional crags, the bootheel south and west of Lordsburg appeals largely to naturalists.

South from Albuquerque

The desert terrain beyond Albuquerque on I-25 doesn't look immediately promising, and there's no escaping to a more scenic frontage road in this stretch. Los Lunas and Belén have their own heritage, in farming and railroads, but in recent years they have become bedroom communities for Albuquerque. By exit 152, though, you can strike out into truly remote New Mexico along the scenic Quebradas Backcountry Byway.

ISLETA PUEBLO

Tiwa-speaking Isleta Pueblo (505/869-3111, www.isletapueblo.com) had a good deal of interaction with the first Spanish settlers and was the only community that didn't participate in the Pueblo Revolt of 1680, during which many of its people fled to Hopi lands and intermarried. Notably, Isleta was home to civil rights hero Miguel Trujillo, who in 1948 successfully sued the New Mexico government for American Indians' right to vote, ending 24 years of the state's disregard for federal law.

Visitors can see the whitewashed St. Augustine Church (71 Tribal Rd. 35), a beautiful example of early mission architecture. Established in 1612, it was rebuilt in 1716, and it now glows with whitewashed walls and a sky-blue back wall. Take exit 215, heading south on Highway 47, then west on Highway 147, to the village. The pueblo celebrates the Feast of St. Augustine (Aug. 28-Sept. 4), with the biggest dances on the first and last days.

BELÉN

An easy outing south from Albuquerque and accessible via the Rail Runner train, Belén has had an eventful past largely due to its proximity to the Rio Grande and its significance as a key stop for cross-country freight rail lines. The handsome **Harvey House Museum** (104 N. 1st St., 505/861-0581, www.harveyhousemuseum.org, noon-5pm Tues.-Fri., 10am-5pm Sat., donation) is over the bridge from the Rail Runner station, across Reinken Avenue. It tells the story of the town's past as a major rail hub and also that of "Harvey Girls" who worked at the Harvey House restaurants that were once commonplace along Santa Fe Railway. Just across the street, **Pete's Café** (105 N. 1st St., 505/864-4811, 11am-8pm Mon.-Thurs., 11am-8:30pm Fri.-Sat., $9) has been open since 1949. Chile con queso—a melty, Velveeta-heavy mess—starts every meal, and there are plenty of familiar New Mexican dishes—try the stuffed sopaipillas and, appetite permitting, a slide of the homemade pie for dessert.

Walk south one block to reach Becker Avenue, Belén's historic main drag. Not much is hopping here, though feminist artist Judy Chicago lives in the old Belen Hotel building and runs the **Through the Flower Art Space** (107 Becker Ave., 505/864-4080, www.throughtheflower.org, noon-5pm Wed.-Sat.) across the street. It's a small space, with one corner devoted to bios of her and her husband, Donald Woodman, a photographer. The main exhibition area has rotating pieces by both of them. There's also a gift shop with lots of books and limited-edition reprints, and the space hosts occasional evening events. You can taste a "Judy Chicago" red wine picked by the artist across the street at the **tasting room** for the highly regarded **Jaramillo Vineyards** (114 Becker Ave., 505/569-9660, noon-5pm Thurs.-Sun.), which is located a few miles away.

A few more blocks east is the **Art League Gallery** (509 Becker Ave., 505/861-0217, noon-4pm Tues.-Sun.), which holds more than a few finds in various mediums by local artists and one block north is **Buckland Pharmacy** (600 Dalies Ave., 505/864-7434, 8:30am-6:30pm Mon.-Fri., 8:30am-3pm Sat.), which runs a nice old-fashioned soda fountain.

Tomé Hill

Midway between Belén and Los Lunas 15 miles to the north and east of I-25 and the Rio Grande, **Tomé Hill** is an important Catholic pilgrimage site, especially on Good Friday; it is topped with three 16-foot-high crosses. A natural lookout point, the hill was a landmark on the Camino Real, and that history is commemorated with a sculpture at the base of the trail. A 20-minute climb gives a good view down the Rio Grande; keep an eye out for petroglyphs on the rocks near the top. Take exit 203 from I-25, head east, then south about three miles on Highway 47 and turn east. Tomé's old town church is across Highway 47 to the west.

QUEBRADAS BACKCOUNTRY BYWAY

This 24-mile dirt road, which runs in a jagged arc down to U.S. 380, just south of Socorro, more than makes up for the previous miles of dreary highway driving. The rounded hills here are striped with rainbow hues, and the scrub desert teems with hawks, mule deer, and foxes. Requiring two to three hours, the route makes a good slow way to or from the Bosque del Apache. Don't attempt the drive if it has rained recently—the route is named for the deep "breaks," or drainage channels it crosses, and the mud in the bottoms can be impossible to pass. Look out for sandy patches at all times, as well as the occasional hardy mountain biker.

Leave I-25 at Escondida (exit 152), then go north for 1.3 miles on the east-side frontage road; turn east at Escondida Lake and continue for 0.8 mile, crossing the river, to Pueblito, where you turn right at a

T-intersection. After about a mile, you see a sign for the byway beginning on your left (west); the road ends on U.S. 380 about 10 miles east of San Antonio and the road to the *bosque.* Coming north, the start is easier to find: From the intersection of the *bosque* road (Highway 1) in San Antonio, in front of the Owl Café, head east on U.S. 380 for just over 10 miles; then turn north on County Road A-129, the beginning of the byway.

Socorro and the Plains of San Agustín

The small town of Socorro is the gateway to the Plains of San Agustín, a prehistoric lake bed transformed into a vast bowl of grazing land that is, in one spot, punctuated by the dramatic sight of enormous white radio telescopes spread across a field, known as the Very Large Array. U.S. 60 used to be a well-used cross-country route. Now this part of the state is seldom visited, except by hunters and ranchers. It is beautiful, expansive landscape, especially after a wet winter or a good summer rainy season, when the plains turn into lush fields of wildflowers. And the same dark skies that aid the VLA's research are also great for amateurs—this is probably the easiest outing from a city for a night or two of stargazing. The tiny communities that mark the west edge of the plains—Datil, Pie Town, and Quemado—are, not coincidentally, a day's horseback ride apart.

SOCORRO

Once a pueblo that offered food to conquistador Don Juan de Oñate, Socorro (Succor, or Relief) now shelters people en route to the Bosque del Apache (about 20 miles south), as well as the students of the **New Mexico Institute of Mining & Technology** (aka New Mexico Tech, 801 Leroy Pl., 575/835-5011, www.nmt.edu), which has been training engineers since 1889. The town has a small time-warp historic plaza, but the mission-style campus is scenic as well. To reach it, turn west from the main north-south route, California Street, onto Bullock Street and follow it toward the hills.

Entertainment

Wet your whistle at the **Capitol Bar** (110 Plaza St., 575/835-1193, noon-2am Mon.-Sat., noon-midnight Sun.), on the plaza, which doesn't seem to have changed much in more than 120 years of doing business—this is one of those creaky-wood-floor saloons that you thought existed only on movie sets. But with friendly bartenders, a great selection of beers on tap, pool tables, and live bands, it also has what every modern bar-goer needs.

Food

For your caffeine fix, **M Mountain Coffeehouse** (110 Manzanares St., 575/838-0809, 7am-6pm daily), just off the plaza, has the necessary espresso, as well as house-made gelato, sandwiches, full breakfasts, and freshly baked muffins. The vibe is distinctly nerdy-intellectual.

No-frills **La Pasadita** (230 Garfield St., 575/835-3696, 10am-8pm Mon.-Fri., $7) has Socorro's best homey New Mexican cuisine, with solidly good red and green chile. Garfield Street is off the southwest corner of the plaza; the restaurant is easy to miss among the other houses on the block.

Out on the main drag, **Yo Mama's Grill** (913 N. California St., 575/838-3962, 11am-9pm Mon. and Wed.-Sat., noon-8pm Sun., $9) has a great range of fresh diner standards, from juicy burgers to a satisfying surf and turf, with house-made potato chips. Vintage Americana fans—or anyone hungry after 9pm—should head for **El Camino** (707 N. California St., 575/835-1180, 24 hours, $6), an all-night diner that's plucked straight from the early faux-wood-paneling era. Its chicken-fried steak and eggs is a good bet at any time of the day.

Accommodations

Socorro has two B&Bs, both small, and both quite nice. **Socorro Old Town B&B** (114 Baca St., 575/418-9454, www.socorrobandb. qwestoffice.net, $125 d), in a renovated 1800s adobe with a nice back patio, has just two rooms and gets high marks for its blueberry muffins. **Dos Casitas en Socorro** (317 Eaton Ave., 575/835-2858, www.doscasitasensocorro. com, $110 d) has two stand-alone cottages, done in bright colors, with gas fireplaces; it is open only in birding season, September-mid-May. Both are an easy walk to the central plaza.

As for the numerous motels, you can choose from the various chain options, and on the low end, **America's Best Value Inn** (1009 N. California St., 575/835-0276, $49 d) is especially nice for the price, with a few chips in its furniture but otherwise well kept up.

Getting There

Socorro is 80 miles south of Albuquerque on I-25, a bit more than an hour's drive. If you're heading west from here on U.S. 60, through Magdalena and on to the Very Large Array, be sure to fill up your gas tank, as there's only one station farther west, in Datil, and it's very expensive.

MAGDALENA

Sleepy to the point of making Socorro feel bustling, Magdalena sits on the edge of the plains, a small clutch of houses under a great sky. Established in 1884, the town was a commercial hub: Ranchers drove cattle here, and miners shipped ore, to be loaded on a rail spur from the main line at Socorro. But the last cattle drive happened in 1970, and the rails were torn out in 1981, and now the place feels a bit wind-swept. Still, it's the largest town along U.S. 60.

For orientation: U.S. 60 becomes 1st Street in town; Main Street runs north-south in the center.

Sights

Follow signs south from U.S. 60 to the **Box Car Museum** (Main St., 575/854-2261, 11am-5pm Tues. and Thurs.-Fri., 10am-3pm Sat., donation), where a small collection of historic artifacts is on display, including some items from the remote Alamo Navajo reservation (29 miles north), next to the former train depot.

Hiking

The little-visited Magdalena Mountains south of town provide a great chance to hike or mountain bike in solitude. A good entry point into the mountains and the surrounding Cibola National Forest is **Water Canyon Campground** (16 sites; free) reached via Forest Road 235 (Water Canyon Rd.), which runs south from U.S. 60, 11 miles east of Magdalena. From the campground you can embark on the moderate to challenging **Copper Canyon Trail** (no. 10), which climbs steadily for over 3,000 feet over the course of five miles, bringing you to a ridge with a rewarding view. From there you can head back, or pick up the **North Baldy Trail** (no. 8) for an additional mile to the Walter Canyon picnic site. Along the way you should be able to spot the white dome of the Magdalena Ridge Observatory, which is operated by New Mexico Tech.

If you're looking to *really* get away, the remote **Bear Trap Campground** (4 sites; free), tucked away in the San Mateo Mountains southwest of Magdalena, makes for an excellent base for hikes into the surrounding wilderness and is also ideal for stargazing. To get there, head west on U.S. 60 out of Magdalena for 12 miles and turn left onto Forest Road 549 (also known as Hwy. 52) for approximately 16 miles. It's in an extremely isolated part of the Cibola National Forest; come prepared and take the drive in slowly.

For info on the trails above and elsewhere in the national forest, visit the **Magdalena Ranger District office** (575/854-2281, 8am-4:30pm Mon.-Fri.), on the east side.

Food and Accommodations

The **Western Motel & RV Park** (404 1st St., 575/412-7278, www.thewesternmotel.com, $56 s, $66 d) has flower boxes and lace curtains in the windows, plus lavish pine paneling for a, yes, Western feel. The bathrooms are small and the rooms don't exactly live up to their names, but it's a pleasant place with an enduring charm.

One block off the main street, the three-story ★ **Magdalena Hall Hotel** (404 2nd St., 575/854-2040, $95 d), built in 1917, recently underwent an extensive and tasteful renovation. The 16 rooms have lots of nice touches that evoke the hotel's historic past and the beds are exceedingly comfortable. The onsite **Kelly's Place Café** (11am-7pm Wed.-Sat., 9am-2pm Sun., $7) is a cheerful spot with good burritos, soup, and tempting desserts.

A fine old relic, the **Golden Spur Saloon** (1st St., 575/854-2558, 10am-2am daily) is worth a stop even if you're not drinking the hard stuff. On summer weekends, it's a popular stop for bikers, but it's really the locals who prop up the bar all week. Look for it just east of Main Street.

To really enjoy Magdalena's light-free solitude, a good option is three miles west of town, at **Rancho Magdalena** (U.S. 60, 575/418-8206, www.ranchomagdalena.com, $115 d). This B&B has three cozy rooms with corner fireplaces, all in a house set on a small rise, overlooking rolling ranch land. The same owners also offer a rental house in Magdalena proper ($175), and two other cabins ($175) farther out. For the B&B, turn south off U.S. 60 near mile marker 109.

Also of note, outside town, is **Concho Hills Guest Ranch** (1522 Remuda Tr., 575/772-5757, www.conchohillsranch.com, $325 pp), a low-key and very pleasant dude ranch where you can ride horses and target-shoot to your heart's content. Rates include all activities and meals.

★ THE VERY LARGE ARRAY

A little more than 20 miles west of Magdalena, strange structures jut out of the Plains of San Agustín. These are the 27 radio telescopes—which look like enormous satellite dishes—that compose the **Very Large Array**, a research center devoted to the study of deep space. Reach the **visitors center** (575/835-7243, www.vla.nrao.edu, 8:30am-sunset daily, $6) by turning south onto Highway 52 and following signs to the VLA access road. The center explains, first of all, just what radio astronomy is, as well as how the telescopes are focused to see deep into the Milky Way and show images as precise as the shading on Mercury's poles that may be ice. Then you can walk up close to one of the telescopes, as large as a baseball diamond and weighing 230 tons; with any luck, the array will be refocusing, and you'll get to see the massive structure slowly, grindingly turn, eerily in synch with all the others stretching up to 20 miles away. The first and third Saturday of the month, there are guided tours at 11am, 1pm, and 3pm.

For a long back-road drive, continue south on Highway 52, passing through a 600-acre private elk reserve and the town of Winston (with a possible detour to the ghost town of Chloride), to eventually connect with I-25 just north of Truth or Consequences.

DATIL

For visitors and Datil's 50 or so locals, life centers on the **Eagle Guest Ranch** (U.S. 60, 575/772-5612, 6am-9pm Mon.-Sat., 9am-5pm Sun.), an all-purpose motel, gas station, taxidermy shop, saloon, and steakhouse. Radio techies from the VLA rub shoulders with hunting parties over thick slabs of meat and a salad bar. The motel rooms ($59 d) will do in a pinch. It's a chummy, frontier-feeling place, but most people blow right through on their way to . . .

PIE TOWN

Aside from Truth or Consequences, no other town name in New Mexico looks as intriguing on a map as Pie Town. In fact, "town" is overstating it, as it has a population of about 45, though its cafés cater to some of Catron County's crustiest ranchers; keep your cool when folks swagger in with guns strapped to their hips. The second weekend in September is the annual **Pie Festival.**

The place got its name in the 1920s, when an entrepreneur began dishing out a sweet pick-me-up to famished homesteaders and, later, intrepid cross-country motorists. But after the federal interstate diverted traffic, the pie market dried up, and the place went pie-less for decades. In 1995, a disappointed visitor to Pie Town took matters into her own hands and opened the ★ **Pie-O-Neer Café** (U.S. 60, 575/772-2711, 11am-4pm Thurs.-Sun. Mar.-Nov., $6), still by far the best of the four pie vendors now in operation. The daily roster of pies—there's nothing else on the menu except what you can wash them down with—is dazzling. There's apple-cranberry, double cherry, coconut cream, and apple with green chile, to name just a few and each one is encased in perfectly flaky crust. So you might want a slice to eat in, and a pie to go. Call ahead to confirm hours—and note that it's closed for several months in winter. It typically opens for the season on, of course, Pi Day (Mar. 14).

For more nourishing food, **Pie Town Café** (U.S. 60, 575/772-2700, 9am-5pm Mon.-Tues. and Fri.-Sun. Mar.-Nov., $7) is another option, with a selection of New Mexican and diner standards along with the sweets; consult the "pie chart" to see what varieties are available that day. With the most generous opening hours, **The Gatherin' Place** (U.S. 60, 575/772-2909, 8am-5pm daily, $9) is more of an all-purpose hangout, with breakfast burritos and lunch specials like veggie curry; pie is a slight afterthought.

QUEMADO

Quemado is little more than a wide spot along the highway, but it does provide some basic services for travelers. The **Largo Motel** (U.S. 60, 575/773-4686, $65 d), on the west edge of town, has comfortable beds. Its **café** (6am-9pm Mon.-Wed., 6am-11pm Thurs.-Sat., 7am-9pm Sun., $10) is decent—its "Mexican cheeseburger" is the stuff of legend, a patty wrapped in a flour tortilla and smothered in green chile and cheese.

★ The Lightning Field

Quemado is also the unlikely starting point for a visit to an elaborate work of land art called *The Lightning Field* (505/898-3335, www.lightningfield.org, May-Oct.). In 1977, sculptor Walter de Maria installed 400 stainless-steel poles in a grid measuring one mile by one kilometer. The light glints off the poles, and summer storms create a field of crackling, brilliant electricity across their pointed tips. De Maria envisioned an immersive experience, in which the viewer, in pure isolation, watches the light shift over the course of the day. To this end, casual visitors are not allowed, and the road to the site is unmarked; you must make reservations for an overnight stay and leave your car in Quemado. At $150 per person ($250 during the prime storm months of July and August), the basic accommodations may seem a bit steep, but this ranks as one of the state's most remarkable places to spend the night, not to mention one of the great places to meditate on New Mexico's phenomenal landscape.

1: the Pie-O-Neer Café in Pie Town **2:** radio telescopes in the Very Large Array

El Camino Real

As I-25 continues south from Socorro, the highway passes alongside Bosque del Apache, one of the largest nature reserves in the United States. Then the Chihuahuan Desert scenery takes over, with dusty grasses occasionally punctuated by yucca trees. Highway 1, the interstate frontage road now designated **El Camino Real National Scenic Byway,** grants a quieter perspective and leads directly to the two major sights in this area: the remains of a Civil War-era fort and a monument to El Camino Real de Tierra Adentro (the Royal Road of the Interior), forged between central Mexico and Santa Fe during the Spanish colonial period. Just one of a network of trade routes through Spanish territory in the Americas, this north-south trail brought fur and silver into the heart of Mexico, from where it was shipped out to seaports.

★ BOSQUE DEL APACHE NATIONAL WILDLIFE REFUGE

Bosque del Apache National Wildlife Refuge, 57,000 acres of wetlands along the river, is the site of a winter sojourn for some 15,000 giant sandhill cranes and hundreds of other migratory species. It's one of the country's top birding destinations as a result, but you don't need an ability to differentiate a great blue heron from a little blue heron to appreciate the spectacle of thousands of birds rising in unison at sunrise.

Access to the *bosque* is via Highway 1, south from U.S. 380, where the small town of **San Antonio,** just a blip on the map, provides a couple of lunch spots for hungry birders. Five miles inside the north border of the reserve, you pass the **visitors center** (575/835-1828, www.friendsofthebosque.org, 8am-4pm daily), where you can pick up maps and find out which birds have been spotted that day.

A bit farther south on Highway 1, a 12-mile paved car loop passes through all the marshlands and the grain fields; at certain points along the drive, you can get out and hike set trails, such as a quarter-mile boardwalk across a lagoon or a trail to the river. Some areas are open to mountain bikers. The **loop drive** ($5/car) through the wetlands opens when birdlife is at its best, one hour before sunrise; cars need to be out by an hour after dark. The so-called Flight Deck adjacent to the *bosque's* main pool is the place to be at dawn; arrive at least 30 minutes before sunrise to ensure an unobstructed view of massive flocks of snow geese taking flight. With all its marshland, the *bosque* could just as well be called a mosquito sanctuary—slather on plenty of repellent before you start your drive.

The biggest event of the year is the arrival of the sandhill cranes—they were the inspiration for the refuge, as their population had dwindled to fewer than 20 in 1941. But now more than 15,000 of these graceful birds with six-foot wingspans winter over in the *bosque*. They're celebrated annually at the five-day **Festival of the Cranes** (www.festivalofthecranes.com) in November, when birders gather to witness the mass morning liftoffs and evening fly-ins.

Food

San Antonio, the nearest town, is best known for its green-chile cheeseburgers, especially at the legendary **Owl Bar & Café** (77 U.S. 380, 575/835-9946, 8am-8pm Mon.-Sat., $6-13), untouched by time—though rival **Buckhorn Burgers** (68 U.S. 380, 575/835-4423, 11am-7:50pm Mon.-Fri., 11am-2:45pm Sat., $5-7), just across the street, is equally renowned for similar fare.

Actually, the Owl gets extra points for historic details: It kept atomic-bomb engineers such as Robert Oppenheimer supplied with cheeseburgers and booze while they worked at Trinity Site, about 20 miles away. And the Owl's wooden bar is salvaged from the world's first Hilton hotel, started here in San Antonio by the father of modern hospitality, magnate Conrad Hilton.

If, for some reason, you're not in the mood for a burger, follow the signs for **San Antonio Crane** (17 Pino St., 575/835-2208, 10am-4pm Tues.-Sat., noon-3pm Sun., $8), one block south off U.S. 380, for homemade New Mexican food (including especially good tamales) served in a tiny dining room. In the winter, during birding season, it opens for breakfast, too.

Just north of San Antonio, **Socorro** has a few good places where you can refuel post-birdwatching, including the all-night diner **El Camino** (707 N. California St., 575/835-1180, 24 hours, $6-9), **M Mountain Coffeehouse** (110 Manzanares St., 575/838-0809, 7am-6pm daily), just off the plaza, and, on the plaza, the old-school **Capitol Bar** (575/835-1193, noon-2am Mon.-Sat., noon-midnight Sun.).

Accommodations

You can stay overnight, either in **San Antonio** at the pleasant **Casa Blanca B&B** (13 Montoya St., 575/835-3027, www. casablancabedandbreakfast.com, $100 d), or just north in **Socorro** a few blocks west of I-25 at **Dos Casitas en Socorro** (317 Eaton Ave.,

575/835-2858, $110 d), which has two cheerful guesthouses with kiva-styled fireplaces.

For camping, **Bosque Birdwatchers RV Park** (575/835-1366, $25) is just 100 yards north of the reserve border on Highway 1.

FORT CRAIG NATIONAL HISTORIC SITE

One of the largest forts in the Southwest and the staging point for the crucial Battle of Valverde during the Civil War, **Fort Craig National Historic Site** (dawn-dusk daily, free) is a long way to drive for precious little to see. Only true military buffs will have the imagination to bring the few building outlines and crumbling earthworks to life.

As a place to stretch your legs, though, you could do worse: The site is near the Rio Grande (a bit of a walk over level ground), in view of Black Mesa to the north. In the days of the Camino Real, this striking landmass was known as the Mesa del Contadero, as its position next to the river formed a natural chute for counting livestock herds. In February 1862, the north side of the mesa saw the Battle of Valverde, in which the fort's forces managed to damage a Confederate supply train, setting the stage for a more decisive

the Bosque del Apache

Union victory in the Battle of Glorieta about a month later.

EL CAMINO REAL HISTORIC SITE

Hidden from view about 2.5 miles east of I-25 (exit 115), **El Camino Real Historic Site** (575/854-3600, www.caminorealheritage.org, 8:30am-5pm Wed.-Sun., $5) is well worth a detour. The stark modern museum stands on a windswept bluff with no sign of human population in sight—a fitting locale for this tribute to the often-difficult Spanish trade route that for centuries linked Zacatecas, Mexico, with the frontier town of Santa Fe. Inside the heritage center, the information-packed exhibits describe the major points along the royal road. Outside are traditional gardens, a dramatic vista on the Chihuahuan Desert, and a six-mile trail north to Fort Craig.

Truth or Consequences

For decades, the town of Hot Springs was just a dot on the map 150 miles south of Albuquerque. In the early 20th century, its bathhouses had been packed with health-seekers enjoying the underground reservoir of mineral-rich water, but by the 1940s, the place had slumped into obscurity. Around this time, the popular radio show *Truth or Consequences* was offering national publicity to any town willing to change its name to match the show's, and the Hot Springs council took the bait. The stunt was completed in the spring of 1950, with host Ralph Edwards and a convoy of press and celebrities on hand. National notoriety faded, but T or C (as it's commonly known) has managed to hang on, acting as a diversion from the interstate for through travelers and a bargain retirement spot for people fleeing frigid Minnesota and Dakota winters.

In the 21st century, the town has received a boost from younger artists who have relocated here from the coasts, helping revive the small downtown area with galleries and hot-springs operations. The British billionaire Richard Branson, whose Virgin Galactic commercial space-flight company is the anchor tenant at the Spaceport America east of town, has been equally influential. While wealthy space tourists have put their money up and await the eventual first launch into low-Earth orbit for just a few minutes, T or C remains a pleasant, if slightly ramshackle, place to spend a night or two. Ideally stop here on a weekend, as many businesses close at least Monday and Tuesday.

ORIENTATION

Drivers enter T or C either at its farthest north end (exit 79), where Highway 181 turns into the long commercial strip known as North Date Street, or on the south side (exit 76), where Highway 187 runs through an adjunct town called Williamsburg. Both routes lead downtown, bounded by Main Street and Broadway. Most of the bathhouses and hotels with springs are on or south of Main Street.

SIGHTS
The Galleries

Of the more than 15 galleries downtown, **RioBravoFineArt** (110 N. Broadway, noon-5pm Wed.-Sun.) is the oldest, representing, among others, the town's best-known painter, Delmas Howe, who made his name with lush murals and homoerotic cowboy portraits. Howe painted the **Civic Center** (W. 4th Ave. between Grape St. and N. Foch St.) in lush flowers. A few blocks to the west, funky **Desert Archaic** (324 N. Broadway St., 503/953-4346, 10am-5pm Fri.-Sun.) features jewelry and woven works by local artists and also hosts live music.

For older artwork, peek in the always-open **post office** (300 Main St.) for a somewhat eerie 1938 mural of an American Indian dance, by Lithuanian immigrant Boris Deutsch.

Truth or Consequences

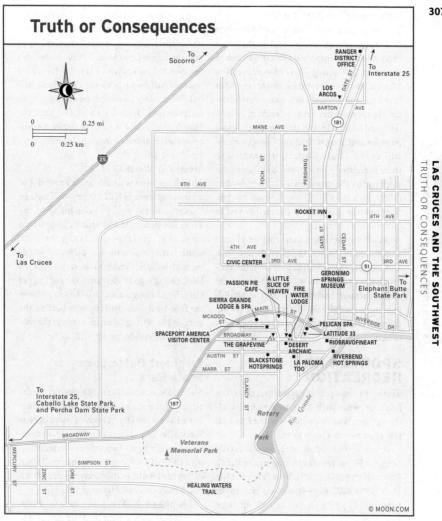

Map labels:

To Socorro
RANGER DISTRICT OFFICE
To Interstate 25
LOS ARCOS
BARTON AVE
DATE ST
181
MANE AVE
FOCH ST
PERSHING ST
8TH AVE
25
0   0.25 mi
0   0.25 km
ROCKET INN
6TH AVE
DATE ST
CEDAR ST
4TH AVE
To Las Cruces
CIVIC CENTER   3RD AVE
3RD AVE
51
GERONIMO SPRINGS MUSEUM
To Elephant Butte State Park
PASSION PIE CAFE
A LITTLE SLICE OF HEAVEN
FIRE WATER LODGE
SIERRA GRANDE LODGE & SPA
MAIN ST
MCADOO ST
RIVERSIDE DR
SPACEPORT AMERICA VISITOR CENTER
BROADWAY
PELICAN SPA
LATITUDE 33
THE GRAPEVINE
DESERT ARCHAIC
RIOBRAVOFINEART
AUSTIN ST
BLACKSTONE HOTSPRINGS
LA PALOMA TOO
RIVERBEND HOT SPRINGS
MARR ST
CLANCY ST
To Interstate 25, Caballo Lake State Park, and Percha Dam State Park
187
Rio Grande
Rotary Park
BROADWAY
Veterans Memorial Park
MERCURY ST
ZINC ST
ORE ST
SIMPSON ST
HEALING WATERS TRAIL
© MOON.COM

Geronimo Springs Museum

T or C's must-see sight is **Geronimo Springs Museum** (211 Main St., 575/894-6600, www.geronimospringsmuseum.com, 9am-5pm Mon.-Sat., noon-5pm Sun., $6). A fantastic small-town collection, it documents both the monumental and the mundane in T or C since its founding. Seven rooms display everything from mammoth skulls to portraits of local bankers to an authentic log cabin. Local rebel Geronimo gets a lot of attention, as does town-maker and radio and TV host Ralph Edwards.

Veterans Memorial Park

On the hill south of downtown is **Veterans Memorial Park** (996 S. Broadway, 575/894-7640, www.torcveteransmemorial.com), which contains a half-scale replica of the Vietnam Memorial in Washington DC, as well as a **museum of military history** (10am-4pm Tues.-Sat., noon-4pm Sun., free).

Spaceport America

For sheer potential, Spaceport America (www.spaceportamerica.com) is thrilling: this is the first commercial space-flight hub in the world. The setting—here in southern New Mexico, with its empty space, history of rocket research, and alleged alien spacecraft activity—is appropriate. Yet the Norman Foster-designed facility, tucked into the desert about 30 miles southeast of Truth or Consequences, still awaits Virgin Galactic passengers, so there is relatively little to see. Still, it's worth stopping by the downtown visitors center (301 S. Foch St., 575/267-888, 8:30am-4:30pm, free) to see displays about the facility and to glimpse what some day might be.

As activity develops, tours may be a better window on this desert industry. Tours (9am and 1pm Sat.-Sun., $50) depart from the visitor center and visit only a small wing of the main Spaceport building and a second building where specialized fire trucks wait for occasional rocket launches by other Spaceport clients.

SPORTS AND RECREATION

Truth or Consequences caters largely to the layabout, what with all the warm baths, although sports aficionados enjoy the artificial lakes just minutes from town.

If you'll be heading west into the Gila National Forest from here, stop by the Black Range Ranger District office (1804 N. Date St., 575/894-6677, 8am-4pm Mon.-Fri.), in the Lakeway Shopping Center, to pick up maps and other info.

Hot Springs

Of the dozen or so spots to take the waters, Riverbend (100 Austin St., 575/894-7625, www.nmhotsprings.com, 8am-10pm daily) is the best if you prefer the open air. Perched at the water's edge, the cascading communal pools ($10/hour) offer a range of water temperatures. If you're feeling less social, opt for one of three private tubs, similarly open-air and facing the river ($15/hour).

For a more historic vibe, head for La Paloma Too (300 Austin St., 575/894-2228, www.lapalomahotspringsandspa.com, 7am-noon and 5pm-11pm Mon.-Thurs., 10am-8pm Sat.-Sun.), also known as Hay-Yo-Kay. This restored bathhouse from the 1920s has small but clean indoor pools for one or two people; rates start at $7 for half an hour. Out back, the "longhouse" is one very large tub in a semi-open shelter, shielded from the weather.

Healing Waters Trail

This three-mile walking route around and a bit out of town is half history, half nature. Downtown, the route passes many of the iconic hot springs and historic buildings, with markers at crucial points. Across the river, southeast of downtown, a dirt trail winds through wetlands and into the scrub-covered hills, giving a good view over the old part of town. Signs along the way tell the story of how the favorite Apache bathing spot became the town of Hot Springs. Pick up a map at the museum or the visitors center on Broadway.

Elephant Butte Lake State Park

Named for a distinctive rock formation in the center of the water, 40-mile-long Elephant Butte Lake is the largest body of water in New Mexico. So long as there's no drought, it maintains a steady buzz of activity in summertime, with the party spilling over to the small town of Elephant Butte, immediately north of Truth or Consequences on Highway 181.

Elephant Butte Lake State Park (575/744-5923, www.emnrd.state.nm.us, $5/car) contains a huge number of campsites ($14) with hook-ups. Follow the frontage road along the west edge of the lake to quieter campsites such as North and South Monticello Point.

Campers and day-trippers alike should stop first at the visitors center (575/744-5421, 7:30am-4:30pm daily) near the south

1: Geronimo Springs Museum 2: Elephant Butte Lake State Park

end, to pay fees and check on current conditions. Major services are here, too, at the marinas or in town. **Marina del Sur** (101 S. Hwy. 195, 575/744-5567, www.marinadelsur. info) rents pontoons ($75/3hrs) and has a general store. In the nearby town of Elephant Butte you can rent kayaks ($39/full day) and stand-up paddleboards ($39/full day) to take on the lake at **Zia Kayak Outfitters** (310 Rock Canyon Rd., 575/744-4185).

Caballo Lake State Park

Smaller **Caballo Lake State Park** (Hwy. 187, 575/743-3942, www.emnrd.state.nm.us, $5/car), 16 miles south of Truth or Consequences, is quieter than Elephant Butte, frequented mainly by anglers out for white bass and walleye. The **Lakeside Campground** has boat access and a few easy hiking trails. The developed sites at **Stallion Campground** ($14), overlooking the lake, are preferable to those at Appaloosa, and the primitive camping area is fairly private; you can also park your car about a mile north of the park entrance and hike in to camp at **Eagle Point.**

South of Caballo Dam, the **Riverside Campground** has fairly attractive developed sites ($14) right on the water, though the spaces are not particularly private-feeling. The best ones are at the far south end of the recreation area.

Percha Dam State Park

Five miles south of Caballo Lake and off Hwy. 187, small **Percha Dam State Park** (Percha Dam Canal Rd., 575/743-3942) is a **birding** hot spot for vermilion flycatchers, among other rare migratory birds. Otherwise, the area is not particularly lush and can feel a little dusty despite the big old cottonwood trees that line the river.

Armendaris and Ladder Reserves

Media magnate and conservationist Ted Turner owns more than half a million acres in southern New Mexico, land that was strictly private property for centuries. That land, now part of the **Armendaris and Ladder Reserves**, is open for tours with Ted Turner Reserves (877/277-7637, www. tedturnerreserves.com). Tours (from $175 pp for a five-hour outing) from the Ladder Reserve including mountain biking, bird-watching, bison roundups, and fishing, while from the Armendaris Reserve in the Chihuahuan Desert, you can visit a bat cave at dusk and take a nature photography workshop. None of the possibilities are cheap, but if you have a hankering to see land that most others have only glimpsed from the interstate, these are exciting options. At the Armendaris Reserve, it's also possible take a nature photography workshop and watch a bat colony of over one million members take flight at night.

ENTERTAINMENT AND EVENTS

T or C's version of nightlife is the outdoor group pool at **Riverbend Hot Springs** (100 Austin St., 575/894-7625, www.nmhotsprings. com, 8am-10pm daily). The most festive night out is the downtown **Second Saturday Art Hop** (Main St. and Broadway, 6pm-9pm), every month, year-round. Doors stay open late, and residents toddle from spot to spot, sharing gossip and free refreshments.

The biggest annual event is the **T or C Fiesta** (www.sierracountynewmexico.info), celebrated with style on the first weekend in May every year since 1950. Ralph Edwards himself attended until 1999, often with assorted TV and movie personalities in tow. Even without him (he died in 2005), the festivities are pretty grand for such a small town, pulling together what feels like all of T or C's disparate population of 6,000, with the Old Time Fiddlers Association marching alongside youngsters dressed as aliens. Expect lots of goofy floats, art cars, Spam-craft contests, and more.

FOOD

Start your day right with an "Elvis waffle" (banana slices and peanut butter sauce), or perhaps even more brilliantly, a waffle with bacon in the batter and real maple syrup on the side. ★ **Passion Pie Café** (406 Main St., 575/894-0008, 7am-3pm daily, $6) is where this magic happens, plus plenty more (including Greek salads, cupcakes, and a "Passionate Pear Wafflewich"—pear, walnut, feta, and honey in a waffle sandwich), all fresh and homemade.

Another good breakfast-lunch option is **The Grapevine Bistro** (413 Broadway, 575/894-0404, 8am-3pm Mon.-Fri., 7am-3pm Sat.-Sun., $8), a cheery one-man operation that serves fresh breakfast burritos (including one with grilled vegetables), creative salads, and killer peanut-butter pie.

To call **Latitude 33** (304 S. Pershing St., 575/740-7804, 11:30am-8pm Tues.- Sun., $12) an "Asian fusion" restaurant conjures up something too grand. This is creative, home-style food that happens to have ingredients like coconut milk and ginger. The cabbage salad is packed with flavor, as is the Thai-style iced tea and the coconut black rice pudding with a generous dollop of whipped cream.

A Little Slice of Heaven (313 N. Broadway, 575/223-8257, noon-10:30pm Thurs.-Sun., $5.50) is a cute and colorful spot that has several vegetarian-friendly options, including a stellar veggie burger. The tacos with mango salsa and homemade desserts, such as mouthwatering brownies, are also good bets.

If you're in the mood for a hefty dry-aged steak, shrimp cocktail, and deep-fried zucchini strips, seek out the time-warp steakhouse ★ **Los Arcos** (1400 N. Date St., 575/894-6200, 5pm-9:30pm Sun.-Thurs., 5pm-10:30pm Fri.-Sat., $17), where the calendar seems never to have changed from opening day in 1970. Nonetheless, the food and wine has kept up with the times just enough to be fresh and satisfying, without turning trendy.

ACCOMMODATIONS

Places with in-room hot springs are all downtown, cheaper options are on North Date Street, and a few chain hotels are very close to the interstate.

Under $75

Just out of the downtown loop, the ★ **Rocket Inn** (605 N. Date St., 575/894-2964, www.rocketinn.net, $74 d) is a very well-tended old motor court from 1948, with an immaculate interior. Sparkling bathrooms, ceiling fans, fantastic beds, microwaves, and refrigerators are all a steal at this price—and the owners are efficient and friendly. You can walk to hot springs downtown (guests get a discount at Riverbend).

$75-100

The lure of the hot springs is hard to resist, and for not too much more per night, **Riverbend Hot Springs** (100 Austin St., 575/894-7625, www.riverbendhotsprings.com) gives you a more efficient commute to its nice outdoor soaking facilities. The "artist rooms" ($95) are their cheapest option, built in mobile homes but with all new furnishings; casitas and suites (from $146) with kitchenettes are also available. Note that kids younger than 12 are not welcome.

The truly luxurious—if less sociable, and with less of a view—option is to have hot-spring water pour directly into your bathroom tub. Of these operations, ★ **Blackstone Hotsprings** (410 Austin St., 575/894-0894, www.blackstonehotsprings.com) is probably the best. Its ten rooms are decorated (tastefully) in retro-TV themes, from the black-and-white Twilight Zone studio ($100) to the 1950s space-age Jetsons suite ($160). Some setups have patios and/or kitchenettes, and every room has a large soaking tub. There's also a theme-less bungalow ($90) across the street from the main property.

In a similar motor-court setting, **Fire Water Lodge** (311 Broadway, 575/740-0315, www.firewaterlodge.com, from $88 d) has 10 rooms, and two cottages painted in jewel tones, with hand-carved furniture and mosaic spring-fed tubs. Two rooms and the two cottages have outdoor pools; some rooms also have kitchens. The decor can be a bit haphazard, but it's a good backup option.

Over $100

By far the ritziest choice in T or C, Ted Turner's **Sierra Grande Lodge & Spa** (501 McAdoo St., 575/288-7637, www.sierragrandelodge. com, $155 d, $285 suite) occupies a historic hotel building, with 16 wood-floor rooms decorated in a spare Southwest style, plus a separate casita. Rooms on the front upstairs have balconies with a view of the mountains. Hotel rates include a one-hour soak in the spa, which has indoor and outdoor baths.

INFORMATION AND SERVICES

Stop in at the helpful **visitors center** (301 S. Foch St., 575/894-1968, www.

sierracountynewmexico.info, 9am-4:30pm Mon.-Sat., noon-4pm Sun.) for a map of the town and scads of brochures to surrounding attractions, including the Geronimo Trail.

For local reads and more, **Black Cat Books and Coffee** (128 Broadway, 575/894-7070, 7:30am-10:30am Tues.-Thurs., 8am-5pm Fri.-Mon.) stocks new and used titles.

GETTING THERE

Truth or Consequences is a little over two hours' drive south of Albuquerque (150 miles), and one hour (75 miles) from Socorro. From Las Cruces, it's 75 miles north on I-25, about 1.25 hours in a car.

The Geronimo Trail

Named for the Apache leader who held out against American forces until 1866, longer than any other Native fighter, the **Geronimo Trail National Scenic Byway** (www. geronimotrail.com) winds through the former territory of his tribe, the Black Range, in what is now Sierra County. This is the longest and most rugged stretch of mountains in the state, where many of the battles between U.S. troops and the Apaches were waged. That period lives on only in such place names as Massacre Canyon. More prevalent are the relics of the short-lived silver boom of the late 19th century. Some of the saloons, general stores, and banks from that era still stand, empty and listing dangerously or propped up and turned into museums.

The route is technically a loop, but the west side of the circuit (Forest Road 150) is 46 miles of rudimentary dirt that's recommended only for those with four-wheel drive, in dry weather. Instead, most people will drive either the northern section to Chloride, Winston, and Monticello or, more commonly, the southern section, through Hillsboro and Kingston, and winding over the pass to Silver City. Many of the more

interesting sights are short side trips off the main trail. Before you head out, fill your tank—there are no gas stations between the interstate and Silver City.

THE NORTHERN ROUTE

Head north out of T or C along the I-25 frontage road, then turn west into the Cuchillo Mountains on Highway 52.

Winston to Beaverhead

The road passes through what was once **Cuchillo,** founded in the 1850s, and then winds up and over the mountains to **Winston,** a clutch of wood buildings set on a wide plain. All the action is at the general store with a gas pump (8am-6pm daily)—fitting, considering Winston took its name from a generous shop-owner who gave credit to residents suffering through the crash of 1893, when silver was devalued and prospectors lost everything. Now Winston is a hub for hunters, who head farther into the wilderness via Highway 52. The last leg of the Geronimo Trail (few people get this far) is Highway 59, a narrow road across the northern reaches of the Gila National Forest, paved all the way to

Beaverhead. The route then turns south, onto gravel, and heads about 10 more miles into the wilderness.

Chloride

In Winston, most drivers turn left at the T-junction (off Highway 52), which takes you to **Chloride,** a highly picturesque little ghost town, maintained as a sort of outdoor museum. Established in 1879, Chloride went bust less than 20 years later. The "hanging tree" still stands in the middle of Wall Street, and, most interesting, the **Pioneer Store Museum** (575/743-2736, www.pioneerstoremuseum.com, 10am-4pm daily, donation) is a fine time capsule. It is stocked almost precisely as it was when it closed in 1923, thanks to an owner who closed for business by simply locking the door and sealing the windows. The current owners have restored the place with tender care, and they also run a gallery and gift shop next door. They can tell you the story behind the few other buildings in town, and advise on nearby trails up to abandoned mines.

The bank building is now the excellent **Chloride Bank Café** (300 Wall St., 575/743-0414, 11am-6pm Thurs.-Sun., $7), with fresh, homemade, and creative food—including new pies and cakes every day. There is also an RV park in town, with five spots ($30).

Monticello

Backtrack on Highway 52 about halfway, then cut east on dirt Tortilla Flats Road (County Rd. 16, but unsigned) to Las Placitas and, farther northwest on Highway 142, **Monticello.** This is a pretty, tiny farming community that was an early Spanish settlement; it is still centered on the traditional plaza established in the 1850s. One farm (www.organicbalsamic.com) specializes in organic lavender, desert-hardy fruit trees, and balsamic vinegar, and one artist in town has the astonishing **PharrWest Gallery** (575/743-0868, by appointment).

You can then return to Truth or Consequences via Highway 142.

THE SOUTHERN ROUTE

Twelve miles south of Truth or Consequences, Highway 152 heads west into the Black Range, passing a couple of old mining towns. The road is serpentine and best driven in the daytime.

Hillsboro

Seventeen miles along the road, Hillsboro has an Old West feel. It became the seat of Sierra County in 1884, then managed to weather the silver devaluation and a bitter murder trial in 1899, as cattlemen's feuds and other range rivalries split the whole region. But in the early 20th century, it suffered floods and the flu epidemic, and after a long legal struggle, lost its county-seat status to Hot Springs (later T or C) in 1936, along with most of its remaining population. Just to be certain there was no going back, the courthouse was dismantled; you can still see its ruins along the "high road" through town.

On the east edge of town, the exceedingly dusty **Black Range Museum** (Hwy. 152, 575/895-5233, call for hours) has been closed for renovations and might merit a poke around if it's open once more. The haphazard collection has included fittings from "The Chinaman's Café" that occupied this building after legendary madam-made-good Sadie Orchard sold the property to Tom Ying. The **Hillsboro Historical Society** (Hwy. 152, 575/895-3321, 11am-4pm Fri.-Sun.) also has a small museum, largely of old photos of the town. There's a farm market here at 10am on Saturday.

The **Hillsboro General Store Café** (10697 Hwy. 152, 575/895-5306, 8am-3pm Fri.-Tues., $7), a homey place in an 1879 building (that still works as a store as well), is good for a filling meal. Road-food standards like steak and eggs, burritos and grilled cheese with green chile are on the menu.

Lake Valley Historic Site

From the main junction in Hillsboro, Highway 27 detours south, out of the mountains and into the rolling hills around **Lake Valley**

Historic Site (9am-4pm Thurs.-Mon.), an especially well-kept relic. The slumping buildings with rusted tin roofs are all the evidence that remains of the richest single silver mine ever discovered, in 1881: a glittering cavern lined with solid ore that prospectors dubbed The Bridal Chamber. The find was marred by typical tragedy for that period, as George Daly, the man who'd led the exploration, was killed by Apaches the same day the trove was unearthed. The strike prompted all the usual expansion, with saloons, stagecoach and railroad service, and plenty of gunfights. Although the silver crash and a catastrophic fire in 1895 ruined this town, Lake Valley was inhabited by a few hardy old-timers until as recently as 1994. As a result, some of the buildings are in recognizable shape, and the schoolhouse is still used for special events.

The site is now operated by the BLM; the Las Cruces District Office (575/525-4300) has the latest information. Stewards might be on-site to give you a walking-tour map and answer questions. Even when the site isn't open, you can drive a dirt road alongside it, with signs explaining the full history of the area.

Highway 27 ends at the intersection with Highway 26 and the welcoming watering hole that is the **Nutt Corner Bar** (19160 Hatch Hwy., 575/267-4567, 10am-8pm Wed.-Thurs., 10am-9pm Fri.-Sat., noon-6pm Sun.). It used to be called the Middle of Nowhere Bar, but the land to the west is now much busier since a solar and wind farm has been installed, so it's not as remote-feeling as it once was. Head east to Hatch (18 miles) or southwest to Deming (28 miles).

Kingston

Back in Hillsboro, continue nine miles west on Highway 152 to where a Dead End sign points to Kingston. A population of more than 7,000 made this the largest town in New Mexico in 1890, when the surrounding

mountains were being stripped of their silver in mines called Ready Pay and Opportunity. Butch Cassidy, Mark Twain, and Billy the Kid all passed through, and Lillian Russell performed in the opera house, but the market panic in 1893 inspired a mass exodus. All that's left now is a community even smaller than Hillsboro, a clutch of buildings along a narrow road. The only one that looks just as it did during the boom years is the faithfully restored 1884 **Percha Bank** (575/895-5652, 11am-3pm Fri.-Sun. June-Aug., free), complete with all the woodwork and fittings, as well as an enormous working vault. A gallery space exhibits local art.

The **Black Range Lodge** (119 Main St., 575/895-5652, www.blackrangelodge.com, from $105 d) is an atmospheric mountain outpost where you'll get a real sense of the outdoors. The main building, with its heavy stone walls and wood ceiling beams, may inspire memories of summer camp. The bedrooms upstairs are far better than bunks, however, with sensible, not-too-frilly antiques, old quilts, and cozy radiant heat in the floors. A separate building showcases the owners' expertise in straw-bale construction; the upstairs guesthouse has a full kitchen and a deck, while the downstairs studio ($135) has a kitchenette. A larger property overlooking a creek across the street ($240) can sleep up to 14. Kids will appreciate the foosball in the game room. Full breakfast (with eggs from the resident chickens) is provided; for dinner, you're welcome to cook your own food in the kitchen.

West to Silver City

After Kingston, Highway 152 snakes up to Emory Pass (elev. 8,228 feet), which was hard hit by the Silver Fire in 2013. The route can be tedious and tiring in even the best of weather. If heavy rain is forecast, better to take the southern route to Silver City; snow often closes the pass entirely.

Continuing to Silver City through the Mimbres Valley, you will pass Chino Mine (see "Trail of the Mountain Spirits" later in this chapter).

1: vestiges of mining history in Chloride **2:** the Pioneer Store Museum in Chloride **3:** the Hillsboro General Store Café

Mesilla Valley

Heading due south from Truth or Consequences on I-25 (or, more scenically, on Highway 187 and Highway 185), you're in the fertile river valley and the heartland of New Mexico's distinctive cuisine. This is chile country, where the bulk of the state's crop is grown and processed. In the summer, the fields are hot and still and solidly green. By the fall harvest, the air is almost noticeably spicy (those with allergies, beware!).

HATCH

This community has earned a much bigger name than its population of 2,000 would suggest. Every Labor Day weekend, the Hatch Chile Festival (www.hatchchilefest.com) celebrates the town's most famous crop. As you'd imagine, food vendors are plentiful, and you can shop for chile-themed crafts and wave to the Chile Festival Queen. The tiny Hatch Museum (149 W. Hall St., 575/267-3638, 9am-3pm Mon.-Fri., donation) should document this a bit more, but instead features locally made doilies and a whole wall full of rocks and minerals.

If your visit doesn't coincide with the fiesta, head to ★ Sparky's (115 Franklin St., 575/267-4222, 10:30am-7pm Thurs.-Sun., $8), which is a festive attraction in its own right—just look for the mass of colorful kitsch at the main town intersection. Its specialties are green-chile (natch) cheeseburgers and barbecue, including a half-pound plate of meat with two sides.

For more home-style New Mexican, visit Valley Café (335 W. Hall St., 575/267-4798, 8am-3pm Mon.-Fri., 8am-3:30pm Sat.-Sun., $6), which makes chiles rellenos and other green-chile standards hot and fast. B&E Burritos (303 N. Franklin St., 575/267-5191, 7am-5pm Mon.-Fri., 7am-3pm Sat., $6), another one of the more esteemed places to eat the hot stuff in Hatch, serves rellenos that are dangerously greasy, but the chile-meat burrito is good. If you like the salsa, you can buy whole jars of it. It's on the right when coming in from I-25, set back a bit at the corner of West Hill Street.

You can buy chile year-round in Hatch, whether freshly roasted in late August and early September, or frozen or dried and ground. Look no further than Hatch Chile Express (657 Franklin St., 575/267-3226, 8am-5pm Mon.-Fri., 9am-3pm Sat.), which also sells all manner of homemade chile products.

FORT SELDEN HISTORIC SITE

Established in 1865, Fort Selden Historic Site (1280 Ft. Selden Rd., 575/526-8911, 8:30am-4:30pm Wed.-Sun., $5), 22 miles south of Hatch and 16 miles north of Las Cruces, was never the site of a dramatic battle—but that doesn't mean a visit here is dull. On the contrary, because the small museum isn't bogged down in troop maneuvers, it has space to dedicate to the humdrum details of life on the 19th-century frontier. Here you learn, for instance, that women often accompanied their husbands to forts, and that a soldier's diet consisted of not much more than flour, bacon grease, and the occasional apple. Recipes, building fixtures, and remnants of letters flesh out the portrait of the soldiers stationed here to escort trading caravans. The adobe fort itself has melted to the outlines of a few walls surrounding a central parade ground; a monument to the Buffalo Soldiers, many of whom were stationed here, sits adjacent.

1: Sparky's restaurant in Hatch 2: chiles, Hatch's most famous crop

Utopia on the Rio Grande

Even before the Hog Farm and other communes were established in the 1960s, New Mexico was a destination for visionaries. In 1882, a New York City dentist named John Newbrough claimed angels had channeled his hands to type almost a thousand pages of revelation in a manuscript he called *Oahspe*. The text lays out an elaborate cosmology in which, among other things, the earth moves along with the sun through different regions of space, each having a spiritual effect on the human race. It also details a plan for dealing with the world's orphans, through the building of a model village called the Shalam Colony that would be dedicated to children's education.

Oahspe's text inspired followers, who called themselves Faithists, and with 20 of these people Newbrough set about realizing Shalam Colony on the banks of the Rio Grande, about a mile from the village of Doña Ana, north of Las Cruces. A wealthy Bostonian put up the money for 1,500 acres of rich farmland, and the Faithists built some 35 buildings, plus innovations such as heated chicken pens, and a grand residence for the children. But farming proved difficult for the inexperienced colonists, and they were able to relocate only about 50 orphans. When Newbrough died of the flu in 1891, Shalam was already suffering. His wife and the Boston investor (who married in 1893) struggled to keep the place afloat, but the group dispersed in 1901, and the few remaining children were shipped to orphanages in Texas and Colorado.

A few Faithists carried on and settled in other parts of the West, but the only remnant of the Shalam Colony's social experiment is a historical marker on Highway 185.

DOÑA ANA

South of Fort Selden, Highway 185 cuts just west of the village of Doña Ana. West of the highway, Shalem Colony Trail leads into the foothills, then via a dirt road to Prehistoric Trackways National Monument (575/525-4300), an area in which the keen-eyed hiker can spot ancient animal tracks that predate the age of the dinosaurs preserved in the red sandstone. Permian Track Road, the final dirt road to the monument, requires 4WD.

East of the highway, via Highway 320, Doña Ana, established in 1842 as a way station along the Camino Real, claims to be the oldest settlement in southern New Mexico. It is home to the lovely old Church of Nuestra Señora de la Candelaria (5525 Cristo Rey St., 575/526-2114, 9am-noon and 1pm-5pm Mon.-Fri.), which resembles a Mexican village church more than it does anything in the northern part of the state. The whitewashed adobe building was carefully restored in 2001; ask at the church office to be let inside to see the beautiful *latilla* wooden ceiling, and the new but compelling woodcarvings. The bells are from the old Shalam Colony nearby.

Las Cruces

Built along the Rio Grande, with mountains jutting up to the east, Las Cruces resembles a miniature Albuquerque in its geography. But this city of 97,000 is distinct in several respects. As the home of New Mexico State University, which has a dedicated Chile Pepper Institute, this is a farm town and proud of it. And while Las Cruces may not literally abut Mexico (El Paso, Texas, 42 miles south, gets in the way), the neighboring country's influence is strongly felt here, in a cross-border culture that's distinct from the Hispano communities in the northern part of the state.

SIGHTS

Las Cruces was founded in 1849. The most notable landmarks are its mural-adorned water towers—you'll see a few coming in from the north on I-25. The largest historic area is the adobe enclave of Mesilla on the city's east side, technically a separate town, though functionally just a particularly scenic neighborhood. Another small section of old Las Cruces, a clutch of old adobe homes, can be found in the scenic Mesquite Historic District: Mesquite, Tornilla, San Pedro, and Campo Streets, between Chestnut and Colorado Avenues. There is also one outlying pueblo, Tortugas, wedged on a patch of land next to I-10; on an average day, there's not much to see, but it does host a great event for the Virgin of Guadalupe at the beginning of December.

Mesilla

For the most scenic approach to Mesilla, drive via University Avenue in the south. Fields line the road, and you'll feel as if you have indeed arrived in a different town when you turn north on Calle de El Paso. The historic village, which has largely preserved its original adobe architecture, centers on a trim plaza that's more sedate than Albuquerque's or Santa Fe's,

but also less plagued with tourist tackiness. The twin-spired Basilica of San Albino (2070 Calle de Santiago, 575/526-9349, 1pm-5pm Wed.-Thurs., 11am-5pm Fri.-Sat., noon-4pm Sun.), which dates from 1906, stands on the north side of the plaza. It replaced an earlier adobe built in the mid-19th century, when the settlement of Mesilla had finally attained, after seven years, some security from Apache raids, as well as legal surety when the Gadsden Purchase settled the dispute over the land on which Mesilla sat.

For more on Mesilla's historic buildings, stop in at the visitors center (2231 Avenida de Mesilla, 575/524-3262 ext. 117, www.oldmesilla.org, 9:30am-4:30pm Mon.-Thurs., 10am-2pm Fri.-Sat.), inside the town hall, for an annotated map. It will point out such venerable spots as the Fountain Theatre, off the southeast corner of the plaza. It was established by Albert Jennings Fountain, the powerful political leader who lived in Mesilla with his Mexican wife; his family performed melodramas on its stage. Fountain later disappeared, along with his young son, a victim of the range wars; his presumed murder prompted a contentious 1899 trial of cattleman Oliver Lee in the town of Hillsboro.

After you've toured around the plaza, walk west, to the residential section, where you'll get an idea of what the all-adobe village looked like 150 years back. (Be respectful when taking photos, though.)

Downtown Museums

The heart of old Las Cruces has been through a lot. It once looked just like Mesilla and the Mesquite District, all old adobes and "modern" mercantiles. But a 1960s urban renewal scheme razed all that and installed a covered pedestrian mall that made the whole area dark and hard to reach. Starting in 2005, this was gradually reversed, and Main Street has emerged into a slightly livelier place, with a

Las Cruces

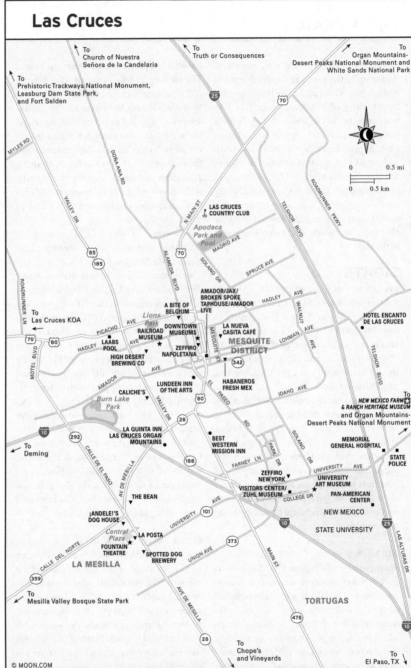

To
Church of Nuestra
Señora de la Candelaria

To
Truth or Consequences

To
Organ Mountains-
Desert Peaks National Monument and
White Sands National Park

To
Prehistoric Trackways National Monument,
Leasburg Dam State Park,
and Fort Selden

0   0.5 mi

0   0.5 km

MYLES RD

DONA ANA RD

VALLEY DR

ROADRUNNER LN

ROADRUNNER PKWY

TELSHOR BLVD

N MAIN ST

ALAMEDA BLVD

SOLANO DR

MADRID AVE

APODACA Park and Pool

LAS CRUCES
COUNTRY CLUB

SPRUCE AVE

HADLEY AVE

WALNUT AVE

LOHMAN AVE

MESQUITE ST

HOTEL ENCANTO
DE LAS CRUCES

To
Las Cruces KOA

MOTEL BLVD

PICACHO AVE

HADLEY

Lions Park

LAABS POOL

RAILROAD MUSEUM

DOWNTOWN MUSEUMS

A BITE OF BELGIUM

AMADOR/JAX/
BROKEN SPOKE
TAPHOUSE/AMADOR
LIVE

LA NUEVA
CASITA CAFÉ

MESQUITE DISTRICT

HIGH DESERT
BREWING CO

ZEFFIRO
NAPOLETANA

AMADOR AVE

AMADOR

Burn Lake Park

CALICHE'S

LUNDEEN INN
OF THE ARTS

VALLEY DR

EL PASEO

HABANEROS
FRESH MEX

IDAHO AVE

NEW MEXICO FARM
& RANCH HERITAGE MUSEUM
and Organ Mountains-
Desert Peaks National Monument

To
Deming

LA QUINTA INN
LAS CRUCES ORGAN
MOUNTAINS

CALLE DE EL PASO

AV DE MESILLA

BEST
WESTERN
MISSION INN

FARNEY LN

PARK DR

SOLANO DR

MEMORIAL
GENERAL HOSPITAL

STATE
POLICE

UNIVERSITY AVE

ZEFFIRO
NEW YORK

VISITORS CENTER/
ZUHL MUSEUM

COLLEGE DR

UNIVERSITY
ART MUSEUM

PAN-AMERICAN
CENTER

THE BEAN

¡ANDELE!'S
DOG HOUSE

Central Plaza

LA POSTA

FOUNTAIN
THEATRE

SPOTTED DOG
BREWERY

UNIVERSITY AVE

UNION AVE

NEW MEXICO
STATE UNIVERSITY

MAIN ST

LAS ALTURAS DR

CALLE DEL NORTE

LA MESILLA

To
Mesilla Valley Bosque State Park

TORTUGAS

AVE DE MESILLA

To
Chope's
and Vineyards

To
El Paso, TX

© MOON.COM

few anchor theaters and a farmers market on Saturday mornings.

The city runs four **museums** (10am-4:30pm Tues.-Fri., 9am-4:30pm Sat., free) in the downtown area. Individually, no one place is notable, but together, they give a good outlook on the area. Three are adjacent downtown. The **Branigan Cultural Center** (501 N. Main St., 575/541-2154) hosts special events and houses a concise history of the city. Next door to the south, the **Las Cruces Museum of Art** (491 N. Main St., 575/541-2137) shows off local talent, and next door to that (doors on both Main Street and Water Street, in the back) is the **Las Cruces Museum of Nature and Science** (411 N. Main St., 575/522-3120), which gives a good overview of the ecosystems in this part of New Mexico, illustrated with terrariums showcasing native reptiles.

A few blocks west is the old Santa Fe depot, now the **Las Cruces Railroad Museum** (351 N. Mesilla St., 575/647-4480), with some nice period details in the furniture. But of course the real fun is in the model-train room, which re-creates the AT&SF line around Las Cruces.

New Mexico State University

Founded in 1888, **New Mexico State University** (NMSU, www.nmsu.edu), home of the Aggies, is on the south side of town in the triangle formed by the intersection of I-10 and I-25, on a modern campus with a few Spanish and Southwestern touches. On the northwest corner, next to the visitors center (where it's easiest to park), look in at the **Zuhl Museum** (775 College Dr., 575/646-3616, 8am-5pm Mon.-Fri., free), a collection of geological items; particularly beautiful are the slabs of petrified wood. In the newly built Devasthali Hall, on University Avenue just east of Solano Drive, the **University Art Museum** (575/646-2545, call for times) is due to occupy a modern space in the spring of 2020 and will replace the University Art Gallery. Just to the west, in Kent Hall, the **University Museum** (575/646-3739, noon-4pm Tues.-Sat., free) displays recent archaeological finds.

★ New Mexico Farm & Ranch Heritage Museum

Even avowed city slickers will find something intriguing at the **New Mexico Farm & Ranch Heritage Museum** (4100 Dripping Springs Rd., 575/522-4100, www.frhm.org, 9am-5pm Mon.-Sat., noon-5pm Sun., $5), on the east edge of town near the Organ Mountain foothills. Indoors, trace the history of agriculture in New Mexico by peeking inside a traditional Mogollon pit house, then hearing the personal histories of homesteaders who replaced the Spanish in the 1860s. Space is given to Blackdom, the African American farmers' settlement begun in the Pecos Valley and relocated to Las Cruces in 1921, as well as the travails of other immigrant groups. Ag geeks can admire giant cotton pickers and learn more about the Spanish acequia system of irrigation. Outside, the museum sprawls for acres, encompassing a dairy barn and goats and longhorn cattle. Look out for demonstrations of sheep shearing, blacksmithing, home canning, and the like. Throughout, the volunteer docents have the zeal of missionaries—you, too, may have a real appreciation for vintage tractors by the time you leave.

SPORTS AND RECREATION

Las Cruces' proximity to the Organ Mountains—now a designated national monument—as well as Doña Ana and Robledo Peaks, both north of the city, makes it an outdoorsy town. The **Southwest Environmental Center** (275 N. Main St., 575/522-5552, www.wildmesquite.org, 9am-6pm Mon.-Fri.) is a great resource for anyone interested in the wild areas around the city. Ask here for trail recommendations, and learn what the latest efforts to protect the desert have yielded.

Hiking

The most accessible day hikes are directly east of Las Cruces in the foothills of the **Organ Mountains-Desert Peaks National**

Monument (575/525-4300, $5/car), a vast and rugged wilderness encompassing parts of the Chihuahuan Desert up to peaks that rise over 9,000 feet. The Dripping Springs Natural Area visitors center (8am-5pm daily), 10 miles east of the city, is the head of the 1.5-mile Dripping Springs Trail, which winds through the ruined buildings of the 19th-century resort that gives the area its name. Just before you reach the visitors center, La Cueva Picnic Area is high enough that it affords a fine view across the basin. The La Cueva Trail from here leads past a cave that was the home of an Italian hermit for a few years in the 1860s, until he was found dead with a knife in his back; his murder was never solved. A spur from the trail leads to a waterfall, rains permitting.

Running six miles up and over the mountains to the east side, Baylor Pass Trail is a more challenging undertaking. It begins in the foothills east of Baylor Canyon Road—look for the turn 1.9 miles south of U.S. 70. After ascending about 1,600 feet to the pass, you have a view of both the Mesilla Valley to the west and White Sands to the east, then the trail descends over two miles to end in Aguirre Springs Recreation Area (575/525-4300, $5/car), a campground on the east side of the mountains. It takes about four hours to traverse; alternatively, you could make a shorter—but steeper—hike by starting on the east (city) side and going only up to the pass and back, about 2.5 hours. From the same campground, you have access to Pine Tree Trail, a 4.5-mile loop that's a little shadier, without much altitude gain—it takes only about three hours to do the circuit.

Biking

Las Cruces is flat and relatively slow-paced, making it easy to get around on two wheels; empty roads and rugged trails nearby cater to any recreational style. Ride On Sports (2001 E. Lohman Ave., 575/521-1686, www.rideonsports.com, 10am-8pm Mon.-Fri., 9am-8pm Sat., 11am-6pm Sun.) is the best local shop, with all kinds of gear and plenty of tips on where to ride.

One of the best-loved mountain biking trails is Robledo Trail (also known as SST Trail, 575/525-4300, www.blm.gov), 6.5 miles of single-track (13 miles round-trip) with lots of technical challenges and little time to catch your breath—definitely not for the faint of heart. It's north of the city, just off Highway 185 west of the Rio Grande, in the same area as Prehistoric Trackways National Monument and a non-contiguous patch of land included in the Organ Mountains-Desert Peak National Monument.

A more accessible circuit, the five-mile-long "A" Mountain Trail (also signed as Tortugas Mountain Trails) starts just 10 minutes east of the NMSU campus and loops around the cone-shaped hill bedecked with a big red capital "A." The counterclockwise route around the low peak is the easier option, though beginning riders might still have to walk in a couple of spots.

For a longer outing, one of the more manageable and scenic rides is the 29-mile Sierra Vista Trail, which follows the Organ Mountains southeast toward Texas, before looping back north of Las Cruces. It's a mix of single-track and dirt roads that wend through a striking desert landscape—mule deer are a common sight. Look for the trailhead off Exit 1 on I-25, about seven miles along University Avenue.

Bird-Watching

Encompassing three miles of wetlands on the west side of the Rio Grande, Mesilla Valley Bosque State Park (5000 Calle del Norte, 575/523-4398, emnrd.state.nm.us, 7:30am-4:30pm daily, $5/car) is a popular birding spot, both for its proximity to the city and for the number of species that can be seen in such a comparatively small area. Entrance is via the visitors center on the northern side,

---

1: historic farm equipment at the New Mexico Farm & Ranch Heritage Museum 2: view from the Dripping Springs Trail

where **guided hikes** go out at 2:30pm on weekends, and birding tours run at 7:30am on Saturday. Take Calle del Norte (Hwy. 359) west from central Mesilla, then drive south 1.2 miles within the park.

Rock Climbing

With the near-vertical Organ Mountains nearby and the granite outcrops of Hueco Tanks State Park closer to El Paso, this is one of the best areas for bouldering and climbing in the United States. The options are too many to detail here; your best bet is to contact **Outdoor Adventures** (1424 Missouri Ave., 575/521-1922, www.outdooradventures-lc.com, 10am-6pm Mon.-Fri., 10am-5pm Sat.) for guidance and maps.

Swimming

Las Cruces has several public pools. **Laabs** (750 W. Picacho Ave., 575/524-3168, 8am-9pm daily, $4) is a modern outdoor pool with slides, open only during the summer. The **Las Cruces Regional Aquatic Center** (1401 E. Hadley St., 575/541-2777, $4) is a year-round indoor facility with slides and multiple pools.

ENTERTAINMENT AND EVENTS

With a student body of more than 16,000, NMSU is a strong influence on local nightlife, so casual bars with free-flowing beer are the norm. Special events highlight the city's ties to Mexican culture.

Nightlife

"None of our beers suck," boasts **High Desert Brewing Co.** (1201 W. Hadley Ave., 575/525-6752, 11am-midnight Mon.-Sat., noon-10pm Sun.), but they needn't set standards so low. This brewpub's products—mainly ales and lagers— are all quite savory, and they wash down good basic bar grub. There's live music on Tuesday, Thursday, and Saturday, though you'd never guess it from the outside of the place, which looks like an office.

It may not be much to look at from the outside, but ★ **Spotted Dog Brewery** (2920 Ave. de Mesilla, 575/650-2729, 11:30am-10:30pm Mon.-Thurs., 11:30am-midnight Fri.-Sat., noon-8:30pm Sun.) consistently brews some of the best beers in the state, particularly for such a relatively small operation. A number of seasonal ales augment the several house beers on tap, including a brown ale and cream ale—perfect pairings to the tasty sandwiches and munchies on the food menu.

On the plaza in Mesilla, **El Patio Cantina** (2171 Calle de Parian, 575/526-9943, 4pm-11pm Mon., 4pm-2am Tues.-Thurs., 2pm-2am Fri.-Sat., noon-midnight Sun.) is a good old-fashioned bar. Wednesday night is jazz night, and weekends are usually booked with classic-rock cover bands that draw a cross section of Las Cruces. A few blocks away, **Palacio Bar** (2600 Avenida de Mesilla, 575/525-2910, 1pm-midnight Tues.-Fri., noon-midnight Sat.-Sun.) is another longtime local legend, tacitly men-only until only a quarter century ago, but now more welcoming and run by the previous owner's daughter. Multiple generations drink here, especially during the day.

Opened in 2019 and occupying a block at the corner of Water and Main streets, **Amador** (302 S. Main St.) is a vast multi-venue complex that has quickly positioned itself at the nexus' of Las Cruces' nightlife. The space holds the rooftop lounge **JAX** (575/541-7417, 11am-11pm Tues.-Sat.), the **Broken Spoke Taphouse** (575/323-8051, 4pm-11pm Mon., 11am-11pm Tues.-Sat.), and a courtyard hosting frequent concerts under the moniker of **Amador LIVE** (575/680-0172).

Performing Arts

Downtown on Main Street the Italianate **Rio Grande Theatre** (211 N. Main St., 575/523-6403, www.riograndetheatre.com), a fine movie palace of yore, was undergoing renovations at the time of writing. It typically hosts live performances and shows classic films. Nearby is the **Las Cruces Community Theatre** (313 N. Main St., 575/523-1200, www.lcctnm.org), set in the historic State Theater, which is the best spot in the city to catch a play or a musical.

Cinema

In Mesilla, the **Fountain Theatre** (2469 Calle de Guadalupe, 575/524-8287, www. mesillavalleyfilm.org, $7) has been open since 1870 and operating as a cinema since 1905. It's a tiny, anonymous adobe building, the anti-movie palace, but a cool place to see a film, as you settle in between walls painted with murals of the Rio Grande. The place is entirely run by volunteers, with all kinds of interesting international films shown nightly at 7:30pm, plus weekend matinees.

Festivals and Events

The city's annual party, a fundraiser for a cancer charity, used to be called the Whole Enchilada, devoted to cooking the world's largest enchilada, but the chef hung up his apron. A few years ago the party (minus the large-scale food) became known as simply **La Gran Fiesta** (www.carelascruces.org), and is held over three days in late September. The festival of *lucha libre* (Mexican wrestling), motorcycle shows, and food vendors takes place downtown.

In December, residents of Tortugas Pueblo host the three-day **Our Lady of Guadalupe Fiesta** (575/526-8171), well worth attending if your schedule allows. On December 10 after sundown and continuing all night, there are Matachines and other dances in front of the Our Lady of Guadalupe Shrine and Parish at the pueblo. On the morning of December 11, a procession climbs nearby Tortugas Mountain (also known as "A" Mountain). On the last day are more dances and a big free community lunch. There are feasts and dances in front of Our Lady of Guadalupe Shrine and Parish, in the pueblo. Like so much culture in southern New Mexico, the event follows Mexican styles more closely than anything in the northern half of the state.

Other city parties reflect the city's Mexican history. Mesilla's plaza celebrates Mexico's victory in the 1862 Battle of Puebla on **Cinco de Mayo,** with fireworks, music, piñatas, and folk-dancing performances on the weekend closest to May 5. Likewise, the **Diez y Seis de**

Septiembre Fiesta commemorates Mexico's independence movement with all the usual fun on the weekend nearest September 16. At the end of October, the colorful fun of **Dia de los Muertos,** the Day of the Dead, gives kids a chance to see a different sort of Halloween.

NMSU's Pan-American Center fills with the blare of trumpets for four days in June, for the **Las Cruces International Mariachi Conference** (www.lascrucesmariachi.org), which draws a long roster of musicians from northern Mexico, California, and across the Southwest.

FOOD
Mesilla

A couple of landmark spots cluster around the plaza, and there are some casual options that are good to know about if you're just out strolling around.

LANDMARK RESTAURANTS

One deservedly famous place is ★ **La Posta** (2410 Calle de San Albino, 575/524-3524, 11am-9pm Mon.-Thurs., 11am-9:30pm Fri., 9am-9:30pm Sat., 9am-9pm Sun., $11), one of those epically large and much beloved old restaurants where families go to celebrate special occasions. From the colorful parrots and macaws in the lobby to the waitstaff in billowing Mexican skirts to the two-page-long margarita menu, it's a party. It occupies an old adobe that was a stop on the Butterfield Overland Mail & Stage route, as well as room upon room in adjacent buildings—unspool a string to find your way back from the bathroom. Considering the scale of the place, the food is unexpectedly good and reliable; the hot empanadas served with ice cream for dessert are a nice touch, too.

The other big special-night-out place is **Double Eagle** (2355 Calle de Guadalupe, 575/523-6700, 11am-10pm Mon.-Sat., 11am-9pm Sun., $24), with a grand old atmosphere of fogged mirrors and chandeliers. But it's best for a drink at the bar and an appetizer, to admire the scenery, rather than a full meal from its fancy-steakhouse menu.

If you're up for a drive, consider the historic roadhouse **Chope's** (Hwy. 28, 575/233-3420, 11:30am-1:30pm and 5:30pm-8:30pm Tues.-Fri., 5:30pm-8pm Sat., $8), in the village of La Mesa, about 20 minutes south of Mesilla. It's worth the effort alone for the chiles rellenos, which have kept people coming back for decades.

NEW MEXICAN

By day, **Double Eagle** is the more casual New Mexican café **Peppers** (575/523-4999, 11am-3pm Mon.-Sat., $12), inside two smaller front rooms. The menu consists mainly of tacos, chile rellenos, salads, chicken-fried steak, and burgers, including a green-chile cheeseburger the size of a dinner plate.

¡Andele!'s Dog House (1983 Calle del Norte, 575/526-1271, 11am-9pm daily, $10) is good for *tacos al carbon* (with meat fresh off the grill), great salsas, and Mexican-style hot dogs (wrapped in bacon and doused in jalapeños and other goodies). And, true to its name, it's canine-friendly and has a nice patio where pooches are welcome. (If you prefer no pets, head to the main restaurant, in the strip mall across the street, another epic warren popular for family celebrations.)

CAFÉS

For both coffee and community, ★ **The Bean** (2011 Avenida de Mesilla, 575/527-5155, 7am-1pm daily, $3) is the most popular place to chill out with a cup of joe. Set in an old gas station, the coffeehouse hosts an array of quirky regulars, while serving up pastries, omelets, and grilled sandwiches.

Las Cruces

Dining options are more varied in Las Cruces proper.

NEW MEXICAN

Chef Alfredo does just about everything at ★ **Habaneros Fresh Mex** (600 E. Amador Ave., 575/524-1829, 8am-8pm Sun.-Thurs., 8am-9pm Fri.-Sat., $6), whipping up gorditas, house-made mole, carne asada fries, and more

in this casual order-at-the-counter place. It's all hot and fresh, and a fantastic bargain—you even get free "welcome soup."

There's nothing new about **La Nueva Casita Café** (195 N. Mesquite St., 575/523-5434, 8am-3pm Sun.-Mon., 8am-7:30pm Tues.-Thurs., 8am-8:30pm Fri.-Sat., $9), an old-school place in the pretty Mesquite Historic District with tile-topped tables, mariachi horns, and plenty of neighbors as customers. The food is homey, with good flautas and enchiladas and plenty of vegetarian options, too.

FRESH AND LOCAL

The downtown **farmers market** (221 N. Main St.) usually has a number of good snack vendors—tamales and more. It sets up on Wednesday and Saturday (8:30am-1pm), with more activity on the latter day.

ITALIAN

As pizza purists demand, it's all about the crust at ★ **Zeffiro Pizzeria Napoletana** (136 N. Water St., 575/525-6757, 11am-2pm and 5pm-8pm Mon.-Thurs., 11am-2pm and 5pm-9pm Fri.-Sat., $9). Pies come out of the wood oven with almost comically blistered and bubbling edges. Toppings run from typical pepperoni to prosciutto and golden potatoes; there are plenty of pasta dishes and calzones, too. The same team runs the student-friendly **Zeffiro New York Pizzeria** (901 University Ave., 575/525-6770, 11am-2pm and 5pm-8pm Mon.-Thurs., 11am-2pm and 5pm-9pm Fri.-Sat.), where you can get a greasier pizza by the slice ($2.95).

INTERNATIONAL

For a break from chile, head to **A Bite of Belgium** (741 N. Alameda Blvd., 575/527-2483, 7am-2pm and 5pm-8pm Wed.-Thurs. and Sun., 7am-2pm and 5pm-9pm Fri.-Sat., $8), where the food is European and the

1: Chope's, a road-food icon south of Las Cruces 2: La Nueva Casita Café 3: the historic La Posta restaurant

service American-friendly, with bottomless cups of coffee to go with your Liège-style waffles or fluffy-custardy French toast. Lunch is soups and sandwiches—try the lamb with caramelized onions.

DESSERTS

On a hot summer night, there's no better place to be than Caliche's (590 S. Valley Dr., 575/647-5066, 11am-10pm daily, $4), which serves frozen custard under pink and blue neon. A caliche (Spanish for hard clay) is the local equivalent of a St. Louis-style concrete, a shake so thick you have to eat with a spoon. Of course there are New Mexican mix-ins such as pine nuts and red chile.

ACCOMMODATIONS

Las Cruces is short on distinctive lodging. Of the numerous chain operations, the most conveniently located ones are on Avenida de Mesilla where it passes under the interstate, before you reach Mesilla proper.

Under $100

Campers can set up at the Las Cruces KOA (814 Weinrich Rd., 575/526-6555, www.koa.com), west of the city just south of U.S. 70, with fantastic views of the mountains, a heated swimming pool, and wireless Internet. Cabins ($59) and tent sites (from $33) are available. You can also camp at Leasburg Dam State Park (Hwy. 157, 575/524-4068, emnrd.state.nm.us), 15 miles north of town adjacent to Fort Selden. The park runs along a series of irrigation canals and is favored by kayakers and bird-watchers; it has 31 developed campsites ($14).

Near Mesilla, La Quinta Inn & Suites Las Cruces Organ Mountains (1500 Hickory Dr., 575/523-0100, www.lq.com, $59 d) is in excellent shape and has a small pool. The Best Western Mission Inn (1765 S. Main St., 575/524-8591, www.bwmissioninn.com, $75 d) is well kept, and its large rooms have nice little Southwestern details like tile mirror frames. Rates include a full breakfast, and you can often get very good online discounts.

$100-150

Walking distance from downtown, the rambling, Spanish-style Lundeen Inn of the Arts (618 S. Alameda St., 575/526-3326, www.innofthearts.com, $89 s, $125 d) has been open for decades, and the walls crowded with paintings reflect that age. The place feels a bit dim and dusty, but the owner, an architect, is interesting, and the history is palpable. Some of the seven rooms have fireplaces.

The city's plushest hotel, Hotel Encanto de Las Cruces (705 S. Telshor Blvd., 575/522-4300, www.hotelencanto.com, $125 d) perches on a hill, affording great views across the valley. Inside, the decor is a rich palette of tan and wine, with a hint of Spanish colonial style, and the beds are particularly comfortable. Request either a west-facing top-floor room for a great sunset view or something on the pool level, where patios open onto the swimming area. The only drawback is that its location on the east side is a bit isolated, and the only place in walking distance is the Mesilla Valley Mall.

INFORMATION AND SERVICES

Las Cruces Convention & Visitors Bureau (336 S. Main St., 575/541-2444, www.lascrucescvb.org, 8am-5pm Mon.-Fri.) has free high-speed Internet service, along with a helpful staff and piles of brochures.

On the old plaza, the excellent Mesilla Book Center (2360 Calle Principal, 575/526-6220, 11am-5:30pm Tues.-Sat., 1pm-5pm Sun.) has perhaps every book you'd ever want to read about the American West and the Mexican border, plus current and classic fiction, guides to horse care and bike repair, and plenty more. Downtown, Coas Books (317 N. Main St., 575/524-8471, 9am-7pm Mon.-Fri., 9am-6pm Sat., noon-5pm Sun.) is crammed with secondhand titles of every kind.

GETTING THERE AND AROUND

By car, Las Cruces is 225 miles (3 hours) south of Albuquerque on I-25 and U.S. 85, and 45 miles (about 45 minutes) north of El Paso, Texas.

South of Las Cruces

Drive south out of Mesilla on Calle de El Paso (Highway 28), and you're almost immediately in lush agricultural land: Pecan orchards, vineyards, and cotton fields sprawl almost all the way to the Texas border. The two-lane road winds by you-pick farms, corn mazes, and other seasonal entertainment. Year-round, you can break up the drive with stops at wineries, such as **Rio Grande Vineyards** (5321 Hwy. 28, 575/524-3985, noon-5:30pm Fri.-Sun.), closest to Mesilla, or **La Viña** (4201 Hwy. 28, 575/882-7632, noon-5pm Thurs.-Tues.), the oldest vineyard in New Mexico, in La Union. Both stock other local products, such as honey and chiles, in addition to wine.

Loop through the little village of La Union (west off Highway 28), then head back north and conclude with a meal at **Chope's** (Hwy. 28, 575/233-3420, 11:30am-1:30pm and 5:30pm-8:30pm Tues.-Fri., 5:30pm-8pm Sat., $8), back close to Las Cruces, in the village of La Mesa. It's a down-at-the-heels roadhouse and restaurant, famous for its heavily egg-battered chiles rellenos, red chile beans, and rural New Mexican ambience. The restaurant is in the house to the south of the parking area. You can also eat in the bar, and even if you don't, you should have a beer there just to people-watch.

From Alamogordo, it's 68 miles (1 hour) west on U.S. 70; from Deming, it's 60 miles (1 hour) east on I-10; and from Truth or Consequences, 75 miles (1.25 hours) south on I-25.

Rather than making the drive from the Albuquerque airport, many visitors to Las Cruces fly into El Paso (ELP). **Las Cruces Shuttle** (575/525-1784, www.lascrucesshuttle.com) runs an airport transport service at least eight times daily. Rates are $50 one-way, or $85 round-trip. Las Cruces International Airport (LRU, 575/541-2471) is only for private aviation—but it does have a large collection of scale-model planes.

The **Greyhound bus** (800/231-2222, www.greyhound.com) stops at the Chucky's convenience store (800 E. Thorpe Rd., 575/524-8518, 7am-11pm daily). Two buses run daily from Albuquerque; five run from El Paso.

RoadRunner Transit (575/541-2500, www.las-cruces.org) is the city bus system, though buses run infrequently, and only until 7pm Monday-Friday, and until 6pm on Saturday, and not at all on Sunday. Fare is $1 (exact change, bills accepted), and buses are equipped with front bike racks. Route No. 40 runs to Mesilla from downtown.

West to the Bootheel

From Las Cruces, I-10 runs west through the flatlands up to the Chiricahua Mountains on the Arizona border. Most of the area is unrelenting desert punctuated by spikes of mountains, such as the Floridas, rising 2,800 feet above the surrounding plain. The area is known for dust storms and shimmering heat, but in the southwestern corner of the state, a little stub of virtually untouched wilderness juts farther south. Jaguars have been spotted here on very rare occasions, and critters like coatimundi, tarantulas, rattlesnakes, and

particularly enormous locusts thrive. By late August, when the summer rains are strong enough, the desert turns a lush green; avoid May and June, however, before the rains have started, as this is the hottest, driest period.

DEMING

"Pure water and fast ducks" boasts Deming of its charms, and surely no other town in the United States can make such a claim to fame. The water comes from a large aquifer under the city of 15,000; as for the speedy birds,

Deming

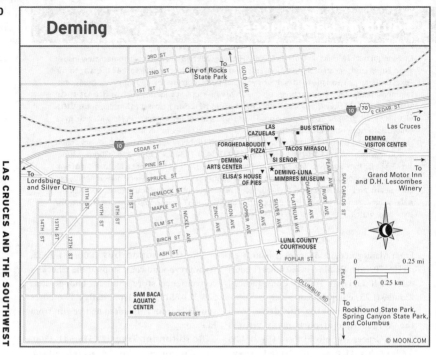

© MOON.COM

they're part of the Great American Duck Race, the city's biggest annual event. The business leaders who came up with the scheme in 1980 (to rival Ruidoso's horse-racing industry) admitted the initial brainstorming session did involve liquor.

Deming is popular with retirees from the upper Midwest, and its greater cityscape is one of RV and trailer parks, as well as truck stops. But its old downtown, south of the intersection of Pine and Gold, is a few blocks of surprising elegance, and it's a great place to pull off the highway for authentic Mexican food or a slice of pie. Street addresses with directionals (SW, NE, etc.) are outside of town, not in central Deming.

Sights

A good place to start is with the **Deming-Luna Mimbres Museum** (301 S. Silver Ave., 575/546-2382, 9am-4pm Mon.-Sat., donation), one block south of Pine Street. Set in a 1917 armory, the museum is the county's

vast repository of historic flotsam, lovingly curated and carefully arranged. Novelty whiskey bottles, nutcrackers, geodes, beautiful Mimbres pottery—it's all here, in incredible detail and profusion.

At the end of South Silver Avenue, the redbrick **Luna County Courthouse** (700 S. Silver Ave), restored in 2006, looks like it would be more at home in Iowa. It was built in 1910, then in 1916 saw the trial of many of Pancho Villa's alleged accomplices in the rebel leader's raid on Columbus, New Mexico; four of the "Villistas" were subsequently hanged on the green lawn in front of the building.

The **Deming Arts Center** (100 S. Gold Ave., 575/546-3663, 10am-4pm Tues.-Sat.) occupies a grand old building at the main crossroads and showcases local artists with a selection of works that changes monthly.

Sports and Recreation

Beat the summer heat at **Sam Baca Aquatic Center** (815 W. Buckeye St., 575/546-7958,

8am-5pm daily mid-May-late Sept., $2), which has three big outdoor pools and a waterslide, with frolicking kids segregated from the lap swimmers.

For a more outdoorsy experience, head southeast to the Florida (Flowering) Mountains, so named for the colorful wildflowers that blanket their steep slopes in springtime. In summer, though, they can feel a bit barren and hot, and nowhere more so than at **Rockhound State Park** (9880 Stirrup Rd. SE, 575/546-6182, www.emnrd. state.nm.us, $5/car). Its setting in the foothills is picturesque, especially around sunset, but a day poking around with a pickax (you're allowed to carry out 15 pounds of finds) is rewarding only for the truly geologically minded. Everyone else will probably be satisfied with the exhibits of geodes and other mineral miracles in the visitors center. The well-equipped and spotless **campground** has more than 50 sites ($14), over half of which have electricity. Two short and fairly moderate **hiking trails** (Jasper and Thunder Egg) lead out from the adjacent picnic area; it's worth combining them into a two-mile loop and taking in some nice views of the area.

For more scenic hiking and good birdwatching, head to **Spring Canyon State Park** (8am-4pm Wed.-Sun.), immediately adjacent to Rockhound. While you're out, you have a slim chance of spotting an ibex, a variety of goat with large curving horns. The Department of Game and Fish imported them from Iran and released them here in 1970, as part of a now-discontinued program to create an exotic game-hunting industry; about 400 of the animals live in the mountains now.

Entertainment and Events

The **D.H. Lescombes Winery,** established by a French family in 1984, occupies 15 acres a few miles outside of town (head east on Pine Street) and is an easy hop off the interstate. This is just part of some 120 acres the group owns, to produce most of the grapes for winemakers all over the state. You can sample a wide range of wines at the tasting room in Deming (1325 De Baca Rd. SE, 575/546-1179, 9am-6pm Mon.-Thurs. and Sat., 10am-8pm 10am-10pm Fri., noon-7pm Sun.); the better ones include the syrah, which does well in the sun here. The winery also has a wine festival in early October.

Deming's annual hoedown is the last weekend in August, when the **Great American Duck Race** (www.demingchamber.com) takes over. In addition to the headline duck sprint, festivities include a cash-prize tortilla toss, outhouse races, a parade with more fake foam beaks than you can count, a duck dance, and a balloon rally.

Food

Deming doesn't look like a promising gourmet stop, but it is a good place to sample some Mexican (as opposed to *New* Mexican) food. **Tacos Mirasol** (309 E. Pine St., 575/544-0646, 10am-10pm Mon.-Sat., $5) is a tiny but sparkling-clean roadside hut that does tacos, of course, but also Mexican-style sandwiches (*tortas*), which consist of a choice of meat on a soft fluffy roll, usually slathered with avocado, mayonnaise, and a thin layer of refried beans. Both come with a tangy-hot tomatillo salsa; cut the heat with a banana milkshake or fresh limeade.

For a heartier meal, head for ★ **Las Cazuelas** (108 N. Platinum St., 575/544-8432, 11am-7pm Tues.-Sat., 11am-4pm Sun., $8), a cheery Mexican restaurant hidden in the back of a butcher and grocery. Of course you can get a big *churrasco* platter of grilled meats, but you can go smaller, with a burger or a spicy soup, as well as burritos and other goodies. Everything's fresh and homemade.

For New Mexican, the time-warp **Si Señor** (200 E. Pine St., 575/546-3938, 9:30am-8pm Mon.-Sat., 10am-3pm Sun., $7) shouldn't be discounted for its walls tiled like a 1970s bathroom. The prices are low, the portions are huge and their specialty is an ingenious platter of chicken-fried steak slathered with green chile and cheese (the "milanesa"). Regulars also recommend the *carne adovada*-stuffed sopaipilla.

In a side alley by the Wells Fargo parking lot, ★ **Elisa's House of Pies & Restaurant** (208 S. Silver Ave., 575/494-4639, 9am-7pm Tues.-Fri., 9:30am-7pm Sat., 9am-4pm Sun., $10) is not messing around: pecan, lemon meringue, millionaire (cream pie with pecans and pineapple), French silk (creamy chocolate), and more make up the daily pie list. Elisa and her husband also dish out a full soul-food menu that includes barbecue ribs, collard greens, and red beans and rice. The sides are good for vegetarians—a nice break from cheese enchiladas.

Finally, if you've got a car full of kids (and/or you just can't face another enchilada), **Forghedaboudit Pizza** (115 Silver Ave., 575/275-3881, 3pm-8pm Mon.-Thurs., 11am-8:30pm Fri., 3pm-8:30pm Sat., 3pm-8pm Sun., $10) is worth a detour. Solo diners can ask for a 12-inch pizza (not on the menu), and the homemade meatball parmigiana has a kick. There are also calzones, subs, and salads.

Accommodations

Travelers seldom plan to spend the night in Deming, but if you're deciding between here and Lordsburg, Deming has a slightly larger selection of upper-end chain hotels (with more chance of a vacancy), and also better options for dinner. For better, non-chain value, though, consider driving south to Columbus—or to the one vintage motel in Lordsburg. Ordinarily, you should have no trouble rolling into Deming without a reservation, but book ahead when the duck races are on at the end of August.

On the east side of town, **Grand Motor Inn** (1721 E. Pine St., 575/546-2632, www.grandhoteldeming.com, $55 d) delivers good value for the money—though, oddly, it charges $1 for toiletries, and breakfast is an extra $4. You get a nice big room, with a mini-fridge, and even a swimming pool.

Information

Make your first stop in town the **Deming Visitor Center** (800 E. Pine St., 575/567-1962, 9am-5pm Mon.-Fri.), where you'll find chatty staff and answers to all your area questions. **Readers Cove Books** (200 S. Copper St., 575/544-2512, 10am-5pm Tues.-Sat.) is a cozy shop with an eclectic selection.

Getting There

By car, Deming is 60 miles (one hour) west of Las Cruces via I-10; it's another 60 miles west to Lordsburg. Silver City is 53 miles (one hour) north via U.S. 180. The **Greyhound bus** (800/231-2222, www.greyhound.com) comes in twice a day from Las Cruces and drops you at the Shell station (420 E. Cedar St., 7am-10pm daily).

CITY OF ROCKS STATE PARK

Bristling out of the flat basin north of Deming, **City of Rocks State Park** (327 Hwy. 61, 575/536-2800, www.emnrd.state.nm.us, $5/car) does indeed resemble a metropolis, as imagined by Dr. Seuss. Hardened lava, eroded over 35 million years, has formed a skyline of towering pinnacles and bulbous growths. With expansive views across the flatlands and all sorts of birds and other wildlife to check out up close, this is a great spot for a picnic and short hike, or an overnight in one of the 52 **campsites** (10 have water and electrical hookups; $14). The visitors center is well equipped, with showers for overnighters. The park is 24 miles from Deming (28 miles from Silver City) on U.S. 180, then 4 miles northeast on Highway 61.

Faywood Hot Springs

On the road to City of Rocks is **Faywood Hot Springs** (165 Hwy. 61, 575/536-9663, www.faywood.com); the springs are much easier to reach than those on the Gila River, as the route here from surrounding towns is a straight highway. Once the site of a posh resort, which was later razed, the pools have been redeveloped in a more natural way. All outdoors, shaded with small trees, they're

---

1: Faywood Hot Springs **2:** Elisa's House of Pies & Restaurant in Deming **3:** the town of Palomas, just south of Columbus (and the border with Mexico)

sealed inside and cleaned regularly. They're perched around a small rise, and surrounded by campsites and cabins.

The public pools (10am-10pm daily, $13/day) are split between clothing-optional and swimsuits-required; private pools ($26/hour) are also available. The very nice **tent sites** ($33 d) and **cabins** ($110) include access to the pools. The visitors center stocks water, snacks, and towels, in case you don't have your own.

COLUMBUS

Devastated in a raid by Pancho Villa in 1916, the border town of Columbus is still not exactly jumping. It's centered on a park and a WPA-built town hall, with most of its commerce and community linked with Mexico in some way. As you drive south from Deming on Highway 11, the terrain grows sandier, more dotted with cactus and yucca, and generally more like what people imagine Mexico to look like. You may see a giant white blimp in the sky—it's an aerostat, a balloon-borne radar system used by the U.S. Border Patrol.

Sights
PANCHO VILLA STATE PARK
The southeast corner of the main crossroads (Highways 9 and 11) in Columbus, formerly a U.S. Army encampment, has been transformed into small **Pancho Villa State Park** (400 W. Hwy. 9, 575/531-2711, www.emnrd. state.nm.us, $5/car). It includes an excellent **museum** (8am-5pm daily, free) dedicated to Villa's 1916 attack, in which 18 of Columbus's 400 residents were killed. The subsequent manhunt for the Mexican rebel leader, led by General John J. Pershing, involved some 2,000 troops traveling by car and airplane—the first mechanized military campaign in history. The museum does a great job of portraying both the personal tragedy felt in Columbus and the impressive scale of Pershing's military operation, which was a crucial training ground for World War I.

South of the museum and a large cactus garden are 79 **campsites** ($14) with good facilities but in somewhat spartan surroundings.

COLUMBUS HISTORICAL SOCIETY MUSEUM
The **Columbus Historical Society Museum** (575/531-2620, 10am-2pm daily, donation) is across the intersection from the state park. Housed in the old depot, it has nifty train paraphernalia, as well as some morbidly interesting items, such as a replica death mask of Pancho Villa and a diorama showing the wreckage of the town in 1916.

PALOMAS
While you're in Columbus, you may as well see a bit of Mexico. Immediately past the customs gates and the dead-straight border fence is a five-block strip of dentist offices, pharmacies, fruit-pop vendors, and taco shops, with the central plaza a couple of blocks to the west. One mega-mart, the impossible-to-miss **Pink Store** (575/545-5206, 9am-6pm daily), sells crafts from all over Mexico, plus the obligatory margaritas at the in-house restaurant.

Crossing the border is usually as easy as being waved through; coming back to American soil, however, you'll need to show your passport, and your car may be subject to X-ray. It's a lot easier to walk over (do take your passport). Free parking is available just before the border, and the Pink Store can arrange a golf-cart escort if you buy too much to carry yourself.

Food and Accommodations
For breakfast and lunch, **Irma's Kitchen** (Hwy. 11 at Hwy. 9, 575/694-4026, 7am-6pm Wed.-Mon., $7), at the main crossroads, is a major gathering spot with excellent red chile and other very homey New Mexican food. The **Patio Café** (211 Broadway, 575/531-2495, 9am-3pm Mon.-Sat., $7) has good burgers and green-chile stew. For dinner, it's practical—and preferable—just to walk to Mexico and have great *barbacoa* and more at the various street carts and restaurants.

In this relative middle of nowhere, there are two good places to sleep. Formerly known as Martha's Place, **Los Milagros** (204 Lima Rd., 575/531-2467, www.losmilagroshotel. com, $49 s, $59 d) is a great surprise—in fact, you might want to make the detour from Deming if you prefer B&Bs. Each of the five sunny, freshly renovated upstairs rooms has a balcony, while the downstairs room has two queen beds. There are also RV sites ($15). Across Highway 11, **Hacienda de Villa** (220 S. Hwy. 11, 575/531-1000, $55 d) is a nicely kept little motel that's a real bargain. The main building used to be the town's museum.

LORDSBURG

Aesthetically, Lordsburg is lacking—a quick cruise around town suggests this is where the chain-link-fence salesman made his first million. It's also a bit tragic economically, as the freight train industry that drove the place has all but died, leaving a desolate strip of 1st Street (now Motel Drive) running parallel to the tracks. Why stop? Well . . .

Sights
LORDSBURG-HIDALGO
COUNTY MUSEUM
The **Lordsburg-Hidalgo County Museum** (710 E. 2nd St., 575/542-9086, 1pm-5pm Mon.-Fri., free) has a fascinating exhibit on the history of POW camps in New Mexico during World War II. One was located near Lordsburg, and German and Italian prisoners were put to work farming. The rest of the museum is a bit of a jumble, though there are some relics from local mines (another defunct Lordsburg industry).

SHAKESPEARE
Two and a half miles south of Lordsburg on Highway 494, the ghost town of **Shakespeare** (575/542-9034, www.shakespeareghosttown. com, $5) is in perhaps the ideal state of repair—just enough to spark the imagination, but not so polished as to seem museum-like.

What's even more interesting is how the typical Old West buildings such as the saloon, the assay office, and the blacksmith's shop are overlaid with the history of the family that has owned and maintained the place since 1935. There's also a dance studio, where a generation of Lordsburg girls took classes, and a shack that the family matriarch squatted in to protest the expansion of I-10. The result is a more poignant monument to the fading American West than you find in most ghost towns.

The place is open one weekend a month—check the schedule online. You can also schedule private tours ($7), which can be booked daily.

Food and Accommodations
For New Mexican food, head into town to **Ramona's** (904 E. Motel Dr., 575/542-3030, 8am-8pm Tues.-Fri., 8am-2pm Sun., $7), a tiny café with pretty curtains in the windows. On Sunday, they serve a fantastic *menudo*.

Thanks to the U.S. Border Patrol setting up headquarters here, Lordsburg's accommodation options are a little better than the town might suggest. Independent, old-style **Holiday Motel** (600 E. Motel Dr., 575/542-3535, $50 d) and the recently renovated **Motel 6** (1303 S. Main St., 575/542-8807, www.motel6.com, $66 d) are both good-value options; the latter has a pool.

RODEO AND INTO ARIZONA

The gateway town, such as it is, to New Mexico's "bootheel" is a string of barely a dozen buildings along Highway 80, fronting now-vanished railroad tracks and the Arizona state line. Rodeo sits in a dramatic bowl between small but spiking mountain ranges; coming over the low pass into the valley affords one of the more awe-inspiring views in southern New Mexico, especially in late afternoon when the sun glints off the crags. This flat terrain, which develops temporary shallow lakes (called playas) in the wet season, is hospitable to a huge range of birds. Nine miles away is Portal, Arizona, world-famous as a birding destination.

Sights

Two miles north of Rodeo proper, the **Chiricahua Desert Museum** (4 Rattlesnake Canyon Rd., 575/557-5757, 9am-5pm daily, $10) is a herper's dream—dedicated to all things reptilian. The entry fee allows access to two rooms full of live, rare rattlesnakes and lizards, as well as a profusion of slithery tchotchkes, from Steve Irwin memorabilia to vintage snake-bite kits. Also on display are beautifully detailed paintings and prints of snakes by noted wildlife illustrator Tell Hicks. For those who get nervous just reading about snakes, there's a large gift shop to browse (plenty of local guides and more) and a garden with rare cacti (free).

Ten miles over the border in Arizona, alongside Highway 80, the **Geronimo Surrender Memorial** is the final chapter to the Apache leader's story, lived so vividly around New Mexico. For nearly 30 years, Geronimo fought against the incursions into Apache lands after Mexicans killed his family; he finally submitted to American terms in 1886, effectively ending the Indian Wars. After his surrender, he was taken prisoner and toured as an exotic attraction, including at the 1904 World's Fair in St. Louis. Just as Geronimo's birth monument is not at the "headwaters of the Gila," but in an accessible parking lot, the stone memorial pillar is placed for convenience by the highway. The actual surrender site is in privately owned **Skeleton Canyon,** in the Peloncillo Mountains, now gated off.

Sports and Recreation

The wilderness areas around here are almost completely devoid of trails; if you fancy adventure (and carrying plenty of water), the **Big Hatchet** and **Animas** ranges to the south await.

1: Hacienda de Villa motel in Columbus 2: a special tour at the ghost town of Shakespeare ending with a shootout

CAVE CREEK CANYON

Take Highway 533 (Portal Road) west from Highway 80, directly across from the Chiricahua Desert Museum for a short drive past Portal and on to **Cave Creek Canyon** in Arizona's Coronado National Forest. Strikingly lush, the canyon is lined with sheer cliffs pocked with caves and the whole place teems with birds, making it one of the best birdwatching spots in the Southwest.

Stop first at the **visitor information center** (Forest Rd. 42, 8am-4pm Fri.-Sun.) for maps and a bird checklist. (Note that Arizona does not observe Daylight Saving Time; in summer, the closing time is really 5pm New Mexico time.)

Up the road a couple of miles is the turn for **South Fork Trail** (no. 243), a birding pilgrimage site because the rare elegant trogon is often in residence along the creek here. Even if you're not interested in our feathered friends, it's hard not to love the elegant trogon, which lives up to its name with its scarlet breast and long chestnut-brown tail. The area is also lovely in the fall, when the maple leaves turn. The full trail is nearly seven miles, with an elevation gain of 2,500 feet, but the first mile or so is level.

For more local information and books, stop off at the **Southwestern Research Station** (520/558-2396, www.amnh.org), an ecologists' camp maintained by the American Museum of Natural History. Its **Chiricahua Nature Shop** (520/558-2396, 8:30-noon and 1pm-4:30pm Wed.-Sat.) is a good place to find out what interesting critters have been spotted here. Farther up the road from here is another good walk, the **Herb Martyr Trail** (no. 247); at 2.8 miles it's much shorter than the South Fork route, but more strenuous.

Food and Accommodations

For meals and a bit of social contact, head to the **Rodeo Grocery & Café** (195 Hwy. 80, 575/557-2295, 7:30am-3pm Mon.-Sat., $7), which posts its food specials for the month—school-cafeteria-style, but so much tastier.

(The grocery is open until 5:30pm, for basic DIY provisions.) For dinner, the **Rodeo Tavern** (209 Hwy. 80, 575/557-2229, 4pm-10pm Tues.-Thurs., 11am-10pm Fri.-Sat., $12) makes excellent fried chicken, and also has a pool table and a varied crew of regulars. In summer, it serves lunch on Friday and Saturday as well.

Reason alone to drive all this way, the lovely ★ **Casa Adobe** (Hwy. 80, 575/557-7777, www.casaadobe.net, $160 d) fulfills every get-away-from-it-all fantasy. Rodeo has no cell phone coverage, and there's no Internet in this beautiful casita, leaving you free to sit and admire the dramatic mountains on either side. The whole house is yours, impeccably decorated with rustic furniture and stocked with goodies like eggs from the hosts' chickens. Similar digs on better-trod paths in the state would cost at least twice as much. There's a two-night minimum.

The **Mountain Valley Lodge RV Park** (223 Hwy. 80, 575/520-3731, www.mountainvalleylodgesite.com) has two rooms ($75) to rent, and two larger cabins with kitchens ($95 and $125).

With 24 hours' notice, you can also eat at the cafeteria at the **Southwestern Research Station** (520/558-2396, www.amnh.org) or stay in the lodge rooms ($90 pp, including meals), if they're not booked by researchers.

Silver City

Called just "Silver" by the locals, this casual mountain town ranks high on quality-of-life lists. It has lured a portion of its 10,000 population from out of state with a near-utopian combination of outdoor activities, an educated populace (Western New Mexico University is here), and beautiful housing stock that dates from the city's boom in the late 19th and early 20th centuries. Unlike more slapdash towns, Silver was built to last, and its stone and cast-iron structures have helped the town maintain its grandeur. Over the decades, it has been home to Billy the Kid, who came here in 1873 at about age 13 and got into trouble from the start, then many wealthy tuberculosis patients in the 1890s.

For decades, the primary industry fueling the town was mining, but as that diminished, creative transplants remade the center of Silver City. Contemporary hippies have set the mellow pace downtown and drive the local food co-op and other local institutions, while rat-race dropouts, young artists, and a small gay and lesbian community have bought up the territorial-style bungalows and downtown storefronts, repainted them in candy colors, and created a distinctive, unpretentious cultural scene.

Navigating Silver City is not immediately intuitive because the main downtown drag is Bullard Street, though Hudson Street, a couple of blocks east, is larger and runs directly south from U.S. 180. The original Main Street, which ran parallel to and between Bullard and Hudson, was washed away in a series of floods between 1895 and 1903, leaving what's evocatively called the Big Ditch. A greenery-filled chasm some 50 feet below the street level, it's an unorthodox park for an unorthodox populace. Most of the rest of Silver's attractions are on the west side of it.

SIGHTS

The first stop in learning about the town, the **Silver City Museum** (312 W. Broadway, 575/538-5921, www.silvercitymuseum.org, 9am-4:30pm Tues.-Fri., 10am-4pm Sat.-Sun., $5 donation) is an intriguing, polished collection in an old Victorian home. You'll see photos of Main Street before and after it became the Big Ditch, a fascinating exhibit on the culture and economy of tuberculosis treatment in New Mexico, and more than you thought you

Silver City

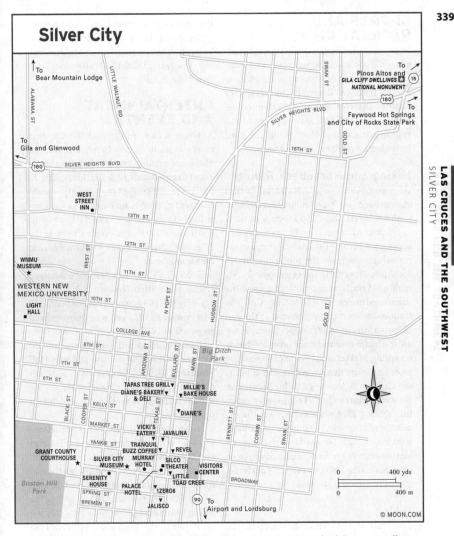

wanted to know about mining history and science. Be sure to climb up to the cupola to take in the view of the whole town.

Just up the hill at the end of Broadway, the **Grant County Courthouse** (201 N. Cooper St.) is a small but elegant building. The highlight is 1934 murals depicting the local ranching and mining industries.

A bit farther afield, the **WNMU Museum** (1000 W. College Ave., 575/538-6386, www. wnmumuseum.org, 9am-4:30pm Mon.-Fri.,

10am-4pm Sat.-Sun., free) has an excellent collection of Mimbres pottery, on which critters such as coatis, turkeys, and pronghorns dance, not to mention a grand antique urinal in the basement men's room. The museum is in the historic Fleming Hall, which recently underwent an extensive renovation that has elevated the overall presentation of the museum's exhibits. Head west on 10th Street; on campus, look for the building near the top of the hill on the right.

SPORTS AND RECREATION

Nearly encircled by the Gila National Forest, Silver City is an outdoorsy town and some of the state's best mountain biking and hiking is at the town's doorstep. The **Silver City Ranger District office** (3005 Camino del Bosque, 575/388-8201, 8am-4:30pm Mon.-Fri.) is just north of U.S. 180 off the 32nd Street Bypass on the east side of town.

Hiking and Horseback Riding

Of course, with the **Gila National Forest** close at hand (see "Gila National Forest" later in this chapter), there's no shortage of trails to fill your day's pursuits. In town, you can stroll up **Boston Hill,** and take in a commanding view from the top at just under 6,400 feet. From there you can choose from a number of trails from a network around the abandoned mines that started Silver City. The trailhead nearest to downtown is at the end of Spring Street, just off Cooper Street. There are trail maps here and at the other trailheads on Spring, Market, and Cheyenne streets. For more immersive excursions consider contacting Chiricahua Apache guide Joe Saenz, who runs **Wolf Horse Outfitters** (Arenas Valley Rd., 575/534-1379, www.wolfhorseoutfitters.com), specializing in low-impact, educational trips into the Gila National Forest. His excellent services range from a half-day hike or horseback ride ($95) to custom packhorse adventures (from $240/day).

Biking

The staff at **Gila Hike & Bike** (103 E. College Ave., 575/388-3222, 9am-5:30pm Mon.-Fri., 9am-5pm Sat., plus 10am-4pm Sun. Mar.-Dec.) are veterans, with lots of tips on where to ride in the area. Ambitious road cyclists can trace some of the routes of the Tour de Gila, while mountain bikers can head to **Little Walnut Picnic Area,** north of town via Little Walnut Road from near the intersection of U.S. 180 and Highway 90. This is the starting point for a couple of short, relatively easy outings, including the gorgeous two-mile **Picnic Loop/Berg Trail** (No. 711), as well as the seven-mile **Wagon Wheel Loop** that's more challenging. You can get detailed trail guides from Gila Hike & Bike.

ENTERTAINMENT AND EVENTS

Although it's a college town, Silver City isn't rowdy at night. A few bars along Bullard give some evening options. Of these, **Little Toad Creek Brewery & Distillery** (200 N. Bullard St., 575/956-6144, 11am-11pm daily, later on Fri.-Sat.) is probably the most consistently busy, with live music, trivia nights, and house-made booze. People also make the 20-minute drive to Pinos Altos for music at the saloon there.

Silver City's excellent new-old downtown cinema is the **Silco Theatre** (311 N. Bullard St., 575/956-6090, www.thesilco.com, $8), first opened in 1923 and was renovated and reopened in 2016. It's under new ownership and shows first-run films. For second-run films and occasional live shows, **Light Hall Theater** (1000 W. College Ave., 575/538-6300, http://movies.wnmu.edu, $2), on the WNMU campus, is another venue with a lot of character.

As for events, Silver City is internationally known for the spring bike race **Tour of the Gila** (www.tourofthegila.com), which, thanks to its winding routes through the surrounding mountains, is known as a warm-up for the Tour de France. If you're a cycling fan and in town late April to early May, this is a great time to see teams sweat up close. Plan well ahead: All hotels are packed for the event, and surrounding highways are restricted on certain days.

Later in May, Silver City's biggest cultural event is the **Silver City Blues Festival** (www.silvercitybluesfestival.org), over Memorial Day weekend. Since 1995, it has gained a strong reputation, and national acts, including Grady Champion and the Dirty Dozen Brass Band, have graced the stage (usually at Gough Park).

In mid-September, the **Gila River Festival** (575/538-8078, www.gilaconservation.org) rallies an excellent roster of musicians and artists for an environment-friendly party. While the center of the action is Silver City, activities such as guided hikes, bird-watching, and archaeological tours take place in the forest to the north. It's a great opportunity to explore less-visited spots in the company of experts. The same organization hosts the **Wild & Scenic Film Festival** (www.wildandscenicfestival.org) in January as well.

FOOD

Silver City has a large number of amazing places to eat, all in the downtown area—so many, it's hard to designate just one as a top pick. Note that most restaurants close early, and some of the best are open only a few days a week.

New Mexican and Mexican

Occupying a string of old storefronts on the south end of downtown, **Jalisco Café** (103 S. Bullard St., 575/388-2060, 11am-8pm Mon.-Sat., 9am-2pm Sun., $12) is the most popular New Mexican joint in town. Along with a small selection of seafood dishes, you'll get all the green- and red-chile-smothered classics, though they're not nearly as hot as the menu warns, and the green chile is typical of southern New Mexico, all mellow and creamy—a relief for some diners, a travesty for others. Everyone can agree on the sopaipillas, though, which are huge and perfectly pillowy.

Cafés

Get your java at **Javalina** (117 W. Market St., 575/388-1350, 6am-7pm daily, $3), a rambling and welcoming coffeehouse with lots of thrift-store sofas and people sitting for hours over a game of chess or the daily paper.

Set in the former Elks Lodge, **Vicki's Eatery** (315 N. Texas St., 575/388-5430, 11am-2:30pm Mon.-Fri., 7am-2:30pm Sat., 8am-2pm Sun., $9) is a prime spot for lunch, with big sandwiches that range from familiar and hearty

(green-chile turkey melt) to the more exotic (turkey and Havarti cheese with chutney).

Millie's Bake House (602 N. Bullard St., 575/597-2253, 7am-3pm Tues.-Sat., $4) is a fantastically home-style operation, with nice sandwiches and salads to balance out the myriad sugar-fix options, including the icebox pie of your dreams.

Quirky and cozy, ★ **Tranquil Buzz Coffee** (112 W. Yankie St., 575/654-2057, 7am-5pm Mon.-Sat., 9am-3pm Sun., $4) serves caffeine with a smile and plenty of baked goods and quiche, too. It's usually full of locals and understandably so—it's an unhurried place with plenty of comfy seats and outside tables.

International and Eclectic

Cheerful ★ **Tapas Tree Grill** (619 N. Bullard St., 575/597-8282, 11am-3pm Mon.-Thurs., 11am-7pm Fri., 11am-4pm Sat., $9), where you can munch on empanadas filled with chorizo and potatoes and nosh on Thai noodle bowls, embodies global fusion food truck cuisine. That means tapas, too, of course, like a Moroccan lamb kefta plate, but the real treats are the savory and sweet crepes—try the one with smoked gouda, greens, strawberries, and nuts—and chompers—twin sliders with all sorts of delectable toppings.

Silver residents love long-established **Diane's** (510 N. Bullard St., 575/538-8722, 11am-2pm and 5pm-9pm Tues.-Fri., 9am-2pm and 5pm-9pm Sat., 9am-2pm Sun., $17). It's the go-to spot for familiar favorites, such as biscuits and gravy, meatloaf and lasagna, in a pleasant atmosphere, and is very popular for brunch. The adjacent "parlor" (from 2pm daily) hosts live music some evenings. They also run a **bakery** and **deli** (601 N. Bullard St., 575/534-9229) that specializes in sandwiches made with homemade bread, European pastries, and exquisite cakes.

Local

With a menu determined by locally sourced and seasonal ingredients, ★ **Revel** (304 N. Bullard St., 575/388-4920, www.eatdrinkrevel.com, 11am-9pm Mon.-Tues. and Thurs.-Fri.,

9am-9pm Sat.-Sun., $18) is Silver City's defining farm to table experience. Fortunately, it's not overly precious about its approach and the focus is squarely on the food, which is consistently flavorful and filling. Expect hearty dishes such as a surf and turf with mashed sweet potatoes and grilled trout with a chickpea salad. Their starters are hard to pass up, especially the white cheddar biscuits with homemade raspberry jam.

ACCOMMODATIONS

Downtown Silver has a couple of excellent lodging options. Most chain hotels and motels are on U.S. 180 on the east side of town (also called Silver Heights Boulevard), which is not walkable to downtown.

Under $100

The **Palace Hotel** (106 W. Broadway, 575/388-1811, www.silvercitypalacehotel.com, $62 s, $82 d) embodies the phrase "faded charm," but it is moderately priced and full of historic ambience—even if the beds can be a bit saggy. Street noise can be a problem; no. 59 ($98), a two-room suite, is one of the quieter options. A basic continental breakfast is included in the rate.

Silver's "newer" historic hotel is the ★ **Murray Hotel** (200 W. Broadway, 575/956-9400, www.murray-hotel.com, $84 d), a glamorous slab of a building erected in the late 1930s. It reopened in 2012, after major renovation, and its rooms are both comfortable and fabulously located. Room 426 has beautiful glass bricks in the bathroom.

$100-150

As for B&Bs, the 1883 **Serenity House** (411 W. Broadway, 575/574-2696) is in a fine location, across from the Silver City Museum. Three sunny rooms upstairs ($120-150) are spacious, with especially nice bathrooms. The cozier downstairs room ($150) has a marble fireplace. Decorating styles range from subdued Victorian to subdued Western. The proprietor is exceedingly helpful, and the breakfast is a real treat.

If you'll be in town for a few nights, or just want the full comforts of home, consider **West Street Inn** (1303 West St., 575/534-2302, www.weststreetinn-nm.com), which contains three well-kept apartments with full kitchens. Casa Bonita ($125) is good for groups or families, with two bedrooms and a yard; the other two apartments ($105) are one-bedrooms with king beds.

Over $150

Set on 178 acres up against the national forest, **Bear Mountain Lodge** (60 Bear Mountain Ranch Rd., 575/538-2538, www.bearmountainlodge.com, $160 d) is a homey retreat where you can get a taste of the Gila in comfort—trails crisscross the land out back. The beautiful adobe main building was built in the mid-1920s. The creative, unpretentious café here is open to non-guests with prior reservations.

INFORMATION

The **Silver City Visitors Center** (201 N. Hudson St., 575/538-5555, www.visitsilvercity.org, 9am-5pm Mon.-Sat. 10am-2pm Sun.) is just east of Big Ditch Park at Broadway. There's info available out front all the time, and its website is very thorough.

GETTING THERE

By car, Silver City is closest to Deming, about 60 miles (1 hour) south via U.S. 180. From Truth or Consequences, the closest town on I-25, it's 88 miles west, but the drive takes more than 2 hours on the winding road over Emory Pass; count on 4.5 hours from Albuquerque via I-25. Tucson, Arizona, is 200 miles (3 hours) west, and El Paso, Texas, is 2.5 hours southeast.

Grant County Airport (SVC), about 10 miles southeast of Silver City, receives flights two or three times daily from Albuquerque, five weekly from Phoenix, and one weekly from Los Angeles on Advanced Air (800/393-7035, www.advancedairlines.com).

1: creatively painted storefronts in Silver City
2: Bear Mountain Lodge

Trail of the Mountain Spirits

A romantic name for the usual driving circuit out of Silver City, the Trail of the Mountain Spirits runs north on Highway 15 through the little town of Pinos Altos, then up to Gila Cliff Dwellings National Monument and many hiking trails into the wilderness. After backtracking from the cliff dwellings, the route continues through the pine forest east on Highway 35, past Lake Roberts, over the Continental Divide to Bear Canyon Lake, and through the village of Mimbres. Highway 152 then leads back west to Silver City via the region's modern mining center around Bayard.

PINOS ALTOS

About seven miles north on Highway 15, a sign points to the optimistically named Pinos Altos Business Loop. In fact, this tiny community offers just a couple of commercial attractions, and that's the way folks like it. "P.A.," as the village is known, is the retreat for those who think Silver is too big and busy.

In terms of sights, you can stop in at the obligatory Log Cabin Curio Shop (33 Main St., 575/388-1882, 11am-5pm daily, $2), an 1860s log cabin packed with cast-iron gewgaws; it sets the tone for the rest of the buildings in the area, which are functional if not always accurate replicas of what used to stand here in the 19th century.

Across the street, the ★ Buckhorn Saloon (32 Main St., 575/538-9911, www.buckhornsaloonandoperahouse.com, 5pm-10pm Mon.-Sat.) serves burgers ($13) and steaks ($33) in a wood-paneled, Wild West setting. The kitchen can be hit or miss, but the excellent old bar oozes character. The place is open for drinks starting at 3pm and continuing past the dinner hour, with very well attended live music starting around 7pm.

Also look for Hearst Church (Golden Ave., 10am-5pm Fri.-Sun. May-Oct.), an odd pitched-roof adobe structure built in 1898 by William Randolph Hearst's mother, Phoebe, who had gained her family fortune from a gold mine in the area. It's west of the main street—follow Historic Route signs as you come into town.

GILA HOT SPRINGS

A small collection of services for wilderness visitors, the village of Gila Hot Springs is the last chance to stock up before heading farther north. Doc Campbell's Post (3796 Hwy. 15, 575/536-9551, 1pm-4pm Mon.-Fri., noon-4pm Sat.-Sun.) sells basic provisions, books, fishing and hunting licenses, and homemade ice cream.

Just south of here are two semi-developed hot springs. Look for a turn labeled Access Road and signs to Gila Hot Springs Campground (http://gilahotspringscampground.com). The three riverside pools ($5 pp for day use only), kept at different temperatures, are lightly developed, and there are a few tent campsites here ($8 pp), which should be reserved ahead. The whole place is quiet and tightly run, with a ban on booze and loud music at the pools.

An earlier right turn, at the four-way intersection down the hill from Highway 15, leads to Wildwood Retreat & Hot Springs (575/536-3600, www.wildwoodhotspringsretreat.com), which is closed in the winter. The springs are channeled into paved pools ($10/day). You can camp here ($15 pp), or stay in a snug cabin ($60 d) or larger straw-bale hogan ($80).

One safety note: To avoid the extremely remote possibility of contracting a fatal infection caused by an amoeba that can live in warm waters such as those in hot springs, keep your head (especially your nose) above water at all times.

★ GILA CLIFF DWELLINGS NATIONAL MONUMENT

The big destination on the byway is the **Gila Cliff Dwellings National Monument** (575/536-9461, www.nps.gov/gicl, 8:30am-5pm daily June-Aug., 9am-4pm daily Sept.-May, free), just past Gila Hot Springs and 44 miles north of Silver City. Compared with the ruins at Bandelier National Monument or Chaco Canyon, these are relatively small and in a less spectacular setting, but if these are the only cliff settlements you'll be near on your trip, don't miss them. The drive up from Silver City, along a narrow road often with no center stripe, takes up to three hours.

Stop in first at the **visitors center** (8am-4:30pm daily), which gives a basic overview of the environment as well as the Mogollon culture that inhabited the cliff dwellings for only a generation near the end of the 13th century, through excavated relics of daily life such as reed mats and mosaic work. The rock cairn in the parking lot is a discreet monument to the Apache chief Geronimo, born far up the canyon ("at the headwaters of the Gila," as he said) in 1829.

A two-mile drive gets you to the pay station at the **trailhead** and a basic nature center, where enthusiastic rangers will let you know what kind of animals are out and about. You reach the **caves** via a mile-long loop trail that takes about an hour to walk. The route is level for the first half, then increasingly steep as it winds up and through the dwellings. The trail passes three of the five caves, which once housed up to 60 people in about 40 rooms; the central one is a large, bilevel arrangement that included the central ceremonial chambers. Much of the wood you see in the rooms is original, preserved perfectly in the dry air; the Mogollon, who did not have steel, shaped it by burning it and hacking it with stone tools.

Recreation

This is the most accessible part of the Gila Wilderness, with some very scenic hiking along canyon bottoms. Set aside time to get the latest on trails and hot springs at the visitors center.

HIKING

The three forks of the Gila River converge near the cliff dwellings, and the canyons formed by the water are usually a nice place to walk. Be prepared, however, for wet and muddy stream crossings, and in summer, plan to hike in the morning, so you're not caught in canyons during afternoon rainstorms.

At 34 miles, the **West Fork Trail** (no. 151) is the longest in the Gila Wilderness. The first three miles provide a pleasantly varied, fairly easy day hike. The trail begins at Scorpion Campground, across from the Gila Cliff Dwellings. Just off the trail to the south after the first river crossing, a small ruined cabin sits next to the grave of one William Grudging, murdered in 1893—eerie evidence of the violent past of this otherwise peaceful setting. Further traces of past inhabitants can be seen at a small cliff dwelling on the west side, which marks the turnaround point for most day hikers. Others do the full length as a multiday backpacking trek.

Given the complex network of trails in this area, it's easy to make a number of loop hikes through varied terrain. Ask for suggestions in the visitors center, where you can also pick up a topographical map.

HOT SPRINGS

A refreshing warm bath in the great outdoors is a fine motivator for a hike, and there are several natural springs in the vicinity of the cliff dwellings' visitors center. The closest ones to the visitors center are **Lightfeather Hot Spring,** just a half-mile up the Middle Fork Trail; however, the water here is scalding hot, and you may have to reroute the river water to dilute it to a usable temperature. The deep pools of **Jordan Hot Springs** are worth the longer hike (about eight miles) up the same trail; you can shorten the trip by starting at the trail behind TJ Corral, farther up the road

to the cliff dwellings, but get precise directions from the visitors center.

LAKE ROBERTS

Heading east from the intersection with Highway 35, you reach pristine Lake Roberts. Shaded heavily by tall pine trees and stocked with trout, it's a popular getaway during the summer months. You can camp above the lake in developed sites ($15) or undeveloped ones ($10) at the aptly named and very pretty Mesa Campground; there are also several lodges in the area.

MIMBRES VALLEY

The wide, green valley surrounding the village of Mimbres is the epicenter of the ancient culture of the same name, best known for its elegant black-on-white pottery designs, done about a thousand years ago. One of the sites where these works were unearthed is the Mimbres Valley Cultural Site (12 Sage Dr., 575/536-3333, 11am-3pm daily Apr.-Oct., 11am-3pm Fri.-Sun. Nov.-Mar., free). There's virtually nothing to see in terms of ancient settlement, but you can also visit the museum set in two more recent (19th-century) homesteads. Look for the turn off the north side of the road.

A Mennonite family runs ★ Three Questions Coffee House (Hwy. 35, 575/536-3267, 7am-noon Tues.-Sat., $6.50), serving a generous all-you-can-eat breakfast and lunch buffet of simple but wholesome food, plus giant cinnamon rolls and other great baked goods.

Mimbres also has a gas station, and the Gila Wilderness Ranger District office (Hwy. 35, 575/536-2250, 8am-4:30pm Mon.-Fri.) is here. Just after the turnoff to the old Spanish settlement of San Lorenzo, Highway 35 dead-ends at Highway 152, which runs west to Silver City.

CHINO MINE

Off the east side of Highway 152, you can't help but notice the monumentally altered landscape around the Chino Mine, the pit of which measures more than a mile across. The oldest continuously mined claim in the United States, it was first known by Apaches, who took copper from the area. In 1799, the Spanish, with the help of convict labor, began extracting copper and sending it to Mexico. Production was so great that the majority of the early 19th-century copper coins from Mexico and Spain can be traced back to Santa Rita del Cobre, as the mine was known then. Open-pit mining began in 1910, eventually swallowing up the town of Santa Rita, which had grown adjacent to the mine.

The hole now reaches 1,600 feet into the ground, dwarfing the trucks and shovels that toil on its terraces, and a good portion of Grant County's population is employed here in some capacity. You can't miss Chino from the road, but if you want an up-close look, stop at the observation point maintained by current owners Freeport-McMoRan, just south of mile marker 6. If you're able to ignore the obvious environmental ravages, you could call it an impressive piece of land art.

FORT BAYARD

Located just after the junction of Highway 152 with U.S. 180, Fort Bayard (575/956-3294, www.fortbayard.org) was built in 1866 by the Ninth Cavalry, some of the Buffalo Soldiers who earned renown fighting the Apaches. During the 1920s, it was a center of tuberculosis treatment for the military, and the tidy rows of white barracks are a product of that period. For decades it was a veterans hospital, but now it has a ghostly feel, as it has been deemed too costly to maintain, and left to ruin—except for a museum (9:30am-1:30pm Sat.-Mon.) in the old officers' quarters. Fort Bayard Days reenactments are in mid-September.

1: Buckhorn Saloon in Pinos Altos 2: Gila Cliff Dwellings National Monument 3: Doc Campbell's Post in Gila Hot Springs 4: the Gila River

Gila National Forest

From Silver City, U.S. 180 runs north about 45 miles to the junction with Highway 12 and the town of Reserve. For much of the drive, the road is surrounded by the **Gila National Forest,** the larger region surrounding the more tightly controlled Gila Wilderness. Its 2.7 million acres stretch west to Arizona and north as far as Quemado. Passing through rolling grassy plains and between mountain peaks, this is a beautiful—and often empty—drive.

GILA

Not to be confused with Gila Hot Springs, the village of Gila is often a jumping-off point for trips into the wilderness area or down the Gila River to the southwest. And as it's less than 30 miles from Silver City, it counts as a sort of suburb.

Set on 90 acres with a stream running through, ★ **Casitas de Gila** (50 Casita Flats, 575/535-4455, www.casitasdegila.com) is a great way to enjoy the area in comfort. Nightly rates go down the longer you stay—and once you get a glimpse of the night sky from the hot tub, you'll probably want to settle in. The apartments, furnished with custom Mexican woodwork, have kiva fireplaces, kitchens stocked with breakfast food, and private patios. Foldout couches in the living rooms make the standard casitas ($170) family-friendly, while a larger two-bedroom option ($225) can sleep six.

SAN FRANCISCO HOT SPRINGS

The **San Francisco Hot Springs** are some of the most beautiful in the area, with a large warm pool tucked in a canyon about 1.5 miles from the trailhead. The hot water bubbles out of the river plain, and the specific pool locations may change from year to year, but the general spot is easy to reach. Look for the turn west off U.S. 180, about five miles south

of Glenwood, around mile marker 58. A dirt road leads to a well-marked trail. Avoid the area during summer rainstorms—not only is there a risk of flash flooding, but the trail is heavy clay that's a slog when wet. If you happen to miss the turn, you can always stop in the Glenwood ranger office and ask directions—and check the status.

GLENWOOD

The road north from Gila skirts the mountains and races through grasslands, reaching the small town of Glenwood after about 30 miles. It's a nice quiet spot to stay the night on this loop.

For info on local trails, stop in at or call the **Glenwood Ranger District office** (Mineral Creek Rd., 575/539-2481, 8am-4:30pm Mon.-Fri.).

Catwalk Trail

A Civilian Conservation Corps project in the 1930s, the **Catwalk Trail** ($3) is a hanging walkway over a stream for the first half of its 1.1 miles, sometimes suspended more than 20 feet above the water and pink canyon walls pressing in close on either side. The catwalk follows the route of a water pipeline built in the 1890s as part of a mining operation. The first, easiest part is also wheelchair-accessible. The turnoff for the trail is in the middle of Glenwood, well marked as Highway 174 (Catwalk Road).

Food and Accommodations

The slices are satisfyingly thick and gooey at **Mario's Pizza** (U.S. 180, 575/539-2316, 4pm-8pm Thurs. and Fri., 2pm-8pm Sat., 2pm-6pm Sun., $7), which also makes calzones and a great Philly cheesesteak sandwich, too.

A few miles south in Pleasanton, **D and D's Organic Haven** (13 Blue Heron Ln., 575/539-2483, http://d-and-d-organic-haven. homestead.com, $80 s, $100 d) is a pretty

Exploring the Gila Wilderness

Covering 558,000 acres, the Gila Wilderness is the largest such protected area in any state but Alaska, and it's also the first. With the adjacent 200,000 acres of the Aldo Leopold Wilderness, plus the Gila National Forest to the south and north, it's an almost overwhelming place to explore. The terrain ranges from piñon forests dotted with spring wildflowers to the flat beds of the three forks of the Gila River. As fires and massive flooding in 2013 burned some trails and changed watercourses, any forays into the wilderness should be preceded by a visit to one of the national forest district offices.

The most common access point to the wilderness is on the south side, via Highway 15 north of Silver City. This serpentine road makes its way up through pine trees to the Gila Cliff Dwellings National Monument and several well-used trailheads.

While you're driving or hiking around, keep your eyes open for the area's rich wildlife. At lower elevations, javelinas (small wild pigs) are plentiful, as are packs of coatimundis. Nimble, raccoon-like animals with long snouts, coatis usually live in more tropical climates; southern New Mexico is the only area they're found in the United States. You might see one scampering across the road or napping in a tree. Less exotic, skunks are plentiful (four different species, in fact), and you'll surely encounter at least the traces of one at some point on your trip. In the higher mountains, you may see herds of mule deer and elk. The eponymous Gila monster, a venomous lizard that can grow up to two feet in length, makes its home here, as do lots of rattlesnakes. Be alert in the springtime, when the snakes have just come out of hibernation and are on the prowl for mates. Wear boots that come above your ankles, and don't place your feet between rocks or in crevices when hiking.

straw-bale hideaway with three rooms, lush gardens, and great food. It's open only March-mid-November.

If you're traveling as a family, you'll appreciate the cute stone cabins at **Los Olmos Lodge** (U.S. 180, 575/539-2224, www.losolmoslodge.com, from $80), with plenty of beds for everyone. There's also an outdoor pool, a creek, a fishing pond, and other activities.

MOGOLLON

Unlike many old mining towns, Mogollon bursts with color and cheer—at least on weekends between May and October, when the businesses up here are open. Its old buildings, including the **Silver Creek Inn** (www.silvercreekinn.com, May-Oct., $110 d), the **Purple Onion Café** (575/539-2710, 9am-5pm Sat.-Sun., $8), and the village archives, are painted in vibrant shades. It's a great place to get away for a night or two, as it feels quite cut off from the world.

In fact it *is* quite cut off from the world, nine miles up Highway 159, which locals call the **Bursum Road.** The road washed out due

to floods in 2013, and it is very often closed with snow in the winter. From a turn east, about three miles north of Glenwood, it starts off easily enough, crossing rolling scrub, but then it ascends steeply into the mountains. About halfway into the climb, the road reduces to a harrowing single lane with steep switchbacks and no guardrails.

But the view across the rolling grasslands below is stunning. Hardier drivers can carry on past Mogollon, where the road grows increasingly rough and enters aspen glades that glow gold in the fall. Wind your way very, very carefully back down the way you came in. Avoid doing this at sundown, however, as the glare just adds to the risk.

ALMA

Once a hideout for Butch Cassidy, this wide spot in the road is the turnoff for the 13-mile point-to-point **Mineral Creek Trail** (no. 201), one of the more gorgeous hikes into the Gila. The first 1.5 miles are an easy family hike along the creek, and the scenery beyond gets even better. Be prepared to cross the creek several times. To reach the trail, turn east in

Alma onto Mineral Creek Road, a dirt track; this turns into Forest Road 701 and dead-ends at the trailhead after 5.5 miles. Just before mile 5, look for **"Cooney's tomb,"** a giant boulder made into the gravesite for miner James Cooney and a few of his men, who were killed here by Apaches in 1880.

Food and Accommodations

On the east side of the road, **Alma Grill** (4592 U.S. 180, 575/539-2233, 6am-3pm Fri.-Wed., $6) serves all the necessary food for a good road trip: enchiladas, biscuits, and more.

A ten-minute drive north of Alma, the ★ **Cosmic Campground** (575/388-8201) has been designated an International Dark Sky Sanctuary—only one of ten such sites in the world—which is to say that, weather permitting, you will see the Milky Way in awe-inspiring detail. The campsites (free) are first come, first served and there are no facilities beyond pit toilets. The sites themselves are nothing special; they do, however, afford unobstructed views of a night sky unpolluted by artificial light. The turnoff to the campground is on the right off Highway 180, eight miles from Alma.

RESERVE

Hunting is big business in **Reserve,** the Catron County seat, with expeditions leaving from here and plenty of taxidermy shops in town. First settled by Mexican homesteaders in the early 1800s, the town is notorious for an 1884 shootout between 80-odd Texan cowboys and the local deputy sheriff, Elfego Baca, who held off the gang for 36 hours, until they ran out of ammunition. In what many saw as a blatantly racist move, Baca was later brought to trial for murdering one of the cowboys; he was finally acquitted when he displayed the bullet-riddled door he'd hidden behind. Look for a memorial to Baca at the main crossroads.

The **Reserve Ranger District office** (575/523-6232, 8am-4:30pm Mon.-Fri.), on Highway 12 just west of town, has information on the Gila National Forest, as well as the wilderness area.

For food, ★ **Adobe Does BBQ** (95A/B N. Main St., 575/533-6145, 7am-8pm Mon., 7am-3pm Tues.-Fri., $8) serves espresso and excellent homemade baked goods in the morning and barbecue, soups, and salads for lunch. The same owners run **Adobe Café and Bakery** (U.S. 180, 575/533-6146, 7am-3pm Mon. and Thurs.-Fri., 7am-8pm Sun., $8), southwest of Reserve, about a quarter-mile from the junction with Highway 12 (you'll pass this first if you're coming from the south). It also has a fresh, varied menu of breakfast goodies, as well as salads and creative sandwiches. The same team also has the adjacent **Hidden Springs Inn** (www.thehiddenspringsinn.com, $69 d), a very good deal, and nicely kept.

For dinner other nights, **Ella's** (96 Main St., 575/533-6111, 7am-8pm Tues.-Sun., $8), in Reserve proper, will do just fine—locals in Carhartts and hats dig in to chicken-fried steak and enchiladas.

Carlsbad Caverns and the Southeast

Barren land stretches between the atypical

tourist sights in southeastern New Mexico: the vast, bat-filled spaces of Carlsbad Caverns, the ghostly gypsum dunes at White Sands, and a museum dedicated to UFOs in Roswell.

You'll find surprising things if you make the drive—and what a long drive it is. The blank expanse the Spanish dubbed the Llano Estacado starts in Fort Sumner (where sharpshooter Billy the Kid finally met his end in 1881) and stretches east and south into Texas. The roads are straight, the horizon unbroken, and soon you can't tell if you've been driving for 20 minutes or two hours. The occasional oil derrick, wind turbine, or herd of cattle breaks up the monotony, and tiny towns—some long abandoned—loom up suddenly and disappear

Highlights

Look for ★ to find recommended sights, activities, dining, and lodging.

★ **International UFO Museum & Research Center:** Mysteries of deep space revealed! Government conspiracies uncovered! Plush alien dolls for sale! Roswell's most popular museum may seem campy, but it takes its mission very seriously (page 369).

★ **Anderson Museum of Contemporary Art:** Roswell is also home to this excellent collection of artwork in every media, which rivals the galleries in Santa Fe in quality and wins for sheer gutsy enthusiasm (page 370).

★ **The Big Room:** Some 600,000 visitors a year tour the main cave at **Carlsbad Caverns National Park**—for good reason. It's amazing in both its vast scale and its smallest details, such as clusters of tiny stalactites as delicate as lace. Silence is requested on the tour—not hard, as you'll be too awed to speak (page 382).

★ **Heart of the Sands:** Visiting the eerie bleached landscape at the center of **White Sands National Park** is like going to the beach and the North Pole both at once. If you're looking to experience sheer solitude—and come prepared—it's hard to imagine a better place (page 395).

★ **Lincoln State Monument:** The late 19th century's "most dangerous town in America" is now a quiet place, half of its main-street buildings preserved as museums that conjure life in Billy the Kid's era, without all the usual Wild West kitsch (page 402).

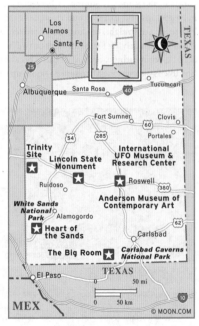

★ **Trinity Site:** You can only visit the stark site of the first atomic bomb blast two days a year. Consider it an essential stop if your visit aligns with the dates (page 405).

in the rear-view mirror just as fast. Portales, center of the "peanut basin of the Southwest," is a rare green spot, thanks to a deep aquifer. Roswell is the area's largest settlement, and perhaps its strangest, as many people are drawn to it solely for an alleged crash-landing of an alien spacecraft here in 1947.

Southwest of Roswell, the Sacramento Mountains spike along the edge of the plains. Here, the resort towns of Cloudcroft and Ruidoso cater to Texans who've fled the flatlands. The steep trails at Ski Apache, with a base elevation of 9,600 feet, provide winter entertainment. At the base of the mountains, orderly Alamogordo is home to the International Space Hall of Fame and is the closest town to White Sands, a 275-square-mile landscape that's fascinating as a natural attraction, but also inextricably linked with the world's first atomic bomb test, which took place in this desert in 1945.

Carlsbad Caverns, another natural wonder, fortunately has no such legacy. Getting there requires the longest drive of all, nearly to the Texas state line in the south. But when you see the so-called Big Room, the vast main cave that drips with stalactites and takes more than an hour to explore, you'll know there's nothing else like it in New Mexico, nor in the whole country.

HISTORY

Hundreds of millions of years ago, southeastern New Mexico's modern history was already set in stone: The dinosaurs that roamed the swampy banks of the sea were eventually transformed into the fossil fuel that many a contemporary Lovingtonian or Artesian makes a living extracting today.

In between, New Mexico's southern plains and mountain ranges saw much the same patterns as the rest of the state. The U.S. Army set upon the resident Indian tribes, and General James Carleton ordered Kit Carson, "All Indian men of that [Mescalero] tribe are to be killed whenever and wherever you can find them." Billy the Kid got up to no good and eventually died here, at the age of 21. And railroad lines and highways (especially the legendary Route 66) brought modern thrills to previously untouched patches of plain.

But a single cataclysmic event really marked the area. Just before sunrise one summer morning in 1945, White Sands was lit brighter than high noon by a towering mushroom cloud—the successful test of the first atomic bomb, which was then deployed over Japan to win World War II. During the Cold War, White Sands was the proving ground for some essential technology in the space race. In this respect, the region is an odd juxtaposition of humankind's most current obsessions against a timeless landscape.

PLANNING YOUR TIME

If you're focusing on Carlsbad, White Sands, and even Cloudcroft or Ruidoso, it can make sense to fly in to El Paso (ELP), then stay in Las Cruces (one hour's drive) your first night; the town of Carlsbad also receives commuter flights from Albuquerque.

Driving from Albuquerque, you could take the leisurely route via the Salinas Pueblo Missions and Carrizozo, reaching Ruidoso or Alamogordo by dinnertime, then carrying on to White Sands the next day—or you could cruise down the interstate and get straight to White Sands by the afternoon. In any case, allow about three hours for a basic visit to the park, or more if you plan to do any hiking or photography. Carlsbad Caverns calls for the better part of a day to see just the basics, though the more adventurous small-group tours are well worth allotting a second day. Both places get busy in the summer, and the caverns can feel crowded; the sands absorb crowds better. At any rate, if you can push your visit until mid-August, you may miss some crowds (as kids head back to school), and also see the landscape a bit greened by summer rains.

Previous: White Sands National Park; the Blue Hole; photo of outlaw Billy the Kid.

Carlsbad Caverns and the Southeast

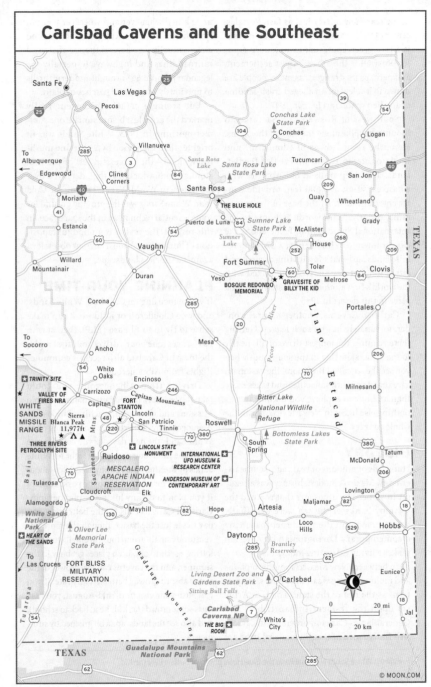

© MOON.COM

East on the Interstate and Route 66

After crossing the pass between the Sandia and Manzano Mountains east of Albuquerque, I-40 heads into the high plains. Get used to the scenery, because it won't change until well into Texas. The wind blows constantly across gold tufts of grass, and the barbed-wire fences are clotted with tumbleweeds. The most exciting thing along this stretch is counting down the billboards to truck stops like the Flyin' C, where you can stock up on everything from moccasins to fireworks. It's not quite the glamour of Route 66 of old, but the combination of tacky signage, big sky, and a whole lot of nothing says "American road trip" like nothing else.

EDGEWOOD

Off exit 187 in Edgewood, **Wildlife West Nature Park** (505/281-7655, www.wildlifewest.org, 10am-6pm daily mid-Mar.-Oct., noon-4pm daily Nov.-mid-Mar., $9) is a better-than-average roadside attraction. This "enhanced zoo" is a 122-acre wildlife sanctuary for wolves, cougars, elk, and other native animals. Throughout the spring and summer the park hosts festivals and special events, perhaps none more popular than periodic chuckwagon dinners ($27), complete with hay rides.

For solid road food at the same exit, **Katrinah's East Mountain Grill** (150 Hwy. 344, 505/281-9111, 7am-8pm Tues.-Sat., 8am-3pm Sun., $8) has a menu of standard diner goodies, from enchiladas to veggie wraps, all made from fresh ingredients. Look for it three miles north of I-40, just past Walmart.

SANTA ROSA

Santa Rosa, a town of 2,500, is easy to cruise past on I-40. But for a refreshing swim, take time out for the "City of Natural Lakes," where cool springs well up alongside the Pecos River. From 1901, the town was a stop on the Chicago, Rock Island & Pacific freight line, and in the 1930s, the place began to grow as Route 66 travelers passed through. John Steinbeck set a scene of *The Grapes of Wrath* here, which was then re-created for film in the town in 1940. Its stretch of the historic highway, which runs parallel to I-40 to the south, is lined with stately old warehouses and lurid neon.

Sights and Recreation
THE BLUE HOLE

Most people come to Santa Rosa for an unexpected natural attraction: **The Blue Hole** (575/472-3763, dawn-dusk daily), an 81-foot-deep pool of water that's a constant 64°F year-round. Only about 80 feet across, it doesn't look like much from the surface, but it's more impressive when you consider that water is gushing from the spring at the bottom at 3,000 gallons per minute (check the overflow channel on the south side to get an idea just what that number means). The steady temperature and perfect clarity of the water makes it a popular place for scuba divers—who create an incongruous image with the tumbleweeds blowing by. The place is popular with local kids, too, who can spend a whole summer day doing cannonballs off the high rocks on one side. (There are less adventurous ways of getting into the water, including cement stairs.)

Admission is free, but to dive you'll need a **permit** ($20 weekly), available from the visitors center or the dive shop, both adjacent to the Blue Hole. To reach the area, get off at exit 278 or 275 and follow signs to Blue Hole Road (also a section of Historic Route 66).

If you want more room to play, backtrack on Blue Hole Road to **Park Lake,** an adjacent natural spring that's the town's biggest recreation spot. Zip down the free waterslide, rent a pedal boat, or just jump into the cool, clear water. (Compared with these natural springs, **Santa Rosa Lake State Park,** the product of a dam on the Pecos River north of town, is quite dull.)

ROUTE 66 AUTO MUSEUM

For car buffs, the **Route 66 Auto Museum** (2866 Historic Rte. 66, 575/472-1966, 7:30am-5:30pm daily Apr.-Oct., $5), on the east side of town, is a showroom of Mother Road paraphernalia and a few dozen curvaceous machines from the heyday of American road-tripping; most are for sale.

Food

Santa Rosa boasts of its PDL chile, a special strain grown just to the south in the village of Puerto de Luna; it's usually eaten in its green form. Unfortunately, there's nowhere reliable to eat it. **Comet II** (1257 Historic Rte. 66, 575/472-3663, 11am-9pm Tues.-Sun., $8), bathed in neon, has potential for simple, diner-style New Mexican, but doesn't always deliver; and the landmark **Joseph's Bar & Grill** (865 Historic Rte. 66, 575/472-3361, 11am-9pm Sun.-Thurs., 11am-10pm Fri.-Sat., $7), is better for its kitschy decor (including its "Fat Man" logo, salvaged from a Depression-era restaurant) than its food, which is spotty. Still, if you're headed east on I-40, this is about your last chance for chile before blander Texan-style fare takes over.

Accommodations

Santa Rosa has the normal chain places, with a couple, such as **Comfort Inn** (2524 Historic Rte. 66, 575/472-5412, www.comfortinn.com, $109 d), in better condition than their counterparts in Tucumcari. If you want a vintage Route 66 motel, **La Mesa Inn** (2415 Historic Rte. 66, 575/472-3021, $45 s, $54 d) is your best bet; it's been in the same family since 1962, though the carpet, bathrooms, and flat-screen TVs are brand new. Still, if your taste runs to vintage, there are better places in Tucumcari.

Information

Next to the Blue Hole, the **Santa Rosa Visitors Center** (1085 Blue Hole Rd., 575/472-3763, www.santarosanm.org, 8am-5pm Mon.-Fri., 9am-noon Sat.) sells dive permits, in addition to stocking a hefty visitors guide and all the usual brochures.

PUERTO DE LUNA

Santa Rosa's historic roots are in this tidy collection of tin-roofed adobe buildings in a protected valley 10 miles south of I-40 on Highway 91. Aside from the **Nuestra Señora del Refugio**, a purpose-built church dating to the 19th century with a brick facade, there's nothing precisely to see here, but, as part of the larger **Mesalands Scenic Byway,** which zigzags across I-40 between Santa Rosa and Tucumcari, it's a pretty way to head south to Fort Sumner, through red-striped rocky hills and chile fields. (The next legs of the byway are U.S. 84 back north to I-40, then Highway 156 from Santa Rosa and Highway 209 north to Tucumcari.)

Founded in the early 1860s, Puerto de Luna was the county seat in the 1880s and later the childhood home of writer Rudolfo Anaya, who described the place in detail in his seminal novel *Bless Me, Ultima*. It's also alleged to be the place Billy the Kid—a supposed frequent visitor—enjoyed his last Christmas dinner, while Pat Garrett was taking him to jail in Lincoln.

SUMNER LAKE STATE PARK

A welcome bit of lushness amid the dry grasses, **Sumner Lake State Park** (Hwy. 203, 575/355-2541, www.emnrd.state.nm.us, $5/car) is an excellent birding spot, as it's on a major migration route (check the canyon below the dam in summer). The **camping** spots ($8-14), spread out in four areas amid cottonwoods and junipers, are very pretty. The state park is midway between Santa Rosa and Fort Sumner, six miles west of U.S. 84 via Highway 203.

FORT SUMNER

A small town bedecked in Old West style, **Fort Sumner** is 42 miles south of I-40 and Santa Rosa via U.S. 84. It's best known as the final resting place of Henry McCarty, aka Henry Antrim, aka William H. Bonney, aka Billy the Kid. It was here in 1881 that Lincoln County sheriff Pat Garrett finally tracked down the gunfighter and shot him (in ambush, in the dark, the Kid's fans will point out), to mete out justice for the 21 men Billy had allegedly killed in his short life—he was only 21, in fact, when he died in a farmhouse kitchen.

For more than a century, this legend of a Wild West antihero had all but obliterated the memory of what Fort Sumner had first been: a failed reservation-turned-concentration-camp for about 9,000 Navajo and 500 Mescalero Apache for five years during the Civil War. In 2005, a state monument finally gave more public recognition to this tragic period in the settling of the American West.

Sights

In town proper, seek out the **WPA murals** in the De Baca County Courthouse (514 Ave. C, 575/355-2601, 8am-4:30pm Mon.-Fri.), just northeast of the main intersection in town. Inside the redbrick building, head upstairs to see vivid images of the taming of the Western frontier. On the main street is the **Billy the Kid Museum** (1435 E. Sumner Ave., 575/355-2380, www.billythekidmuseumfortsumner.com, 8:30am-5pm daily mid-May-Sept., 8:30am-5pm Mon.-Sat. Oct.-mid-May, $5), a tourist outpost of the highest order: room upon room of gewgaws, a gift shop, and a replica of Billy's grave.

The real deal is down the road: Head 3 miles east of town on U.S. 84, then 3.5 miles south on Billy the Kid Road, and you reach the *real* **gravesite of Billy the Kid** (free), in a desolate little cemetery behind **Old Fort Sumner Museum** (closed for renovations). Fitting, due to his repeated jailbreaks in life, William Bonney is now penned in by a wrought-iron fence as well as cemented over, along with a couple of his "pals." (Really, the fencing is to deter grave robbers.) Also buried nearby is Lucien B. Maxwell, owner of the enormous Maxwell Land Grant in northern New Mexico, as well as this property, after the fort was decommissioned. It was in Maxwell's son's home, less than a mile away, that Billy the Kid was fatally shot. The museum offers yet another collection of Old West relics and plenty more detail about the young star of the Lincoln County War.

BOSQUE REDONDO MEMORIAL

Immediately south on the road from here, the **Bosque Redondo Memorial** (3647 Billy the Kid Rd., 575/355-2573, www.nmhistoricsites.org, 8:30am-4:30pm Wed.-Sun., $3) is a long-overdue museum and monument to the exceptional misery endured by most of the Navajo and a handful of Mescalero Apache, beginning in 1863. Force-marched in to this reservation at Fort Sumner from the northern corners of the state, the people endured what the Navajo came to call the Long Walk, a midwinter trek of hundreds of miles, during which the weakest were shot for holding up the group and many women and children were sold into slavery.

The two bands, which had little in common culturally and shared only a history of raiding each other, were penned in here and told to make a life together. But the allotted stretch of river basin was not enough land to support so many, so crops failed and disease tore through the overcrowded communities. The Mescalero Apache defied the U.S. military and left as a group two years into the terrible experiment. Nearly 3,000 Navajo—almost a third of the tribe—died in what they named H'weeldi (Place of Suffering) before they were allowed to return to their homelands.

The museum is a conceptual modern building—Navajo hogan meets Apache tepee—with a detailed exhibit on the camp, plus extra room for rotating displays on other low points in human rights history. Opt for the audio tour to explore the path out back, leading past the site where the Navajo leaders finally signed the treaty that released them (and established the Navajo Nation) in 1868, and into the greenery alongside the river, where the fort itself used to stand. It's a deceptively pretty setting.

Food

Choices to grab a bite to eat in town are few. The best option by a comfortable margin is the **Rodeo Grill** (451 W. Sumner Ave., 575/355-8000, 7:30am-2pm Sun.-Fri., $9), a few blocks east of the main intersection. Options range from sizable burgers and hand-cut fries to nice breakfast burritos, heated on the grill until the tortilla gets crispy, in a casual room hung with lariats and saddles.

Sadie's (257 Sumner Ave., 575/355-1461, 11am-2pm and 5pm-8pm Mon. and Thurs.-Fri., 8am-2pm and 5pm-8pm Sat.-Sun., $7) is good for New Mexican food—especially on Saturday, when the Rodeo Grill is closed. The Navajo tacos are enchiladas are among the tastier options on the menu.

Information

Visit the **De Baca Chamber of Commerce** (707 N. 4th St., 575/355-7705, www.fortsumnerchamber.net, 9am-4pm Mon.-Fri.) for all the basic tourist details.

TUCUMCARI

For the California-bound on Route 66, Tucumcari was the first real stop on New Mexico's stretch of the Mother Road. "Tucumcari Tonite!" urged the billboards leading up to the town strip—and they still do today. The neon glow is not as bright as it once was, but Americana buffs should get off the highway here, to see the Tepee Curios shop and other architectural oddities, and bunk down in one of the well-preserved old motor courts. Dinosaur freaks will find a great museum.

Tucumcari's existence predates Route 66: Main Street is oriented with the old railroad depot, north of the highway. When the tracks were being laid, this spot on the plains was dubbed Six-Shooter Siding, but the gunplay quieted down once regular trade got going, and the place took the name of nearby Tucumcari Mountain. The railroad provided steady employment until it closed operations here in 1999. But the residents of the sturdy, low bungalows that line the wide side streets have kept the town

from being blown away in the wind—they are stubborn and dedicated to keeping the place alive.

Sights

After you've cruised the neon signs on Historic Route 66 (aka Tucumcari Boulevard), stop in the **New Mexico Route 66 Museum** (1500 W. Rte. 66 Blvd., 575/461-3064, www.nmrt66museum.org, 9am-5pm Mon., Fri.-Sat., 9am-1pm Tues.-Thurs., $3), in a back room of the Tucumcari Convention Center. The museum displays vintage photos, a juke box, gas pumps, and a few honeys, including a couple Studebakers and a classic Model A. If your cruise isn't complete, check out the *other* main drag: Turn north on 1st Street and drive about eight blocks up to **Main Street** and the train depot; along the way, elaborate photo-realistic **murals,** most by a husband-and-wife team, adorn many buildings.

The surprisingly spiffy **Mesalands Dinosaur Museum** (222 E. Laughlin St., 575/461-3466, www.mesalands.edu, 10am-6pm Tues.-Sat. Mar.-Aug., noon-5pm Tues.-Sat. Sept.-Feb., $8) is in this area, too, just east of 1st Street and two blocks north of Tucumcari Boulevard. The exhibit hall contains a huge number of beautiful bronze casts of dinosaur skeletons (neat, because you're allowed to touch them), as well as some dinosaur eggs and lots of other fossils. It also owns a rare, nearly complete 40-foot-long skeleton of the giant carnivore *Torvosaurus,* and has an interactive, augmented reality sandbox where kids can manipulate the topography.

Two blocks farther north (look for the windmill), the **Tucumcari Historical Museum** (416 S. Adams St., 575/461-4201, 9am-3pm Tues.-Sat. Sept.-May, 9am-6pm Tues.-Sat. June-Aug., $5) takes up an entire two-story redbrick house with old saddles, slot machines, and Indian relics, then spills over

---

1: Tucumcari's vintage roadside architecture 2: the Odeon Theater in Tucumcari 3: the Blue Swallow Motel in Tucumcari

into a yard full of vintage boxcars, Route 66 paraphernalia, and more.

Sports and Recreation

In the summer, locals decamp to one of New Mexico's bigger reservoirs, Conchas Lake State Park (575/868-2270, www.emnrd.state. nm.us, $5/car), northwest of town 34 miles on Highway 104. It stretches for about 25 miles, its coastline weaving along many inlets, sandy beaches, and canyons. The setting is rather austere, however, and there's very little shade—it's nicer to visit in the cooler spring or fall, when crowds are lighter as well.

In town, the public pool (415 W. Hines St., 575/461-4582) is open summers only, and closes as soon as school is in session, by the third week in August.

Entertainment

Built in 1936, the elegant deco-style Odeon Theater (123 S. 2nd St., 575/461-0100, $7) is a small-town treasure, with a modest but cool pink neon sign, offset with yellow zia symbols. Shows are Tuesday and Thursday-Sunday at 7pm, and also at 3pm on Sunday. The concession stand includes hot dogs, in case you want to make a dinner of it (only the Pow Wow Restaurant is open after the movie lets out).

Food

Look for the big fiberglass steer above the sign at Del's (1202 E. Route 66 Blvd., 575/461-1740, 11am-9pm Mon.-Sat., $10), where you'll find full diner menu, which features a mighty fine chicken-fried steak (lovely crunchy batter, with rich mashed potatoes on the side), as well as a nicely appointed soup-and-salad bar. It's been serving locals since 1956, and feels like a chummy living room because of it.

Because it's open late and has a full bar, Pow Wow Restaurant & Lizard Lounge (801 W. Route 66 Blvd., 575/461-2587, 7am-9pm Mon.-Thurs., 7am-10pm Fri.-Sun., $9) is a major town hangout—there are portraits of locals, such as the magistrate judge, on the walls to prove it. The restaurant serves sandwiches and plenty of New Mexican dishes.

For lunch, the friendly Cornerstone Deli (711 E. Route 66 Blvd., 575/461-3326, 10am-9pm Mon.-Thurs., 10am-10pm Fri.-Sat., $6) serves filling sandwiches with ingredients from the local small-scale Tucumcari Mountain Cheese Factory (check out the factory store at 823 E. Main St.), as well as homemade potato chips and super-creamy frozen custard.

For breakfast, it's hard to beat Kix on 66 (1102 E. Route 66 Blvd., 575/461-1966, 6am-2pm daily, $6), where you can smell the bacon from the parking lot. For less than you might expect, the old-style diner slings hash browns, biscuits, and other morning standards to regulars in teal vinyl booths or at the long Formica counter. It has the same owners as Del's—you'll recognize the white gravy.

Accommodations

Tucumcari has a handful of excellent-value retro motels—worth a stop just to enjoy a taste of the past. A relic of the Route 66 days, the pink-and-turquoise ★ Blue Swallow Motel (815 E. Route 66 Blvd., 575/461-9849, www. blueswallowmotel.com, $75 s, $85 d), on the east side of town, dates from 1939, making it perhaps the oldest standing motel on Route 66. The 12 rooms are cozy, with honeycomb-tiled bathrooms and chenille bedspreads; rotary phones heavy enough to be weapons round out the historic feel. Several rooms have adjacent garages, and the Lillian Redman Suite ($130), named after the longtime owner of the motel, has a claw-foot tub for soaking. If you stop just for a photo op, it's polite to ask for permission.

If you prefer your retro style in the form of midcentury groovy, head to the jaunty cinderblock court of the Motel Safari (722 E. Route 66 Blvd., 575/461-1048, www.themotelsafari. com, $70 d), with firm beds and flat-panel TVs, plus mod, spindly legged furniture that conjures 1959. One suite nods to Wanda Jackson, the queen of rockabilly ($99).

Just a tiny bit later in the timeline of motel architecture, the excellent-value Historic Route 66 Motel (1620 E. Route 66 Blvd.,

575/461-1212, www.rte66motel.com, $45 d) conjures Palm Springs in Tucumcari, and its owners have maintained the minimalist style. It might not have a fabulous neon sign, but all rooms have floor-to-ceiling windows, and most have very cool turquoise vinyl ranch chairs original to the 1963 motel.

Information

The **Tucumcari-Quay County Chamber of Commerce** (404 W. Route 66 Blvd., 575/461-1694, www.tucumcarinm.com, 8:30am-5pm Mon.-Fri.) has the usual assortment of information.

Getting There

By car, Tucumcari is 59 miles (less than one hour) east along I-40 from Santa Rosa, 176 miles (three hours) east from Albuquerque, and 113 miles (two hours) west from Amarillo, Texas. By bus, **Greyhound** (800/231-2222, www.greyhound.com) stops in Tucumcari three times a day, at the McDonald's (2608 S. 1st St., 575/461-1350, 5am-8pm daily).

The Llano

Texans refer to these barren plains as the Llano, and much of this area could be mistaken for the neighboring state, from the fields of cattle (for both beef and dairy) to the oil derricks that dot the horizon. "West West Texas" rarely sees tourists, but some of this land is exceptionally pretty: South on Highway 209 from Tucumcari, for instance, takes you closer to the mesas and leaves the visual clutter of billboards and semitrucks behind. Scored by deep channels, the red earth is studded with cholla cactus and yucca, as well as black, brushy mesquite. The occasional farmhouse—often built only feet away from a ruined homestead from 50 years ago—shows the optimism required to live in this windy, harshly beautiful landscape. (If you jog west toward Fort Sumner, you'll see the state actually profiting from the rough climate here, through a field of wind turbines that feed the electricity grid.)

CLOVIS

Busy as it is with rail freight, cattle auctions, and the adjacent Cannon Air Force Base, Clovis doesn't really court tourists. It had its big moment in the national spotlight in 1957, when Buddy Holly recorded "That'll Be the Day" in a music studio here. And even though its population is nearly 40,000 and growing, it feels like a fairly small town,

especially along its wide, brick-paved Main Street, which dead-ends at the rail yard. The downtown area sports some stylish **art deco buildings,** including the glamorous Hotel Clovis, once the tallest building between Dallas and Albuquerque, recently converted to lofts, but now overshadowed by grain silos.

Sights

No one talks about it much today, but in the late 1950s, the "Clovis Sound" was an unmistakable, and deeply influential, musical phenomenon. It was the product of a single recording studio here on the edge of the Texas plains, and it's commemorated in the small but thorough **Norman & Vi Petty Rock & Roll Museum** (105 E. Grand Ave., 575/763-3435, 8am-noon and 1pm-5pm Mon.-Fri., by appointment Sat., $5). The displays of ephemera tell the story of how local boy Norm Petty and his wife, Vi, scored a hit with their smooth version of "Mood Indigo," then returned here to build a recording studio. Norm was an acoustic obsessive, and his attention to detail came through when he helped an aspiring country star named Buddy Holly, from Lubbock, Texas, revamp his tunes into pop hits. After Holly shot to stardom, other hopeful artists beat a path to Clovis to work with the Pettys.

Clovis

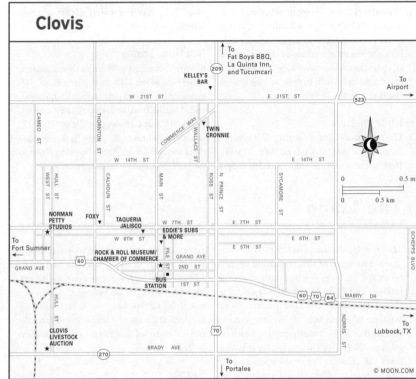

The Beatles, who saw Holly in concert in 1958, were indelibly marked by the big, clean Clovis Sound, and the young Rolling Stones covered "Rave On." Norman Petty helped launched the careers of Roy Orbison and Waylon Jennings, and kept producing through the 1960s (as rockabilly bands morphed into psychedelia) and the 1970s, and died in 1984.

The museum also contains a re-creation of the studios that made the Clovis Sound. But if your schedule allows, call ahead to arrange a tour of the actual **Norman Petty Recording Studios** (1313 W. 7th St., 575/356-6422, donation). You get to hold the mic Buddy Holly used and see where he and The Crickets lived, in a small apartment at the back of the studio. If you're lucky, an old-timer who sang backup tracks at the studio will be there to serenade you.

Otherwise, Clovis's attractions are just the regular business activities: You can watch the cattle changing hands every Wednesday morning and, less frequently, horses being sold at the **Clovis Livestock Auction** (504 S. Hull St., 575/762-4422), south of the tracks at the corner of Brady. Or follow the freight trains' comings and goings from the bridge over Hull Street.

Entertainment and Events

Local country acts play at **Kelley's Bar** (2208 N. Prince St., 575/762-0044, 11am-10pm Mon.-Tues., 11am-11pm Wed., 11am-1am Thurs., 11am-2am Fri.-Sat.), the only real bar in town. The annual Petty-inspired jam has morphed into the **Clovis Draggin' Main Music Festival** (575/763-3435, www.dragginmain.org), a week-long celebration of throwback rockabilly, roots, and rock acts and

The *Llano Estacado*

The early explorers on Francisco Vásquez de Coronado's first excursion through the West, in 1541, referred to the stretch east from the Sacramento Mountains as the *llano estacado*, describing the place as an endless sea of green, with grass as high as their horses' bellies. It's an evocative image, but it doesn't explain exactly what the conquistadors may have meant by the word *estacado*.

The common translation is "stockaded" or "staked" plains, which hardly clarifies the issue. Some academics have reasoned that the great green expanse was as disorienting as being at sea, so the Spanish horsemen pounded stakes in the ground to mark their way. Meanwhile, those in the "stockaded" camp reason that the Spanish thought the mesas that punctuated the flatlands—particularly the 300-foot-high Caprock Escarpment near Tucumcari—stood up, straight-walled, like defensive stockades. A third, far less common interpretation proposes that in 16th-century Spanish, *estacado* also had the meaning of "covered in spikes." That is, these were the "stickered plains," due to the spiny yucca plants and thorn-covered mesquite bushes that flourish here. Whatever the case, although the "sea of green" that Coronado traversed is not so green today, the mesas remain as stark and straight.

all things cars. The Norman Petty studio is also open during that weekend.

Food

For Mexican, head to **Taqueria Jalisco** (217 W. 7th St., 575/763-1865, 7am-9:30pm Sun.-Thurs., 7am-10pm Fri.-Sat., $8), where you can get a huge slab of steak and homemade flour tortillas, as well as deep-fried gorditas, stuffed *tortas*, and creamy, cinnamon-spiked *horchata* to drink—far more food than you can eat, served with style (the trompe l'oeil mural takes you right to Mexico's Pacific coast), at astonishingly low prices.

Downtown, a popular spot for the noon meal is **Eddie's Subs & More** (517 N. Main St., 575/762-6911, 10:30am-4pm Mon.-Fri., $7), good for hamburgers and green-chile stew—in addition to a number of the aforementioned heroes, served on fresh-baked bread.

Then there's the category of 1950s-style drive-in restaurants, the likes of which are seldom seen these days—especially not of this caliber. ★ **Foxy** (720 W. 7th St., 575/763-7995, 7am-10pm Mon.-Sat., 8am-10pm Sun., $5) excels at crispy taquitos and steak fingers; there are also plenty of burgers, hot dogs, and ham sandwiches to choose from. Buddy Holly and The Crickets would eat lunch here when recording just down the

street at Norman Petty Recording Studios. **Twin Cronnie** (709 Commerce Way, 575/763-5463, 7am-9pm Mon.-Wed., 7am-10pm Thurs.-Fri., 7:30am-10pm Sat., $5) is the home of a tasty combination involving two hot dogs, chili, and a round bun, among a million other menu items.

If you're staying on the north side of town, **Fat Boys BBQ** (901 E. Llano Estacado Blvd., 575/763-9543, 11am-8pm Mon., 11am-9pm Tues.-Sat., 11am-3pm Sun., $12) is a handy dinner spot, with a broader menu than just smoked meat (you can even get a salad!). But it's not quite so stupendous that it's worth a drive north for its own sake.

Accommodations

Most of the cheaper motels in Clovis are on Mabry Drive, parallel to the very busy railroad tracks through town—which can make for a bad night's sleep if you're sensitive to noise. If you're willing to pay more, go for the town's branch of **La Quinta** (4521 N. Prince St., 575/763-8777, www.lq.com, $124 d), one of a few chain options on the north side of town, with a nice indoor pool and well-kept, suite-layout rooms.

Information

The Clovis **chamber of commerce** (105 E. Grand Ave., 575/763-3435, www.clovisnm.

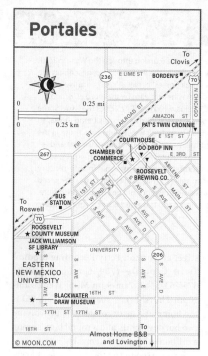

Portales

E LIME ST — BORDEN'S

To Clovis

236

70

N CHICAGO

RAILROAD ST

AMAZON ST

PAT'S TWIN CRONNIE

COURTHOUSE

E 1ST ST

DO DROP INN

E 3RD ST

ABILENE

CHAMBER OF COMMERCE

ROOSEVELT BREWING CO.

267

FIR ST

W 1ST ST

W 2ND ST

BUS STATION

AVE B

AVE C

AVE A

MAIN ST

70

To Roswell

ROOSEVELT COUNTY MUSEUM

JACK WILLIAMSON SF LIBRARY

AVE F

AVE E

AVE D

AVE C

AVE E

AVE D

EASTERN NEW MEXICO UNIVERSITY

UNIVERSITY ST

206

AVE K

BLACKWATER DRAW MUSEUM

16TH ST

17TH ST — 17TH ST

18TH ST

To Almost Home B&B and Lovington

© MOON.COM

0 — 0.25 mi

0 — 0.25 km

org, 8am-5pm Mon.-Fri.) has its offices downtown, in the same building as the Petty Museum.

Getting There

By car, Clovis is 85 miles (1.5 hours) south from Tucumcari zigzagging on Highway 209, 110 miles (2 hours) northeast from Roswell on U.S. 70, 3.5 hours from Albuquerque, and 2 hours from Lubbock, Texas. Fort Sumner is 60 miles (1 hour) west on U.S. 84.

Clovis Municipal Airport (CVN), six miles east of town, receives three flights daily from Dallas on **Boutique Air** (855/268-8478, www.boutiqueair.com). **Greyhound** (800/231-2222, www.greyhound.com) stops at Cortez Gas (2207 S. Prince St., 575/762-4584, 9am-5pm Mon.-Sat.); buses come from Las Cruces once a day.

PORTALES

Anchored by **Eastern New Mexico University,** Portales is also home to some prairie chickens and a whole lot of peanut farmers. The farmland surrounding Portales may produce a mere 24 million pounds of legumes a year—less than 1 percent of the nation's peanut crop—but that accounts for 90 percent of the exceptionally tasty red-skinned Valencia variety. Its downtown, fanning out from a deco-goes-West courthouse (look for the cowboy friezes above the windows), is slowly being revitalized, and the most attractive area of town is the campus of brick buildings and green lawns in the southwest corner of town. On the 21-mile drive down from Clovis, you might see the biggest tumbleweeds of your trip—just slow down and let 'em roll on by.

Sights

Three collections on the ENMU campus merit a quick look, depending on your interests. Another is impossible to miss from the road.

BLACKWATER DRAW MUSEUM

The **Blackwater Draw Museum** (Lea Hall, 1500 S. Ave. K, 575/562-2202, 9am-5pm Mon.-Sat., noon-5pm Sun. June-Aug., closed Mon. Sept.-May, $3) tells the story of a major discovery in ancient history that happened nearby. In the 1940s and 1950s, archaeologists discovered fluted spearheads embedded in a mammoth carcass, effectively proving the existence of humans in North America at the end of the last ice age, in roughly 11,300 BCE. Clovis Man, as this "type site" was dubbed (now known as the Blackwater Draw National Historic Landmark), is still the oldest known culture in the New World—or at least the oldest one that researchers can agree on. The museum displays the site findings, which also include later layers of occupation: Remnants of the later Folsom Man culture were stacked atop the Clovis points, with early agricultural efforts on top of that. Your museum admission also gives you access to the site, about eight miles north of town. Ask for directions at the museum.

ROOSEVELT COUNTY MUSEUM

Featuring an interesting assortment, **Roosevelt County Museum** (575/562-2592, 8am-noon and 1pm-5pm Mon.-Fri., free) is a very manageable size, with some great paintings (see the cowboy's ode to the mountain lion in the main hall) and cool dioramas, along with items from Japan and Peru, donated by well-traveled locals. The museum is at West 2nd Street and University Place. Weekend hours in summer may vary—call ahead.

JACK WILLIAMSON SCIENCE FICTION COLLECTION

Upstairs at Golden Library is the voluminous **Jack Williamson Science Fiction Library** (8am-5pm Mon.-Fri.), more than a dozen long shelves of sci-fi and fantasy work collected by Williamson, both a fan and author (his lifetime achievement Nebula Award is on display) who happened to live in Portales, and donors from elsewhere in the state. Fittingly, the library's style is a bit midcentury space-age—it's a rare place where you can settle into a low-slung lounge chair and flip through a 1963 *Science Fiction* back issue.

PEANUTS

If you're tempted by the thought of fresh Valencia peanuts, stop in at **Borden's** (620 E. Lime St., 575/356-8545, 9am-5pm Mon.-Fri.), which has a lot of other locally made snacks as well.

Festivals and Events

Near the end of October, ENMU and the chamber of commerce sponsor the long-running **Peanut Valley Festival** (575/356-8541). It's not *completely* peanut-obsessed, what with distractions like local musicians, a big craft fair, funnel-cake booths, and the like, but it is a lively time to be in town.

Food and Accommodations

Sample Portales's produce in a deliciously creamy peanut-butter shake at ★ **Pat's Twin Cronnie** (100 N. Chicago Ave., 575/356-5841,

10am-9pm Mon.-Fri., 10am-10pm Fri.-Sat., noon-8pm Sun., $5), where you can also fill up on taquitos, burgers, chili dogs, and all manner of fried sides.

On the plaza, the **Do Drop Inn** (123 S. Main St., 575/226-5282, 7am-4pm Mon.-Fri., 10am-6pm Sat., $4) is a chummy little café that serves supremely gooey homemade baked goods and assorted sandwiches; their breakfast club on a bagel makes for a great start to the day.

Just across the street, ★ **Roosevelt Brewing Co.** (201 S. Main Ave., 575/226-2739, 11:30am-9pm Tues.-Sun., $10) serves a more substantial meal, using local farm products in the timeless combo of wood-oven pizza, house-brewed beer, and killer craft-brew-inspired cupcakes.

Along with a couple of chain hotels, there's **Almost Home Bed and Breakfast** (8168 Hwy. 206, 575/356-0011, www.almosthomebedandbreakfast.com, $89 d), a ranch-style home on the outskirts of town. The rooms are simple but clean, with private entrances. Be prepared to chat with the owners over breakfast.

Information

The **Roosevelt County Chamber of Commerce** (100 S. Avenue A, 800/635-8036, www.portales.com, 8am-5pm Mon.-Fri.) can help you out with maps and brochures.

Getting There

By car, Portales is 21 miles (20 minutes) southwest of Clovis on U.S. 70; it's about 90 miles (1.5 hours) northeast of Roswell, and 228 miles (3.5 hours) southeast from Albuquerque. **Greyhound** (800/231-2222, www.greyhound.com) drops passengers at McDonald's (1020 W. 1st St.); buses come from Las Cruces once a day.

LOVINGTON

The seat of Lea County, Lovington has a handsome art deco courthouse and tidy streets. The town-operated **Lea County Museum** (103 S. Love St., 575/396-4805, www.

leacountymuseum.org, 9am-5pm Tues.-Sat., free), across from the courthouse, contains all the usual pioneer-era items. In addition, one room is dedicated to Western writer Max Evans, who lived until the age of 12 in nearby Humble City, now all but vanished (Evans rechristened the place Starvation, Texas, in one of his novels).

If you're hungry in Lovington, hit the **Lazy 6** (102 S. 1st St., 575/396-5066, 10am-2pm Mon.-Thurs., 10am-8pm Fri., $6), where the knickknack-to-customer ratio is 10 to 1, even when the place is packed for lunch. Don't let it distract you from the satisfying home cooking, though. It's one block west of Main Street.

HOBBS

Yet another oil town with the smell of, shall we say, "money" in the air, Hobbs is just five miles from the Texas border and the largest settlement in Lea County, with more than 37,000 residents. It's a destination only for people working in the industry (of which there are many), students at New Mexico Preparatory College and the College of the Southwest, and fans of gliding—the flat land and empty skies are ideal for delicate sailplanes.

Wild West fanatics will want to pay their respects at the **Western Heritage Museum and Lea County Cowboy Hall of Fame** (5317 Lovington Hwy., 575/492-2678, www. nmjc.edu/museum, 10am-5pm Tues.-Sat., 1pm-5pm Sun., $5), a sleek bit of architecture that renders an oil derrick in green glass. The complex on the north edge of town honors rodeo champions (Lea County has a disproportionately high number) and all-around good local citizens. It also gives an interesting overview of the region's history, from dinosaur stomping ground to homesteaded territory to modern source of black gold, first tapped in 1927.

1: Roosevelt County courthouse in Portales
2: metal art in Lovington 3: oil derricks at work in Artesia

ARTESIA

To quote the travel cliché, Artesia is a town of contrasts. One of the most discordant views of New Mexico can be had at the junction of U.S. 285 and U.S. 82 in Artesia. Look west and you'll see an attractive, modernized Main Street that boasts a concert hall, a revamped movie palace, shops, and sturdy old buildings. Look east and you'll see the state's largest oil refinery, all concrete towers, blinking lights, and plumes of steam and smoke. More practically, Artesia is less than an hour's drive from Carlsbad, and it has two decent hotels—so you could conceivably sleep here, for slightly better value, before or after visiting the caverns. But don't stay here if you're up to no good—Artesia is all about law-abiding behavior, thanks to the presence of the Federal Law- Enforcement Training Center.

Sights

If you keep your back to the refinery, you can spend a pleasant hour or two (or more, if you go to a movie) checking out the **Artesia Historical Museum & Art Center** (505 W. Richardson Ave., 575/748-2390, www. artesianm.gov, 9am-5pm Tues.-Fri., 1pm-5pm Sat., free), in a pretty area two blocks south of Main Street. It houses a large collection of historical photos of the area and hosts art exhibits.

Larger-than-life bronze statues dot the main drag, including a very cool series of life-size figures in the midst of a cattle-rustling operation, arranged across three intersections. Stroll by the **Artesia Public Library** (205 W. Quay St., 575/746-4252, 9:30am-6pm Mon.-Sat.) to see a 46-foot-long fresco by New Mexico painter Peter Hurd, installed here in late 2015 after being saved from demolition in its original home in Houston. The lush farm scene is the focal point of the new building; it's visible from the street through floor-to-ceiling windows.

If your schedule allows, attend a show at the **Ocotillo Performing Arts Center** (310 W. Main St., 575/746-4212, www.

artesiaartscouncil.com), a stately theater that draws touring musicians.

Food

For caffeine, a cinnamon roll, or a hearty sandwich, head to **Kith+Kin Roasting Co.** (105 N. 5th St., 575/746-9494, 7am-8pm Mon.-Thurs., 7am-9pm Fri., $8), the new name for Artesia's longest-running coffee shop (formerly the Jahva House). There's a long list of house coffee drinks—and several matcha drinks as well.

For dinner, pickings are limited. The clear standout is the perennially packed ★ **Adobe Rose** (1614 N. 13th St., 575/748-3082, 4pm-10pm Mon.-Tues., 11am-10pm Wed.-Thurs., 11am-midnight Fri., 3pm-midnight Sat.), which has a menu that changes seasonally and features exceptional meals made with local ingredients; there are also flavorful takes on familiar standbys such as chicken-fried steak. **Piccolino** (201 N. 1st St., 575/748-1100, 10:30am-9pm Mon.-Sat., $11) does passable red-sauce Italian (stick to the pastas). Portions are generous, though service can be glacial. Or head to **The Wellhead** brewpub (332 W. Main St., 575/746-0640, 11am-9pm Mon.-Sat., $11) for livelier atmosphere; the menu is pretty standard bar food, though.

Accommodations

Heritage Inn (209 W. Main St., 575/748-2552, www.artesiaheritageinn.com, $139 d) is a historic hotel with modern bathrooms, comfy beds, Wi-Fi and a continental breakfast. The glitzier **Hotel Artesia** (203 N. 2nd St., 888/746-2066, www.hotelartesia.com, $137 d) looks like it has been beamed in from Miami. The 52 spacious rooms are done in a somewhat generic sleek modern style, with every convenience for business travelers. The lobby lounge is popular after work.

The **Adobe Rose Inn** (1614 N. 13th St., 575/748-3082, from $109 d), attached to the eponymous restaurant, has five comfortable and spacious rooms, each with welcoming touches and microwaves and refrigerators. There's also a pool and laundry facilities.

Information

Stop in at the **Artesia Chamber of Commerce** (107 N. 1st St., 575/746-2744, www.artesiachamber.com, 9am-5pm Mon.-Fri.), in the old train depot, for additional info.

Kith+Kin Roasting Co. is the spot for a caffeine fix in Artesia.

Roswell

Launched into national notoriety in 1947 by an alleged UFO crash (and subsequent government cover-up) on a ranch northwest of town, Roswell has been marked indelibly by odd events. Popular fascination was renewed with "truth-seeking" exposés in the 1980s, and the town has become a pilgrimage site for true believers and kitsch seekers alike. The city seal sports an alien, the green streetlamps have eyes, and the McDonald's resembles a spaceship about to lift off. In short, Roswell embraces its unconventional and extraterrestrial past for outsiders.

But there's a lot more to this city of 48,000, the largest metro area in this region. Founded in 1870, it has its roots in ranching, then agriculture, after an artesian well was discovered in 1890; Chaves County is the largest dairy producer in the state. The 1910 courthouse has a tall, green-tiled dome, built by Isaac Hamilton Rapp, who was also instrumental in designing Santa Fe's zoning codes to create a homogenous downtown.

Over the long term, Roswell has probably been more influenced by the Rapp-designed New Mexico Military Institute, established in 1891. There's a conservative streak, to the point it's hard to find a bar at night. As if to balance the scales, Roswell has hosted a small clan of contemporary artists every year since the mid-1960s, which has fostered strong arts appreciation and two excellent museums. These disparate elements can keep a visitor entertained for a day or two.

SIGHTS

The central intersection is at North Main Street (U.S. 285) and West 2nd Street (U.S. 70/380), also the location of the UFO museum. Like debris around a crash site, space-themed gift shops and other attractions dot the surrounding blocks.

★ International UFO Museum & Research Center

Most visitors to Roswell make a beeline to the **International UFO Museum & Research Center** (114 N. Main St., 800/822-3545, www.roswellufomuseum.com, 9am-5pm daily, $5), a converted movie theater where the events of July 1947 are dissected with obsessive care. The mass of data—newspaper clippings, affidavits, faded photos—is a little overwhelming and presented with a minimum of gloss; an audio tour only heaps on more detail. Related issues such as ancient alien cults, Area 51, abductions, and crop circles get the same thorough documentary treatment.

The mood lightens a bit with a section about Roswell in the movies and an "alien autopsy." And be sure to press the button for special effects on the central installation of four gawky aliens below a silver disc. Space is also given over to promoting the CW series *Roswell, New Mexico,* which began airing in 2019.

Roswell Museum and Art Center

The wide-ranging **Roswell Museum and Art Center** (100 W. 11th St., 575/624-6744, www.roswellmuseum.org, 9am-5pm Tues.-Sat., 1pm-5pm Sun., free) is a real treasure. The original gallery space, built in 1937 as a WPA project, is an attraction in itself, with high viga ceilings and tin chandeliers; it contains work by local luminaries like Peter Hurd and Henriette Wyeth, as well as a beautiful collection of Western paraphernalia, such as finely wrought spurs.

The place celebrates science, too, with an exhibit on space-flight visionary Robert Goddard, who moved from Massachusetts to Roswell in the 1930s to continue his work on liquid-fueled rockets in a less populated

Roswell

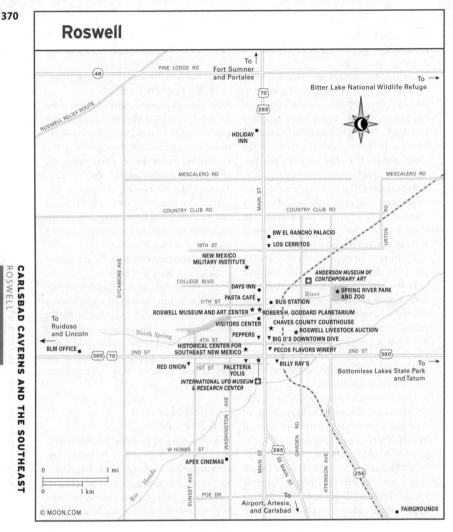

area—his workshop has been re-created, piece by piece, in one room. Adjacent to the main museum, the **Robert H. Goddard Planetarium** (912 N. Main St.), the second-largest in the state, has several public shows a month; call the museum for the schedule.

★ Anderson Museum of Contemporary Art

As good as the Roswell Museum is, it's no match for the 22,000-square-foot **Anderson Museum of Contemporary Art** (409 E. College Blvd., 575/623-5600, www. roswellamoca.org, 9am-4pm Mon.-Fri., 1pm-5pm Sat.-Sun., free), an invigorating collection borne out of the Roswell Artist-in-Residence Program from the past four decades, in media ranging from oil paintings to wood inlay. The works on view are representative samples from the program, established in 1967 by oilman Donald Anderson, whose work is also displayed. Since then it has hosted luminaries like abstract expressionist Milton Resnick and sculptor Luís Jiménez (best known for his *Blue Mustang* outside the Denver airport), along with scores of others still working and developing their reputations.

In the museum, more than 400 products of the "gift of time" (as the foundation calls the residency) fill the walls alongside photos of the artists. They're posed in the compound they're granted on the fringes of town—a sort of yearbook photo, which also pegs the art to a certain period. It's an unorthodox approach to contemporary art, and it lends an exuberance to the place that's hard to resist, even if you generally prefer older, less experimental artwork.

General Douglas L. McBride Military Museum

A visit to the array of military paraphernalia at the **General Douglas L. McBride Military Museum** (800/421-5376, www. nmmi.edu/museum, 8am-4pm Mon.-Fri., free) is an excuse to get inside the giant fortress that is the New Mexico Military Institute, on North Main Street at College Boulevard. The institution has about 1,000 high school students from all over the country, and alumni include newscaster Sam Donaldson, hotelier Conrad Hilton, historian Paul Horgan, painter Peter Hurd, actor Owen Wilson, and even Miss New Mexico 2001. The museum entrance is in the back of the main building; head west on College, then turn right on Kentucky, then through the gates at Duty Street.

Historical Center for Southeast New Mexico

The trials of pioneer living are detailed at the **Historical Center for Southeast New Mexico** (200 N. Lea Ave., 575/622-8333, www. roswellnmhistory.org, 10am-4pm daily, free), a 1910 Prairie-style brick bungalow filled with period furniture and mannequins. You can pick up a brochure for a walking tour around Roswell's other historic houses, in a variety of styles.

SPORTS AND RECREATION

A big park in town caters to kids, while a state park to the east offers a few opportunities for swimming and mountain biking. Overall, though, the flat terrain around Roswell doesn't lend itself to exciting outdoor activities. The **BLM Roswell field office** (2909 W. 2nd St., 575/627-0272, 8am-4:30pm Mon.-Fri.), on the far west edge of town, is the contact point for questions about nearby public lands.

Spring River Park and Zoo

Like many small-town zoos, the animal component of **Spring River Park and Zoo** (1306 E. College Blvd., 575/624-6760, 9am-6pm Wed.-Mon. in summer, 9am-5pm Wed.-Mon. in winter, free) might be a little distressing—although the massive prairie dog village (allegedly the largest in the state) is always a crowd-pleaser, and there's a fishing hole just for kids. And, the 1926 carousel costs just a quarter, as does the miniature train that loops around the grounds. The park is the head of the **Spring River Trail,** a five-mile paved route to the town golf course.

Bottomless Lakes State Park

The pools at **Bottomless Lakes State Park** (575/624-6058, www.emnrd.state.nm.us, $5/car), just east of Roswell, are a rare phenomenon in New Mexico. Like the Blue Hole in Santa Rosa, they began as water-filled caverns, then the ceilings collapsed. Lea Lake, the deepest and largest of the pools here, plunges 90 feet. It's also the only lake open for swimming and diving, but it's a pretty small patch of water for the crowds that descend on it in the summertime.

There's tent **camping** at Cottonwood Lake, adjacent to the park office. (If you're interested in archaeology, ask here for directions to **Garnsey Arroyo,** a barely excavated bison "kill site" from about 500 years ago.) You'll find RV sites and additional, more secluded, campsites with hookups farther down the access road at Lea Lake.

New Mexico's Alien Obsession

New Mexico's extreme weather may account for some UFO sightings.

In 1947, strange objects were spotted in American skies. First an incident was reported in Washington State, then another in Idaho. When the next one happened, less than a month later, in Roswell, it was all over the press, with stories of a "flying disc," complete with alien crew, crashing on a ranch outside of town. No sooner did journalists descend than stories were revised, the military got involved, and a haze of confusion swirled up around the event.

The military's denial of the event did not squash the story, and soon enough, the United States seemed to be in the grip of a UFO frenzy, as scores of sightings were reported. A 1950 book titled *Behind the Flying Saucers,* by a reporter for *Variety,* Frank Scully, described yet another strange encounter in New Mexico: In March 1948, just nine months after the Roswell incident, the residents of Aztec, near Farmington, apparently had a similar occurrence in their own backyard—although no one actually saw the disc in the sky or at the crash site, as all but a scrap had been whisked away by the military. In fact, Scully was the first to investigate the crash, when he was in the area looking into the "Farmington Armada" spotted earlier in the year.

Two years later, it came out that the spaceship wreckage Scully had seen was actually the work of Silas Newton and Leo Gebauer, who had been seeking investors in their device for finding oil. The crash had been their backstory for the alien technology that allegedly drove their gadget, and they hoped to secure investors in their scheme. The two con men were convicted of fraud in 1953.

That didn't stop UFO enthusiasts from reviving the Aztec story in the 1980s, along with the Roswell incident, which became the subject of fresh fascination. Now both towns have a respectable alien-inspired tourism industry. The general perception in New Mexico toward these and other events (such as the creepy cattle mutilations in the 1970s, and not-uncommon tales of alien abductions) is not one of feverish conviction, nor of outright dismissal. It's more an attitude of resigned acceptance—as if the UFOs are just one more weird happening in a very weird state.

Skidmarks Trail, good for biking or hiking, runs for a little more than three miles over some of the limestone bluffs on the north edge of the park area. Wildflowers bloom here in the spring, and you'll see lots of waterbirds. Look for the trailhead just as you turn onto the loop road around the park (if you get to Lazy Lagoon, you've gone too far).

To reach the park, head east of Roswell 12 miles on U.S. 380, then turn south on Bottomless Lakes Road, which loops around the lakes after about 3 miles.

Bitter Lake National Wildlife Refuge

Established in 1937, the **Bitter Lake National Wildlife Refuge** (4067 Bitter Lakes Rd., 575/622-6755) encompasses nearly 25,000 acres of grasslands, dunes, and wetlands around the Pecos River. As at Bottomless Lakes, there are a number of freshwater sinkholes. The area draws a few hundred species of migrating birds and is therefore great for birding, as well as for spotting more than 90 species of colorful dragonflies and damselflies, best viewed in late summer. There's even a **Dragonfly Festival** in early September. To reach the refuge headquarters, from North Main Street (U.S. 70/285), turn east onto East Pine Lodge Road and follow it until it turns into Bitter Lakes Road and runs into the park. The visitors center is open weekdays only (8am-4pm).

ENTERTAINMENT AND EVENTS

You're lucky to find even a restaurant open past 8pm in Roswell, much less a bar. The city lets loose for a couple of annual parties, though. **Apex Cinemas** (900 W. Hobbs St., 575/208-2810, www.iconcinemas.com), the south side of town, shows the latest blockbusters. Given the limited nightlife in Roswell, it's usually pretty packed. For a glimpse of local business, visit the **Roswell Livestock Auction** (900 N. Garden St., 575/622-5580, www.roswelllivestockauction.com, 9am Mon.); feel free to walk in and take a seat in the bleachers.

Nightlife

Roswell is pretty tame at night, and almost completely dry. **Stellar Coffee** (315 N. Main St., 575/623-3711, 7am-9pm Mon.-Fri., 8am-9pm Sat., 8am-7pm Sun.) is one of the livelier places, with a small stage for acoustic acts. If you're looking for a rowdier scene, check out **Billy Ray's** (118 E. 3rd St., 575/627-0997, 11am-midnight Tues.-Sat.), which is popular for its karaoke and live music on the weekends.

It's not strictly nightlife, as the tasting bar shuts at 5pm, but **Pecos Flavors Winery & Bistro** (113 E. Third St., 575/627-6265, 10am-7pm Mon.-Thurs., 10am-8pm Sat.-Sun.) does give you a chance to sample local vino. Thanks to its bistro, which boasts a handsome antique wood bar and a convivial atmosphere, this feels more like a town hangout than a formal tasting room, and it's a nice place to put your feet up after walking around downtown. It also stocks other local bounty, such as salsas and pistachios, and occasionally hosts live music in the evenings.

Festivals and Events

The town dedicates Fourth of July weekend to visitors from space, as well as around the world, for the **Roswell UFO Festival** (www.ufofestivalroswell.com), which melds serious science with all the geekiness of a *Star Trek* convention. More than 50,000 space fans gather for an alien costume contest, screenings of vintage sci-fi films, a nighttime disc-golf tourney, and lectures by scientists and assorted actors. By contrast, the **Eastern New Mexico State Fair & Parade** (575/623-9411, www.enmsf.com), at the fairgrounds on the southeast side of town in early October, seems pretty mundane. Still, it's well attended and it kicks off with a parade down Main Street.

FOOD
New Mexican

Peppers (500 N. Main St., 575/623-1700, 11am-10pm Mon.-Sat., $10) fills up with locals nightly. It feels a bit like a family-owned Chili's, with an all-over-the-place menu. It's strongest on meat, from fajitas to baby-back ribs, but there's also a good vegetarian burrito and some other solid New Mexican dishes. Get a seat on the patio if you can, and wash it all down with a microbrew.

Mexican

A nice dose of Mexico can be had at the **Red Onion** (1400 W. 2nd St., 575/622-3232, 8am-3pm Tues.-Fri., 7am-3pm Sat.-Sun., $7),

which transports you south of the border for breakfast or lunch, with big platters of *migas* (scrambled eggs with tortilla bits mixed in) and other standards and Jarritos sodas to wash it down. It also has a surprisingly appetizing lunch buffet 11am-1pm. Look for it in a half-empty strip mall a bit out of the center on the west side.

Los Cerritos (2103 N. Main St., 575/622-4919, 7am-9pm Mon.-Sat., 7am-5pm Sun., $9) is more mainstream mash-up Mexican. The place has all the interior charm of a Denny's, but it does great fresh table-side guacamole and giant refreshing *micheladas* (beer, spicy tomato juice, and lime).

Cafés
Stellar Coffee (315 N. Main St., 575/623-3711, 7am-9pm Mon.-Fri., 8am-9pm Sat., 8am-7pm Sun.) supplies both caffeine and sociability, with plenty of room to lounge.

Diners
Don't be fooled by the name, the casual order-at-the-counter setup, and the walls covered with New Mexico license plates: ★ **Big D's Downtown Dive** (505 N. Main St., 575/627-0776, 11am-9pm Mon.-Sat., $7) is no dive at all, but a gourmet operation in fast-food disguise. "Bergs" (burgers) have toppings like sautéed mushrooms and sherry mayonnaise, salads burst with goodies like toasted pine nuts, the waffle fries are sprinkled with garlic, and even the water is elevated, in this case with cucumber and lime. Look out for weekly dinner specials, which can include burgers for $5.

Italian
As one of the few places serving on a Sunday night, **Pasta Café** (1208 N. Main St., 575/624-1111, 11am-9pm daily, $13) does solid Italian. Despite the name, the place is a bit more formal than a café, and the menu's not just pasta—it also has well-executed

favorites like a delectably light eggplant Parmesan and a blackened ribeye with Cajun seasoning.

Desserts
For afternoon refreshment, head to ★ **Paleteria Yolis** (107 W. 6th St., 11am-9pm daily, $2) for a fresh-fruit ice pop or other cold treat. The place feels straight out of Mexico in the best possible way, from the sparkling pink-and-white decor to the case full of flavors like tamarind and *fresas con crema* (strawberries and cream). The *mangoneada,* mango sorbet doused in sweet-tart-hot sauce and chile, is a taste sensation. Everything's made fresh (and translated into English).

ACCOMMODATIONS
Most of the motels are along the northern section of Main Street (U.S. 70/285); unfortunately, the only respectable options are national chains.

Under $100
Of the chains, the **Best Western El Rancho Palacio** (2205 N. Main St., 575/622-2721, www.bestwestern.com, $76 d) almost always can be booked for under $100. "Palace" may be stretching it, but the rooms, which open onto exterior hallways, are in good shape and fairly modern feeling; those upstairs have nice higher ceilings. Breakfast is included, and there's an outdoor pool.

For about the same price, the **Days Inn** (1310 N. Main St., 575/578-3594, www.daysinn.com, $76 d) is admittedly not quite as sturdy-feeling; walls and ceilings are a bit thin, breakfast is skimpier, and the pool is smaller. But it is well kept, and it's located a bit closer to the center of town, so is a good option if you prefer to walk around, rather than drive.

$100-150
In this price bracket, the **Holiday Inn** (3620 N. Main St., 575/623-3216, www.holidayinn.com, $107 d) is functional and modern with

1: Roswell welcome sign 2: the Roswell UFO Festival 3: Big D's Downtown Dive 4: the International UFO Museum & Research Center

a standard range of amenities. The lobby has a full restaurant—a fine option if you want to stay in. Guests get discounts on breakfast there, too.

INFORMATION AND SERVICES

The Roswell Visitors Center (426 N. Main St., 575/623-3442, www.roswell-nm.gov, 9am-5pm Tues.-Fri., 9am-4pm Sat., 10am-3pm Sun.-Mon.) has info on all parts of the state and free wireless Internet access.

GETTING THERE AND AROUND

By car, Roswell is 40 miles (40 minutes) north of Artesia on U.S. 285, 185 miles (3.25 hours) northeast of Las Cruces via U.S. 54

and U.S. 70, and 200 miles (3 hours) southeast of Albuquerque. American Airlines (800/443-7300, www.aa.com) operates two flights daily, sometimes more, from Dallas, Texas, and Phoenix, Arizona, to Roswell (ROW). The airport is five miles south of town. Greyhound (800/231-2222, www.greyhound.com) runs one bus a day from Las Cruces to the station (1100 N. Virginia Ave., 575/622-2510, 8am-4pm Mon.-Fri., 11:30am-3:30pm Sat.).

In town, Roswell has a surprisingly good bus system, Pecos Trails Transit (575/624-6766, www.roswell-nm.gov). The most useful bus for visitors is no. 1, which runs up and down Main Street roughly every half hour; the no. 2 bus runs west along 2nd Street. Fare is $0.75.

Carlsbad

Tourists rarely hear the word Carlsbad without "caverns" tacked on the end, which means that few people come to see the town itself (the national park is 30 miles farther south on U.S. 62/180). But the place is pleasant enough, thanks to an orderly plan laid out in 1888 and the broad ribbon of the Pecos River. Shaded with old trees, the river makes a great place to swim. You'll be excused if you make a beeline for the caves, though.

SIGHTS

Canal Street is the big north-south route now, but the historic main drag was Canyon Street, which still has a few cute shops, galleries, and antiques stores, as well as a Pueblo Revival-style courthouse, its front door bordered with cattle brands. The Pecos River glides along the east side. On the north edge of town, the Pecos River Flume, erected in wood in 1890 then rebuilt more permanently in 1903, brings irrigation water to farm plots; it was the largest concrete structure in the world at the time.

Carlsbad Museum & Art Center

The town's Carlsbad Museum & Art Center (418 W. Fox St., 575/887-0276, 10am-5pm Tues.-Sat., free) holds a small trove of excellent Southwestern art, including some beautiful pieces by Ernest Blumenschein and other early Taos painters, and rotating exhibits by local artists. There are also a few early photographs of the caverns, a real stagecoach, and lots of local arrow points and pottery, as well as a whole array of Peruvian crafts and textiles, donated by a local collector.

Living Desert Zoo and Gardens State Park

Immediately north of Carlsbad, off U.S. 285, the zoo and gardens at Living Desert Zoo and Gardens State Park (1504 Miehls Dr. N., 575/887-5516, www.emnrd.state.nm.us, 8am-5pm daily June-Aug., 9am-5pm daily Sept.-May, $5) is a great place to familiarize yourself with flora and

Carlsbad

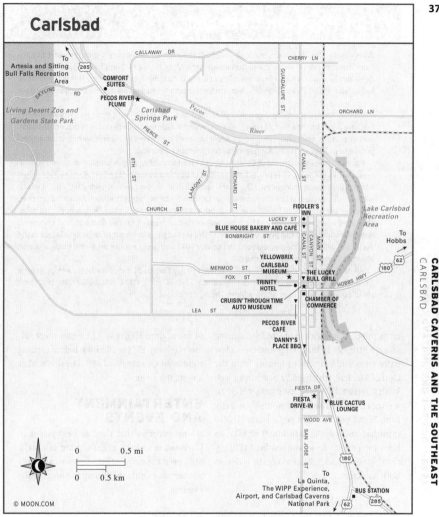

fauna endemic to the Chihuahuan Desert, which extends south into Mexico for several hundred miles. You can learn about native cacti, grasses, and yucca along the 1.3-mile interpretive trail. The place also keeps a few rescued animals in cages, so you can get an up-close look at elk, peccary, and even bobcats and a black bear. Last entrance is 3:30pm.

SPORTS AND RECREATION

Essential when the temperature climbs above 90°F in the summer, Carlsbad offers a number of ways to cool off.

Pecos River

The great **Lake Carlsbad Recreation Area,** at the end of Church Street, is essentially the

Hot Rocks in Carlsbad

When many New Mexicans think of Carlsbad, they think of an entirely different sort of cave from the ones preserved in the national park here. More than 2,000 feet below ground is a vast, deep salt bed into which 16 square miles of storage halls have been carved. This is the Waste Isolation Pilot Plant (WIPP), a dump for transuranic nuclear waste that sits 26 miles east of town, south of the highway to Hobbs.

Bitterly fought from the day it was proposed in 1979 until after it opened in 1999, the site became a symbol of a sort of New Mexican fatalism. Judging from decades of prior oafishness, corner-cutting, and corruption, most people believed New Mexican leaders were just too incompetent to pull off such a tricky, potentially dangerous operation.

For years, the Department of Energy site operated smoothly, and expansion was even considered, thanks to the jobs the project offered. But critics' fears were realized in February 2014, when a barrel in the repository burst. (The barrel was full of an organic, wheat-based kitty litter, which was incorrectly used at Los Alamos National Laboratory to absorb plutonium-contaminated salts, typical of the kinds of radioactive waste products trucked here from Los Alamos and from other DOE sites across the country.) The room was sealed to prevent further damage, and engineers have since improved the poor ventilation in the rest of the site (thought to be one factor in the accident). WIPP resumed operations in January 2017 and is once more receiving nuclear waste, albeit at a slower pace than it once did.

While this debate rages, the Department of Energy Carlsbad field office hosts a chipper little exhibit in its lobby about the current operation, The WIPP Experience (4021 National Parks Hwy., 800/336-9477, 8am-3:30pm Mon.-Thurs., free).

city's public pool, with protected swimming areas, a little island for diving, and even a few palm trees and seagulls (migrants from the Gulf of Mexico), which lend a beachfront feel. With Carlsbad Cruise Lines (800/976-3021, www.carlsbadcruises.com, noon-8pm daily June-Sept.), you can rent pedal boats ($10/30 minutes) and kayaks ($10/hour) or take an hour-long cruise on a pontoon boat ($10). A river walk runs 4.5 miles along the water on both banks.

Sitting Bull Falls

West of town, the 130-foot cascade of Sitting Bull Falls (9am-5pm daily Oct.-Mar., 8:30am-6pm daily Apr.-Sept., gate closes to incoming traffic an hour before close, $5/car) is a nice spot for an easy and short hike on a paved path, a picnic, and a dip in the small, icy pool. Sixteen miles of longer dirt trails also wind through the recreation area (though fire damage from 2011 is still visible), including the intermediate 10-mile-long Loop Trail, which encircles the area and requires some scrambling. Look for the turn 12 miles north

of town, onto Highway 137. From there follow Highway 137 for 20 miles, before turning right onto County Road 409. The drive takes about 50 minutes.

ENTERTAINMENT AND EVENTS

It's no surprise that the two best places in Carlsbad to enjoy a night out are in hotels. Still, even the daily influx of visitors and area workers does little to liven up the town in the evening.

Nightlife

As for evening drinks, Trinity Hotel & Suites (201 S. Canal St., 575/234-9891, 5pm-9pm Mon.-Sat.) is a popular place, with a long wood bar in a high-ceilinged room. Only beer, wine (from around New Mexico, including the hotel owner's own label), and faux cocktails are served, but there's a good selection of snacks. For a rowdier night out,

---

1: Living Desert Zoo and Gardens State Park
2: Sitting Bull Falls 3: Lake Carlsbad Recreation Area

the **Blue Cactus Lounge** (1829 S. Canal St., 575/887-2851, 3pm-10pm Mon.-Sat.), in the Best Western Stevens Inn, is the place to go for occasional live music, and an illuminating cross section of Carlsbadians.

Festivals and Events

If you're in Carlsbad in the winter, don't miss **Christmas on the Pecos** (575/887-6516, www.christmasonthepecos.com, $15 Sun.-Thurs., $20 Fri.-Sat.), an extravaganza of twinkling lights, leaping reindeer, and even glowing margarita glasses strung across more than a hundred homes along the river. View the spectacle from a pontoon boat gliding along the water; the whole ride takes an hour. The city has obligingly extended the "Christmas" season from Thanksgiving to New Year's Eve, and you should book tickets in advance, especially on weekends.

FOOD

While Carlsbad isn't bursting with choices, there are enough good options to ensure you'll have a satisfying meal before you travel onwards. Most places are on or very near Canal Street.

Breakfast and Lunch

Good for a quick coffee and morning pastry, or for a more leisurely meal in the yard, the ★ **Blue House Bakery & Café** (609 N. Canyon St., 575/628-0555, 6am-noon Mon.-Sat., $6) is relaxing and comfortable, tucked away in a residential area. The menu ranges from homemade granola to daily soups and sandwiches, including a very tasty egg, cheese, and green chile croissant.

Pecos River Café (409 S. Canal St., 575/887-8882, 6:30am-2pm Mon.-Fri., $8) is much better than its architecture (a former Pizza Hut) might suggest. Thanks to its spicy green-chile enchiladas and other New Mexican platters, and its killer cinnamon rolls, it gets packed; try to avoid the noon lunch rush.

Barbecue

The eponymous owner of ★ **Danny's Place BBQ** (902 S. Canal St., 575/885-8739, 11am-9pm Wed.-Mon., $10) is obsessive, in a good way. He earned a reputation for quality 'cue while operating a pit off the side of the Dairy Queen he managed. Now on his own, he keeps not much more on the menu than smoked meat in a sweet-hot sauce (though the meat's so succulent, it's fine plain) and burgers. There are the usual sides, including some great bacon-y pinto beans and fried okra.

Fine Dining

For a slightly dressed-up dinner scene, the **Trinity Hotel Restaurant** (201 S. Canal St., 575/234-9891, 7am-1:30pm and 5pm-8:30pm Mon.-Sat., $16-28) has a familiar menu of pastas, Italian dishes, and steaks at dinner, and a mix of sandwiches for lunch. It doesn't break any new ground, but it's better than a chain restaurant and consistently good. The split-level, high-ceilinged dining room buzzes with conversation while chandeliers add to the elegant ambience. At breakfast, there are fresh pastries and sun shining in through the big front windows. There's a free New Mexico wine tasting daily (3pm-7pm).

The **Lucky Bull Grill** (220 W. Fox St., 575/725-5444, 11am-9pm Mon.-Sat., $18) is a laid-back steakhouse with a sports-bar vibe. Locals rave about the oversized burgers, especially the namesake, which is topped with pepper jack, bacon, green chile, and a fried egg.

Set in a butter-yellow craftsman bungalow, **Yellowbrix** (201 N. Canal St., 575/941-2749, 11am-9pm Mon.-Fri., 9am-10pm Sat., 9am-9pm Sun., $9) is Carlsbad's toniest lunch spot, with dishes like French onion soup and poached-pear salad. At night, it aspires to fine dining, which isn't particularly inspired or worth the money ($23 or so for mains)—but there's a good green-chile cheeseburger on the menu, which is a fine excuse to sit out on the front patio, which often has live music.

ACCOMMODATIONS

The lodging situation in Carlsbad is the most difficult in the state to negotiate. Hotels have a captive clientele, between executives from the oil and gas industry and the half-million visitors to the caverns every year. Room availability and prices reflect that—there is no decent room here under $100, and many hideous rooms go for $200. A few of the chains have spiffy new places, but the independent scene hasn't caught up. Almost all hotels are on Canal Street and its continuation, National Parks Highway (U.S. 62/180), for an easy start on the drive to the caverns. You might consider staying up the highway in Artesia—although you'll have to allot an extra hour of driving time.

On the north end of town, Comfort Suites (2600 W. Pierce St., 575/689-8222, www.choicehotels.com, $179 d) is a perfectly good modern hotel with spacious rooms. Connecting doors are a convenience for groups traveling together, but a bit of a noise sieve for those who aren't. On the south end of town, La Quinta (4020 National Parks Hwy., 575/236-1010, www.laquintacarlsbadnm.com, $199 d) offers similar amenities in a location closer to the caverns. Both were built in 2014.

There are two bright spots in Carlsbad's dreary hotel scene; they're both pricier than anywhere else in town, though not by much, and both vastly nicer. Trinity Hotel & Suites (201 S. Canal St., 575/234-9891, www.thetrinityhotel.com, $239 d) occupies a stately old bank building downtown. Within the historic setting, rooms are thoroughly modern, with sleek black furniture and all the tech trimmings, set under high ceilings. Opt for an upstairs room, as those on the ground floor have large windows facing the street, so you need to keep the drapes shut for privacy. Also note that only two of the nine rooms have more than one bed.

The one B&B in town, Fiddler's Inn (705 N. Canyon St., 575/725-8665, www.fiddlersinnbb.com, $209 d) opened in 2015 and takes a pleasant modern approach. The four rooms are airy and lace-free, and you don't have to worry about pressure to chat over breakfast—it's served two doors down, at the excellent Blue House Bakery & Café. One suite ($229) has a full kitchen; another, two bedrooms ($239).

INFORMATION AND SERVICES

Stop in at the Carlsbad Chamber of Commerce (302 S. Canal St., 575/887-6516, www.carlsbadchamber.com, 8am-5pm Mon.-Fri.) for a visitors guide and a detailed map.

GETTING THERE

By car, Carlsbad is 37 miles (40 minutes) south of Artesia on U.S. 285, and 207 miles (3.5 hours) east of Las Cruces by the fastest route, I-10 south to U.S. 62/180 east via El Paso, Texas (165 miles; 3 hours). From Albuquerque, it's 275 miles (4.25 hours). Greyhound (800/231-2222, www.greyhound.com) buses come through from Albuquerque and El Paso, Texas, once a day, stopping at Food Jet (3102 National Parks Hwy., 575/628-0768, 5am-midnight daily).

Boutique Air (855/268-8478, www.boutiqueair.com) flies in to Carlsbad airport (CNM) from Albuquerque and Dallas. The airport is south of town on U.S. 62/180.

Carlsbad Caverns National Park

One of the country's most awesome natural wonders, Carlsbad Caverns is mesmerizing, even in a two-hour stroll around the biggest cavern. But you could easily spend days here (your entrance ticket is good for three days) visiting ever more obscure underground worlds. Aboveground, the Chihuahuan Desert is especially scenic here, studded with spiky plants; you may also want to make time for a bit of a drive through the terrain.

VISITING THE PARK

The park is 23 miles south of the town of Carlsbad and 7 miles in on a winding access road. In prime conditions, it takes about 45 minutes to get to the **visitors center** (727 Carlsbad Caverns Hwy., 575/785-3137, www.nps.gov/cave, 8am-7pm daily June-Aug., 8am-5pm daily Sept.-May, $15). In the summer months, allow an extra hour of waiting time at the visitors center. Probably the best time to go is in December, before the holidays, or in January and February, because you'll have the whole place to yourself, in near ghostly silence. Still, there are two reasons to consider a spring or summer visit: Hundreds of thousands of bats fly out every evening, and the 56°F temperature underground is a relief.

Always pack a sweater, no matter how hot it is outside, and wear sturdy shoes, even if you're only going on the main self-guided tours. You might want to pack a lunch, too, as the cafeteria at the caverns is pretty institutional. Fill your gas tank in Carlsbad, as once you head south you're at the mercy of one pricey station in White's City.

★ The Big Room

The basic entrance ticket gives you access to two major parts of the cave: the **Natural Entrance Trail** (last entrance 3:30pm daily June-Aug., 2pm daily Sept.-May), which descends about 800 feet in the course of a mile, on a paved trail dense with switchbacks, and **The Big Room** (last entrance 5pm daily June-Aug., 3:30pm daily Sept.-May), the largest cave in the Carlsbad complex. If you don't want to hike down, an elevator will whisk you 754 feet down to the cavern floor.

the Big Room at Carlsbad Caverns

Guided Tours in Carlsbad Caverns

The tour schedule varies by season. Times given here are typical for low season; additional tours are offered in summer. Please confirm at www.nps.gov/cave or www.recreation.gov.

TOUR	Cost	Duration	Length	Age Limit	Schedule
King's Palace	$8	1.5 hours	1 mile	4 and up	9:30am, 11:30am, 1pm daily
Left Hand Tunnel	$7	2 hours	0.5 mile	6 and up	10:30am daily
Lower Cave	$20	3 hours	1 mile, plus 60-foot descent on rope ladders	12 and up	8:30am Mon., Thurs., Fri.
Slaughter Canyon Cave	$15	5.5 hours, including driving time	1.75 miles, including steep 0.5-mile hike to entrance	8 and up	8:30am Tues., Sat.
Hall of the White Giant	$20	4 hours	1 mile, very strenuous	12 and up	8:30am Wed.
Spider Cave	$20	4 hours	1 mile, very strenuous	12 and up	8:30am Sun.

Instead of floors, the display panel shows 50-foot increments. The 1.5-hour walk down is preferable, as it gives you a better sense of what it must have been like for cowboy Jim White to first explore this place in the early 20th century. It also gives an idea of the scale you'll be dealing with once you get underground—at one point, you have to hike for about 30 minutes around Iceberg Rock, a 200,000-ton boulder.

The Big Room is lit in tasteful white lights and glows like a natural cathedral: The ceiling soars up into the dark, and the space is 1.25 miles long. If you think of caves as claustrophobia-inducing, this one will change your mind. (But it's not all natural—there's still a snack bar down on the cave floor, as well as restrooms, discreetly hidden behind rock formations.)

Scientists theorize that The Big Room—and many of the other caverns in this network—began to form more than 20 million years ago, as the petroleum deposits under the Guadalupe Mountains reacted with groundwater to create sulfuric acid, which ate through the stone to form vast hollow spots under the ground. These spaces started to fill with stalagmites and stalactites about 500,000 years ago, and now the intricate formations—still growing in some spots—range from hulking towers that ripple like clay to delicate needles that look more like icicles than stone.

For both routes, you can rent an **audio tour** for $5—it includes some interesting information, but don't get too caught up in listening to every entry. It's just as rewarding to let your imagination roam.

Ranger-Led Tours

These small-group side tours are an alternative to the crowds in The Big Room. You get a little more quiet and, of course, see a lot more of the caverns. During peak season, reservations are necessary (877/444-6777, www.recreation.gov); it's advisable to make your reservations at least 48 hours in advance. Be sure to ask what time to arrive; some tours require hour-long hikes in to the departure point. Note that if you'd like to see more once you're down in The Big Room, you have to come back up to the surface to buy the extra ticket.

The easiest addition to your itinerary, **King's Palace** is the deepest part of the caves open to the public. Limited to 75 participants, the tour passes giant formations as well as tiny details such as a bat's skeleton grown into a stalagmite. Best of all, it includes a few minutes with the lights turned off, when you get to stand in the cool, smothering black. Unlike all the other ranger-led tours, the trail is paved and not particularly steep except at the entrance.

Left Hand Tunnel is best for a sheer sense of discovery. On the trek, limited to 15 people, you carry just a flickering lantern through fantastic rock formations—made all the more bizarre as they loom up out of the darkness. **Lower Cave** requires a bit more exertion, starting with a clamber down 50 feet of rope and narrow ladders. The formations

here include toothpick-like stalactites and the perfectly round and white formations called "cave pearls."

Slaughter Canyon Cave is the only spot not accessible through the visitors center. Instead, you have to drive five miles south of White's City, then turn west onto a well-signed county road; there's also a steep hike to the entrance. Once in the cave, though, the walk isn't too difficult, and it goes past formations like the glittering, crystal-covered column dubbed "The Christmas Tree."

Finally, for people who aren't afraid of tight spaces, **Hall of the White Giant** and **Spider Cave** are strenuous but rewarding trips. Each one takes about four hours, and you have to bring batteries and gloves (the rangers provide headlamps and helmets). Expect to wiggle through some very narrow tunnels and get muddy in the process.

Special Events

Late May-mid-October, hundreds of thousands of bats rush out from the depths of the caverns and into the bug-filled twilight. Half an hour before sunset, at an amphitheater at the top of the Natural Entrance Trail, rangers give a short talk about the bats (ask at the visitors center or call 575/785-3012 for times;

Bat Flight amphitheater at Carlsbad Caverns

free). When the **Bat Flight** begins, you hear the soft flapping of their wings and feel the rush of air as they pass overhead.

Most are of the Brazilian free-tail variety, which migrate to Mexico in the winter. Another group of larger cave *Myotis* live in the Lake of the Clouds, the deepest point in the cave system; they too come out every night, and if you're at the underground cafeteria near closing time, you might feel them whir through. Whether you're underground or at the amphitheater, keep your camera stowed—the flash and auto-focus devices disorient the animals.

Throughout the summer, the park also hosts monthly **Star Party** (www.nps.gov/cave) events, with rangers on hand with telescopes. From late spring until early fall, you can also go on a **Star Walk** and a **Moon Hike**. The former involves hiking half a mile along an area trail when the night sky is especially clear, while the latter follows a 1.5-mile trail during a full moon.

WHITE'S CITY

This so-called town at the junction of U.S. 62/180 and Highway 7 is an unreconstructed tourist trap—there's a bad restaurant, two hopelessly dumpy hotels, a wildly overpriced gas station, and a junk-filled gift shop. Blindfold your kids as you drive past the giant waterslide (for hotel guests only), or you'll never hear the end of it. The **Greyhound** bus can be prevailed upon to pull up here, though it's not a regularly scheduled stop.

GUADALUPE MOUNTAINS NATIONAL PARK

Adjacent to the caverns land and just over the border in Texas, **Guadalupe Mountains National Park** (915/828-3251, www.nps.gov/gumo, $5) is mentioned here because it's where people usually camp ($15) when visiting Carlsbad Caverns. The largest area, with both tent and RV sites (but no hookups), is **Pine Springs Campground,** near the visitors center, about 35 miles south of White's City on U.S. 62/180. In the park's northern section, **Dog Canyon Campground** (no hookups), is smaller, more pleasant, and generally cooler.

You can also hike the exceptionally scenic **McKittrick Canyon,** where a 6.8-mile out-and-back trail leads through a narrow limestone canyon thick with deciduous trees—truly stunning in late October when the leaves turn, though often crowded. The park also encompasses **Salt Basin Dunes,** a glittering landscape similar to White Sands National Park, but more isolated.

Cloudcroft

The closest mountains to the Texas flatlands, the Sacramentos have drawn vacationers with a drawl since 1899, when a local railroad man built a resort at Cloudcroft, now accessible by U.S. 82, due west of Artesia. The village is still barely more than a cluster of rustic cabins and a few gift shops—but the view, looking down as far as White Sands, is majestic, especially when the clouds are gathering below you. The view straight up is great, too—hence the location of a major solar observatory nearby.

SIGHTS

Burro Avenue, the main street in town and just north of U.S. 82, is where you'll find a row of Old West-style false-front buildings along a wooden boardwalk.

Sacramento Mountains Historical Museum

Across the street from the chamber of commerce, the local **Sacramento Mountains Historical Museum** (U.S. 82, 575/682-2932, www.cloudcroftmuseum.com, 10am-4pm

Mon.-Tues. and Fri.-Sat., 1pm-4pm Sun. in summer, 10am-4pm Fri.-Sat. in winter, $5) has the usual assortment of memorabilia from the past, plus a "pioneer village" made up of several old log cabins, furnished with antique tools and furniture. The site hosts occasional events, including lectures and arts and crafts festivals.

Sunspot

Sixteen miles south of Cloudcroft on Highway 6563 (named for the wavelength of the orange-red light we associate with images of the sun; most people call it Sunspot Highway), **Sunspot National Solar Observatory** and privately owned Apache Point Observatory take advantage of the high altitude and clear skies to spy on deep space. The Sunspot **visitors center** (575/434-7190, 9am-5pm daily Mar.-Jan.) explains how the telescopes work. Since a 2018 incident that involved the FBI and a dwindling need to keep it operational, the observatory's days feel numbered. Before making the drive, check at the visitors center first to see if it's open and if a guided tour (typically at 2pm on Saturday and Sunday in summer; $3) is possible.

Even if you're not interested in the science side, the highway is a pretty drive, with dramatic vistas down to White Sands, and you'll pass **Karr Canyon,** another nice place for a picnic. Look for signs en route labeled with the names of planets—they're placed along the road according to their relative distance to one another, at a scale of 1:250 million.

SPORTS AND RECREATION

The opportunities for outdoor activities around Cloudcroft are exceptional year-round. As long as you're adjusted to the altitude, the hiking trails are not too strenuous. Check current conditions with the **Sacramento Ranger District office** (4 Lost Lodge Rd., 575/682-2551, 8am-4pm Mon.-Fri.), one mile up Highway 130 toward the Sunspot Highway.

Hiking

The old railroad that used to zigzag up the mountain is gone, but the rail bed makes for excellent hiking on the well-maintained 8-mile **Switchback Trail.** The **Cloud-Climbing Trestle Trail** is the best introduction—it's just 1.3 miles and leads to the picturesque (and vertigo-inducing) Mexican Canyon trestle, built in 1899. The trail starts on the west edge of town, off the south side of the road, by a replica of the original train depot. For a map on the rest of the rails-to-trails network, stop in at the chamber of commerce.

Another popular route is **Osha Trail** (no. 10), maintained by the National Forest Service. It runs three miles through relatively level, shaded forest that's especially pretty when the leaves change in the fall. The trailhead is on the opposite side of the road from the Mexican Canyon trestle.

Mountain Biking

The 28-mile multi-use **Rim Trail** is legendary for its amazing views as it winds along the spine of the mountains, roughly parallel to Sunspot Highway (Hwy. 6563). It climbs about a thousand feet over the course of the whole ride, though it has some zippy downhill sections, as well as some jarring rocky terrain. Only the first 13 or so miles are official Forest Service trail (no. 105), but it runs all the way to Sunspot, then down to Forest Road 90 to the southeast. You can cut in at the observatory and take the paved road back downhill. The trailhead is just off Highway 6563—look for parking on the right side almost immediately after you make the turn from Highway 130.

A handful of other loop trails start in town and nearby. Stop in at the chamber of commerce or the exceptionally helpful **High Altitude Outfitters** (310 Burro Ave., 575/682-1229, 10am-5:30pm Mon.-Thurs., 10am-6pm Fri.-Sat., 10am-5pm Sun.), a shop that also

---

1: Cloudcroft's old railroad trestle, now a walking trail **2:** Mad Jack's, offering Texas barbecue in New Mexico

organizes a race, the High Altitude Classic, every August for maps and other guidance.

Winter Sports

Two miles east of town on U.S. 82, **Ski Cloudcroft** (575/682-2333, www. skicloudcroft.net, $45 full-day lift ticket) has modest ski runs as well as a tubing area ($20/2 hours). With no snowmaking abilities, the ski area is highly weather dependent. There's more reliable winter fun in town, at **Cloudcroft Ice Rink** (751 James Canyon Hwy., 575/644-5525, 3:30pm-9:30pm Tues.-Fri., 10am-9pm Sat.-Mon.) at the west end of Zenith Park, and tubing all over the hills. Many of the town's rail trails are suitable for **cross-country skiing.** Another good bet is the **Fir Trail** (no. 122), which is just under 2 miles long and is groomed for cross-country skiing. Trail access is off Highway 244 near the Silver Campground, northeast of town.

FOOD

Cloudcroft's unofficial social center, the **Western Bar & Café** (304 Burro Ave., 575/682-9910, 6am-9pm daily, $7) satisfies just about every social need, whether you want a breakfast omelet, a cold beer, or a crazy night of karaoke (the bar is open until 10pm on Mon. and 2am Tues.-Sat.). The vibe is friendly and the crowd is eclectic.

Up the hill at The Lodge, **Rebecca's** (575/682-3131, 7am-10:30am, 11:30am-2:30pm, and 5:30pm-9pm Mon.-Sat., 8am-2pm Sun.) has historic ambience, though the prices for fairly average sandwiches and steaks are high ($12 at lunch, $25 and up at dinner). But it's a good spot for a drink and a snack.

For barbecue that wins approving nods from the Texas crowds—and rightly so, as the owner is from Lockhart—stop in at ★ **Mad Jack's** (105 James Canyon Hwy., 575/682-7577, 11am-3pm Thurs.-Sun., $8). The menu focuses on barbecue cuts by the pound, including angus beef ribs, pulled pork, and sandwiches, such as the signature gut-busting Mad Jack—sliced brisket, jack cheese and grilled onions and peppers.

ACCOMMODATIONS

The main type of accommodation in town is a rustic cabin. Location isn't too essential, considering how small the town is.

Under $100

Halfway down the mountain on the way to Tularosa, the excellent ★ **Cloudcroft Mountain Park Hostel** (1049 U.S. 82, 575/682-0555, www.cloudcrofthostel.com) has two rooms with eight bunks each ($19 pp), as well as two basic private rooms ($37) and one big family room (from $42), all with access to shared baths and a big common area and kitchen. Everything's clean and colorfully painted, with a casual but orderly atmosphere.

Summit Inn (Chipmunk Ave. at Curlew Pl., 575/682-2814, www.summitinn-nm.com, $62.50 s, $86 d) has clean and tidy, if dated, rooms, with tiny kitchenettes, vintage TVs, and showers (no tubs). Don't bother with the cabins, though—they're relatively expensive (from $106) and short on charm.

At the east end of town, **Spruce Cabins** (100 Lynx Ave., 575/682-2381, www. sprucecabins.com, $60 d) are pleasant enough standalone apartments with a faintly rustic feel. The wood paneling has a certain 1970s mobile home vibe, but that's offset by attractive quilts on the beds, cozy wood-burning fireplaces, and a great nightly rate.

Burro Street Boardinghouse (608 Burro Ave., 575/682-3601, $99) has just three rooms, but each one is very nicely done, with choice antiques and details like vanity sinks. The building is a big, airy, pine-paneled A-frame, and the owner is an old Cloudcroft hand.

$100-150

At the top of the hill, **The Lodge** (601 Corona Pl., 800/395-6343, www.thelodgeresort.com, $125 d) is a fairly well-restored relic from the early railroad era. The current structure, with its vaguely Tyrolean look, was built in 1911 by the Alamogordo & Sacramento Railway. With lots of chintz, brocade, and dark wood, the style may be historically accurate, but some of the 58 rooms can feel cramped, especially the standard queens. Rooms in the Retreat wing (from $315) are newer construction and have fireplaces and whirlpool tubs. Down the hill, the Pavilion is the oldest section, a large wood cabin with a wraparound porch—the rooms here are a bit more rustic, and rates (from $145) include breakfast at Rebecca's, the resort's main restaurant.

INFORMATION

Cloudcroft's **chamber of commerce** (U.S. 82, 575/682-2733, www.coolcloudcroft.com, 10am-4pm Mon.-Sat.) occupies a tiny cabin on the east side of town and has just about any info on the town you could need.

GETTING THERE

Cloudcroft is 20 miles (30 minutes) by car east from Alamogordo via U.S. 82 and 90 miles (1.5 hours) west from Artesia.

Alamogordo

For most visitors, Alamogordo functions as the gateway to the stunning White Sands National Park, the largest field of pure gypsum in the world. It also has a couple of interesting sights of its own. Founded in 1899 as a railroad stop, the town has been shaped more by the early space industry and Holloman Air Force Base, which also trains German pilots. It fits between the railroad tracks and the foothills of the Sacramento Mountains, with some 31,000 residents in a low-rise sprawl.

SIGHTS

Navigating Alamogordo is straightforward: Almost everything is located on or very near White Sands Boulevard (U.S. 54/70), which runs roughly north-south through town. On New York Avenue, one block east, is Alamogordo's historic downtown, along a couple of blocks south of 10th Street. The space museum is far up in the foothills, but it's visible from a long way off.

New Mexico Museum of Space History

The state-run **New Mexico Museum of Space History** (Hwy. 2001, 575/437-2840, www.nmspacemuseum.org, 10am-5pm Mon. and Wed.-Sat., noon-5pm Sun., $8) began in 1976 as a hall of fame for astronauts, including the first chimpanzee in space, who's buried here. Then it expanded into this comprehensive look at space exploration—which in many ways got its start in rocket tests in the Tularosa Basin below. Working your way down through four floors, you pass assorted relics from the space race, a chunk of moon rock, and more. But perhaps the most interesting items are those that hint at what everyday life in zero gravity is like, such as the space station interior model and a space-shuttle food system. It's a surprisingly un-high-tech museum. The cobbled-together rockets and patched-up spacesuits serve as a reminder of just how mechanical and hardware-driven space exploration has been—not a sleek, digital process at all.

The current state of space exploration looks a little slicker: The bottom floor of the museum is devoted to the X Prize, which encourages commercial space flights, and a hangar outside contains a model of the first winner: glossy, bulbous SpaceShipOne, covered in corporate-sponsor logos. Next to it, a 1940s accelerator for testing G-forces looks brutally primitive.

Toy Train Depot

You can't miss Alamogordo's nifty miniature train: It runs straight through town, parallel to White Sands Boulevard. The northern endpoint is the **Toy Train Depot** (1991 N. White Sands Blvd., 575/437-2855, noon-5pm Wed.-Thurs.

Alamogordo

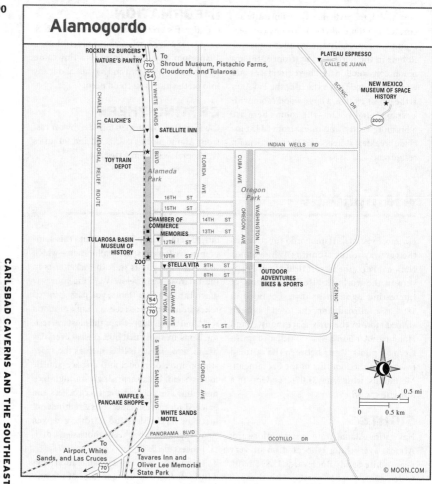

ROCKIN' BZ BURGERS ▼
NATURE'S PANTRY ▼

To
Shroud Museum, Pistachio Farms,
Cloudcroft, and Tularosa

PLATEAU ESPRESSO
▼ CALLE DE JUANA

NEW MEXICO
MUSEUM OF SPACE
HISTORY
★

SCENIC DR

(2001)

CHARLIE LEE MEMORIAL RELIEF ROUTE

N WHITE SANDS

CALICHE'S ■ ★ SATELLITE INN

INDIAN WELLS RD

BLVD

TOY TRAIN DEPOT ★

Alameda Park

FLORIDA AVE

CUBA AVE

Oregon Park

WASHINGTON AVE

OREGON AVE

16TH ST
15TH ST

CHAMBER OF COMMERCE ★
14TH ST
MEMORIES ▼
13TH ST
TULAROSA BASIN MUSEUM OF HISTORY ■ ★
12TH ST
10TH ST
ZOO ★

▼ STELLA VITA 9TH ST
8TH ST

OUTDOOR
ADVENTURES ■
BIKES & SPORTS

NEW YORK AVE

DELAWARE AVE

(54)
(70)

1ST ST

SCENIC DR

S WHITE SANDS BLVD

FLORIDA AVE

0   0.5 mi
0   0.5 km

WAFFLE & PANCAKE SHOPPE ▼

WHITE SANDS MOTEL ●

PANORAMA BLVD

OCOTILLO DR

To
Airport, White
Sands, and Las Cruces

To
Tavares Inn and
Oliver Lee Memorial
State Park

© MOON.COM

and Sun., 10am-5pm Fri.-Sat., $5), the model-train collection of a retired rocket scientist. One of the layouts shows the old route up to Cloudcroft. But the real fun is outside on the larger-scale tracks, where two trains run down to Alameda Park and back, and a smaller-gauge one runs loops around the yard ($5). Kids might get to drive it themselves, if they're well behaved.

Tularosa Basin Museum of History

The usual assortment of pioneer gear and old furniture is on display at the brilliantly white

Tularosa Basin Museum of History (1004 N. White Sands Blvd., 575/434-4438, https://alamogordonmtrue.com/tularosa-basin-museum, 10am-4pm Mon.-Sat., $3); the highlight of the collection is an American flag with 47 stars. There's also some information about Trinity Site, as well as the older Hispano community of La Luz, just north of Alamogordo.

Alameda Park and Zoo

Alameda Park and Zoo (1321 N. White Sands Blvd., 575/439-4290, 9am-5pm daily, $4) is the oldest in the Southwest. It has about

90 species on view, including some frisky otters and even some kangaroos, which don't look too out of place in this desert. There's also a nice shaded picnic area inside. The entrance is on 10th Street just west of White Sands Boulevard.

Shroud Exhibit and Museum

Alamogordo's most surprising attraction is undoubtedly the **Shroud Exhibit and Museum** (923 N. New York Ave., 575/921-3505, 1pm-5pm Mon.-Tues. and Fri.-Sat., 2pm-4pm Sun., free), devoted to a photo-replica of the Shroud of Turin, the work of a group of researchers based in New Mexico, who examined the shroud in 1978 using state-of-the-art imaging technology.

Pistachios

Just north of Alamogordo, past the turn to Cloudcroft, are two places focused on the area's proudest agricultural accomplishment: pistachios. **McGinn's Pistachioland & Arena Blanca Winery** (7320 Hwy. 54/70, 800/368-3081, 9am-5pm daily) is home to the world's largest pistachio, making it a hugely popular stop for roadside attraction devotees. Just next door is **Heart of the Desert Pistachios and Wine at Eagle Ranch** (7288 Hwy. 54/70, 575/434-0035, 8am-6pm Mon.-Sat., 9am-6pm Sun.), known for its green-chile pistachios.

SPORTS AND RECREATION

For general info on trails and other recreation, stop in at the **Lincoln National Forest** supervisor's office (3463 Las Palomas Rd., 575/434-7200, 8am-4pm Mon.-Fri.) or **Outdoor Adventures Bikes & Sports** (1516 10th St., 575/434-1920, 10am-6pm Mon.-Fri., 10am-5pm Sat.), where you can also rent mountain bikes ($25/24 hours).

Hiking

The one big rec area nearby is **Oliver Lee Memorial State Park** (409 Dog Canyon Rd., 575/437-8284, www.emnrd.sate.nm.us, $5/car), at the base of the Sacramento Mountains 12 miles southeast of Alamogordo. The 5.5-mile **Dog Canyon Recreational Trail** begins at the visitors center and leads through a surprisingly lush canyon where you'll see everything from moss to orchids growing, if you look closely. It then heads up to a ridge with sweeping views of the desert basin—a strenuous climb, with an elevation gain of 3,100 feet; many hikers just go about 2.5 miles in to a 19th-century stone cowboy cabin, then turn around. There are also more than 40 developed **campsites** ($8-14)—the closest camping to White Sands National Park.

FOOD

It's slim pickings for distinctive dining in Alamogordo—and no surprise most people wind up eating at the chain restaurants on White Sands Boulevard.

For a pick-me-up after the space museum, **Plateau Espresso** (2724 N. Scenic Dr., 575/434-4466, 6am-9pm daily) will do the trick nicely, with a strong selection of coffee drinks and baked goods. Take your order outside and enjoy the awesome views over the city from the patio.

Diners with text anxiety might not like the ordering system at **Rockin' BZ Burgers** (3005 N. White Sands Blvd., 575/434-2375, 11am-8pm Tues.-Sat., 11am-3pm Sun., $7), which involves filling out a form to select burger toppings and sides. If in doubt, go for the signature half-pound Champ burger, which has made an excellent showing in the state fair green-chile cheeseburger cook-off in recent years; it adds grilled onions to the mix. Another nice touch: buttered buns.

For a healthy lunch, the deli counter at the back of **Nature's Pantry** (2909 N. White Sands Blvd., 575/437-3037, 10am-6pm Mon.-Sat., $7) makes vegetarian-friendly wraps and sprout-stuffed sandwiches, which you can wash down with a shot of wheatgrass juice or a smoothie—a great antidote to standard road food.

Caliche's (2251 N. White Sands Blvd., 575/439-1000, 11am-10pm daily, $4) is an

outpost of the frozen-custard specialist in Las Cruces. It's no balanced meal, but given the options in Alamogordo, you're excused if you have a hot dog with all the trimmings and a thick shake for dinner.

If nothing else, the **Waffle & Pancake Shoppe** (950 S. White Sands Blvd., 575/437-0433, 6am-1pm daily, $7) lives up to its name. Fortunately, the waffles and pancakes don't disappoint and are a clear cut above what you'd get from a chain. There's also quite a bit more on the menu, including breakfast and lunch diner standards, as well as a few New Mexican staples.

It requires a 20-minute drive to the south edge of Tularosa, but ★ **Casa de Sueños** (35 St. Francis Dr., 575/585-3494, 11am-8pm Mon.-Thurs., 11am-8:30pm Fri.-Sat., 10:30am-8pm Sun., $12) is a big step up from Alamogordo dining. Red-chile-rubbed pork chops are just one of several tasty (and very meaty) dishes on the menu. You can also get the usual enchiladas and rellenos, as well as burritos to go. The ambience is warmly lit, with a pretty patio out back.

ACCOMMODATIONS

A rare case in which an eye-catching neon sign actually points to quality lodging, ★ **White Sands Motel** (1101 S. White Sands Blvd., 575/437-2922, www.whitesandsmotel.com, $55 s, $65 d) is a tidy little shell of an old motel court, nicely updated inside. The rooms are snug, but they're kept clean, and many are well back from the main road, for slightly less traffic noise. Rooms all have mini-fridges, microwaves, and wireless Internet. A decent continental breakfast is included as well.

On the south edge of town, **Tavares Inn** (153 San Pedro Dr., 575/437-8779, www.tavaresinn.com, $105 d) puts the "breakfast" back in bed-and-breakfast, with a massive morning spread. The three rooms ooze character and are in a rambling white ranch house, with an indoor pool, horses, and more out back.

INFORMATION

The **Alamogordo Chamber of Commerce** (1301 N. White Sands Blvd., 575/437-6120, www.alamogordo.com, 8am-5pm Mon.-Fri.) dispenses a very detailed free map. The associated visitors center is open daily.

GETTING THERE AND AROUND

By car, Alamogordo is 68 miles (1.25 hours) northeast from Las Cruces via U.S. 70, and 215 miles (3.25 hours) from Albuquerque via I-25, then U.S. 380 and U.S. 54. Cloudcroft is about 20 miles (30 minutes) due east up the mountains, and Ruidoso is 50 miles (1 hour) northeast. **Greyhound** (800/231-2222, www.greyhound.com) connects Alamogordo to Las Cruces once a day, stopping at the station on the north side (3500 N. White Sands Blvd., 575/437-3050, 7am-11am and 4pm-8pm Mon.-Fri., 7am-9am and 5pm-8pm Sat.-Sun.).

1: a roadside photo op with the world's biggest pistachio at McGinn's, just north of Alamogordo 2: White Sands Motel 3: the New Mexico Museum of Space History

White Sands National Park

TOP EXPERIENCE

White Sands, 275 square miles of blinding, shimmery gypsum, is a surreal and magnificent place. At every turn, you have to remind yourself what you're really looking at. In the summer, temperatures exceed 100°F, but the sand looks like no desert you've ever seen. On a cool winter day, especially after rainwater has pooled along the road, your brain can't stop thinking snow and ice. For the best photography, as well as a break from the heat, you'll probably want to visit either early or late in the day—but there is also something undeniably overwhelming about this featureless landscape at high noon.

Although the barren dunes at the core of the park are the most popular image of the place, there's a surprising amount of life here, from tiny kangaroo mice to the beleaguered tufts of skunkbush sumac that are the last holdouts as the sand shifts around them. A number of nature trails lead off the 16-mile-long Dunes Drive, and if you have time, you should definitely join one of the ranger-led walks—usually near sunset. There are periodic—and sometimes short-notice—closures due to testing at the nearby White Sands Missile Range, so check ahead.

VISITORS CENTER

Stop in at the pleasant **visitors center** (575/479-6124, www.nps.gov/whsa, $20) at the main gate to check the schedule of ranger tours and maybe pick up a plastic sled, for sliding down the dunes, at the gift shop. Among the ranger outings is a car trip to **Lake Lucero** ($8, reserve ahead), the crystal-filled lake bed that's the source of the sands, as well as occasional full-moon **hikes** and outings for **sunrise and sunset photography** (each $8). If you plan to do any backcountry hiking, you'll need to get a permit at the center ($3)—there's only one designated hike-in camping area, about a mile from the road, so check for a vacancy.

Hours for the visitors center and the park vary substantially month to month. You can count on at least 9am-5pm year-round, but it's also open from 8am during the holidays in December and early January. In the shoulder

sunset at White Sands National Park

seasons (mid-Mar.-mid-May and mid-Sept.-Nov.), it's open 9am-6pm. Mid-May-mid-September, it's open 8am-7pm.

DUNES DRIVE

The loop through the park leads from the shaggy, brush-covered hills at the edge of the white desert into the pure dunes at the center. In between is the transition area, where hills are being carved away by wind, and yuccas teeter on lone sand pedestals. As long as you park in one of the designated pullouts, you're welcome to walk wherever you like, but make careful note of landmarks; even in the areas with lots of vegetation, it's easy to wind up walking in circles—a very dangerous prospect, particularly in the middle of the day.

The first stop on the drive, **Playa Trail** runs 500 yards along the border where the gypsum meets the regular desert terrain, ending up at a playa, the term for a depression that forms a temporary lake after rainfall. These playas are all over White Sands, as well as in the desert areas of the rest of New Mexico. Of all the trails, this may be the least remarkable—skip it if you're not planning to spend all day here.

The one-mile-long **Dune Life Nature Trail** does a quick loop up to the top of a dune and past the most typical types of vegetation. At least stop to pick up one of the trail guides, which can help you identify animal tracks. The **Interdune Boardwalk** is another quick trail—a very easy way to check out some of the more common plants, without trudging through sand.

★ HEART OF THE SANDS

Waves of gypsum dunes stretch out before you to mountains looming far in the distance—this is the park's most mesmerizing section. You can set up camp in one of the mod metal picnic shelters (which include grills), then go out to clamber, slip, and slide down the pristine white hills. (There are also restrooms out here, but no water.) From the end of the parking area, the **Alkali Flat Trail** is a 5-mile loop into the most austere part of the dunes; signs of life are few and far between. This can be extremely disorienting—heed the stern warnings to turn back if you can't see the orange trail markers, which periodically get covered with sand. Allow about three hours for the whole hike, and be sure to register at the trailhead before you proceed.

Ruidoso

North of Alamogordo and east on U.S. 70, Ruidoso (Spanish for "noisy") is named for the audible stream that flows through a canyon in the town center. Like Cloudcroft, it's a patch of Texas in the high mountains—but it's quite a bit bigger and, at least in spots, substantially more upscale. It's very much a resort town, dedicated to golf (there are six courses in the immediate area), horse racing, and skiing on southern New Mexico's highest mountain, Sierra Blanca Peak. Don't go for culture, but for cool air and a cabin in the woods. And brace yourself for cutesy kitsch—the number of tree-trunk bear sculptures is higher per capita than anywhere else in the state.

On the drive up on U.S. 70, you pass through the Mescalero Apache reservation, established in 1883 on some 463,000 acres. The tribe (which got its name from the Spanish, who remarked on its ritual use of peyote, or mescal) operates the ski area as well as a resort and casino about a 20-minute drive south of town.

SIGHTS

Ruidoso's main drags are Sudderth Drive (east-west) and Mechem Drive, running north from the west end of Sudderth, to form a big L. The town is divided into districts by the major intersections. Uptown is lower Mechem and

Ruidoso

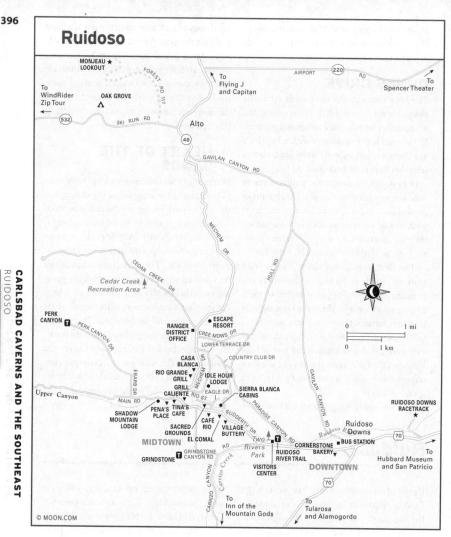

© MOON.COM

the west end of Sudderth (higher address numbers); Midtown, the densest business area, refers to the stretch of Sudderth from up near Mechem to Carrizo Canyon Road. Finally, Downtown is the east end of Sudderth (the lowest street numbers), and "the Y" is the junction of Sudderth and U.S. 70, where most of the chain businesses are. Farther east along U.S. 70, Ruidoso Downs is technically a separate town, but there is no physical gap between it and its neighbor.

Hubbard Museum of the American West

The small **Hubbard Museum of the American West** (26301 U.S. 70 W, 575/378-4142, www.hubbardmuseum.org, 9am-5pm Thurs.-Mon., $7), the only real "sight" in Ruidoso, is the collection of a local woman who loved all things equine and had good taste in Native American crafts. Her assortment of horse-drawn carriages, from a sulky to a chuckwagon to a hearse, fills the downstairs. Upstairs is space for temporary, Western-themed exhibitions.

SPORTS AND RECREATION

For details on nearby national forest areas, contact the **Smokey Bear Ranger District office** (901 Mechem Dr., 575/257-4095, 8am-4pm Mon.-Fri.). Birders should keep an eye out for hummingbirds, which summer in the area in great numbers.

Sure, there are *real* golf courses in the area, but **Funtrackers** (101 Carrizo Canyon Rd., 575/257-3275, 10am-9pm daily in summer, Sat.-Sun. in winter) has 18 miniature holes ($7), as well as go-carts ($6/5 minutes), an arcade, a human-scale maze, and more. Even Ruidoso's **public swimming pool** (515 Sudderth Dr., 575/257-5030, noon-4:45pm, $4) is pretty fun, with a giant loop-de-loop slide; but it closes when the school year starts, in mid-August.

Hiking and Biking

Ruidoso is particularly prone to wildfire and much of the forest surrounding the town is still recovering from intense wildfires in 2012. As a result, recreation is somewhat limited while the area recovers. In town, the **Ruidoso River Trail** in Two Rivers Park, right behind the **visitors center** (720 Sudderth Dr.), is a 1.25-mile paved trail along the river all the way into Upper Canyon, sometimes so far below the main road level that you forget you're in the middle of town.

Handy **Perk Canyon Trail** begins basically in people's backyards and runs steadily up about three miles across streams and to some open meadows. To get to the trailhead, follow Main Road to Ebarb Drive (next to Story Book Cabins); turn right, go about 0.3 mile to Perk Canyon Road, and turn left. The paved road dead-ends at the trailhead.

Off Highway 48 a few miles to the west of the town center, the heavily wooded **Cedar Creek Recreation Area** (May-Oct.) in the Lincoln National Forest has over 30 miles of multi-use trails popular with bikers and hikers from spring until fall.

The International Mountain Biking Association designed the 18-mile **Grindstone Trail System** (575/257-4905) with cyclists in mind, but is the five trails are good for running and walking too. Take Grindstone Canyon Road to park at Grindstone Lake for trail access.

Horse Racing

Memorial Day-Labor Day, **Ruidoso Downs** (26225 U.S. 70, 575/378-4431, www.raceruidoso.com) hosts races Friday-Monday, starting at 1pm. There are a few thoroughbred meets, but historically Ruidoso has been a quarter-horse track. The All-American Futurity, which draws nearly 20,000 people to town over Labor Day weekend, has been dubbed the World's Richest Quarter Horse Race, thanks to its purse of more than one million—not bad money for 21 seconds of running. (As in any futurity, owners start the gambling early—they buy into the race as soon as a horse is born, with incremental payments over the next two years.)

Winter Sports

Head 18 miles north to **Ski Apache** (575/464-3600, www.skiapache.com, $75 full-day lift ticket), which can get more than 15 feet of snow a year. Of the 55 trails, 40 percent are advanced, with a vertical drop of 1,900 feet across the mountain. Snowboarders have the run of the trails, as well as the Boneyard, a special park with all kinds of rails and jumps. Don't go driving up here just on a lark, though—Ski Run Road is dangerously narrow, so uphill traffic is banned 3pm-6pm during ski season.

The **Apache Wind Rider ZipTour** (575/464-3633, $75) gives thrill seekers a way to enjoy the mountain year-round. Parallel ziplines stretch just under nearly 9,000 feet, making the system one of the longest in the world, and riders can get going up to 65 miles per hour. The whole

excursion, starting with a gondola ride up the mountain, takes about 1.5 hours.

ENTERTAINMENT

Midtown is the place to be at night, but the track is where the action is on weekend afternoons. In Alto, **Flying J Ranch** (575/336-4330, www.flyingjranch.com, June-Aug.) is unapologetically cheesy, but it may be just the thing if you have kids to delight. Expect pony rides, staged gunfights, and gold panning, followed by a whole lotta grub and a wholesome, Opry-style stage show. The price is actually relatively old-timey too: $28 for adults, $16 for kids.

Nightlife

For margaritas and mules, **Casa Blanca** (501 Mechem Dr., 575/257-2495, 11am-8:30pm Mon.-Thurs., 11am-9pm Fri.-Sat., 11am-8pm Sun.) is the top spot, enhanced by a great patio surrounded by tall pines. After the first round of drinks and dinner, action usually moves to the two dueling mega-bars in Midtown: **The Quarters** (2535 Sudderth Dr., 575/257-9535, 11am-2am daily) and **Win, Place and Show** (2516 Sudderth Dr., 575/257-9982, 7am-1:30am Mon.-Sat., 7am-11pm Sun.), which play both kinds of music (that'd be country *and* western) to inspire some speedy two-stepping around the dance floors. The Quarters also has pool tables.

Spencer Theater for the Performing Arts

Just up the road from Ruidoso in the satellite community of Alto, the 514-seat **Spencer Theater for the Performing Arts** (108 Spencer Rd., 575/336-4800, www.spencertheater.com) hosts touring musical productions as well as local performers. The building alone, a white wedge jutting from the plain, is an attraction; the architect is New Mexican Antoine Predock, who

designed buildings as diverse as the UNM architecture school and the Hotel Santa Fe at Euro Disney. The interior features a number of Dale Chihuly glass sculptures. Call to book a free tour.

FOOD

Ruidoso's best dining is at the casual end. Many places cater to more delicate Texan palates—you'll see green chile on the menu, but it's the mildest possible form.

New Mexican

Prepare to be tempted by an assortment of New Mexican classics for breakfast and lunch at ★ **Tina's Café** (2825 Sudderth Dr., 575/257-8930, 7am-3pm Tues.-Sun., $6), as well as house specials, such as shrimp tostadas and poached salmon. They also make a satisfying chicken-fried steak and have plenty of lighter fare, including salads and soups. The wait can be long, but it's well worth it.

Mexican

El Comal (2117 Sudderth Dr., 575/258-1397, 10am-7pm Sun.-Mon. and Wed.-Fri., 11am-3:30pm Sat., $9) is known for its tamales and its *enmoladas*, tortillas doused in rich mole sauce. Look for it in the Gazebo shopping center, and enjoy a seat on the back porch.

Brewhouse

The menu at **Rio Grande Grill and Taproom** (441 Mechem Dr., 575/808-8456, 11am-9pm Tues.-Thurs. and Sun., 11am-10pm Fri.-Sat., $16) has a little bit of everything—steaks, burgers, and sandwiches—but the craft brews are the real stars here. Sierra Blanca Brewery owns the place, offering its own beers and others from around New Mexico. Their nut brown ale and pilsner are two of the standouts; they have seasonal ales as well.

Cafés

Hidden away at the small traffic circle where Sudderth Drive turns into Main Road, tiny **Peña's Place** (2963 Sudderth Dr., 575/257-4135, 7am-2pm Thurs.-Sat., 7am-1pm Sun.,

1: equine sculpture by artist Dave McGary at the Hubbard Museum of the American West **2:** Sierra Blanca Cabins **3:** Ruidoso's tree-trunk art

$8) is a homey operation, a labor of love where the owner made the wood-slab tables himself. Like just about everywhere in Ruidoso, the chile on the huevos rancheros packs exactly zero punch, but it's balanced out by stupendous blueberry-pecan whole-wheat pancakes. It's small, so go early or be prepared to wait.

Cornerstone Bakery & Café (359 Sudderth Dr., 575/257-1842, 7am-3pm Mon.-Fri., 7am-4pm Sat.-Sun., $8) helps you start the day right—with French toast, for instance, a BEST sandwich (bacon, eggs, spinach, and tomatoes), or a super-sticky sweet roll. This is many residents' and regular visitors' morning favorite, so the atmosphere is chummy, and you see a good slice of the town.

Sacred Grounds Coffee and Tea House (2704 Sudderth Dr., 575/257-2273, 7am-6pm Sun.-Thurs., 7:30am-10pm Fri.-Sat., $8) is an all-around crowd pleaser on the main drag. It's a go-to for healthy soups, wraps, and salads, plus a huge selection of baked goods and gelato. If you're up early, you can help yourself to coffee service on an honor system before the official opening time, and it stays open later than most places for dessert and coffee.

Good thing **Village Buttery** (2107 Sudderth Dr., 575/257-9251, 10:30am-2:30pm Mon.-Sat., $8) doesn't open too early, or you might be tempted to start your day with pie. For lunch, you can get hearty soups, quiches, and sandwiches with a Texan twist (pimento cheese, say) before you embark on a pie-case tour. They're best known for a dense and fairly irresistible buttermilk pie and they also have a small selection of stellar cheesecakes.

Italian

For pizza, head to super-casual **Café Rio** (2547 Sudderth Dr., 575/257-7746, 11am-8pm Sun.-Thurs., 11am-9pm Fri.-Sat., $8), which earns the local vote for best pie. All the usual toppings are on offer, along with rarer treats like artichoke hearts and capers, and the rest of the menu reflects the owners' quirky outlook, with items like shrimp jambalaya and Portuguese kale soup. You can wash it all down with a milkshake and indulge in a hot fudge sundae. It often closes Wednesday in spring and fall. Cash only.

ACCOMMODATIONS

The signature lodging of Ruidoso is the cozy wood cabin, with kitchen and fireplace, and most of these are in what's called Upper Canyon, on Main Road, which follows the river up a narrowing route. If country-cute is not to your taste, you might prefer the guesthouses at the Hurd La Rinconada Gallery in San Patricio, 20 miles east of town. The majority of the chain hotels are at the east end of town, around the Y, but it's hard to find anything decent for less than $100.

Under $100

The cheapest lodging in Ruidoso is camping. Follow Highway 48 north out of town and turn left onto Highway 532 for five miles to the **Oak Grove Campground** (mid-May-Sept., $6), with 30 sites, including a few walk-in spots that are wonderfully secluded under oak trees; you'll have to bring your own water.

$100-150

Set on the river in the Midtown area, **Sierra Blanca Cabins** (215 Country Club Rd., 575/257-2103, www.ruidoso.net/sbcabins, $139 d) are nicely outfitted one- and two-bedroom cabins that have lovely views, and a prime location not too far from Sudderth.

A key feature of **Idle Hour Lodge** (112 Lower Terrace Dr., 575/808-8484, www.idlehourlodge.com, $139 d) is its location, tucked away from the main roads yet still easy walking distance to a grocery store and restaurants in Uptown. The 12 cabins come in one- and two-bedroom configurations with full kitchens, and, in typical Ruidoso style, with wood paneling, quilts on the beds, and little porches out front.

Of the cabins in Upper Canyon, **Shadow Mountain Lodge** (107 Main Rd., 575/257-4886, www.smlruidoso.com, $139) is conveniently located at the near end, so you can easily walk into town, if you're so inclined.

You have a choice of 19 rooms in the central lodge or in four standalone cabins. All are geared to couples, with king beds in the pine-paneled lodge and queens in the cabins, which are more modern but still rustic enough. There are fireplaces and kitchenettes in all the rooms.

$150-250

There are only two alternatives to mountain-cabin style in town and neither are exactly cheap. **Escape Resort** (1016 Mechem Dr., 575/258-1234, www.theescaperesort. com, $229 d) is a cluster of five minimalist-Southwest-style casitas. Each one is enormous, with a full living room, a small kitchen, and a patio, in addition to a lavish bedroom (or two) and bath with separate tub and steam shower. Yes, it's definitely Ruidoso's upper end—but a bargain compared with what you'd pay for such digs in Santa Fe.

The other alternative is **Inn of the Mountain Gods** (287 Carrizo Canyon Rd., 800/545-9011, www.innofthemountaingods. com, $159 d, $349 suite), run by the Mescalero Apache. The guest rooms are sleek, with dark-wood furniture and modern art; some have lake views. In-house dining options are plentiful, including a pub, steakhouse, and barbecue grill. The resort's casino and theater are also popular entertainment spots that can draw national acts.

INFORMATION

The Ruidoso tourism department operates a very cheery **visitors center** (313 Cree Meadows Dr., 877/784-3676, www. discoverruidoso.com) in the village hall, positively bursting with information and helpful staff.

GETTING THERE

By car, Ruidoso is 74 miles (1.25 hours) west from Roswell on U.S. 70, 170 miles (3 hours) from Albuquerque via I-25 south and east on U.S. 380, and 115 miles (2 hours) northeast from Las Cruces via U.S. 70. **Greyhound** (800/231-2222, www.greyhound.com) stops at Apache Motel (344 Sudderth Dr., 575/257-2660) once a day from Las Cruces.

Billy the Kid National Scenic Byway

This scenic 84-mile driving route forms a triangle with Ruidoso, Tinnie, and Capitan at the points. The loop is an easy day's drive, meandering through orchards, horse farms, and deep forest. If you're feeling thorough, you can stop first at the **Billy the Kid Interpretive Center** (U.S. 70, 575/378-5318, 10am-5pm Thurs.-Tues.) in Ruidoso Downs, next to the Hubbard Museum. November-April, it closes at 4:30pm.

SAN PATRICIO

This bucolic village in a valley 20 miles east of Ruidoso glows with the sort of light painters praise—no surprise, then, that it was the home of artists Peter Hurd and Henriette Wyeth, daughter of N. C. Wyeth. Their son owns the family ranch and operates ★ **Hurd**

La Rinconada Gallery (100 Rinconada Ln., 800/658-6912, www.wyethartists.com, 9am-5pm Mon.-Sat.), which displays the family's work. It also rents some beautiful guest homes, scattered over the Wyeth land. These are an excellent alternative to staying in Ruidoso—the smallest ones ($140) are much larger and more attractive overall than what you'd find in town, furnished with original art and antiques. The original Wyeth House ($310) has an especially lovely sunroom for breakfast (but note you'll have to bring your own groceries, as breakfast is not provided, and there are no restaurants nearby).

HONDO

The **Hondo Iris Farm** (575/635-4062, 8am-5pm Tues.-Fri., 8am-4pm Sat.) is a lovely garden oasis, dedicated in part to growing iris bulbs. But just as important is the owner's gallery of dramatic handmade jewelry, all of pewter. It's a pretty place to shop and enjoy the greenery. The farm is also open on Monday during May for the iris bloom.

★ LINCOLN STATE MONUMENT

More of an open-air museum than a town, Lincoln State Monument is an artfully preserved Old West village where many of the buildings have been turned into public monuments. A stroll up and down the road is a chance to meditate on history without the distraction of souvenir vendors.

During the Lincoln County War (1878-1881), when the area was wracked by retaliatory killings triggered by a struggle to control the town dry-goods business, the national press dubbed this "the most dangerous town in America." The local feud also put Billy the Kid, who'd been causing low-grade trouble around New Mexico, in the spotlight. He burnished his outlaw reputation when he took sides with the upstart Tunstall faction and the band of "Regulators" who later sought vengeance for Tunstall's murder. Near the end of the war, Billy made a daring escape from the town jail, killing two guards in the process.

Anderson-Freeman Visitors Center & Museum

You can learn all about the Kid's exploits—as well as the Mexican families who first settled the town in 1846, and the Buffalo Soldiers who bunked at nearby Fort Sumner—at the Anderson-Freeman Visitors Center & Museum (U.S. 380, 8:30am-4:30pm daily, $5). Then tour the other buildings in town, which have been filled with period furnishings and small historical displays. (A couple of them are open only April-October and are generally open 9am-5pm daily.) The Tunstall Store—which started the whole fracas—is kitted out with 19th-century stock, and you can see the holes in the courthouse wall where Billy the Kid fired bullets as he made his getaway.

Food and Accommodations

"No guests gunned down in over 100 years," boasts the Wortley Hotel (U.S. 380, 575/653-4300, www.wortleyhotel.com, $125 d), which was formerly owned by Sheriff Pat Garrett. The historic building is smack in the middle of town, so after visiting the museums, you can toddle over here and settle into a rocking chair on the porch, and feel like you're part of the exhibit. The five whitewashed rooms, all with corner fireplaces, are simply furnished with appropriate antiques; there's also a suite ($199) and two larger family rooms (from $125). New owners as of 2016 gave the place a fresh coat of paint and serve an exceptional breakfast.

The beautiful Dolan House (U.S. 380, 575/653-4670, 9am-3:30pm Fri.-Tues., $10), a restored adobe in the center of the village, also serves a good breakfast and lunch with a salad buffet in the summer. It also has a single room for overnight stays ($100).

In a stone house with blue trim, Annie's Little Sure Shot (1068 Calle La Placita, 575/653-4045, 10am-5pm Tues.-Sat., $4), is a funky coffeehouse and art gallery. Stop in for a pick-me-up latte, Italian soda, or lavender lemonade to sip while strolling.

FORT STANTON

A well-signed detour off U.S. 380 on Highway 220, Fort Stanton is one of the largest historic military outposts in the West. Its buildings were made of stone, rather than adobe, so the complex looks remarkably intact, and the tree-shaded grounds are pleasant for a picnic. A small but interesting museum (575/354-0341, 10am-4pm Mon.-Sat., noon-4pm Sun. Mar.-Dec., 11am-3pm Mon.-Thurs., 10am-4pm Fri.-Sat., noon-4pm Sun. Jan.-Feb., free) details the fort's myriad uses, from staging ground for the Indian Wars to a tent hospital for tuberculosis patients to internment camp for hundreds of German sailors in World War II (alas, the swimming pool these industrious men built is in ruins). It stops short of more recent uses—as a women's prison and drug-rehab center—before it was made a state monument in 2007.

Fort Stanton-Snowy River Cave National Conservation Area

About 1.5 miles before reaching the fort on Highway 220 is the **Fort Stanton-Snowy River National Conservation Area** (575/354-0099), a wilderness reserve most remarkable for being set over the state's third-largest cave system, though it's currently closed to protect bat life. More accessibly, the area is cut through with over 70 miles of horse and hiking trails, including a two-mile-long trail that passes by a rock marked by petroglyphs made by the Jornada Mogollon people who lived in the area more than 2,000 years ago. There's a kiosk with trail maps at the **Rob Jaggers Campground** (developed sites $5), one of two campgrounds within the reserve; you can also pick up a trail map at the fort museum.

CAPITAN

Capitan is all about Smokey Bear, the tiny cub discovered clinging to a tree after a fire raged across 17,000 acres in the Capitan Mountains in 1950. Badly burned, the cub was nursed back to health, dubbed "Smokey," and eventually shipped off to the National Zoo in Washington DC, where a generation of schoolkids got to visit the living symbol of fire prevention. (The image of Smokey Bear

was invented in 1944—but the campaign didn't catch on until the real, adorable bear took over the mantle.) Smokey died in 1976, but, like Elvis, his spirit lives on, especially here in Capitan, where he's buried, and where nearly every business name is some ursine pun. The place really goes crazy for **Smokey Bear Days** (www.smokebeardays.com), on the first weekend in May.

The state forestry office operates **Smokey Bear Historical Park** (118 W. Smokey Bear Blvd., 575/354-2748, www.smokeybearpark. com, 9am-5pm daily, $2). It's a bit dry, in a 1970s-education way, though kids will probably be impressed by the displays of forest-fighting gear, and adults might be interested to see how the fire-prevention ads have changed over the years. There's also a short walking trail to Smokey's grave.

Food

A lovely surprise in this tiny town, **Renee's Real Food** (435 Smokey Bear Blvd., 575/973-0351, 10am-3pm Tues.-Sat., $7) is just that—an eclectic, unpretentious menu cooked from scratch. Depending on the chef's whim, you may encounter shrimp po'boys, meatball sandwiches, and, at weekend brunch, crème brûlée French toast. One constant is handmade bagels, hot and fresh at opening time, and pizza on Thursday.

Northern Tularosa Basin

Both U.S. 70 and U.S. 380 descend to meet U.S. 54, which runs north through a broad, dry valley between the Sacramento and San Andres Mountains. Much of it is part of the White Sands Missile Range, which does industrial and military testing.

THREE RIVERS PETROGLYPH SITE

Five miles off U.S. 54, in an unremarkable stretch between Tularosa and Carrizozo, the BLM-managed **Three Rivers Petroglyph Site** (575/525-4300, 8am-7pm daily Apr.-Oct., 8am-5pm Nov.-Mar., $5/car) is easy enough to drive right past. A trail leads up to a series of low hills, marked by volcanic rock that appears to cover the ridgeline like scabs. Look carefully, and you'll soon see why these 50 acres are protected: The dark rocks are scored with thousands of intricate designs—lizards, mountain goats, snakes, checkerboards, spirals. Because it's so far from any modern settlement, the area has barely been marred by more recent carving (as the West Mesa in Albuquerque has). Archaeologists estimate that the inscriptions here date from between 900 and 1400, when the Mogollon people had a settlement nearby (a separate short trail leads to its remnants), and the farther off the trail you go, the more carvings you'll see.

Farther down County Road B-30 about eight miles, just at the base of massive Sierra Blanca, **Three Rivers Campground** ($7-18) is a very pretty place with tent and RV sites, a creek running nearby, and trails up into the hills. Unlike high-elevation campgrounds, this one is open year-round, and it's rarely crowded.

CARRIZOZO

The seat of Lincoln County, Carrizozo was a booming railroad town until the early 1950s, but now is most notable for its gallery scene. **Gallery 408** (408 12th St., 575/648-2598, 10am-5pm Mon. and Fri.-Sat., noon-5pm Sun.) exhibits fine abstract and modern art and is responsible for the painted burros around town. **Tularosa Basin Gallery of Photography** (401 12th St., 575/937-1489, 10am-5pm Mon. and Thurs.-Sat., noon-5pm Sun.) is the largest photography gallery in the state. All works are by New Mexico photographers and of the Land of Enchantment. **Carrizozo Heritage Museum** (103 12th St., 575/937-6555, 10am-2pm Thurs.-Sun. Mar.-Nov.) has a small collection devoted to local history, some model trains, and a very large collection of barbed wire.

At the corner of Central Avenue and Airport Road, one block south of the intersection of U.S. 54 and U.S. 380, the **chamber of commerce** (575/648-2732, www.carrizozochamber.org, 10am-2pm Fri.-Sun.) has its office in a vintage caboose. If it's not open, you can grab brochures from the display outside—one is a very detailed walking/driving tour of all the old buildings in town.

VALLEY OF FIRES NATIONAL RECREATION AREA

Four miles west of Carrizozo on U.S. 380, the little-visited **Valley of Fires National Recreation Area** (575/648-2241, $3 pp or $5/car) is far smaller than the more commonly visited El Malpais National Monument, west of Albuquerque. But the geology is striking because it's the product of a more recent explosion, just 1,500 years ago; the rocks here are still shiny, craggy, and often a very dramatic black, unlike the duller, almost purple hue of older volcanic stone. Up close, you'll be surprised at how much scrubby greenery has managed to grow—a short paved **nature trail** leads around part of the site.

The **campground** ($7-18) has 19 sites, most with electricity hookups, as well as showers and restrooms. The tent sites are in a very nice secluded gully.

★ TRINITY SITE

Deep within the Jornada del Muerto desert, this portion of White Sands Missile Range, where the first atomic bomb was detonated on July 16, 1945, is open to the public only on the first Saturday in April and October. The gate is open 8am-2pm; the site closes at 3:30pm. If this happens to coincide with your schedule, do try to go. At first, it doesn't seem there's much to see beyond the ranch house where the bomb was assembled and the small depression left by the explosion, but then small details, such as shards of the green glassy substance that the heat of the bomb created on the desert floor, pop out as you look around. Perhaps the most disturbing thing about the place is just how normal it looks.

Access is via the Stallion Gate to the missile range, off U.S. 380, at a southbound turn 53 miles west of Carrizozo or 12 miles east of San Antonio. Contact the missile range public affairs office (575/678-1134, www.wsmr.army.mil) to confirm dates and directions. A car convoy makes the 72-mile drive from Alamogordo, starting in the Tularosa High School parking lot; contact Alamogordo's chamber of commerce (575/437-6120) for details.

WHITE OAKS

It's worth the nine-mile detour to White Oaks for a lesson in impermanence: Unbelievably, this used to be the second-largest city in New Mexico, after Las Vegas, and now it's a rough settlement of a couple dozen hardy creative types. Its social heart is the No Scum Allowed Saloon (575/648-5583, 6pm-9pm Wed., 4pm-9pm Thurs., noon-2am Fri.-Sat., noon-6pm Sun.), cheerier than its name suggests and also well worth the drive—you might stumble on amazing fiddle playing or a biker bash.

The bar is open year-round, but the rest of this former mining settlement is near-silent in the off-season. At the end of April, it opens with its annual artist studio tour. The most intriguing buildings—such as spooky, fenced-off Hoyle's Castle to the south, and the equally looming Gumm House, on the north side—are closed to visitors, but the brick schoolhouse and a little miner's home both contain small museums open weekends in the summer. In June, Gold Rush Days offers a parade, vendors, and exhibitions.

Look for the turn for White Oaks off U.S. 54 three miles north of Carrizozo; head east on Highway 349.

Background

The Landscape

Sharp peaks, deep gorges, harsh desert, sweeping plains—everything about New Mexico's landscape is dramatic. The light glints off surfaces at surprising angles, and the scenery can change at any bend in the road. The altitude ranges from around 2,800 feet down by the Texas border to more than 13,000 at Wheeler Peak north of Taos, but the average is about 5,700 feet, more than a mile high. So even if the scenery doesn't make you gasp for breath, the thin air might.

GEOGRAPHY AND GEOLOGY

Much of New Mexico's landscape is the product of volcanic activity that ceased (at least for now) around the year AD 500. The main mountain ranges, which form part of the **Continental Divide**, are relatively young, pushed up in the Eocene era between 55 million and 34 million years ago, when shock waves from the collision of the North American plate and the Farallon plate caused the continent to heave.

Just a few million years later, the **Rio Grande Rift**—one of the biggest rift valleys in the world—formed, as eras' and eras' worth of accumulated rock was pulled apart by shifting faults, leaving the perfect path for the Rio Grande when it began to flow about three million years ago. The water carved deep canyons, such as the 800-foot-deep gorge west of Taos. These canyons are perfect slices of geologic time, layers of limestone, sandstone, clay, and lava neatly stacked up.

A million years ago, a volcano's violent eruption and subsequent collapse created the huge **Valles Caldera**, and the jagged edges of the crater have barely softened in the intervening time. Only 1,500 years ago, in the Tularosa basin, molten lava hardened into black badlands. One tangible benefit of the state's volcanic activity is the numerous hot springs, especially in the young Jemez Mountains (15 million years old).

Beneath all this is evidence of a more stable time. For some four billion years, the land was completely underwater, then spent hundreds of millions of years supporting prehistoric sealife—hence the marine fossils found at the top of the Sandia Mountains, 10,000 feet above the current sea level. Dinosaurs, too, flourished for a time. One of the first, the nimble meat-eater *Coelophysis*, lived during the Triassic period around Abiquiu, but all of them were apparently killed at once, perhaps by a flash flood. Another product of the dinosaur age (specifically, the Jurassic) was the lurid red, pink, and orange sandstone. It began as a vast desert, then petrified into the very symbol of the American Southwest, and is visible around Abiquiu as well as Jemez Pueblo.

CLIMATE

For the most part, altitude determines the climate in New Mexico, where central Albuquerque, in the river valley, can be crisp and cloudless while Sandia Peak, 20 miles away and almost 5,000 feet up, is caught in a blinding snowstorm. (Yes, it snows plenty in New Mexico.) Nowhere, though, is it a particularly gentle climate; expect sudden changes in weather and temperature extremes.

At the lower elevations, winter is cold—days usually between 40°F and 55°F—but rarely cloudy, with a few snowstorms that never add up to as much moisture as people hope. Come spring, which starts in late April or May, the number of wildflowers that dot the hills is a direct reflection of the previous winter's precipitation. The higher the elevation, the later the spring: At 8,500 feet, snow could still be on the ground in May. Little rain falls in May and June, typically the hottest and windiest months of the year, with temperatures climbing into the 90s—though it can still drop to the 50s at night.

By early or mid-July, the so-called monsoon season brings heavy, refreshing downpours and thunderstorms every afternoon for a couple of months. If you're out hiking in this season, steer clear of narrow canyons and arroyos during and after rains, as they can fill with powerful, deadly flash floods in a matter of minutes. Summer nights are rarely too warm.

September, October, and November are again dry, with the temperature dipping lower each month. Snow can often start falling in late October or November, although in recent years, overall winter precipitation has

---

Previous: Valley of Fires National Recreation Area.

been quite low, so it takes months for a good base layer to build up at the ski areas.

ENVIRONMENTAL ISSUES

For thousands of years, New Mexicans have faced a water shortage. In prehistoric times, farming in the river valley was relatively easy, if subject to flooding. But at higher elevations, mountain streams had to be channeled into irrigation ditches. This system was perfected by Spanish settlers, who called their ditches *acequias,* a word they'd learned from the Arabs (*as-saqiya*), who used the system to cultivate the Iberian Peninsula.

Today, as an ever-growing population demands more amenities, traditional ways of managing water have given way to more complex legal wranglings and outright hostility (*No chingen con nuestra agua*—don't f—k with our water—reads a bumper sticker on some trucks in northern New Mexico). Some 49 billion gallons are pumped out of the middle Rio Grande aquifer every year, and only a portion of that is replenished through mountain runoff. Albuquerque

started using filtered river water in late 2008. "Smart growth" gets lip service in city council meetings, although construction continues apace on Albuquerque's arid West Mesa. Neo-homesteaders install cisterns to catch rain, as well as systems to reuse gray water, but these features are still far from standard.

Years of relative drought can make tinderboxes of the forests. In a few weeks in the summer of 2012, for instance, the Whitewater-Baldy fire in the Gila National Forest burned almost 300,000 acres, the largest recorded fire in New Mexico history (almost double the scale of the previous record-setter, near Los Alamos the year before).

Visitors to New Mexico can help by following local environmental policies: Take scrupulous care with fire in the wilderness (no campfires, of course), and follow drought measures such as keeping showers short. Golfers may want to consider curtailing their play here. New courses, improbably, have been installed at every new casino resort and high-end residential development, despite the fact that they're intense draws on the water table.

Plants and Animals

Just as humans have managed to eke a life out of New Mexico, so have plants and animals—and a rather large variety of them. The state supports the fourth most diverse array of wildlife in the country.

PLANTS

Although much of the plant growth in New Mexico is nominally evergreen, the landscape skews toward brown, until you get up to the wetter alpine elevations.

Vegetation Zones

Below 4,500 feet, New Mexico's **Lower Sonoran** zone, in the river valleys in the southern part of the state, is dotted with cactus, yucca, and scrubby creosote bushes. The

Upper Sonoran zone, covering the areas between 4,500 and 7,000 feet, is the largest vegetation zone in the state and includes the high plains in the northeast and most of Albuquerque and Santa Fe, where the Sandia and Sangre de Cristo foothills are covered with juniper and piñon trees. The **Transition** zone, 7,000-8,500 feet, sees a few more stately trees, such as ponderosa pine, and the state's more colorful wildflowers: orange Indian paintbrush, bright red penstemon, purple lupine. Above 8,500 feet, the **Mixed Conifer** zone harbors that sort of tree, along with clusters of aspens. The **Subalpine** zone, starting at 9,500 feet, is home to Engelmann spruce and bristlecone pine, while 11,500 feet marks the tree line in most places and the beginning

Leave No Trace

So as not to upset the rather precarious environmental balance in much of New Mexico, you should internalize the ethic of "leave no trace"—even on a short stroll. Let the phrase first guide your trip in the **planning** stages, when you equip yourself with good maps and GPS tools or a compass, to avoid relying on rock cairns or blazes. Backpackers should repackage food and other items to minimize the waste to pack out. And everyone should try to keep group size under six people; pets should not go in wild areas.

On the trail, resist the urge to cut across switchbacks. Stick to the center of the trail, even if it has been widened by others trying to avoid mud. Be quiet, to avoid disturbing wildlife and other hikers. Leave what you find, whether plants, rocks, or potsherds.

Camp only where others have, in durable areas, at least 200 feet from water sources; dig cat holes 200 feet away, too. Pack out your toilet paper and other personal waste, and scatter dishwater and toothpaste. Safeguard food in "bear bags" hung at least 15 feet off the ground. Campfires are typically banned in New Mexico—please honor this policy, and keep a close eye on camp stoves. Pack out all cigarette butts.

Day hikers should also maintain a strict policy regarding litter. Tossing an orange peel, apple core, or other biodegradable item along the trail may not cause an environmental disaster, but it reminds other hikers that humans have been there and intrudes on the natural solitude of New Mexico's wilderness.

For more information, contact **Leave No Trace** (http://lnt.org).

of the **Alpine** zone, where almost no greenery survives. At 11,973 feet, the top of Sierra Blanca, near Ruidoso, is the southernmost example of this zone in the United States.

Trees and Grasses

Trees are the clearest marker of elevation. In low areas—such as the Chihuahuan Desert outside of Las Cruces—you'll see almost no trees, only assorted cacti, such as the common **cane cholla;** the spiky **yucca** plant, which produces towering stalks of blooms in May; and the humble **tumbleweed.** Along the Rio Grande and the Pecos River, thirsty **cottonwoods** provide dense shade; the biggest trees, with their gnarled, branching trunks, are centuries old. In spring, their cotton fills the air—hell for the allergic, but the source of a distinctive spicy fragrance—and in fall, their leaves turn pure yellow. Willow and olive are also common.

Everywhere in the foothills grows **piñon** (also spelled "pinyon"), the scrubby state tree that's slow-growing and drought-resistant, evolved to endure the New Mexican climate. When burned, its wood produces the scent of a New Mexico winter night, and its cones yield tasty nuts. Alongside piñon is **shaggy-bark juniper,** identifiable by its loose strips of bark, sprays of soft needles, and branches that look twisted by the wind. In season, it's studded with purple-gray berries—another treat for foraging humans and animals alike. At ground level in the foothills, also look for clumps of sagebrush and bear grass, which blooms in huge, creamy tufts at the ends of stalks up to six feet tall.

Up in the mountains, the trees are a bit taller. Here you'll find the towering **ponderosa pine,** with its thick, almost crusty chunks of reddish-black bark; the crevices smell distinctly of vanilla. At slightly higher elevations, dense stands of **aspens** provide a rare spot of fall color in the evergreen forests. The combination of their golden leaves and white bark creates a particularly magical glow, especially in the mountains near Santa Fe. The highest mountain areas are home to a number of dense-needled hardy pines, such as blue-green **Engelmann spruce, corkbark fir, bristlecone pines,** and **subalpine fir,** with its sleek, rounded pinecones. Hike your way up to stands of these, which are tall but with sparse branches, and you'll know you're close to the peak.

ANIMALS

As with plants, what you see depends on whether you're down in the desert or up on the mountain slopes. And you'll have to look carefully, because a lot of the animals that have survived here this long are the sort that blend in with their surroundings—which means there are a lot of brown critters.

Mammals

In the open, low-elevation areas on Albuquerque's fringes (and sometimes in the occasional vacant urban lot), look for **prairie dogs,** which live in huge underground warrens. When you're camping, the first creatures you'll meet are **squirrels** and **chipmunks**—at higher elevations, look out for Abert's squirrel, with its tufted ears and extra-fluffy tail. Long-haunched, clever, and highly adaptable, **coyotes** roam the lower elevations and are not shy about nosing around backyards; they make a barking yelp at night.

On the plains, you may see **pronghorns** (often called pronghorn antelope, though they are not related to true antelope) springing through the grasses, while long-eared **mule deer** flourish in mountain forests, such as the Pecos Wilderness. Herds of **elk** live in the high valleys; Rocky Mountain elk are common, thanks to an aggressive reintroduction effort in the early 20th century to make up for overhunting. A group of the largest variety, Roosevelt elk, whose fanlike antlers are the stuff of dreams for trophy hunters, roams in Valles Caldera. **Bighorn sheep** live in the mountains around Taos and in the Gila Wilderness.

Taos is also a hot spot for **North American river otters,** which were reintroduced in the rivers in Taos Pueblo starting in 2008—after their absence from the whole state for some 55 years. The small aquatic mammals seem to be flourishing and can now be spotted in the Rio Grande and tributaries, from the Colorado border to Cochiti Dam.

Black bears crash around the forests, though their name is misleading—at any given time, they can be brown, cinnamon-red, or even nearly blond. (Smokey Bear, the mascot of the National Forest Service, was from New Mexico, a cub rescued from a forest fire in the southern town of Capitan.) Drought often drives the omnivorous beasts into suburban trash cans to forage, with tragic results for both people and the animals. Campers are strongly urged to pack food in bear-proof canisters.

And then there's the elusive **jackalope,** a jackrabbit sporting elaborate antlers. Alas, it seems now to appear only on postcards, although you may occasionally see a taxidermied head in a curio shop.

Birds

New Mexico's state bird is the impressive **roadrunner:** It grows up to two feet long, nests in the ground, feeds on insects and even rattlesnakes, and has feet specially adapted to racing on sandy ground. It can be spotted at lower desert elevations. Blue-and-black **Steller's jays** and raucous all-blue **piñon jays** are common in the foothills and farther up in the mountains, where you can also see **bluebirds, black-masked mountain chickadees,** and **Clark's nutcrackers,** which hoard great stashes of piñon nuts for winter. Also look around for **woodpeckers,** including the three-toed variety, which lives at higher elevations. On the highest peaks are **white-tailed ptarmigans,** which blend in with their snowy environment. But you can't miss the yellow-and-red **western tanager,** a vivid shot of tropical delight in the Transition zone forests.

In late summer, keep an eye out for tiny, red-throated **rufous hummingbirds** on their way to Mexico for the winter, along with hundreds of other birds that use the center of the state as a migratory corridor. The Sandia Mountains and the Las Vegas National Wildlife Refuge, among other spots, are on the flight path for **red-tailed hawks, eagles,** and other raptors, especially numerous in the springtime.

With more than 450 species spotted in New Mexico, this list is only scraping the surface. If you're a dedicated birder, first contact the **Randall Davey Audubon Center** in Santa Fe, which leads bird walks, or the **Rio Grande Nature Center** in Albuquerque. **Bosque del Apache National Wildlife Refuge,** south of Albuquerque, is a must in the winter when thousands of **sandhill cranes**—and even the occasional rare **whooping crane**—rest in the wetlands. In the southeast near Roswell, the **Bitter Lake National Wildlife Refuge** is an annual stop for hundreds of migrating birds. Bill West of **WingsWest Birding** (505/989-3804, www.wingswestbirding. com) is a reputable guide who has been leading groups around New Mexico since 1996. Tours range from half-day options to multiday outings.

Fish

Trout is the major endemic fish, found in the cold waters of the Rio Grande as well as the San Juan, Chama, and Pecos Rivers. The cutthroat is particularly beloved in New Mexico—the only variety of trout originally found on the eastern side of the Continental Divide. (The more aggressive rainbow and brown trout are interlopers.) The Rio Grande cutthroat, the official state fish, is now quite uncommon. Another local fish in jeopardy is the **Rio Grande silvery minnow,** listed as endangered since 1994. The last of the Rio Grande's five native fish, it's in such a dire state that biologists have scooped them out of the water individually during dry spells and taken them to the Albuquerque aquarium for safekeeping.

Reptiles

One can't step foot in the desert without thinking of **rattlesnakes,** and New Mexico has plenty of them, usually hidden away under rocks and brush, but very occasionally sunning themselves in full view. The predominant species in the Rio Grande Valley, the **Western diamondback,** can grow to be seven feet long. Although its venom is relatively weak, it has an impressive striking distance of almost three feet. Around Taos and Santa Fe, the main species is the **prairie rattlesnake,** which is only four feet long at most; the threatened **New Mexico ridgenose** is only about two feet long. The snakes you're more likely to encounter, however, are **bull snakes.** Though often mistaken for rattlesnakes due to similar size and colorings, they're not venomous.

More benign cold-blooded critters include **lizards,** such as the **short-horned lizard** (aka horny toad), a miniature dinosaur, in effect, about as big as your palm. Look for it in the desert and the scrubby foothills.

Insects and Arachnids

Because it's so dry, New Mexico isn't teeming with bugs. The ones that are there, however, can be off-putting, particularly if you chance upon the springtime **tarantula migration,** usually in May around Albuquerque. It's not a true seasonal relocation, just the time when males come out of their dens to prowl for mates. The fist-size spiders move hundreds at a time, and occasionally back roads are closed to let them pass. If you'll be camping in the desert in the spring, ask the ranger's office about the status. Though they're big and hairy, they're not venomous.

Scorpions, though, can be more dangerous, if very rarely deadly. In the southern desert areas, the most common variety is the bark scorpion, which nestles in rock crevices and woodpiles and can find its way into your shoes or the bottom of your sleeping bag. Its sting can cause anything from severe pain to difficulty breathing and should be treated with antivenin as soon as possible. Hardshelled, segmented **desert centipedes** are another local creepy-crawly; they're often out at night and can grow up to nine inches long.

History

The historical and cultural continuity in New Mexico is remarkable. The state has been transformed from ice-age hunting ground to home of the atom bomb, but many people claim roots that stretch back hundreds, even thousands, of years.

ANCIENT AND ARCHAIC CIVILIZATION

New Mexico was one of the first places to harbor humans after the end of the last ice age. Archaeological findings indicate that some 12,000 years ago, people were hunting mastodons and other big game across the state. Mammoth bones, arrowheads, and the remains of campfires have been found in the Sandia Mountains east of Albuquerque; Folsom, in northeastern New Mexico; and Clovis, in the south. Sometime between 8000 and 5000 BC, these bands of hunters formed a small temporary settlement just north of Albuquerque, but it was not enough to stave off the decline of that ancient culture, as climatic shifts caused the big game to die off. Nomadic hunter-gatherers, seeking out smaller animals as well as seeds and nuts, did better in the new land, and by 1000 BC, they had established communities built around clusters of pit houses—sunken, log-covered rooms dug into the earth.

Along with this new form of shelter came an equally important advance in food: Mexican people gave corn kernels (maize) and lessons in agriculture to their neighbors, the Mogollon, who occupied southern New Mexico and Arizona. By AD 400, the Mogollon had begun growing squash and beans as well and had established concentrated communities all around the southern Rio Grande basin. This culture, dubbed the Basketmakers by archaeologists, also developed its own pottery, another skill learned from the indigenous people of Mexico. So when the Mogollon made contact with the Ancestral Puebloans (also known as the Anasazi) in the northern part of the state, they had plenty to share.

THE PUEBLOS

The year 700 marks the beginning of what archaeologists call the Pueblo I phase, when disparate groups began to form larger communities in the upland areas on either side of the northern Rio Grande. Pit houses were still in use, but aboveground buildings of clay and sticks were erected alongside them. Increasingly, the pit houses were sacred spaces, chambers in which religious ceremonies were carried out; these are now known as kivas and are still an integral part of pueblo life.

The Pueblo II era began in 850 and is distinguished by the rise of Pueblo Bonito in Chaco Canyon, northwest of Santa Fe, into a full-scale city and perhaps capital of a small state. It was home to an estimated 1,500 people ruled by a religious elite. But Chaco abruptly began to crumble around 1150, perhaps due to drought, famine, or warfare. This shift marked the Pueblo III period, when the people who were to become today's Puebloans began building their easily defended cliff dwellings—most famously in the Four Corners area, at Mesa Verde in present-day Colorado, but also farther south, on the Pajarito Plateau in what's now Bandelier National Monument, and in Puyé, on Santa Clara Pueblo land. A drought at the end of the 13th century cleared out the Four Corners at the start of the Pueblo IV era, provoking the population to consolidate along the Rio Grande in clusters of sometimes more than a thousand interconnected rooms. These communities dotted the riverbank, drawing their sustenance both from the river water and from the mountains behind them.

THE SPANISH ARRIVE

These settlements were what the Spanish explorer Francisco Vásquez de Coronado and his crew saw when they first ventured into the area in 1540. Their Spanish word for the villages, *pueblos*, stuck and is still the name for both the places and the people who live in them. Coronado wasn't impressed, however, because the pueblos were made out of mud, not gold as he had been hoping. So after two years and a couple of skirmishes with the natives, the team turned around and headed back to Mexico City.

It took another 50 years for the Spanish to muster more interest in the area. This time, in 1598, Don Juan de Oñate led a small group of Spanish families to settle on the banks of the Rio Grande, at a place they called San Gabriel, near Ohkay Owingeh (which they called San Juan Pueblo). About a decade later, the settlers moved away from their American Indian neighbors, to the new village of Santa Fe. The territory's third governor, Don Pedro de Peralta, made it the official capital of the territory of Nuevo México, which in those days stretched far into what is now Colorado and Arizona.

This time the colonists, mostly farmers, were motivated not so much by hopes of striking it rich but simply of making a living. Moreover, they were inspired by Catholic zeal, and Franciscan missionaries accompanied them to promote the faith among the Puebloans. It was partly these missionaries and their ruthless oppression of the native religion that drove the Indians to organize the Pueblo Revolt of 1680. The Franciscans' "conversion" strategy involved public executions of the pueblos' medicine men, among other violent assaults on local traditions. But the Spanish colonists were no help either. In their desperation to squeeze wealth out of the hard land, they exploited the only resource they had, the slave labor of the Indians, who were either conscripts or stolen from their families. (The Indians did some poaching from Spanish families, too, creating a violent sort of cultural exchange program.)

The leader of the Pueblo Revolt was a man named Popé (also spelled Po'pay), from San Juan Pueblo. Using Taos Pueblo as his base, he traveled to the other communities, secretly meeting with leaders to plan a united insurrection. Historians theorize he may have used Spanish to communicate with other Puebloans who did not speak his native Tewa, and he distributed among the conspirators lengths of knotted rope with which to count down the days to the insurrection. Although the Spanish captured a few of the rope-bearing messengers (Isleta Pueblo may never have gotten the message, which could explain its being the only pueblo not to participate), they could not avert the bloodshed. The Puebloan warriors killed families and missionaries, burned crops, and toppled churches. Santa Fe was besieged, and its population of more than 1,000 finally evacuated in a pitiful retreat.

The Spanish stayed away for 12 years, but a new governor, Diego de Vargas, took it upon himself to reclaim the area. He managed to talk many pueblos into peaceful surrender, meeting resistance only in Taos and Santa Fe, where a two-day fight was required to oust the Indians from the Palace of the Governors; in Taos, violence ground on for an additional four years. The Spanish strategy in the post-revolt era was softer, with more compromise between the Franciscans and their intended flock, and a fair amount of cultural and economic exchange. The threat of raiding Comanche, Apache, and Navajo also forced both sides to cooperate. Banding together for defense, they were finally able to drive the Comanche away, culminating in a 1778 battle with Chief Cuerno Verde (Green Horn). The decisive victory is celebrated in the ritual dance called Los Comanches, still performed in small villages by Hispanos and Puebloans alike.

The other bonding force was trade. The Spanish maintained the Camino Real de Tierra Adentro (Royal Road of the Interior), which linked Santa Fe with central Mexico—the route follows roughly the line carved by

I-25 today. Caravans came through only every year or two, but the profit from furs, pottery, textiles, and other local goods was enough to keep both cultures afloat, if utterly dependent on the Spanish government.

MEXICAN INDEPENDENCE AND THE FIRST ANGLOS

Spain carefully guarded all of its trade routes in the New World, even in a relatively unprofitable territory like Nuevo México. The only outside trade permitted was through the Comancheros, a ragtag band who traded with Comanche and other Plains Indians, working well into what would later be Oklahoma and even up to North Dakota. The Spanish governor encouraged them because their tight relationship with the Comanche helped protect New Mexico and Texas against intruders.

Interlopers were not welcome. Only a few enterprising fur trappers, lone mountain men in search of beaver pelts, slipped in. Spy-explorer Zebulon Pike and his crew were captured (perhaps intentionally, so Pike could get more inside information) and detained in Santa Fe for a spell in 1807. But in 1821, Mexico declared independence from Spain, liberating the territory of Nuevo México along with it. One of the first acts of the new government was to open the borders to trade. Initially just a trickle of curious traders came down the rough track from St. Louis, Missouri, but soon a flood of commerce flowed along the increasingly rutted and broad Santa Fe Trail, making the territory's capital city a meeting place between Mexicans and Americans swapping furs, gold, cloth, and more.

THE MEXICAN-AMERICAN WAR AND AFTER

Pike's expedition gave the U.S. government new details about the locations of Spanish forts. Just as important, Pike, who returned not long after Lewis and Clark completed their march across the Louisiana Purchase, helped fuel the country's expansionist fervor. In the next few decades, "manifest destiny" became the phrase on every American's lips, and the government was eyeing the Southwest. It annexed Texas in 1845, but New Mexico, with its small population and meager resources, didn't figure heavily in the short-lived war that followed. The Mexican governor surrendered peacefully to General Stephen Kearny when he arrived in Santa Fe in 1846. In Taos, the transition was not accepted so readily, as Hispano business leaders and Taos Pueblo Indians instigated a brief but violent uprising, in which the first American governor, Charles Bent, was beheaded.

During the Civil War, New Mexico was in the way of a Texan Confederate strategy to secure the Southwest, but the rebels were thwarted in 1862 at the Battle of Glorieta Pass. The territory stayed in the hands of the Union until the end of the war, and people were more concerned with the local, increasingly brutal skirmishes caused by the arrival in Santa Fe of Bishop Jean-Baptiste Lamy, a tyrannical—or at least very thoughtless—Frenchman who tried to impose a European vision of the Catholic Church on a populace that had been beyond centralized control for centuries.

Even more significant to New Mexico's development was the arrival of the railroad in 1880, as it was laid through Raton Pass, near Santa Fe, and close to Albuquerque. Virtually overnight, strange goods and even stranger people came pouring into one of the remoter frontier outposts of the United States. Anglo influence was suddenly everywhere, in the form of new architecture (red brick was an Eastern affectation) and new business. Albuquerque, almost directly on the new railway tracks, boomed, while Santa Fe's fortunes slumped and Taos all but withered away, having peaked back in the late days of the Camino Real.

But while wheeler-dealers were setting up shop in central New Mexico, some more intrepid souls were poking around in the less-connected areas farther north. These tourists were artists who valued New Mexico not for its commercial potential but for its dramatic landscapes and exotic populace who seemed untouched by American ways. From the early 20th century on, Santa Fe and Taos were cultivated as art colonies, a function they still fulfill today.

FROM STATEHOOD TO WORLD WAR II

Based on its burgeoning economy, New Mexico became the 47th state in the union in 1912, effectively marking the end of the frontier period, a phase of violence, uncertainty, and isolation that lasted about 300 years, longer here than anywhere else in the United States. In addition to the painters and writers flocking to the new state, another group of migrants arrived: tuberculosis patients. Soon the state was known as a health retreat, and countless people did stints in its dry air to treat their ailing lungs.

One of these patients was J. Robert Oppenheimer, whose mild case of TB got him packed off to a camp near Pecos for a year after high school. He loved northern New Mexico and got to know some of its more hidden pockets. So when the U.S. Army asked him if he had an idea where it should establish a secret base for the Manhattan Project, he knew just the place: a little camp high on a plateau above Santa Fe, named Los Alamos. This was the birthplace of the atomic bomb, a weird, close-knit community of the country's greatest scientific minds (and biggest egos), working in utter secrecy. Only after the bomb was tested at White Sands and Fat Man and Little Boy were dropped over Japan was the mysterious camp's mission revealed.

CONTEMPORARY HISTORY

The A-bomb ushered New Mexico into the modern era. Not only was it world-changing technology, but it also boosted the local economy. High-paying support staff jobs at Los Alamos and Kirtland Air Force Base in Albuquerque pulled some of the population away from subsistence farming and into a life that involved cars and electricity. But even so, the character of the state remained conservative and closed, so when the 1960s rolled around and New Mexico's empty space looked like the promised land to hippies, the culture clash was fierce. Staunch Catholic farmers took potshots at their naked, hallucinogen-ingesting neighbors who fantasized about getting back to the land but had no clue how to do it. After a decade or so, though, only the hardiest of the commune-dwellers were left, and they'd mellowed a bit, while the locals had come to appreciate at least their enthusiasm. Even if the communes didn't last, hippie culture has proven remarkably persistent in New Mexico. Even today, distinctly straight Hispanos can be heard saying things like, "I was tripping out on that band, man," and the state still welcomes Rainbow Gatherings, would-be Buddhists, and alternative healers.

The end of the 20th century saw unprecedented growth in both Albuquerque and Santa Fe. As usual, Albuquerque got the practical-minded development, such as the Intel chip-manufacturing plant and the services headquarters for Gap Inc., while Santa Fe was almost felled by its own artsiness, turned inside-out during a few frenzied years in the early 1990s when movie stars and other moneyed types bought up prime real estate. In just a matter of months, rents went up tenfold and houses started selling for more than $1 million. Santa Fe has yet to work out the imbalance between its creative forces, which did save the city from utter decline, and economic ones, though it implemented a living-wage law in 2009. The state's capital has drawn both praise and ire for standing firm in its stance as a sanctuary city, even in the face of possible cuts in federal funding as a result.

Meanwhile, Taos has grown slowly but steadily, as have the pueblos, thanks to the legalization of gambling on their lands, but all of these communities still have an air of old New Mexico, where the frontier flavor and solitude can still be felt.

Government and Economy

New Mexico doesn't look so good on paper—in national rankings of income, education, and more, it often ranks 49th or 50th. "New Mexico is a third-world country" is a common quip, at least among an older generation that has seen a lifetime of nepotism and incompetence. But these issues have also inspired a good deal of activist sentiment, and politics are lively.

GOVERNMENT

New Mexico's political scene is as diverse as its population, though the cities tend to vote Democrat. Still, Republican Susana Martinez became New Mexico's first woman governor in 2010 (her opponent was also a woman, incidentally), and was reelected in 2014. It didn't take the state long to elect its second woman governor: the Democrat Michelle Lujan Grisham began her term in 2019. In the 2016 presidential election, counties skewed extremely red or blue; former governor and Libertarian Gary Johnson took 9 percent of the vote, his highest stake in the nation.

New Mexico is notable for its equitable Hispanic representation in every level of government, including the state legislature, where it consistently matches the state Hispanic population, just under 50 percent. This has helped keep the immigration debate at a relatively polite pitch—unlike in neighboring Arizona and Texas, where the Hispanic population is underrepresented in the government.

Each American Indian pueblo (as well as Navajo, Zuni, and Apache lands elsewhere in the state) acts as a sovereign nation, with its own laws, tax regulations, police forces, and government. Indians vote in U.S. and state elections, while in the pueblos, most domestic issues are decided by a tribal governor, a war chief, and a few other officials elected by a consensus of men in the kiva.

The Navajo Nation, with more than 250,000 people to manage, as well as a substantial cache of natural resources, does practice direct democracy, open to both men and women. In its system, the reservation, which reaches into Arizona and Utah, is divided into "chapters," and their elected representatives participate in the Navajo Council, which convenes in the capital at Window Rock, Arizona. Since a reform in 1991, the Navajo system has had three branches, like the American one. In 2006, Lynda Lovejoy was the first woman to run for nation president; she ran again in 2010, losing by a small margin. The 2014 election brought up a different issue, when one candidate was disqualified for failing to demonstrate fluency in the Navajo language, a legal requirement for holding the position.

Deb Haaland, of the Laguna Pueblo and former chair of the New Mexico Democratic Party, became one of the first Native Americans to serve in the United States Congress, when she was sworn in to the House of Representatives in 2019.

ECONOMY

In New Mexico, roughly 20 percent of the population lives below the poverty level, compared with national averages around 15 percent. It's also near the bottom in the number of high school and college graduates per capita. Statistics in the pueblos and reservations have historically been grimmer, with up to 50 percent unemployment in some areas—but this has changed due to casino-fueled development. The Navajo Nation has extensive landholdings, but with an infrastructure that's more 19th than 21st century, businesses seldom invest. The same could in fact be said for many of the rural sections of the state, on Indian land or not.

The unemployment rate, however, is often lower than the national average, in part because Albuquerque continues to be a manufacturing center for computer chips, mattresses, specialty running shoes, and more. And the city where Microsoft was founded (Bill Gates and Paul Allen later moved back to Seattle to be close to their families) does foster technology development. As well, the Sandia and Los Alamos national laboratories are the state's biggest employers—together they employ over 23,000 people. Aerospace manufacturing parks are growing outside Albuquerque and Las Cruces. Despite heady optimism, private spaceflights are, however, still some ways from taking off from Spaceport America near Truth or Consequences.

Outside the cities, significant profits from coal, copper, oil, and natural gas—most in the southern part of the state, as well as in the northwest—keep the economy afloat. That's the big money, but the agricultural sector, from dairy cows in the south to apple orchards along the Rio Grande to beef jerky from the numerous cattle ranches, contributes a decent amount to the pot. And Santa Fe's arts sector

shouldn't be overlooked—galleries post sales of $200 million every year, though they're criticized for sending much of that money right back to artists who live and work out of state. Thanks to tax rebates, the film industry, nicknamed "Tamalewood," has flourished. Albuquerque Studios is one of the largest production facilities in the country and in the fall of 2018 was bought by Netflix, a deal which is expected to see a huge upturn in the studio's output. To the north, Santa Fe Studios has been the site of a number of film and TV productions in the relatively short time since it was founded.

Even if the economic situation isn't ideal, it's nothing New Mexicans aren't used to. Low income has been the norm for so long that a large segment of the population is, if not content with, at least adapted to eking out a living from very little (the median family income is only around $46,744, compared with the U.S. median of $60,336). In this respect, the state hasn't lost its frontier spirit at all.

Local Culture

New Mexico's 1.8 million people have typically been described as a tricultural mix of Indians, Spanish, and Anglos. That self-image has begun to expand as residents have delved deeper into history and seen that the story involves a few more threads.

DEMOGRAPHY

The labels of Indian, Spanish, and Anglo are used uniquely in New Mexico. First, Indian: This is still a common term, as "Native American" never fully caught on. You'll see "American Indian" in formal situations, but even the "American" part is a bit laughable, considering "America" wasn't so named until Christopher Columbus made his voyage west. "Indian" refers to a number of different peoples who do not share a common culture or language: Navajo on the west side of the state, Jicarilla and Mescalero Apache, and

the Puebloans of the Rio Grande and west as far as Acoma and Zuni. "Pueblo" refers not to a particular tribe, but to a larger group of people who speak four distinct languages but are banded together by a common way of living. Typically, people will identify themselves by their particular tribe: Santa Clara, for instance, or Taos. With about 10.2 percent of the population claiming American Indian ancestry (nearly 10 times the national average, and second only to Alaska), traditions are still strong.

Spanish really means that: the people, primarily in northern New Mexico, whose ancestors were Spaniards, rather than the mestizos of Mexico. For many families, it's a point of pride similar to that of *Mayflower* descendants. Over the years, particularly during the 20th century, a steady influx of Mexican immigrants blurred racial distinctions a bit, but it also reinforced the use of Spanish as a daily language and inspired pride in the culture's music and other folkways. In some circles, the word **Hispano** is used to label New Mexico's distinct culture with centuries-old Iberian roots, which includes the **Basques,** who came here both during the conquest (Don Juan de Oñate, the first Spanish governor, was Basque) and in the early 20th century as sheepherders. The discovery of families of **crypto-Jews** (Spanish Jews who nominally converted to Catholicism but fled here to avoid the Inquisition) has added another fascinating layer to the Spanish story, along with the knowledge that many of the first Spanish explorers likely had Arab blood as well.

Anglo is the most imprecise term, as it can mean anyone who's not Spanish or Indian. Originally used to talk about traders of European descent who came to hunt and sell furs and trade on the Santa Fe Trail, it still refers to people who can't trace their roots back to the conquistadors or farther. If you're a Vietnamese immigrant, a Tibetan refugee, or an African American whose family settled a farm here after the Civil War, you could be, at least in jest, Anglo. (As of 2014, about 38.9 percent of the population was non-Hispanic Caucasian; Asians were only 1.7 percent, and African Americans made up 2.5 percent.) But all Anglo culture is shot through with Spanish and Indian influence, whether among the organic garlic farmers from California who rely on their acequias for water or the New Age seekers who do sweat-lodge rituals.

Even with a liberal application of "Anglo," the tricultural arrangement is limiting, as it doesn't assign a place to contemporary immigrants from Mexico and other Latin American countries, and their numbers are growing steadily. It also doesn't acknowledge the strong Mexican American **Chicano** culture that's shared across the Southwest, from Los Angeles through Texas. The U.S. census form lumps both newer arrivals and old Spanish under "Hispanic"—a category (distinct from race) that made up 47.7 percent of the population in 2014, the highest in the country.

RELIGION

Four hundred years after the arrival of the Franciscan missionaries, New Mexico is still a heavily **Catholic** state—even KFC offers a Friday-night fish fry during Lent. But the relative isolation of the territory produced some variances that have disturbed the Vatican. In both Indian and Spanish churches, the pageantry of medieval Christianity is preserved. Las Posadas, the reenactment of Mary and Joseph's search for lodging in Bethlehem, is a festive torch-lit tradition every December, and during the annual Holy Week pilgrimage to Chimayó, devoted groups stage the stations of the cross, complete with 100-pound wood beams and lots of fake blood.

The Pueblo Indians play on church-as-theater, too: During Christmas Eve Mass, for instance, the service may come to an abrupt end as the priest is hustled off the pulpit by face-painted clowns making way for the parade of ceremonial dancers down the aisle. In both cultures, the Mexican Virgin of Guadalupe is highly revered, and a number of saints are honored as intercessors for all manner of dilemmas, from failing crops to false imprisonment.

Eastern religions have a noticeable presence in New Mexico as well, and even a bit of political clout. A community of primarily American-born converts to **Sikhism** in Española, for example, is a major donor to both parties. Santa Fe is home to a substantial number of **Buddhists,** both American converts and native Tibetan refugees who have relocated to this different mountainous land. Stupas can be found up and down the Rio Grande.

LANGUAGE

English is the predominant language, but **Spanish** is very commonly used—about 30 percent of the population speaks it regularly. Spanish-speakers in northern New Mexico were for centuries only the old

New Mexico's Penitentes

a *morada* in Abiquiu

Most Hispano villages in northern New Mexico have a modest one-story building called a *morada*—the meeting place of **Los Hermanos Penitentes** (The Penitent Brothers), a lay Catholic fraternity with deep roots in medieval Spain and a history that has often put it at odds with the church.

The Penitentes developed in New Mexico in the early colonial era and were at the height of their influence during the so-called Secular Period (1790-1850), when the Franciscans had been pushed out by church leaders in Mexico but no new priests were sent to the territory. Members of the brotherhood cared for the ill, conducted funerals, and settled petty disputes and even elections. They maintained the spiritual and political welfare of their villages when there were no priests or central government to do so.

The Penitentes are best known for their intense religious rituals, which are rumored to still include self-flagellation, bloodletting, and mock crucifixion—activities that took place in public processions for centuries but were driven underground in the late 19th century following official church condemnation. The secrecy, along with sensational journalism by visitors from the East Coast, fueled gruesome rumors. For their crucifixion reenactments, it was said Penitentes used real nails, and the man drawn by lot to be the *Cristo* had a good chance of dying—though no eyewitness ever recorded the practice on paper. One well-documented ritual involves pulling *la carretera del muerte*, an oxcart filled with rocks and a wooden figure of Doña Sebastiana, Lady Death. Morbid imagery bred morbid curiosity: Photos in a *Harper's* magazine story from the early 1900s show Anglos looking on agog as Penitentes clad in white pants and black hoods whip themselves.

In 1947, after years of concerted lobbying (but not an official renunciation of its rituals), the Penitentes were again accepted into the fold of the Catholic Church. The *hermanos mayores* (head brothers) from all of the *moradas* convene annually in Santa Fe, and the group, which has an estimated 3,000 members, functions as a political and public-service club.

The rituals do continue, most visibly during Holy Week, when the group's devotion to the physical suffering of the human Jesus is at its keenest. The Penitentes reenact the stations of the cross and the crucifixion, and although ketchup is more prevalent than real blood and statues often stand in for the major players, the scenes are solemn and affectingly tragic. On some days during Holy Week, the *morada* is open to non-Penitentes—a rare chance for outsiders to see the meeting place of this secretive group.

Hispano families, communicating in a variant of Castilian with a distinct vocabulary that developed in isolation. This "Quixotic" dialect changed little until the early 1900s, when immigrants arrived from Mexico and elsewhere in Latin America. For much of the 20th century, English was the only permissible classroom language, although many school districts required Spanish as a foreign language. Since the 1990s, education policy has shifted to include bilingual classrooms.

Additionally, you'll occasionally hear Indians speaking their respective languages. Of the four main Pueblo tongues, **Tewa, Tiwa,** and **Towa** are part of the Tanoan family of languages, which are also spoken by Plains Indians. They are related but mutually unintelligible, roughly equivalent to, say, French, Spanish, and Italian. Tewa is the most widely spoken, used in all of the pueblos just north of Santa Fe: Ohkay Owingeh, San Ildefonso, Santa Clara, Pojoaque, Tesuque, and Nambé. Four pueblos speak Tiwa—Taos and Picurís share one dialect, while Isleta and Sandia, in an odd pocket near Albuquerque, speak a different dialect. Towa is now spoken only at Jemez Pueblo. Part of the greater Athabaskan family, the **Navajo** and **Apache** languages are related to but distinct from one another.

Keresan (spoken in Laguna, Acoma, Cochiti, Kewa, San Felipe, Santa Ana, and Zia) and **Zuni** (spoken only at that pueblo) are what linguists call "isolates." Like Basque, they are not connected to neighboring languages, nor to any other language.

Additionally, each Keresan-speaking pueblo has developed its own dialect, so immediately adjacent communities can understand each other, but those farthest apart cannot.

One interesting characteristic of the Pueblo languages is that they have remained relatively pure. Tewa vocabulary, for instance, is still less than 5 percent loan words, despite centuries of Spanish and English influence. This is probably due to the way speakers have long been forced to compartmentalize, using Tewa for conversation at home and switching to English or Spanish for business and trade. For centuries, the Franciscan priests, then the U.S. government, attempted to stamp out Native American languages. Following the Civil War, Puebloan children were moved forcibly to boarding schools, where they were given Anglo names and permitted to speak only English, a policy that continued for decades.

Only in 1990, with the passage of the **Native American Languages Act,** were American Indian languages officially permitted in government-funded schools—indeed, they are now recognized as a unique element of this country's culture and encouraged. In Taos, where the Tiwa language is a ritual secret that outsiders are not permitted to learn, one public school has Tiwa classes for younger students, open only to tribe members and taught by approved teachers; as an added measure against the language being recorded, the classroom has no chalkboard. Less-formal instruction within the pueblos as well as on the Navajo Nation has also helped the Indian languages enjoy a renaissance.

The Arts

New Mexico is a hotbed of creativity, from Santa Fe's burgeoning contemporary art scene to traditional Spanish folk artists working in remote villages, using the same tools their great-grandfathers did, to whole American Indian villages, such as Zuni and Acoma, devoted to the production of fine silverwork and pottery, respectively. Here's what to look for in the traditional arenas of pottery, weaving, jewelry, and wood carving.

POTTERY

New Mexico's pottery tradition thrives, drawing on millennia of craftsmanship. About 2,000 years ago, the Mogollon people in the southern part of the state began making simple pots of brown, coiled clay. A thousand years later, the craft had developed into the beautiful black-on-white symmetry of the Mimbres people. Later, each of the pueblos developed its own style.

By the 20th century, some traditions had died out, but almost all felt some kind of renaissance following the work of San Ildefonso potter María Martinez in the first half of the 20th century. Along with her husband, Julian, Martinez revived a long-lost style of lustrous black pottery with subtle matte decoration. The elegant pieces, which looked at once innovative and traditional, inspired Anglo collectors (who saw the couple's work at the 1934 Chicago World's Fair, among other places) as well as local potters. Today, many artists make their livings with clay.

The various tribal styles are distinguished by their base clay, the "slip" (the clay-and-water finish), and their shape. Taos and Picurís pueblos, for instance, are surrounded by beds of micaceous clay, which lends pots a subtle glitter. (It also helps them withstand heat well; they're renowned for cooking beans.) Acoma specializes in intricate black designs painted on thin white clay. Pottery from Ohkay Owingeh (formerly San Juan) is typically reddish-brown with incised symbols. And Santa Clara developed the "wedding jar," a double-neck design with a handle. If a particular style catches your eye in city galleries, then you can visit the specific pueblo, where you may be able to buy directly from the artisan and perhaps see where the piece was made.

TEXTILES

After pottery, weaving is probably the state's most widespread craft. Historically, Indian and Spanish weaving styles were separate, but they have merged over the centuries to create some patterns and styles unique to the Rio Grande Valley. The first Spanish explorers marveled at the Navajo cotton blankets, woven in whole panels on wide looms; Spaniards had been working with narrow looms and stitching two panels together. Spanish weavers introduced the hardy Churro sheep, with its rough wool that was good for hand-spinning, as well as new dyes, such as indigo (although the blue-tinted rugs are often called Moki rugs, using a Navajo word).

In the early 1800s, in an attempt to make a better product for trade, the Spanish government sent Mexican artists north to work with local weavers. Out of this meeting came the distinctive Saltillo styles (named for the region the Mexican teachers came from), such as the running-leaf pattern, which Rio Grande weavers alternated with solid-color stripes. In the 1880s, New Mexican artisans first saw quilts from the eastern United States, and they adapted the eight-pointed star to their wool rugs. Another popular motif from the 19th century is a zigzag pattern that resembles lightning.

One item that shows up in antiques shops is the Chimayó blanket, an invention of the tourist age in the early 20th century, when Anglo traders encouraged local Hispano weavers to make an affordable souvenir to

Luminarias or *Farolitos*?

luminarias in Santa Fe ... where most people would call them *farolitos*

The cultural differences between Santa Fe and Albuquerque don't apply just to the number of art galleries per square block and whether you eat posole or rice with your enchiladas. Every Christmas, a debate rears its head: What do you call a paper bag with a bit of sand in the bottom and a votive candle inside? These traditional holiday decorations, which line driveways and flat adobe rooftops in the last weeks of December, are commonly known as luminarias in Albuquerque and most towns to the south, and as *farolitos* in Santa Fe and all the villages to the north.

To complicate matters, another holiday tradition in Santa Fe and other northern towns is to light small bonfires of piñon logs in front of houses. And Santa Feans call these little stacks of wood ... luminarias. *Farolitos,* they argue, are literally "little lanterns," an accurate description of the glowing paper bags—and under this logic, use of the term *farolito* has spread a bit in Albuquerque, at least among people who weren't raised saying luminaria from birth.

Albuquerqueans do have Webster's on their side, however; the dictionary concurs that luminarias are paper-bag lanterns and notes the tradition comes from Mexico, where the bags are often colored and pricked with holes. Because this author's loyalties are to Santa Fe—and the city does have a hugely popular annual event named after them—the argument is settled, at least in these pages: *Farolito* it is.

sell to visitors looking for "Indian" blankets. They're handsome, single-width rugs with a strong central motif, perhaps the iconic Southwestern-look rug.

Also look for *colcha* work, a Spanish style in which a loose-weave rug is decorated with wool embroidery. It was revived in the 1930s by Mormons, and you will occasionally see beautiful examples from this period in collectors' shops. Contemporary weaving can draw on any and all of these innovations and is practiced just as often by a young Anglo as

a Hispano grandmother. A strong small-batch wool industry in New Mexico helps the scene tremendously—expect to see vivid color-block contemporary pieces alongside the more traditional patterns.

JEWELRY

Despite a long native tradition, the familiar forms of jewelry seen today date only from the mid-19th century, when the Navajo of western New Mexico pioneered silversmithing (it's thought they learned it during their internment at Fort Sumner) and taught it to the Pueblo Indians. The most iconic piece of Southwestern jewelry, a signature Navajo design, is the turquoise-and-silver **squash-blossom necklace,** a large crescent pendant decorated with flowerlike silver beads. Actually derived from Spanish pomegranate decorations, rather than native plant imagery, it's seen in every Southwest jewelry store.

Look also for shell-shaped **concha belts** (also spelled "concho"), silver "shells" linked together or strung on a leather belt, and the San Felipe specialty, *heishi,* tiny disks made of shell and threaded to make a rope-like strand. The Zuni carve small animal **fetishes**—bears, birds, and more—often strung on necklaces with *heishi.* In addition to turquoise, opals are a popular decorative stone, along with brick-red coral, lapis lazuli, and black jet and marble. Whatever you buy, the gallery or artisan should supply you with a written receipt of its components—which stones, the grade of silver, and so forth.

Turquoise

Although New Mexico's turquoise is all mined out, the stone is still an essential part of local jewelry-making; most of it is imported from mines in China. It is available in shades from lime-green to pure sky-blue, and much of it has been subjected to various processes to make it stabler and more versatile, which affects the price.

Rare gem-grade turquoise is the top of the line—a high-quality piece with complex spiderwebbing from now-empty mines like Lander or Lone Mountain can cost $350 per carat. "Gem-grade" applies only to **natural stones** (those that have not been chemically treated in any way) and is based on the piece's luster, hardness, and matrix, the term for the web of dark veins running through it, which you should be able to feel in any natural turquoise, regardless of grade. Highest-quality stones from still-functioning mines in China or Tibet will cost significantly less ($10-20 per carat) but will be of the same quality as some premium American stones. Slightly less splendid natural stones are graded jewelry-quality, high-quality, or investment-quality—but they are not quite hard enough to guarantee they will not change color over decades. They cost $2-5 per carat. For any natural stone, the seller must provide you with a written certificate of its status.

Because good natural turquoise is increasingly difficult to come by and turquoise is such an unreliable stone, various treatments are a common and acceptable way of making a great deal of the stuff usable. **Treated turquoise** refers to any stone that has added resins, waxes, or other foreign elements. A certain proprietary treatment, **enhanced turquoise,** also called "Zachary process turquoise," is usually applied to medium-grade or higher stones.

Turquoise that has been **stabilized,** or submerged in epoxy resin to harden it and deepen the color, makes up the bulk of the market. Because it's less expensive, it allows for a little waste in the carving process, and good-quality stabilized turquoise is often found in expensive jewelry with elaborate inlay. Average-quality stabilized stone, the next grade down, is used by perhaps 70 percent of American Indian artisans—it can stand up to being carved and is very well priced. Though it ranks relatively low in the range of turquoise available, it produces an attractive piece of jewelry—perhaps not with the elaborate spiderwebbing of a rare piece, but with an overall good color and luster.

Below this are low-quality stabilized stones that have been artificially colored (often called "color shot," or, more confusing, "color stabilized"). **"Synthetic"** stones are actually real turquoise—small chunks mixed with a binding powder of ground turquoise or pyrite, then pressed into shapes and cut. The result is surprisingly attractive, with natural spiderwebbing, but it should be clearly labeled as synthetic. And of course there is the turquoise that isn't at all—plastic stuff that can be quite convincing.

Aside from the synthetic stuff, don't worry too much about getting "bad" or "cheap" turquoise—because each stone is different, the more important thing is to find a piece that's attractive to you and is priced to reflect its quality. Just remember that the words "genuine," "authentic," or "pure" have no real meaning—only "natural" is legally defined. Likewise, the phrase "authentic Indian handmade" is a legal one—any variation on this wording (such as "Indian crafted") is likely some kind of ruse. Shopping in New Mexico provides many opportunities to buy direct from the artisan—under the portal at the Palace of the Governors in Santa Fe, for instance. Otherwise, just avoid shopping in too-good-to-be-true stores that are perpetually "going out of business" or "in liquidation."

WOOD AND TINWORK

When Spanish colonists arrived in New Mexico, they had few resources, little money, and only the most basic tools. A group of settlers would typically include one carpenter, whose skills helped fill everyone's houses with heavy wood furniture (still made today). But the carpenter also helped the group to worship—for chief among the wood-carvers was (and is) the *santero* or *santera,* who carves

images of saints. These so-called santos can be either flat (*retablos*) or three-dimensional (*bultos*) and are typically painted in lively colors, though some outstanding work has been produced in plain, unpainted wood.

Santo styles have shown remarkable continuity over the centuries. The most notable break from tradition was by Patrocinio Barela, whose WPA-sponsored work in the 1930s was almost fluid, utilizing the natural curves and grains of the wood. His sons and grandsons practice the art today. For centuries, the piousness of the *santero* was valued at least as much as his skill in carving, though many contemporary carvers do their work for a large market of avid collectors. One popular figure is San Isidro, patron saint of farmers, from 12th-century Spain.

Look also for straw marquetry, another product of hard times in the colonial period, in which tiny fibers of "poor man's gold" replaced precious metals as inlay to make elaborate geometric designs on dark wood. Tinwork is another ubiquitous craft, found in inexpensive votive-candle holders as well as elaborately punched and engraved mirror frames and chandeliers.

Essentials

Transportation

GETTING THERE
Air

Albuquerque International Sunport (ABQ; 505/244-7700, www.
cabq.gov/airport) is the main access point to the region. It's served
by the three major U.S. air carriers, plus Southwest Airlines, JetBlue,
Alaska Airlines, Allegiant Air, and Frontier. Fares fluctuate on the
same schedule as the rest of the country, with higher rates in summer and over holidays; in the winter, it's wise to choose a connection

through a more temperate hub, such as Dallas (American) or Salt Lake City (Delta).

Small **Santa Fe Municipal Airport** (SAF; 121 Aviation Dr.; 505/955-2900, www.santafenm.gov/airport), west of the city, receives direct flights from Dallas and Phoenix with American Eagle, and from Denver with United. For visiting the southern half of the state, you might find it easier to fly into **El Paso International Airport** (ELP; 915/780-4749, www.elpasointernationalairport.com), in Texas, just an hour's drive from Las Cruces.

Train

Amtrak (800/872-7245, www.amtrak.com) runs the *Southwest Chief* daily between Chicago and Los Angeles, stopping in **Raton, Las Vegas, Lamy** (18 miles from Santa Fe), **Albuquerque,** and **Gallup.**

Amtrak's *Sunset Limited* train, from Florida to Los Angeles via the southern edge of the state, is less useful—it runs every other day and requires a bus transfer from El Paso to **Las Cruces,** and makes stops in **Deming** and **Lordsburg.**

Arriving in Albuquerque, you're in the middle of downtown, in a depot shared with Greyhound. There are lockers here (occasionally full), and city buses are available just up the block. Lamy (the stop nearest Santa Fe) is no more than a depot—though it is a dramatic and wild-feeling place to get off the train. Amtrak provides an awkwardly timed shuttle service to Santa Fe hotels (passengers arriving on eastbound trains must wait for passengers from the westbound train, an hour later). From Chicago, Amtrak pads its schedule heavily between Lamy and Albuquerque—so if the train is running behind, you'll be late arriving in Lamy but generally will still get to Albuquerque on schedule.

Bus

Greyhound (800/231-2222, www.greyhound.com) connects New Mexico with adjacent states and Mexico. Routes run roughly along I-40 and I-25, with little service to outlying areas. If you're coming from elsewhere in the Southwest, you may want to investigate **El Paso-Los Angeles Limousine Express** (915/532-4061 in El Paso, 626/442-1945 in Los Angeles, 505/247-8036 in Albuquerque, www.eplalimo.com), a long-established operator that originally served the Mexican immigrant population. Its route runs east-west from El Paso to Los Angeles, stopping in Las Cruces and Deming; it also connects Denver to Santa Fe and Albuquerque.

Car

Conveniently, New Mexico is crisscrossed by interstates: **I-40** and **I-10** run east-west, and **I-25** cuts roughly down the center, north-south. Denver, Colorado, to Santa Fe is 450 miles, about a 6-hour drive; add another hour to reach Albuquerque. El Paso, Texas, to Albuquerque is 275 miles, about 4 hours. Coming from Flagstaff, Arizona, Albuquerque is 325 miles along I-40, about 4.5 hours; from Amarillo, Texas, it's just slightly less distance in the other direction.

Southwest road-trippers often combine New Mexico with southwestern Colorado, in which case **U.S. 550** makes a good route south from Durango. Other southern Colorado options to consider include **U.S. 84** from Pagosa Springs and **U.S. 285,** which runs from Alamosa to Carlsbad. From Tucson, Arizona, a nice route into New Mexico is to cut north off I-10 at Lordsburg, following Highway 90 to Silver City and winding through the mountains northeast to reach I-25 to Albuquerque.

GETTING AROUND

Practically speaking, you will need a car. Traveling between towns by bus or train is feasible, but it certainly limits what you can see. Within Albuquerque and Santa Fe, you can often get around by walking,

---

Previous: the Rail Runner, connecting Albuquerque and Santa Fe.

Driving Distances

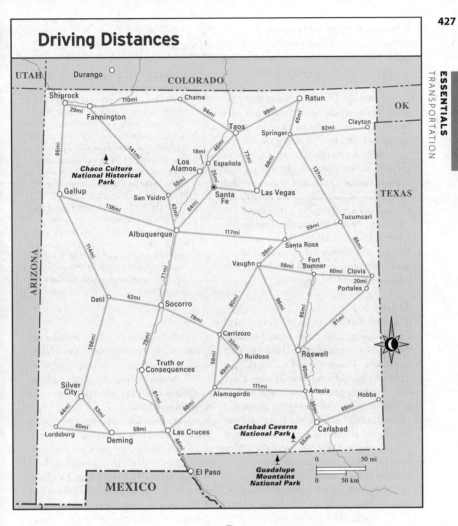

biking, or public transport, but getting to or around anywhere smaller requires your own wheels.

Regional Airlines

To cover the longer distances, flying is a possibility, albeit a limited one: **Boutique Air** (855/268-8478, www.boutiqueair.com) flies from Albuquerque to Carlsbad (connecting on to Dallas). At the time of writing, no other regional airlines were operating flights between points within the state.

Bus

Between Santa Fe and Taos (and communities around and in between, including the pueblos), the **North Central Regional Transit District** (866/206-0754, www.ncrtd.org) offers commuter bus service. It's not very frequent, but it's free, and it covers a lot of area, making it an option for the hard-core no-car traveler.

Another option is the weekday **Park & Ride** (866/551-7433, https://dot.state. nm.us) service offered by the New Mexico

Department of Transportation. It covers stops as far south as Las Cruces and the White Sands Missile Range and as far north as Los Alamos and Española, with several points in between.

The **Navajo Transit System** (928/729-4002, www.navajotransit.navajo-nsn.gov) can get you around the northwest and into Arizona—with *a lot* of planning.

Greyhound (800/231-2222, www.greyhound.com) connects Albuquerque with Santa Fe and Las Cruces, as well as a few other midsize towns. Anything off the interstate in the southeast will require a transfer in Las Cruces. **El Paso-Los Angeles Limousine Express** (1611 Central Ave. SW, Albuquerque, 505/247-8036, www.eplalimo.com) offers good alternative service to Las Cruces from Albuquerque and Deming.

Train

The **Rail Runner** (866/795-7245, www.riometro.org) commuter train connects Belén, Albuquerque, and Santa Fe, with convenient downtown stations, making a car-free visit quite feasible, or even a day trip. The train passes through odd pockets of Albuquerque and stunning, untouched pueblo lands. Tickets are based on a zone system; the 90-minute ride between downtown Albuquerque and Santa Fe costs $9, or $10 for a day pass. (Kids: Listen for the "meep-meep!" warning as the doors close!)

Via **Amtrak** (800/872-7245, www.amtrak.com), Gallup, Raton, and Las Vegas are feasible destinations from Albuquerque.

Car

Driving New Mexico's scenic byways is definitely one of the pleasures of traveling here. On the other hand, parking in Santa Fe can be difficult, or at least expensive—and you can get around the center of town very easily on foot. So, ideally, you would rent a car only for the days you plan to go out of the city. Central Taos is small, but sights are spread out on the fringes, and only the most dedicated can manage without a car. In Albuquerque,

Riding the Rails

Traveling by train in New Mexico, if you have the time to do it, is a rewarding experience. You'll get a great sense of the state's emptiness—as well as what a dramatic change the railroad made when it arrived in 1880. Going by train does rule out some parts of the state, but it also opens up whole areas you would never see by car. And nothing's more relaxing than watching the scenery roll by. In the words of one Amtrak fan, "It's like having your own chauffeur!"

The **Belen Main Street** organization (www.belenmainstreet.org) publishes a map with major sites of train history, along with a suggested seven-day all-train itinerary, visiting Belén, Gallup, Santa Fe, and Las Vegas. It's feasible because Amtrak departs Albuquerque midday, so you arrive at a reasonable hour.

you can live without a car for a few days, but it requires planning and rules out a few of the sights. All of the major car-rental chains are at Albuquerque's airport, in a single building; see the respective city chapters for other rental companies and offices.

All but a few roads are passable year-round. You won't need four-wheel drive, but be prepared in winter for ice and snow anywhere other than central Albuquerque and the southernmost section of the state. Also check your car-rental agreement for restrictions on driving on dirt roads—a rare clause in the United States, but occasionally employed by smaller companies. Needless to say, this is a liability, as it's almost impossible to go anywhere interesting in New Mexico without winding up on a dirt road.

Get in the habit of topping off your tank. In the southern half of the state, especially along the Mexican border and anywhere away from I-10 and I-25, there are long stretches of smaller roads without gas stations, and prices can range by as much as $0.50 per gallon between convenient city locations and more remote areas. Contrary to logic, fuel is vastly more expensive in the southeastern side of the state around Hobbs and Artesia, where the terrain is dotted with oil derricks.

Bike

With beautiful vistas, often deserted roads, and a strong community of both road cyclists and mountain bikers, New Mexico can be a great place to get around on two wheels, as long as it's not your main form of transport. Whether you'll be riding your own bike or renting one here, always pack a patch kit, and consider installing tire liners. Goathead thorns and broken glass are particular scourges of the highway shoulder.

Central Albuquerque and Santa Fe are both manageable by bicycle, with separate lanes. Las Cruces is moderately accommodating. In Taos, traffic on the main road can be unpleasantly heavy and fast. But services such as the Rail Runner, Taos Express, and Park & Ride have space for bicycles, so it's possible to take your wheels with you from town to town.

Food

New Mexicans love their food so much, they have been known to enshrine it on lottery tickets, with scratch cards named Chile Cash, Chips and Salsa, and Sopaipilla Dough (promising "lots of honey and plenty of money"). The state cuisine is a distinctive culinary tradition that shouldn't be confused with Tex-Mex, Californian Mex, or south-of-the-border Mexican—even though most locals will say they're going out for "Mexican" when they mean they want a bowl of purely *New* Mexican green-chile stew. (But if you're eating mole or ceviche, that's *"Mexican* Mexican," and you can get more of it the farther south you drive.) New Mexican cuisine doesn't typically do bean-and-meat chili, certainly not mango-flavored anything, and only rarely guacamole—you can get it, but avocados are expensive here.

ALL CHILE, ALL THE TIME

The cuisine's distinguishing element is the New Mexico chile pepper. The best-known variety is the Hatch chile, named for the southern New Mexican town that's the center of the industry. In the north, Chimayó is another big chile-producing town, with its own heirloom strain, usually picked red.

When the chile is picked green, it is roasted and peeled, then used whole to make chiles rellenos (stuffed with cheese and fried in batter), or cut into chunks and cooked in sauces or used as the base of a meaty green-chile stew. In northern New Mexico, that sauce is pure chile, maybe thinned with chicken broth; in some towns in the southern part of the state, it's more like a green-chile cream gravy, often with a base of cream-of-mushroom soup.

When the New Mexico chile is left to ripen, then dried in the sun, it turns turn dark red and leathery. These dry red chiles are stored whole, in long chains called *ristras*, or ground into flakes (*chile caribe*) or finer powder to be the base of a sauce or marinade. The heartiest red-chile dish is *carne adovada*, chunks of pork shoulder stewed with pure red sauce.

Most other items—enchiladas, burritos, and eggs (huevos rancheros), to name a few—can be ordered with either variety of chile, so a standard query in restaurants (and now enshrined as the official state question) is "Red or green?" You can have both, splitting the plate half-and-half, a style many people call "Christmas," though old-timers still call it "Mexican flag."

The chile is often coupled with the traditional Native American triad of corn, squash, and beans. The beans are typically brown, meaty pintos, served whole in a stew or mashed up and "refried" (not actually fried twice—the term is a mistranslation

Red-Chile Sauce

Use only freshly ground New Mexico red chile for this sauce—not the "chile powder" sold in most grocery stores. The sauce will keep in the refrigerator for a month, and you can use it to top eggs or steaks, or devote the whole batch to a tray of enchiladas. (If you're doing the latter, you'll want to keep the sauce relatively thin, so you can easily coat the tortillas with sauce before filling them.) The flavor is best if it is prepared ahead and left to sit overnight.

Yield: 2 cups
½ c. New Mexico red chile powder
½ tsp. ground cumin (optional)
1 tsp. ground coriander (optional)
2 Tbsp. all-purpose flour
2 Tbsp. lard (or vegetable oil)
2 or 3 cloves garlic, crushed or minced
2 c. chicken stock or water
1 tsp. dried oregano (optional)

Measure the chile, cumin, coriander, and flour into a heavy-bottomed saucepan and place over medium-high heat. Stir continuously until the spices are just fragrant and the flour has darkened slightly. Remove the chile-flour mix to a small bowl. Heat the lard or oil in the pan, and add the garlic and stir until fragrant. Then stir the chile-flour mix into the oil-garlic mixture—you will have a very coarse paste. Stirring constantly, slowly add half of the stock or water. Continue stirring, and the mixture will thicken and become velvety. Add the remaining stock or water and the oregano, mix well, turn heat to low, and let sauce simmer for about 20 minutes, until it is somewhat reduced and thickened to your liking. If the mixture becomes too thick, simply add more water.

of the Spanish *refrito*, which means "really fried"). Corn takes the form of tortillas as well as hulled kernels of hominy, called posole here and often cooked into a stew with chile, oregano, and meat. Ground corn paste (masa) is whipped with lard (or Crisco, if you're "healthy") and wrapped around a meaty filling, then tied in a corn husk and steamed to make a **tamale.** Squash comes in a common side dish called *calabacitas,* sautéed with onions and a touch of green chile. Spanish settlers brought lamb, which finds its way into tacos and stews.

American Indian cuisine isn't so distinct from what everyone else eats—its one major element is **fry bread,** a round of deep-fried dough served with honey or filled with ground meat, cheese, and lettuce to make an "Indian taco"; a "Navajo taco" often uses shredded lamb or mutton in place of ground beef. Bread baked in a traditional domed adobe *horno* oven is also popular, and the Zuni make a distinctive sourdough this way. In pueblos and on the reservations, you'll see these mud ovens in most yards. Game meat, such as deer, is also a major component of American Indian cooking, though you'll rarely see it in restaurants.

Green chile makes its way into standard American fare as well. It's a popular pizza topping (great with pepperoni or ham), and the **green-chile cheeseburger** is a top choice everywhere. Also look out for **breakfast burritos,** big flour tortillas filled with scrambled eggs, hash browns, and some kind of meat—bacon, crumbled sausage, or sometimes Mexican chorizo, a spicy pork sausage. Some places sell them as to-go food, wrapped in foil with green chile added to the mix. At sit-down places, you get the whole construction smothered in either red or green chile.

Sopaipillas are another New Mexican specialty. They're palm-sized pillows of deep-fried dough, used to mop up chile and beans during the main meal, then slathered with honey for dessert. In a disturbing trend, some restaurants now offer a honey-flavored corn syrup, because it's cheaper and doesn't crystallize—if you encounter this, complain at top volume.

Bizcochitos, little anise-laced cookies, are the state's official sweet treat. Wash it all down with a margarita, which purists insist should involve only lime, tequila, and triple sec and be served on the rocks in a salt-rimmed glass. (Restaurants with only a beer-and-wine license often offer an agave-wine margarita—decent flavor, but pretty weak.)

HOW TO TAKE THE HEAT

When your server plunks down a heavy white ceramic plate covered in chile and melted cheese, the words "this plate is very hot" cover only half of the story. Every year the harvest varies a bit, and the chile can be mild or so spicy as to blister lips and produce a dizzying (and addictive) endorphin rush. Locals look back on particularly incendiary seasons with that mixture of awe, fear, and longing that junkies reserve for their best scores. In general, green chile tends to be hotter than red, but it's best to ask your server what to expect—some restaurants specialize in one or the other.

You can protect yourself against chile-heat by ordering a side of sour cream with your enchiladas or burrito—although be warned that many consider this a "Texan" affectation, and you may be derided by your fellow diners. Locals usually just reach for a sopaipilla, the starch from which can absorb some of the chile oils. Don't gulp down water, which only spreads the searing oils around your mouth. Beer is a marginal improvement, and margaritas are at least distracting.

FINE DINING AND WINE

While there are plenty of time-warp diners and mom-and-pop hole-in-the-wall joints in New Mexico, dining can also be very sophisticated, keeping pace with the national trend toward local and organic produce. This movement hasn't been such a huge leap here: Many small family farms didn't have to "go organic," because they were never very industrialized in the first place. At white-tablecloth places, Southwestern fusion is still common, with chile working its way into foie gras appetizers and even high-concept desserts.

The fine dining scene is enhanced by a burgeoning wine industry, initiated by Spanish settlers in the 17th century but enjoying a resurgence since the 1980s. Gruet Winery in Albuquerque is the best-known New Mexico producer, especially for its excellent sparkling wine. This makes for a nice little perk of New Mexico dining: You can get inexpensive bubbly by the glass almost everywhere. The New Mexico Wine & Grape Growers Association (www.nmwine.com) has information on more wineries, and you can read more about the high-end and organic food scene in *Local Flavor* (www.localflavormagazine.com), a monthly tabloid, and the periodic *Edible New Mexico* guides (www.ediblenm.com).

VEGETARIAN FOOD

New Mexican food isn't meat-centric, but strict vegetarians will have to be vigilant, as many chile dishes are traditionally made with beef or chicken stock as well as lard for flavoring. The closer you get to Texas, the more likely it is that red chile sauce will contain bits of meat. Decades of hippie influence, though, have resulted in many menus stating clearly whether the chile is meatless. Some restaurants have an unreconstructed 1970s worldview, with alfalfa sprouts and squash casseroles galore.

Religious Retreats

One quirk of New Mexico is that the area harbors an exceptionally high number of religious retreats of all stripes, set in some of the most scenic, quiet areas. Most of them welcome guests, with no religious strings attached. Facilities are usually basic but comfortable, and rates (suggested donations, officially) are very reasonable, especially for solo travelers, and often include meals. Look for the following properties:

· **Bodhi Manda Zen Center:** Buddhist retreat in Jemez Springs (page 83)

· **Quaker Meeting House:** A single charming guesthouse, in Santa Fe (page 131)

· **Ghost Ranch:** A large Presbyterian retreat in Abiquiu, the most secular-feeling of the bunch (page 153)

· **Christ in the Desert Monastery:** Very remote, outside Abiquiu (page 153)

· **Pecos Benedictine Monastery:** In the town of Pecos (page 218)

· **The Monastery of Our Lady of the Desert:** in the northwest, east of Farmington (page 283)

Christ in the Desert Monastery

Accommodations

Throughout this guide, distinctive choices—bed-and-breakfasts, lodges, and small, independently owned hotels and motels—are emphasized over chain options as much as possible. Just because the chains are not listed doesn't mean they're not available—and in many small towns, they're the only solid option.

The prices listed are the official high-season rack rates—that is, what you'd pay if you just walked in off the street, with no discounts; tax is not included. Most often, the numbers are the least expensive room for one person in one bed (a single, abbreviated s) and two people in two beds (a double, abbreviated d). **High season** is usually June-August. **Ski season** is January-March; prices in Taos and Santa Fe don't completely bottom out—but they are still cheaper than summer. Expect higher rates in the week following Christmas and during special events, such as Indian Market in Santa Fe and Balloon Fiesta in Albuquerque, but overall you will be able to secure lower rates than those listed simply by looking online or calling the hotel directly.

Note that while many hotels tout their swimming pools, they are often forced to leave them empty due to water restrictions imposed during droughts. If you've booked at a hotel specifically for the pool, call to check the status before your trip, so you don't wind up paying a premium for a service you can't use. Santa Fe is the strictest area in the state, and it also limits hotels to changing towels and bed linens only every four days during your visit.

Travel Tips

WHAT TO PACK

The contents of your suitcase will be determined largely by the time of year, but be prepared for a **wide range of temperatures**—with a variety of layers—whenever you visit. Many people wrongly assume that New Mexico's desert setting means heat all day, all year round. In fact, due to the altitude in much of the state, you may encounter severe cold. Winter temperatures can dip well below freezing even in the relatively low elevations of central Albuquerque and further south. If you think you'll attend pueblo ceremonial dances during the winter, pack mittens, long underwear, double-thick wool socks, and a hat with earflaps—there will be a lot of standing around outside.

Spring is mud season—if you hike or head to rural areas during this time, save a clean pair of shoes for around town. Summers are hot by day (July's average temperature is 92°F), but as soon as the sun dips below the horizon, the temperature can drop up to 30°F, especially outside of city centers; always keep a sweater on hand. Brief afternoon "monsoons" in July and August sometimes warrant an umbrella or rain slicker. In the strong sun, you'll be more comfortable if you cover up, in long-sleeve, light-colored shirts and pants in silk or cotton. In fact, you should guard against the sun any time of year, as the thin atmosphere at this altitude means you'll burn more quickly than you're used to. You should never be without **sunglasses,** heavy-duty **sunscreen,** and a **brimmed hat.**

As for style, anything goes. If you'll be hobnobbing with Santa Fe's upper echelon, you might want to pack something dressy—the local formalwear for men is clean jeans, shined cowboy boots, and a bolo tie. Otherwise, though, New Mexicans are very casual. But note that when visiting churches and pueblos, it's respectful to not show excessive skin—women should avoid obvious cleavage and super-short skirts.

TOURIST INFORMATION

For pre-trip inspiration, the New Mexico Tourism Board publishes the monthly *New Mexico* magazine (www.newmexico.org/ nmmagazine), which does an excellent job covering both mainstream attractions and more obscure corners of the state.

Many smaller towns' chambers of commerce can also be extremely helpful.

If you plan to do a lot of hiking, you can order detailed topographical maps from the **National Forest Service** office in New Mexico (505/842-3292) or from the Bureau of Land Management's **Public Lands Interpretive Center** (301 Dinosaur Tr., 505/954-2002, www.publiclands.org) in Santa Fe. Also, in Santa Fe, **Travel Bug** (839 Paseo de Peralta, 505/992-0418, 7:30am-5:30pm Mon.-Sat., 11am-4pm Sun.) bookstore has an extensive selection of maps as do the **REI** stores in Santa Fe (500 Market St., 505/982-3557, 10am-8pm Mon.-Fri., 10am-7pm Sat., 11am-6pm Sun.) and Albuquerque (1550 Mercantile Ave. NE, 505/247-1191, 10am-9pm Mon.-Fri., 9am-7pm Sat., 11am-7pm Sun.).

Telephone and Internet

Albuquerque, Santa Fe, Los Alamos, Gallup, and Farmington use the area code 505, while the rest of the state's numbers start with 575.

For mobile phone reception, the corridor between Albuquerque and Santa Fe is fine, but in rural areas, phones on the GSM network (AT&T, T-Mobile) get very poor or no reception. Data service is equally spotty. If you'll be spending a lot of time outside of the cities or counting on your phone for emergencies, you might consider a CDMA phone (Verizon is best). Likewise, don't count on data service on your smartphone.

Internet access is widespread, though DSL and other high-speed service is still not necessarily the norm, and thick adobe walls can be a hindrance for wireless signals. Rural areas still rely on satellite Internet, which can be poor in bad weather. In the cities, cafés often have hotspots, and the city of Albuquerque even maintains a few free ones in public spaces, such as the Old Town plaza.

Time Zone

New Mexico is in the **mountain time** zone, one hour ahead of the West Coast of the United States and two hours behind the East Coast. It's -7 GMT (Greenwich Mean Time) during the winter and -6 GMT in summer, when Daylight Saving Time is followed statewide.

Note that neighboring Arizona does not follow Daylight Saving Time, which can lead to confusion around the border.

CONDUCT AND CUSTOMS

New Mexico is a part of the United States, but it can sometimes feel quite foreign, particularly in the high mountain Spanish villages and in the Indian pueblos. Regardless, basic courtesy rules and, in smaller communities, modest dress are appreciated, especially at the older Catholic churches.

Some Pueblo Indians, as well as Navajo, find loud voices, direct eye contact, and firm handshakes off-putting and, by the same token, may not express themselves in the forthright way a lot of visitors are used to. Similarly, a subdued reaction doesn't necessarily mean a lack of enthusiasm.

New Mexico is not a wealthy state, and the gap between rich and poor can be wide. In general, people don't appreciate conspicuous displays of wealth, and it's doubly rude to flash cash, fancy gadgets, and jewelry in tiny villages and pueblos (and public cell-phone use is still considered tacky most places). Be thoughtful when taking photos, particularly of people's homes—always ask permission, and consider that some of the more "scenic"

elements of New Mexico are also the products of poverty, which some people may not be proud to have captured on film.

You can help the local economy by favoring New Mexican-owned businesses, rather than chain operations, and buying directly from artisans wherever possible. In these situations, don't get too bent on bargaining. The item you're buying represents not just raw materials and hours of work, but a person's particular talent, skill, and heritage. Insisting on an extra-low price belittles not just the item, but the artisan as well.

Pueblo and Reservation Etiquette

When visiting pueblos and reservations, remember that you are not at a tourist attraction—you are walking around someone's neighborhood. So peeking in windows and wandering off the suggested route isn't polite. If you want to take photos, you'll usually need a camera permit, for an additional fee. Always ask permission before taking photos of people, and ask parents, rather than children, for their consent. All pueblos ban alcohol.

Some pueblos are more welcoming than others. San Ildefonso, for instance, is open year-round, whereas Jemez is completely closed except for some feast days. So it's flawed logic to seek out the less-visited places or go in the off times in order to have a less "touristy" experience. In fact, the most rewarding time to visit *is* on a big feast day—you may not be the only tourist there, but you have a better chance of being invited into a local's home.

CLASSES AND VOLUNTEERING

From afternoon cooking workshops to intensives on adobe building techniques, the opportunities to learn in New Mexico are broad.

General Education

Look first into the art, music, and outdoors programs at **Ghost Ranch** (877/804-4678, www.ghostranch.org), the beautiful property in Abiquiu. Santa Fe and Albuquerque are both home to renowned alternative healing, herbal medicine, and massage schools, more than can be listed here; visit **Natural Healers** (www.naturalhealers.com) for a list.

Arts and Crafts

Taos in particular is a hotbed for art classes. **Fechin Art Workshops** (575/751-0647, www.fineartservices.info) are five-day live-in retreats that have been running for more than two decades; they are based in Taos Ski Valley. The equally long-established **Taos Art School** (575/758-0350, www.taosartschool. org) focuses on landscape techniques, in six-day painting or photo workshops that include hiking and rafting options.

For crafts, Taos is also the place to be: **Weaving Southwest** (575/758-0433) gives three-day workshops on Navajo frame looms. **Taos School of Metalsmithing and Lapidary Design** (575/758-0207, www. taosjewelryschool.com) covers a range of jewelry-making topics, starting with half-day sessions. Just north of Tierra Amarilla, in the tiny community of Los Ojos, the long-running **Río Grande Weaving School** (575/588-7231, www.handweavers.com) offers five-day weaving workshops and three-day natural dye classes, among other classes.

The excellent **Santa Fe Photographic Workshops** (505/983-1400, www. santafeworkshops.com) offers nationally-recognized photography classes in its campus in the Sangre de Cristo Mountains, just outside the city. Workshops range from three days onsite to longer field programs around New Mexico.

In Albuquerque, **Casa Flamenca** (505/247-0622, www.casaflamenca.org) offers classes in flamenco dance and classical Spanish guitar.

Music

Two of the best places to learn music in the state teach courses for music that New Mexico isn't all that well known for. Las Cruces Ukes hosts the annual **UkeFest** (https://lascrucesukefest.com) in spring, which includes several classes that focus on learning how to play the ukulele. Throughout the year, the highly regarded **New Mexico Jazz Workshop** (nmjazz.org) in Albuquerque offers a variety of jazz-focused courses, from improvisation to singing.

Cooking

Santa Fe School of Cooking (125 N. Guadalupe St., 505/983-4511, www. santafeschoolofcooking.com) offers day classes in contemporary Southwestern cuisine, as well as traditional Native American cooking and New Mexican standards; nice farmers market trips and restaurant walking tours are offered, too.

In Dixon, **Comida de Campos** (505/852-0017, www.comidadecampos.com) offers classes on cooking in a traditional outdoor *horno,* and occasionally on clay-pot cooking, all in a beautiful farm setting.

Permaculture and Alternative Construction

In Albuquerque, **The Old School** (www. abqoldschool.com) teaches skills such as canning, quilting, and building solar phone chargers. If you're interested in New Mexico's solar architecture movement, you can enroll in the monthlong intensive **Earthship Academy** (575/751-0462, www.earthship.org), a crash course in building the off-the-grid rammed-earth houses that have their roots in Taos. The Earthship Biotecture organization also accepts volunteers. For more on local building styles, look into the semester-long classes in adobe construction at **Northern New Mexico College** (575/581-4115, www.nnmc. edu).

FOREIGN TRAVELERS

As for any destination in the United States, check before departure whether you'll need a **visa** to enter; most European nationals do not need one.

New Mexico uses the **United States dollar,** and currency exchange is available at most banks as well as in better hotels, though the rates in the latter case will not be as good. For the best rates and convenience, withdraw cash from your home account through **automatic teller machines** (ATMs); check first, though, what fee your home bank and the ATM's bank will charge you for the transaction, including any fee for a foreign-currency transaction.

Tipping is similar to elsewhere in the country: 15 percent to cab drivers, and 15-20 percent on restaurant bills. For larger groups, often restaurants will add 18 percent or so to the bill; this is suggested, and you may refuse it or write in a lower amount if service was poor. Add $1 or so per drink when ordered at the bar; $1 or $2 to staff who handle your luggage in hotels; and $3-5 per day to housekeeping in hotels—envelopes are often left in rooms for this purpose. **Bargaining** is acceptable only if you're dealing directly with an artisan, and even then, it is often politely deflected. But it doesn't hurt to ask, nicely, if the quoted price is the best possible one.

Electricity is 120 volts, with a two-prong, flat-head plug, the same as Canada and Mexico.

ACCESS FOR TRAVELERS WITH DISABILITIES

Wheelchair access can be frustrating in some historic properties and on the narrower sidewalks of Santa Fe and Taos, but in most other respects, travelers with disabilities should find no more problems in New Mexico than elsewhere in the United States. Public buses are wheelchair accessible, an increasing number of hotels have ADA-compliant rooms, and you can even get out in nature a bit on paved trails such as the Santa Fe Canyon Preserve loop and the Paseo del Bosque in Albuquerque.

If you'll be visiting a number of wilderness areas, consider the National Park Service's **Access Pass** (888/467-2757, www. nps.gov), a free lifetime pass that grants admission for the pass-holder and three adults to all national parks, national forests, and the like, as well as discounts on interpretive

services, camping fees, fishing licenses, and more. Apply in person at any federally managed park or wilderness area; you must show medical documentation of blindness or permanent disability.

TRAVELING WITH CHILDREN

Though the specific prices are not listed in this guide, admission at major attractions is almost always lower for children than for adults. Your little ones will be welcome in most environments, the only exceptions being a few of the more formal restaurants in Santa Fe and Albuquerque. Kids are sure to be fascinated by ceremonial dances at the pueblos, but be prepared with distractions, because long waits are the norm. Prep children with information about American Indian culture, and brief them on the basic etiquette at dances, which applies to them as well. Kids will also enjoy river rafting (relaxing "floats" along placid sections of the Rio Grande and Rio Chama are good for younger ones). For skiing, Taos Ski Valley has a very strong program of classes for youngsters.

SENIOR TRAVELERS

Senior discounts are available at most museums and other attractions. If you'll be visiting a number of wilderness areas, look into a **Senior Pass** ($10), a lifetime pass for people 62 and older that grants free admission for the pass-holder and three additional adults to national parks, National Forest Service lands, and many other areas, as well as discounts on activities such as camping and boat-launching. The pass can be purchased in person at any federally managed wilderness area, or online with an additional $10 processing fee; for more information, contact the **National Park Service** (888/467-2757, www.nps.gov).

Road Scholar (800/454-5768, www. roadscholar.org) runs more than 20 reasonably priced group trips in New Mexico, from a five-day general introduction to Santa Fe history and a week-long exploration of top draws in southern New Mexico to more focused tours on the history of crypto-Jews, for instance, and ancestral Puebloan culture.

GAY AND LESBIAN TRAVELERS

Gay marriage was legalized in New Mexico in late 2013, but Santa Fe has been one of the major gay capitals in the United States for decades, second only to San Francisco in the per-capita rates of same-sex coupledom. There are no designated "gay-borhoods" (unless you count RainbowVision Santa Fe, a retirement community) or even particular bar scenes. Instead, gay men and lesbian women are well integrated throughout town, running businesses and serving on the city council. The city's Pride parade is usually in late June, and is preceded by several big events.

Albuquerque also has a decent gay scene, especially if you want to go clubbing, which is not an option in quieter Santa Fe. As for smaller towns and pueblos, they're still significantly more conservative.

Gay culture in the state isn't all about cute shops and cabarets. One big event is the annual **Zia Regional Rodeo,** sponsored by the **New Mexico Gay Rodeo Association** (505/720-3749, www.nmgra.org). It takes place every summer in Santa Fe, with all the standard rodeo events, plus goat dressing and a wild drag race.

Health and Safety

Visitors to New Mexico face several unique health concerns. First and foremost are the environmental hazards of **dehydration, sunburn,** and **altitude sickness.** The desert climate, glaring sun, and thinner atmosphere conspire to fry your skin and drain you of all moisture. (On the plus side, sweat evaporates immediately.) Apply SPF 30 sunscreen daily, even in winter, and try to drink at least a liter of water a day, whether you feel thirsty or not. (Request water in restaurants—it's usually brought only on demand, to cut down on waste.) By the time you start feeling thirsty, you're already seriously dehydrated and at risk of further bad effects: headaches, nausea, and dizziness, all of which can become full-blown, life-threatening **heatstroke** if left untreated. Heatstroke can happen even without serious exertion—just lack of water and very hot sun. So if you're feeling at all woozy or cranky (another common symptom), head for shade and sip a Gatorade or similar electrolyte-replacement drink.

Staying hydrated also staves off the effects of the high elevation, to which most visitors will not be acclimated. The mildest reaction to being 7,000 feet or more above sea level is lethargy or light-headedness—you will probably sleep long and soundly on your first night in New Mexico. Some people do have more severe reactions, such as a piercing headache or intense nausea, especially if they engage in strenuous physical activity. Unfortunately, there's no good way to judge how your body will react, so give yourself a few days to adjust, with a light schedule and plenty of time to sleep.

More obscure hazards include **West Nile virus** (wear a DEET-based insect repellent if you're down along the river in the summer); **hantavirus,** an extremely rare pulmonary ailment transmitted by rodents; and the even rarer **bubonic plague** (aka the Black Death), the very same disease that killed millions of Europeans in the Middle Ages. Luckily, only a case or two of the plague crops up every year, and it's easily treated if diagnosed early. **Lyme disease** is almost as rare, as deer ticks do not flourish in the mountains.

If you'll be spending a lot of time hiking or camping, take precautions against **giardiasis** and other waterborne ailments by boiling your water or treating it with iodine or a SteriPen (www.steripen.com), as even the clearest mountain waterways may have been tainted by cows upstream. Snake bites are also a hazard in the wild, so wear boots that cover your ankles, stay on trails, and keep your hands and feet out of odd holes and cracks between rocks. Only the Western diamondback rattlesnake is aggressive when disturbed; other snakes typically will not bite if you simply back away quietly.

General outdoor safety rules apply: Don't hike by yourself, always register with the ranger station when heading out overnight, and let friends know where you're going and when you'll be back. Pack a good topographical map and a compass or GPS device; people manage to get lost even when hiking in the foothills, and if you're at all dehydrated or dizzy from the altitude, any disorientation can be magnified to a disastrous degree. Also pack layers of clothing, and be prepared for cold snaps and snow at higher elevations, even in the summer.

CRIME AND DRUGS

Recreational drug use is not uncommon in New Mexico—generally in a relatively benign form, with marijuana fairly widespread. (Former governor and Republican presidential candidate Gary Johnson, though no longer a user himself, has been a strenuous advocate for its legalization.) But as in much of the rural United States, crystal methamphetamine is an epidemic, and some villages in northern New Mexico have also been devastated by heroin use, with overdose deaths at a rate several hundred times higher than the national average. None of this affects travelers, except that petty theft, especially in isolated areas such as trailheads, can be an issue. Always lock your car doors, and secure any valuables in the trunk. Don't leave anything enticing in view.

Drinking and driving is unfortunately still common, especially in rural areas; be particularly alert when driving at night. A distressing number of crosses along the roadside (*descansos*) mark the sites of fatal car accidents, many of which had alcohol involved.

Resources

Glossary

abierto: Spanish for "open"

acequia: irrigation ditch, specifically one regulated by the traditional Spanish method, maintained by a *mayordomo,* or "ditch boss," who oversees how much water each shareholder receives

adobe: building material of sun-dried bricks made of a mix of mud, sand, clay, and straw

arroyo: stream or dry gully where mountain runoff occasionally flows

asado: stew (usually pork) with red-chile sauce

atrio: churchyard between the boundary wall and the church entrance, usually used as a cemetery

bizcochito: anise-laced shortbread, traditionally made with lard

bosque: Spanish for "forest," specifically the cottonwoods and trees along a river

bulto: three-dimensional wood carving, typically of a saint

caldera: basin or crater formed by a collapsed volcano

canal: water drain from a flat roof; pl. *canales*

carne adovada: pork chunks marinated in red chile, then braised; meatier and drier than *asado*

cerrado: Spanish for "closed"

chicharrón: fried pork skin, usually with a layer of meat still attached

chile: not to be confused with Texas chili, Cincinnati chili, or any other American concoction; refers to the fruit of the chile plant itself, eaten green (picked unripe and then roasted) or red (ripened and dried)

chimichanga: deep-fried burrito; allegedly invented in Arizona

colcha: style of blanket, in which loom-woven wool is embellished with long strands of wool embroidery

concha belt: belt made of stamped, carved silver medallions; *concha* is Spanish for "shell"; also concho

convento: residential compound adjoining a mission church

enchilada: corn tortilla dipped in chile sauce, filled with cheese or meat, and topped with more chile; can be served either rolled or flat (stacked in layers)

farolito: in Santa Fe and Taos, a luminaria

GCCB: common abbreviation for green-chile cheeseburger

genízaro: during Spanish colonial times, a detribalized Indian (usually due to having been taken as a slave) who lived with Spaniards and followed Catholic tradition

gordita: a variation on the taco, with a thicker tortilla-like shell, sometimes deep-fried; these are a more traditionally Mexican dish (though in that case rarely fried) and are available only in the southern part of the state

heishi: fine disk-shaped beads carved from shells

horno: traditional dome-shaped adobe oven

jerga: Spanish-style wool blanket or rug, loosely woven and barely decorated, meant for daily use

kachina: ancestral spirit of the Pueblo people as well as the carved figurine representing the spirit; also spelled "katsina"

kiva: sacred ceremonial space in a pueblo, at least partially underground and entered by a hole in the ceiling *latillas:* thin saplings cut and laid across vigas to make a solid ceiling

lowrider: elaborately painted and customized car with hydraulic lifts

luminaria: in Albuquerque, lantern made of a sand-filled paper bag with a votive candle set inside; in Santa Fe and Taos, refers to small bonfires lit during the Christmas season

menudo: tripe soup, said to be good for curing a hangover

morada: meeting space of the Penitente brotherhood

nicho: small niche in an adobe wall, usually meant to hold a santo

Penitente: member of a long-established Catholic brotherhood in northern New Mexico

petroglyph: rock carving

pictograph: painting on a rock surface

piñon: any of several fragrant varieties of pine tree that grow in New Mexico

portal: the covered sidewalk area in front of a traditional adobe structure; pl. *portales*

posole: stew of hulled corn (hominy), pork, and a little chile, either green or red

pueblo: Spanish for "village," referring to the various communities of American Indians settled in the Rio Grande Valley, as well as the larger land area owned by the community (preferable to the term "reservation"); also, capitalized, the people themselves, though they speak several different languages

rajas: rough-hewn slats laid over vigas to form a ceiling; also, strips of roasted chile

ramada: simple structure built of four sapling posts and topped with additional saplings laid flat to form a shade structure and a place to hang things to dry

reredos: altar screen, usually elaborately painted or carved with various portraits of Christ and the saints

retablo: flat portrait of a saint, painted or carved in low relief, usually on wood

ristra: string of dried red chiles

santero/santera: craftsperson who produces santos

santo: portrait of a saint, either flat (a *retablo*) or three-dimensional (a *bulto*)

sipapu: hole in the floor of a kiva, signifying the passage to the spirit world

sopaipilla: square of puffed fried dough, served with the main meal for wiping up sauces and with honey for dessert

tamale: corn husk filled with masa (hominy paste) and a dab of meat, vegetables, or cheese, then steamed; usually made in large quantities for holidays

terrón: building material of bricks cut out of sod and dried in the sun, similar to adobe, but less common

Tewa: language spoken by the majority of Pueblo Indians; others in the Rio Grande Valley speak Tiwa, Towa, and Keresan

torreón: round defensive tower built in Spanish colonial times

vato: cool Chicano, usually driving a lowrider

viga: ceiling beam made of a single tree trunk

zaguán: long central hallway

Suggested Reading

ART AND CULTURE

Clark, Willard. *Remembering Santa Fe.* Layton, UT: Gibbs Smith, 2004. A small hardback edition of selections from the Boston artist who stopped off in Santa Fe in 1928. He stayed to learn printmaking and produce this series of etchings depicting city life.

Eaton, Robert. *The Lightning Field.* Boulder, CO: Johnson Books, 1995. Eaton served as a forest ranger in Chaco Canyon for five years, so his eye is for the empty and the starkly beautiful destinations around the state, including the art installation of the title (in Quemado, in western New Mexico). His essays, each focusing on a different destination, combine history and strong description. Seek this title out if you want to get well off the usual track.

Lamadrid, Enrique. *Hermanitos Comanchitos: Indo-Hispano Rituals of Captivity and Redemption.* Albuquerque: University of New Mexico Press, 2003. Fascinating documentation, in descriptive prose and rich black-and-white photos, of the traditional Spanish dances of northern New Mexico, such as Los Comanches and Los Matachines.

Lummis, Charles F. *A Tramp Across the Continent.* Lincoln, NE: University of Nebraska Press, 1982. In 1884, fledgling journalist Lummis decided to walk from Cincinnati to his new job in Los Angeles; this book chronicles his trip. The sections on New Mexico shine, and Lummis was so entranced that he later moved to the territory. He was the first to write stories about the Penitente brotherhood in the national press.

Myers, Joan. *Pie Town Woman: The Hard Life and Good Times of a New Mexico Homesteader.* Albuquerque: University of New Mexico Press, 2001. The biography of a woman captured in famous Farm Security Administration photos from 1940, this book also muses on the power of memory and photography.

Padilla, Carmella, and Juan Estevan Arellano. *Low 'n Slow: Lowriding in New Mexico.* Santa Fe, NM: Museum of New Mexico Press, 2005. Lovingly lurid color photographs by Jack Parsons are the centerpiece of this book, which pays tribute to New Mexico's Latino car culture—an art form that has even landed a Chimayó lowrider in the Smithsonian.

Parhad, Elisa. *New Mexico: A Guide for the Eyes.* Los Angeles: EyeMuse Books, 2009. Informative short essays on the distinctive things you see in New Mexico and then wonder what the backstory is: concha belts, beat-up pickup trucks, blue sky. The richly illustrated book makes good pre-trip reading or a souvenir when you return.

Price, Roberta. *Across the Great Divide: A Photo Chronicle of the Counterculture.* Albuquerque: University of New Mexico Press, 2010. Documentary photographer Price "went native" with a Colorado commune in the 1960s and visited several groups in New Mexico. She also wrote the narrative *Huerfano: A Memoir of Life in the Counterculture* (Amherst: University of Massachusetts Press, 2004).

Price, V. B. *Albuquerque: A City at the End of the World.* Albuquerque: University of New Mexico Press, 2003. Journalist and poet Price writes a travel guide to New Mexico's biggest metropolis but disguises it as a discourse on urban theory, recommending his favorite spots in the context of the city's unique position and growth processes. Black-and-white photographs by Kirk Gittings highlight the stark landscape.

Robinson, Roxana. *Georgia O'Keeffe: A Life.* Lebanon, NH: University Press of New England, 1998. A strong and intimate biography, focusing on the celebrated painter's role as a protofeminist and her difficult relationships.

FOOD

Feucht, Andrea. *Food Lovers' Guide to Santa Fe, Albuquerque & Taos.* Guilford, CT: Globe Pequot, 2012. A good companion for adventurous eaters, with especially good coverage of Albuquerque's more obscure ethnic restaurants.

Frank, Lois Ellen. *Foods of the Southwest Indian Nations.* Berkeley, CA: Ten Speed Press, 2002. Beautiful photographs are a highlight of this thorough documentation of a little-covered cuisine. They help make an ancient culinary tradition accessible and modern without subjecting it to a heavy-handed fusion treatment. For good reason, it earned a James Beard Award.

Jamison, Cheryl and Bill. *Rancho de Chimayo Cookbook: The Traditional Cooking of New Mexico.* Guilford, CT: Lyons Press, 2014. Like the famous namesake restaurant in a village north of Santa Fe, this engaging cookbook expertly captures the essence of New Mexican cuisine.

Kagel, Katharine. *Cooking with Café Pasqual's: Recipes from Santa Fe's Renowned Corner Cafe.* Berkeley, CA: Ten Speed Press, 2006. Re-create your best meals from the legendary restaurant that set the standard for Santa Fe fusion cooking. Chef Kagel is a charming contrarian, too, which makes for great reading.

HISTORY

Childs, Craig. *House of Rain: Tracking a Vanished Civilization Across the American Southwest.* New York: Little, Brown, 2007. The story of the Ancestral Puebloans (Anasazi), as told by a curious naturalist, becomes less a solution to an archaeological puzzle than a meditation of why we romanticize "lost" civilizations. His more recent book, *Finders Keepers: A Tale of Archaeological Plunder and Possession* (Little, Brown, 2010), takes the drama to the academy, with tales of scholarly intrigue.

Egan, Timothy. *The Worst Hard Time: The Untold Story of Those Who Survived the Great American Dust Bowl.* New York: Mariner Books, 2006. The town of Clayton features a bit in the pages of this highly readable history that conveys the misery and environmental folly of the period.

Held, E. B. *A Spy's Guide to Santa Fe and Albuquerque.* Albuquerque: University of New Mexico Press, 2011. A former CIA agent reveals nefarious Cold War intrigue—fascinating details, if not so grippingly told.

Hordes, Stanley. *To the End of the Earth: A History of the Crypto-Jews of New Mexico.* New York: Columbia University Press, 2008. An exhaustive but intriguing account of the Jewish families who fled the Inquisition and lived in the Southwest as Catholic converts. The communities, some still practicing distinctly Jewish rituals, came to light only a few decades ago.

Horgan, Paul. *Great River.* Middletown, CT: Wesleyan University Press, 1991. Two enormous tomes (*Vol. 1: The Indians and Spain* and *Vol. 2: Mexico and the United States*) won the Pulitzer Prize for history. They're packed with drama, on a base of meticulous analysis of primary sources.

Martinez, Esther. *My Life in San Juan Pueblo.* Champaign, IL: University of Illinois Press, 2004. Born in 1912, Martinez has a lot of stories to tell. This free-flowing book incorporates her memories with larger pueblo folklore, and a CD with recordings of some of her stories is included.

Poling-Kempes, Lesley. *Valley of Shining Stone: The Story of Abiquiu.* Tucson, AZ: University of Arizona Press, 1997. Georgia O'Keeffe fans will like the personal stories of those in her circle in the 1930s, while historians will appreciate the detailed, linear second half of the book, about the transformation of this remote valley into an artists' haven.

Sides, Hampton. *Blood and Thunder: An Epic of the American West.* New York: Doubleday, 2006. Working from the story of Kit Carson and the campaign against the Navajo, including the Long Walk, Sides tells the gripping story of the entire American West. He's an excellent storyteller, and the 480 pages flow by in a rush of land grabs, battles on horseback, and brutality on all sides.

Simmons, Marc. *New Mexico: An Interpretive History*. Albuquerque: University of New Mexico Press, 1988. The state's historian laureate presents an easy, concise overview of the major historical events. Also look into his more specialized titles, such as *The Last Conquistador: Juan de Oñate and the Settling of the Far Southwest* (Norman: University of Oklahoma Press, 1993).

Smith, Mike. *Towns of the Sandia Mountains*. Charleston, SC: Arcadia, 2006. This slim volume of vintage photographs and juicy stories in extended captions is about a very specific region, but it could tell the story of much of New Mexico in its shift to modernity.

Usner, Donald J. *Sabino's Map: Life in Chimayó's Old Plaza*. Santa Fe, NM: Museum of New Mexico Press, 1995. A balanced and gracefully written history of the author's hometown, illustrated with fond photos of all the craggy-faced characters involved.

LITERATURE AND MEMOIR

Anaya, Rudolfo. *Bless Me, Ultima*. New York: Warner, 1994. Anaya's story of a young boy coming of age in New Mexico in the 1940s is beautifully told. The book, first published in 1973, launched Anaya into his role as Chicano literary hero; his later books, such as *Alburquerque* (1992), are not quite so touching, but they have a lot of historical and ethnic detail.

Blume, Judy. *Tiger Eyes*. New York: Delacorte, 2010. A young girl with family troubles relocates to Los Alamos, giving a great teen's-eye view on the landscape of New Mexico.

Connors, Philip. *Fire Season: Field Notes from a Wilderness Lookout*. New York: Ecco, 2012. In the tradition of Edward Abbey, this memoir recounts life in a remote fire tower in the Gila Wilderness.

Evans, Max. *Hi-Lo to Hollywood: A Max Evans Reader*. Lubbock, TX: Texas Tech University Press, 1998. Prolific Western author Evans coined the term "Hi-Lo Country" for the "high lonesome" eastern plains of New Mexico, and all of his works, whether essay or fiction, somehow reflect the rolling expanse and the particular dilemmas of the modern cowboys who work on them. A ranch kid himself, he has an eye for detail and a direct and affectionate tone; this reader includes many of his own favorite pieces.

Goodman, Tanya Ward. *Leaving Tinkertown*. Albuquerque: University of New Mexico Press, 2013. A poignant memoir of growing up in the wondrous folk-art assemblage outside Albuquerque. The author's father, Ross Ward, died of early-onset Alzheimer's disease, and this book logs that medical tale, unflinchingly, alongside the larger-than-life artist's own story.

Hillerman, Tony. *Skinwalkers*. New York: HarperTorch, 1990. Hillerman's breakout detective novel, set on the Navajo Nation, weaves a fascinating amount of lore into the plot—which comes in handy when Tribal Affairs police Joe Leaphorn and Jim Chee investigate homicides. Hillerman spun Leaphorn and Chee into a successful franchise, and all of the books show the same cultural depth.

Nichols, John. *The Milagro Beanfield War*. New York: Owl Books, 2005. A comic novel about water rights, set in a northern New Mexico village. Nichols's visionary environmental nonfiction in *On the Mesa* (Layton, UT: Gibbs Smith, 2005) is also stunning.

Pillsbury, Dorothy. *Roots in Adobe*. Santa Fe, NM: Lightning Tree Press, 1983. Pillsbury's charming stories capture the strangeness and warmth of Santa Fe culture in the 1940s. The author tells hilarious stories of settling into her little home and the characters she meets.

Quade, Kirstin Valdez. *Night at the Fiestas.* New York: W. W. Norton, 2015. Quade, who grew up in New Mexico, sets many of the short stories in this collection in tiny Hispano towns, amid the most intense belief and ritual. A great mix of cultural detail and poignant characters.

Silko, Leslie Marmon. *Ceremony.* New York: Penguin, 1988. Silko's classic novel about the impact of the atomic bomb on Native Americans' worldview (and that of all Americans) is brutal, beautiful, and bleak.

NATURE AND THE ENVIRONMENT

Coltrin, Mike. *Sandia Mountain Hiking Guide.* Albuquerque: University of New Mexico Press, 2005. A print version of Coltrin's meticulously maintained website (www.sandiahiking.com), with thorough trail descriptions, GPS coordinates, and a foldout map of the east and west slopes of the mountain.

Julyan, Robert, and Mary Stuever, eds. *Field Guide to the Sandia Mountains.* Albuquerque: University of New Mexico Press, 2005. A thorough guide illustrated with color photographs, detailing birds, animals, plants, even insects of the Sandias. Most of it applies to the Santa Fe area, too.

Kavanagh, James. *New Mexico Nature Set: Field Guides to Wildlife, Birds, Trees & Wildflowers of New Mexico.* Dunedin, FL: Waterford Press, 2017. This collection of three pocket guides provides a handy means to identify and better understand what you're likely to see out in the wild on hikes across the state.

Kricher, John. *A Field Guide to Rocky Mountain and Southwest Forests.* New York: Houghton Mifflin Harcourt, 2003. A

Peterson Field Guide, covering both flora and fauna: trees, birds, mammals, you name it. It's illustrated with both color photos and drawings. It's not encyclopedic, but it's a great basic reference. Peterson guides are also available for narrower categories such as reptiles and amphibians or butterflies.

McFarland, Casey, and S. David Scott. *Bird Feathers: A Guide to North American Species.* Mechanicsburg, PA: Stackpole Books, 2010. While not New Mexico-specific, it is the only guide of its kind, and its authors grew up in the state and know the birdlife well. Great for serious birders and curious hikers, with detailed photographs.

Price, V. B. *The Orphaned Land: New Mexico's Environment Since the Manhattan Project.* Albuquerque: University of New Mexico Press, 2011. Journalist Price examines New Mexico's droughts and other trials—in the same vein as Reisner's *Cadillac Desert.*

Reisner, Marc. *Cadillac Desert: The American West and Its Disappearing Water.* New York: Penguin, 1993. Not specifically about New Mexico, but an excellent analysis of the Southwest's water shortage and how the U.S. government's dam-building projects exacerbated it. Apocalyptic, sarcastic, and totally compelling.

Sibley, David Allen. *The Sibley Field Guide to Birds of Western North America.* New York: Knopf, 2003. The New Mexican birder's book of choice, with 810 species listed, about 4,600 color illustrations, and a handy compact format. Generally beats out Peterson's otherwise respectable series.

Tekiela, Stan. *Birds of New Mexico: Field Guide.* Cambridge, MN: Adventure Publications, 2003. A great book for beginning birders or curious visitors, with 140 of the state's most common species listed, many illustrated with photographs.

Happy Trails!

See New Mexico through a focused lens, with these specialized guides to the state.

- **Birding Trail** (http://wildlife.state.nm.us): A map and road signs for feathered friends
- **Brewery Trail** (www.nmbeer.org): Features a downloadable map to breweries across the state
- **Clay Arts Trail** (www.clayfestival.com): A guide to the "creative economy of clay" in the southwest corner of the state
- **Green Chile Cheeseburger Trail** (www.newmexico.org): Between this and a breakfast burrito trail (same site), you'll never go hungry again.
- **Film Trails** (www.newmexico.org): Filming locations for more than a dozen films, plus *Breaking Bad*
- **Space Trail** (www.nmspacemuseum.org): Locations where rockets were launched
- **Trails in New Mexico State Parks** (www.emnrd.state.nm.us): Alphabetized list and summaries of some of the best hikes in state parks

Internet Resources

TRAVEL INFORMATION

Albuquerque Convention and Visitors Bureau
www.visitalbuquerque.org
The official intro to the city and surrounding areas, with events listings as well as hotel-booking services.

ExploreNM
https://explorenm.com
An extensive, if barebones, repository of user reviews of hikes and campgrounds around New Mexico.

Four Corners Geotourism
www.fourcornersgeotourism.com
A directory of sustainable tourism, sponsored by *National Geographic.*

Hiking in the Sandia Mountains
www.sandiahiking.com
Mike Coltrin hiked every trail in the Sandias over the course of a year, covering about 250 miles. He detailed each hike, complete with GPS references, here.

New Mexico Board of Tourism
www.newmexico.org
The best of the official sites, this one has thorough maps and suggested itineraries.

Public Lands Information Center
www.publiclands.org
Buy USGS, Forest Service, and other topographical maps online from the Bureau of Land Management's well-organized website. Good stock of nature guides and other travel books, too.

Sangres.com
www.sangres.com
Scores of travel details about the mountain communities, culture, and history of northern New Mexico, as well as southern Colorado. Not regularly updated, however.

Taos Vacation Guide
www.taos.org
A thorough directory and events listings.

Tourism Santa Fe
www.santafe.org
Near-exhaustive listings of tourist attractions and services on this slickly produced site.

Visit Las Cruces
www.lascruces.cvb.org
Comprehensive listings of a wide variety of attractions, restaurants, and accommodations, all easy to navigate.

Visit Los Alamos
www.visitlosalamos.org
Colorful and helpfully arranged with suggestions based on the time you have available.

NEWS AND CULTURE

Albuquerque Journal
www.abqjournal.com
The state's largest newspaper is available free online after answering survey questions.

Alibi
www.alibi.com
This free weekly has been cracking wise since 1992, taking a critical look at politics and culture. Its annual "Best of Burque" guide is usually reliable.

Chasing Santa Fe
www.chasingsantafe.blogspot.com
The glamorous Santa Fe lifestyle, lovingly documented: local chefs, events, new shops, and fashion spotting.

Las Cruces Sun-News
www.lcsun-news.com
The paper of record in Las Cruces, covering issues all across the southern half of the state, especially border debates.

New Mexico Political Report
http://nmpoliticalreport.com
Non-profit news site that covers New Mexico politics thoroughly and unearths stories you're not likely to find anywhere else.

New Mexico Politics with Joe Monahan
www.joemonahansnewmexico.blogspot.com
Political analyst Joe Monahan's obsessive, snarky blog charts the circus that is state politics.

Santa Fe New Mexican
www.santafenewmexican.com
Santa Fe's main newspaper. The gossip column *El Mitote* documents celebs in Santa Fe, and the Roundhouse Roundup does roughly the same—but with politicians.

Santa Fe Reporter
www.sfreporter.com
Santa Fe's free weekly is politically sharp and often funny. Get opinionated reviews and news analysis here.

Smithsonian Folkways
www.folkways.si.edu
Prep for your road trip at this enormous online music archive, which has a number of traditional treasures from the state, including the excellent *Music of New Mexico: Hispanic Traditions* and *New Mexico: Native American Traditions*.

Taos News
www.taosnews.com
The town paper is a weekly, but its website has daily updates and an events calendar.

Index

List of Maps

Photo Credits

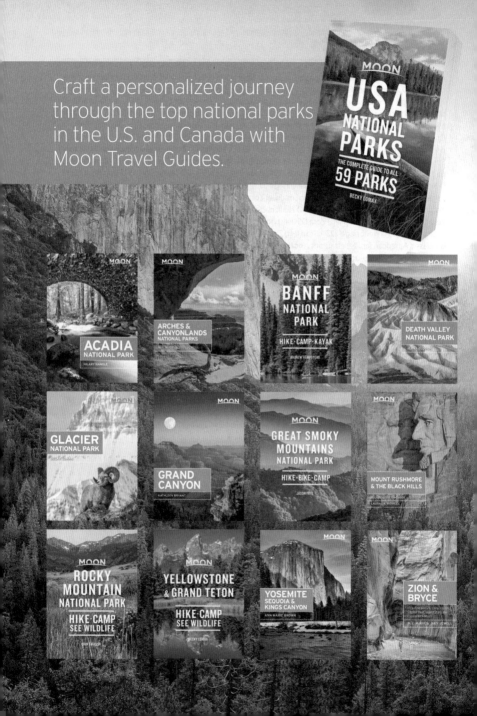

Craft a personalized journey through the top national parks in the U.S. and Canada with Moon Travel Guides.

MAP SYMBOLS

═══ Expressway	○	City/Town	✗	Airport	⚲	Golf Course	
─── Primary Road	◉	State Capital	✗	Airfield	🅿	Parking Area	
─── Secondary Road	⊛	National Capital	▲	Mountain	▰	Archaeological Site	
···· Unpaved Road	★	Point of Interest	✦	Unique Natural Feature	⬧	Church	
─── Feature Trail	•	Accommodation			🗲	Gas Station	
---- Other Trail	▼	Restaurant/Bar	🕊	Waterfall		Glacier	
···· Ferry	■	Other Location	▲	Park		Mangrove	
═══ Pedestrian Walkway	Δ	Campground	🚩	Trailhead		Reef	
▥▥▥ Stairs			🎿	Skiing Area		Swamp	

CONVERSION TABLES

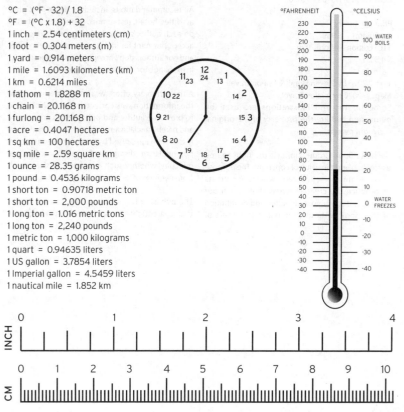

$°C = (°F - 32) / 1.8$

$°F = (°C \times 1.8) + 32$

1 inch = 2.54 centimeters (cm)
1 foot = 0.304 meters (m)
1 yard = 0.914 meters
1 mile = 1.6093 kilometers (km)
1 km = 0.6214 miles
1 fathom = 1.8288 m
1 chain = 20.1168 m
1 furlong = 201.168 m
1 acre = 0.4047 hectares
1 sq km = 100 hectares
1 sq mile = 2.59 square km
1 ounce = 28.35 grams
1 pound = 0.4536 kilograms
1 short ton = 0.90718 metric ton
1 short ton = 2,000 pounds
1 long ton = 1.016 metric tons
1 long ton = 2,240 pounds
1 metric ton = 1,000 kilograms
1 quart = 0.94635 liters
1 US gallon = 3.7854 liters
1 Imperial gallon = 4.5459 liters
1 nautical mile = 1.852 km

MOON NEW MEXICO
Avalon Travel
Hachette Book Group
1700 Fourth Street
Berkeley, CA 94710, USA
www.moon.com

Editor and Series Manager: Kathryn Ettinger
Acquiring Editor: Nikki Ioakimedes
Copy Editor: Kelly Lydick
Graphics Coordinator: Rue Flaherty
Production Coordinator: Rue Flaherty
Cover Design: Faceout Studios, Charles Brock
Interior Design: Domini Dragoone
Moon Logo: Tim McGrath
Map Editor: Albert Angulo
Cartographers: John Culp and Andrew Dolan
Indexer: Greg Jewett

ISBN-13: 978-1-64049-761-0

Printing History
1st Edition — 1989
11th Edition — April 2020
5 4 3 2 1

Front cover photo: Shiprock © Brad Mitchell / Alamy Stock Photo

Back cover photo: cactus in Organ Mountains-Desert Peaks National Monument © Martha Marks | Dreamstime.com

Printed in China by RR Donnelley